THE SELECTED WORKS OF ANDREW LANG

VOLUME I

THE SELECTED WORKS OF ANDREW LANG

VOLUME I

Anthropology:
Fairy Tale, Folklore,
the Origins of Religion,
Psychical Research

EDITED BY
Andrew Teverson, Alexandra Warwick
and Leigh Wilson

EDINBURGH
University Press

© Andrew Teverson, Alexandra Warwick
and Leigh Wilson, 2015

Edinburgh University Press Ltd
The Tun – Holyrood Road, 12(2F) Jackson's Entry,
Edinburgh EH8 8PJ

www.euppublishing.com

Typeset in 10.5 pt Monotype Bembo
by Isambard Thomas, and
printed and bound in Great Britain by
CPI Group (UK) Ltd, Croydon CR0 4YY

A CIP record for this book is available from the British Library

ISBN 978 1 4744 0021 3 (hardback)
ISBN 978 1 4744 0022 0 (webready PDF)
ISBN 978 1 4744 0449 5 (epub)

The right of Andrew Teverson,
Alexandra Warwick and Leigh Wilson
to be identified as Editors of this work
has been asserted in accordance
with the Copyright, Designs and Patents Act 1988,
and the Copyright and Related Rights Regulations 2003
(SI No. 2498).

CONTENTS

General Introduction

When Andrew Lang died in 1912, and for some time after, even the most sympathetic commentators remarked on the disappointment inherent in his now completed *oeuvre*. The most scathing was Henry James, writing to Edmund Gosse in November 1912:

> Where I can't but feel he <u>should</u> be brought to justice is in the matter of his whole 'give-away' of the wonderful chance he so continually enjoyed (enjoyed thanks to certain of his very gifts, I admit!) give-away, I mean by his <u>cultivation</u>, absolutely, of the puerile imagination and fourth-rate opinion, the coming round to that of the old apple-woman on the corner as after all the good and the right as to any of the mysteries of mind or of art.[1]

Both were publically more generous to Lang, as were the many obituaries and commemorative writings, but in introducing the published versions of the first ten years of the Andrew Lang Lectures,[2] Adam Blyth Webster, Professor of English Literature at St Andrews, admits that:

> Through much, through most, of what had been written about him there ran the admission that he had done many things gracefully and some exceedingly well, but also the wonder, regretful or complaining, not that he should have done so much but that, it seemed, he had failed to do more.[3]

For many, though, it was not so much that they wished Lang had done more, rather that he had done less, and concerned himself with just one area; usually, for each commentator, the area that most concerned themselves. His friend George Saintsbury wrote of Lang's ability:

It may be that in one way it did not concentrate itself enough—did not leave two or three big books instead of thirty or forty little ones; and in another concentrated itself too much by writing not very small books on subjects which might have been adequately treated in not very long essays.[4]

Saintsbury concluded his assessment:

'Selections', of course, suggest themselves and have been suggested. It would be possible to conceive not merely one but more than one which would supply reading of the most refreshing kind. But it would be an extraordinarily difficult job; and while selections often fail to satisfy their readers, this selection would be so unlikely to satisfy the selector that he would probably never get it finished.[5]

Saintsbury's words indicate the sense that is present over and over again in those who discuss Lang, that he is, simply, unmanageable, both in the volume of his production and in its variety. The volume is undeniable: he started his career as a reviewer for *The Academy* in 1874 and he wrote for the *Daily News*, the *Morning Post* and the *Saturday Review* producing hundreds of reviews over more than two decades.[6] For *Longman's Magazine* (with which he was so closely associated that he repeatedly had to tell readers that he was not the editor), he wrote 240 columns, occasional articles, poetry and fiction; he produced more than 500 columns for the *Illustrated London News*, as well as essays for the *Cornhill Magazine*, *Fraser's Magazine*, the *Fortnightly Review*, the *Contemporary Review*, *Blackwood's Edinburgh Magazine*, *Harper's*, *Macmillan's*, the *St. James's Gazette*, *The Pilot*, *The Critic* and numerous others. His work was also published in American journals and newspapers and was widely syndicated in the English-language press around the world.

Aside from the periodical and newspaper work, Roger Lancelyn Green, Lang's only biographer, lists more than 200 publications under Lang's name: poetry and fiction, translations, histories, biographies, collections, works on anthropology, mythology, folklore, literature and many introductions to works by others, including every volume of the complete works of Scott and Dickens.[7] The range and variety seems to have defeated possible critics as well as potential editors. After the commemorative pieces that appeared in 1912 and 1913 and the personal notes in the autobiographies of those that knew him, only the Lang Lectures kept his work in view and even they became intermittent after 1934. The centenary of his birth in 1944 drew some brief articles and a radio programme was broadcast on the fiftieth anniversary of his death.[8] John Gross, one of the few later twentieth-century critics that mentions Lang, called him 'a don lost to journalism'[9] and in 1984 Harold Orel, in his book on Victorian literary critics, concludes in almost the same words as writers sixty years earlier: 'For all his wisdom and gracefulness of style, Lang's legacy to our age is … a disappointment, and less than it might have been.'[10] In the 1980s Marysa Demoor carried out invaluable work on his letters[11] and while there was a smattering of works on Lang,[12] on the whole most twentieth-century scholars tacitly agreed with his obituaries, and no collections or editions of his work have ever appeared.[13]

There is, however, an indication of what might be the real reason for the neglect in the first Lang Lecture, delivered by George Gordon in 1927. He says that:

> It is worthwhile to observe how instinctively Lang settled, in the studies of his time, on the adventurous, the mysterious, the problematic; on the frontier of subjects, where new work was being done, and on sciences in the making … the conditions of his performance have not always been understood.[14]

In the late nineteenth century the sciences and other disciplines were struggling for definition, working for greater clarity of boundaries and objects of study rather than less. Lang's refusal of such segregation placed him awkwardly in the intellectual milieu of his own time and further stranded his work as those boundaries between academic disciplines hardened in the twentieth century. It is only recently that it has become possible, in George Gordon's words, to understand the conditions of Lang's performance. Firstly, the digitisation of catalogues and material (particularly periodicals) has made the location of his sprawling mass of work far easier, but more importantly over the last forty years or so, the *fin de siècle*, the period of his prime, has become one of particular interest for scholars from a number of disciplines. The developing interest in the gothic, in the construction and rise of consumer capitalism, in the histories of science and technology, in the genealogies of modernism, in the constructions of modern identities around, in particular, gender, sexuality and ethnicity, in the development of the idea of professionalisation, all have given a preeminence to the period as the origin of a particular kind of modernity and have found significance in exactly the adventurous, the mysterious and the problematic topics that fascinated him. Thus we can see Lang anew as the complicated and sometimes contradictory scholar that he was, both a Victorian man of letters and one who worked in and on the boundaries between subjects in a way that anticipated the interdisciplinary studies of the later twentieth century.

Fittingly for a man at the intersection of so many fields, he was born at the edges of two nations, in the Border country of Scotland. Lang's nationality has been rather scornfully treated by some; Henry James, in his correspondence with Gosse, accuses Lang of affecting an 'extraordinary voulu Scotch provincialism'[15] and more recently Margaret Beetham has suggested that he 'performed' Scottishness in a way that was typical of the English upper class.[16] Neither of these views is true; Lang felt himself to be a Scot, a member, as he puts it, of a 'small nationality'[17] and never entirely at home in England. He spent as much time as he could in Scotland and gathered a good deal of folkloric material as well as accounts of contemporary and historical psychic phenomena. Though his longer works on Scottish history were published later in his career, beginning in the1890s, there is Scottish material throughout his work, indeed, among his first published pieces was a collection of Scottish nursery tales.[18]

The same longevity is apparent in his other interests too. In 1863, the same year as the nursery tale collection, he also published a piece on 'Spiritualism Mediaeval and Modern', and it was decades later, in 1911, when he became President of the Society for Psychical Research. He studied classics at Balliol and became a Fellow of Merton in 1868 and while there he published poetry and worked on translations of Aristotle and Homer, but the Merton library records show that he also read the newest work in other subjects, such as anthropology. He read E. B. Tylor's important work *Primitive Culture* (1871) in 1872 and he met Tylor in the same year.[19] At the end of his life he was still researching and writing on the same topics. *The World of Homer* came out in 1910, in which he offered further evidence in support of his assertion that the *Odyssey* and the *Iliad* were the work of a single author, against the dominant view that they were patchwork texts by several hands, and *Method in the Study of Totemism* was published in 1911. He was also translating folk and fairy tales long before the first of his highly popular Fairy Books came out in 1889, and the last of the series of twelve appeared only two years before his death.

It was after his unexplained departure from Oxford,[20] however, that he began the career that brought him to public attention and to a central place in late nineteenth-century literary life. His contemporaries admired his wit and learning, even those like George Bernard Shaw whose political positions were far from Lang's own,[21] and the *Daily News* had a list of subscribers who wanted only issues with Lang's articles sent to them.[22] He soon became a powerful figure, dominating journals and newspaper columns, instrumental in the careers of other writers (such as Henry Rider Haggard) and popular with the reading public. It was also in this arena that the debates occurred that perhaps did the most damage to Lang's reputation as a literary critic. His review of Thomas Hardy's *Tess of the D'Urbervilles* in 1892, his criticism of the work of Émile Zola and his long-running skirmish with W. D. Howells and others over the value of Romance led to the caricature of him that James articulates to Gosse: of dismissing important new novelists and willfully cultivating 'puerile imagination and fourth-rate opinion' in his many readers.[23]

There may have been resentment of Lang's success in the turn against him that occurs in the 1890s; James and Gosse were not the only writers jealous of their status in the competitive literary world. Publically Lang continued to engage confidently in sharp debates in all the areas of his interests, but privately he expressed increasing lack of certainty about his own worth. In this, as in so much else, Lang is a contradictory figure. He was a very public man and by no means isolated from the social world. Among many connections that he made, he originally introduced James to Gosse, and both to Robert Louis Stevenson. He was also one of the first to notice

Rudyard Kipling, introducing him to Haggard, and he brought together George Saintsbury and Austin Dobson. His reserve, however, is a striking feature of all accounts of him,[24] and he demonstrates an almost pathological privacy. He consistently advised his correspondents to destroy his letters – 'Burn this or some beast will publish it, some day, for ten bob'[25] – and was insistent that no biography of him should be written, instructing his wife to destroy all his papers after his death.[26] He seems to have found socialising painful and upsetting; a remark in a letter to Haggard is typical of many such comments that he makes: 'I came back a week ago [to London] – I hate the place as much as ever, and have no craving for Society; a lot of people I don't want, and who don't want me. I envy Robinson Crusoe.'[27]

His personal and social diffidence translated into an insistence on his outsider status in relation to the subjects on which he wrote. In his letters it is often difficult to tell whether he considers himself a great writer and thinker or a talentless and shallow mind, and in his 1890 essay *How to Fail in Literature* (see Volume 2, pp. 275–90), the failure that he details is actually the description of a highly successful career not unlike his own. The tacking back and forth between these positions is found not just in his journalism but in his writings on other subjects too. In his historical and anthropological work he often stresses his amateur status and suggests that he has no real right to be intervening in the debate, while simultaneously asserting his position in confident terms and questioning the place of those apparently better qualified. In his correspondence this is also evident; a letter to his friend Anna Hills in 1891 is typical:

> I'm doing a book on Homer, and nobody will ever read it, even if I finish it.
> I have to do over again, and more systematically most that I did last year.
> This is dull work, and impels me to vivacities of expression about the
> German commentators. Of all the bustards, the blind owls, the German
> Homeric critic is the most bewilderingly imbecile. We were at a dance last
> night: I don't dance and I knew nobody (and do not wish to do either).[28]

He expresses lack of confidence in the eventual success of his work, switches to assertion of the stupidity of existing authorities and then drops immediately into a social scene that exactly mirrors the exclusion yet superiority of his scholarly position.

In the light of this, Lang's attitude to the institutions of culture is unsurprising. When, in the 1890s, there was agitation for the formation of an authoritative cultural body similar to the Académie française, Lang mocked the idea, yet in 1906 he accepted election to a Fellowship of the British Academy, which had finally been established in 1902. When the Academic Committee of the Royal Society of Literature was formed in 1910[29] Lang was among the original group selected (and he accepted), but he wrote to Clement Shorter; 'Thanks for electing me an Academician, but my place, if anywhere, is in the Anthropology lot',[30] while elsewhere he despairs that he will be remembered only for 'totems'.[31] Similarly, writing to Oliver Lodge after the Society for Psychical Research asked Lang to be their President for 1911, he makes light of his credentials for the job, suggesting that they amount only to his need for 'something' about which to 'jaw', and saying that he is 'a mere <u>littérateur</u> (as the hap'ny papers say)'.[32] It would seem that he used the range of his disciplinary interests to disclaim full membership of any of them, but it is exactly in this borderline position that the value of Lang's work appears. It also perhaps explains the lack of attention to his legacy; his refusal of allegiance meant that no school saw him as 'one of their own' and continued to tend to his memory.

Although public recognition continued to be offered and his writing continued at an enormous rate, in his last years Lang, who had always been physically rather frail, became much more so and seemingly beset with depression and anxiety. According to Marie Belloc Lowndes, Mrs Lang had found her husband's behaviour strange:

> He declared that awful calamities were about to befall Europe, and that almost everything for which he cared would be destroyed, especially university buildings and libraries. He further said the little money they possessed would probably be taken from them … even when he was dying, he had tried to make her promise she would leave the old world and settle in America.[33]

At the same time Charles Longman wrote to Haggard concerned for Lang's health and his 'strange depression about public affairs', particularly the strikes that were taking place.[34] The melancholic tendency noted by his friends and his often-stated aversion to 'politics' converged, with his wife claiming only two days after his death 'it was really the strikes that killed him.'[35] Whatever the personal reasons and political conservatism that this might show, it also shows that Lang recognised the change that was happening and saw the shape of the twentieth century: European wars, a greater social democracy and America as the future. Born on a geographical borderland, he died in a temporal one and his work illuminates much of the intellectual conditions of the emergence of the new world from the old.

On the death of his brother Lang wrote 'I know it is for the best, not to survive ourselves',[36] and that wish was almost fulfilled. His house in St Andrews has no plaques, there is no memorial to him, even his gravestone in the old cathedral precincts of St Andrews does not have his name on it. His vast body of work is little known and he is consistently relegated to the footnotes of all the disciplines in which he wrote. These two volumes of selections of his writings are an attempt to address that neglect and to enable his work to be read in a new light; one that shows him in a crucial place in turn-of-the-century intellectual life. Mindful of Saintsbury's prediction that a selection from Lang 'would be so unlikely to satisfy the selector that he would probably never get it finished', and given that a Complete Works would probably occupy about fifty volumes, much has necessarily been omitted from the current volumes. The principle of the selection has been to pick out the pieces most representative of Lang's originality and complexity, and to illustrate his position on contemporary topics of debate. We have not included any of Lang's own poetry or fictional writing, his newspaper leaders or reviews. He also wrote many essays on individual writers and, with the exception of the piece on Zola and the more general surveys in Volume 2, these too have been excluded. Enthusiasts of golf, cricket and fishing will be disappointed at the omission of his many pieces on those subjects. His journalism has been selected where it bears more directly on particular topics, such as Scotland or the business of writing, and where longer essays are also presented, but there remains a great deal of more general interest that does not appear here. A number of the longer pieces included have, in addition, been edited to eliminate repetition and to show the range of his ideas more clearly in relation to each other. It is our hope that the reader *will* be unsatisfied and so look further into the wealth of material that remains.

Andrew Teverson
Alexandra Warwick
Leigh Wilson

Introduction to Volume 1

In a column in the *Illustrated London News* in 1893 on the eerie effects of disturbing a Viking's bones, Andrew Lang begins:

> To aid in the Restoration of Superstition, what a glorious task that would be for a man! At various times, in various places, with some subtlety and tact, I hope, I have laboured towards this noble end. In the essay on 'Apparitions' in the *Encyclopaedia Britannica* I have attempted to place ghosts in a favourable light, for which some scientific characters have upbraided me. I have defended wraiths and fetches from the telepathic and far-fetched subjective hypothesis of the Psychical Society. 'A ghaist's a ghaist for a' that.'[1]

Here, in a column that constituted much of Lang's wider reputation during the last decades of the nineteenth century, his position is a strange one. He is resisting the disenchanting effects of research, learning and investigation – against the main thrust of nineteenth-century intellectual culture – yet has set out his stall to this effect in the *Encyclopaedia Britannica*, in which his entry on 'Apparitions' first appeared in the ninth edition (1875–89). This edition quickly became known as 'the scholar's edition' and was critically praised for its rigour and learning. The ninth edition was seen as an exemplar of nineteenth-century scholarship – methodical, sceptical, 'scientific' – yet Lang used it, he says here, to defend ghosts from science.

As the work included in this volume shows, Lang's relations to the discourses of science reveal a shifting and seemingly paradoxical attitude. Over and over again in his work on myth, folklore, the origins of religion and psychical research, Lang destroys his opponents (and sometimes his allies) by a precise and assiduous concern for the primacy of scientific method. He castigates them for their poor attention to detail, their lack of logic and their woolly methods. Neither James Frazer nor Alfred Russel Wallace, neither Grant Allen nor Anatole France, are spared his steely eye for lapses in logic and the misuse of evidence.[2] But, and with Lang there is often a 'but', so often he uses the methods of science to question what were becoming the fundamental assumptions of science. In his chapter 'Science and "Miracles"', in *The Making of Religion* (1898), Lang charts the 'scientific' approach to what he calls 'the X region' – the boundary where science and phenomena which so far have eluded scientific explanation meet – from ancient Greece onwards in order to reproach contemporary science for its failure to take these phenomena seriously. Lang takes apart Hume's argument in his 'Of Miracles' section in *An Enquiry Concerning Human Understanding* (1748) because he is 'guilty of denouncing the investigation of apparent facts. No attitude can be less scientific than his'.[3] His assertion throughout is that evidence has to be taken seriously, however uncomfortable or embarrassing it may be:

> We cannot now discard evidence as necessarily false because it clashes with our present ideas of the possible, when we have to acknowledge that the very same evidence may safely convey to us facts which clashed with our fathers' notions of what is possible, but which are now accepted. Our notions of the possible cease to be a criterion of truth or falsehood … [4]

Lang's work in the areas covered by this volume, then, seems to veer between an assertion of the marvellous and the miraculous for its own sake, beyond the abilities of science to prove or disprove, and an assertion that the methods of science are *the* way to assess everything that occurs, no matter how strange or unlikely.

The complex relation between facts, evidence and belief, between the empirical and the epistemological, between science and religion, between superstition and modernity which Lang's work so insistently reveals, has, in the last few years, returned to scholarly attention. This return has marked a growing sense that the nature and shape of these relations are not as settled as we had perhaps begun to assume.[5] The revisionism of recent scholarship has begun to see the complex and tangled nature of the relations between science and religion, fact and belief, the material and the marvellous, as productive rather than as merely the site of embarrassing error, and scholars have begun to insist, not just that the late nineteenth and early twentieth centuries can be seen as anxiously in denial about the nature of these relations, but that a number of important figures from the period themselves used to rich ends the entanglements between the modern and the non-modern, between science, religion and magic.

It is in this context, then, of a growing sense of the complexity of the relation between modernity and its supposed others, indeed of the growing sense that modernity itself is shot through with those very things against which it attempts to construct itself, that Lang's work in the areas covered in this volume can be considered significant. Taken in this context, what is most striking about Lang is his centrality to a number of the discourses of the late nineteenth century, such as anthropology, historical studies, folklore and psychical research, where the 'modern' and the 'non-modern' faced each other most starkly. What is more striking still is the extent to which Lang's insistences in all of these areas illuminate his profound interest in the nature of belief.

Lang's obsession with the nature, effects and shape of all kinds of beliefs differs from that of his fellow British anthropologists, however. For E. B. Tylor and Sir James Frazer, for instance, the encyclopaedic gathering and analysis of beliefs and the practices they provoke and justify are concerned with making distinctions between 'us' and 'them', between 'savage' and 'civilised', between non-modern and modern. For Frazer, the very practice of anthropology distinguishes the modern from the non-modern.[6] For Andrew Lang, however, the arena of magical beliefs, stories and phenomena, although in part presenting a fertile ground for intellectual ambition and prowess, also held out a challenge to modernity's busy, systematising project. While the variety of areas through which Lang concerned himself with anthropology were central to his reputation and were considered by him as consisting of his most important work, his engagement with the discipline constituted a challenge to its very basis. This can be seen in particular in the way that the different configurations and demands of the different areas within anthropology produced different effects and challenges in Lang's work, some of them contradictory.

Lang's interest in anthropology began while he was at St Andrews, where the records of his reading in the university library show a passion for accounts of past practices and beliefs, and in particular an interest in magic.[7] One of his earliest published essays, from 1863, in the university's undergraduate magazine, was titled 'Spiritualism Medieval and Modern'.[8] By end of his life his anthropology was, he believed, his most important contribution. In a letter to the literary critic Clement Shorter, he claimed that his place, 'if anywhere, is in the Anthropology lot'.[9] Lang's developing sense of the subject was fuelled by the very earliest attempts at legitimising it as a coherent academic and 'scientific' discipline. He read Tylor's book *Primitive Culture* (1871), one of the founding texts of the academic discipline of anthropology, the year after its original publication and met Tylor in the same year.[10] However, Lang's relation to Tylor was never one of uncritical disciple. In his essay on Tylor included in a collection to celebrate Tylor's 75th birthday, Lang implies, at best, that he took suggestions not followed through in Tylor's work and developed them and, at worst, that he disagreed with Tylor. A mixture of the two can be seen in particular in Lang's attitude to Tylor's position on the relation between 'savage' practices and beliefs and contemporary spiritualism:

With his habitual caution and open-mindedness, Mr. Tylor remarked that a careful and scientific observation of some of the new or revived marvels 'would seem apt to throw light on some most interesting psychological questions', beyond the scope of his inquiry ... Mr. Tylor's affair was to discover great numbers of ethnological parallels to the *speciosa miracula* of spiritualism, and to leave the matter there for the present; while the savage animistic explanation led up to the whole vast subject of Animism.[11]

However, in his later work, when Lang took issue with some of Tylor's central claims, he did still acknowledge Tylor as his model and Tylor's work as instituting the most authoritative and systematic methods of the subject. In *The Making of Religion* (1898), for example, Lang acknowledges that some anthropology deserves the criticism levelled against it by the philologist Friedrich Max Müller, and that it 'is mainly for this reason that the arguments presently to follow are strung on the thread of Mr. Tylor's truly learned and accurate book, "Primitive Culture."'[12] As an anthropologist, then, from the very beginning Lang maintained a complex and ambiguous relation to the discipline.

At the same time, at the heart of Lang's contribution to anthropology was his insistence on the comparative method begun by Tylor, which asserted that material from cultures separated by time and space could be used together to understand and explain human behaviour. Lang defends the comparative method as logical and scientific in a number of places and across a range of his interests, but his central question when using the method was always around what people believed and why. Lang's sense of the importance of belief differs from that of Tylor and the other early anthropologists. For Lang, the beliefs that people shared across time and space were more significant than those which divided them. These questions over sameness and difference, over what divided different human cultures and what they shared, can be seen at the very beginning of anthropology as a discipline. Its origin, while clearly enmeshed with colonialism, also contains this assertion of a shared humanity. The Ethnological Society of London (ESL), founded in 1843, was descended from the Aborigines Protection League – founded six years before – whose motto was *ab uno sanguine*, 'of one blood'.[13]

The work of one of the central figures of the ESL, James Cowles Prichard, an Evangelical Anglican from Quaker stock, asserted 'monogenism' against the increasingly influential 'polygenism'. This was in part so that his account could accord with those in the Old Testament[14] – all human beings must necessarily be the descendants of Adam and Eve – but its effect was also to assert, as Henrika Kuklick tells us, a challenging account of human difference and sameness:

Prichard initially thought original humans were persons of colour, and linked skin lightening to elevated behavioural standards; ultimately, he speculated that racial variations might be associated with different environments. Regardless, he consistently sought to trace humans' dispersion and establish relationships among populations, relying primarily on linguistic affinities.[15]

Here, racist assumptions – the linking of lightened skin and 'civilised' behaviour – are entwined with an assertion of a common humanity which challenged the idea that humans could belong to different 'races'.

The effects and outcomes of the ESL position were thrown into relief by the founding, in 1863, of the Anthropological Society of London (ASL). The ASL expounded polygenism, was anti-Darwinian in that it rejected the role of environment in the development of species, and its central members were, politically, the antithesis of the ESL's liberal reformism. The ASL backed the South in the American Civil War, and backed Governor Eyre's brutal suppression of an uprising by black farmers in Jamaica in 1866.[16] The ASL and ESL were amalgamated in 1871 to make the Anthropological Institute of Great Britain and Ireland, with John Lubbock as President. This amalgamation on the whole represented the victory of the ESL, and pre-pared a place institutionally for what Kuklick calls 'a core idea of late-nine-teenth-century anthropology – the "psychic unity" of all varieties of hu-mankind'.[17] However, as Kuklick goes on to suggest, while the idea that human beings constitute a single species was becoming the orthodoxy in anthropology in the second half of the nineteenth century, ideas of what constituted the most important kinds of similarity shifted away from Prichard's assertion of common ancestors. For Prichard, resemblances be-tween human groups 'revealed processes of diffusion', whereas for Tylor they 'instead emphasized similarities resulting from independent invention', par-ticularly in non-modern cultures.[18] Lang shared Tylor's position, arguing for a 'solution in original, independent, and coincidental invention', rather than the 'theories of unity of race' espoused by 'popular writers' – a group Lang always disdained.[19] But here too Lang's work is paradoxical; he is both more credulous and more materialist than his anthropological peers. His belief that humans are always the same is not in the end to do with either essence or biology, but rather he asserts again and again that, in given material cir-cumstances, people will do and believe the same things.[20] Lang acknowl-edged that Tylor made it possible to see that 'savages' are as human as 'we' are, and repeatedly he asserted that early man was already a philosopher, artist and full human being.[21] While he shared the revisions Tylor made to Prichard's arguments, then, Lang retained the underlying sense that human beings shared something vital, and this made it impossible for him to follow many of the evolutionary 'laws' deduced by anthropologists from their evi-dence. Indeed, Lang's scepticism towards totalising theories, his insistence on the centrality of facts and his developing sense of a different relation between early culture and the modern produced his most important inter-ventions in the developing discipline – that is, his challenge to the philolog-ical theories of Max Müller and to both the 'ghost theory' of Herbert Spencer and Tylor's theory of animism.

Folklore, myth and fairy tale

As with his interest in anthropology more generally, Lang's interest in folk-lore was already in evidence whilst he was a student at St Andrew's University. In April 1863, in the first volume of the *St Andrew's University Magazine*, he published two narratives, both in Scottish dialect, that he had collected 'as a boy' from his maternal great aunt, Margaret Craig of Darliston in Elgin: 'Rashin Coatie', a 'Scotch *Cinderella*', in which an ill-treated heroine mar-ries a prince with the help of a red calf she has been given by her dead mother; and 'Nicht, Nought, Nothing', a 'Scotch *Jason*', in which a young man is aided in his escape from a giant by the giant's own daughter.[22] Throughout the 1860s and the early 1870s, moreover, Lang was reading widely in French popular culture and ballad-lore, a period of study that culminated in his collection of poems modelled on traditional French poetry, *Ballads and Lyrics of Old France* (1872), and his long essay published in the first volume of *The Folk-Lore Record*, 'The Folk-Lore of France' (1878). Together, these early publications testify to the younger Lang's interest in national folklores (of Scotland and France respectively) and to a passion for the collection and recording of items of original folklore. Simultaneously, however, Lang was also becoming interested in anthropological arguments about the universal, and therefore transnational, characteristics of folklore, and in the extent to which folklore collection was expressive of universal motifs, rather than national particularities. It was these latter interests, as Richard Dorson observes, that increasingly dominated Lang's writing on the subject, and that formed the basis of his major contributions to Victorian folkloristics: the essay collection *Custom and Myth* (1884), his introduction to Margaret Hunt's translation *Grimms' Household Tales*, 'Household Tales; Their Origin, Diffusion, and Relations to the Higher Myths' (1884), and his two-volume opus *Myth, Ritual and Religion* (1887).

In these works of the 1880s, Lang began to explore, and to supply an-swers for, what he regarded as the principle questions confronting folklorists in the late nineteenth century, as formulated in the essay 'Household Tales': How can the international diffusion of traditional tales of similar types be explained? What is the origin of popular traditional tales? And how is it possible to explain the distinctive continuities between the plots and inci-dents found in folk tales and those found in Medieval Romances and Greek and Vedic mythological texts?[23] Several theories purporting to solve these problems were already current when Lang entered the field of enquiry, but two in particular had gained a general currency: firstly, the theory proposed by the German Sanskrit scholar Theodor Benfey in the introduction to his translation of the *Panchatantra* (1859), and later developed by the French folklorist Emmanuel Cosquin in his introduction to *Contes populaires de Lorraine* (1887), that all folk tales had originated in India, and been spread throughout the world as a result of slow transmission; and secondly, the theory introduced by the Grimms, and later elaborated by the German philologist Friedrich Max Müller, that folk tales were the degenerate remains of a mythological system developed by the Aryan ancestors of Indo-European peoples.[24] According to the former theory, folk tales had a single place of origin (India) and had been disseminated initially as a result of migration and textual transmission. According to the latter, folk tales had originated in a single culture and had been spread throughout the Indo-European region when the Aryan tribes had dispersed.[25] Lang staked his claim in mythological studies by contesting both of these reigning arguments. He rejected the theory of Indian origin on the basis that many of the tale types that are supposed to have originated in India can also be shown to exist in cultures and at periods when they could not have been borrowed from Indian sources. The presence of folk tales in the surviving literature of ancient Egypt, for instance, or in the '*Märchen* of Homeric Greece', supply clear evidence for Lang that India was not the sole or even primary reservoir of folk tales, rather that such tales had always been widely dispersed.[26] This argument is made concisely by Lang in the conclusion of his introduction to the *contes* of Perrault:

> [The] Indian theory ... correctly states that many stories were introduced into Europe, Asia, and Africa from India, in the middle ages, but brings no proof that *contes* could only have been invented in India, first of all. Nor does it account for the stories which were old in Egypt, and even mixed up with the national mythology of Egypt, before we knew anything about India at all ... [I]t is not shown that the *ideas* in the *contes* are peculiar to India; almost the only example adduced is the *gratitude of beasts*. But this notion might occur to any mind, anywhere, which regarded the beasts as on the same intellectual and moral level as humanity. Moreover, a few examples have been found of *Märchen* among American races, for example, in early Peru, where there is no reason to believe that they were introduced by the Spaniards.[27]

Lang also contests Cosquin's efforts to trace specific narrative types to an Indian source. In his introduction to Perrault's tales he pokes fun at Cosquin's efforts to claim an Indian origin for 'Puss in Boots' solely on the basis that the moral of the story seems faintly 'Buddhistic';[28] and in his introduction to an edition of William Adlington's translation of Apuleius's story of Cupid and Psyche, *The Most Pleasant and Delectable Tale of the Marriage of Cupid and Psyche* (1887), he opposes Cosquin's contention that versions of the tale type found in India supply certain evidence that 'India was the birthplace of the primitive form of *Cupid and Psyche*, and that where the tale occurs elsewhere, it has been borrowed from India of the historic period'.[29] Such precise identification, Lang avers, is impossible, and cannot be supported by any firm evidence:

> It will be enough for us to try to detect the oldest *ideas* that occur in the tale, to exhibit them as they inspire the *incidents*, and to seek for the origin of the ideas in certain demonstrable conditions of human intellect, human manners, and human society. Beyond this it would be desirable, were it possible, to

trace the wanderings of the legend from its original birthplace (if that could be discovered), or to show that the essential parts of the narrative might (at a certain stage of human culture) have been separately invented anywhere.[30]

In parallel with his contestation of the ideas of Benfey and Cosquin, Lang also tackled the arguments of the Aryanists – particularly the contention advanced by Müller that folk tales were the degraded remains of once coherent Aryan mythologies that encoded the now obscured and forgotten sun worship of these distant ancestors. This contention of Müller's was first disputed by Lang in his inaugural essay on folklore theory, 'Mythology and Fairy Tales' which appeared in the *Fortnightly Review* in May 1873.[31] Here Lang proposed that Müller's core thesis that *Märchen* are the 'detritus' of the 'higher mythology' of the Aryan race founders on the evidence produced by contemporary anthropologists.[32] In folk tales collected by anthropologists and ethnographers, Lang argues, recurrent 'references to Shamanism, to cannibalism, to kinship with the beasts' are an indication that these fictions have emerged from savage societies in which these practices and beliefs had been shown to be current.[33] In myths and sagas, by contrast, these beliefs and practices are relatively rare or have been obscured, indicating that these fictions are later developments, in which savage elements have gradually been omitted by virtue of the narrative's passage 'through the refining atmosphere of a higher civilisation'.[34] On this basis, Lang proposes, the empirical data indicates that folk tales emerge first, and myths evolve from folk tales in the course of the progress of civilisation from a low state of savagery to the state of advancement reflected in classical Greek and Vedic culture, and not, as Müller had proposed, the other way round.

These ideas were restated by Lang six years later in the preface he was asked to write to the second volume of the *Folk-Lore Record* (subsequently the *Folk-Lore Journal*). Here Lang defines the 'science of Folk-Lore' precisely as the examination of 'the things that are the oldest, and most permanent, and most widely distributed, in human institutions' and proceeds to outline his core ideas:

> Man started from a savage origin, in a savage state he gave his fancy free play, and devised many curious and cumbrous rites. As he rose to civilisation he never wholly laid aside anything he had once acquired. His barbarous legends were polished into epics and national traditions, his rude ritual became the basis of a more polished cult. But all men did not advance with equal rapidity, and the peasant class retained something very much nearer the old savage legends than the cultivated and elaborate myths. These peasant legends survived as *märchen* in the mouths of old nurses, and even now, while they often resemble in plot and incident the greater myths of Greece, retain a still closer likeness to the legends of Zulus and Bechuanas.[35]

'If this view be correct,' he adds:

> the germ of Greek and other great mythologies is to be sought in the known qualities of the savage fancy, and in the habits of the savage mind, not in a

fancied stage of society in which everybody spoke allegorically about the sun and the clouds, and then forgot the meaning of what he had said.[36]

This final thrust at Müller's ideas unmistakably announced that the Folk-Lore Society and its journal were to be broadly anthropological in orientation rather than Aryanist. It also heralded a period of intensive scholarly attack by Lang upon solar mythology in all its manifestations. This attack began with the essay 'Mr. Max Müller's Philosophy of Mythology' in *Fraser's Magazine* for August 1881, in which Lang takes issue with the solar mythologist's focus upon the etymology of the names of mythological characters. One of Müller's principal methods had been to subject the names of mythological characters to philological analysis with a view to demonstrating that these characters originally represented a solar phenomenon. Thus he argues in the essay 'Comparative Mythology' that the figure of Urvasi in the Vedas represents the coming of day because her name can be shown to derive from the Sanskrit words meaning 'widely pervading', which Müller identifies as an epithet of the dawn.[37] Lang's response is to point out that the stories under analysis exist in multiple forms in multiple cultures, and in many cases have protagonists with different names. This being the case, he asks rhetorically of Müller: 'How are you to be certain that the story was *originally* told of the god or hero whose name you analyse by the aid of philology?'[38]

Lang restates this argument three years later in *Custom and Myth,* and extends it further to accommodate not just the work of Müller but that of other key mythologists of the day who sought to use philology to discover nature myths in traditional tales. Here Lang points particularly to the fact that the philological interpreters of myths, using the same methods on the same materials, come up with divergent results: Müller sees the myth of Urvasi and Pururavas in the *Rig Veda* as a narrative that 'expresses the identity of the morning dawn and the evening twilight'; Adalbert Kuhn sees the same story as a fire myth; Rudolf von Roth discovers a sexual allegory.[39] Lang concludes:

> No better example could be given to illustrate the weakness of the
> philological method, … Kuhn sees fire everywhere, and fire-myths; Mr.
> Müller sees dawn and dawn-myths; [Wilhelm] Schwartz sees storm and
> storm-myths, and so on. As the orthodox teachers are thus at variance, so
> … there is no safety in orthodoxy.[40]

In the same year this position is restated in the essay 'Household Tales', which takes as its focus the arguments of both Müller and his English disciple George William Cox, who adopted and to some extent adapted Müller's ideas in his two-volume opus *The Mythology of the Aryan Nations* (1870). In this long essay, Lang expresses what is arguably at the heart of his disagreement with the Aryanists: that their system is highly speculative, lacks the surety of verification by objective data and ignores the existence of much more reliable data upon popular traditional materials that was being supplied in increasing quantities by anthropologists, ethnologists and folklorists working in the field. It is this position that Lang revisits in various forms over the next fifteen years, most prominently in the chapter on 'Heroic and Romantic Myths' in *Myth, Ritual and Religion* (1899) (which also restates and extends the arguments concerning Benfey and Cosquin's theory), and in the late book *Modern Mythology* (1897), written in reply to Müller's critique of 'the ideas and methods of the anthropological school of mythologists' in *Contributions to the Science of Mythology* (1897).[41] By this point, however, the argument against Müller had long since been established and won, and Lang's energies seem misdirected – as he appears to concede in the opening sentence of the work when he notes that '[i]t may well be doubted whether works of controversy serve any useful purpose'.[42]

Philological analysis and solar theory never recovered from their critique by Lang.[43] From the publication in 1856 of Müller's seminal essay 'Comparative Mythology' until the appearance of Cox's vast and eloquent summation of the Aryan position in 1870, the school of Müller had dominated mythological studies. By the late 1880s, however, after the publication of Lang's *Custom and Myth* and 'Household Tales', there were few mythologists still willing to endorse the solar argument. There is no more eloquent testimony to this development, Eric Lawrence Montenyohl observes, than the fact that when the editors of the ninth edition of the *Encyclopaedia Britannica* were looking for a contributor to write the entry on 'Mythology' it was not Müller they asked, as they almost certainly would have done a decade earlier, but Lang.[44] The answers to the 'sphinx of popular tales' provided by solar mythology were discredited, and in their place were the answers given by Lang: first, that folk tales originate when society is at a savage stage of its development and reflect the ideas and customs that predominate at that stage; second, that folk tales are disseminated throughout the world in part (but not solely) because all societies pass through similar stages of culture, and so develop similar codifications of savage rites; and third, that folk tales are primary narrative forms and evolve first into 'household tales' and later into the 'higher mythologies' as societies become more civilised and, in the process of civilisational advancement, successively remove savage elements from their storytelling.[45]

In formulating his arguments about folklore and myth Lang relied heavily upon ideas about society and culture being developed by nineteenth-century anthropologists such as Tylor and J. F. McLennan ('without the work of Mr. Tylor and Mr. McLennan,' Lang acknowledged, 'the whole hypothesis would never have occurred to me'[46]). One idea in particular derives directly from these sources: the central hypothesis upon which Lang's method rests, that all societies pass through the same stages of culture in a progressive development from 'savagery' through 'barbarism' towards 'civilisation'. Tylor supplies the seminal expression of this theory of 'cultural evolution' in

Primitive Culture (1871), in which, after caveats and qualifications, he proposes that:

> the savage state in some measure represents an early condition of mankind, out of which the higher culture has gradually developed or evolved, by processes still in regular operation as of old, the result showing that, on the whole, progress has far prevailed over relapse.[47]

From this core proposition there follows a further concept that Lang also borrows from Tylor: the doctrine of 'survivals', which holds that there are certain elements of savage practice which survive into the periods of civilisation, where, out of their original context, their meaning becomes obscure.[48] The role of the anthropologist when confronted by such survivals in the modern world, Tylor argued, was to compare them with equivalent practices at the earlier stages of culture in order to reconstruct their original meanings.[49]

While elsewhere in his work, and in particular in his psychical research, as we shall see, Lang implicitly challenged Tylor's version of the 'survival', from this comparative practice derives Lang's 'method of folklore' as expressed in *Custom and Myth*. When 'an apparently irrational and anomalous custom' is encountered in the mythology of a civilised nation, Lang argues, the folklorist seeking to explain this custom should look for equivalent practices in savage communities 'where the practice is no longer irrational and anomalous, but in harmony with the manners and ideas of the people among whom it prevails'.[50] The explanation of the custom in its savage context may then be given as a rationale for the origin of the same, apparently inexplicable, custom in the civilised country, on the assumption that the civilised country has at some point in its past been through the same stage of culture as the savage tribe and developed the custom for similar reasons. Thus, to explain the proposed sacrifice of Phrixus and Hellê in the story of Jason and the Golden Fleece, Lang compares this episode in the myth to equivalent episodes in Samoyed, Epirote and Zulu folk tales, each of which involve the threat of cannibalism, and argues that these paradigms reveal that the sacrificial threat in the Greek tale must be a 'survival' from a savage stage of culture when cannibalism was practised.[51] Similarly in *Custom and Myth*, to explain the prohibition against the bride seeing the bridegroom in the Greek tale of Cupid and Psyche, Lang compares the narrative motif as it appears in Lucius Apuleius's *Metamorphoses* with equivalent motifs in stories from Breton, Ojibway, Zulu and Welsh folk traditions and argues that these latter reveal that the motif must first have arisen to illustrate, sanction or caution against breaking a primitive 'law of nuptial etiquette'.[52] '[W]e think it a reasonable hypothesis,' Lang concludes, 'that tales on the pattern of "Cupid and Psyche" might have been evolved wherever a curious nuptial taboo required to be sanctioned, or explained, by a myth.'[53]

Many of the assumptions Lang makes in developing his method of folklore are subject to the same criticisms that have been made of Tylor's brand of 'cultural evolutionism' from within the discipline of anthropology. This critique was first made by Franz Boas in an article for *Science* titled 'The Limitations of the Comparative Method of Anthropology' published in December 1896.[54] Lang is not mentioned by name here – Boas focuses primarily upon the prominent anthropologists D. G. Brinton, Adolf Bastian, Herbert Spencer and Tylor – but the arguments made can readily be applied to Lang's approach to folklore. Boas begins the article by summarising the core beliefs of the comparativist school: that common traits (or 'analoga') in different cultures supply evidence of 'the uniform working of the human mind', which notion implies the possibility of discovering a coherent set of 'laws ... which govern the development of society'.[55] 'The point of view is taken,' Boas writes,

> that if an ethnological phenomenon has developed independently in a
> number of places its development has been the same everywhere; or,
> expressed in a different form, that the same ethnological phenomena are
> always due to the same causes. This leads to the still wider generalisation
> that the sameness of ethnological phenomena found in diverse regions is
> proof that the human mind obeys the same laws everywhere.[56]

These generalisations, however, are according to Boas open to 'a very fundamental objection:' that '[e]ven the most cursory review shows that the same phenomena may develop in a multitude of ways'.[57] For instance, comparative observation reveals that diverse primitive societies use geometrical designs in art; but anthropological research within the societies that use these designs demonstrates that the designs have developed in different ways for different reasons: that they have 'originated either from naturalistic forms which were gradually conventionalised or from technical motives, or that they were primarily geometrical or that they were derived from symbols'.[58] 'From all these sources the same forms have developed,' Boas concludes, so they cannot be regarded as essentially comparable phenomenon. This critique of the assumption of the fundamental comparability of similar phenomenon by Boas also extends to the assumption that it is possible to discover 'the laws and the history of the evolution of human society'.[59] For the comparativists,

> [t]he fact that many fundamental features of culture are universal, or at least
> occur in many isolated places, interpreted by the assumption that the same
> features must always have developed from the same causes, leads to the
> conclusion that there is one grand system according to which mankind has
> developed everywhere; that all the occurring variations are no more than
> minor details in this grand uniform evolution[60]

If the principle that the same phenomena are always due to the same causes is abandoned, however, then this assumption must also be abandoned, and 'ingenious attempts at constructions of a grand system of the evolution of society' must be regarded as being 'of very doubtful value'.[61] In its place, Boas proposes an alternative method of proceeding – a method that was to do for Tylor's brand of cultural evolutionism what Lang had done for solar mythology: guarantee its near total eclipse. 'We have a method, which in many respects is much safer,' Boas announces:

> A detailed study of customs in their bearings to the total culture of the tribe practicing them, and in connection with an investigation of their geographical distribution among neighbouring tribes, afford us almost always a means of determining with considerable accuracy the historical causes that led to the formations of the customs in question and to the psychological processes that were at work in their development.[62]

Within the discipline of anthropology, this critique of the endeavour to discover 'a grand system of evolution of society' has subsequently been broadened to suspicion of all attempts to argue for ahistorical and universal patterns of transformation across cultures. Anthropologists would now widely agree that society does not change in uniform or homogeneous ways, neither does it 'progress' in a unilinear manner; rather, change in societies must be understood as a complex phenomenon that arises from specific historical conditions. Ideas of unilinear progression, moreover, become profoundly problematic if they are used, as they were widely in the nineteenth century, to reinforce culturally imperialist discourses concerning the superiority of 'western civilisation' over so-called 'savage' or 'primitive' peoples. Lang's relationship to such arguments is tangential and ill-defined. In some ways his arguments work to puncture European cultural suprem-acism by pointing to continuities between European culture and the culture of Native Americans or Aboriginal Australians. In other respects, however, Lang's belief in ascribing relative values to cultures that he conceives to be at different stages of development – as, for instance, when he draws a dis-tinction between 'the civilised races' and 'the lower races of South America, and other worse than barbaric peoples' – clearly endorses the kinds of thinking that were being used in other circles to justify and legitimatise the imperial mission.[63]

Two further, and related, reservations about Lang's approach to folklore arise from anthropological critiques of the comparative method. The first, emerging directly from Boas's charge that comparitivists underestimate the importance of specific histories, is that Lang's method seeks to emphasise superficial similarities between folkloric practices at the expense of under-standing the cultural specificities of those practices and their relation to the cultural identity of the group more generally.[64] Lang's treatment of the Scottish tale 'Nicht, Nought, Nothing' that he himself had collected from Margaret Craig is a case in point. Some thirty years after he had first pub-lished this story, Lang observed in passing that it had a fascinating Scottish genealogy. Margaret Craig's family was Lowland Scottish, he recalled, 'con-nected with the Craigs of Riccarton':

> But, behind Miss Craig, comes the Celtic figure of Miss Nelly McWilliam,
> whose young romance was stained with loyal blood in the Forty-Five. Miss
> Nelly was the family heroine, a *Celte Celtisante*, and it would not be
> surprising if these particular versions of two tales came into a Lowland Scots
> household from a Celtic source.[65]

The stories, for Lang, thus tell a tale about the Scottish past: they identify continuities between Lowland tradition and its Highland roots, and
they forge a connection with a history of Jacobite struggle against the
English throne. Yet when Lang came to write about this story in his essay
'A Far-Travelled Tale' in *Custom and Myth* (1884), there was no mention
of Miss Nelly McWilliam, the *Celte Celtisante*, or the revolt of Forty-Five,
only of the story's international distribution, and the likelihood that it had
been spread around the world as a result of human migration.[66] The reason
for this is not hard to determine: Lang neglected to investigate the story's
associations with Scottish history and culture because the theoretical orientation of his scholarship disinclined him to emphasise national and cultural
particularity and led him instead towards the abstraction of items of folklore
from their cultural contexts. As a Scot and a folklore collector, he was passionately interested in local items of folk narrative such as those provided
by Margaret Craig; but as a folklore theorist his primary objective was to
prove, in Dorson's words, that 'folklore in all cultures develops along much
the same lines,' and so cannot be, in its essentials, different from nation to
nation.[67] Such was his desire to win the argument for his anthropological
approach that he allowed the latter argument to overwhelm and obscure
his interests in particular cultural identities.

The second objection to Lang's folklore method that arises from critiques of Tylor's anthropological theory is that, in locating the meaning of
elements of tradition in a savage past that has been outgrown, Lang effectively argues that these elements of tradition do not have meaning for society in the present. Folklore in the so-called civilised nations is, according
to Lang's method, a vestigial remainder of a social reality that has passed.
Yet most folklorists now would see items of folklore not as a set of dead
relics, but as a living practice. They would also regard the survival of folkloric practice as evidence of the fact that these practices continue to be
socially meaningful. Survival, in short, is an indication of persistent relevance, not of protracted obsolescence. This objection to Lang's argument
was broached relatively early on by Joseph Jacobs, in a reflection upon
interpretations of 'Cinderella' at the International Folk-Lore Congress of
1891. Initially Jacobs praises Lang, as the president of the Congress he was
addressing, for his annihilation of the solar mythological school's interpretations of the story. Having stated his praise, however, Jacobs proceeds to
argue that Lang, 'while getting rid of one substituted bride' had 'only succeeded in introducing another false claimant':

> Anthropology takes the place nowadays that Mythology once usurped, and the poor Folk-tale is set the task of finding 'survivals' for her envious sister Anthropology. We are to study *Cinderella* on this method in order to discover traces of the old manorial custom of Borough English, in which the youngest child, and not the eldest, succeeds, or to find traces of animal metamorphosis, or to find other things interesting enough in their way, but having extremely little to do with *Cinderella* as a tale. Now, all these 'survivals' are of interest in their way; I am even guilty myself of having written something on Borough English in some of the most ancient of folk-tales. But to study *them* is not to study the tale … [68]

Instead Jacobs makes a case that the meaning of folklore lies not in the past, but in the present; that the folklorist can learn as much about folklore from the contemporary music hall as he can from 'survivals'.[69] Jacobs's argument here would later find magnification in the work of Bronislaw Malinowski who, in the 1930s contested the doctrine of survivals on the basis that 'customs, institutions or moral values' in societies are rarely of a 'necrotic or irrelevant character', but persist because they have a current, living function for the society in which they are found.[70]

This objection to Lang's method of folklore draws attention to a degree of conflict between his theoretical work as an anthropological folklorist of the comparative school and his practice as an occasional folklore collector and as a mediator of folk and fairy tales for the reading public in late nineteenth- and early twentieth-century Britain. There is surely some irony in the fact that Lang, who championed the view that the meaning of folklore should be sought in the savage stages of man's journey, also did more than any other individual of his age to make folk tales and fairy tales meaningful and relevant for his contemporaries.[71] In 1889 he published his first anthology of tales, *The Blue Fairy Book*, containing thirty-seven stories taken from various sources, but primarily from the collections of Grimm, Charles Perrault, Marie-Catherine d'Aulnoy, Antoine Galland, Robert Chambers, Jorgen Moe and Peter Asbjornsen, and the English chapbook tradition.[72] This collection was followed in 1890 by *The Red Fairy Book* published, like the *Blue,* for the Christmas market, and this contained a further thirty-seven stories, this time with a number of more unusual folk tales, such as the stories 'The Norka' and 'The Death of Koschei the Deathless', both taken from W. R. S. Ralston's English translation of Alexander Afanas'ev's collection of Russian folk tales. Ten further fairy books had ensued by 1910 (up to *Lilac*) – establishing Lang's status as the primary mediator of popular narrative tradition for late-Victorian and Edwardian readers. He also published five works of fiction of his own that were strongly influenced by folklore:[73] a picture-book titled *The Princess Nobody, A Tale of Fairyland* (1884), for which the text was devised by Lang to complement a series of paintings by the illustrator Richard Doyle;[74] a children's novella set in the borders in the sixteenth century about transactions with fairy-folk titled *The Gold of Fairnilee* (1888); and three parodic works, influenced by W. M.

Thackeray's *The Rose and the Ring* (1855), about the imaginary Kingdom of Pantouflia: *Prince Prigio* (1889), *Prince Ricardo of Pantouflia* (1893) and *Tales of a Fairy Court* (1907). Both Lang's fairy anthologies and his Pantouflia books (published together as *The Chronicles of Pantouflia* in 1932) enjoyed considerable success in the late nineteenth and early twentieth centuries. Nearly 70,000 copies of *The Blue Fairy Book* had been printed by Lang's death, and 60,000 of the *Red*; and both collections, but especially the *Blue*, had received enthusiastic reviews.[75] Lang's Pantouflia trilogy also sold rapidly, and was still selling rapidly well into the next century, as Roger Lancelyn Green records:

> The bookshops at Christmas 1943 displayed whole shelves of the latest reprint of *Chronicles of Pantouflia* – shelves that were not full for many days; while 1945 had exhausted the newly-illustrated edition of *Prince Prigo* some months before the year's end.[76]

In each case, however, Lang presented these works as if they were distractions, 'old things' made in the interests purely of entertainment. Time and again in his prefaces to the fairy books, Lang emphasises the durability of the folk or fairy tale, but simultaneously disclaims their relevance to the present. The fairy books were published for children, he says, because they were invented by savages when the world was young, and 'children … represent the young age of man.' [77] Likewise, Lang presents *The Gold of Fairnilee*, in a letter to Henry Rider Haggard , as 'only a lot of childish reminiscences of old times in a better place than 1 Marloes Road'.[78] The significance of such folkloric fiction is, in other words, for states that are early and outgrown, and if they do remain significant for adults, they remain significant because they remind adults of their childhood, just as romance functions to remind modern man of his distant past, not to engage him with current affairs.[79] This attitude is in part a result of Lang's self-presentation as a talented amateur; but the view also coincides with his understanding of the functions of folklore as it is presented in *Custom and Myth*: that it held meaning for a savage (or childish) mindset, but had become recondite in the civilised world, still to be enjoyed because of the 'ancestral barbarism of our natures', but fundamentally of the past in significance.[80] The success of Lang's fairy-tale project, however, clearly contradicts this denial of relevance. In fact, Lang's books were popular not because fairy tales are the universally durable entertainment of the primitive and the young, but because they struck specific chords with the present. One instance of this is given by Sara Hines in her essay 'Collecting Empire: Andrew Lang's Fairy Books (1889–1910)'. Here Hines argues that Lang's efforts to collate and hold together the narratives of many nations spoke directly to the imperial imagination at the end of the nineteenth century.[81] Another instance of the immediacy of Lang's uses of fairy tales may be found in his novel the *Gold of Fairnilee*, in which border transitions between the world of humans and the world of fairies are echoed in, and so become a means of negotiating, parallel transitions over the English and Scottish border. The significance of such an investigation of border identities for Lang himself, as a man of the borders, must at the very least cast doubt upon his assertion that the novel has no current relevance for the inhabitants of 1 Marloes Road. In these respects, we witness a disjunction between Lang's ideas about fairy tale and his achievements as a practitioner. As a theorist he follows Tylor in projecting the meaning of folklore into the distant past and identifying its persistence into the present as an act of survival; as a practitioner, he invests items of popular tradition with current meanings and current value, and he shows that the meaning of elements of tradition is to be found in the specific culture and the specific contexts within which those elements have purchase. It is almost certainly for this latter reason, and not because of the eternal durability of the folk tale, that Lang flourished as a folklorist and a fairy tale writer. It is also for this reason that his practice as a folklorist still speaks powerfully today of the later Victorian era.

The origins of religion

Lang's relations to the idea of survivals and to the assumptions of cultural evolutionism more generally are perhaps even more complex in the areas of anthropology that follow most closely from Tylor's own work, that is, in his work on the origins of religion and in his assessment of the continuity of psychical phenomena from early cultures into the present. As is acknowledged in a popularising work by Grant Allen – the kind of work so often disparaged by Lang – by the 1890s an assumption that the origin and development of religious belief and practices was now fully accounted for had spread beyond anthropological circles to the lay reader. In 1893 Allen asserted as 'proved almost beyond the possibility of doubt Mr. Herbert Spencer's luminous theory of the origin of polytheism from ghost worship and ancestor worship'.[82] Lang's most important anthropological contribution during the 1890s, however, and arguably until his death, was his assertion that such theories, rather than finally illuminating religion's origins, in fact were guilty of ignoring many of the facts. Lang's work in this area was seen as important at the time for suggesting that all was not solved in relation to these questions, and is significant too for the revealing ways it negotiates late nineteenth-century science's assertions around the relation between facts and the truth. Lang's work on the origins of religion, and his interest in psychical research that is so closely allied to it, challenges rather than accepts Tylor's 'survivals' and uses the past precisely to challenge assumptions about the present.

Spencer first articulated his 'ghost theory' in an article for the *Fortnightly Review* in 1870, and then set it out more fully in volume 1 of his *Principles of Sociology* (which appeared in three volumes, published between 1874 and

1896). Spencer argued that those things that seemed unaccountable and absurd in 'savage' beliefs and practices in fact show that people in early and traditional societies thought logically with the material at their disposal. He suggested that savage beliefs and practices – hallucinations, possession, the belief in the animation of the inanimate, and the belief in spirits – had their origin in traditional people's observation of the dead and of reflections in water, and in their experience of altered states of consciousness. All of these led early people to assume that humans have a 'second personality', a double, distinct from the physical body, which survives death and can travel across distance and time.[83] This 'ghost theory', then, provides the basis of all beliefs in non-material beings and occurrences for Spencer, and for him constitutes the origin of religious belief per se. Belief in this double and its consequences evolved, he argues, eventually into what anthropology defined as religious belief.

At around the same time as Spencer fully elaborated his theory in the *Principles of Sociology*, Tylor was arguing too in *Primitive Culture* for a version of the ghost theory. His concept of 'Animism' describes 'the deep-lying doctrine of Spiritual Beings, which embodies the very essence of the Spiritualistic as opposed to Materialistic philosophy'.[84] Tylor asserted explicitly that animism underlay all religious belief, calling it 'the groundwork of the Philosophy of Religion, from that of savages to that of civilized men'.[85] For Tylor too the beginnings of animism were in early people's misunderstanding of dreams, abnormal states of consciousness and dead bodies.[86] In both Spencer and Tylor, these accounts of the origins of religious belief were set, sometimes explicitly and sometimes more implicitly, within an evolutionary model which saw 'progress' from magical beliefs, through religious belief, and finally arriving at science's true view of the world.[87] For Spencer and Tylor, and later James Frazer, magical and religious beliefs *were* rooted in facts, but in the misreading of them, and this changed only when science, the result of progress in human understanding, could eventually read these facts correctly.

In Lang's earlier work in anthropology, in *Custom and Myth* (1884) and the first edition of *Myth, Ritual and Religion* (1887), he was still taking the ghost theory for granted. However, by the early 1890s there is evidence that he was beginning to change his mind. The final chapter of his book written for the general reader on the evidence for psychical phenomenon, *Cock Lane and Common Sense* (1894), first set out a challenge to anthropological accounts of the origin and development of religious thought. Here it is clear that Lang's resistance to the theories of Spencer and Tylor is based on a sense of human experience as less rigid and schematised than theirs: 'Thus the elements of religion are universally distributed in all degrees of culture, though one element is more conspicuous in one place or mood, another more conspicuous in another.' Lang suggests that the beliefs of 'savages' and the beliefs of the Catholic Church are comparable, rather than a clear line of evolution being traceable from 'low' to 'high' beliefs and practices.[88] More than this, Lang makes it clear here that his challenge to the 'ghost theory' is in part a challenge to its notion of the status of facts. Both Spencer and Tylor argued that early people deduced incorrect conclusions from their observation of the world around them, but Lang asks what if the 'savage' did not misinterpret 'normal facts', but rather started from 'abnormal facts – from facts which science does not yet recognise at all – then it is possible that the conclusions of the savage, though far too sweeping and in parts undeniably erroneous, are yet, to a certain extent, not mistaken.'[89] This argument set out in *Cock Lane and Common Sense* was first articulated for those within the discipline of anthropology in *The Making of Religion* (1898). The suggestions made in the final chapter of *Cock Lane and Common Sense* form the basic structure of the later work. As Lang acknowledged in his preface to the second edition, *The Making of Religion* was a work in two halves;[90] the first concerned to show, through evidence widely dispersed spatially and temporally, that psychical experiences may indeed have their bases in 'abnormal facts', and the second to show, again through a mass of evidence, that early peoples possessed a belief in a creator god, an 'All Father', Lang's 'High Gods of Low Races', *before* they developed magical beliefs and practices. For Lang, to investigate whether the beliefs of early peoples were indeed based on 'facts or fancies' was crucial to the credibility of the ghost theory and of animism, and from *Cock Lane and Common Sense* on he criticises Tylor in particular for his lack of interest in this question.[91] Lang frequently asserts that the evidence for these 'abnormal facts', being more then either error or fraud, passes the 'anthropological test of evidence' equally well as those things which have passed into the orthodoxies of the discipline.[92]

The challenge to the theories of both Tylor and Spencer in the 1890s seems to have brought out fully Lang's scepticism about theory per se. While his work in folklore, as we have seen, is guilty of such universalising tendencies, his anthropological work on religion is very different. Lang derided James Frazer's tendency to explain everything by fertility laws as much as he did Müller's explanation of all myth as a 'disease of language'. In his chapter 'Anthropology and Religion' in the *Making of Religion* (1898), for example, Lang says that anthropology, when still excluded from science and treated with intellectual suspicion, was often done by men who were 'intellectual outlaws, people of one idea'.[93] The totalising theory, then, was both a symptom of anthropology's exclusion from science and provided a reason for it. Lang often said he had no theory, but only asserted the need to consider all facts and to be wary of the effects of all-inclusive theories.[94] For example, in the preface to the 1893 edition of *Custom and Myth*, Lang challenges critics of the first edition who accused him of believing that the same myths found among different peoples at different times were independently evolved. He argues, instead, that it varies by case and the anthropologist must look carefully at the particular setting and form of mythic content.[95]

In 1899, the year following publication of *The Making of Religion*, Lang published his revised edition of the two volumes of *Myth, Ritual and Religion*, rewritten to incorporate his challenge to the ghost theory. Lang knew that such work put him at odds with some of the fundamental assertions of British anthropology, but made clear his belief that the rational method claimed by Tylor and others must be itself subject to the rational, and that this subjection could produce surprising results:

> I am rationalist about the rationalism of most of my masters and teachers, and deserve to be an outcast from the church anthropological of Mr. Tylor, Mr. Huxley, Mr. Herbert Spencer, Sir Alfred Lyall, and Mr. Grant Allen. But I have summarised the facts on which my opinion is based, and, for the rest, have gone where the *logos* led me.[96]

The challenge to the theory set out fully in *The Making of Religion* delighted many Christians – Lang had some of his most positive reviews in Catholic journals[97] – and led many to believe that Lang shared Müller's idea that humans possess an inherent sense of the infinite or the numinous (a theory Lang had explicitly challenged in the chapter 'Fetichism and the Infinite' from *Custom and Myth*, even before the development of his anti-ghost theory). Lang was, however, keen to dispel this reading of his book. As he indicated in a letter to the anthropologist R. R. Marett in 1900, he was anxious that his theories should seem 'in no way mystical'.[98] The theories set out in *The Making of Religion* rather challenge both anthropological orthodoxy and the orthodoxy of its main rival at this time, the philology of Müller. While it is possibly the case that Lang privately retained his Christian beliefs, in this anthropological work no special case is made for Christianity and Lang makes clear his view that Christianity has been shaped by the same experiences and material realities as other beliefs. In particular, Lang's evidence for the existence of an early 'All Father' resists the sometimes crude evolutionary thinking of anthropology that led to non-European and non-Christian cultures being seen as less developed, less sophisticated and less human.[99]

As is clear from his late essay, 'Theories of the Origins of Religion' (1908), Lang was disappointed with the reception of his challenge to the ghost theory and to animism, and with Tylor's response in particular.[100] Lang did, however, retain his respect for Tylor, and directed his most waspish criticism rather at Tylor's disciple, James Frazer. Lang's attitude to the first edition of Frazer's *The Golden Bough* (1890) had been mainly positive. He wrote to Rider Haggard, suggesting that the subject of its first chapter – that of the priest who acquired his position by murdering the previous priest, and would himself be slain by his successor – would make a good subject for a novel by Haggard.[101] Lang and Frazer corresponded during the second half of the 1890s and Lang's side of the correspondence is friendly and informal in tone, offering information, references and gossip.[102] It is the case, though, that Lang's attitude was from the beginning mixed, as is clear in the preface to a new edition of *Custom and Myth* in 1893:

> In Mr. Frazer's *Golden Bough* … the student will find a carefully conceived argument, and a large collection of testimonies, bearing on the wide diffusion, among savages and civilised peoples, of ancient rites and ancient ideas … To push a theory too far is the common temptation of mythologists, and perhaps Mr. Frazer's cornstalk does rather threaten to overshadow the whole earth and exclude the light of sun and sky. But the reader, whatever his opinions, will find great pleasure and profit in Mr. Frazer's remarkable studies … [103]

The balance of Lang's opinion, however, shifted as time went on. Despite the friendly correspondence through the late 1890s, Lang was eventually in part responsible for the less enthusiastic reception of the second edition of *The Golden Bough* in 1900. He first expressed his reservations in the *Fortnightly Review* in 1899[104] and Lang's *Magic and Religion* (1901) is devoted in great part to the refutation of Frazer's theories following the second edition of *The Golden Bough*, in which Frazer articulated for the first time in his preface his argument that magic is both opposed to and prior to religion in human development, and that magic is fundamentally about the control of nature.

The crux for both Frazer and Lang was the relation between religion and magic. The anthropologist R. R. Marett has suggested that in his conversation and correspondence with Lang, they 'never got to grips' with the distinction between them, although Marett assumed that Lang followed Tylor and Frazer in this, despite his criticisms of both.[105] However, Lang explicitly challenges Frazer's definition of religion in Chapter 3 of *Magic and Religion*. Here he seems broadly to concur with Frazer with regards to magic, but he sharply criticises Frazer's definition of religion.[106] Of course, though, the two are closely linked, and in effect Lang's redefinition of religion challenges Frazer's attitude to both. For Frazer both magic and religion are ways of controlling the world; while different, they could be viewed as two steps on the way to discovering the correct way of controlling the world, that is, through science. As Lang acknowledges, for Frazer religion is the 'despair of magic'; it is what is turned to once the inefficacy of magic as a way of controlling nature is realised.[107] However, based on the evidence he presents, for Lang neither belief in magical phenomena nor belief in a monotheistic god are at bottom functionalist, but are ways of responding to actual experiences in the world. In other words, Lang reads these beliefs for what they might tell us about what is true about the world, rather than seeing them as trying to control the world but in an erroneous way.

In *Magic and Religion*, then, Lang attempted to show that Frazer's theories were often groundless, and he repeated his assertion that much evidence exists for religious beliefs that pre-existed magical practice. His chapter 'The Ghastly Priest' offers an alternative theory that could account for the practices that Frazer takes hundreds of pages to explain. Frazer begins *The Golden Bough* with an account of the role and fate of the priest at Nemi in Ancient Greece, whose job was to guard the tree of the golden bough in Diana's grove and to defend himself against his murderer, who would in turn become the priest and suffer the same fate. This priesthood, Frazer claims, 'has no parallel in classical antiquity' and cannot therefore be explained by it. '[T]o find an explanation we must go farther afield,' Frazer states, and so begins his long and circuitous route through the myths and magical practices of many peoples and places.[108] In *Magic and Religion* Lang not only suggests an alternative theory but suggests too the possibility that such a search for a single underlying cause is itself mistaken:

> I hope that my bald prosaic theory, abjectly Philistine as it is, has the characteristics of a scientific hypothesis. But … this attempt to explain the office of the ghastly priest is but a conjecture. The affair is so singular that it may have an isolated cause in some forgotten occurrence.[109]

Privately, Lang was more scathing. In a letter to his friend Anna Hills, his opinion is unconstrained:

> That is the most learned and the most inconceivably and demonstrably silly book of recent times. To criticize it is really too like hitting a child. And the gifted author thinks he has exploded all of christianity that Mrs. Ward has left. I'll 'learn him to be a toad.' One laughs out loud, in bed, at the absurdity of it.[110]

While there is undoubtedly a sense here that Lang's gentlemanly values are irked by Frazer's implicit suggestion in his work that Christianity is merely the latest in a long line of errors, all of which must eventually be superseded by the clear vision of science, Lang's opposition is more than just conservative anxiety. His commitment in his anthropological writing is always to the facts, however far they may take him from the secure positions of anthropological orthodoxy. In his anthropology Lang uses facts against the positivists to challenge their certainty, their totalising theories and the arrogance of their claim to be the possessors of a unique vision of the truth, and to retain for human experience areas resistant to the explanatory powers of science.

Frazer was outraged by Lang's challenges.[111] As is often the case with Lang's work, not the least of its disruptions was the way that it undid easy demarcations of insider and outsider. Frazer, like Tylor, had a somewhat attenuated relationship to the institutions of the English elite. Tylor was brought up a Quaker, and therefore was excluded from the most prestigious public schools and from taking a first degree at either Oxford or Cambridge. Frazer, like Lang, was Scottish, and therefore also somewhat distanced from the political and academic elite. Frazer had, again like Lang, risked much in moving from his original discipline, Classics, to anthropology. Most classicists of the period considered any comparison between the ancients and 'primitives' as demeaning to the former.[112] In his lecture on Lang from 1927, George Gordon remembered the

> chill air of disapproval with which most of the classical instructors of my
> youth regarded [Lang's] parallels from anthropology ... . The suggestion
> that there could be anything in common between the minds and customs
> of such people and the habits of ancient Greece seemed to these gentlemen
> rather a violation of decency than a contribution to the study of man.[113]

Unlike Tylor or more particularly Frazer, Lang did not directly challenge the bases of Christianity, and his position is far from the sceptical and re-forming ones they took. However, as is clear from Gordon's memory, his work did challenge the opinions of the intellectual elite, and his challenge to the work of both Tylor and Frazer around the relations between religion and magic, the relations between 'savage' and contemporary experiences of psychical phenomenon, and the nature of early religious belief undid assumptions about the movement from 'low' to 'high', from 'primitive' to 'civilised' which came from their use of evolutionary models. In his essay 'Australian Problems' (1907), for example, Lang sets out the difficulty of establishing whether any aspect of a culture is evidence of early forms or of those which are degenerating. In *Magic and Religion*, contra Frazer, he insists that the practices of early peoples are often more civilised than later religions' practices: 'So far it cannot be doubted that, as man advanced in social progress, he became more deeply stained with religious cruelty.'[114] In his late essay from 1908 he goes so far as to suggest in relation to Aboriginal culture in Australia – considered by many anthropologists, in-cluding Frazer, to represent the 'lowest' form of human culture – that 'if any man "lives up to" [the Aboriginal Australians'] best moral ideas, he will be an excellent citizen, or not a bad socialist, as you please to put it'.[115]

Many anthropologists gave only partial and sometimes grudging admis-sion to the importance of Lang's work. It took another figure poised un-comfortably, for him and his subsequent reputation, on the borders of modernity and its supposed others to recognise its significance. G. K. Chesterton, in an obituary for Lang, held up his anthropological work as challenging 'the distant and frigid study of savage belief'. For Chesterton the mystery of Lang's own beliefs – in the sense of either his own religious faith or his final beliefs on the origins of religion – added to the value of his work, rather than detracting from it:

> he really kept real agnosticism alive. His open and accessible temper in
> dealing with tales of gods or spirits was all the more valuable because he
> never himself seems to have reached any final belief. If he could not believe
> in gods, he would at least believe in man, and this concession
> revolutionised anthropology.[116]

Anthropology and psychical research

In some ways, Lang's most provocative and influential contribution to anthropology after his critique of Müller – that is, his challenge to the idea
that religious belief originates in a belief in ghosts – sits strangely with his
own interest in 'spooks'. As R. R. Marett pointed out in his 1929 Andrew
Lang Lecture, in Lang's challenge to the ghost theory and to animism 'the
real question is whether a genuine theism can arise apart from a preoccupation with spooks'.[117] In his anthropology Lang is keen to deny the role
of the belief in the ghosts of the dead given to the development of religion
by both Spencer and Tylor, yet elsewhere he insists repeatedly that accounts
of such phenomena have to be taken seriously. However, Lang's interest in
such phenomena is motivated by his assertion that they are linked, not to
actual communication with the dead, but are 'facts', actual experiences,
which can tell us something as yet unknown about human capacities and
possibilities. In Tylor, and even more so in Frazer, the location of the origin
of religious belief in magical thinking was, however implicitly, meant to
lead the reader to suspect that contemporary religious belief was as much
an error as belief in the abilities of the medicine man. In Lang, a desire to
investigate and indeed venerate belief led to two lines of thought which
seem contradictory – his assertion that religious belief did not begin in
magic and only eventually lead to monotheism, and his assertion that the
phenomena of 'savage' magic and of heterodox modern belief has something in it. It was bringing these two together that led Lang to another
assertion which again situated him as an outsider, and which again muddied
what was fast becoming a clear separation of research areas – the claim that
anthropology and psychical research had much in common, and should
share each other's evidence and methods.

In relation to his work on psychical phenomenon, Lang's insistence on
the comparative method for anthropology went beyond what had become
its normative limits as the discipline formed itself. Time after time he castigates anthropology for ignoring a class of evidence which he believed
could transform the subject – contemporary accounts of magical phenomena.[118] For Lang's own anthropology in the 1890s and beyond, the relation
between evidence from non-modern cultures and evidence from contemporary modernity is of the essence. As we have seen, in *The Making of
Religion* the fundamental evidence for Lang's challenge to what had become
the orthodox account of the development of religion is in part provided by
the evidence of contemporary experiences of, for example, crystal gazing,
the animation of the supposedly inanimate, use of the divining rod, and
possession and clairvoyance – that is, phenomena more usually investigated
by psychical research. So while in Lang's folklore, his notion of survivals
closely follows Tylor's own, in his consideration of psychical phenomena
he went beyond Tylor. Psychical phenomena in the present day, Lang be-

lieved, as evidenced in *The Making of Religion*, are not anomalous traces of the past; rather they are abnormal facts, the consideration of which had the potential to reveal new and exciting human capacities. Lang concluded from this that anthropology needed to be interested in *modern* beliefs and practices as much as in non-modern – but this was anathema to anthropology and contributed to his own attenuated relation to the discipline. Underlying the development of social anthropology was the investigation of difference – the difference between, in the end, the 'scientific' claims of anthropology and the superstitious beliefs of the objects of its scrutiny[119] – and the inclusion of modern beliefs and experiences would threaten that assertion of difference.

Lang was certain that psychical research needed to go beyond its own evidence base and use the comparative method to think about evidence from the past and from different cultures. This was anathema to psychical researchers, who were not interested in historical or non-modern evidence because they were unable to subject it to the discipline's central methods of investigation, based, as they were, on the science of the laboratory. As Lang acknowledges in his preface to the second edition of *The Making of Religion* (1900), then, his hopes for this collaboration were disappointed. His freer expression in a number of letters makes his frustration clear. In a letter of the late 1890s to Henry Sidgwick, one of the founders of the Society for Psychical Research, Lang wrote that: 'Of course my Psychics are very unpopular, but Tylor brought them in, and left them in, and left them hanging in air, and did little to the civilized side of them. This was hardly scientific in my opinion.'[120] On the other side, in a letter to the journalist and spiritualist W. T. Stead written in the the early 1890s, Lang complained that 'The S.P.R. people "don't even know their own silly old business", as far as its history is concerned.'[121] A third letter acknowledges the effects of all this on Lang's own position. Writing to William Blackwood in 1894, he suggested that his writings on the psychical were 'too sceptical for the credulous, and too serious, in spots, for the sceptical'.[122]

Lang's insistence that anthropology needed to take seriously the evidence and methods of psychical research, however, can give a misleading impression of his own relations with both psychical research and its main institution, the Society for Psychical Research (SPR). The SPR had been founded in 1882 by, among others, the Cambridge classicist and moral philosopher Henry Sidgwick and the Cambridge classicist and poet Frederic Myers. Apart from Sidgwick and Myers, the most important figures in the Society in the 1880s and 1890s were Eleanor Sidgwick, wife of Henry and sister of the future Conservative Prime Minister Arthur Balfour, and Edmund Gurney, like Myers and Henry Sidgwick also an alumnus of Trinity College Cambridge. Lang may have been introduced to the tight Cambridge circle at the heart of the SPR through his collaboration with Walter Leaf and Ernest Myers on their translation of the *Iliad* (1883). Myers was the younger brother of Frederic Myers, and Walter Leaf was a member of the SPR and a frequent contributor to its *Proceedings*. Lang's correspondence through the 1890s with both Oliver Lodge, also a central figure in the SPR, and William James, one of the founders of the American SPR (see this volume, pp. 314–27, 328–31) makes clear the extent of his interest in the subject, but he did not join the Society until 1904.[123] Even at the time of his presidency in 1911, Lang was not one of those most closely associated with the SPR itself, although his interest in the subject was widely known. Often in his journalism he made sceptical, if not disparaging, remarks about the Society. In his many columns in the *Illustrated London News* from 1895 Lang clearly attempts to construct an impartial, outsider's position vis-à-vis the Society, castigating it for its lapses in sense and logic, while also defending it against scientific intolerance. In a column on 'Premonitions' in 1896, Lang criticises the work of his friend Frederic Myers for the SPR on the subject: 'In the new number of the "Proceedings of the Psychical Society," Mr. Myers gives a crowd of modern instances which, somehow, fail to beget conviction.'[124] In 'Ghosts Up To Date' (1894), in *Blackwood's Edinburgh Magazine*, published the same year as *Cock Lane and Common Sense*, in which Lang asserted the necessary link between anthropology and psychical research, he opens his article with despair at the effects of psychical research:

> The most frivolous pastimes have now a habit of degenerating into scientific exercises … ghost stories, the delight of Christmas Eve, have been ravaged and annexed by psychology. True, there are some who aver that the science of the Psychical Society does not hold water; but, in any case, it is as dull and difficult as if it were some orthodox research dear to Mr Herbert Spencer. To prove this fact, I had marked for quotation some remarks, by eminent ghosthunters, on the provinces and parts of the brain, on the subjective and the objective, the conscious, the reflex, the automatic, – *tout le tremblement*, as we may well say, – which would frighten off the most intrepid amateurs. 'The oldest aunt' would forget 'the saddest tale,' if plied with remarks on the 'dextro-cerebral hemisphere' of the brain.[125]

Despite these complaints, however, Lang then goes on in the main body of the article to discuss ghosts with exactly the language and methods of psychical research. At the same time as Lang was writing in an ambiguous way about psychical research in *the Illustrated London News* and in *Blackwood's*, and practising his assertion of the mutual need between anthropology and psychical research in *Cock Lane and Common Sense*, he was making his initial contributions to SPR publications. Lang's first writing within the institutions of the SPR was in 1895, with articles in both the *Proceedings* and the *Journal*.[126] Significantly, though, both of these pieces originated in Lang's historical work, the very place he insisted psychical research needed to go to make its evidence and methods complete.

Notwithstanding Lang's criticism of psychical research and his somewhat attenuated relation to the early history of the Society, Lang was publicly and privately involved in three of the most important investigations of the SPR during the late nineteenth and early twentieth centuries – those of the mediums Mrs Leonora Piper and Eusapia Palladino, and the long investigation into the so-called cross-correspondences. His involvement in these reveals the fundamental ambiguity of his position and the extent to which this ambiguity produced new positions and viewpoints. In 'The Three Seeresses (1880–1900, 1424–1431)', published in *The Anglo-Saxon Review* in 1900, Lang compares Mrs Piper (along with the Swiss medium Hélène Smith who had been made famous by the psychologist Theodore Flournoy in the same year) to Jeanne d'Arc. Leonora Piper, from Boston in the US, had been 'discovered' for psychical research by William James in the mid-1880s. She was investigated both in the US and in the UK numerous times over the following two decades. A trance medium who communicated with the dead via a number of 'controls', Mrs Piper seemed to many, including her main investigator, the psychical researcher Richard Hodgson, to provide the most convincing evidence yet for survival beyond death and the possibility of communicating with the dead. Lang's argument in 'The Three Seeresses' is not that those things claimed for both Piper and Smith were not possible, just that they do not provide them. For Jeanne d'Arc, on the other hand, Lang claims not that she was supernatural, but that if we can accept as fact what is known about her, then we must readjust our sense of the natural.

Indeed, Lang's writing on Jeanne d'Arc demonstrates in miniature much that makes his work surprising, confusing and significant (see Volume 2, pp. 236–58). Similarly, Lang's valuing of Jeanne over both Mrs Piper and Hélène Smith is certainly part of his general denigration of the present over the past, but the manner of his valuation makes him modern while transforming the very idea of the modern. As Louis Cazaman noted in his lecture on Lang in 1931, Lang's various ripostes to the work of Anatole France on the figure of Jeanne blurred the assumed boundaries between the pre-modern and the modern, between magical thinking and scientific thought. Lang, says Cazaman, counters Anatole France's rationalism not with mysticism, but with rigorous historical method, which he believes leads to a sense of the natural that 'must not be fixed immovably by a narrow sectarianism of reason'.[127] Similarly, in writing sceptically about both Mrs Piper and Eusapia Palladino, as he does in many places in his letters and published work (see this volume, pp. 314–27, 328–31), Lang uses the language and methods of science to show that the trouble with them both is that they were just not marvellous or miraculous enough.

The difficult effects of such a position for Lang are often apparent in his writing on psychical phenomenon and psychical research. Lang urged anthropologists, as we have seen, to consider accounts of contemporary psychical phenomena, as they might suggest causality beyond their own sense of the 'error' of 'savages'; but often too, when writing of these contemporary cases Lang insists that his interest is 'purely anthropological'.[128] In other words, he evades the question of the truth status of Mrs Piper's phenomenon by retreating to exactly the position for which he criticises anthropology. Lang does very occasionally give explicit indications of his own beliefs,[129] but on the whole, while he repeats the assertion that these different areas need to be thought of together, when the consequences of his demands become too uncomfortable, he restores the disciplinary boundaries.

What Lang avoids most often, and disavows, is the possession of a theory – he states his position again and again, explaining that he has no theory but can present only the facts, and that these facts must be acknowledged.[130] For Lang, the importance of psychical research lay in establishing facts *as* fact, that is, in being able to state that these things do happen, rather than necessarily to account for or explain them. It is possible that psychical research's location in what Lang called the 'unofficial, unstaked waste of Science' was precisely its attraction for him.[131] It gave him an opportunity to remain at the point of ascertaining and establishing 'facts', rather than committing himself to any more solid claims. However, it is also the case that his resistance to totalising theories – such of those of Max Müller and James Frazer – and his attempt to expand the category of the 'fact' had the effect of upsetting and undoing many of the developing certainties of late nineteenth-century intellectual culture.

Chronology of the life and major works of Andrew Lang

1844
Born (31 March) in Selkirk on the Scottish Borders to John Lang and Jane Plenderleath Sellar Lang.

c.1852–4
Attends Selkirk Grammar School.

1854–61
Attends the Edinburgh Academy.

1861–3
Attends St Andrews University.

1863
Co-founds and edits the *St Leonards Magazine* at St Andrews University.

1863–4
Transfers to the University of Glasgow to compete for the Snell Exhibition Scholarship to Oxford University. Awarded scholarship.

1865–8
Attends Balliol College, Oxford University, reading Classics under Benjamin Jowett. Graduates first class in 'Classical Moderations' (1866) and 'Greats' (1868).

1869–75
Fellow at Merton College, Oxford University.

1872
Ballads and Lyrics of Old France (poetry collection).

1872
Reads E. B. Tylor's *Primitive Culture*.

1872–4
Spends winters on the French Riviera to recover from a lung infection.
Meets Robert Louis Stevenson (31 Jan 1874).

1873
(May) Publishes his first scholarly essay on folklore, 'Mythology and Fairy
Tales' in the *Fortnightly Review*.

1874
Begins writing regularly for *The Academy*.

1875–*c.*1895
Writes regular leaders in the *Daily News* and the *Saturday Review*.

1875–1911
Contributes entries for the *Encyclopaedia Britannica*, eventually writing for
the ninth, tenth and eleventh editions.

1875
(17 April) Marries Leonora Blanche Alleyne.

1875
Leaves Merton College and settles in London at 1 Marloes Road,
Kensington.

1877
Publishes letters in *The Academy* (1 and 15 December) concerning the
foundation of a Folk-Lore Society.

1878
Foundation of the Folk-Lore Society, and publication of the first volume
of the *Folk-Lore Record* (subsequently the *Folk-Lore Journal*) with Lang's
long essay 'The Folk-Lore of France'.

1879
Publishes with S. H. Butcher the translation *The Odyssey of Homer Rendered into English Prose*.

1882
Helen of Troy (epic poem).
The Black Thief (play).

1883
Publishes with Ernest Myers and Walter Leaf *The Iliad of Homer, a prose translation*.

1884
Publishes his first book on folklore, *Custom and Myth*.
The Princess Nobody: A Tale of Fairyland (children's book, using drawings by Richard Doyle).
Ballads and Verses Vain (poetry collection).
Introduces Margaret Hunt's translation *Grimms' Household Tales* with the Essay 'Household Tales'.

1885
Rhymes à la Mode (poetry collection).

1886–1905
Writes the monthly column 'At the Sign of the Ship' in *Longman's Magazine*.

1886
Books and Bookmen (literary essays).
Letters to Dead Authors (epistolary literary criticism and pastiche).
In the Wrong Paradise (stories).
The Mark of Cain (novel).

1887
First edition of the anthropological work *Myth, Ritual and Religion*.
Publishes *He* anonymously with Walter Herries Pollock, a parody of Henry Rider Haggard's novel *She*.
Publishes an edition of William Adlington's translation of Apuleius, *The Most Pleasant and Delectable Tale of the Marriage of Cupid and Psyche*, with a substantial introduction.

1888

Grass of Parnassus (poem collection).
The Gold of Fairnilee (children's book).
Editor of *Perrault's Popular Tales* (1888), which includes a substantial introductory essay.

1888–9

President of the Folk-Lore Society.

1889–1910

Publishes twelve anthologies of fairy tales known as the 'coloured fairy books' beginning with *The Blue Fairy Book* (1889) and *The Red Fairy Book* (1890).

1891–7 & 1905–12

Regular contributor to the *Illustrated London News*.

1889

Prince Prigio (children's fantasy novel, first of the 'Chronicles of Pantouflia').
Letters on Literature (epistolary literary criticism).
Lost Leaders (selected journalism).

1890

The World's Desire (novel, with Henry Rider Haggard).
Publishes his first biography, *The Life, Letters, and Diaries of Sir Stafford Northcote*.
How to Fail in Literature (satirical advice for writers).

1891

The International Folk-Lore Congress is held in London with Lang as President.
Essays in Little.

1892–1912

Regular contributor to *Blackwood's (Edinburgh) Magazine*.

1892–4

Editor of the *Waverley Novels* by Walter Scott (48 vols).

1893

Homer and the Epic (classical literary criticism).
Prince Ricardo of Pantouflia (children's fantasy novel, second of the 'Chronicles of Pantouflia').
Collaborates with Rider Haggard on the novel *Montezuma's Daughter*.
Publishes an edition of *Kirk's Secret Commonwealth* with a substantial introduction.

1894

Ban and Arrière Ban (poetry collection).
Publishes his first book-length investigation of spiritualism *Cock Lane and Common Sense*.

1895

My Own Fairy Book (collected children's stories).

1896

A Monk of Fife (novel; historical romance).
The Life and Letters of John Gibson Lockhart (biography).

1897

The Book of Dreams and Ghosts (history of psychical phenomena).
Publishes his investigation of the identity of the spy for the English codenamed 'Pickle', *Pickle the Spy; or the Incognito of Prince Charles*.
Modern Mythology (study of mythological interpretation).
Editor of *The Works of Charles Dickens* (34 vols).

1898

The Making of Religion (anthropological study on the origins of religion).
Parson Kelly (novel, with A. E. W. Mason).

1899

The Homeric Hymns (translation).
Second edition of *Myth, Ritual and Religion*, revised and enlarged.

1900–7

Publishes four volumes of *A History of Scotland from the Roman Occupation to the Suppressing of the Last Jacobite Rising*.

1900

Prince Charles Edward Stuart (biography).

1901

The Mystery of Mary Stuart (historical study).
Magic and Religion (anthropological study).
Alfred Tennyson (biography).

1902

James VI and the Gowrie Mystery (historical study).
The Disentanglers, last single authored novel.

1903

The Valet's Tragedy, and Other Studies in Secret History (accounts of historical mysteries).
Social Origins (anthropological study).
Collaborates with Rider Haggard on the novel *Stella Fregelius*.

1904

(22 June) Made honorary Doctor of Letters by Oxford University and appointed Ford Lecturer in English History.

1905

John Knox and the Reformation (historical study).
The Secret of the Totem (anthropological study).
Adventures Among Books (literary criticism and autobiography).

1906

The Story of Joan of Arc (historical study for children).
New and Old Letters to Dead Authors (epistolary literary criticism).
Life of Sir Walter Scott (biography).
Portraits and Jewels of Mary Stuart (study in art history).
Homer and his Age (classical literary criticism and history).
Elected Fellow of the British Academy.

1907

Tales of a Fairy Court (children's book).

1908

The Maid of France: Being the Story of the Life and Death of Jeanne d'Arc (biographical and historical study).

1910

The World of Homer (classical literary criticism and history).
Sir Walter Scott and the Border Minstrelsy (literary history and criticism).
Elected founding member of the Academic Committee of the Royal Society of Literature.

1911

Method in the Study of Totemism (anthropological study).
Elected president of the Society for Psychical Research.
A Short History of Scotland.

1912

A History of English Literature (literary history/criticism).
Shakespeare, Bacon and the Great Unknown (literary history/criticism).
Sees his family's death omen, a ghostly cat.
(20 July) Dies at Banchory in Aberdeenshire aged 68 of a heart attack.

1923

Posthumous publication of *The Poetical Works* (4 vols) edited by
Leonora Lang.

A Note on the Text

The first published version of the text has been used for all pieces reproduced here, with two exceptions. Lang rarely revised his work, even
when it was published multiple times and in multiple locations. The exceptions are *Myth, Ritual and Religion* (first published 1887, second edition 1899)
and *The Making of Religion* (first published 1898, second edition 1900), where
Lang did revise the second editions. As his changes are useful indications of
the development of his thought, the second edition of each has been used
here, with the changes made indicated in endnotes.

Lang's spelling and punctuation have been kept, as have the original
styles of presentation, which vary according to the practice of the publisher, journal or newspaper in which the work appeared. The only exception
to this is the consistent editorial use of single inverted commas throughout.
Obvious typesetting errors have been silently corrected, but other editorial interventions are indicated in square brackets.

Where Lang has used languages other than English, we give translations
in the endnotes, except in those instances where words or phrases are very
familiar to English speakers, or where Lang has given his own translation.

Original footnotes have been retained except where ommissions are
indicated in endnotes. Where they are correct, no additional information
has been added. Where they are incorrect, or if Lang's use of different editions is confusing, the correct or additional information is given in endnotes.
In particular, Lang seems to have used different editions of E. B. Tylor's
Primitive Culture without indicating which. For ease of reference, citations
of the first edition (1871) have been provided on those occasions where
Lang paraphrases or directly quotes from it.

Of the letters included included here, only the letters to William James have been previously published (in Marysa Demoor, *Friends Over the Ocean: Andrew Lang's American correspondents, 1881–1912*, Ghent: Rijksuniversiteit Gent, 1989). Others are reproduced from the manuscript copy. Dating of the letters reproduced and those referred to in the introductions is speculative. Lang never put a year on his letters, and frequently no month or date either. Some letters remain with original envelopes bearing legible postmarks, but otherwise internal evidence has been used to date previously unpublished letters.

Lang's poor handwriting obstructs certainty about all words in the letters, and where words are truly illegible, this is indicated in square brackets. Where there is some uncertainty about a word, the most likely reading of it has been given and a question mark in square brackets follows it.

Where it will assist in the identification of the stories Lang refers to, 'tale type' references have been given in the section headings and endnotes. These refer to entries in the tale type indexing system developed by Antti Aarne and Stith Thompson in the early twentieth century, and reworked by Hans-Jörg Uther in 2004. As is conventional, the tale type reference numbers are given with the prefix ATU (Aarne/Thompson/Uther), and in every case the citation may be found in Uther, *The Types of International Folk Tales*, FF Communications 284 (Helsinki: Suomalainen Tiedeakatemia Scientiarum Fennica, 2004). Frequently mentioned proper names of people or groups do not have a footnote, but can be found in detail in the appendices.

Acknowledgements

Thanks to the following for their generous help: Susan Halpert and Heather Cole, Houghton Library, Harvard University; Elaine Miller, Catriona Foote and Dr Norman Reid, Special Collections, University of St Andrews; Dr Chris Morton and Philip Grover, Pitt Rivers Museum, University of Oxford; Jonathan Smith, Trinity College Library, Cambridge; Peter Meadows, Department of Manuscripts, Cambridge University Library; Moira Marsh at the Wells Library, Indiana University; staff of London Library; staff of the British Library; staff of Senate House Library, University of London.

Thanks to the Department of English, Linguistics and Cultural Studies, University of Westminster and to the Research Capability Fund of the Faculty of Arts and Social Sciences, Kingston University for their generous financial contributions.

Thanks also to: Simon Avery, Monica Germanà, Louise Sylvester and Martin Willis for well-timed encouragement; Jackie Jones for her support during a difficult beginning; Bill Gray for his thorough reading and good advice; Debra Kelly and Valerie Chambon for help with the French; Catriona Macdonald; Jonathan Metzer for help with the Greek; Kate Simpson for shared frustration with Lang's handwriting; Diane Stafford for care with the copy-editing; Izzie Thomas for care with the typesetting; Em Warwick for biographical notes; Simone Coxall, David Cunningham and Toby Litt.

For permission to reproduce Lang's letters to Oliver Lodge, William James and E.B. Tylor, thanks to: SPR archive, Cambridge University Library; Houghton Library, Harvard University; Manuscript Collection, Pitt Rivers Museum, University of Oxford.

I

THE METHOD
OF FOLKLORE

The two extracts included in this section deal with Lang's methodological approach to folklore analysis as it is developed and demonstrated in his first published book on the subject, *Custom and Myth* (London: Longmans, Green and Co.,1884). *Custom and Myth* is made up of fourteen essays, some previously published, some original; each essay seeks to demonstrate that popular tradition incorporates elements which may be regarded as survivals from the savage state Lang believed all civilisations to have passed through.

'The Method of Folklore', as the first essay in the collection, sets out to explicate the comparative method of analysis to be used throughout the work, and in so doing presents the founding principles of the anthropological argument. As such it serves as an excellent introduction to Lang's proposed treatment of folklore and mythology.

'Cupid, Psyche, and the "Sun-Frog"', also included here, is the fourth essay in the collection. Here Lang applies the system outlined in 'The Method of Folklore' to a selection of international tale types, including ATU425 'The Search for the Lost Husband', ATU402 'The Animal Bride' and ATU440 'The Frog King'. The essay is notable for its spirited critique of the interpretations of these tale types that have been offered by scholars of the solar mythological school and for its careful explication of Lang's views concerning independent invention.

'The Method of Folklore',
Custom and Myth
(London: Longmans, Green and Co., 1884)

After the heavy rain of a thunderstorm has washed the soil, it sometimes happens that a child, or a rustic, finds a wedge-shaped piece of metal or a few triangular flints in a field or near a road. There was no such piece of metal, there were no such flints, lying there yesterday, and the finder is puzzled about the origin of the objects on which he has lighted. He carries them home, and the village wisdom determines that the wedge-shaped piece of metal is a 'thunder-bolt,' or that the bits of flint are 'elf-shots,'[1] the heads of fairy arrows. Such things are still treasured in remote nooks of England, and the 'thunder-bolt' is applied to cure certain maladies by its touch.

As for the fairy arrows, we know that even in ancient Etruria they were looked on as magical, for we sometimes see their points set, as amulets, in the gold of Etruscan[2] necklaces. In Perugia the arrow-heads are still sold as charms. All educated people, of course, have long been aware that the metal wedge is a celt, or ancient bronze axe-head, and that it was not fairies, but the forgotten peoples of this island who used the arrows with the tips of flint. Thunder is only so far connected with them that the heavy rains loosen the surface soil, and lay bare its long hidden secrets.

There is a science, Archæology, which collects and compares the material relics of old races, the axes and arrow-heads. There is a form of study, Folklore, which collects and compares the similar but immaterial relics of old races, the surviving superstitions and stories, the ideas which are in our time but not of it. Properly speaking, folklore is only concerned with the legends, customs, beliefs, of the Folk, of the people, of the classes which have least been altered by education, which have shared least in progress. But the student of folklore soon finds that these unprogressive classes retain many

of the beliefs and ways of savages, just as the Hebridean people use spindle-whorls of stone,³ and bake clay pots without the aid of the wheel, like
modern South Sea Islanders, or like their own prehistoric ancestors.*⁴ The
student of folklore is thus led to examine the usages, myths, and ideas of
savages, which are still retained, in rude enough shape, by the European
peasantry. Lastly, he observes that a few similar customs and ideas survive
in the most conservative elements of the life of educated peoples, in ritual,
ceremonial, and religious traditions and myths. Though such remains are
rare in England, we may note the custom of leading the dead soldier's horse
behind his master to the grave, a relic of days when the horse would have
been sacrificed.† We may observe the persistence of the ceremony by which
the monarch, at his coronation, takes his seat on the sacred stone of Scone,⁵
probably an ancient fetich stone. Not to speak, here, of our own religious
traditions, the old vein of savage rite and belief is found very near the surface
of ancient Greek religion. It needs but some stress of circumstance, something answering to the storm shower that reveals the flint arrow-heads, to
bring savage ritual to the surface of classical religion. In sore need, a human
victim was only too likely to be demanded; while a feast-day, or a mystery,
set the Greeks dancing serpent-dances or bear-dances like Red Indians, or
swimming with sacred pigs, or leaping about in imitation of wolves, or
holding a dog-feast, and offering dog's flesh to the gods. […] Thus the student of folklore soon finds that he must enlarge his field, and examine, not
only popular European story and practice, but savage ways and ideas, and
the myths and usages of the educated classes in civilised races.

[…]

The science of Folklore, if we may call it a science, finds everywhere,
close to the surface of civilised life, the remains of ideas as old as the stone
elf-shots, older than the celt of bronze. In proverbs and riddles, and nursery
tales and superstitions, we detect the relics of a stage of thought, which is
dying out in Europe, but which still exists in many parts of the world. Now,
just as the flint arrow-heads are scattered everywhere, in all the continents
and isles, and everywhere are much alike, and bear no very definite marks
of the special influence of race, so it is with the habits and legends investigated by the student of folklore. The stone arrow-head buried in a Scottish
cairn is like those which were interred with Algonquin chiefs. The flints
found in Egyptian soil, or beside the tumulus on the plain of Marathon,

---

* A study of the contemporary stone age in Scotland will be found in Mitchell's
Past and Present.

† About twenty years ago, the widow of an Irish farmer, in Derry, killed her
deceased husband's horse. When remonstrated with by her landlord, she said,
'Would you have my man go about on foot in the next world?' She was quite in
the savage intellectual stage.

nearly resemble the stones which tip the reed arrow of the modern Samoyed. Perhaps only a skilled experience could discern, in a heap of such arrow-heads, the specimens which are found in America or Africa from those which are unearthed in Europe. Even in the products of more advanced industry, we see early pottery, for example, so closely alike everywhere that, in the British Museum, Mexican vases have, ere now, been mixed up on the same shelf with archaic vessels from Greece. In the same way, if a superstition or a riddle were offered to a student of folklore, he would have much difficulty in guessing its *provenance*, and naming the race from which it was brought. Suppose you tell a folklorist that, in a certain country, when anyone sneezes, people say 'Good luck to you,' the student cannot say *a priori* what country you refer to, what race you have in your thoughts. It may be Florida, as Florida was when first discovered; it may be Zululand, or West Africa, or ancient Rome, or Homeric Greece, or Palestine. In all these, and many other regions, the sneeze was welcomed as an auspicious omen. The little superstition is as widely distributed as the flint arrow-heads. Just as the object and use of the arrow-heads became intelligible when we found similar weapons in actual use among savages, so the salutation to the sneezer becomes intelligible when we learn that the savage has a good reason for it. He thinks the sneeze expels an evil spirit. Proverbs, again, and riddles are as universally scattered, and the Wolufs puzzle over the same *devinettes*[6] as the Scotch schoolboy or the Breton peasant. Thus, for instance, the Wolufs of Senegal ask each other, 'What flies for ever, and rests never?'— Answer, 'The Wind.' 'Who are the comrades that always fight, and never hurt each other?'—'The Teeth.' In France, as we read in the 'Recueil de Calembours,'[7] the people ask, 'What runs faster than a horse, crosses water, and is not wet?'—Answer, 'The Sun.' The Samoans put the riddle, 'A man who stands between two ravenous fishes?'—Answer, 'The tongue between the teeth.' Again, 'There are twenty brothers, each with a hat on his head?'—Answer, 'Fingers and toes, with nails for hats.' This is like the French *'un père a douze fils?'*—*'l'an.'*[8] A comparison of M. Rolland's 'Devinettes'[9] with the Woluf conundrums of Boilat,[10] the Samoan examples in Turner's 'Samoa,'[11] and the Scotch enigmas collected by Chambers,[12] will show the identity of peasant and savage humour.

A few examples, less generally known, may be given to prove that the beliefs of folklore are not peculiar to any one race or stock of men. The first case is remarkable: it occurs in Mexico and Ceylon — nor are we aware that it is found elsewhere. In *Macmillan's Magazine** is published a paper by Mrs. Edwards, called 'The Mystery of the Pezazi.' The events described in this narrative occurred on August 28, 1876, in a bungalow some thirty miles from Badiella. The narrator occupied a new house on an estate called Allagalla. Her native servants soon asserted that the place was haunted by a

---

*   Nov. 1880.

Pezazi. The English visitors saw and heard nothing extraordinary till a certain night: an abridged account of what happened then may be given in the words of Mrs. Edwards:—

Wrapped in dreams, I lay on the night in question tranquilly sleeping, but gradually roused to a perception that discordant sounds disturbed the serenity of my slumber. Loth to stir, I still dozed on, the sounds, however, becoming, as it seemed, more determined to make themselves heard; and I awoke to the consciousness that they proceeded from a belt of adjacent jungle, and resembled the noise that would be produced by some person felling timber.

Shutting my ears to the disturbance, I made no sign, until, with an expression of impatience, E--- suddenly started up, when I laid a detaining grasp upon his arm, murmuring that there was no need to think of rising at present—it must be quite early, and the kitchen cooly was doubtless cutting fire-wood in good time. E--- responded, in a tone of slight contempt, that no one could be cutting fire-wood at that hour, and the sounds were more suggestive of felling jungle; and he then inquired how long I had been listening to them. Now thoroughly aroused, I replied that I had heard the sounds for some time, at first confusing them with my dreams, but soon sufficiently awakening to the fact that they were no mere phantoms of my imagination, but a reality. During our conversation the noises became more distinct and loud; blow after blow resounded, as of the axe descending upon the tree, followed by the crash of the falling timber. Renewed blows announced the repetition of the operations on another tree, and continued till several were devastated.

It is unnecessary to tell more of the tale. In spite of minute examinations and close search, no solution of the mystery of the noises, on this or any other occasion, was ever found. The natives, of course, attributed the disturbance to the *Pezazi*, or goblin. No one, perhaps, has asserted that the Aztecs were connected by ties of race with the people of Ceylon. Yet, when the Spaniards conquered Mexico, and when Sahagun[13] (one of the earliest missionaries) collected the legends of the people, he found them, like the Cingalese, strong believers in the mystic tree-felling. We translate Sahagun's account of the 'midnight axe'[14]:—

When so any man heareth the sound of strokes in the night, as if one were felling trees, he reckons it an evil boding. And this sound they call *youaltepuztli* (*youalli*, night; and *tepuztli*, copper), which signifies 'the midnight hatchet.' This noise cometh about the time of the first sleep, when all men slumber soundly, and the night is still. The sound of strokes smitten was first noted by the temple-servants, called *tlamacazque*, at the hour when they go in the night to make their offering of reeds or of boughs of pine, for so was their custom, and this penance they did on the neighbouring hills, and that when the night was far spent. Whenever they heard such a sound as one makes when he splits wood with an axe (a noise that may be heard afar off), they drew thence an omen of evil, and were afraid, and said that the sounds were part of the witchery of Tezeatlipoca,[15] that often thus dismayeth men who journey in the night. Now, when tidings of these things came to a certain brave man, one exercised in war, he drew near, being guided by the sound, till he came to the very cause of the hubbub. And when he came upon it, with difficulty he caught it, for the thing was hard to catch: natheless at last he overtook that which ran before him; and behold, it was a man without a heart, and, on either side of the chest, two holes that opened and shut, and so made the noise. Then the man put his hand within the breast of the figure and grasped the breast and shook it hard, demanding some grace or gift.

As a rule, the grace demanded was power to make captives in war. The curious coincidence of the 'midnight axe,' occurring in lands so remote as Ceylon and Mexico, and the singular attestation by an English lady of the actual existence of the disturbance, makes this *youaltepuztli* one of the quaintest things in the province of the folklorist. But, whatever the cause of the noise, or of the beliefs connected with the noise, may be, no one would explain them as the result of community of *race* between Cingalese and Aztecs. Nor would this explanation be offered to account for the Aztec and English belief that the creaking of furniture is an omen of death in a house. Obviously, these opinions are the expression of a common state of superstitious fancy, not the signs of an original community of origin.

Let us take another piece of folklore. All North-country English folk know the *Kernababy*.[16] The custom of the 'Kernababy' is commonly observed in England, or, at all events, in Scotland, where the writer has seen many a kernababy. The last gleanings of the last field are bound up in a rude imitation of the human shape, and dressed in some tag-rags of finery. The usage has fallen into the conservative hands of children, but of old 'the Maiden' was a regular image of the harvest goddess, which, with a sickle and sheaves in her arms, attended by a crowd of reapers, and accompanied with music, followed the last carts home to the farm.* It is odd enough that the 'Maiden' should exactly translate Κόρη,[17] the old Sicilian name of the daughter of Demeter.[18] 'The Maiden' has dwindled, then, among us to the rudimentary kernababy; but ancient Peru had her own Maiden, her Harvest Goddess. Here it is easy to trace the natural idea at the basis of the superstitious practice which links the shores of the Pacific with our own northern coast. Just as a portion of the yule-log and of the Christmas bread were kept all the year through, a kind of nest-egg of plenteous food and fire, so the kernababy, English or Peruvian, is an earnest that corn will not fail all through the year, till next harvest comes. For this reason the kernababy used to be treasured from autumn's end to autumn's end, though now it com-

---

* 'Ah, once again may I plant the great fan on her corn-heap, while she stands smiling by, Demeter of the threshing floor, with sheaves and poppies in her hands' (Theocritus, [*Idylls*] vii. 155–157).

monly disappears very soon after the harvest home. It is thus that Acosta[19] describes, in Grimston's old translation (1604), the Peruvian kernababy and the Peruvian harvest home:—

This feast is made comming from the chacra or farme unto the house, saying certaine songs, and praying that the Mays (maize) may long continue, the which they call *Mama cora*.[20]

What a chance this word offers to etymologists of the old school: how promptly they would recognise, in *mama* mother—μήτηρ,[21] and in *cora*—κόρη, the Mother and the Maiden, the feast of Demeter and Persephone! However, the days of that old school of antiquarianism are numbered. To return to the Peruvian harvest home:—

They take a certaine portion of the most fruitefull of the Mays that growes in their farmes, the which they put in a certaine granary which they do calle Pirua, with certaine ceremonies, watching three nightes; they put this Mays in the richest garments they have, and, being thus wrapped and dressed, they worship this Pirua, and hold it in great veneration, saying it is the Mother of the Mays of their inheritances, and that by this means the Mays augments and is preserved. In this moneth they make a particular sacrifice, and the witches demand of this Pirua, 'if it hath strength sufficient to continue until the next yeare,' and if it answers 'no,' then they carry this Mays to the farme to burne, whence they brought it, according to every man's power, then they make another Pirua, with the same ceremonies, saying that they renue it, to the ende that the seede of the Mays may not perish.[22]

The idea that the maize can speak need not surprise us; the Mexican held much the same belief, according to Sahagun:—

It was thought that if some grains of maize fell on the ground, he who saw them lying there was bound to lift them, wherein, if he failed, he harmed the maize, which plained itself of him to God, saying, 'Lord, punish this man, who saw me fallen and raised me not again; punish him with famine, that he may learn not to hold me in dishonour.'[23]

Well, in all this affair of the Scotch kernababy, and the Peruvian *Mama cora*, we need no explanation beyond the common simple ideas of human nature. We are not obliged to hold, either that the Peruvians and Scotch are akin by blood, nor that, at some forgotten time, they met each other, and borrowed each other's superstitions. Again, when we find Odysseus sacrificing a black sheep to the dead,* and when we read that the Ovahereroes in South Africa also appease with a black sheep the spirits of the departed, we do not feel it necessary to hint that the Ovahereroes are of Greek descent, or have borrowed their ritual from the Greeks. The connection between the colour black, and mourning for the dead, is natural and almost universal.

★   *Odyssey*, xi. 32.

Examples like these might be adduced in any number. We might show how, in magic, negroes of Barbadoes make clay effigies of their enemies, and pierce them, just as Greeks did in Plato's time, or the men of Accad[24] in remotest antiquity. We might remark the Australian black putting sharp bits of quartz in the tracks of an enemy who has gone by, that the enemy may be lamed; and we might point to Boris Godunof[25] forbidding the same practice among the Russians. We might watch Scotch, and Australians, and Jews, and French, and Aztecs spreading dust round the body of a dead man, that the footprints of his ghost, or of other ghosts, may be detected next morning. We might point to a similar device in a modern novel, where the presence of a ghost is suspected, as proof of the similar workings of the Australian mind and of the mind of Mrs. Riddell.[26] We shall later turn to ancient Greece, and show how the serpent-dances, the habit of smearing the body with clay, and other odd rites of the mysteries, were common to Hellenic religion, and to the religion of African, Australian, and American tribes.

Now, with regard to all these strange usages, what is the method of folklore? The method is, when an apparently irrational and anomalous custom is found in any country, to look for a country where a similar practice is found, and where the practice is no longer irrational and anomalous, but in harmony with the manners and ideas of the people among whom it prevails. That Greeks should dance about in their mysteries with harmless serpents in their hands looks quite unintelligible. When a wild tribe of Red Indians does the same thing, as a trial of courage, with real rattlesnakes, we understand the Red Man's motives, and may conjecture that similar motives once existed among the ancestors of the Greeks. Our method, then, is to compare the seemingly meaningless customs or manners of civilised races with the similar customs and manners which exist among the uncivilised and still retain their meaning. It is not necessary for comparison of this sort that the uncivilised and the civilised race should be of the same stock, nor need we prove that they were ever in contact with each other. Similar conditions of mind produce similar practices, apart from identity of race, or borrowing of ideas and manners.

Let us return to the example of the flint arrow-heads. Everywhere neolithic arrow-heads are pretty much alike. The cause of the resemblance is no more than this, that men, with the same needs, the same materials, and the same rude instruments, everywhere produced the same kind of arrow-head. No hypothesis of interchange of ideas nor of community of race is needed to explain the resemblance of form in the missiles. Very early pottery in any region is, for the same causes, like very early pottery in any other region. The same sort of similarity was explained by the same resemblances in human nature, when we touched on the identity of magical practices and of superstitious beliefs. This method is fairly well established and orthodox when we deal with usages and superstitious beliefs; but may we apply the same method when we deal with myths?

Here a difficulty occurs. Mythologists, as a rule, are averse to the method of folklore. They think it scientific to compare only the myths of races which speak languages of the same family, and of races which have, in historic times, been actually in proved contact with each other. Thus, most mythologists hold it correct to compare Greek, Slavonic, Celtic, and Indian stories, because Greeks, Slavs, Celts, and Hindoos all speak languages of the same family. Again, they hold it correct to compare Chaldæan and Greek myths, because the Greeks and the Chaldæans were brought into contact through the Phœnicians, and by other intermediaries, such as the Hittites. But the same mythologists will vow that it is unscientific to compare a Maori or a Hottentot or an Eskimo myth with an Aryan story,[27] because Maoris and Eskimo and Hottentots do not speak languages akin to that of Greece, nor can we show that the ancestors of Greeks, Maoris, Hottentots, and Eskimo were ever in contact with each other in historical times.

Now the peculiarity of the method of folklore is that it will venture to compare (with due caution and due examination of evidence) the myths of the most widely severed races. Holding that myth is a product of the early human fancy, working on the most rudimentary knowledge of the outer world, the student of folklore thinks that differences of race do not much affect the early mythopœic faculty.[28] He will not be surprised if Greeks and Australian blacks are in the same tale.

In each case, he holds, all the circumstances of the case must be examined and considered. For instance, when the Australians tell a myth about the Pleiades very like the Greek myth of the Pleiades,[29] we must ask a number of questions. Is the Australian version authentic? Can the people who told it have heard it from a European? If these questions are answered so as to make it apparent that the Australian Pleiad myth is of genuine native origin, we need not fly to the conclusion that the Australians are a lost and forlorn branch of the Aryan race. Two other hypotheses present themselves. First, the human species is of unknown antiquity. In the moderate allowance of 250,000 years, there is time for stories to have wandered all round the world, as the Aggry beads of Ashanti have probably crossed the continent from Egypt, as the Asiatic jade (if Asiatic it be) has arrived in Swiss lake-dwellings, as an African trade-cowry is said to have been found in a Cornish barrow, as an Indian Ocean shell has been discovered in a prehistoric bone-cave in Poland.[30] This slow filtration of tales is not absolutely out of the question. Two causes would especially help to transmit myths. The first is slavery and slave-stealing, the second is the habit of capturing brides from alien stocks, and the law which forbids marriage with a woman of a man's own family. Slaves and captured brides would bring their native legends among alien peoples.

But there is another possible way of explaining the resemblance (granting that it is proved) of the Greek and Australian Pleiad myth. The object of both myths is to account for the grouping and other phenomena of the constellations. May not similar explanatory stories have occurred to the ancestors of the Australians, and to the ancestors of the Greeks, however remote their home, while they were still in the savage condition? The best way to investigate this point is to collect all known savage and civilised stellar myths, and see what points they have in common.[31] If they all agree in character, though the Greek tales are full of grace, while those of the Australians or Brazilians are rude enough, we may plausibly account for the similarity of myths, as we accounted for the similarity of flint arrow-heads. The myths, like the arrow-heads, resemble each other because they were originally framed to meet the same needs out of the same material. In the case of the arrow-heads, the need was for something hard, heavy, and sharp—the material was flint. In the case of the myths, the need was to explain certain phenomena—the material (so to speak) was an early state of the human mind, to which all objects seemed equally endowed with human personality, and to which no metamorphosis appeared impossible.

In the following essays,[32] then, the myths and customs of various peoples will be compared, even when these peoples talk languages of alien families, and have never (as far as history shows us) been in actual contact. Our method throughout will be to place the usage, or myth, which is unintelligible when found among a civilised race, beside the similar myth which is intelligible enough when it is found among savages. A mean term will be found in the folklore preserved by the non-progressive classes in a progressive people. This folklore represents, in the midst of a civilised race, the savage ideas out of which civilisation has been evolved. The conclusion will usually be that the fact which puzzles us by its presence in civilisation is a relic surviving from the time when the ancestors of a civilised race were in the state of savagery. By this method it is not necessary that 'some sort of genealogy should be established' between the Australian and the Greek narrators of a similar myth, nor between the Greek and Australian possessors of a similar usage. The hypothesis will be that the myth, or usage, is common to both races, not because of original community of stock, not because of contact and borrowing, but because the ancestors of the Greeks passed through the savage intellectual condition in which we find the Australians.

[...]

'Cupid, Psyche, and the "Sun-Frog"', *Custom and Myth*

(London: Longmans, Green and Co., 1884)

'Once upon a time there lived a king and a queen,' says the old woman in Apuleius, beginning the tale of Cupid and Psyche[1] with that ancient formula which has been dear to so many generations of children. In one shape or other the tale of Cupid and Psyche, of the woman who is forbidden to see or to name her husband, of the man with the vanished fairy bride, is known in most lands, 'even among barbarians.' According to the story the mystic prohibition is always broken: the hidden face is beheld; light is brought into the darkness; the forbidden name is uttered; the bride is touched with the tabooed metal, iron, and the union is ended. Sometimes the pair are re-united, after long searchings and wanderings; sometimes they are severed for ever. Such are the central situations in tales like that of Cupid and Psyche.

In the attempt to discover how the ideas on which this myth is based came into existence, we may choose one of two methods. We may confine our investigations to the Aryan peoples, among whom the story occurs both in the form of myth and of household tale. Again, we may look for the shapes of the legend which hide, like Peau d'Ane[2] in disguise, among the rude kraals[3] and wigwams, and in the strange and scanty garb of savages. If among savages we find both narratives like Cupid and Psyche, and also customs and laws out of which the myth might have arisen, we may provisionally conclude that similar customs once existed among the civilised races who possess the tale, and that from these sprang the early forms of the myth.

In accordance with the method hitherto adopted,[4] we shall prefer the second plan, and pursue our quest beyond the limits of the Aryan peoples.

The oldest literary shape of the tale of Psyche and her lover is found in the Rig Veda (x. 95).[5] The characters of a singular and cynical dialogue in that poem are named Urvasi and Pururavas. The former is an Apsaras, a kind of fairy or sylph, the mistress (and a *folle maîtresse*,[6] too) of Pururavas, a mortal man.[*] In the poem Urvasi remarks that when she dwelt among men she 'ate once a day a small piece of butter, and therewith well satisfied went away.'[7] This slightly reminds one of the common idea that the living may not eat in the land of the dead, and of Persephone's tasting the pomegranate in Hades.[8]

Of the dialogue in the Rig Veda it may be said, in the words of Mr. Toots, that 'the language is coarse and the meaning is obscure.'[9] We only gather that Urvasi, though she admits her sensual content in the society of Pururavas, is leaving him 'like the first of the dawns'; that she 'goes home again, hard to be caught, like the winds.' She gives her lover some hope, however—that the gods promise immortality even to him, 'the kinsman of Death' as he is. 'Let thine offspring worship the gods with an oblation; in Heaven shalt thou too have joy of the festival.'[10]

In the Rig Veda, then, we dimly discern a parting between a mortal man and an immortal bride, and a promise of reconciliation.

The story, of which this Vedic poem is a partial dramatisation, is given in the Brahmana of the Yajur Veda. Mr. Max Müller has translated the passage.[†] According to the Brahmana, 'Urvasi, a kind of fairy, fell in love with Pururavas, and when she met him she said: Embrace me three times a day, but never against my will, and let me never see you without your royal garments, *for this is the manner of women*.'[‡] The Gandharvas, a spiritual race, kinsmen of Urvasi, thought she had lingered too long among men. They therefore plotted some way of parting her from Pururavas. Her covenant with her lord declared that she was never to see him naked. If that compact were broken she would be compelled to leave him. To make Pururavas break this compact the Gandharvas stole a lamb from beside Urvasi's bed: Pururavas sprang up to rescue the lamb, and, in a flash of lightning, Urvasi saw him naked, contrary to the *manner of women*. She vanished. He sought her long, and at last came to a lake where she and her fairy friends were playing *in the shape of birds*. Urvasi saw Pururavas, revealed herself to him, and, according to the Brahmana, part of the strange Vedic dialogue was now spoken. Urvasi promised to meet him on the last night

---

[*]   That Pururavas is regarded as a mortal man, in relations with some sort of spiritual mistress, appears from the poem itself (v. 8, 9, 18). The human character of Pururavas also appears in R. V. i. 31, 4.

[†]   *Selected Essays*, i. 408.

[‡]   The Apsaras is an ideally beautiful fairy woman, something 'between the high gods and the lower grotesque beings,' with 'lotus eyes' and other agreeable characteristics. […]

of the year: a son was to be the result of the interview. Next day, her kins-folk, the Gandharvas, offered Pururavas the wish of his heart. He wished to be one of them. They then initiated him into the mode of kindling a certain sacred fire, after which he became immortal and dwelt among the Gandharvas.

It is highly characteristic of the Indian mind that the story should be thus worked into connection with ritual. In the same way the Bhagavata Purana has a long, silly, and rather obscene narrative about the sacrifice offered by Pururavas, and the new kind of sacred fire. Much the same ritual tale is found in the Vishnu Purana[11] (iv. 6, 19).

Before attempting to offer our own theory of the legend, we must ex-amine the explanations presented by scholars. The philological method of dealing with myths is well known. The hypothesis is that the names in a myth are 'stubborn things,' and that, as the whole narrative has probably arisen from forgetfulness of the meaning of language, the secret of a myth must be sought in analysis of the proper names of the persons. On this principle Mr. Max Müller interprets the myth of Urvasi and Pururavas, their loves, separation, and reunion. Mr. Müller says that the story 'express-es the identity of the morning dawn and the evening twilight.'[*][12] To prove this, the names are analysed. It is Mr. Müller's object to show that though, even in the Veda, Urvasi and Pururavas are names of persons, they were originally 'appellations'; and that Urvasi meant 'dawn,' and Pururavas 'sun.' Mr. Müller's opinion as to the etymological sense of the names would be thought decisive, naturally, by lay readers, if an opposite opinion were not held by that other great philologist and comparative mythologist, Adalbert Kuhn. Admitting that 'the etymology of Urvasi is difficult,' Mr. Müller derives it from '*uru*, wide (ευρύ), and a root *as* = to pervade.' Now the dawn is 'widely pervading,' and has, in Sanskrit, the epithet urûkî, 'far-going.' Mr. Müller next assumes that 'Eurykyde,' 'Eurynome,' 'Eurydike,' and other heroic Greek female names, are 'names of the dawn'; but this, it must be said, is merely an assumption of his school. The main point of the argu-ment is that Urvasi means 'far-going,' and that 'the far and wide splendour of dawn' is often spoken of in the Veda. 'However, the best proof that Urvasi was the dawn is the legend told of her and of her love to Pururavas, a story that is true only of the sun and the dawn' (i. 407).

We shall presently see that a similar story is told of persons in whom the dawn can scarcely be recognised, so that 'the best proof' is not very good.

The name of Pururavas, again, is 'an appropriate name for a solar hero.' … Pururavas meant the same as Πολυδεύκης, 'endowed with much light,' for, though *rava* is generally used of sound, yet the root *ru*, which means originally 'to cry,' is also applied to colour, in the sense of a loud or crying

---

★   *Selected Essays*, i. p. 405.

colour, that is, red.* Violet also, according to Sir G. W. Cox,† is a loud or
crying colour. 'The word (ιος), as applied to colour, is traced by Professor
Max Müller to the root *i*, as denoting a "crying hue," that is, a loud colour.'
It is interesting to learn that our Aryan fathers spoke of 'loud colours,' and
were so sensitive as to think violet 'loud.' Besides, Pururavas calls himself
Vasistha, which, as we know, is a name of the sun; and if he is called Aido,
the son of Ida, the same name is elsewhere given‡ to Agni, the fire. 'The
conclusion of the argument is that antiquity spoke of the naked sun, and of
the chaste dawn hiding her face when she had seen her husband. Yet she
says she will come again. And after the sun has travelled through the world
in search of his beloved, when he comes to the threshold of Death and is
going to end his solitary life, she appears again, in the gloaming, the same
as the dawn, as Eos in Homer, begins and ends the day, and she carries him
away to the golden seats of the Immortals.'§

Kuhn objects to all this explanation, partly on what we think the inadequate ground that there is no necessary connection between the story of
Urvasi (thus interpreted) and the ritual of sacred fire-lighting.[13] Connections
of that sort were easily invented at random by the compilers of the Brahmanas
in their existing form. Coming to the analysis of names, Kuhn finds in
Urvasi 'a weakening of Urvankî (*uru* + *anc*), like *yuvaça* from *yuvanka*, Latin
juvencus ... the accent is of no decisive weight.' Kuhn will not be convinced
that Pururavas is the sun, and is unmoved by the ingenious theory of 'a
crying colour,' denoted by his name, and the inference, supported by such
words as *rufus*, that crying colours are red, and therefore appropriate names
of the red sun. The connection between Pururavas and Agni, fire, is what
appeals to Kuhn—and, in short, where Mr. Müller sees a myth of sun and
dawn, Kuhn recognises a fire-myth. Roth, again (whose own name means
red), far from thinking that Urvasi is 'the chaste dawn,' interprets her name
as *die geile*, that is, 'lecherous, lascivious, lewd, wanton, obscene'; while
Pururavas, as 'the Roarer,' suggests 'the Bull in rut.'[14] In accordance with
these views Roth explains the myth in a fashion of his own.¶

Here, then, as Kuhn says, 'we have three essentially different modes of
interpreting the myth,'** all three founded on philological analysis of the

---

*   Cf. *ruber, rufus*, O. H. G. *rôt, rudhira*, ερυθρός; also Sanskrit, *ravi*, sun.

†   *Myth. Ar. Nat.* [*The Mythology of the Aryan Nations*] ii. 81.

‡   R. V. iii. 29, 3.

§   The passage alluded to in Homer does not mean that dawn 'ends' the day, but
'when the fair-tressed Dawn brought the full light of the third day' (*Od.* v. 390).

¶   Liebrecht (*Zur Volkskunde* [To Folklore], 241) is reminded by Pururavas (in
Roth's sense of *der Brüller* [the roarer]) of loud-thundering Zeus, ἐρίγδουπος
[Erigdupus].

**   *Herabkunft des Feuers*, p. 86–89.

names in the story. No better example could be given to illustrate the weakness of the philological method. In the first place, that method relies on names as the primitive relics and germs of the tale, although the tale may occur where the names have never been heard, and though the names are, presumably, late additions to a story in which the characters were originally anonymous. Again, the most illustrious etymologists differ absolutely about the true sense of the names. Kuhn sees fire everywhere, and fire-myths; Mr. Müller sees dawn and dawn-myths; Schwartz sees storm and storm-myths,[15] and so on. As the orthodox teachers are thus at variance, so that there is no safety in orthodoxy, we may attempt to use our heterodox method.

None of the three scholars whose views we have glanced at—neither Roth, Kuhn, nor Mr. Müller—lays stress on the saying of Urvasi, 'never let me see you without your royal garments, *for this is the custom of women.*'[16] To our mind, these words contain the gist of the myth. There must have been, at some time, a custom which forbade women to see their husbands without their garments, or the words have no meaning. If any custom of this kind existed, a story might well be evolved to give a sanction to the law. 'You must never see your husband naked: think what happened to Urvasi—she vanished clean away!' This is the kind of warning which might be given. If the customary prohibition had grown obsolete, the punishment might well be assigned to a being of another, a spiritual, race, in which old human ideas lingered, as the neolithic dread of iron lingers in the Welsh fairies.[17]

Our method will be, to prove the existence of singular rules of etiquette, corresponding to the etiquette accidentally infringed by Pururavas. We shall then investigate stories of the same character as that of Urvasi and Pururavas, in which the infringement of the etiquette is chastised. It will be seen that, in most cases, the bride is of a peculiar and perhaps supernatural race. Finally, the tale of Urvasi will be taken up again, will be shown to conform in character to the other stories examined, and will be explained as a myth told to illustrate, or sanction, a nuptial etiquette.

The lives of savages are bound by the most closely-woven fetters of custom. The simplest acts are 'tabooed,'[18] a strict code regulates all intercourse. Married life, especially, moves in the strangest fetters. There will be nothing remarkable in the wide distribution of a myth turning on nuptial etiquette, if this law of nuptial etiquette proves to be also widely distributed. That it is widely distributed we now propose to demonstrate by examples.

The custom of the African people of the kingdom of Futa is, or was, even stricter than the Vedic *custom of women*—'wives never permit their husbands to see them unveiled for three years after their marriage.'*

In his 'Travels to Timbuctoo' (i. 94), Caillié[19] says that the bridegroom 'is

---

*   Astley, *Collection of Voyages*, ii. 24. […]

not allowed to see his intended during the day.' He has a tabooed hut apart, and 'if he is obliged to come out he covers his face.' He 'remains with his wife only till daybreak'—like Cupid—and flees, like Cupid, before the light. Among the Australians the chief deity, if deity such a being can be called, Pundjel, 'has a wife whose face he has never seen,' probably in compliance with some primæval etiquette or taboo.*

Among the Yorubas 'conventional modesty forbids a woman to speak to her husband, or even to see him, if it can be avoided.'[†] Of the Iroquois Lafitau says: 'Ils n'osent aller dans les cabanes particulières où habitent leurs épouses que durant l'obscurité de la nuit.'[‡][20] The Circassian women live on distant terms with their lords till they become mothers.[§] Similar examples of reserve are reported to be customary among the Fijians.

In backward parts of Europe a strange custom forbids the bride to speak to her lord, as if in memory of a time when husband and wife were always of alien tribes, and, as among the Caribs, spoke different languages.

In the Bulgarian 'Volkslied,'[21] the Sun marries Grozdanka, a mortal girl. Her mother addresses her thus:—

> Grozdanka, mother's treasure mine,
> For nine long years I nourished thee,
> For nine months see thou do not speak
> To thy first love that marries thee.[22]

M. Dozon, who has collected the Bulgarian songs, says that this custom of prolonged silence on the part of the bride is very common in Bulgaria, though it is beginning to yield to a sense of the ludicrous.[¶] In Sparta and in Crete, as is well known, the bridegroom was long the victim of a somewhat similar taboo, and was only permitted to seek the company of his wife secretly, and in the dark, like the Iroquois described by Lafitau.

Herodotus tells us (i. 146) that some of the old Ionian colonists 'brought no women with them, but took wives of the women of the Carians, whose fathers they had slain. Therefore the women made a law for themselves, and handed it down to their daughters, that they should never sit at meat with their husbands, and *that none should ever call her husband by his name.*' In precisely the same way, in Zululand the wife may not mention her husband's name, just as in the Welsh fairy tale the husband may not even know the name of his fairy bride, on pain of losing her for ever.[23] These ideas about

---

* Brough Smyth, [*The Aborigines of Victoria*] i. 423.

† Bowen, *Central Africa*, p. 303.

‡ Lafitau, [*Moeurs des Sauvages Amériquains* (Customs of the American Indians)] i. 576.

§ Lubbock, *Origin of Civilisation* (1875), p. 75.

¶ *Chansons Pop. Bulg.* [*Chansons Populaires Bulgares*], p. 172.

names, and freakish ways of avoiding the use of names, mark the childhood of languages, according to Mr. Max Müller,* and, therefore, the childhood of Society. The Kaffirs call this etiquette 'Hlonipa.'[24] It applies to women as well as men. A Kaffir bride is not called by her own name in her husband's village, but is spoken of as 'mother of so and so,' even before she has borne a child. The universal superstition about names is at the bottom of this custom. The Aleutian Islanders, according to Dall, are quite distressed when obliged to speak to their wives in the presence of others.[25] The Fijians did not know where to look when missionaries hinted that a man might live under the same roof as his wife.† Among the Turkomans, for six months, a year, or two years, a husband is only allowed to visit his wife by stealth.[26]

The number of these instances could probably be increased by a little research. Our argument is that the widely distributed myths in which a husband or a wife transgresses some 'custom'—sees the other's face or body, or utters the forbidden name—might well have arisen as tales illustrating the punishment of breaking the rule. By a very curious coincidence, a Breton sailor's tale of the 'Cupid and Psyche'[27] class is confessedly founded on the existence of the rule of nuptial etiquette.‡

In this story the son of a Boulogne pilot marries the daughter of the King of Naz—wherever that may be. In Naz a man is never allowed to see the face of his wife till she has borne him a child—a modification of the Futa rule. The inquisitive French husband unveils his wife, and, like Psyche in Apuleius, drops wax from a candle on her cheek. When the pair return to Naz, the king of that country discovers the offence of the husband, and, by the aid of his magicians, transforms the Frenchman into a monster. Here we have the old formula—the infringement of a 'taboo,' and the magical punishment—adapted to the ideas of Breton peasantry. The essential point of the story, for our purpose, is that the veiling of the bride is 'the custom of women,' in the mysterious land of Naz. 'C'est l'usage du pays: les maris ne voient leurs femmes sans voile que lorsqu'elles sont devenues mères.'[28] Now our theory of the myth of Urvasi is simply this: 'the custom of women,' which Pururavas transgresses, is probably a traditional Aryan law of nuptial etiquette, *l'usage du pays*, once prevalent among the people of India.

If our view be correct, then several rules of etiquette, and not one alone, will be illustrated in the stories which we suppose the rules to have suggested. In the case of Urvasi and Pururavas, the rule was, not to see the husband naked. In 'Cupid and Psyche,' the husband was not to be looked upon at all. In the well-known myth of Mélusine, the bride is not to be seen naked.

---

* *Lectures on [the Science of] Language*, Second Series, p. 41.

† J. A. Farrer, *Primitive Manners*, p. 202, quoting Seemann.

‡ Sébillot, *Contes Pop. de la Haute-Bretagne*, p. 183.

Mélusine tells her lover that she will only abide with him *dum ipsam nudam non viderit.*[*][29] The same taboo occurs in a Dutch *Märchen.*[†][30]

We have now to examine a singular form of the myth, in which the strange bride is not a fairy, or spiritual being, but an animal. In this class of story the husband is usually forbidden to perform some act which will recall to the bride the associations of her old animal existence. The converse of the tale is the well-known legend of the Forsaken Merman. The king of the sea permits his human wife to go to church. The ancient sacred associations are revived, and the woman returns no more.

> She will not come though you call all day
> Come away, come away.[31]

Now, in the tales of the animal bride, it is her associations with her former life among the beasts that are not to be revived, and when they are reawakened by the commission of some act which she has forbidden, or the neglect of some precaution which she has enjoined, she, like Urvasi, disappears.

The best known example of this variant of the tale is the story of Bheki, in Sanskrit. Mr. Max Müller has interpreted the myth in accordance with his own method.[32] His difficulty is to account for the belief that a king might marry a frog. Our ancestors, he remarks, 'were not idiots,' how then could they tell such a story? We might reply that our ancestors, if we go far enough back, were savages, and that such stories are the staple of savage myth. Mr. Müller, however, holds that an accidental corruption of language reduced Aryan fancy to the savage level. He explains the corruption thus: 'We find, in Sanskrit, that Bheki, the frog, was a beautiful girl, and that one day, when sitting near a well, she was discovered by a king, who asked her to be his wife. She consented, *on condition that he should never show her a drop of water.* One day, being tired, she asked the king for water; the king forgot his promise, brought water, and Bheki disappeared.' This myth, Mr. Müller holds, 'began with a short saying, such as that "Bheki, the sun, will die at the sight of water," as we should say that the sun will set, when it approaches the water from which it rose in the morning.' But how did the sun come to be called Bheki, 'the frog'? Mr. Müller supposes that this name was given to the sun by some poet or fisherman. He gives no evidence for the following statement: 'It can be shown that "frog" was used as a name for the sun. Now at sunrise and sunset, when the sun was squatting on the water, it was called the "frog."' At what historical period the Sanskrit-speaking race was settled in seats where the sun rose and set in water, we do not know, and 'chapter and verse' are needed for the statement that 'frog' was actually a name of the sun. Mr. Müller's argument, however, is that the sun was called 'the frog,' that

---

[*] Gervase of Tilbury, [*Otia Imperialia* 1.15. 4-6]

[†] Kuhn, *Herabkunft*, p. 92.

people forgot that the frog and sun were identical, and that Frog, or Bheki, was mistaken for the name of a girl to whom was applied the old saw about dying at sight of water. 'And so,' says Mr. Müller, 'the change from sun to frog, and from frog to man, which was at first due to the mere spell of language, would in our nursery tales be ascribed to miraculous charms more familiar to a later age.' As a matter of fact, magical metamorphoses are infinitely more familiar to the lowest savages than to people in a 'later age.' Magic, as Castren observes, 'belongs to the lowest known stages of civilisation.'[33] Mr. Müller's theory, however, is this—that a Sanskrit-speaking people, living where the sun rose out of and set in some ocean, called the sun, as he touched the water, Bheki, the frog, and said he would die at the sight of water. They ceased to call the sun the frog, or Bheki, but kept the saying, 'Bheki will die at sight of water.' Not knowing who or what Bheki might be, they took her for a frog, who also was a pretty wench. Lastly, they made the story of Bheki's distinguished wedding and mysterious disappearance. For this interpretation, historical and linguistic evidence is not offered. When did a Sanskrit-speaking race live beside a great sea? How do we know that 'frog' was used as a name for 'sun'?

We have already given our explanation. To the savage intellect, man and beast are on a level, and all savage myth makes men descended from beasts; while stories of the loves of gods in bestial shape, or the unions of men and animals, incessantly occur. 'Unnatural' as these notions seem to us, no ideas are more familiar to savages, and none recur more frequently in Indo-Aryan, Scandinavian, and Greek mythology. An extant tribe in North-West America still claims descent from a frog. The wedding of Bheki and the king is a survival, in Sanskrit, of a tale of this kind. Lastly, Bheki disappears, when her associations with her old amphibious life are revived in the manner she had expressly forbidden.

Our interpretation may be supported by an Ojibway parallel.[34] A hunter named Otter-heart, camping near a beaver lodge, found a pretty girl loitering round his fire. She keeps his wigwam in order, and 'lays his blanket near the deerskin she had laid for herself. "Good," he muttered, "this is my wife."' She refuses to eat the beavers he has shot, but at night he hears a noise, 'krch, krch, as if beavers were gnawing wood.' He sees, by the glimmer of the fire, his wife nibbling birch twigs. In fact, the good little wife is a beaver, as the pretty Indian girl was a frog. The pair lived happily till spring came and the snow melted and the streams ran full. Then his wife implored the hunter to build her a bridge over every stream and river, that she might cross dry-footed. 'For,' she said, 'if my feet touch water, this would at once cause thee great sorrow.' The hunter did as she bade him, but left unbridged one tiny runnel. The wife stumbled into the water, and, as soon as her foot was wet, she immediately resumed her old shape as a beaver, her son became a beaverling, and the brooklet, changing to a roaring river, bore them to the lake. Once the hunter saw his wife again among her beast kin. 'To thee I sacrificed all,' she said, 'and I only asked thee to help me dry-footed over the waters. Thou didst cruelly neglect this. Now I must remain for ever with my people.'

This tale was told to Kohl[35] by 'an old insignificant squaw among the Ojibways.'* Here we have a precise parallel to the tale of Bheki, the frog-bride, and here the reason of the prohibition to touch water is made perfectly unmistakable. The touch magically revived the bride's old animal life with the beavers. Or was the Indian name for beaver (*temaksê*) once a name for the sun?

[…]

Here, then, we have many examples of the disappearance of the bride or bridegroom in consequence of infringement of various mystic rules. Sometimes the beloved one is seen when he or she should not be seen. Sometimes, as in a Maori story, the bride vanishes, merely because she is in a bad temper.† Among the Red Men, as in Sanskrit, the taboo on water is broken, with the usual results. Now for an example in which the rule against using *names* is infringed.‡

This formula constantly occurs in the Welsh fairy tales published by Professor Rhys.§[36] Thus the heir of Corwrion fell in love with a fairy: 'They were married on the distinct understanding that the husband was not to know her name, … and was not to strike her with iron, on pain of her leaving him at once.' Unluckily the man once tossed her a bridle, the iron bit touched the wife, and 'she at once flew through the air, and plunged headlong into Corwrion Lake.'

A number of tales turning on the same incident are published in 'Cymmrodor,' v. I. In these we have either the taboo on the name, or the taboo on the touch of iron. In a widely diffused superstition iron 'drives away devils and ghosts,' according to the Scholiast on the eleventh book of the 'Odyssey,' and the Oriental Djinn also flee from iron.¶ Just as water is fatal to the Aryan frog-bride and to the Red Indian beaver-wife, restoring them to their old animal forms, so the magic touch of iron breaks love between the Welshman and his fairy mistress, the representative of the stone age.

In many tales of fairy-brides, they are won by a kind of force. The lover in the familiar Welsh and German *Märchen*[37] sees the swan-maidens throw

---

*   *Kitchi Gami*, p. 105.

†   Taylor, *New Zealand* [*Te Ika a Maui: Or, New Zealand and Its Inhabitants*], p. 143.

‡   Liebrecht gives a Hindoo example, *Zur Volkskunde*, p. 239.

§   *Cymmrodor*, iv. pt. 2.

¶   [E. B. Tylor], *Primitive Culture*, i. 140.

off their swan plumage and dance naked. He steals the feather-garb of one of them, and so compels her to his love. Finally, she leaves him, in anger, or because he has broken some taboo. Far from being peculiar to Aryan mythology, this legend occurs, as Mr. Farrer[38] has shown,[*] in Algonquin and Bornoese tradition. The Red Indian story told by Schoolcraft in his 'Algic Researches'[39] is most like the Aryan version, but has some native peculiarities. Wampee was a great hunter, who, on the lonely prairie, once heard strains of music. Looking up he saw a speck in the sky: the speck drew nearer and nearer, and proved to be a basket containing twelve heavenly maidens. They reached the earth and began to dance, inflaming the heart of Wampee with love. But Wampee could not draw near the fairy girls in his proper form without alarming them. Like Zeus in his love adventures, Wampee exercised the medicine-man's power of metamorphosing himself. He assumed the form of a mouse, approached unobserved, and caught one of the dancing maidens. After living with Wampee for some time she wearied of earth, and, by virtue of a 'mystic chain of verse,' she ascended again to her heavenly home.

Now is there any reason to believe that this incident was once part of the myth of Pururavas and Urvasi? Was the fairy-love, Urvasi, originally caught and held by Pururavas among her naked and struggling companions? Though this does not appear to have been much noticed, it seems to follow from a speech of Pururavas in the Vedic dialogue [...] (x. 95, 8, 9). Mr. Max Müller translates thus: 'When I, the mortal, threw my arms round those flighty immortals, they trembled away from me like a trembling doe, like horses that kick against the cart.'[†] Ludwig's rendering[40] suits our view—that Pururavas is telling how he first caught Urvasi—still better: 'When I, the mortal, held converse with the immortals who had laid aside their raiment, like slippery serpents they glided from me, like horses yoked to the car.' These words would well express the adventure of a lover among the naked flying swan-maidens, an adventure familiar to the Red Men as to Persian legends of the Peris.

To end our comparison of myths like the tale of 'Cupid and Psyche,' we find an example among the Zulus. Here[‡] the mystic lover came in when all was dark, and felt the damsel's face. After certain rites, 'in the morning he went away, he speaking continually, the girl not seeing him. During all those days he would not allow the girl (*sic*), when she said she would light a fire. Finally, after a magical ceremony, he said, "Light the fire!" and stood before her revealed, a shining shape.'[41] This has a curious resemblance to the myth of Cupid and Psyche; but a more curious detail remains. In the Zulu story of Ukcombekcansini, the friends of a bride break a taboo and kill a tabooed

---

[*]   *Primitive Manners*, p. 256.

[†]   *Selected Essays*, i. 411.

[‡]   *Callaway*, p. 63.

animal.[42] Instantly, like Urvasi and her companions in the Yajur Veda, the bride and her maidens disappear *and are turned into birds!*[*] They are afterwards surprised in human shape, and the bride is restored to her lover.

Here we conclude, having traced parallels to Cupid and Psyche in many non-Aryan lands. Our theory of the myth does not rest on etymology. We have seen that the most renowned scholars, Max Müller, Kuhn, Roth, all analyse the names Urvasi and Pururavas in different ways, and extract different interpretations. We have found the story where these names were probably never heard of. We interpret it as a tale of the intercourse between mortal men and immortal maids, or between men and metamorphosed animals, as in India and North America. We explain the separation of the lovers as the result of breaking a taboo, or law of etiquette, binding among men and women, as well as between men and fairies.

The taboos are, to see the beloved unveiled, to utter his or her name, to touch her with a metal 'terrible to ghosts and spirits,' or to do some action which will revive the associations of a former life. We have shown that rules of nuptial etiquette resembling these in character do exist, and have existed, even among Greeks—as where the Milesian, like the Zulu, women made a law not to utter their husbands' names. Finally, we think it a reasonable hypothesis that tales on the pattern of 'Cupid and Psyche' might have been evolved wherever a curious nuptial taboo required to be sanctioned, or explained, by a myth. On this hypothesis, the stories may have been separately invented in different lands; but there is also a chance that they have been transmitted from people to people in the unknown past of our scattered and wandering race. This theory seems at least as probable as the hypothesis that the meaning of an Aryan proverbial statement about sun and dawn was forgotten, and was altered unconsciously into a tale which is found among various non-Aryan tribes. That hypothesis again, learned and ingenious as it is, has the misfortune to be opposed by other scholarly hypotheses not less ingenious and learned.

As for the sun-frog, we may hope that he has sunk for ever beneath the western wave.

---

[*]   *Ibid.*, p. 119.

2

ANTHROPOLOGY AND FOLKLORE

The impact of recent anthropological thought and practice upon Lang's approach to folklore is further exemplified in the two following pieces. The first, 'New System Proposed', is taken from *Myth, Ritual and Religion*, 2 vols (1887; Longmans, Green and Co., second edition 1899) – a major two-volume study that sets out to provide scholarly explanations for the existence of apparently irrational elements in mythological and religious traditions. Lang surveys 'past systems of mythological interpretation' (p. 29) from the classical period through to the nineteenth century that have sought to explain away irrational elements in religion by resolving 'nonsense and blasphemy' into 'some harmless or even praiseworthy explanation' (p. 17). 'Each of these systems had its own amount of truth,' Lang judges, 'but each certainly failed to unravel the whole web of tradition and of foolish faith' (p. 30). In the second chapter, extracted in this section, he begins to unfold his own view, supported by recent anthropological research, that these irrational elements are in fact 'survivals' from the period of savagery.

Myth, Ritual and Religion was first published in August 1887; the text was then revised – significantly in some places – for the 'Silver Library' edition of February 1899. The objective of the revisions was to incorporate newly available anthropological research, to reflect developments in Lang's own thinking, and to excise a 'fragment or two of controversy' (p. xv; for discussion see Richard Dorson, *The British Folklorists: A History* (Chicago: University of Chicago Press, 1968), pp. 170-1). The passage extracted here is taken from the second edition. Lang made some minor changes to the 1887 text. Typographic changes and changes to punctuation have not been noted here, but textual changes are recorded in endnotes.

The second piece in this section is from Lang's extended essay, 'Household Tales; Their Origin, Diffusion, and Relations to the Higher Myths', which prefaces the two-volume translation of the *Grimm's Household Tales* (London: George Bell and Sons, 1884) published by Margaret Hunt. It is one of Lang's most important works on folk narrative for two reasons: first because of its comprehensive examination and critique of the arguments of the solar mythological school of thought represented by Max Müller and George Cox; second for its detailed presentation of Lang's alternative theory of the folk narrative: that folk tales originate when man is in the savage state, that they are transformed by the progressive development of civilisation into household tales and higher myths, and that they are spread by a mixture of independent invention and slow transmission. Because of its significance, this essay is included here in almost complete form.

Lang does not include subheadings in the original essay, but supplies a breakdown of the argument in advance. For ease of reading, the present edition uses Lang's 'argument' as a basis for section divisions.

'New System Proposed',
Myth, Ritual and Religion
(Longmans, Green and Co., second edition, 1899)

[...]

[**A**] new science has come into existence, the science which studies man in the sum of all his works and thoughts, as evolved through the whole process of his development. This science, Comparative Anthropology, examines[1] the development of law out of custom; the development of weapons from the stick or stone to the latest repeating rifle; the development of society from the horde to the nation. It is a study which does not despise the most backward nor degraded tribe, nor neglect the most civilised, and it frequently finds in Australians or Nootkas the germ of ideas and institutions which Greeks or Romans brought to perfection, or retained, little altered from their early rudeness, in the midst of civilisation.

It is inevitable that this science should also try its hand on mythology. Our purpose is to employ the anthropological method—the study of the evolution of ideas, from the savage to the barbarous, and thence to the civilised stage—in the province of myth, ritual, and religion. It has been shown that the light of this method had dawned on Eusebius in his polemic with the heathen apologists. Spencer, the head of Corpus, Cambridge (1630–93), had really no other scheme in his mind in his erudite work on Hebrew Ritual.* Spencer was a student of man's religions generally, and he came to the conclusion that Hebrew ritual was but an expurgated, and, so to speak, divinely 'licensed' adaptation of heathen customs at large. We do but follow his guidance on less perilous ground[2] when we seek for the original forms of classical rite and myth in the parallel usages and legends of the most backward races.

---

*   *De Legibus Hebræorum Ritualibus*, Tubingae, 1732.

Fontenelle, in the last century, stated, with all the clearness of the French intellect, the system which is partially worked out in this essay—the system which explains the irrational element in myth as inherited from savagery. Fontenelle's paper (*Sur l'Origine des Fables*)[3] is brief, sensible, and witty, and requires little but copious evidence to make it adequate. But he merely threw out the idea, and left it to be neglected.[4]

Among other founders of the anthropological or historical school of mythology, De Brosses should not be forgotten. In his *Dieux Fétiches* (1760) he follows the path which Eusebius indicated—the path of Spencer and Fontenelle—now the beaten road of Tylor and McLennan and Mannhardt.

In anthropology, in the science of Waitz, Tylor, and McLennan, in the examination of man's faith in the light of his social, legal, and historical conditions generally, we find, with Mannhardt, some of the keys of myth. This science 'makes it manifest that the different stages through which humanity has passed in its intellectual evolution have still their living representatives among various existing races. The study of these lower races is an invaluable instrument for the interpretation of the survivals from earlier stages, which we meet in the full civilisation of cultivated peoples, but whose origins were in the remotest fetichism and savagery.'[5]

It is by following this road, and by the aid of anthropology and of human history, that we propose to seek for a demonstrably actual condition of the human intellect, whereof the puzzling qualities of[6] myth would be the natural and inevitable fruit. In all the earlier theories which we have sketched, inquirers took it for granted that the myth-makers were men with philosophic and moral ideas like their own—ideas which, from some reason of religion or state, they expressed in *bizarre* terms of allegory. We shall attempt, on the other hand, to prove that the human mind has passed through a condition quite unlike that of civilised men—a condition in which things seemed natural and rational that now appear unnatural and devoid of reason, and in which, therefore, if myths were evolved, they would, if they survived into civilisation, be such as civilised men find strange and perplexing.

Our first question will be, Is there a stage of human society and of the human intellect in which facts that appear to us to be monstrous and irrational—facts corresponding to the wilder incidents of myth—are accepted as ordinary occurrences of everyday life? In the region of romantic rather than of mythical invention we know that there is such a state. Mr. Lane, in his preface to the *Arabian Nights*,[7] says that the Arabs have an advantage over us as story-tellers. They can introduce such incidents as the change of a man into a horse, or of a woman into a dog, or the intervention of an Afreet[8] without any more scruple than our own novelists feel in describing a duel or the concealment of a will. Among the Arabs the agencies of magic and of spirits are regarded as at least as probable and common as duels and concealments of wills seem to be thought by European novelists. It is obvious that we need look no farther for the explanation of the supernatural events in Arab romances. Now, let us apply this system to mythology. It is admitted that Greeks, Romans, Aryans of India in the age of the Sanskrit commentators, and Egyptians of the Ptolemaic and earlier ages, were as much puzzled as we are by the mythical adventures of their gods. But is there any known stage of the human intellect in which similar adventures, and the metamorphoses of men into animals, trees, stars, and all else that puzzles us in the civilised mythologies, are regarded as possible incidents of daily human life? Our answer is, that everything in the civilised mythologies which we regard as irrational seems only part of the accepted and natural order of things to contemporary savages, and in the past seemed equally rational and natural to savages concerning whom we have historical information.[9] Our theory is, therefore, that the savage and senseless element in mythology is, for the most part, a legacy from the fancy of[10] ancestors of the civilised races who were once in an intellectual state not higher, but probably lower, than that of Australians, Bushmen, Red Indians, the lower races of South America, and other worse than barbaric peoples. As the ancestors of the Greeks, Aryans of India, Egyptians and others advanced in civilisation, their religious thought was shocked and surprised by myths (originally dating from the period of savagery, and natural in that period, though even then often in contradiction to morals and religion)[11] which were preserved down to the time of Pausanias by local priesthoods, or which were stereotyped in the ancient poems of Hesiod and Homer, or in the Brahmanas and Vedas of India, or were retained in the popular religion of Egypt. This theory recommended itself to Lobeck. 'We may believe that ancient and early tribes framed gods like unto themselves in action and in experience, and that the allegorical softening down of myths is the explanation added later by descendants who had attained to purer ideas of divinity, yet dared not reject the religion of their ancestors.'* The senseless element in the myths would, by this theory, be for the most part a 'survival'; and the age and condition of human thought whence it survived would be one in which our most ordinary ideas about the nature of things and the limits of possibility did not yet exist, when all things were conceived of in quite other fashion; the age, that is, of savagery.

It is universally admitted that 'survivals' of this kind do account for many anomalies in our institutions, in law, politics, society, even in dress and manners. If isolated fragments of earlier ages abide in these, it is still more probable that other fragments will survive in anything so closely connected as is mythology with the conservative religious sentiment and tradition. Our object, then, is to prove that the 'silly, savage, and irrational' element in the myths of civilised peoples is, as a rule, either a survival from the period of savagery, or has been borrowed from savage neighbours by a

---

* *Aglaoph[amus].*, i. 153. [...]

cultivated people, or, lastly, is an imitation by later poets of old savage *data*.'[12] For example, to explain the constellations as metamorphosed men, animals, or other objects of terrestrial life is the habit of savages,[†] —a natural habit among people who regard all things as on one level of personal life and intelligence. When the stars, among civilised Greeks or Aryans of India, are also popularly regarded as transformed and transfigured men, animals and the like, this belief may be either a survival from the age when the ancestors of Greeks and Indians were in the intellectual condition of the Australian Murri; or the star-name and star-myth may have been borrowed from savages, or from cultivated peoples once savage or apt to copy savages; or, as in the case of the *Coma Berenices*,[13] a poet of a late age may have invented a new artificial myth on the old lines of savage fancy.

This method of interpreting a certain element in mythology is, we must repeat, no new thing, though, to judge from the protests of several mythologists, it is new to many inquirers. We have seen that Eusebius threw out proposals in this direction; that Spencer, De Brosses, and Fontenelle unconsciously followed him; and we have quoted from Lobeck a statement of a similar opinion. The whole matter has been stated as clearly as possible by Mr. E. B. Tylor:—

'Savages have been for untold ages, and still are, living in the myth-making stage of the human mind. It was through sheer ignorance and neglect of this direct knowledge how and by what manner of men myths are really made that their simple philosophy has come to be buried under masses of commentator's rubbish … '.[‡] Mr. Tylor goes on thus (and his words contain the gist of our argument): 'The general thesis maintained is that myth arose in the savage condition prevalent in remote ages among the whole human race; that it remains comparatively unchanged among the rude modern tribes who have departed least from these primitive conditions, while higher and later civilisations, partly by retaining its actual principles, and partly by carrying on its inherited results in the form of ancestral tradition, continued it not merely in toleration, but in honour'.[§] Elsewhere Mr. Tylor points out that by this method of interpretation we may study myths in various stages of evolution, from the rude guess of the savage at an explanation of natural phenomena, through the systems of the higher barbarisms,

---

[*]   We may be asked why do savages entertain the irrational ideas which survive in myth? One might as well ask why they eat each other, or use stones instead of metal. Their intellectual powers are not fully developed, and hasty analogy from their own unreasoned consciousness is their chief guide. Myth, in Mr. Darwin's phrase, is one of the 'miserable and indirect consequences of our highest faculties'. *Descent of Man*, p. 69.

[†]   See *Custom and Myth*, 'Star-Myths'.

[‡]   *Primitive Culture*, 2nd edit., i. p. 283.

[§]   *Op. cit.*, p. 275.

or lower civilisations (as in ancient Mexico), and the sacerdotage[14] of India, till myth reaches its most human form in Greece. Yet even in Greek myth the beast is not wholly cast out, and Hellas by no means 'let the ape and tiger die'.[15] That Mr. Tylor does not exclude the Aryan race from his general theory is plain enough.* 'What is the Aryan conception of the Thunder-god but a poetic elaboration of thoughts inherited from the savage stage through which the primitive Aryans had passed?'

The advantages of our hypothesis (if its legitimacy be admitted) are obvious. In the first place, we have to deal with an actual demonstrable condition of the human intellect. The existence of the savage state in all its various degrees, and of the common intellectual habits and conditions which are shared by the backward peoples, and again the survival of many of these in civilisation, are indubitable facts. We are not obliged to fall back upon some fanciful and unsupported theory of what 'primitive man' did, and said, and thought. Nay, more; we escape all the fallacies connected with the terms 'primitive man'. We are not compelled[16] to prove that the first men of all were like modern savages, nor that savages represent primitive man. It may be that the lowest extant savages are the nearest of existing peoples to the type of the first human beings. But on this point it is unnecessary for us to dogmatise. If we can show that, whether men began their career as savages or not, they have at least passed through the savage *status* or have borrowed the ideas of races in the savage *status*, that is all we need. We escape from all the snares of theories (incapable of historical proof) about the really primeval and original condition of the human family.

Once more, our theory naturally attaches itself to the general system of Evolution. We are enabled to examine mythology as a thing of gradual development and of slow and manifold modifications, corresponding in some degree to the various changes in the general progress of society. Thus we shall watch the barbaric conditions of thought which produce barbaric myths, while these in their turn are retained, or perhaps purified, or perhaps explained away, by more advanced civilisations. Further, we shall be able to detect the survival of the savage ideas with least modification, and the persistence of the savage myths with least change, among the classes of a civilised population which have shared least in the general advance. These classes are, first, the rustic peoples, dwelling far from cities and schools, on heaths or by the sea; second, the conservative local priesthoods, who retain the more crude and ancient myths of the local gods and heroes after these have been modified or rejected by the purer sense of philosophers and national poets. Thus much of ancient myth is a woven warp and woof of three threads: the savage *donnée*,[17] the civilised and poetic modification of the savage *donnée*, the version of the original fable which survives in popular tales and in the 'sacred chapters' of local priesthoods. A critical study of these

---

★   *Primitive Culture*, 2nd edit., ii. 265.

three stages in myth is in accordance with the recognised practice of science. Indeed, the whole system is only an application to this particular province, mythology, of the method by which the development either of organisms or of human institutions is traced. As the anomalies and apparently useless and accidental features in the human or in other animal organisms may be explained as stunted or rudimentary survivals of organs useful in a previous stage of life, so the anomalous and irrational myths of civilised races may be explained as survivals of stories which, in an earlier state of thought and knowledge, seemed natural enough. The persistence of the myths[18] is accounted for by the well-known conservatism of the religious sentiment—a conservatism noticed even by Eusebius. 'In later days, when they became ashamed of the religious beliefs of their ancestors, they invented private and respectful interpretations, each to suit himself. For no one dared to shake the ancestral beliefs, as they honoured at a very high rate the sacredness and antiquity of old associations, and of the teaching they had received in childhood.'*

Thus the method which we propose to employ is in harmony both with modern scientific procedure and with the views of a clear-sighted Father of the Church. Consequently no system could well be less 'heretical' and 'unorthodox'.

The last advantage of our hypothesis which need here be mentioned is that it helps to explain the *diffusion* no less than the *origin* of the wild and crazy element in myth. We seek for the origin of the savage factor of myth in one aspect of[19] the intellectual condition of savages. We say 'in one aspect' expressly; to guard against the suggestion that the savage intellect has no aspect but this, and no saner ideas than those of myth. The *diffusion* of stories practically identical in every quarter of the globe may be (provisionally) regarded as the result of the prevalence in every quarter, at one time or another, of similar mental habits and ideas. This explanation must not be pressed too hard nor too far. If we find all over the world a belief that men can change themselves and their neighbours into beasts, that belief will account for the appearance of metamorphosis in myth. If we find a belief that inanimate objects are really much on a level with man, the opinion will account for incidents of myth such as that in which the wooden figure-head of the Argo speaks with a human voice.[20] Again, a widespread belief in the separability of the soul or the life from the body will account for the incident in nursery tales and myths of the 'giant who had no heart in his body,'[21] but kept his heart and life elsewhere. An ancient identity of mental status and the working of similar mental forces at the attempt to explain the same phenomena will account, without any theory of borrowing, or transmission of myth, or of original unity of race, for the world-wide diffusion of many mythical conceptions.

---

*   *Praep. E. [Praeparatio Evangelica]*, ii. 6, 19.

But this theory of the original similarity of the savage mind everywhere and in all races will scarcely account for the world-wide distribution of long and intricate mythical *plots*, of consecutive series of adroitly interwoven situations. In presence of these long romances, found among so many widely severed peoples, conjecture is, at present, almost idle. We do not know, in many instances, whether such stories were independently developed, or carried from a common centre, or borrowed by one race from another, and so handed on round the world.

[...]

Dr. Tiele writes:[22] 'If I were obliged to choose between this method' (the system here advocated) 'and that of comparative philology, it is the former that I would adopt without the slightest hesitation. This method alone enables us to explain the fact, which has so often provoked amazement, that people so refined as the Greeks, ... or so rude, but morally pure, as the Germans, ... managed to attribute to their gods all manner of cowardly, cruel and disorderly conduct. This method alone explains the why and wherefore of all those strange metamorphoses of gods into beasts and plants, and even stones, which scandalised philosophers, and which the witty Ovid played on for the diversion of his contemporaries. In short, this method teaches us to recognise in all those strange stories the survivals of a barbaric age, long passed away, but enduring to later times in the form of religious traditions, of all traditions the most persistent. ... Finally, this method alone enables us to explain the origin of myths, because it endeavours to study them in their rudest and most primitive shape, thus allowing their true significance to be much more clearly apparent than it can be in the myths (so often touched, retouched, augmented and humanised) which are current among races arrived at a certain degree of culture.'[23]

[...]

'Household Tales; Their Origin, Diffusion, and Relations to the Higher Myths', Introduction to Margaret Hunt's *Grimm's Household Tales*

(London: George Bell and Sons, 1884)

Problems Suggested by the Study of Household Tales

Till shortly before the time of the Brothers Grimm the stories which they gathered (*Kinder- und Hausmärchen*)[1] had been either neglected by men of learning or treated as mere curiosities. Many collections had been made in Sanskrit, Arabic, Italian, French, but they were made for literary, not scientific purposes. The volumes of the Brothers Grimm following on several other scientific collections, and the notes of the Grimms (now for the first time reproduced in English), showed that popular tales deserved scientific study. The book of the Grimms has been succeeded by researches made among all Aryan peoples.[2] We have tales from the Norse, French, Breton, Gaelic, Welsh, Spanish, Scotch, Romaic, Finnish, Italian, in fact, the topic of Household Tales is almost obscured by the abundance of material. Now the least careful reader of these collections must notice certain facts which constitute the problem of this branch of mythology.

In the first place the incidents, plots, and characters of the tales are, in every Aryan country, almost identical. Everywhere we find the legends of the ill-treated, but ultimately successful younger daughter; of the triumphant youngest son; of the false bride substituted for the true; of the giant's wife or daughter who elopes with the adventurer, and of the giant's pursuit; everywhere there is the story about the wife who is forced by some mysterious cause, to leave her husband, or of the husband driven from his wife, a story which sometimes ends in the reunion of the pair. The coincidences of this kind are very numerous, and it soon becomes plain that most Aryan Household Tales are the common possession of the peoples which speak an Aryan language. It is also manifest that the tales consist of but few incidents, grouped together in a kaleidoscopic variety of arrangements.

In the second place, it is remarked that the incidents of household tales are of a monstrous, irrational, and unnatural character, answering to nothing in our experience. All animate and inanimate nature is on an intellectual level with man. Not only do beasts, birds, and fishes talk, but they actually intermarry, or propose to intermarry, with human beings.

Queens are accused of giving births to puppies and the charge is believed. Men and women are changed into beasts. Inanimate objects, drops of blood, drops of spittle, trees, rocks, are capable of speech. Cannibals are as common in the rôle of the villain as solicitors and baronets are in modern novels. Everything yields to the spell of magical rhymes or incantations. People descend to a very unchristian Hades, or home of the dead. Familiar as these features of the Household Tale have been to us all from childhood, they do excite wonder when we reflect on the wide prevalence of ideas so monstrous and crazy.

Thirdly, the student of *märchen* soon notices that many of the Household Tales have their counterparts in the higher mythologies of the ancient civilised races, in mediæval romance and saintly legend. The adventure of stealing the giant's daughter, and of the flight, occurs in the myth of Jason and Medea, where the giant becomes a wizard king.[3] The tale of the substituted bride appears in the romance of *Berthe aux grans piés*.[4] The successful younger son was known to the Scythians.[5] *Peau d'Ane* became a saint of the Irish Church,[6] and the 'supplanted bride' developed into St. Tryphine.[7] The smith who made hell too hot for him is Sisyphus in Greek.[8] The bride mysteriously severed from her lord in fairy tales, is Urvasi in the Rig Veda.[9] Thus it is clear that there is some connection, however it is to be explained, between Aryan household tales and the higher Aryan mythology. The same plots and incidents are common to both myth and *märchen*.

These three sets of obvious facts introduce us to the three-fold problem of 'storyology,' of the science of nursery tales.

The first discovery – that these tales among the most widely severed Aryan peoples are the same in plot and incident – leads us to inquire into the cause of this community of fable. How are we to explain the *Diffusion* of Household Tales?

The second feature we observed, namely, the crazy 'irrational,' monstrous character of the incidents leads us to ask, how did such incidents ever come to be invented, and almost exclusively selected for the purpose of popular fiction? What, in fact, is the *Origin* of Household Tales?

The third observation we made on the resemblances between household tales and Greek and Vedic myths, and mediæval romances, compels us to examine into *the Relations between* märchen *and the higher mythologies*.

Taking these three topics in their order, we must first look at what can be said as to the *diffusion* of Household Tales, Why do people so far apart, so long severed by space, and so widely different in language as Russians and Celtic Highlanders, for example, possess the same household stories? There are three, or perhaps we should say four, possible explanations. There is the theory of conscious borrowing. The Celts, it might be averred, read Russian folk tales and acclimatised them. The French took their ideas from the modern Greeks. This hypothesis, thus nakedly stated, may be at once dismissed. The peasant class, which is the guardian of the ancient store of legends, reads little, and travels scarcely at all. Allied to the theory of borrowing, but not manifestly absurd, is the theory of slow transmission. We may be as convinced as Sir George Cox (*Aryan Mythology*, vol. i. 109) that the Aryan peoples did not borrow consciously from each other. We may agree with Mr. Max Müller that 'nursery tales are generally the last things to be borrowed by one nation from another' (*Chips* ii. 216). But we cannot deny that 'in the dark backward and abysm of Time,' in the unrecorded wanderings of Man, Household Tales may have drifted from race to race. In the shadowy distance of primitive commerce, amber and jade and slaves were carried half across the world by the old trade-routes and sacred ways. It is said that oriental jade is found in Swiss lake-dwellings, and that an African trade cowry has been discovered deep in a Cornish barrow.[10] Folk tales might well be scattered abroad in the same manner by merchantmen gossiping over their Khan fires, by Sidonian mariners chatting in the sounding *loggia* of an Homeric house,[11] by the slave dragged from his home and passed from owner to owner across Africa or Europe, by the wife who, according to primitive law, had to be chosen from an alien clan. Time past is very long, land has lain where the sea roars now; we know not how the ancestors of existing races may have met and mixed before Memphis was founded, or Babylon. Thus the hypothesis of the transmission of Household Tales cannot absolutely be set aside as in every case without possible foundation.

The Need for Caution in the Examination of Household Tales: 'The Wolf and the Kids'

Before examining theories of the Diffusion and Origin of Household Tales, and of their relations to the higher mythologies, something must be said about the materials we possess. A strict criticism of the collections of tales offered to the inquirer, a strict avoidance of theory founded on hasty analogies is needful. We must try to distinguish as far as possible what is ancient and essential, from what is relatively modern and accidental in each tale. We must set apart scientific and exact collections from merely literary collections in which the traditional element is dressed up for the sake of amusement. Grimms' collection of Household Tales or *Märchen* is among the earliest of those which were made for scientific purposes. Sanskrit stories, Arab and Egyptian stories, Italian stories, French stories, had been gathered long before into the garners of Somadeva, *The Thousand and One Nights*, Straparola, the Queen of Navarre, Perrault,[12] and others. But to bring together popular narratives merely to divert the reader is an aim which permits the collector to alter and adorn his materials almost as much as he pleases. Consequently the old compilations we have named, however delightful as literature, must be used with great caution for purposes of comparative science. Modern touches, as will be seen, occur freely even in such collections as the Grimms'. Science accepts these narratives (when it can get them unadulterated) as among the oldest productions of the human fancy, as living evidence to the character of the early imaginative faculty. But we must be quite certain that we do not interpret late additions to the tales, as if these incidents were of the primitive essence. An example of this error may be taken from Grimms' Legend (No. 5), 'The Wolf and the Kids.'[13] Here a wolf deceives seven little kids, and eats them all except the youngest, who hides […] 'in the clock-case.' The bereaved old she-goat comes home; finds that only the youngest kid survives, and goes in quest of the wolf. The wolf is found asleep: the old goat cuts him open, and out frisk all the little kids. They then fill the wolf's stomach with stones, and sew up the orifice they had made. When the wolf awakens he is thirsty, and goes to drink, but the heavy stones make him lose his balance, he falls into the well, and is drowned. […]

A story in some ways like that of the 'Wolf and the Kids,' is common among the negroes of Georgia. In a Kaffir tale (Theal) the arts of the wolf are attributed to a cannibal.[14] Apparently the tale (as the negroes tell it) is of African origin, and is not borrowed from the whites.[15] Old Mrs. Sow had five little pigs, whom she warned against the machinations of Brer Wolf. Old Mrs. Sow died, and each little pig built a house for itself. The youngest pig built the strongest house. Brer Wolf, by a series of stratagems, which may be compared to those in Grimms' *Märchen*, entrapped and devoured the four elder pigs. The youngest pig was the wisest, and would not let Brer Wolf come in by the door. He had to enter by way of the chimney, fell into a great fire the youngest pig had lighted, and was burnt to death. Here we have only to note the cunning of the wolf, and his final defeat by the youngest of the pig family, who, as in almost all household tales, is wiser and more successful than his elder brethren. In the same way Grimms' youngest kid was the kid that escaped from the wolf.

The incident on which the revenge turns, the swallowing of the victims and their escape alive, though missing in the negro version, is of almost universal occurrence.

It is found in Australia, in Greece it has made its way into the legend of Cronus, in Brittany into the legend of Gargantua.[16] Callaway's collection gives us Zulu examples: in America it is familiar to the Indians of the North, and to those of British Guiana.[17] Grimm gives some German variants in his note; Bleek's *Bushman Folklore* contains several examples of the incident.[18] The Mintiras of Malay have introduced the conception of swallowing and disgorging alive into a myth, which explains the movements of sun, moon, and stars (Tylor's *Primitive Culture*, i. 338, 356).

In the tale of the Wolf and the Seven Kids, then, the essence is found in the tricks whereby the wolf deceives his victims; in the victory of the goat, in the disgorging of the kids alive, and the punishment of the wolf (as of Cronus in Hesiod)[19] by the stone which he is obliged to admit into his system. In these events there is nothing allegorical or mystical, no reference to sunrise or storms. The crude ideas and incidents are of world-wide range, and suit the fancy of the most backward barbarians. But what is clearly modern in Grimm's tale is the introduction of the clock-case. That, obviously, cannot be older than the common use of tall clocks. If, then, we interpret the tale by regarding the clock-case as its essential feature, surely we mistake a late and civilised accident for the essence of an ancient and barbarous legend. Sir G. W. Cox lays much stress (*Aryan Mythology*, i. 358 [note 1]) on the affair of the clock-case. 'The wolf,' he says, 'is here the Night, or the Darkness, which tries to swallow up the seven days of the week, and actually swallows six. The seventh, the youngest, escapes by hiding herself in the clock-case; in other words, the week is not quite run out, and, before it comes to an end, the mother of the goats unrips the wolf's stomach, and places stones in it in place of the little goats who come trooping out, as the days of the week begin again to run their course.'

This explanation rests on the one obviously modern feature of the story. If the explanation is correct, the state of mind in which Night could be conceived of as a wolf, and as capable of being slit open, loaded with stones, and sewn up again, must have lasted and remained intelligible, till the quite recent invention of clock-cases. The clock-case was then intelligently introduced into the legend. This seems hard to believe, though Mr. Tylor writes (*Primitive Culture*, i. 341) thus, 'We can hardly doubt there is a quaint touch of sun-myth in a tale which took its present shape since the invention of clocks.'[20]

Surely a clock-case might seem […] a good hiding-place, even to a mind not occupied at all with the sun. What makes the whole interpretation the more dubious is, that while with Sir George Cox the Wolf is the Night, with M. Husson[21] (in the similar tale of the swallowing of Red Riding Hood) the Wolf is the Sun. And this is proved by the peculiar brilliance of the wolf's fur, a brilliance recognised by Sir G. Cox when he wants the sun to be a wolf.

On the whole, then, the student of *märchen* must avoid two common errors. He must not regard modern interpolations as part of the mythical essence of a story. He must not hurry to explain every incident as a reference to the natural phenomena of Dawn, Sunset, Wind, Storm, and the like. The points which are so commonly interpreted thus, are sometimes modern interpolations; more frequently they are relics of ancient customs of which the mythologist never heard, or survivals from an archaic mental condition into which he has never inquired. Besides, as Mr. Tylor has pointed out, explanations of the elemental sort, all about storm and dawn, are so easy to find that every guesser can apply them at will to every *märchen*. In these inquiries we must never forget that 'rash inferences which, on the strength of mere resemblances, derive episodes of myth from episodes of nature, must be regarded with utter distrust, for the student who has no more stringent criterion than this for his myths of sun, and sky, and dawn, will find them wherever it pleases him to seek them' (*Primitive Culture*, i. 319). This sort of student, indeed, finds his myths of sun, and sky, and dawn all through the Grimms' Collection.

Sir George Cox's Hypothesis Concerning the Origin and Meaning of Household Tales

We have now set forth the nature of the problems which meet the inquirer into Household Tales, and we have tried to illustrate the necessity of a critical method, and the danger of being carried away by faint or fancied resemblances and analogies. Our next step is to examine the theory of the diffusion and origin of Household Tales set forth by Sir George Cox in his *Mythology of the Aryan Nations* (1870). This theory was suggested by, and, to a certain extent, corresponds with the mythological philosophy of Mr. Max Müller, as published in *Oxford Essays* (1856), and more recently in *Selected Essays* (1881). There are, however, differences of detail and perhaps of principle in the systems of these two scholars. As to the *diffusion* of identical folk tales among peoples of Aryan speech, Sir George Cox (dismissing theories of borrowing or adaptation) writes:

'The real evidence points only to that fountain of mythical language from which have flowed all the streams of Aryan epic poetry, streams so varied in their character yet agreeing so closely in their elements. The substantial identity of stories told in Italy, Norway and India can but prove that the treasure-house of mythology was more abundantly filled before the dispersion of the Aryan tribes than we had taken it to be.'[22] Sir George proceeds to remark on resemblances between German and Hindoo tales, which shew 'the extent to which the folk lore of the Aryans was developed while they still lived as a single people' (*Mythol. Aryan*, i. 145). Thus Sir George Cox accounts, on the whole, for the majority of the resemblances among Aryan household tales, by the theory that these tales are the common inheritance of the Aryan race, such narratives the Aryans possessed 'while they still lived as a single people.' The difficulties in which this theory lands the inquirer will afterwards be set forth. Here it may be observed that people who are not Aryans none the less possess the stories.

So much for the *Diffusion* of Aryan Household Tales. They are widely scattered (the theory goes), because the single people which possessed them in its common seat has itself been scattered widely, from Ceylon to Iceland.

Next, what is Sir George Cox's hypothesis as to the *Origin* of Household Tales? We have seen how he supposes they were diffused. We have still to ask how such crazy legends were originally evolved. Why are all things animate and inanimate on a level with man in the tales; why do beasts and trees speak; why are cannibalism, metamorphosis, magic, descents into Hades, and many other impossible incidents so common? What, in short, is the Origin of Household Tales?

Here it is not easy to be brief, as we have to give a summary of Sir George Cox's theory of the intellectual human past, from which he suppos- es these tales to have been evolved. In the beginning of things, or as near the beginning as he can go, Sir George finds men characterised by 'the selfishness and violence, the cruelty and slavishness of savages.' Yet these cruel and violent savages had the most exquisitely poetical, tender, and sympa- thetic way of regarding the external world (*Mythol. Ar.* i. 39), 'Deep is the tenderness with which they describe the deaths of the sun-stricken dew, the brief career of the short-lived sun, and the agony of the Earth-mother mourning for her summer child.' Not only did early man cherish these passionate sympathies with the fortunes of the sun and the dew, but he cherished them almost to the exclusion of emotions perhaps more obvious and natural as we moderns hold. Man did not get used to the dawn; he was always afraid that the sun had sunk to rise no more, 'years might pass, or ages, before his rising again would establish even the weakest analogy.'[23] Early man was apparently much more difficult to satisfy with analogies than modern mythologists are. After the sun had set and risen with his accus- tomed regularity, 'perhaps for ages,' 'man would mourn for his death as for the loss of one who might never return.'[24]

While man was thus morbidly anxious for the welfare of the sun, and tearfully concerned about the misfortunes of the dew, he had, as we have seen, the moral qualities of the savage. He had also the intellectual confusion, the perplexed philosophy of the contemporary savage. Mr. Tylor, Mr. Im Thurn, Mr. Herbert Spencer,[25] and most scientific writers on the subject, have observed that savages draw no hard and fast line between themselves and the animal or even the inanimate world. To the mind of the savage all things organic or inorganic appear to live and to be capable of conscious movement and even of speech. All the world is made in the savage's own image. Sir George Cox's early man was in this savage intellectual condition, 'He had life, and therefore all things else must have life also. The sun, the moon, the stars, the ground on which he trod, the clouds, storms, and light- nings were all living beings: could he help thinking that, like himself, they were conscious beings also?'[26]

As man thought of all things as living, so he spoke of them all as living. He could not get over the idea that any day living clouds might spring up and choke the living sun, while he had the most unaffected sympathy with the living dawn and the living dew. 'In these spontaneous utterances of thoughts awakened by outward phenomena, we have the source of the myths which must be regarded as primary' (*Myth. Ar.* i. 42). In all this period, 'there was no bound or limit to the images suggested by the sun in his ever varying aspects.' Man, apparently, was almost absorbed in his interest in the sun, and in speculations about the dew, the cloud, the dawn.

We now approach another influence on mythology, the influence of language. While man was in the conditions of mind already described by Sir George Cox, he would use 'a thousand phrases to describe the actions of the beneficent or consuming sun, of the gentle or awful night, of the playful or furious wind, and every word or phrase became the germ of a new story, *as soon as the mind lost its hold on the original force of the name.*'[27] Now the mind was always losing its hold on the original force of the name, and the result would be a constant metamorphosis of the remark made about a natural phenomenon, into a myth about something denoted by a term which had ceased to possess any meaning. These myths, caused by forgetfulness of the meaning of words (as we understand our author), were of the *secondary* class, and a third class came into existence through folk-etymologies, as they are called, popular guesses at the derivations of words. We have now briefly stated Sir George Cox's theory of the origins of myths, and of the mental condition and habits through which myths were evolved. But how does this theory explain the origin of Household Tales?

This question ought to lead us to our third problem, what are the relations of Household Tales to the higher mythologies? But it may suffice to say here that in Sir George Cox's opinion, most of the Household Tales are, in origin, myths of the phenomena of day and night. They are versions of the myths about the dark Night-powers stealing the golden treasure of Day; about Dawn loving the Dew; about the Birth and Death of the Sun; about the fortune of the Clouds, and so forth. Briefly, to illustrate the theory, we have a primary myth when early man says the (living) sun (Kephalos) loves the (living) dew (Prokris),[28] and slays her by his arrows (that is, his rays).
We have a secondary myth where it is forgotten that Kephalos only meant the sun, and Prokris only meant the dew, and when Kephalos is taken for a shepherd swain, and Prokris for a pretty nymph. Lastly, we have a tertiary myth when Apollo Lycæus (whose name meant Apollo of the Light) is supposed – by a folk-etymology – to be Apollo the Wolf,[29] and is said to have been born from a were-wolf.*

Household Tales are these myths in the making, or these myths filtered down through the memories and lips of uncounted generations (*Myth. Ar.* i. 165). It is on these principles that Sir George seeks to explain the irrational and unnatural element so powerful in folk tales.

---

* In these examples Sir G. Cox's theories are only accepted for the sake of argument and illustration.

Criticism of the Theories of Cox and Müller

We must now briefly criticise Sir George's system as a whole. Next we must see how the system is applied by him, and, lastly, we must approach the theory which we propose to substitute for that set forth in *Mythology of the Aryan Peoples*.[30]

The point most open to criticism in Sir George Cox's statement of his views, and in the similar views of Husson, De Gubernatis,[31] and many other mythologists is the very inadequate evidence. The framers of Primary Myths, in Sir George Cox's system are (apparently) savages. Of savages they have the moral qualities and the Intellectual habits. 'The prominent characteristics of that early time were the selfishness, the violence, the cruelty and harshness of savages.'[32] So much for morality. As for intellect, of the several objects which met his eye, says our author, mythopoeic[33] man had no positive knowledge, whether of their origin, their nature, or their proper ties. But he had life, and therefore all things else must have life also. This mental stage 'Animism,' 'personalism,'[34] or whatever we may call it, is also characteristic of savages. Now when we come in our turn to advance a theory of the origin of Household Tales, many points in these tales will be deduced from the cruelty and from the 'Animism'[35] of men like the framers of Sir George Cox's 'Primary Myths.' But Sir George's evidence for the savage estate of early myth-making man is mainly derived from the study of language.* This study has led him to views of the barbarism of the myth-makers with which we are glad to agree, yet he dissents here from his own chief authority, Mr. Max Müller. In the third chapter of the first volume of *Mythology of the Aryan Races*, the chapter which contains evidence for the intellectual condition of early humanity, Sir George Cox quotes scarcely any testimony except that of Mr. Max Müller.

The most important result of the whole examination as conducted by Sir George Cox, is that mythopoeic man, knowing nothing of the conditions of his own life or of any other, 'invested' all things on the earth or in the heavens with the same vague idea of existence. But while Sir George Cox makes this 'Animism' – this investing of all things with life – the natural result of man's *thought*, Mr. Max Müller ascribes the habit to the reflex action on thought of man's *language*. Man found himself, according to Mr. Müller (*Selected Essays*, i. 360), speaking of all objects in words which had 'a termination expressive of gender, and this naturally produced in the mind the corresponding idea of sex,' and, as a consequence, people gave 'some-

---

★   When *The Mythology of the Aryan Nations* was written, philologists were inclined to believe that their analysis of language was the true, perhaps the only key, to knowledge of what men had been in the pre-historic past. It is now generally recognised (though some scholars hold out against the opinion) that the sciences of Anthropology and Archæology also throw much light on the human past, which has left no literary documents. […]

thing of an individual, active, sexual, and at last personal character' to the objects of which they spoke. Mr. Müller is aware that the 'sexual character of words reflects only the quality of the child's mind,' but none the less he attributes the 'animism' of mythopoeic man to the reflex influence of man's language, whereas Sir George Cox attributes it to the direct influence of man's thought. Thus Sir George deserts the authority from which he derives his evidence, and it is not here alone that he differs from Mr. Müller. Sir George's framers of 'primary myths' are savages, morally and intellectually; Mr. Müller's mythopoeic men, on the other hand, are practically civilised. Man, in Mr. Müller's 'mythopoeic age,' had the modern form of the Family, had domesticated animals, was familiar with the use of the plough, was a dweller in cities, a constructor of roads, he was acquainted with the use of iron as well as of the earlier metals. (*Selected Essays.* vol. i. 'Comparative Mythology.'*) There is thus no escaping from the conclusion that, though Mr. Müller's evidence is nearly the sole basis of Sir George Cox's theories, yet from that evidence Sir George draws inferences almost the reverse of those attained by Mr. Müller. Yet starting from the same evidence, and from different inferences, the two authors arrive at much the same conclusion in the long run.

We have complained of the inadequate evidence for Sir George Cox's system. It is, as we have seen, derived from Mr. Max Müller's analysis of the facts of language. But there is another sort of evidence which was germane to Sir George's purpose, and which he has almost absolutely neglected. That evidence is drawn from the study of the manners and customs of men, and is collected and arranged by the science of Anthropology. The materials of that science are found in the whole of human records, in history, in books of travel, in law, customs, superstition. A summary of the results so far attained by anthropology and ethnology is to be studied by English readers in Mr. Tylor's *Primitive Culture* and *Early History of Man.*[36] These works deal with the evolution of human institutions of every kind from their earliest extant forms found among savages. We are thus enabled, by the science of students like Mr. Tylor, to understand what the ideas and institutions of savages are, and how far they survive, more or less modified, in civilisation. Now Sir George Cox's makers of primary myths were in the savage state of culture, or, as he himself puts it, 'The examination of our language carries us back to a condition of thought not many degrees higher than that of tribes which we regard as sunk in hopeless barbarism' (*Myth. Ar.* i. 35). But his description of the intellectual and moral condition of the primary myth-makers shows that really Sir George's mythopoeic men were in no higher degree of 'culture' than Red Indians and Maoris (*Myth. Ar.* i. 39-41). As this is the case, it would surely have been well to investigate what history has to say about the mental habits of savages. As the makers of primary

---

★   Mr. Müller has stated this proposition, but a note in *Selected Essays* proves that he now admits the uncertainty of the early use of iron.

myths were savages, it would have been scientific to ask, 'How do contemporary savages, and how did the savages of history, regard the world in which they find themselves, and of what character are their myths?' Sir George Cox, however, leaves on one side and practically unnoticed all evidence except philological evidence as to the general habits of men in the same intellectual condition as his own makers of primary myths. Herein lies, we think, the original error of his system.

Instead of examining the natural history of savages to see how men like his primary myth-makers regard the universe, Sir George Cox describes the prevalence among mythopoeic men of what we must regard as a purely fanciful mental attitude. Sir George's myth-makers, as we have seen, lived in a tremulous and passionate sympathy with nature, and with the fortunes of the day and the year, of the dawn and the dew. 'Perhaps for ages they could not believe that the sun would rise again in the morning.' From every stage in the sun's progress the myth-makers derived thrilling excitement. They threw themselves with their whole souls into the love affairs and distresses of the dew. They mourned for the setting sun, 'as for the loss of one who might never return.'[37]

Now does Sir George give any evidence, drawn from the natural history of man, for all this sentimental, yet sincere, primitive excitement about the processes of nature? None, or next to none. We do find summer-feasts and winter-fasts, rituals of regret and rejoicing for the coming and departing of summer among many races. […] But as to this all absorbing, all-pervading tender and poetic habit of primitive sympathy with natural phenomena, we find no proof of it anywhere. Savages, like civilised people, are much more interested in making love, making war, making fun, and providing dinner, than in the phenomena of nature.* But in Sir George Cox's system of mythology the enormous majority of myths and of household tales are simply the reflections of the supposed absorbing and passionate early sympathy of savages with the processes of nature. For the existence to the necessary extent of that sympathy we find no evidence. In all ages men must have been more concerned about earthly gold and mortal young women than about the 'dawn gold' or 'the dawn maiden,' yet in myths where gold or girls occur, Sir George sees the treasures of the light, or the radiant maiden of the morn. This is natural, while he is convinced that the makers of primary myths were so intensely absorbed in sympathy with clouds, and dew, and sunshine. But we ask again for sufficient evidence that these sentiments existed in a degree capable of exercising an exclusive influence on myths.

Turning from the theory of the primary to that of the secondary myths, we again note the absence of convincing testimony, or indeed of any valid testimony at all.

---

* Inferences drawn from the Vedas are not to the point, as the Vedas contain the elaborate hymns of an advanced society, not (except by way of survival) the ideas of early myth-makers.

Primary myths arose, Sir George says, from thought; secondary myths from language. They came into existence because 'a thousand phrases would be used to describe the action of the beneficent or consuming sun,' and so forth, 'and every word or phrase became the germ of a new story, as soon as the mind lost its hold on the original force of the name' (*Myth. Ar.* i. 42). This application of dozens of names and phrases to the same object is called *Polyonymy* by Mr. Max Müller, and the converse use of one name for a vast variety of objects (which become 'homonyms') he calls *Synonymy*.[38] It is Mr. Müller's opinion that, in the mythopoeic age, people might call the sun (let us say) by some fifty names expressive of different qualities (this is *polyonomy*), while some of these names would be applicable to other objects also. These other objects would then be *homonyms* of the sun, would be called by the same names as the sun was called by. (This is *synonymy*). The meaning of all these names would be lost in perhaps three generations, but the names and the phrases in which the names occurred would survive after their significance was lost. It is clear that if ever such a state of language prevailed, the endless consequent misunderstandings might well blossom into myths. For example, the grandfather (in the mythopoeic age) observes the rush of the ascending sun, and calls him 'the lion.' The father, being accustomed to the old man's poetic way, understands his meaning perfectly well, and the family style the sun 'the lion,' as they also, *ex hypothesi*,[39] call him by forty-nine other names, most of which they moreover apply to other objects, say to the tide, the wind, the clouds. But the grandson finds this kind of talk hopelessly puzzling (and no wonder), and he, forgetting the original meanings, comes to believe that the sun *is* a lion, and the night (perhaps) a wolf, and so he tells stories about the night-wolf, the sun-lion, and so on.

[...]

Sir George Cox has borrowed *Polyonymy* and its effects from Mr. Müller, though he gives no evidence to prove that it was ever a large factor in mythology. At first the processes of *polyonymy* and oblivion seem superfluous in Sir George's system, because he has already (in the intellectual condition of his primary myth-makers) sufficient myth-making power. While his early men regarded all things as living and personal, they would account for all natural processes on that hypothesis, and the explanations thus given would be nature-myths of the class current among savages. For example, if Sir George's early men thought (as they did) that the sun was alive, they might well marvel at the regularity of his movements; why did he not run about the sky at random as a brute runs about the woods? Why did he go, like a driven beast, in a regular round? To answer this question the New Zealanders and North American Indians have evolved a story that Maui or Tcha-ka-betch once set traps for the sun,[40] caught him, beat him, and made him move for the future with orderly propriety. This is an undeniable nature-myth, and savage mythology, like that of Greece and of the Veda, is full of similar mythic explanations of natural phenomena. To explain such myths no processes of *polyonymy, synonymy*, and oblivion are needed. Why then are those processes required in the system of Sir George Cox? For this reason; he is not content with the myths which declare themselves to be nature-myths. He wishes to prove that epic and romantic legends, which say nothing about sun, moon, stars, and wind, are nature-myths in disguise. Here the processes of *polyonymy* and oblivion become useful.

For example, we have the myth which tells how Jason sought the golden fleece in an eastern land, how he won the treasure and the daughter of its owner, how he returned home, deserted Medea, wedded Glauce, and died.[41] Now nothing is openly said in this legend about natural phenomena, except that the Colchian Royal House belongs to the solar race [...] How, then, can the Jason legend be explained on a nature-myth? By the aid of Polyonymy, thus: The sun had countless names. The names for sun, and dawn, and cloud, lost (in Sir George's opinion) their original sense, and became names of heroes, ladies, gods and goddesses. The original sense of the names was half remembered and half forgotten. Athene is 'the dawn goddess' (*Myth. Ar.* ii. [118]). Phrixus, the child of Nephele, is the son of the cloud.[42] Hellê, the drowned girl of the fable, is 'the bright clear air illumined by the rays of the sun.' When we are told that she was drowned, no more was originally meant than that 'before the dawn can come the evening light must die out utterly' (*Myth. Ar.* ii. 273). Here let us pause and reflect. In the myth, Phrixus and Hellê, children of Nephele, escaped being sacrificed by flying away on a winged ram with a golden fleece. Hellê fell off and was drowned. How does Sir George Cox explain all this? Nephele is the cloud, so far all is plain sailing. The cloud has two children, one 'the frigid Phrixus;' the other, 'the bright clear air illuminated by the rays of the sun;' or again, 'the evening light.' Early men, we are to suppose, said that the cloud produced cold, and also bore the warm evening air. Why do the warm air and the cold air go off together eastward on a golden flying ram? This we do not see that Sir George explains, but the fleece of the ram (after that animal has been slain) becomes the treasure of the light, which is sought in the east by Jason. But who is Jason? His name 'must be classed with the many others, Jasion, Janus, Iolaos, Iaso, belonging to the same root'[43] (*Myth. Ar.* i. 150, *note* 1). And what is the root? Well (ii. 81 [note 2]) Iamus, from the same root, means 'the violet child;' he was found among violets. Now 'ιον (violet) applies to the *violet* coloured sunset clouds, and ἰός also means a spear, and 'represents the far-darting rays of the sun.' 'The word as applied to colour is traced by Prof. Max Müller to the root *i*, as denoting a crying hue, that is, a loud colour'.[*44] Thus, whether we take ἰός to mean a spear, or violet, or what you please, Jason's name connects him with the sun. The brain reels in the attempt to

---

*   The 'violet shrinking meanly' of Miss Bunion's poem, has a 'loud,' or 'crying' colour!

make sense of the cold air and the hot air, children of the cloud, going eastward, on a ram covered with the treasures of the light, and when we come to the warm air dying, and the light being stripped (in the east) from the ram, and being sought for by a man whose name more or less means violet, and who comes from the west, and when all this is only the beginning of the tale, we are absolutely perplexed. Who ever told such tales? Yes, we say, if ever men were deep in the perplexing processes of polyonymy, synonymy and oblivion, if ever the grandfather used countless allegorical phrases, which the grandchild piously retained, while he quite forgot their sense, then, indeed, this kind of muddled and senseless nature-myth may have been evolved. But we have vainly asked for evidence of the existence and activity of polyonymy, synonymy, and oblivion. The first and last of the three factors are useful, however, to Sir George Cox, when he tries to show that myths which do not give themselves out for nature-myths are nature-myths in disguise after all. But we have observed no evidence (except the opinion of some philologists) for the theory on which the whole demonstration depends. Again, M. Decharme, with just as much reason, makes Phrixus 'the demon of thunder,' and Hellê, 'a goddess of lightning!'[45] This kind of philosophy is too facile. To opinions like those which Sir George Cox has advanced with so much earnestness, and in such a captivating style of eloquence, it has always been objected that there is an improbable monotony in the theory which resolves most of old romance into a series of remarks about the weather.

[…]

Mr. Tylor […] writes (*Primitive Culture*, i. 319), 'No legend, no allegory, no nursery rhyme is safe from the hermeneutics of a thorough-going mythologic theorist. Should he, for instance, demand as his property the nursery "Song of Sixpence," his claim would be easily established: obviously the four-and-twenty blackbirds are the four-and-twenty hours, and the pie that holds them is the underlying earth covered with the over-arching sky: how true a touch of nature is it that "when the pie is opened," that is, when day breaks, "the birds begin to sing," the King is the Sun, and his "counting out his money," is pouring out the sunshine, the golden shower of Danae; the Queen is the Moon, and her transparent honey the moonlight. The maid is the "rosy-fingered" Dawn, who rises before the Sun, her master, and "hangs out the clothes" (the clouds) across the sky; the particular blackbird who so tragically ends the tale by "snipping off her nose," is the hour of sunrise. The time-honoured rhyme really wants but one thing to prove it a sun-myth, that one thing being a proof by some argument more valid than analogy.' Mr. Tylor easily shows that historical persons may be disposed of no less readily than the characters of Nursery Rhymes as solar-myths. Analogy is usually the one argument advanced for this scheme, and the analogies (as will be shown) are often so faint as to be practically non-existent. What 'false analogies' can be made to prove, Mr. Max Müller has demonstrated (*Selected Essays*, ii. p. 449). Mr. Müller has also gently censured (*Selected Essays*, i. 564, 565) the ready way in which M. Husson shows that Red Riding Hood was the Dawn: 'It would be a bold assertion to say that the story of Red Riding Hood was really a metamorphosis of an ancient story of the rosy-fingered Eos, or the Vedic Ushas with her red horses.'[46] In Mr. Müller's opinion 'there is but one safe path to follow in these researches into the origin of words or stories. … In addition to the coincidences in characteristic events, we have the evidence of language. Names are stubborn things,' and more to the same purpose. Here we touch one of the differences between Sir George Cox and Mr. Max Müller. Mr. Müller, like Sir George Cox, is of opinion that all the stories of princesses imprisoned, and delivered by young bright heroes, 'can be traced back to mythological tradition about the spring being released from the bonds of winter.' But in each case Mr. Müller asks for names of characters in the story, names capable of being analysed into some equivalent for powers of nature, sun, wind, night, or what not. Now, we have elsewhere tried to show that, in mythological interpretation, scarcely any reliance can be placed on analysis of the names of the characters.*[47] It seems more than probable that in most cases the stories are older than the names. Again, the custom of giving to real persons names derived from forces and phenomena of nature is widely prevalent in early society. Men and women are styled 'cloud,' 'sun,' 'wind,' and so forth. These names, then, even when they can be traced in myths, offer no surer ground for a theory than the analysis of such names as Jones and Thompson would do in a novel. Having to name the characters in his tale, the early story-teller might naturally give such personal titles as were common in his own tribe, such terms as 'Wind,' 'Cloud' 'Sun,' and so forth. Thirdly, the best philologists differ widely from each other as to the roots from which the names spring, and as to the sense of the names. But feeble as is the method which relies on analysis of mythical names, it is at all events less casual than the method which is satisfied with mere 'coincidence in characteristic events.' The simple argument of many mythologists may be stated thus. 'The dawn is a maiden, therefore all maidens in myths are the dawn.' 'The sun is golden, therefore all gold in myths must be solar.' These opinions are derived, in the long run, from the belief that the savage primary myth-makers were so much preoccupied with the daily phenomena of nature, and again from belief in the action of polyonymy and oblivion. We have attempted to show that there is no evidence given to prove either that early man was in passionate, ceaseless anxiety about nature, or that 'polyonymy' and oblivion ever existed in such strength as to produce the required effects on myths. As a rule, a real nature-myth avows itself for what it is, and attempts to give a reason (unsci-

---

★   Fraser's Magazine. *Mythological Philosophy of Mr. Max Müller.*

entific of course) for this or that fact, or assumed fact, in nature. Such tales though wild, and based on misconception, are intelligible and coherent. We have already seen how far from coherent or intelligible is Sir George Cox's explanation of part of the Jason legend as nature-myth.

Criticism of the Solar-Mythological Interpretation of 'The Frog King'

We promised that, after criticising Sir George Cox's theory of the Origin of Myths and Household Tales, we would examine his method of interpreting individual stories. Let us see how Mr. Müller, followed by Sir George, handles a tale with which we are all familiar. In Grimm's *Frosch König* (vol. i. Tale i.), a frog (who in Grimm turns out to be a disguised prince) is betrothed to a princess.[48] 'How came such a story,' asks Mr. Max Müller, 'ever to be invented? Human beings were, we may hope, at all times sufficiently enlightened to know that a marriage between a frog and the daughter of a Queen was absurd. … We may ascribe to our ancestors any amount of childlike simplicity, but we must take care not to degrade them to the rank of mere idiots.'

Mr. Müller thus explains the frog who would a-wooing go. As our ancestors were not mere idiots, the frog story must have had a meaning which would now seem rational. In old times (Mr. Müller says) the sun had many names. 'It can be shown that "frog" was an ancient name for the sun.' But though it can be shown, Mr. Müller never shows it. He observes 'this feminine Bheki (frog) must at one time have been used as a name for the sun.' But though he himself asks for 'chapter and verse from the Veda,' he gives us no verse and no chapter for his assertions (*Chips*, ii. 201, 247). His theory is that tales were told of the sun, under his frog name, that people forgot that the frog meant the sun, and that they ended by possessing an irrational tale about the frog going a-wooing.

The Frog-sun* whose existence is established on this scanty testimony, is a great favourite with Sir George Cox, and occurs no fewer than seven times in his *Mythology of the Aryan Peoples*. Nay, this frog is made to explain the presence of many of the wonderful talking animals in Myth and Household Tale. 'The frog prince or princess is only one of the thousand personifications of names denoting originally the phenomena of day and night. As carrying the morning light from the east to the west the sun is the Bull bearing Eurôpê from the purple land (Phoinikia), and the same changes which converted the Seven Shiners into the Seven Sleepers of Ephesus, or the "Seven Sages" (of Greece?), or the Seven Champions of Christendom, or the Seven Bears, transformed the sun into a wolf, a bear, a lion, a swan.' (*Ar. Myth.* i. 105.)[49]

★   See […] 'Cupid and Psyche' in the author's *Custom and Myth*.

Here we have the old use of analogies. Because of a theory (probably incorrect) that the Seven Bears of Indian stellar myth were originally seven shiners, all sorts of people in sets of seven twinkle off as 'shiners' also, stellar or solar shiners. In the same way the theory of the sun-frog (without chapter or verse as it is) proves that all animals in Household Tales are the sun.

As the appearance of beasts with human qualities and accomplishments is one of the most remarkable features of Household Tales, we may look at another statement of Sir George Cox's views on this subject. Metamorphosis of men into animals and of animals into men is as common in Household Tales as a sprained ankle is in modern novels. Sir George Dasent (*Popular Tales*, p. cxix) pointed out that the belief in such metamorphoses 'is primeval, and the traditions of every race tell of such transformations.'[50] Sir George Cox takes one of Sir George Dasent's numerous examples, and remarks 'if this be an illustration, it accounts for all such transformation but it does so in a way which is completely subversive of any hypothesis of nature-worship. *Such myths may all be traced to mere forgetfulness of the original meaning of words.*'[51] As proof, Sir George Cox adduces the well worn 'seven shiners,' and the supposed confusion between λευκός, *shining*, and λύκος, *a wolf*, 'so named from the glossiness of his "coat,"'[52] as if wolves had coats so peculiarly glossy. By these examples alone (omitting the frog-sun) Sir George Cox contests the plain straight-forward theory of Sir George Dasent, that men everywhere naturally believe in metamorphosis and lykanthropy. Sir George Cox wishes to trace lykanthropy to a confusion between λύκος and λευκός. On this point Sir Alfred Lyall,[53] after long observation of Indian beliefs, says, 'To those who live in a country where wicked people and witches are constantly taking the form of wild beasts, the explanation of lykanthropy by a confusion between *Leukos* and *Lukos* seems wanton.' (*Fortnightly Review*.)[54]

Wantonly or not, Sir George Cox traces 'all such myths to mere forgetfulness of the original meaning of words.' For this prodigiously sweeping generalisation no evidence except evidence like that of the supposed frog-sun and 'seven shiners' and *Leukos* and *Lukos* is afforded (*Ar. Myth.* i. 140-141, note 1). 'Bears, wolves, foxes, ducks, swans, eagles, ants, all these are names under which the old mythical language spoke of the clouds, or the wind, or of the light which conquers the darkness.'[55] Here again we have, by way of supporting evidence, the 'seven shiners,' and 'the wolf in the stories of Phoibos Lykeios.'[56] As the belief in metamorphosis, and in beasts which are rational and loquacious, is world wide, and is the natural result of the ideas of 'primary myth-makers,' or savages, Sir George Cox's theory, that such notions are all to be traced to forgetfulness of the meaning of words denoting natural phenomena, is too narrow, and is too devoid of evidence. Another explanation will presently be offered.

The Anthropological Theory of the Origin and Meaning
of Household Tales

We may now leave Sir George's theories of the diffusion and origin of
Household Tales. They are widely diffused, he thinks, because the race
which originally evolved them is also scattered far and wide, and has carried
them everywhere in its wanderings. The stories originated, again, in man's
early habit of imaginatively endowing all things with life, in his almost exclusive preoccupation with the changes of the day and the year, and in
'polyonymy,' and forgetfulness of the meaning of language. The third problem, as we saw, is to explain the relations between Household Tales and the
higher mythologies. Are children's *märchen* the *detritus*, the last worn relics
of the higher myths, as these reached the peasant class, and passed through
the fancy of nurses and grandmothers? Or do the Household Tales rather
represent the oldest forms of the Romantic myths, and are the heroic legends of Greece, India, Finland, Scandinavia, Wales, merely the old nursery
stories elaborated and adorned by the arts of minstrels and priests? On the
former hypothesis, *märchen* are a *detritus*; on the latter *märchen* are rather the
surviving shapes of the original germs of myths. On this topic Sir George
Cox, as far as we have ascertained his meaning, appears to hold what is
perhaps the most probable opinion, that in certain cases the Household Tale
is the decaying remnant of the half-forgotten myths, while in other cases it
rather represents the original *näif* form out of which the higher myth has
been elaborated (*Ar. Myth.* i. 123). Possibly we have not succeeded here in
apprehending the learned author's sense. As a rule, however, writers on these
subjects believe in the former hypothesis, namely, that Household Tales are
the *detritus* of the higher myths; are the old heroic coins defaced and battered
by long service. Thus, about the time when the Grimms were collecting
their stories, Scott wrote (in a note to the *Lady of the Lake*), 'The mythology
of one period would appear to pass into the romance of the next, and that
into the nursery tales of subsequent ages.'[57] Mr. Max Müller expresses the
same idea (*Chips*, xi. 243), 'The gods of ancient mythology were changed
into the demigods and heroes of ancient epic poetry, and these demigods
again became at a later age the principal characters in our nursery tales.'[58]
The opposite of this theory might be expressed thus, 'Stories originally told
about the characters of savage tales were finally attracted into the legends of
the gods of ancient mythology, or were attributed to demigods and heroes.'
The reasons for preferring this view (the converse of Mr. Müller's) will
presently be explained. In the meantime Mr. Müller's hypothesis 'has great
allies' in Scott; and in Von Hahn, who holds that myths are imaginative descriptions of the greater elementary powers and changes of nature; that the
Saga or heroic epic localises the myths in real places, and attributes the adventures to supposed ancestral heroes, and, finally, 'that the *Märchen*, or

Household Tale is the last and youngest form of the *saga*' (*Griechische Märchen, p. 5*).[59]

Starting from this point, namely, from the doubt as to whether *märchen* are the youngest (Von Hahn. Max Müller), or rather, as we shall attempt to show, the oldest extant form of the higher myths, we will endeavour to explain our theory of the whole subject. That theory must first be stated as briefly and clearly as possible.

With regard (1) to the *Origin* of the peculiar and irrational features of myth and *märchen* we believe them to be derived and inherited from the savage state of man, from the savage conditions of life, and the savage way of regarding the world. (2) As to the *Diffusion* of the tales, we think it impossible at present to determine how far they may have been transmitted from people to people, and wafted from place to place, in the obscure and immeasurable past of human antiquity, or how far they may be due to identity of human fancy everywhere. (3) As to the relations between Household Tales and Greek or other civilised myths, we prefer the following theory, which leaves room for many exceptions. The essence both of *märchen* and myths is a number of impossible and very peculiar incidents. These incidents are due to the natural qualities of the savage imagination. Again, the incidents are combined into various romantic arrangements, each of these arrangements being a *märchen*. The *märchen* were originally told, among untutored peoples, about anonymous heroes, – a boy, a girl, a lion, a bear, – such were the leading characters of the earliest tales. As tribes became settled, these old stories were localised, the adventures (originally anonymous) were attributed to real or imaginary named persons or gods, and were finally adorned by the fancy of poets like the early singers of Greece. Thus, while a savage race has its *märchen* (in which the characters are usually beasts or anonymous persons), the civilised race (or the race in a state of higher barbarism) has the same tale, developed and elaborated into a localised myth, with heroes rejoicing in such noble names as Perseus, Odysseus, Jason, Leminkainen,[60] or Maui. But while the progressive classes in civilised countries are acquainted with the named heroes, and the elaborate forms of the legends, the comparatively stationary and uneducated classes of shepherds, husbandmen, wood-men, and fishers, retain a version but little advanced from the old savage story. They have not purified away the old ferocious and irrational elements of the tale, or at most they have substituted for the nameless heroes, characters derived from history or from Christian records. Thus the Household Tales of the European peasantry occupy a mean position between the savage story, as we find it among African tribes, and the elaborate myth which, according to our theory, poets and priests have evolved out of the original savage *data*.

To sum up the theory thus briefly stated:

1. The origin of the irrational element in myth and tale is to be found in the qualities of the uncivilised imagination.

2. The process of *Diffusion* remains uncertain. Much may be due to the identity everywhere of early fancy: something to transmission.

3. Household Tales occupy a middle place between the stories of savages and the myths of early civilisations.

There are probably *märchen*, however, especially among the tales of modern Greece, which are really the *detritus*, or worn and battered relics of the old mythologies.

Supporting Evidence for the Anthropological Argument

Nothing is easier than to advance new theories. The difficulty begins when we try to support them by argument and evidence. It may be as well to show how the system which we have just explained occurred to the mind of the writer. It was first suggested, years ago, by the study of savage *märchen*. If Bushmen and Samoyeds, and Zulus, and Maoris, and Eskimo, and Odjibwas, and Basutos have household tales essentially identical with European *märchen*, how, we asked, is this to be explained? Mr. Max Müller and Sir G. W. Cox had scouted the idea of borrowing. Then, was it to be supposed that all the races with Household Tales had once shared the capacious 'cradle of the Aryan Race?' That seemed hard to demonstrate.* To account for the identity of savage and Indo-European *märchen*, there remained the process of slow filtration and transmission on one hand, and the similarity of the workings of the human mind (especially in its earlier stages) on the other hand. But Mr. Max Müller had already discredited the hypothesis that *märchen* 'might have been invented more than once' (*Chips*, ii. 233).[61] 'It has been said,' writes Mr. Müller, 'that there is something so natural in most of the tales, that they might well have been invented more than once. This is a sneaking argument, but has nevertheless a certain weight. It does not apply, however, to our fairy tales. They surely cannot be called "natural." They are full of the most unnatural conceptions. ...'[62] Among these unnatural conceptions, Mr. Müller noted the instance of a frog wooing a maiden; and he went on, as we have already seen, to explain such ideas on the hypothesis that they resulted from 'a disease of language,' from forgetfulness of the meaning of words. Now some little anthropological study had shown us that the ideas (so frequent in Household Tales), which Mr. Müller calls *unnatural*, were exactly the ideas most *natural* to savages. So common and so natural is the idea of animal kinship and matrimonial alliance with animals to the savage mind, that stories turning on these *data* are, of all stories, the most likely to have been invented in several places.† We do not say

---

* This appears, however, to be the theory by which Sir George Cox would prefer to account for the diffusion of myths possessed by the Aryan race among the Indians of Labrador [...]

† Ὁμοίως που ανέμιξαν θηρία καί ανθρώπους, says Porphyry, speaking of the founders

that they were thus separately invented, but only that the belief on which they turn is, of all beliefs, the most widely diffused. Having once attained this point, we soon discovered that other essential incidents in *märchen*, incidents which seem unnatural to civilised men, are common and accredited parts of the savage conception of the world he lives in. When this was once ascertained, the rest of our theory followed on the ordinary lines of the evolution of human institutions. To take an example in another province. Savages of a certain degree of culture make hand-turned pots of clay. Civilised races use the wheel. Peasants in remote districts of civilised countries make hand-turned pots of clay much like those of savages. The savage tale answers to the savage pipkin. The vase from Vallauris[63] answers to the civilised myth. The hand-turned pot from Uist or Barra,[64] answers to the peasant *märchen*; pot and *märchen* both surviving, with modifications, from the savage state, among the non-progressive class in civilised countries.

Such pipkins from the Hebrides (where Mr. Campbell collected his *Tales*) resemble much more the prehistoric and savage pot than they resemble our Vallauris vase, with its classic shape, ornament, and balance. Just in the same way, the West Highland or Russian *märchen* is much more akin to the Zulu story than to the civilised myth of Greece, which turns on the same ideas. In both the material and the imaginative product, you have the same process of evolution. You have the rude stuff, clay and small flints and shells for the savage pot, savage ideas for the savage tale. You have the refined, selected clay for the civilised vase, the ingenious process of fabrication, the graceful form and ornament. In the realm of imagination these answer to the plastic fancy of old minstrels, and of Homer or Apollonius Rhodius, refining and modifying the rude stuff of savage legend. Finally, among the non-progressive crofters of the Hebrides you have (in manufacture) the rude clay, the artless *façon*,[65] the ornament incised with the nails; and you have, in the imaginative province, tales almost as wild as the working of Bushman or Zulu imagination. (Campbell's *Tales of the West Highlands*).

Here then is an example, and dozens might be given of the process of evolution, which is the mainspring of our system. Another example may be taken from the realm of magic. All over the world savages practise spells, divinations, superstitious rites; they maim images to hurt the person whom the image resembles; they call up the dead; they track the foot-prints of ghosts in ashes; they tie 'witch-knots;'[66] they use incantations; they put sharp objects in the dust where a man has trodden that the man may be lamed. Precisely the same usages survive everywhere in the peasant class, and are studied by amateurs of folk-lore. But among the progressive classes of civilisation those practices do not occur at all; or if they do occur, it is by way of revival and recrudescence. On the other hand, the magical ideas are found much elaborated, in the old myths of civilisation, in the sagas of Medea and

of the old Religions; 'they mixed up men and beasts indiscriminately.' [Porphyry quoted in Eusebius, *Praeparationis Evangelicae*] iii. 4.

Circe, of Odin and Loki.[67] Probably it will now be admitted that we have established the existence of the process of evolution on which our theory depends. It is a *vera causa*,[68] a verifiable working process. If more examples are demanded, they may be found in any ethnological museum. In General Pitt Rivers's anthropological collection,[69] the development may be traced. Given stone, clay, the tube, or blow-pipe, and the throwing-stick, and you advance along the whole line of weapons and projectiles, reaching the boomerang, the bow, the stone-headed arrow, the metal arrow-head, the dagger, the spear, the sword, and, finally, the rifle and bayonet. The force which works in the evolution of manufactured objects works also in the transmutation of custom into law, of belief into tale, and of tale into myth, with constant minute modification, and purification, degradation, and survival.

If we have established the character of our theory, as one of a nature acknowledged and accepted by science, we have still to give evidence for our facts. The main purpose of our earlier pages was to show that the popular mythological theory of Sir G. W. Cox, had either no evidence, or scanty evidence, or evidence capable of a more correct interpretation than it receives from its friends. The evidence for our own theory will be closely scrutinised: let us examine its nature and extent. First, Have savages Household Tales, and do they correspond with those of the Aryan race?

The questions raised by the similarity between Aryan folk-tales on the one hand, and African folk-tales on the other, have not yet been seriously considered by mythologists.[70] When Mr. Max Müller wrote (*Chips*, ii. 211) on Dr. Callaway's Zulu *Märchen*, he had only the first part of the collection before him. As the learned writer observed, much more material was required; we wanted more Zulu tales, and other tales from members of the same great South African race, for purposes of comparison. We still need, for comparative purposes, much larger collections of savage instances than we possess. But those collections are amassed slowly, and it has seemed well, for our present end, to make use of the materials at hand. If comparatively scanty in quantity, they are very remarkable in character. From Africa we have 'Nursery Tales, Traditions, and Histories of the Zulus, in their own words, with a translation into English, and notes,' by the Rev. Canon Callaway, M.D. (Trübner, London, 1868.) We have also Dr. Bleek's *Bushman Folk-lore* (Trübner, 1875), and his *Reynard the Fox in Africa*, and Steere's *Swahili Tales*.[71] Madagascar is represented by the collections of the Rev. James Sibree,[72] published in the *Folk Lore Record* (1883). Some Basuto tales are given by Casalis *(Les Bassoutos, ou 23 ans de séjour au sud de l'Afrique*, 1860).[73] Some Ananzi stories from West Africa are printed in Sir George Dasent's *Tales from the Norse* (1859).[74] From the Kaffirs we derive Theal's *Kaffir Folk-lore* (Sonnenschein, London, *n.d.*).[75] Mr. Gill has given us some South Sea examples in his *Myths and Songs from the South Pacific*. (London, 1876).* The

---

* Turner's *Samoa* (*1884*) also contains some South Sea Märchen.

Folk Lore Society of South Africa,[76] in a little periodical now extinct, gave other African examples. Jülg's *Kalmückische Märchen[77]* are Indian in origin. Schoolcraft and his associates collected North American Indian examples in *Algic Researches.*[78] Samoyed *Märchen* have been published by Castren (*Ethnologische Vorlesungen*, St. Petersburg, 1857); and examples of *Märchen*, magnified and elaborated, occur in Japanese mythology (*Transactions of Asiatic Society of Japan*, vol. x.);[79] in New Zealand Myths (Taylor's *New Zealand*);[80] and in the accounts of Melanesian and Andaman myth, by Mr. Codrington and other writers, in the *Journal of the Anthropological Institute.*[81] While Mr. Mitford[82] has given us *Tales of Old Japan*, Prof. Hartt has collected the *Märchen* of the Indians on the Amazon.[83] Rink has published those of the Eskimo; and scattered examples are to be found in Bancroft's large compilation on the *Native Races of the Pacific*,[84] and in the old *Relations* of the Jesuit fathers and other missionaries.[85] Thus there are gleanings which may be provisionally used as samples of a large harvest of savage children's tales. The facts already in our possession are important enough to demand attention, particularly as the savage tales (in Africa especially) correspond, as will be shewn, so closely with the European and Aryan examples.

Here then, in the volumes named, we have a gleaning at least, from the harvest of savage *Märchen*. The names of most of the collectors will be to anthropologists, if not to all etymologists, a guarantee of their accuracy. Here, too, it may be observed, that a race so non-Aryan as the ancient Egyptians possessed Household Tales identical (in 'unnatural' incident, and to a great extent in plot) with our own (Maspero, *Contes Egyptiens*).[86]

It will be shown later that the ideas, stock incidents and even several of the plots of savage and other non-Aryan Household Tales are identical with the ideas, incidents, and plots of Aryan *Märchen*. It will also be shown that in the savage *Märchen*, the ideas and incidents are the inevitable result of the mental habits and beliefs of savages. The inference will be that the similar features in European tales are also derived from the savage conditions of the intellect. By 'savages' we here mean all races from the Australians and Bushmen to such American tribes as the Algonquins, and such people as the Maoris. In this great multitude of stocks there are found many shades of nascent civilisation, many degrees of 'culture.' But the races to whom we refer are all so far savage, that they display the characteristic feature of the savage intellect.

Before taking another step, we must settle the question of evidence as to savage ideas. We have ourselves criticised severely the evidence offered by certain mythologists, without, however denying that they may possess more than they offer. It is natural and necessary that we, in turn, should be asked for trustworthy testimony. How do we know anything about the ideas of savages? How can we pretend to understand anything about the nature of the savage imagination? The philological school of mythologists, about whose scanty show of proof we have complained, are conscientiously desir-

ous that our evidence should be full and trustworthy. Now, according to Mr.
Max Müller, the materials which we possess for the study of savage races
'are often extremely untrustworthy' (*India and what it can Teach us*).[87] This
remark, or its equivalent, is constantly repeated, when any attempt is made
to study the natural history of man. M. Reville, on the other hand, declares
with truth that our evidence is chiefly embarrassing by the very wealth of
documents. (*Les religions des Peuples non Civilisés*).[88] We naturally side with
M. Reville.

Consider for a moment what our evidence as to the life and ideas of
savages is; our evidence, in the first place, from the lips of civilised eyewit-
nesses. It begins with the Bible, which is rich in accounts of early religious
ideas, animal worship, stone worship, ritual, taboos on articles of food; marriage customs and the like. Then we have Herodotus, with his descriptions
of savage manners, myths, and customs. Next come all the innumerable
Greek and Roman geographers, and many of the historians and general
writers, Aristotle, Strabo, Pliny, Plutarch, Ptolemy,[89] and dozens of others.
For the New World, for Asia, for Africa, we have the accounts of voyagers,
merchants, missionaries, from the Arab travellers in the East to Marco Polo,
to Sahagun, to Bernal Diaz, to Garcilasso de la Vega, to Hawkins,[90] to all the
Spanish travellers, and the Portuguese, to Hakluyt's men;[91] we have the
Jesuits, with their *Relations Edifiantes*;[92] we have evangelists of every Christian
church and sect; we have travellers of every grade of learning and ignorance,
from shipwrecked beech-combers [*sic*] to Nordenskiöld and Moseley.[93]
Now from *Leviticus*[94] to the *Cruise of the Challenger*,[95] from Herodotus to
Mariner,[96] nay, from the Rig-Veda[97] to Fison and Howitt, we possess a series
of independent documents on savage customs and belief, whether found
among actual savages or left as survivals in civilisation. These documents all
coincide on certain points, and establish, we venture to say, with evidence
that would satisfy any jury, the ancient existence of certain extraordinary
savage customs, myths, ideas, and rites of worship. These ideas and rites are
still held and practised by savages, and seem natural to their state of mind.
Thus the coincident testimony of a cloud of witnesses, through three thousand years, establishes the existence of certain savage beliefs and rites, in
every quarter of the globe. Doubtless in each instance the evidence must be
carefully scrutinised. In matters of religion, missionaries may be witnesses
biassed in various ways, they may want to make out that the savage has no
religion at all, or that he is a primitive methodist.[98] The scientific explorer
may have a sceptical bias: the shipwrecked mariner who passes years with a
savage tribe, may be sceptical or orthodox, or may have his report tinged by
the questions put to him on his return to civilisation. Again, savages take
pleasure in hoaxing their catechists, and once more, the questions put by the
European may suggest answers appropriate but wholly false. Therefore in
examining the reports as to savage character, we must deal cautiously with
the evidence. If our witness be as candid, logical, and fair as Dr. Bleek, Mr.

Codrington, Mr. Orpen, Mr. Gill, Egede, Dr. Rink, Dobrizhoffer,[99] or a score of other learned missionaries and explorers, we may yield him some confidence. If he be tinged and biassed more or less by scientific theories, philological or anthropological, let us allow somewhat for the bias; probably we must allow still more in our own case. If the witness be unlearned, we have, at least, the probability that he is not transplanting to Otaheite or to Queensland ideas and customs which he has read about in Herodotus or Strabo,[100] or theories of Müller or McLennan.[101] Lastly, if all evidence from all quarters and all ages, evidence learned and unlearned, ancient, mediæval, and modern agrees in certain points, and if many of the witnesses express surprise at the occurrence of customs and notions, which our reading shows to be almost universal, then let the undesigned coincidence itself stand for confirmation.

[...]

Such, then, are our tests of reported evidence. Both the quantity and the quality of the testimony seem to justify an anthropological examination of the origin of myths and *märchen*. As to the savage ideas from which we believe these *märchen* to spring we have yet stronger evidence.[102]

We have the evidence of institutions. It may be hard to understand what a savage *thinks*, but it is comparatively easy to know what he does. Now the whole of savage existence, roughly speaking, is based on and swayed by two great institutions. The first is the division of society into a number of clans or stocks. The marriage laws of savages depend on the conception that these stocks descend from certain plants, animals, or inorganic objects. As a rule no man and woman believed to be connected by descent and blood kinship with the same animal, plant, stone, natural phenomenon, or what not, can intermarry. This law is sanctioned by severe, sometimes by capital, punishment. Now about the evidence for this institution there can be no mistake. It has been observed by travellers in North and South America, in Australia, Samoa, India, Arabia, in Northern Asia, and in West and South Africa. The observations were obviously made without collusion or intention to support a scientific theory, for the scientific importance of the institution was not perceived till about 1870.*

The second institution of savage life, from which the nature of savage ideas may be deduced, is the belief in magic and in 'medicine-men.' Everywhere we find Australians, Maoris, Eskimo, old Irish, Fuegians, Brazilians, Samoyeds, Iroquois, and the rest, showing faith in certain jugglers or wizards of their own tribe. They believe that these men can turn themselves or their neighbours into animal shapes; [103] that they can go down into the abodes of

---

* The first writer who collected examples of these facts was Mr. McLennan. ('The Worship of Plants and Animals,' *Fortnightly Review,* [6–7] 1869).

the dead; that they can move inanimate objects by incantations; that they can converse with spirits, and magically cure or inflict diseases. This belief declares itself in the institutions of untutored races; the sorcerer has a considerable share in what may be called political and priestly power.

We have now unfolded the character of our evidence. It is based, first on the testimony of innumerable reports corroborated by recurrence or coincidence; next on the testimony of institutions.

[…]

We are now able to prove, from the social and political institutions of savages, their belief in human descent from animals, in kinship with animals, in powers of metamorphosis, in the efficacy of incantations, and in the possibility of communion with the dead. Savages also believe in the possibility of 'personal intercourse between man and animal', 'the savage man's idea of the nature of those lower animals is very different from the civilised man's' (Tylor, *Primitive Culture*, i. 467; ii. 230).[104] Mr. Tylor gives many curious observances, as proofs of the existence of these wild conceptions. We may add that savages believe the human soul passes into animal shapes at death, and that women may bear animal children.

Similar views prevail about inanimate nature. 'To the savage all nature seems animated, all things are persons.' We have already seen that Sir George Cox assumed this state of thought in the makers of his 'primary' myths. 'To the Indian all objects animate and inanimate seem exactly of the same nature, except that they differ in the accident of bodily form' (Im Thurn, *Indians of Guiana*, p. 350).

Other savage ideas may be briefly explained. Among savages many harmless and necessary acts are 'taboo'd' or forbidden for some mystic or ceremonial reason.

Again, the youngest child in polygamous families is apt to be the favourite and heir. Animals of miraculous power are supposed to protect men and women. Cannibalism is not unknown in practice, and, as savages seldom eat members of their own tribe, alien tribes are regarded as cannibals. Further, various simple moral ideas are inculcated in savage tales. We may now offer a short list of savage ideas, and compare each idea with an incident in a savage and in a civilised Household Tale.

1 SAVAGE IDEA.

Belief in kinship with Animals

Savage Tale.	*European Tale.*
Woman marries an elephant.	Man weds girl whose brothers are ravens.
Woman marries a whale.	Queen accused of bearing puppies or cats.
Woman gives birth to crows.	Girl marries a frog.
Man marries a beaver.	Girl marries a tick.
Girl wooed by frog.	Man marries a frog.
Girl marries serpent.	

2 SAVAGE IDEA.

Belief in Metamorphosis.

Savage Tale.	*European Tale.*
Hero becomes Insect.	Hero becomes Worm.
Hero becomes Bird.	Heroes become Birds.
Hero becomes Mouse.	Hero becomes Roebuck.
Girls become Birds.	Girls become Birds.

3 SAVAGE IDEA.

A. Inanimate objects obey incantations, and speak.

Savage Tale.	*European Tale.*
Hero uses incantations with success.	Hero uses incantations with success.

B. Inanimate objects may speak.

Savage Tale.	*European Tale.*
Drops of spittle speak.	Drops of spittle speak.

4 SAVAGE IDEA.

Animals help favoured Men and Women.

Savage Tale.	*European Tale.*
Hero is helped by Ox.	Heroine is helped by Bull.
Heroes helped by Wolf.	Heroine is helped by Sheep.
	Hero is help by various Beasts.

5 SAVAGE IDEA.

Cannibals are a constant danger.

Savage Tale.	*European Tale.*
Hero and Heroine are captured by Cannibals.	Hero and Heroine are captured by Cannibals.
Hero or Heroine flees from home to being eaten.	Hero or Heroine flees from home to avoid being eaten.

6 SAVAGE IDEA.

The belief in possible descents into Hades, a place guarded by strange beasts, and where living men must not eat.

Savage Tale.	European Tale.
Descent by a Melanesian.	Descent of Psyche
His adventures.	Her similar adventures.
Descent by an Odjibwa.	
His adventures.	

7 SAVAGE custom.

Husband and wife are forbidden to see each other, or to name each other's names.

Savage Tale.	European Tale.
Wife disappears (but not apparently because of infringement of taboo). Wife disappears after infringement of taboo.	Husband or wife disappear when seen, or when the name is named. (These acts being prohibited by savage custom.)

8 SAVAGE custom.

The youngest son in the Polygamous family is the heir.

Savage Tale.	European Tale.
King's youngest son, as heir, is envied and ill-treated by his brothers.	Youngest son or daughter succeeds where the elders fail, and is betrayed by jealousy of the elders.

9 SAVAGE idea.A

Human strength, or soul, resides in this or that part of the body, and the strength of one man may be acquired by another who secures this part.

Savage Tale.	European Tale.
Certain Giants take out their hearts when they sleep, and are overcome by men who secure the hearts.	The Giant who has no heart in his body. The man whose life or force depends on a lock of hair, and is lost when the hair is lost.

SAVAGE idea.B

Souls of dead enter animal forms.

Savage Tale.	European Tale.
Dead Boy becomes a Bird.	Dead Boy becomes a Bird.

The lists now furnished exhibit several of the leading and most 'unnatural' ideas in European Household Tales.[105] It has been shown that these ideas are also found in savage Household Tales. It has further been demonstrated that the notions on which these incidents are based are as natural to, and as common among, savages as they seem 'unnatural' to the modern civilised student of Aryan dialects. The conclusion appears to follow inevitably, that the incidents of savage stories are derived from the beliefs and ideas of savages, while the identical incidents in civilised tales are an inheritance, a survival from a past of savagery.

[…]

The Myth of Jason Examined According to Anthropological Theories

We may now examine, as briefly as possible, a famous myth of the classical world, and point out its component parts and stock ideas, which are scattered through the Household Tales of the civilised and barbarous races. For our present purpose the myth of Jason is as well suited as any other.[*]

If our system be correct, the Jason myth is a heroic legend, with a plot composed of incidents now localised, and with characters now named, but the events were originally told as happening in no particular place, and the characters were originally mere 'somebodies.' The Jason myth starts from the familiar situation common in Household Tales. A Boeotian king (Athamas) has a wife, Nephele, and two children, a boy and a girl, named Phrixus (or Phryxus) and Helle.[106] But Athamas takes a new wife or mistress, Ino, and she conspires against her step-children. By intrigues, which it is needless to explain, Ino procures a decree that Phrixus and Helle shall be sacrificed to Zeus, this feature being a survival from the age of human sacrifice in Greece. As Phrixus stood at the altar, Nephele brought forward a golden ram which could speak. Phrixus and Helle mounted on the ram; the beast flew eastwards; Helle fell off, and was drowned in the Hellespont; Phrixus reached Colchis, sacrificed the ram, dedicated the golden fleece in a temple, and became the eponymous, or name-giving hero of Phrygia (Apollodorus, [*Bibliotheca*], I.ix.i). The Scholiast, on *Iliad* vii. 86, quotes the story, with some unimportant variations from Philostephanus.[107] He says that the ram met Phrixus and revealed to him the plot against his life.

[…]

The classical writers were puzzled by the talkative ram, but to students of Household Tales the surprise would be if the ram did *not* speak. According to De Gubernatis, the ram is the cloud or the sun, or a mixture; 'the sun in the cloud butts with its rays until it opens the stable and its horns come out.'[108] And so forth.

We may now compare Household Tales which contain *unlocalised* versions of the early incidents in the Jason myth. The idea of the earlier inci-

---

[*]   See 'A Far Travelled Tale' in the author's *Custom and Myth*.

dents is that children, oppressed or threatened at home, escape by aid of an animal, or otherwise, and begin a series of adventures.[109] The peculiar wrong from which the children escape, in the classic and heroic myth, is human sacrifice. In the Household Tales, on the other hand, they usually run away to escape being eaten. As human sacrifice is generally a survival of cannibalism, and is often found clinging to religion after cannibalism has died out of custom, it is only natural that the religious rite should be found in the classic myth, the savage custom in savage tales, and in the household stories which we regard as survivals of savagery. In the following Household Tales, the children flee from home like Phrixus and Helle, to escape being eaten, sometimes by a step-mother, sometimes by a mother, while in the most civilised version they only run away from a step-mother's ill-treatment.

Our first example is from *Samojedische Märchen* (Castren, p. 164).[110] Here the childless wife intends to devour the daughters of her rival, whom she has slain. The daughters escape, and when they reach the sea, they are carried across not by a golden ram, but by a beaver. The Epirote version of the story is given by Von Hahn (*Gr. Mär.* [*Griechische und Albanesische Märchen*] i. 65). A man brings home a pigeon for dinner, the cat eats it; the wife, to conceal the loss of the pigeon, cooks one of her own breasts; the husband relishes the food, and proposes to kill his own two children and eat them. Exactly as the ram warned Phrixus, according to Philostephanus, so the dog warns the boy hero of the Epirote *märchen*, and he and his sister make their escape. The tale then shades off into one of the *märchen* of escape by magical devices, which are the most widely diffused of all stories. But these incidents recur later in the Jason legend. Turning from the Samoyeds and the Epirotes to Africa, we find the *motif* (escape of brother and sister) in a Kaffir tale, 'Story of the Bird that made Milk.'[111] Here the children flee into the desert to avoid the anger of their father, who had 'hung them on a tree that projected over a river.' The children escape in a magical manner, and intermarry with animals (Theal's *Kaffir Folk Lore*, p. 36). Finally, among the Kaffirs, we find a combination of the form of the stories as they occur in Grimm (ii. 15). Grimm's version opens thus, 'Little brother took his little sister by the hand and said, "Since our mother died our step-mother beats us every day … come, we will go forth into the wide world."'[112] The Kaffir tale (Demane and Demazana)[113] tells how a brother and sister who were twins and orphans were obliged on account of ill-usage to run away from their relatives. Like Hänsel and Grethel they fall into the hands of cannibals, and escape by a ruse. In their flight they are carried over the water, neither by a ram nor a beaver, but by a white duck.

Here, then, we see how widely diffused are the early ideas and incidents of the Jason cycle. We see, too, that they are consistent with the theory of a savage origin, if cannibalism be a savage practice, and if belief in talking and protective animals be a savage belief.

The Jason myth proceeds from the incidents of the flight of the children, and enters a new cycle of ideas and events. We come to incidents which may be arranged thus:

> 1. The attempt to evade prophecy. (Compare *Zulu Tales*, p. 41).
> 2. The arrival of the true heir.
> 3. Endeavour to get rid of the heir by setting him upon a difficult or impossible adventure. (Callaway's *Zulu Tales*, p. 170).
> 4. The hero starts on the adventure, accompanied by friends possessed of miraculous powers. (Compare *Kalewala*).

In the Jason Legend the true heir is Jason himself. His uncle, Pelias, the usurper of his kingdom, has been warned by prophecy to guard against a one-shoe'd man. Jason has lost one shoe crossing the river. His uncle, to get rid of him, sends him to seek, in far away Colchis, the golden fleece of the talking ram. He sets forth in a boat with a talking figure-head, and accompanied by heroes of supernatural strength, and with magical powers of seeing, hearing, and flying.

All these inventions are natural, and require no comment. The companions of the hero, 'Quick Sight,' 'Fine Ear' and the rest, are well known in European Household Tales, where their places are occasionally taken by gifted beasts.[114] The incident of the expedition, the companions and the quest in general, recurs in the *Kalewala*, the national poem of the Finns.[115] When Jason with his company arrive in Colchis, we enter on a set of incidents perhaps more widely diffused than any others in the whole of folklore.

Briefly speaking, the situation is this: an adventurer comes to the home of a powerful and malevolent being. He either is the brother of the wife of this being, or he becomes the lover of his daughter. In the latter case, the daughter helps the adventurer to accomplish the impossible tasks set him by her father. Afterwards the pair escape, throwing behind them, in their flight, various objects which detain the pursuer. When the adventurer is the brother of the wife of the malevolent being, the story usually introduces the 'fee fo, fum' formula, – the husband smells the flesh of the stranger. In this variant, tasks are not usually set to the brother as they are to the lover. The incidents of the flight are much the same everywhere, even when, as in the Japanese and Lithuanian myths a brother is fleeing from the demon-ghost of his sister in Hades, or when, as in the Samoyed tale, two sisters are evading the pursuit of a cannibal step-mother. The fugitives always throw small objects behind them, such as a comb, which magically turns into a forest, and so forth.[116]

We have already alluded to the wide diffusion of these incidents, which recur, in an epic and humanised form, in the Jason myth. By way of tracing the incidents from their least civilised to their Greek shape, we may begin with the Nama version. It is a pretty general rule that in the myths of the lower races, animals fill the *rôles* which, in civilised story, are taken by human beings. In Bleek's *Hottentot Fables and Tales*, p. 60, the incidents turn on the visit of brothers to a sister, not on the coming of an adventurous lover.[117] The sister has married, not a wizard king, nor even a giant, but an elephant. The woman hides her brothers, the elephant 'smells something.' In the night, the woman escapes, with all the elephant's herds except three kine, which she instructs to low as loud as if they were whole flocks. These beasts then act like the 'talking spittle,' in Gaelic and Zulu, and like the chattering dolls in the Russian tale.[118] The woman bids a rock open, she and her brothers enter, and when the elephant comes the rock closes on him, like the 'Rocks Wandering,' or clashing rocks, in the Odyssey, and he is killed. In the Eskimo Tale (Rink, 7) two brothers visit a sister married to a cannibal, but she has become a cannibal too.[119] A tale much more like the Hottentot story of the Nama woman is the Eskimo 'Two Girls' (Rink 8).[120] One of the girls married, not an elephant, but a whale. To visit her, her two brothers built a boat of magical speed. In their company the woman fled from the whale. But instead of leaving magical objects, or obediently lowing animals behind her, she merely tied the rope by which the whale usually fastened her round a stone. The whale discovered her absence, pursued her, and was detained by various articles which she threw at him. Finally she and her brothers escaped, and the whale was transformed into a piece of whale-bone. In the Samoyed story (Castren. 11) the pursuit of the cannibal is delayed by a comb which the girl throws behind her, and which becomes 'a thick wood;' other objects tossed behind become rivers and mountains.[121] The same kind of feats are performed during the flight, in a story from Madagascar (*Folk-lore Record*, Aug. 1883),[122] a story which, in most minute and curious detail of plot, resembles the Scotch 'Nicht, Nocht, Nothing,'[123] the Russian 'Tsar Morskoi,'[124] and the Gaelic 'Battle of the Birds.'[125]

[...]

It is scarcely necessary to show how the incidents which we have been tracing are used in the epic of Jason. He himself is the adventurer; the powerful and malevolent being is the Colchian King Æetes, the daughter of the king, who falls in love with the adventurer, is Medea. Hard tasks, as usual, are set the hero; just as in the *Kalewala*, Ilmarinen is compelled to plough the adder-close with a plough of gold, to bridle the wolf and the bear of Hades, and to catch the pike that swims in the waters of forgetfulness.[126] The hard tasks in the Highlands and in South Africa may be compared. (Campbell, ii. 328; Callaway, 470).[127] Instead of sowing dragons' teeth, the Zulu boy has to 'fetch the liver of an Ingogo,' a fabulous monster. When the tasks have been accomplished, the adventurer and the king's daughter, Jason and Medea, flee, as usual, from the wrath of the king, being aided (again as usual) by the magic of the king's daughter. And what did the king's daughter throw behind her in her flight, to delay her father's pursuit? Nothing less than the mangled remains of her own brothers. Other versions are given: that of

Apollonius Rhodius (iv. 476, cf. *Scholia*) contains a curious account of a savage expiatory rite performed by Jason.[128] But Grote (ed. 1869, i. 232)[129] says, 'So revolting a story as that of the cutting up of the little boy cannot have been imagined in later times.'

[…]

Conclusion

We have now examined a specimen of the epic legends of Greece. We have shown that it is an arrangement, with local and semi-historical features, of a number of incidents, common in both savage and European Household Tales. Some moments in the process of the arrangement, for example, the localising of the scene in Colchis, and the attachment of the conclusion to the fortunes of the Corinthian House, are discussed by Grote (i. 244). Grote tries to show that the poetic elaboration and arrangement were finished between 600 and 500 B.C. Whatever the date may have been, we think it probable that the incidents of the Jason legend, as preserved in *märchen*, are much older than the legend in its epic Greek form. We have also shown that the incidents for the most part occur in the tales of savages, and we believe that they are the natural expressions of the savage imagination. We have not thought it necessary to explain (with Sir George Cox) the mutilation of the son of Æetes as a myth of sunset (*Ar. Myth*, i. 153) 'a vivid image of the young sun as torn to pieces among the vapours that surround him, while the light, falling in isolated patches on the sea, seems to set bounds to the encroaching darkness.'[130] Is the 'encroaching darkness' Æetes? But Æetes, in myth, was the son of the Sun, while Sir George Cox recognises him as 'the breath or motion of the air.'[131] Well, Jason was (apparently) the Sun, and Apsyrtus is the young Sun, and Medea is the Dawn, and Helle is the evening Air, and Phryxus is the cold Air, and the fleece is the Sunlight, and Æetes is the breath of the air, and the child of the Sun, and why they all behave as they do in the legend is a puzzle which we cannot pretend to unravel.

Did space permit, we might offer analyses of other myths. The Odyssey we have dealt with in the introduction to our prose translation (Butcher and Lang ed. 1883). The myths of Perseus and of Urvasi and Pururavas may be treated in a similar way.* As to the relations between the higher myths and *Märchen*, civilised or savage, there is this to be said: where the *Märchen* is diffused among many distinct races, while the epic use of the same theme is found only among one or two cultivated peoples, it is probable that the *Märchen* is older than the cultivated epic. Again, when the popular tale retains references to the feats of medicine men, to cannibalism, to metamorphosis,

---

* See 'Cupid, Psyche, and the Sun-frog' in the author's *Custom and Myth*.

and to kinship with beasts, all of which are suppressed or smoothed down in the epic form of the story, these omissions strengthen the belief that the epic is later than the tale, and has passed through the refining atmosphere of a higher civilisation.

As to the origin of the wild incidents in Household Tales, let any one ask himself this question: Is there anything in the frequent appearance of cannibals, in kinship with animals, in magic, in abominable cruelty, that would seem unnatural to a savage? Certainly not; all these things are familiar in his world. Do all these things occur on almost every page of Grimm? Certainly they do. Have they been natural and familiar incidents to the educated German mind during the historic age? No one will venture to say so. These notions, then, have survived in peasant tales from the time when the ancestors of the Germans were like Zulus or Maoris or Australians.

Finally, as to the *diffusion* of similar *incidents* in countries widely severed, that may be, perhaps, ascribed to the identical beliefs of early man all over the world. But the diffusion of *plots* is much more hard to explain, nor do we venture to explain it, except by the chances of transmission in the long past of human existence. As to the 'roots' or 'radicals' of stories, the reader who has followed us will probably say, with Mr. Farrer[132] (*Primitive Manners*, p. 257) 'We should look, not in the clouds, but upon the earth; not in the various aspects of nature, but in the daily occurrences and surroundings,' he might have added, in the current opinions and ideas, 'of savage life.'

3

FAIRY TALES

Lang wrote numerous introductions to works concerned with fairy tales in the 1880s and 1890s, including introductions to William Adlington's translation of Apuleius, *The Most Pleasant and Delectable Tale of the Marriage of Cupid and Psyche* (London: Nutt, 1887), a reprint of the poem *Beauty and the Beast* attributed to Charles Lamb (London: Field and Tuer, 1887), Marian Roalfe Cox's groundbreaking work of tale-type analysis *Cinderella: Three Hundred and Forty-Five Variants* (London: Nutt, 1893), and K. Langloh Parker's *Australian Legendary Tales* (London: Nutt, 1895) and *More Australian Legendary Tales* (London: Nutt, 1898). The following pieces are taken from two introductions by Lang that examine the uses of popular tradition as a basis for the creation of literary fictions. The first is Lang's introduction to Clara Bell's 1895 translation of the allegorical children's adventure story *De kleine Johannes* by the Dutch psychiatrist Frederik van Eeden (1860–1932) (*Little Johannes*, London: William Heinemann, 1885). It is especially interesting as an account of Lang's approach to 'the history of the Fairy Tale in modern literature', though, as so often with Lang's introductions, he has very little to say about the work in hand, and instead uses the opportunity of the introduction to pursue his own concerns. The second set of extracts is taken from Lang's introduction to his own 1888 edition of Charles Perrault's *Histoires ou Contes du Temps Passé, avec des Moralitéz (Stories or Tales of Times Passed, with Morals)* and *Contes en vers (Tales in Verse)*, published as *Perrault's Popular Tales* (Oxford, Clarendon, 1888). This introduction, substantial enough to be reckoned a book-length critical study in its own right, includes a biography of Perrault, an account of the courtly context in which the tales were written, and essays on each of Perrault's prose tales, complete with detailed comparative data about each narrative type. The selection here includes Lang's account of the appearance of the tales, and his comparative analysis of the story 'Puss in Boots' (ATU545) and its variants. Also included is Lang's brief conclusion, in which he offers a concise summary of existing theories concerning narrative transmission, states his objections to these theories, and formulates his own views on the problem.

Lang's highly popular anthologies of international fairy tales, known as the 'coloured fairy books', were published at regular intervals from 1889 to 1910. There were twelve volumes in total, published in London by Longmans, Green and Co.: *The Blue Fairy Book* (1889), *The Red Fairy Book* (1890), *The Green Fairy Book* (1892), *The Yellow Fairy Book* (1894), *The Pink Fairy Book* (1897), *The Grey Fairy Book* (1900), *The Violet Fairy Book* (1901), *The Crimson Fairy Book* (1903), *The Brown Fairy Book* (1904), *The Orange Fairy Book* (1906), *The Olive Fairy Book* (1907) and *The Lilac Fairy Book* (1910). The hardcover limited first editions of the first two fairy books (*Blue* and *Red*, published in only 113 copies each) included substantial introductions, which do not appear in subsequent editions. Extracts from both of these introductions are included in this section. All subsequent coloured fairy books include relatively short prefaces, retained in later editions, which are represented here by extracts from *Green*, *Yellow*, *Pink* and *Lilac*. These materials provide an opportunity to see how Lang reframes his fairy tale scholarship for the benefit of a popular readership, and offer insights into the principles Lang adopted as an editor and compiler.

'Literary Fairy Tales', Introduction to Frederik van Eeden's *Little Johannes*, trans. Clara Bell

(London: William Heinemann, 1895)

The *Märchen*, or child's story, is a form of literature primevally old, but with infinite capacity of renewing its youth. Old wives' fables, tales about a lad and a lass, and a cruel step-mother, about three adventurous brothers, about friendly or enchanted beasts, about magical weapons and rings, about giants and cannibals, are the most ancient form of romantic fiction. The civilised peoples have elaborated these child-like legends into the chief romantic myths, as of the Ship Argo, and the sagas of Heracles and Odysseus. Uncivilised races, Ojibbeways, Eskimo, Samoans, retain the old wives' fables in a form far less cultivated, — probably far nearer the originals. European peasants keep them in shapes more akin to the savage than to the Greek forms, and, finally, men of letters have adopted the *genre* from popular narrative, as they have also adopted the Fable.

Little Johannes, here translated from the Dutch of Dr. Frederik van Eeden, is the latest of these essays, in which the man's fancy consciously plays with the data and the forms of the child's imagination. It is not my purpose here to criticise *Little Johannes, an Allegory of a Poet's Soul*, nor to try to forestall the reader's own conclusions. One prefers rather to glance at the history of the Fairy Tale in modern literature.

It might, of course, be said with truth that the Odyssey, and parts of most of the world's Epics are literary expansions of the *Märchen*, but these, we may be confident, were not made of set literary purpose. Neither Homer, nor any poet of the French *Chansons de Geste*,[1] cried, 'Here is a good plot in a child's legend, let me amplify and ennoble it.' The real process was probably this: adventures that from time immemorial had been attributed to the vague heroes of *Märchen* gradually clustered round some half divine or heroic name, as of Heracles or Odysseus, won a way into national traditions, and were finally sung of by some heroic poet. This slow evolution of romance is all unlike what occurs when a poet chooses some wild-flower of popular lore, and cultivates it in his garden, when La Fontaine, for example, selects the Fable; when the anecdote is developed into the *fabliau* or the *conte*,[2] when Apuleius makes prize of *Cupid and Psyche* (a *Märchen* of world-wide renown),[3] when Fénelon moralises the fairy tale, or Madame d'Aulnoy touches it with courtly wit and happy humour, or when Thackeray burlesques it, with a kindly mockery, or when Dr. Frederik van Eeden, or Dr. Macdonald,[4] allegorises the nursery narratives. To moralise the tale in a very ancient fashion: Indian literature was busy to this end in the Buddhist Jatakas or Birth-stories, and in the *Ocean of the Stream of Stories*.[5] Mediæval preachers employed old tales as texts and as illustrations of religious and moral precepts. But the ancient popular fairy tale, the salt of primitive fancy, the drop of the water of the Fountain of Youth in modern fiction, began its great invasion of literature in France, and in the reign of Louis XIV. When the survivors of the *Précieuses*,[6] when the literary court ladies were some deal weary of madrigals, maxims, *bouts-rimés*,[7] 'portraits,' and their other graceful bookish toys, they took to telling each other fairy tales.*

On August 6, 1676, Madame de Sévigné tells her daughter that at Versailles the ladies *mitonnent*,[8] or narrate fairy tales, concerning the Green Isle, and its Princess and her lover, the Prince of Pleasure, and a flying hall of glass in which the hero and heroine make their voyages. It is not certain whether these exercises of fancy were based on memories of the *Pentamerone*,[9] and other semi-literary Italian collections of Folk-Tales, or whether the witty ladies embroidered on the data of their own nurses. As early as 1691, Charles Perrault, inventing a new *genre* of minor literature, did some Folk-Tales into verse, and, in 1696, he began to publish his famous *Sleeping Beauty*, and *Puss in Boots*, in Moetjens's miscellany, printed at the Hague. In 1696 Mlle. L'Héritière put forth a long and highly embroidered fairy tale, *Les Enchantements de l'Eloquence*, in her *Bizarrures Ingénieuses* (Guignard), while Perrault's own collected *Contes de ma Mère l'Oye* were given to the world in 1697 (Barbin, Paris).

The work of Mlle. L'Héritière was thoroughly artificial, while the immortal stories of Perrault have but a few touches of conscious courtly wit, and closely adhere to the old nursery versions. Perrault, in fact, is rather the ancestor of the Grimms and the other scholarly collectors, than of the literary letters of fairy tales. The Fairy Godmothers of modern *contes* play quite a small part in Perrault's works (though a larger part than in purely popular narrative) compared with their rôle in Madame d'Aulnoy, and all her successors. Much more truly than la Comtesse de M— (Murat),[10] author of *Contes des Fées* (1698), Madame d'Aulnoy is the true mother of the modern

---

* Part of what follows I have already stated in a reprint of *Perrault's Popular Tales*, Clarendon Press, Oxford, 1888.

fairy tale, and the true Queen of the *Cabinet des Fées*.[*][11] To this witty lady of all work, author of *Mémoires de la Cour d'Espagne*, and of many novels, a mere hint from tradition was enough. From such hints she developed her stories, such as *Le Mouton, Le Nain jaune, Finette Cendron, Le Bon petit Souris*,[12] and very many others. She invented the modern Court of Fairyland, with its manners, its fairies — who, once a year, take the forms of animals, its Queens, its amorous, its cruel, its good, its evil, its odious and its friendly *fées*; illustrious beings, the counsellors of kings, who are now treated with religious respect, and now are propitiated with ribbons, scissors, and sweetmeats.

The Fairies are as old as the Hathors of Egypt, the Moerae who came to the birth of Meleager, the Norns of Scandinavian myth.[13] But Madame d'Aulnoy first developed them into our familiar *fées* of fairy tale. Her *contes* are brilliant little novels, gay, satirical, full of hits at courts and kings. Yet they have won a way into true popularity: translated and condensed, they circulate as penny scrap-books, and furnish themes for pantomime.[†] It is from Madame d'Aulnoy that the *Rose and the Ring* of Thackeray derives its illustrious lineage. The banter is only an exaggeration of her charming manner. It is a pity that Sainte-Beuve, in his long gallery of portraits,[14] found no space for Madame d'Aulnoy. The grave Fénelon follows her in his *Rosimond et Braminte*, by no means the worst effort of the author of *Télémaque*.[‡] From Madame d'Aulnoy, then, descend the many artificial stories of the *Cabinet des Fées*, and among these the very prolix novel out of which *Beauty and the Beast* has been condensed takes a high place.[15] The tales of the Comte de Caylus[16] have also humour, wit, and a pleasant invention.[§]

The artificial fairy tale was in the eighteenth century a regular literary *genre*, a vehicle, now for satire, now for moralities. The old courtly method has died out, naturally, but the modern *Märchen* has taken a hundred shapes, like its own enchanters. We have Kingsley's *Water Babies*,[17] a fairy tale much too full of science, and of satire not very intelligible to children, and not always entertaining to older people, but rich in tenderness, poetry, and love of nature. We have the delightful *Rose and the Ring*, full of characters as real to us, almost, as Captain Costigan, or Becky Sharpe.[18] Angelica is a child's Blanche Amory; Betsinda is a child's Laura Bell, Bulbo is the Foker of the

---

[*]   In forty-one volumes, Paris, 1785-89.

[†]   There are complete English translations of the eighteenth century. Many of the stories have been retold by Miss M. Wright, in the *Red* and *Blue Fairy Books*.

[‡]   I am unacquainted with the date of composition of this story about a Ring more potent than that of Gyges. (It is printed in the second volume of *Dialogues des Morts*, Paris, 1718).

[§]   From one of these tales by Caylus the author, who but recently made their acquaintance, finds that he has unconsciously plagiarised an adventure of Prince Prigio's.

nursery,[19] and King Valoroso a potentate never to be thought of without respectful gratitude. How noble is his blank verse.

— 'He laid his hands on an anointed king,
    Hedzoff! and floored me with a warming pan!'[20]

Then we have the Phantastes of Dr. Macdonald,[21] which the abundant mysticism does not spoil, a book of poetic adventure perhaps too unfamiliar to children. To speak of Andersen is superfluous, of Andersen so akin in imagination to the primeval popular fancy; so near the secret of the heart of childhood. The *Tin Soldier*, the *Ugly Duckling* and the rest, are true *Märchen*, and Andersen is the Perrault of the North, more grave, more tender, if less witty, than the kind Academician who kept open for children the gardens of the Louvre.[22] Of other modern *Märchen*, the delightful, inimitable, irresponsible nonsense of *Alice in Wonderland* marks it the foremost. There has been, of course, a vast array of imitative failures: tales where boisterousness does duty for wit, and cheap sentiment for tenderness, and preaching for that half-concious moral motive, which, as Perrault correctly said, does inform very many of the true primeval *Märchen*. As an inveterate reader of good fairy tales, I find the annual Christmas harvest of them, in general, dull, imitative, — *Alice* is always being imitated, — and, in brief, impossible. Mere vagaries of absurdity, mere floods of floral eloquence, do not make a fairy tale. We can never quite recover the old simplicity, energy, and romance, the qualities which, as Charles Nodier said, make Hop o' my Thumb, Puss in Boots, and Blue Beard 'the Ulysses, the Figaro and the Othello of children.'[23] There may possibly be critics or rather there are certain to be critics, who will deny that the modern and literary fairy tale is a legitimate *genre*, or a proper theme of discussion. The Folklorist is not unnaturally jealous of what, in some degree, looks like Folk-Lore. He apprehends that purely literary stories may 'win their way,' pruned of their excrescences, 'to the fabulous,'[24] and may confuse the speculations of later mythologists. There is very little real danger of this result. I speak, however, not without sympathy; there was a time when I regarded all *contes* except *contes populaires*[25] as frivolous and vexatious. This, however, is the fanaticism of pedantry. The French *conteurs*[26] of the last century, following in the track of Hop o' my Thumb, made and narrated many pleasing discoveries, if they also wrote much that was feeble and is faded. To admit this is but common fairness; literary fairy tales may legitimately amuse both old and young, though 'it needs heaven-sent moments for this skill.'[27] The *conteurs*, like every one who does not always stretch the bow of Apollo till it breaks,[28] had, of course, their severe censors. To listen to some persons, one might think that gaiety was a crime. You scribble light verses, and you are solemnly told that this is not high poetry, told it by worthy creatures whose rhymes could be uncommonly elevated, if mere owl-like solemnity could make poetry and secure elevation. You make a fairy tale, and you are told that the incidents border on the impossible, that analysis of character, and the discussion of grave social and theological problems are conspicuously absent. The old *conteurs* were met by those ponderous objections. Madame d'Aulnoy, in *Ponce de Léon*, makes one of her characters defend the literary *Märchen* in its place. 'I am persuaded that, in spite of serious critics, there is an art in the simplicity of the stories, and I have known persons of taste who sometimes found in them an hour's amusement. ... He would be ridiculous who wanted to hear and read nothing but such legends, and he who should write them in a pompous and inflated style, would rob them of their proper character, but I am persuaded that, after some serious occupation, l'on peut badiner avec.' 'I hold,' said Mélanie,' that such stories should be neither trivial nor bombastic, that they should hold a middle course, rather gay than serious, not without a shade of moral, above all, they should be offered as trifles, which the listener alone has a right to put his price upon.'[29]

This is very just criticism of literary fairy tales, made in an age when we read of a professional *faiseur des contes des fées vieux et modernes*.[30]

Little Johannes is very modern, and, as Juana says in *Ponce de Léon*: 'Vous y mettrez le prix qu'il vous plaira, mais je ne peux m'empêcher de dire que celui qui le compose est capable de choses plus importantes, quand il veut s'en donner la peine.'[31]

'Perrault's Popular Tales',
Introduction to *Perrault's Popular Tales*

(Oxford: Clarendon, 1888), pp.vii–cvx

'Madame Coulanges, who is with me till to-morrow, was good enough to tell us some of the stories that they amuse the ladies with at Versailles. They call this *mitonner*, so she *mitonned* us, and spoke to us about a Green Island, where a Princess was brought up, as bright as the day! The Fairies were her companions, and the Prince of Pleasure was her lover, and they both came to the King's court, one day, in a ball of glass. The story lasted a good hour, and I spare you much of it, the rather as this Green Isle is in the midst of Ocean, not in the Mediterranean, where M. de Grignan might be pleased to hear of its discovery.'

So Madame de Sévigné writes to her daughter, on the 6th of August, 1676.[1]

The letter proves that fairy tales or *contes* had come to Court, and were in fashion, twenty years before Charles Perrault published his *Contes de Ma Mère l'Oye*, our 'Mother Goose's Tales.' The apparition of the simple traditional stories at Versailles must have resembled the arrival of the Goose Girl, in her shabby raiment, at the King's Palace.* The stories came in their rustic weeds, they wandered out of the cabins of the charcoal burners, out of the farmers' cottages, and, after many adventures, reached that enchanted castle of Versailles. There the courtiers welcomed them gladly, recognised the truant girls and boys of the Fairy world as princes and princesses, and arrayed them in the splendour of Cinderella's sisters, 'mon habit de velours rouge, et ma garniture d'Angleterre; mon manteau à fleurs d'or et ma barrière de diamans qui n'est pas des plus indifférentes.'[2] The legends of

---

* Grimm, *Kinder- und Hausmärchen*. No. 89.

the country folk, which had been as simple and rude as *Peau d'Ane*[3] in her scullion's disguise, shone forth like *Peau d'Ane* herself, when she wore her fairy garments, embroidered with the sun and moon in thread of gold and silver. We can see, from Madame de Sévigné's letter, that the *Märchen* had been decked out in Court dress, in train and feathers, as early as 1676. When the Princess of the Green Isle, and the Prince of Pleasures alighted from their flying ball of crystal, in Madame Coulanges' tale, every one cried, 'Cybele[4] is descending among us!' Cybele is remote enough from the world of fairy, and the whole story, like the stories afterwards published by Madame d'Aulnoy, must have been a highly decorated and scarcely recognisable variant of some old tradition.

How did the Fairy-tales get presented at Court, and thence win their way, thanks to Perrault, into the classical literature of France? Probably they were welcomed partly in that spirit of sham simplicity, which moved Louis XIV and his nobles and ladies to appear in Ballets as shepherds and shepherdesses.* In later days the witty maidens of Saint Cyr[5] became aweary of sermons on *la simplicité*. They used to say, by way of raillery, 'par simplicité je prends la meilleure place,' 'par simplicité je vais me louer,' 'par simplicité je veux ce qu'il y a de plus loin de moi sur une table.'[6] This, as Madame de Maintenon[7] remarked, was 'laughing at serious things,' at sweet simplicity, which first brought Fairy Tales to the Œil de Bœuf.[8]† Mlle. L'Heritier in *Bigarrures Ingénieuses* (p. 237)[9] expressly says, 'Les Romances modernes tâchent d'imiter la simplicité des Romances antiques.'[10] It is curious that Madame de Maintenon did not find this simplicity simple enough for her pupils at St. Cyr. On the 4th of March, 1700, when the fashion for fairy tales was at its height, she wrote to the Comte d'Ayen on the subject of harmless literature for *demoiselles*,[11] and asked him to procure something, 'mais non des contes de fées ou de *Peau d'Ane*, car je n'en veux point.' [12] ‡

Indeed it is very probable that weariness of the long novels and pompous plays of the age of Louis XIV made people find a real charm in the stories of *Cendrillon*, and *La Belle au Bois Dormant*.[13] For some reason, however, the stories (as current in France) existed only by word of mouth, and in oral narrative, till near the end of the century. In 1691 Charles Perrault, now withdrawn from public life, and busy fighting the Battle of the Books with Boileau, published anonymously his earliest attempt at story telling, unless we reckon *L'Esprit Fort*,[14] a tale of light and frivolous character. The

---

★　*Ballet des Arts, dansé par sa Majesté; le 8 Janvier*, 1663. A Paris. Par Robert Ballard. M.DC.LXIII.

†　*Madame de Maintenon d'après sa Correspondance*. Geffroy, ii. 211. Paris, 1887.

‡　*Madame de Maintenon d'après sa Correspondance*. Geffroy, i. 322.

new story was *La Marquise de Salusses, ou la Patience de Griselidis, nouvelle*.[15]*
Griselidis is not precisely a popular tale, as Perrault openly borrowed his
matter from Boccaccio,[16] and his manner (as far as in him lay) from La
Fontaine. He has greatly softened the brutality of the narrative as Boccaccio
tells it, and there is much beauty in his description of the young Prince lost
in the forest, after one of those Royal hunts in Rambouillet or Marly[17]
whose echoes now scarce reach us, faint and fabulous as the horns of Roland
or of Arthur.† Nay, there is a certain simple poetry and sentiment of Nature,
in *Griselidis*, which comes strangely from a man of the Town and the Court.
The place where the wandering Prince encounters first his shepherdess

> 'Clair de ruisseaux et sombre de verdure
> Saisissait les esprits d'une secrete horreur;
> La simple et naive nature
> S'y faisoit voir si belle et si pure,
> Que mille fois il benit son erreur.'[18]

So the Prince rides on his way

> 'Rempli de douces reveries
> Qu'inspirent les grands bois, les eaux et les prairies.'[19]

The sentiment is like Madame de Sévigné's love of her woods at Les
Rochers, the woods where she says goodbye to the Autumn colours, and
longs for the fairy *feuille qui chante*,[20] and praises 'the crystal October days.'
Of all this there is nothing in Boccaccio. Perrault, of course, does not repeat
the brutalities of the Italian tyrant, in which Boccaccio takes a kind of pleasure, while Chaucer veils them in his kindly courtesy.[21]

To *Griselidis* Perrault added an amusing little essay on the vanity of
Criticism, and the varying verdicts of critics. In this Essay, Perrault appar-
ently shews us the source from which he directly drew his matter, namely
Boccaccio in the popular form of the chap-books called *La Bibliothèque
Bleue*.[22] 'If I had taken out everything that every critic found fault with,' he
says, 'I had done better to leave the story in its blue paper cover, where it
has been for so many years.'[23] Thus Perrault borrowed from the Bibliothèque
Bleue, not the Bibliothèque Bleue, as M. Maury[24] fancied, from Perrault.‡

---

* Paris: de l'imprimerie de Jean Baptiste Coignard, imprimeur du Roy et de
l'Académie Françoise [from the press of Jean Baptiste Coignard, printer to the King
and the French Academy], rue Saint Jacques, la Bible d'or, 1691. The Bibliothèque
Nationale and the Arsenal possess copies of this duodecimo of 58 pages. One of the
copies is inscribed *Donné par Lautheur* [given by L'autheur] 1691. (Lefèvre. *Contes de
Charles Perrault*, p. 167. Paris, *s. a.*)

† Paul de Saint Victor, *Les Contes des Fées*, in *Hommes et Dieux*, p. 475. Paris,
1883.

‡ *Les Fées du Moyen Age*, p. 101. Paris, 1843.

In 1694 Moetjens, the bookseller at The Hague, began to publish a little Miscellany, or Magazine, in the form of the small Elzevir collection,[25] called *Recueil de pièces curieuses et nouvelles, tant en prose qu'en vers.*[26] Perrault had already published *Les Souhaits Ridicules,*[27] in a Society paper, *Le Mercure Galant* (Nov. 1693). He now reprinted this piece, with *Griselidis* and *Peau d'Ane*, in Moetjens' *Recueil.** These versified tales caused some discussion, and were rather severely handled by anonymous writers in the *Recueil*. In 1694, Perrault put forth the three, with the introductions and essay, in a small volume. Probably each tale had appeared separately, but these treasures of the book-hunter are lost. Another edition came out, with a new preface, in 1695.†

This is the early bibliographical history, as far as it has been traced by M. André Lefèvre,[28] of the stories in verse. They received a good deal of unfriendly criticism, and Perrault was said, in *Peau d'Ane*, to have presented the public with his own natural covering. This witticism, rather lacking in finish, is attributed to Boileau in an epigram published in Moetjens' *Recueil*. Boileau was still irritated with Perrault for his conduct in the great Battle of the Books between the Ancients and Moderns. By a curious revenge Perrault, who had blamed Homer for telling, in the Odyssey, old wives' fables, has found, in old wives' fables, his own immortality. In the *Parallèle,*[29] iii. p. 117, the Abbé quotes Longinus, and his admiration of certain hyperboles in Homer. The Chevalier, another speaker in the dialogue, replies, 'this sort of Homeric hyperbole is only imitated by people who tell stories like *Peau d'Ane*, and introduce Ogres in seven-leagued boots (*bottes à sept lieues*).' The 'seven-leagued boots' are in the Chevalier's fancy an apt parallel to the prodigious bounds made by the horses of Discord, in the Iliad. Thus, even before Perrault began to write fairy-tales, he and Boileau had a very pretty quarrel about *Peau d'Ane*. Boileau happened to remember that Zoilus[30] of old had reviled Homer for his *contes de Vieilles*,[31] and thus he could conscientiously treat Perrault as a new Zoilus. In the fifth volume of his works (Paris, 1772), in which these amenities are republished, there is a Vignette by Van der Meer[32] representing Homer, very old and timid, cowering behind a shield which Boileau, like Ajax, holds up for his protection, while Perrault, in a sword and cocked hat, throws arrows at the blind bard of Chios.[33] The strange thing is that they were all in the right. The Odyssey, as Fénelon's Achilles tells Homer in Hades, and as Perrault knew, is a mass of popular tales, but then these are moulded by the poet's art into an epic which Boileau could not over-praise.‡

In the edition of his stories in verse, published in 1695, Perrault replied

---

* Recueil, 1694. *Peau d'Ane*, p. 50. *Les Souhaits Ridicules*, p. 93. *Griselidis*, p. 233.

† Coignard Veuve. Paris.

‡ *Dialogues des Morts par feu Messire François de Salignac de la Motte Fénelon*, vol. i. p. 23. Paris, 1718. […]

to the criticisms that reached him, 'I have to do,' he said, 'with people who can only be moved by Authority, and the example of the Ancients;'[34] meaning Boileau and the survivors of the great literary feud. Perrault therefore adduces old instances of classical *contes*, the *Milesian Tales*, and *Cupid and Psyche* in Apuleius. 'The Moral of *Cupid and Psyche*,' he says, 'I shall compare to that of *Peau d'Ane*, when once I know what it is.'[35] Then he declares that his Contes have abundance of moral, which is true, but there are morals even in *Cupid and Psyche*. He sketches, very pleasantly, the enjoyment of children in those old wives' fables; 'on les voit dans la tristesse et dans l'abattement tant que le héros ou l'héroine du conte sont dans le malheur, et s'écrier de joie quand le temps de leur bonheur arrive.'[36] Indeed this was and is the best apology for M. Perrault of the French Academy, when he stooped his great perruque to listen to his little boy's repetition of his nurse's stories, and recorded them in the chronicles of Mother Goose.

Had Perrault only written *contes* in verse, it is probable that he would now be known chiefly as an imitator of La Fontaine. Happily he went further, and printed seven stories in prose. It is by these that he really lives, now that his architectural exploits, his sacred poems, his Defence of the Moderns, are all forgotten save by the learned. His Fairies have saved him from oblivion, and the countless editions and translations of his *Contes de Ma Mère L'Oye*, have won him immortality.*

The tales in prose appeared in Moetjens' *Recueil* in the following order: In 1696, in the second part of volume V, came *La Belle au Bois Dormant* (our 'Sleeping Beauty'); and in 1697 (vol. V. part 4), came *Le Petit Chaperon Rouge* ('Red Riding Hood'), *La Barbe Bleue* ('Blue-beard'), *Le Maistre Chat, ou le Chat Botté* ('Puss in Boots,' or 'The Master Cat'), *Les Fées* ('The Fairy'), *Cendrillon, ou la petite pantoufle de verre* ('Cinderilla,' in the older English versions, now 'Cinderella'), *Riquet à la Houppe* ('Riquet of the Tuft'), and *Le Petit Poucet* ('Hop o' My Thumb, Little Thumb').

While Moetjens was producing these in his Miscellany, there was published in Paris, at Perrault's bookseller's (Guignard), a little volume called *Bigarrures Ingénieuses, ou Recueil de diverses Pièces galantes en prose et en vers*. The author was Mlle. L'Heritier de Villaudon, a relation of Perrault's. It is to his daughter, a Mademoiselle Perrault, that she addresses her first piece, *Marmoisan ou l'Innocente Tromperie*.[37] The author says she was lately in a company where people began to praise M. Perrault's *Griselidis*, *Peau d'Ane* and *Les Souhaits*. They spoke also of 'the excellent education which M. Perrault gives his children, of their ingenuity, and finally of the *Contes naifs* which one of his young pupils has lately written with so much charm. A few of these stories were narrated and led on to others.'[38] *Marmoisan* is one of the others, and Mlle. L'Heritier says she told it, 'avec quelque broderie qui me vint sur le champ dans l'esprit.'[39] The tale is, indeed, all embroidery, beneath

---

* Contes de Ma Mère L'Oye is the title on the frontispiece. [...]

which the original stuff is practically lost.[40] But the listener asked the narrator to offer it 'à ce jeune Conteur, qui occupe si spirituellement les amusemens de son enfance.'[41]

In a later page she wonders that the Contes should have been 'handed to us from age to age, without any one taking the trouble to write them out.'[42] Then she herself takes the trouble to write the story of Diamonds and Toads, a story known in a rough way to the Kaffirs[43]—and hopelessly spoils it by her *broderie*, and by the introduction of a lay figure called *Eloquentia Nativa* (*Les Enchantemens de l'Eloquence*, ou *Les Effets de la Douceur*).[44] One has only to compare Mlle. L'Heritier's literary and embroidered *Eloquentia* with Perrault's *Les Fées* (the original of our *Diamonds and Toads*), to see the vast difference between his manner, and that of contemporary *conteurs*. Perrault would never have brought in a Fairy named *Eloquentia Nativa*. Mlle. L'Heritier's *Eloquentia* (1696) was in the field before Perrault's unembroidered version, *Les Fées*, which appeared in Moetjens' *Recueil* in 1697. The Lady writes:

'Cent et Cent fois ma Gouvernante
Au lieu de Fables d'animaux[45]
M'a raconté les traits moraux
De cette Histoire surprenante.'[46]

Here, then, is Mlle. L'Heritier speaking of one of Perrault's children who has written the fairy tales, 'with so much charm.' At this very time (1696–1697), fairy-tales, 'written with much charm,' in prose, and without the author's name, were appearing in Moetjens' *Recueil*. In 1697 these prose *contes* were collected, published, and declared to be by P. Darmancour, Perrault's little boy, to whom the *Privilége du Roy*[47] is granted.*

Critics have often declared that Perrault merely used the boy's name as a cover for his own, because it did not become an Academician[48] to publish fairy-tales, above all in prose. It may be noted that Perrault did not employ his usual publisher, Coignard, but went to Barbin. There might also have been a hope that little Perrault Darmancour, while shielding his father, 'fit parfaitement bien sa Cour en même tems,'[49] like *Le Petit Poucet*. Considering how Perrault's other works are forgotten, and how his Tales survive, and regarding his boy as partly their author, we may even apply to him the Moral of *Le Petit Poucet*.

---

* *Histoires ou Contes du Tem[p]s Passé, avec des Moralités*. A Paris. Chez Claude Barbin, [...]. Avec Privilége de sa Majesté, 1697. The frontispiece, by Clouzier, represents an old woman spinning, and telling tales to a man, a girl, a little boy, and a cat which, from its broad and intelligent grin, naturalists believe to be of the Cheshire breed. On a placard is written
CONTES
DEMA
MERE
LOYE. [...]

'Quelquefois, cependant, c'est ce petit Marmot
Qui fera le bonheur de toute la famille!'[50]

The dedication, signed P. Darmancour, is addressed to Mademoiselle, and contains very agreeable flattery of the sister of the future Regent.[*] These motives would, indeed, account for Perrault's use of his boy's name. But it had occurred to me, before discovering the similar opinion of M. Paul Lacroix,[51] that P. Darmancour really was the author of the *Contes*, or at least a *collaborateur*.[†] The naïveté, and popular traditional manner of their telling, recognised by all critics, and the cause of their popularity, was probably given by the little lad who, as Mlle. L'Heritier said, a year before the tales were published, 'a mis depuis peu les Contes sur le papier avec tant d'agrément.'[52] The child, according to this theory, wrote out, by way of exercise, the stories as he heard them, not from *brodeuses*[53] in Society, but from his Nurse, or from old women on his father's estates. The evidence of Madame de Sévigné and of Mlle. L'Heritier, as well as the testimony of the *contes* which ladies of rank instantly took to printing, shews how the stories were told in Society. Allegorical and other names were given to the characters, usually nameless in *Märchen*. Historical circumstances were introduced, and references to actual events in the past. *Esprit*[54] raged assiduously through the narratives. Moreover the traditional tales were so confounded that Madame d'Aulnoy, in *Finette Cendron*, actually mixes *Cinderella* with *Hop o' My Thumb*.[‡]

Contrast with these refinements, these superfluities, and incoherences, the brevity, directness, and simplicity of *Histoires et Contes du Tem[p]s passé*.[55] They have the touch of an intelligent child, writing down what he has

---

[*] Mademoiselle was Elizabeth Charlotte d'Orleans, born 1676, sister of Philippe, Duc de Chartres, later Duc d'Orleans, and Regent. See Paul Lacroix in *Contes de Perrault*, Paris, s. d. (1826.)

[†] In the introduction to the Jouaust edition of 1876 M. Paul Lacroix has probably gone too far in attributing to Perrault's son the complete authorship of the Tales. It is true that the title of the Dutch reprint of 1697 describes the book as 'par le fils de Monsieur Perrault' [by the son of Mr Perrault]. The Abbé de Villiers, however, in his *Entretiens sur les Contes des Fées* (à Paris chez Jacques Collombat, 1699), makes one of his persons praise the stories 'que l'on attribue au fils d'un célèbre Académicien,' ['which is attributed to the son of a celebrated Academician'] for their freshness and imitation of the style of nurses. Another speaker in the dialogue, The Parisian, replies, 'quelque estime que j'aie pour le fils de l'Académicien, j'ai peine à croire que le père n'ait pas mis la main à son ouvrage' [notwithstanding the respect I have for the son of the Academician, I can hardly believe that the father has not put his hand to the work] p. 109. This opinion is probably correct. [...]

[‡] Even in the popular mouth almost any formula may glide into almost any other, and there is actually a female Hop o' My Thumb in Aberdeenshire folklore. But Madame d'Aulnoy's seems a wanton confusion. The Aberdeen female *Hop o' My Thumb* is *Mally Whuppy*, Folk Lore Journal, p. 68, 1884. For *Finette Cendron*, see *Nouveaux Contes des Fées*, par Madame D——, Amsterdam, Roger, 1708.

heard told in plain language by plain people. They exactly correspond, in this respect, to the Hindoo folk tales collected from the lips of Ayahs by Miss Maive Stokes,[56] who was a child when her collection was published.

But, if the little boy thus furnished the sketch, it is indubitable that the elderly Academician and *beau esprit*[57] touched it up, here toning down an incident too amazing for French sobriety and logic, there adding a detail of contemporary court manners, or a hit at some foible or vanity of men. 'Livre unique entre tous les livres,' cries M. Paul de St. Victor, 'mêlé de la sagesse du vieillard et de la candeur de l'enfant!'[58] This delightful blending of age and youth (which here *can* 'live together') is probably due to the collaboration we describe.

Were it a pious thing to dissect Perrault's *Contes*, as Professors of all nations mangle the sacred body of Homer, we might actually publish a text in which the work of the original Darmancour and of the paternal *Diaskeuast*[59] should be printed in different characters. Without carrying mere guess-work to this absurd extent, cannot one detect the older hand in places like this,—the Ogre's wife finds that her husband has killed his own children by misadventure: 'Elle commença par s'évanouir (car c'est le premier expédient que trouvent presque toutes les femmes en pareilles rencontres)'?[60] One can almost see the Academician writing in that sentence on the margin of the boy's copy. Again, at the end of *Le Petit Poucet*, we read that he made a fortune by carrying letters from ladies to their lovers, 'ce fut là son plus large gain. Il se trouvoit quelques femmes qui le chargeoient de lettres pour leurs maris, mais elles le payoient si mal, et cela alloit à si peu de chose, qu'il ne daignoit mettre en ligne de conte ce qu'il gagnoit de ce côté-là.'[61] That is the Academician's jibe, and it is he who makes Petit Poucet buy Offices 'de la nouvelle création pour sa famille.'[62] 'You never did that of your own wit,'[63] as the Giant says to the Laddie in the Scotch story, *Nicht, Nought, Nothing*. But 'Anne, ma sœur Anne, ne vois–tu rien venir?' 'Je ne vois rien que le Soleil qui poudroye et l'herbe qui verdoye!' or 'Tire la chevillette, le bobinette cherra,' or 'Elle alla donc bien loin, bien loin, encore plus loin';[64] *there* the child is listening to the old and broken voice of tradition, mumbling her ancient burden while the cradle rocks, and the spinning-wheel turns and hums.

It is to this union of old age and childhood, then, of peasant memories, and memories of Versailles, to this kindly handling of venerable legends, that Perrault's *Contes* owe their perennial charm. The nursery tale is apt to lose itself in its wanderings, like the children in the haunted forest; Perrault supplies it with the clue that guides it home. A little grain of French common sense ballasts these light minions of the Moon, the elves; with a little toss of Court powder on the locks, *pulveris exigui jactu*,[65] he tames the wild *fée* into the Fairy Godmother, a grande dame de par le monde, with an agate crutch-handle on her magic wand. 'His young Princesses, so gentle and so maidenly, have just left the convent of Saint Cyr. The King's sons have the proud courtesy of Dauphins of France: the Maids of Honour, the Gentlemen of the Bed-chamber, the red-nosed Swiss guards, sleep through the slumber of the *Belle au Bois Dormant*.*

They are all departed now, Dukes and Vicomtes and Princes, the Swiss Guards have gone, that made the best end of any, the hunting horn is still, and silent is the spinning wheel. The great golden coaches have turned into pumpkins again, the coachman has jumped down from his box, and hidden in his rat-hole, the Dragoon and the Hussar have clattered off for ever, the Duchesses dance no more in the minuet, nor the fairies on the haunted green. But in Perrault's enchanted book they are all with us, figures out of every age, the cannibal ogre that little Zulu and Ojibbeway children fear not unreasonably; the starving wood-cutter in the famines Racine deplored; the Princess, so like Mademoiselle; the Fairy Godmother you might mistake for Madame d'Epernon;[66] the talking animals escaped from the fables of days when man and beast were all on one level with gods, and winds, and stars. In Perrault's fairy-land is room for all of them, and room for children too, who wander hither out of their own world of fancy, and half hope that the Sleeping Beauty dwells behind the hedge of yew, or think to find the dangerous distaff in some dismantled chamber.

[...]

'Notes on the Several Tales by Perrault, and Their Variants'

[...]

LE MAISTRE CHAT, OU LE CHAT BOTTÉ.
Puss in Boots.

Everybody knows Puss in Boots. He is, as Nodier says,[67] the Figaro of the nursery, as Hop o' My Thumb is the Ulysses, and Blue Beard the Othello; and thus he is of interest to all children, and to all men who remember their childhood. Ulysses himself did not travel farther than the story of the patron of the Marquis de Carabas has wandered, and few things can be more curious than to follow the Master-Cat in his migrations. For many reasons the history of *Puss in Boots*, though it has been rather neglected, throws a good deal of light on that very dark question, the diffusion of popular tales. As soon as we read it in Perrault, we find that Monsieur Perrault was at a loss for a moral to his narrative. In fact, as he tells it, there is *no* moral to the Master-Cat. Puss is a perfectly unscrupulous adventurer who, for no reason

---

★   Paul de Saint Victor, *Hommes et Dieux*, p. 474.

but the fun of the thing, dubs the miller's son marquis, makes a royal marriage for him, by a series of amusing frauds, and finally enriches him with the spoils of a murdered ogre. In the absence of any moral Perrault has to invent one—which does not apply.

> 'Aux jeunes gens pour l'ordinaire,
> L'industrie et le savoir-faire
> Valent mieux que des biens acquis.'[68]

Now the 'young person,' the cat's master, had shown no 'industry' whatever, except in so far as he was a *chevalier d'industrie*,[69] thanks to his cat. These obvious truths pained Mr. George Cruikshank[70] when he tried to illustrate *Puss in Boots*, and found that the romance was quite unfit for the young. 'When I came to look carefully at that story, I felt *compelled* to rewrite it, and alter the character of it to a certain extent, for, as it stood, the tale was a succession of successful falsehoods—a *clever* lesson in lying, a system of *imposture* rewarded by the greatest worldly advantages. A *useful* lesson, truly, to be impressed upon the minds of children.'[71] So Mr. Cruikshank made the tale didactic, showing how the Marquis de Carabas was the real heir, 'kep' out of his own' by the landgrabbing ogre, and how puss was a gamekeeper metamorphosed into a cat as a punishment for his repining disposition. This performance of Mr. Cruikshank was denounced by Mr. Dickens in *Household Words* as a 'fraud on the fairies,' and 'the intrusion of a whole hog of unwieldy dimensions into the fairy flower-garden.'*[72]

The Master-Cat probably never made any child a rogue, but no doubt his conduct was flagrantly immoral. And this brings us to one of the problems of the science of nursery tales. When we find a story told by some peoples *with* a moral, and by other peoples *without* a moral, are we to suppose that the tale was originally narrated for the moral's sake, and that the forms in which there is *no* moral are degenerate and altered versions? For example, the Zulus, the Germans, the French, and the Hindoos have all a nursery tale in which someone, by a series of lucky accidents and exchanges, goes on making good bargains, and rising from poverty to wealth. In French Flanders this is the tale of *Jean Gogué*; in Grimm it is *The Golden Goose*; in Zulu it is part of the adventures of the Hermes of Zulu myth, Uhlakanyana. In two of these the hero possesses some trifling article which is injured, and people give him something better in exchange, till, like Jean Gogué, for example, he marries the king's daughter.† Now these tales have no moral. The hero is thought neither better nor worse of because of his

---

* George Cruikshank had also turned *Hop o' My Thumb* and *Cinderella* into temperance tracts. See Cruikshank's *Fairy Library*, G. Bell and Sons.

† The French version is in M. Charles Deulin's *Contes du Roi Gambrinus*. The German (Grimm, 64) omits the story of the exchanges, but ends like *Jean Gogué*. The Zulu is in Dr. Callaway's *Inzinganekwane* [*Nursery Tales, Traditions and Histories of the Zulus*], pp. 38-40.

series of exchanges. But in modern Hindostan the story *has* a moral. The rat, whose series of exchanges at last win him a king's daughter, is held up to contempt as a warning to bargain-hunters. He is not happy with his bride, but escapes, leaving his tail, half his hair, and a large piece of his skin behind him, howling with pain, and vowing that 'never, never, never again would he make a bargain.'* Here then is a tale told with a moral, and *for* the moral in India, but with no moral in Zululand and France. Are we to suppose that India was the original source of the narrative, that it was a parable invented for the moral's sake, and that it spread, losing its moral (as the rat lost his tail), to Europe and South Africa? Or are we to suppose that originally the narrative was a mere *Schwank*,[73] or popular piece of humour, and that the mild, reflective Hindoo moralised it into a parable or fable? The question may be argued either way; but the school of Benfey and M. Cosquin, holding that almost all our stories were invented in India, should prefer the former alternative.

Now *Puss in Boots* has this peculiarity, that out of France, or rather out of the region influenced by Perrault's version of the history, a moral usually does inform the legend of the Master-Cat, or master-fox, or master-gazelle, or master-jackal, or master-dog, for each of these animals is the hero in different countries. Possibly, then, the story had originally what it sadly lacks in its best-known shape, a moral; and possibly *Puss in Boots* was in its primitive shape (like *Toads and Diamonds*) a novel with a purpose. But where was the novel first invented?

We are not likely to discover for certain the cradle of the race of the Master-Cat—the 'cat's cradle' of *Puss in Boots*. But the record of his achievements is so well worth studying, because the possible area from which it may have arisen is comparatively limited.

There are many stories known all the world over, such as the major part of the adventures of *Hop o' My Thumb*, which might have been invented anywhere, and might have been invented by men in a low state of savagery. The central idea in *Hop o' My Thumb*, for example, is the conception of a hero who falls into the hands of cannibals, and by a trick makes the cannibal slay, and sometimes eat, his own kinsfolk, mother, or wife, or child, while the hero escapes. This legend is well known in South Africa, in South Siberia, and in Aberdeenshire; and in Greece it made part of the Minyan legend of Athamas and Ino,[74] murder being substituted for cannibalism. Namaquas, in Southern Africa; Eskimo, in Northern America, and Athenians (as Aeschylus shows in the *Eumenides*, 244), are as familiar as Maoris, or any of us, with the ogre's favourite remark, 'I smell the smell of a mortal man.'

Now it is obvious that these ideas—the trick played by the hero on the cannibal, and the turning of the tables—might occur to the human mind

---

★   *Wide-awake Stories*. A collection of tales told by little children, between sunset and sunrise, in the Punjaub and Kashmir. Steel and Temple, London, 1884, p. 26.

wherever cannibalism was a customary peril: that is, among any low savages. It does not matter whether the cannibal is called a *rakshása*[75] in India, or an *ogre* in France, or a *weendigo*[76] in Labrador, the notion is the same, and the trick played by the hero is simple and obvious.* Therefore *Hop o' My Thumb* may have been invented anywhere, by any people on a low level of civilisation. But *Puss in Boots* cannot have been invented by savages of a very backward race or in a really 'primitive' age. The very essence of *Puss in Boots* is the sudden rise of a man, by aid of a cunning animal, from the depths of poverty to the summit of wealth and rank. Undeniably this rise could only occur where there were great differences of social status, where rank was a recognised institution, and where property had been amassed in considerable quantities by some, while others went bare as lackalls.

These things have been of the very essence of civilisation (the more's the pity), therefore *Puss in Boots* must have been invented by a more or less civilised mind; it could not have been invented by a man in the condition of the Fuegians or the Digger Indians. Nay, when we consider the stress always and everywhere laid in the story on snobbish pride and on magnificence of attire and equipment, and on retinue, we may conclude that *Puss in Boots* could hardly have been imagined by men in the middle barbarism; in the state, for example, of Iroquois, or Zulus, or Maoris. Nor are we aware that *Puss in Boots*, in any shape, is found among any of these peoples. Thus the area in which the origin of *Puss in Boots* has to be looked for is comparatively narrow.

Puss in Boots, again, is a story which, in all its wonderfully varying forms, can only, we may assume, have sprung from one single mind. It is extremely difficult to assert with confidence that any plot can only have been invented once for all. Every new successful plot, from *Dr. Jekyl* [sic] to *She*, from *Vice Versa* to *Dean Maitland*,[77] is at once claimed for half a dozen authors who, unluckily, did not happen to write *She* or *Dr. Jekyl*. But if there can be any assurance in these matters, we may feel certain that the idea of a story, wherein a young man is brought from poverty to the throne by aid of a match-making and ingenious beast, could only have been invented once for all. In that case *Puss in Boots* is a story which spread from one centre, and was invented by one man in a fairly civilised society. True, he used certain hereditary and established *formulæ*; the notion of a beast that can talk, and surprises nobody (except in the Zanzibar version) by this accomplishment, is a notion derived from the old savage condition of the intellect, in which beasts are on a level with, or superior to, humanity. But we can all use these *formulæ* now that we possess them. Could memory of past literature be wholly wiped out, while civilisation still endured, there would be no talking and friendly beasts in the children's tales of the next

---

*   [Richard] Andree, *Die Anthropophagie* [The Cannibals], 'Überlebsel im Volksglauben.' ['Survivals in Popular Beliefs'] Leipzig, 1887.

generation, unless the children wrote them for themselves. As Sainte-Beuve says, 'On n'inventerait plus aujourd'hui de ces choses, si elles n'avaient été imaginées dès longtemps.'[78]*

If we are to get any light on the first home of the tale—and we cannot get very much—it will be necessary to examine its different versions. There is an extraordinary amount of variety in the incidents subordinate to the main idea, and occasionally we find a heroine instead of a hero, a Marquise de Carabas, not a marquis. Perhaps the best plan will be to start with the stories near home, and to pursue puss, if possible, to his distant original tree. First, we all know him in English translations, made as early as 1745, if not earlier, of Perrault's *Maître Chat, ou Chat botté*, published in 1696-7. Here his motives are simple fun and friendliness. His master, who owns no other property, thinks of killing and skinning puss, but the cat prefers first to make acquaintance with the king, by aid of presents of game from an imaginary Marquis de Carabas; then to pretend his master is drowning and has had his clothes stolen (thereby introducing him to the king in a court suit, borrowed from the monarch himself); next to frighten people into saying that the Marquis is their *seigneur*; and, finally, to secure a property for the Marquis by swallowing an ogre, whom he has induced to assume the disguise of a mouse. This last trick is as old as Hesiod,[†79] where Zeus persuades his wife to become a fly, and swallows her.

The next neighbour of the French *Puss in Boots* in the north is found in Sweden[‡80] and in Norway.[§81] In the Swedish, a girl owns the cat. They wander to a castle gate, where the cat bids the girl strip and hide in a tree; he then goes to the castle and says that his royal mistress has been attacked by robbers. The people of the palace attire the girl splendidly, the prince loses his heart to her, the queen-mother lays traps for her in vain. Nothing is so fine in the castle as in the girl's château of Cattenburg. The prince insists on seeing that palace, the cat frightens the peasants into saying that all the land they pass is the girl's; finally, the cat reaches a troll's house, with pillars of gold. The cat turns himself into a loaf of bread and holds the troll in talk till the sun rises on him and he bursts, as trolls always do if they see the sun. The girl succeeds to the troll's palace, and nothing is said as to what became of the cat.

Here is even less moral than in *Puss in Boots*, for the Marquis of Carabas, as M. Deulin says, merely lets the cat do all the tricks,[82] whereas the Swedish girl is his active accomplice. The change of the cat into bread (which can talk), and the bursting of the ogre at dawn, are very ancient ideas, whether

---

*   *Causeries du Lundi* [Monday Conversations], December 29, 1851.

†   *Schol. ad. Theog.* 885.

‡   Thorpe's *Palace with Pillars of Gold*.

§   Dasent's *Lord Peter*.

they have been tacked later on to the *conte* or not. In *Lord Peter* the heroine gives place to a hero, while the cat drives deer to the palace, saying that they come from Lord Peter. The cat, we are not told how, dresses Lord Peter in splendid attire, kills a troll for him, and then, as in Madame d'Aulnoy's *White Cat*, has its head cut off and becomes a princess. Behold how fancies jump! All the ogre's wealth had been the princess's, before the ogre changed her into a cat, and took her lands. Thus George Cruikshank's moral conclusion is anticipated, while puss acts as a match-maker indeed, but acts for herself. This form of the legend, if not immoral, has no moral, and has been mixed up either with Madame d'Aulnoy's *Chatte Blanche*, or with the popular traditions from which she borrowed.

Moving south, but still keeping near France, we find *Puss in Boots* in Italy. The tale is told by Straparola.[83]* A youngest son owns nothing but a cat which, by presents of game, wins the favour of a king of Bohemia. The drowning trick is then played, and the king gives the cat's master his daughter, with plenty of money. On the bride's journey to her new home, the cat frightens the peasants into saying all the land belongs to his master, for whom he secures the castle of a knight dead without heirs.

Here, once more, there is no moral.

In a popular version from Sicily,[†84] a fox takes the cat's place, *from motives of gratitude*, because the man found it robbing and did not kill it. The fox then plays the usual trick with the game, and another familiar trick, that of leaving a few coins in a borrowed bushel measure to give the impression that his master does not *count*, but measures out his money. The trick of frightening the peasants follows, and finally, an ogress who owns a castle is thrown down a well by the fox. Then comes in the new feature: the *man is ungrateful and kills the fox*; nevertheless he lives happy ever after.

Now, at last, we have reached the moral. A beggar on horseback will forget his first friend: *a man will be less grateful than a beast.*

This moral declares itself, with a difference (for the ingrate is coerced into decent behaviour), in a popular French version, taken down from oral recitation.‡

Here, then, even among the peasantry of Perrault's own country, and as near France as Sicily, too, we have *Puss in Boots* with a moral: that of human ingratitude contrasted with the gratitude of a beast. May we conclude, then, that *Puss in Boots* was originally invented as a kind of parable by which this moral might be inculcated? And, if we may draw that con-

---

*   *Piacevoli Notti*, xi. 1, Venice, 1562. Crane's *Italian Popular Tales*, p. 348.

†   Pitré, No. 188; Crane, p. 127. Gonzenbach, 65, *Conte Piro*. In Gonzenbach, the man does not kill the fox, which pretends to be dead, and is bilked of its promised reward, a grand funeral.

‡   Lou Compaire Gatet, 'Father Cat,' *Revue des Langues Romanes*, iii. 396. See Deulin, *Contes de Ma Mère L'Oye*, p. 205.

clusion, where is this particular moral most likely to have been invented, and enforced in an apologue?

As to the first of these two questions, it may be observed that the story with the moral, and with a fox in place of a cat, is found among the Avars, a Mongolian people of Mussulman faith, on the northern slopes of the Caucasus.[85] Here the man is ungrateful, but the fox, as in Sicily, coerces him, in this case by threatening to let out the story of his rise in life.* In Russia, too, a fox takes the cat's *rôle*, and the part of the ogre is entrusted to the Serpent Uhlan, a supernatural snake, who is burned to ashes.†

It is now plain that the tale with the moral, whether that was the original motive or not, is more common than the tale without the moral. We find the moral among French, Italians, Avars, Russians; among people of Mahommedan, Greek, and Catholic religion. Now M. Emmanuel Cosquin is inclined to believe that the moral—the ingratitude of man contrasted with the gratitude of beasts,—is Buddhistic. If that be so, then India is undeniably the original cradle of *Puss in Boots*. But M. Cosquin has been unable to find any *Puss in Boots* in India; at least he knew none in 1876, when he wrote on the subject in *Le Français* (June 29, 1876).[86] Nor did the learned Benfey, with all his prodigious erudition, know an Indian *Puss in Boots*.‡ Therefore the proof of this theory, that Buddhistic India may be the real cat's cradle, is incomplete; nor does it become more probable when we actually do discover *Puss in Boots* in India. For in the Indian *Puss in Boots*, just as in Perrault's, *there is no moral at all*, and the notion of gratitude, on either the man's side or the beast's, is not even suggested.

There could scarcely be a more disappointing discovery than this for the school of Benfey which derives our fairy tales from Buddhism and India. First, the tale which we are discussing certainly did not find a place in the *Pantschatantra*, the *Hitopadesa*,[87] or any other of the early Indian literary collections of *Märchen* which were translated into so many Western languages. Next, the story does not present itself, for long, to European students of living Indian folk-lore. Finally, when puss *is* found in India, where the moral element (if it was the original element, and if its origin was in Buddhist fancy) should be particularly well preserved, there is not any moral whatever.

The Indian *Puss in Boots* is called *The Match-making Jackal*, and was published, seven years after M. Cosquin had failed to find it, in the Rev. Lal Behari Day's *Folk Tales of Bengal* (Macmillan).[88] Mr. Day, of the Hooghly College, is a native gentleman well acquainted with European folk-lore.

---

* *Boukoutchi Khan*, translated into German by Schiefner. *Mémoires de l'Académie de St. Pétersbourg*, 1873. With Dr. Köhler's Notes.

† Gubernatis. *Zoological Mythology*, ii. 136. Quoting Afanassieff, iv. 11. Compare a similar snake in Swahili.

‡ *Pantschatantra* [(Leipzig: Brodhaus, 1859)], i. 222.

Some of the stories in his collection were told by a Bengali Christian woman, two by an old Brahman, three by an old barber, two by a servant of Mr. Day's, and the rest by another old Brahman. Unluckily, the editor does not say which tales he got from each contributor. It might therefore be argued that *The Match-making Jackal* was perhaps told by the Christian woman, and that she adapted it from *Puss in Boots*, which she might have heard told by Christians. Mr. Day will be able to settle this question; but it must be plain to any reader of *The Match-making Jackal* that the story, as reported, is too essentially Hindoo to have been 'adapted' in one generation. It is not impossible that a literary Scandinavian might have introduced the typically Norse touches into the Norse *Puss in Boots*, but no illiterate woman of Bengal could have made Perrault's puss such a thoroughly Oriental jackal as the beast in the story we are about to relate.

There was once a poor weaver whose ancestors had been wealthy men. The weaver was all alone in the world, but a neighbouring jackal, 'remembering the grandeur of the weaver's forefathers, had compassion on him.'[89] This was pure sentiment on the jackal's part; his life had not been spared, as in some European versions, by the weaver. There was no gratitude in the case. 'I'll try to marry you,' said the jackal, off-hand, 'to the daughter of the king of this country.' The weaver said, 'Yes, when the sun rises in the west.' But the jackal had his plan. He trotted off to the palace, many miles away, and on the road he plucked quantities of the leaves of the betel plant. Then he lay down at the entrance of the tank where the princess bathed twice a day, and began ostentatiously chewing betel-leaves. 'Why,' said the princess, 'what a rich land this jackal must have come from. Here he is chewing betel, a luxury that thousands of men and women among us cannot afford.' The princess asked the jackal whence he came, and he said he was the native of a wealthy country. 'As for our king, his palace is like the heaven of Indra; your palace here is a miserable hovel compared to it.' So the princess told the queen, who at once, and most naturally, asked the jackal if his king were a bachelor. 'Certainly,' said the jackal, 'he has rejected princesses from all parts.' So the queen said *she* had a pretty daughter, still *zu haben*,[90] and the jackal promised to try to persuade his master to think of the princess. The jackal returned on his confidential mission, telling the weaver to follow his instructions closely. He went back to court, and suggested that his master should come in a private manner, not in state, as his retinue would eat up the substance of his future father-in-law. He returned and made the weaver borrow a decent suit of clothes from the washermen. Then he made interest with the king of the jackals, the paddy-birds, and the crows, each of whom lent a contingent of a thousand beasts or birds of their species. When they had all arrived within two miles of the palace, the jackal bade them yell and cry, which they did so furiously that the king supposed an innumerable company of people were attending his son-in-law. He therefore implored the jackal to ask his master to come quite alone. 'My master will come alone in undress,' said the jackal; 'send a horse for him.' This was done, and the jackal explained that his master arrived in mean clothes that he might not abash the king by his glory and splendour. The weaver held his tongue as commanded, but at night his talk was of looms and beams, and the princess detected him. The jackal explained that his philanthropic prince was establishing a colony of weavers, and that his mind ran a good deal on this benevolent project.

Here the *Puss in Boots* character of the tale disappears. The weaver and the princess go home, but the jackal does *not* cajole anyone out of a castle and lands. He has made the match, and there he leaves it. The princess, however, has fortunately a magical method of making gold, by virtue of which she builds the weaver a splendid palace, and 'hospitals were established for diseased, sick, and infirm animals,' a very Indian touch. The king visits his daughter, is astonished at her wealth, and the jackal says, 'Did I not tell you so?'

Here, as we said, there is no moral, or if any moral, it is the gratitude of man, as displayed in founding hospitals for beasts, not, as M. Cosquin says, 'l'idée toute bouddhique de l'ingratitude de l'homme opposée à la bonté native de l'animal.'[91] Plainly, if any moral was really intended, it was a satire on people who seek great marriages, just as in the story of *The Rat's Wedding*,[92] the moral is a censure on bargain-hunters.

The failure of the only Indian *Puss in Boots* we know to establish a theory of an Indian origin, does not, of course, prove a negative. We can only say that puss certainly did not come from India to Europe by the ordinary literary vehicles, and that, when he is found in India, he does not preach what is called the essentially Buddhist doctrine of the ingratitude of man and the gratitude of beasts.

There remains, however, an Eastern form of the tale, an African version, which is of morality all compact. This is the Swahili version from Zanzibar, and it is printed as *Sultan Darai*, in Dr. Steere's *Swahili Tales,*[93] *as told by Natives of Zanzibar* (Bell and Daldy, London, 1870). If a tale first arose where it is now found to exist with most moral, with most didactic purpose, then *Puss in Boots* is either Arab or Negro, or a piece in which Negroes and Arabs have collaborated. For nowhere is the *conte* so purposeful as among the Swahilis, who are by definition 'men of mixed Negro and Arab origin.'[94]

There may be Central African elements in the Swahili tales, for most of them have 'sung parts,' almost unintelligible even to the singers. 'I suppose,' says Dr. Steere, 'they have been brought down from the interior by the slaves, and perhaps corrupted by them as they gradually forgot their own language.'[95] Thus Central Africa may have contributed to the Swahili stories, but the Swahili *Puss in Boots*, as it at present exists, has been deeply modified by Mussulman ideas.

Sultan Darai, the Swahili *Puss in Boots*, really contains two tales. The first is about a wicked step-mother; the second begins when the hero, losing his wife and other kinsfolk, takes to vicious courses, and becomes so poor that he passes his time scratching for grains of millet on the common dustheap. While thus scratching he finds a piece of money, with which he buys a gazelle. The gazelle has pity on him, and startles him by saying so: 'Almighty God is able to do all things, to make me to speak, and others more than I.'[96] The story comes, therefore, through narrators who marvel, as in the fairy world nobody does marvel, at the miracle of a speaking beast.

The gazelle, intent on helping the man, finds a splendid diamond, which he takes to the sultan, just as puss took the game, as 'a present from Sultan Darai.' The sultan is much pleased; the gazelle proposes that he shall give his daughter to Sultan Darai, and then comes the old trick of pretending the master has been stripped by robbers, 'even to his loin-cloth.' The gazelle carries fine raiment to his master, and, as in the French popular and traditional form, bids him speak as little as may be. The marriage is celebrated, and the gazelle goes off, and kills a great seven-headed snake, which, as in Russia, is the owner of a rich house. The snake, as he travels, is accompanied (as in the Kaffir story of *Five Heads*)[97] by a storm of wind, like that which used to shake the 'medicine lodges' of the North American Indians, puzzling the missionaries. The snake, like the ogre in all *Hop o' My Thumb* tales, smells out the gazelle, but is defeated by that victorious animal. The gazelle brings home his master, Sultan Darai, and the Princess to the snake's house, where they live in great wealth and comfort.

Now comes in the moral: the gazelle falls sick, Sultan Darai refuses to see it, orders coarse food to be offered it; treats his poor benefactor, in short, with all the arrogant contempt of an ungrateful beggar suddenly enriched. As the ill-used cat says in the *Pentamerone*—

> De riche appauvri Dieu te gard'
> Et de croquant passé richard![98]

Finally the gazelle dies of sorrow, and Sultan Darai dreams that he is scratching on his old dustheap. He wakens and finds himself there, as naked and wretched as ever, while his wife is wafted to her father's house at home.

The moral is obvious, and the story is told in a very touching manner, moreover all the world takes the side of the gazelle, and it is *mourned with a public funeral*.

Here, then, in Zanzibar we have decidedly the most serious and purposeful form of *Puss in Boots*. It is worth noting that the animal hero is *not* the Rabbit who is the usual hero in Zanzibar as he is in Uncle Remus's tales. It is also worth noticing that a certain tribe of Southern Arabians do, as a matter of fact, honour all dead gazelles with seven days of public mourning. 'Ibn al-Moghâwir,' says Prof. Robertson-Smith, in *Kinship in Early Arabia* (p. 195), 'speaks of a South Arab tribe called Beni Hârith or Acârib, among whom if a dead gazelle was found, it was solemnly buried, and the whole tribe mourned for it seven days…. The gazelle supplies a name to a clan of the Azd, the Zabyân.' Prof. Robertson-Smith adds (p. 204), 'And so when we find a whole clan mourning over a dead gazelle, we can hardly but conclude that when this habit was first formed, they thought that they were of the gazelle-stock' or Totem kindred.

It is quite possible that all these things are mere coincidences. Certainly we shall not argue, because the most moral form of *Puss in Boots* gives us a gazelle in place of a cat, and because a certain Arab clan mourns gazelles, while the gazelle hero is found in the story of a half-Arab race, that, therefore, the Swahili gazelle story is the original form of *Puss in Boots*, and that from Arabia the tale has been carried into Russia, Scandinavia, Italy, India, and France, often leaving its moral behind it, and always exchanging its gazelle for some other beast-hero.

This kind of reasoning is only too common, when the object is to show that India was the birthplace of any widely diffused popular fiction. In India, people argue, this or that tale has a moral. Among Celts and Kamschatkans it has *no* moral. But certain stories did undeniably come from India in literary works, like the stories of Sindibad. Therefore this or that story also came from India, dropping its moral on the way. Did we like this sort of syllogism,[99] we might boldly assert that *Puss in Boots* was originally a heroic myth of an Arab tribe with a gazelle for Totem. But we like not this kind of syllogism. The purpose of this study of *Puss in Boots* is to show that, even when a tale has probably been invented but once, in one place, and has thence spread over a great part of the world, the difficulty of finding the original centre is perhaps insuperable. At any time a fresh discovery may be made. Puss *may* turn up in some hitherto unread manuscript of an old missionary among Mexicans or Peruvians.*

[...]

'Conclusion'

The study of Perrault's tales which we have made serves to illustrate the problems and difficulties of the subject in general. It has been seen that similar and analogous *contes* are found among most peoples, ancient and modern. When the resemblances are only in detached ideas and incidents, for example, the introduction of rational and loquacious beasts, or of magical powers, the difficulty of accounting for the diffusion of such notions is comparatively slight. All the backward peoples of the world believe in magic, and in the common nature of men, beasts, and things. The real problem is to explain the coincidence in *plot* of stories found in ancient Egypt, in Peru, in North America, and South Africa, as well as in Europe. In

---

* The work of M. Cosquin's referred to throughout is his valuable *Contes de Lorraine*, Paris, 1886. [...]

a few words it is possible to sketch the various theories of the origin and diffusion of legends like these.

I. According to what may be called the Aryan theory (advocated by Grimm, M. André Lefèvre,[100] Von Hahn, and several English writers), the stories are peculiar to peoples who speak languages of the Aryan family. These peoples, in some very remote age, before they left their original seats, developed a copious mythology, based mainly on observation of natural phenomena, Dawn, Thunder, Wind, Night, and the like. This mythology was rendered possible by a 'disease of language,'[101] owing to which statements about phenomena came to appear like statements about imaginary persons, and so grew into myths. *Märchen*, or popular tales, are the *débris*, or *detritus*, or youngest form of those myths, worn by constant passing from mouth to mouth. The partisans of this theory often maintain that the borrowing of tales by one people from another is, if not an impossible, at least a very rare process.

II. The next hypothesis may be called the Indian theory. The chief partisan of this theory was Benfey, the translator and commentator of the *Pantschatantra*. In France M. Cosquin, author of *Contes Populaires de Lorraine*, is the leading representative. According to the Indian theory, the original centre and fountain of popular tales is India, and from India of the historic period the legends were diffused over Europe, Asia, and Africa. Oral tradition, during the great national movements and migrations, and missions,— the Mongol conquests, the crusades, the Buddhist enterprises, and in course of trade and commerce, diffused the tales. They were also in various translations,—Persian, Arabic, Greek,—of Indian literary collections like the *Pantschatantra* and the *Hitopadesa*, brought to the knowledge of mediæval Europe. Preachers even used the tales as parables or 'examples' in the pulpit, and by all those means the stories found their way about the world. It is admitted that the discovery of *contes* in Egypt, at a date when nothing is known of India, is a difficulty in the way of this theory, as we are not able to show that those *contes* came from India, nor that India borrowed them from Egypt. The presence of the tales in America is explained as the consequence of importations from Europe, since the discovery of the New World by Columbus.

Neither of these theories, neither the Aryan nor the Indian, is quite satisfactory. The former depends on a doctrine about the 'disease of language' not universally accepted. Again, it entirely fails to account for the presence of the *contes* (which, *ex hypothesi*,[102] were not *borrowed*) among non-Aryan peoples. The second, or Indian theory, correctly states that many stories were introduced into Europe, Asia, and Africa from India, in the middle ages, but brings no proof that *contes* could only have been invented in India, first of all. Nor does it account for the stories which were old in Egypt, and even mixed up with the national mythology of Egypt, before we knew anything about India at all, nor for the *Märchen* of Homeric Greece. Again it is not shown that the *ideas* in the *contes* are peculiar to India; almost the only example adduced is the *gratitude of beasts*. But this notion might occur to any mind, anywhere, which regarded the beasts as on the same intellectual and moral level as humanity. Moreover, a few examples have been found of *Märchen* among American races, for example, in early Peru, where there is no reason to believe that they were introduced by the Spaniards.*

In place of these hypotheses, we do not propose to substitute any general theory. It is certain that the best-known popular tales were current in Egypt under Ramses II,[103] and that many of them were known to Homer, and are introduced, or are alluded to, in the *Odyssey*. But it is impossible to argue that the birthplace of a tale is the country where it is first found in a literary shape. The stories must have been current in the popular mouth long before they won their way into written literature, on tablets of clay or on papyrus. They are certainly not of literary invention. If they were developed in one place, history gives us no information as to the region or the date of their birth. Again, we cannot pretend to know how far, given the ideas, the stories might be evolved independently in different centres. It is difficult to set a limit to chance and coincidence, and modern importation. The whole question of the importation of stories into savage countries by civilised peoples has not been studied properly. We can hardly suppose that the Zulus borrowed their copious and most characteristic store of *Märchen*, in plot and incident resembling the *Märchen* of Europe, from Dutch or English settlers. On the other hand, certain Algonkin tales recently published by Mr. Leland[104] bear manifest marks of French influence.

Left thus in the dark without historical information as to the 'cradle' of *Märchen*, without clear and copious knowledge as to *recent* borrowing from European traders and settlers, and without the power of setting limits to the possibility of *coincidence*, we are unable to give any general answer to the sphinx of popular tales. We only know for certain that there is practically no limit to the chances of transmission in the remote past of the race. Wherever man, woman, or child can go, there a tale may go, and may find a new home. Any drifted and wandering canoe, any captured alien wife, any stolen slave passed from hand to hand in commerce or war, may carry a *Märchen*. These processes of transmission have been going on, practically, ever since man was man. Thus it is even more difficult to limit the possibilities of transmission than the chances of coincidence. But the chances of coincidence also are numerous. The *ideas* and *situations* of popular tales are all afloat, everywhere, in the imaginations of early and of pre-scientific men. Who can tell how often they might casually unite in similar wholes, independently combined?

---

* *Rites of the Yncas*, Francisco de Avila. Hakluyt Society.

'Introduction',
The Blue Fairy Book
(Longmans, Green and Co., 1889)

The taste of the world, which has veered so often, is constant enough to fairy tales. The children to whom and for whom they are told represent the young age of man. They are true to his early loves, they have his un-blunted edge of belief, and his fresh appetite for marvels. The instinct of economy so works that we are still repeating to the boys and girls of each generation the stories that were old before Homer sang, and the adventures that have wandered, like the wandering Psyche, over all the world. We may alter now and again the arrangement of incidents, but these always remain essentially the same, and of all the combinations into which they can be fitted, the oldest combinations are still the favourites.

These truisms have been for some time recognised even by Science, and the study of nursery tales, of their wanderings, their antiquity, their origin, has long been a diversion of the learned. This, however, is not the place to repeat the familiar antiquarian theories, nor to attempt any new variety of conjecture. Even a child (this preface is not meant for children) must rec-ognise, as he turns the pages of the *Blue Fairy Book*, that the same adventures and something like the same plots meet him in stories translated from di-fferent languages. The Scotch 'Black Bull of Norroway,' for example, must remind the very youngest reader of 'East of the Sun and West of the Moon,' a tale from the Norse.[1] Both, again, have manifest resemblances to 'Beauty and the Beast,' and every classical student has the fable of 'Eros and Psyche'[2] brought back to his memory, while every anthropologist recollects a similar *Märchen* among Kaffirs and Bassutos. These resemblances and analogies recur on every page. Our 'Bronze Ring,'[3] from the Levant, with the mice which make the Jew sneeze by tickling his nose, has a variant among Mongolian tribes. The Finns, the Santhals, the Kaffirs have a Cinderella of their own, like the Scotch and the Celts.[4] Parts of 'Hop o' my Thumb' ('The Little Thumb') are current in Tartary; the incident of the changed crowns and the murder by the ogre of his own children is part of that ancient Minyan legend of Athamas, Phrixus, and Hellê.[5] The tale of Jason was old when the 'Odyssey' was composed — old and 'familiar' (like the ship Argo) 'to all men.' Here we have a shadow of its main events in 'The Master Maid,' and there are other echoes in Samoa, and among the red men of the North American continent.[6] The papyri of the second Rameses contain fairy tales recognisably like ours;[7] there is no speech nor land where their voice is not heard.

To explain these curious correspondences, these echoes out of some far-off time, is the object of the science of the lower mythology — call it Folk-Lore, or by what name we will. But that science does not at all exhaust the interest of nursery stories. It struggles with their history, asks — Have they come from a common source? have they been independently invented in various centres? have mankind inherited them all from faraway first ancestors? or have they been scattered like the seeds of flowers in the course of commerce, slavery, marriage with strange wives, and war? To answer, or at least to put, these questions is the business of science, of that science which is concerned with origins, popular antiquities, the earlier developments of human thought, life, and art. We shall not say over again here what we have already repeated, perhaps too frequently, concerning these problems.*

They are problems of science, or of a study with scientific aims, rather than of literary criticism. Perhaps it seems almost as cruel to apply the methods of literary criticism as of science to Nursery Tales. He who would enter into the Kingdom of Faery should have the heart of a little child, if he is to be happy and at home in that enchanted realm. But I trust that one may have studied fairy tales both scientifically and in a literary way, without losing the heart of childhood, as far as those best of childish things are concerned. May one be forgiven the egotism of confessing, that in the reading and arranging of these old wives' fables, one has felt perhaps as much pleasure as the child who reads them, or hears them, for the first time? Children, as we know, like to hear a tale often, and always insist that it shall be told in the same way.

Decies repetita placebit![8]

'Blue Beard,' that little tragic and dramatic masterpiece, moves me yet; I still tremble for Puss in Boots when the ogre turns into a lion; and still one's heart goes with the girl who seeks her lost and enchanted lover, and wins

---

* The writer's own ideas may be found in the preface to Mrs. Hunt's translations of Grimm's 'Kinder- und Hausmärchen,' in *The Marriage of Cupid and Psyche*, in the Clarendon Press edition of Perrault's *Contes de ma Mère l'Oye*, in the last chapter of *Myth, Ritual, and Religion*, and the preface to Mr. Tuer's edition of the rhyme of 'Beauty and the Beast,' attributed to Charles Lamb.

him again in the third night of watching and of tears. This may not seem a taste to be proud of, but it is a taste to be grateful for, like the love of any other thing that is old and plain, and dallies with the simplicity of love.

'They all went to bed again, and the damsel began singing as before —

'Seven lang years I served for thee,
The glassy hill I clamb for thee,
The bluidy shirt I wrang for thee,
And wilt thou not wauken and turn to me?'[9]

They will not waken and turn to us, our lost loves, our lost chances, not for all our service, all our singing, not for all our waiting seven or twice seven long years. But, in the fairy tale, he heard, and he turned to her. 'And she told him a' that had befa'en her, and he told her a' that had happened to him.'[10] Where have we heard these simple words before, and known the long lost, the long divided, the reunited hearts, brought 'to the rites of their ancient bed,'[11] and telling each other all the story of their sorrow? It is at the close of the 'Odyssey,' and Homer is the story-teller.

By private experience, then, one is led to hope and believe that much reading of nursery stories, even through the microscope of science and the spectacles of literature, need not make one incapable of relishing the old and friendly narratives. We do not forget our old nurse, the *Märchen*. If any one differs, it is easy for him to pass over these few pages, only placed in front of a limited edition of the *Blue Fairy Book*, only meant for grown-up people, and never for children. [...]

'Introduction',
The Red Fairy Book
(Longmans, Green and Co., 1890)

There is no end of the scientific research into fairy tales, or, indeed, into anything else. A beetle or two may occupy the whole working life of a specialist, and to exhaust the knowledge – literary, anthropological, religious, antiquarian, moral, – of our nursery stories might also be the occupation of a career. Matter is said to be infinitely divisible; and so is the stuff of a *Märchen*. As specialism advances, we may see young men, spectacled from the cradle, and bald from their birth, voyage into middle age and extreme eld, still pouring over 'Cinderella' or 'Puss in Boots'. They will trace these narratives to Aryans and barbarians; they will find lunar, solar, stellar myths in them; or will prove that 'Puss in Boots' was originally the Spirit of Vegetation, or a prehistoric parable of the Gulf Stream. In a book of stories gathered together for children we have little to do with all this erudition. For now twenty mortal years the Editor has been grubbing in the science of fairy tales. Twenty years ago, soon after taking his degree, it occurred to him that the old theories were to be turned upside down, that old wives' fables represented the oldest known romances of the world, and that the classical legends which resemble them in plot were literary amplifications of early popular stories. The more he looked at this idea, the more he liked it; the more he read, the more he saw that the fancies in Grimm or Perrault were, at first, the fancies natural to untutored races and still surviving among them. This doctrine was only an expansion of the theory of the Grimms, and Mannhardt had been at work on one side of it, while it had been stated, in passing, by Fontenelle and other French writers of the last century. For twenty years one has been preaching this belief, in season, and, probably, out of season, as the root of the matter. It has constantly been corroborated, as new tales from alien lands came in – from New Guinea, Samoa, the Eskimo,

South Africa, the Soudan, and Japan. The opinion is now before the world, to take or to leave, to hold that nursery tales embody early fancies of un-taught races, and have been preserved by changeless peasant tradition, or to regard them as corruptions of literary romances. My hypothesis, long ago so exciting to myself, and still, to my mind, so plausible, admits, doubtless, of exceptions, and may be ridden to death like any other theory – indeed, it may even become a weariness, and a jaded intellect may ask whether it has been worth taking so much trouble about, whether quite enough fair paper has not been blackened with lucubrations, for it and against it. However, the questions connected with old wives' fables were among the riddles of the Sphinx of History, and, more than most of her enigmas, were capable of being answered. Fairy tales were part of the ancient human legacy, and are either older than the separation of races, or were communicated by tribe to tribe in dateless days of caravans and canoes, or were spontaneous-ly evolved almost everywhere by the natural action of similar minds, with similar ideas, engaged in the task of story-telling. Later exchanges of the romances, borrowings and barterings, there may well have been, but the foundation is antique, and even savage. That seems to be the conclusion at present most in favour. But, numerous as the stories are, and widely as they are diffused, all are not equally good reading, especially for children. The *Märchen* of New Guinea and Zululand would only perplex little boys and girls: we choose our tales, therefore, from the shapes they have taken among European peoples – Germans, Russians, Roumanians, Finns, French, and others. [...] Nothing has been introduced which is merely a scientific curi-osity or an anthropological fact. The attempt has been to select stories which, as stories, are interesting, humorous, or dramatic. The right critics of them will be children, whose taste, in such matters, is classically excellent and pure. If they cry, 'Tell us that again,' and yet again, the purpose of the Editor will have been attained. If they waken, even in a few little boys and girls, the love of reading, if they open the door into a fairyland, not of science but of fancy, they have reached their proper aim and end. Stories like these will live, or will revive, when, in the changes of human fortunes, science has been lost, when electricity, and steam, and chemistry are buried with their engines and their crucibles beneath the ruins of a world and under the ac-cumulations of innumerable earthworms. Faiths, and Empires, and Philosophies have crumbled and faded, and left the fairy folk happy still in their kingdom beyond the river which runs knee deep with blood. In all generations the Fairy Queen will have her lovers, and carry them off, like True Thomas,[1] to her twilit realm, whence they will issue again with those legends of her domain. These will be heard when the steam whistle is silent, and when the crack of the rifle, the roar of the canon, are sounds forgotten and unknown. Again they will inspire poetry, again be the warp and woof of romance, immortal while man lives, and only to be forgotten when the chill ball of earth rolls round a frozen sun. They are our oldest legacy, they will be our last bequest, flitting from mouth to mouth when the printing press is in ruins and the alphabet has to be re-invented.

But this is taking long views, which are not conducive to mirth; long views which any eye may perceive in the past, and any fancy may feign about the future. So remote, indeed, are these dreams from the topic of nursery tales, that their dreamer may fairly be accused of having no more to say on that matter. To science the tales are inexhaustibly interesting; of literature, of imaginative literature, they are the beginning, the dawn, and it is quite conceivable that they may prove the end and the sunset. They have charmed man in his nonage,[2] and for children, and people in whom the child is not quite dead, we may say of a good nursery story, *Decies repetita placebit.*[3] This is praise to which perhaps no other compositions, except the very highest poems, are entitled.

'Preface',
The Green Fairy Book
(Longmans, Green and Co., 1892)

This is the third, and probably the last, of the Fairy Books of many colours. First there was the *Blue Fairy Book*; then, children, you asked for more, and we made up the *Red Fairy Book*; and, when you wanted more still, the *Green Fairy Book* was put together. The stories in all the books are borrowed from many countries; some are French, some German, some Russian, some Italian, some Scottish, some English, one Chinese. However much these nations differ about trifles, they all agree in liking fairy tales. The reason, no doubt, is that men were much like children in their minds long ago, long, long ago, and so before they took to writing newspapers, and sermons, and novels, and long poems, they told each other stories, such as you read in the fairy books. They believed that witches could turn people into beasts, that beasts could speak, that magic rings could make their owners invisible, and all the other wonders in the stories. Then, as the world became grown-up, the fairy tales which were not written down would have been quite forgotten but that the old grannies remembered them, and told them to the little grandchildren: and when they, in their turn, became grannies, they remembered them, and told them also. In this way these tales are older than reading and writing, far older than printing. The oldest fairy tales ever written down were written down in Egypt, about Joseph's time, nearly three thousand five hundred years ago. Other fairy stories Homer knew, in Greece, nearly three thousand years ago, and he made them all up into a poem, the *Odyssey*, which I hope you will read some day. Here you will find the witch who turns men into swine, and the man who bores out the big foolish giant's eye, and the cap of darkness, and the shoes of swiftness, that were worn later by Jack the Giant-Killer. These fairy tales are the oldest stories in the world, and as they were first made by men who were childlike for their own amusement, so they amuse children still, and also grown-up people who have not forgotten how they once were children.

Some of the stories were made, no doubt, not only to amuse, but to teach goodness. You see, in the tales, how the boy who is kind to beasts, and polite, and generous, and brave, always comes best through his trials, and no doubt these tales were meant to make their hearers kind, unselfish, courteous, and courageous. This is the moral of them. But, after all, we think more as we read them of the diversion than of the lesson. There are grown-up people now who say that the stories are not good for children, because they are not true, because there are no witches, nor talking beasts, and because people are killed in them, especially wicked giants. But probably you who read the tales know very well how much is true and how much is only make-believe, and I never yet heard of a child who killed a very tall man merely because Jack killed the giants, or who was unkind to his stepmother, if he had one, because, in fairy tales, the stepmother is often disagreeable. If there are frightful monsters in fairy tales, they do not frighten you now, because that kind of monster is no longer going about the world, whatever he may have done long, long ago. He has been turned into stone, and you may see his remains in museums. Therefore, I am not afraid that *you* will be afraid of the magicians and dragons; besides, you see that a really brave boy or girl was always their master, even in the height of their power.

[...]

'Preface',
The Yellow Fairy Book
(Longmans, Green and Co., 1894)

The Editor thinks that children will readily forgive him for publishing another Fairy Book. We have had the Blue, the Red, the Green, and here is the Yellow. If children are pleased, and they are so kind as to say that they *are* pleased, the Editor does not care very much for what other people may say. Now, there is one gentleman who seems to think that it is not quite right to print so many fairy tales, with pictures, and to publish them in red and blue covers. He is named Mr. G. Laurence Gomme, and he is president of a learned body called the Folk Lore Society.[1] Once a year he makes his address to his subjects, of whom the Editor is one, and Mr. Joseph Jacobs (who has published many delightful fairy tales with pretty pictures)* is another. Fancy, then, the dismay of Mr. Jacobs, and of the Editor, when they heard their president say that he did not think it very nice in them to publish fairy books, above all, red, green, and blue fairy books![2] They said that they did not see any harm in it, and they were ready to 'put themselves on their country,' and be tried by a jury of children. And, indeed, they still see no harm in what they have done; nay, like Father William in the poem,[3] they are ready 'to do it again and again.'

Where is the harm? The truth is that the Folk Lore Society—made up of the most clever, learned, and beautiful men and women of the country—is fond of studying the history and geography of Fairy Land. This is contained in very old tales, such as country people tell, and savages:

'Little Sioux and little Crow,
Little frosty Eskimo.'[4]

---

* You may buy them from Mr. Nutt, in the Strand.

These people are thought to know most about fairyland and its inhabitants. But, in the Yellow Fairy Book, and the rest, are many tales by persons who are neither savages nor rustics, such as Madame D'Aulnoy and Herr Hans Christian Andersen. The Folk Lore Society, or its president, say that *their* tales are not so true as the rest, and should not be published with the rest. But *we* say that all the stories which are pleasant to read are quite true enough for us; so here they are, with pictures by Mr. Ford,[5] and we do not think that either the pictures or the stories are likely to mislead children.

As to whether there are really any fairies or not, that is a difficult question. Professor Huxley thinks there are none.[6] The Editor never saw any himself, but he knows several people who have seen them—in the Highlands—and heard their music. If ever you are in Nether Lochaber, go to the Fairy Hill, and you may hear the music yourself, as grown-up people have done, but you must go on a fine day. Again, if there are really no fairies, why do people believe in them, all over the world? The ancient Greeks believed, so did the old Egyptians, and the Hindoos, and the Red Indians, and is it likely, if there are no fairies, that so many different peoples would have seen and heard them? The Rev. Mr. Baring-Gould saw several fairies when he was a boy, and was travelling in the land of the Troubadours.[7] For these reasons, the Editor thinks that there are certainly fairies, but they never do anyone any harm; and, in England, they have been frightened away by smoke and schoolmasters. As to Giants, they have died out, but real Dwarfs are common in the forests of Africa. Probably a good many stories not perfectly true have been told about fairies, but such stories have also been told about Napoleon, Claverhouse,[8] Julius Cæsar, and Joan of Arc, all of whom certainly existed. A wise child will, therefore, remember that, if he grows up and becomes a member of the Folk Lore Society, *all* the tales in this book were not offered to him as absolutely truthful, but were printed merely for his entertainment. The exact facts he can learn later, or he can leave them alone.

[...]

'Preface',
The Pink Fairy Book
(Longmans, Green and Co., 1897)

All people in the world tell nursery tales to their children. The Japanese tell them, the Chinese, the Red Indians by their camp fires, the Eskimo in their dark dirty winter huts. The Kaffirs of South Africa tell them, and the modern Greeks, just as the old Egyptians did, when Moses had not been many years rescued out of the bulrushes. The Germans, French, Spanish, Italians, Danes, Highlanders tell them also, and the stories are apt to be like each other everywhere. A child who has read the Blue and Red and Yellow Fairy Books will find some old friends with new faces in the Pink Fairy Book, if he examines and compares. But the Japanese tales will probably be new to the young student; the Tanuki[1] is a creature whose acquaintance he may not have made before. [...] Here, then, are fancies brought from all quarters: we see that black, white, and yellow peoples are fond of just the same kinds of adventures. Courage, youth, beauty, kindness, have many trials, but they always win the battle; while witches, giants, unfriendly cruel people, are on the losing hand. So it ought to be, and so, on the whole, it is and will be; and that is all the moral of fairy tales. We cannot all be young, alas! and pretty, and strong; but nothing prevents us from being kind, and no kind man, woman, or beast or bird, ever comes to anything but good in these oldest fables of the world. So far all the tales are true, and no further.

'Preface',
The Lilac Fairy Book
(Longmans, Green and Co., 1910)

'What cases are you engaged in at present?' 'Are you stopping many teeth just now?' 'What people have you converted lately?' Do ladies put these questions to the men—lawyers, dentists, clergymen, and so forth—who happen to sit next them at dinner parties?

I do not know whether ladies thus indicate their interest in the occupations of their casual neighbours at the hospitable board. But if they do not know me, or do not know me well, they generally ask 'Are you writing anything now?' (as if they should ask a painter 'Are you painting anything now?' or a lawyer 'Have you any cases at present?'). Sometimes they are more definite and inquire 'What are you writing now?' as if I must be writing something—which, indeed, is the case, though I dislike being reminded of it. It is an awkward question, because the fair being does not care a bawbee what I am writing; nor would she be much enlightened if I replied 'Madam, I am engaged on a treatise intended to prove that Normal is prior to Conceptional Totemism'—though that answer would be as true in fact as obscure in significance. The best plan seems to be to answer that I have entirely abandoned mere literature, and am contemplating a book on 'The Causes of Early Blight in the Potato,' a melancholy circumstance which threatens to deprive us of our chief esculent root. The inquirer would never be undeceived. One nymph who, like the rest, could not keep off the horrid topic of my occupation, said 'You never write anything but fairy books, do you?' A French gentleman, too, an educationist and expert in portraits of Queen Mary, once sent me a newspaper article in which he had written that I was exclusively devoted to the composition of fairy books, and nothing else. He then came to England, visited me, and found that I knew rather more about portraits of Queen Mary than he did.[1]

In truth I never did write any fairy books in my life, except 'Prince Prigio,' 'Prince Ricardo,' and 'Tales from a Fairy Court'[2] — that of the aforesaid Prigio. I take this opportunity of recommending these fairy books — poor things, but my own — to parents and guardians who may never have heard of them. They are rich in romantic adventure, and the Princes always marry the right Princesses and live happy ever afterwards; while the wicked witches, stepmothers, tutors and governesses are *never* cruelly punished, but retire to the country on ample pensions. I hate cruelty: I never put a wicked stepmother in a barrel and send her tobogganing down a hill. It is true that Prince Ricardo *did* kill the Yellow Dwarf; but that was in fair fight, sword in hand, and the dwarf, peace to his ashes! *died in harness*.

The object of these confessions is not only that of advertising my own fairy books (which are not 'out of print'; if your bookseller says so, the truth is not in him), but of giving credit where credit is due. The fairy books have been almost wholly the work of Mrs. Lang, who has translated and adapted them from the French, German, Portuguese, Italian, Spanish, Catalan, and other languages.

My part has been that of Adam, according to Mark Twain, in the Garden of Eden.[3] Eve worked, Adam superintended. I also superintend. I find out where the stories are, and advise, and, in short, superintend. *I do not write the stories out of my own head.* […]

Let ladies and gentlemen think of this when they sit down to write fairy tales, and have them nicely typed, and send them to Messrs. Longman & Co. to be published. They think that to write a new fairy tale is easy work. They are mistaken: the thing is impossible. Nobody can write a *new* fairy tale; you can only mix up and dress up the old, old stories, and put the characters into new dresses, as Miss Thackeray did so well in 'Five Old Friends.'[4] If any big girl of fourteen reads this preface, let her insist on being presented with 'Five Old Friends.'

But the three hundred and sixty-five authors who try to write new fairy tales are very tiresome. They always begin with a little boy or girl who goes out and meets the fairies of polyanthuses and gardenias and apple blossoms: 'Flowers and fruits, and other winged things.' These fairies try to be funny, and fail; or they try to preach, and succeed. Real fairies never preach or talk slang. At the end, the little boy or girl wakes up and finds that he has been dreaming.

Such are the new fairy stories. May we be preserved from all the sort of them!

[…]

4

ANTHROPOLOGY, AND THE ORIGINS OF RELIGION

Anthroplogy is the area of Lang's work for which he perhaps most wished to be remembered, and certainly his work was taken seriously by fellow anthropologists and by others interested in anthropology in the period. Sigmund Freud cites Lang's work with approval many times in *Totem and Taboo* (first published in a single volume as *Totem und Tabu*, Leipzig and Vienna: Heller, 1913), for example. Lang wrote on most of the central interests of late nineteenth-century anthropology – kinship structures and exogamy, totemism, magic and religion – but it was his interventions into the debate about the origin of religion that was most influential at the time and of most interest now. These debates disappeared from anthropological interest in the early twentieth century, when anthropologists turned firmly towards the importance of fieldwork and towards the synchronic investigation of discrete cultures, but Lang's interventions are significant still for the way that they illuminate the complex relations within and consequences of late nineteenth-century thinking on 'race', belief, cultural change and the evolution of cultural practices.

'Anthropology and Ancient Literature' is a letter written by Lang in response to an earlier letter from T. W. Rhys Davids to *The Academy*, itself responding to letter in the previous issue (565 (3 March 1883), p. 152) by the anthropologist and folklorist Edward Clodd. Davids is clearly a supporter of the philologist Friedrich Max Müller's position against anthropology, and the letters of both Clodd and Lang are written in support of the comparative anthropology begun by E. B. Tylor's important work, *Primitive Culture: Researches into the Development of Mythology, Pholosophy, Religion, Languages, Art and Customs*, 2 vols (London: John Murray, 1871). Lang makes the case for comparative anthropology often in his work – for example in *Custom and Myth* (London: Longmans, Green and Co., 1884), in *Myth, Ritual and Religon*, 2 vols (London: Longmans, Green and Co., 1887; second edition 1899), and *The Making of Religion* (London: Longman's, Green and Co., 1898; second edition 1900) – arguing again and again that the evidence upon which it is based is more credible than that of philology. In this letter, Lang gives a cogent synopsis of his position, and shows clearly too his continued assertion that all human culture recognisable as such is complex and cannot be called 'primitive'. At this time Lang still accepts Spencer's 'ghost theory', and has not yet reached the realisation, as seen for example in 'Australian Problems', that cultures such as the Aborignine contain complex and sophisticated concepts.

'Fetichism and the Infinite' was first published in *Custom and Myth* (1884). Later editions of *Custom and Myth* were published in 1893, 1904 and 1910. Although Lang added a new preface to the 1893 edition, and a new introduction to the 1904 edition (also reproduced in the 1910 edition), he made no changes at all to the chapters themselves. While adding evidence, the new preface and introduction claim that his arguments from 1884 have in the main been confirmed. This essay is a review of Müller's theory that an inherent sense of the infinite in human beings is the origin of religion.

Lang contests this, and in so doing defends again the kinds of evidence on which the anthropological method depends.

Lang gave the Gifford lectures at St Andrews in the winters of 1888–9 and 1889–90. The series, which began in 1888, was initiated by a bequest of the jurist Lord Gifford to four Scottish universities (Edinburgh, Aberdeen, Glasgow and St Andrews) with the intention of founding a series of annual lectures on 'natural theology'. Müller gave Gifford lectures at the University of Glasgow between 1888 and 1892. Lang's lectures, the first in the series to be delivered at St Andrews, formed the basis for his *The Making of Religion*. The work, as Lang admits in his preface to the second edition, is in two parts. The first part – chapters 2 to 8 – uses the comparative method to compare accounts of supernatural occurrences across time and space, crucially showing that accounts of early and non-European peoples have their parallels in the European past and present. Lang uses this to suggest that the way such accounts have been treated in anthropology (as erroneous explanations of actual events) may be wrong. In the second part – chapters 9 to 13 – Lang sets out in detail for the first time his challenge to Herbert Spencer's 'ghost theory' and Tylor's 'animism' as accounts of the origin of religion. Lang gives detailed evidence that very early peoples had mono-theistic, all-powerful, creator gods, so that it could not be the case that such beliefs always evolved from, and therefore followed, the belief in ghosts and ancestor worship. 'On Religion' consists of a selection of extracts from chapters in the second part of the second edition of *The Making of Religion*.

'Anthropology and Religon I' is taken from the third chapter of the second edition of *The Making of Religion*, from 1900. I have indicated where this version differs from the 1898 edition. Another extract from this chapter is included in the section on 'Anthropology and Psychical Research'. The extract presents one of Lang's most detailed and cogent arguments for the method of comparative anthropology.

'Science and Superstition' and 'First-fruits and Taboos' are chapters 1 and 14 respectively of *Magic and Religion* (London: Longmans, Green and Co., 1901). The book was a direct response to the second edition of James Frazer's *The Golden Bough: A Study in Magic and Religion*, 2nd edition, 3 vols (London: Macmillan, 1900). While Lang had praised the first edition (a two-volume work with the subtitle 'A Study in Comparative Religion, published in 1890) and had corresponded with Frazer, he believed that the second edition was seriously flawed. In *Magic and Religion* Lang challenges Frazer's central explanation of the ritual of the slaying of the priest of the wood of Nemi, and more broadly challenges Frazer's implicit suggestion that totalising the-ories are possible and credible, and his argument of a straightforward evo-lution of human cultures from magic, to religion, to science.

'Australian Problems' is a relatively late work, from 1907, and shows how Lang's attitude to non-European cultures developed and matured. He is still challenging anthropological orthodoxy here, and the essay makes clear his appreciation for the complexity and subtlety of the cultures he is studying.

'Anthropology and Ancient Literature', *The Academy* 566

(10 March 1883), pp. 170–1

A few words may perhaps be added to what Mr. Clodd has said about anthropology and the Vedas. Anthropologists are not really anxious (I hope) to devise reasons for evading the study of the Vedas.[1] They are only anxious that Vedic texts should not be brought forward as proofs on the whole of what man's religious ideas were in the beginning, or near the beginning, of religion. That the Vedas contains some extremely backward notions they are ready, and even anxious, to admit. The Vedic myths of the fire-stealer, of the making of things out of the mangled Purusha,[2] of the stars, and of certain divine adventures tally with the myths of savages, and are probably survivals from a very rude and remote past. But the lofty, moral, and, so to speak, metaphysical speculations of the Vedas look like the speculations of an advanced civilisation. We are told that the ancestors of the Vedic Indians were practically civilised before Sanskrit was a language – before the Aryan separation. We cannot, therefore, regard elaborate hymns of such an old civilisation, hymns elaborately preserved by a careful teaching, as illustrative (save in certain survivals) of a very early condition of human thought. Prof. Max Müller says, 'If we mean by primitive the people who have been the first of the Aryan race to leave behind literary relics of their existence on earth, then I say the Vedic poets are primitive.'[3] But no anthropologist dreams of applying the word 'primitive' to a literary, and an elaborately literary, set of poets. Indeed, the word 'primitive' might well be discarded from the anthropological vocabulary. The rudest savage with a language, a bow, and a fire has probably travelled farther from primitive life than we have travelled from savagery. We do not find fault (as we are said to do) because the Vedas 'do not represent primitive men exactly as we think they ought to have been.'[4] We only find fault when we are told that the Vedas represent primitive men at all. They represent men in a highly interesting state of civilisation, but not exempt from survivals of savage ideas – ideas, to quote Mr. Müller, 'as rude and crude as any palaeolithic weapon.'[5] It is so difficult to get any consistent account of what is in the Vedas! Mr. Müller says, in his *Cambridge Lectures* (p. 97), 'That the Veda is full of child-ish, silly, even, to our minds, monstrous conceptions, who would deny?' Again, he speaks (p. 108) of the great majority of the Vedic hymns as being 'nearly free from all that can be called irrational or mythological.'[6] Probably in the former sentence the Veda includes all the Vedic lore; but even the hymns do appear, to an anthropologist, to contain much that is mytholog-ical, 'rude and crude,' and, from a modern point of view, irrational. Again, we are told that, if we care to know about 'the first attempts at regulating family life, village life, and State life, as founded on religion, ceremonial, traditions, and contract,'[7] we must attend to the Vedas as we do to the clas-sic literature. But were not family life, and village life, and State life duly regulated even before the Aryan separation? What, then, can the infinitely later Vedas tell us about 'the *first attempts*' at regulating them?

In Mr. Müller's new volume a chapter (v.)[8] is partly dedicated to Aryan ancestor worship. Mr. Herbert Spencer had complained of statements (whose he does not say) that 'no Indo-European or Semitic nation seems to have made a religion of the worship of the dead.'[9] It is not easy to imagine how such a statement could have been made. But in the whole of the *Hibbert Lectures* on 'The Origin and Growth of Religion' it would be difficult to find one page on ancestor worship.[10] This reticence about so early a form of religion may have misled some anthropologists.

Probably the anthropological view of the Vedas could not be more clear-ly stated than in Mr. Müller's own words (*Hibbert Lectures*, p. 232): 'There are in the Veda thoughts as rude and crude as any palaeolithic weapon, but by the side of them we find thoughts with all the sharpness of iron and all the brilliancy of bronze.'[11] Now the anthropologist finds in the myths of his savage friends enormous quantities of 'thoughts as rude and crude as any palaeolithic weapon;' and these he places in his collections on the same level as the crude and rude thoughts in the Veda, which they very closely resem-ble. He attributes them to makers in the savage stage of thought, and sup-poses they were preserved by religious conservatism after the Aryans became polite. But the bright and brilliant thoughts of the Vedas he scarcely ever finds among really low savages; and, therefore, the anthropologist is inclined to attribute these (when found in the Vedas) to a later age of ancient Aryan civilisation. There seems nothing unscientific in this tendency, if it is held in check by watchful self-criticism in each instance. One remark of Mr. Müller's (*What can India Teach Us?* p. 112) is scarcely intelligible to the anthropologist: 'If we find that people three thousand years ago were familiar with ideas that seem novel and nineteenth-century-like to us, well, we must somewhat modify our conceptions of the primitive savage ...'[12] Why? [...]

'Fetichism and the Infinite',
Custom and Myth

(Longmans, Green and Co., 1884)

W hat is the true place of Fetichism, to use a common but unscientific term, in the history of religious evolution? Some theorists have made fetichism, that is to say, the adoration of odds and ends (with which they have confused the worship of animals, of mountains, and even of the earth), the first moment in the development of worship. Others, again, think that fetichism is 'a corruption of religion, in Africa, as elsewhere.' The latter is the opinion of Mr Max Müller, who has stated it in his 'Hibbert Lectures,' on 'The Origin and Growth of Religion, especially as illustrated by the Religions of India.'[1] It seems probable that there is a middle position between these two extremes. Students may hold that we hardly know enough to justify us in talking about the *origin* of religion, while at the same time they may believe that Fetichism is one of the earliest traceable steps by which men climbed to higher conceptions of the supernatural. Meanwhile Mr. Max Müller supports his own theory, that fetichism is a 'parasitical growth,' a 'corruption' of religion, by arguments mainly drawn from historical study of savage creeds, and from the ancient religious documents of India.

These documents are to English investigators ignorant of Sanskrit 'a book sealed with seven seals.' The Vedas are interpreted in very different ways by different Oriental scholars. It does not yet appear to be known whether a certain word in the Vedic funeral service means 'goat' or 'soul'! Mr. Max Müller's rendering is certain to have the first claim on English readers, and therefore it is desirable to investigate the conclusions which he draws from his Vedic studies. The ordinary anthropologist must first, however, lodge a protest against the tendency to look for *primitive* matter in the Vedas. They are the elaborate hymns of a specially trained set of poets and philosophers,

living in an age almost of civilisation. They can therefore contain little testimony as to what man, while still 'primitive,' thought about God, the world,
and the soul. One might as well look for the first germs of religion, for
primitive religion strictly so called, in 'Hymns Ancient and Modern' as in the
Vedas. It is chiefly, however, by way of deductions from the Vedas, that Mr.
Max Müller arrives at ideas which may be briefly and broadly stated thus:
he inclines to derive religion from man's sense of the Infinite, as awakened
by natural objects calculated to stir that sense. Our position is, on the other
hand, that the germs of the religious sense in early man are developed, not
so much by the vision of the Infinite, as by the idea of Power. Early religions,
in short, are selfish, not disinterested. The worshipper is not contemplative,
so much as eager to gain something to his advantage. In fetiches, he igno-
rantly recognises something that possesses power of an abnormal sort, and
the train of ideas which leads him to believe in and to treasure fetiches is
one among the earliest springs of religious belief.

Mr. Müller's opinion is the very reverse: he believes that a contemplative
and disinterested emotion in the presence of the Infinite, or of anything that
suggests infinitude or is mistaken for the Infinite, begets human religion,
while of this religion fetichism is a later corruption.

[...]

The first step in Mr. Max Müller's polemic was the assertion that Fetichism
is nowhere unmixed. We have seen that the fact is capable of an interpretation that will suit either side. Stages of culture overlap each other. The
second step in his polemic was the effort to damage the evidence. We have
seen that we have as good evidence as can be desired. In the third place he
asks, What are the antecedents of fetich-worship? He appears to conceive
himself to be arguing with persons (p. 127) who 'have taken for granted
that every human being was miraculously endowed with the concept of
what forms the predicate of every fetich, call it power, spirit, or god.'[2] If
there are reasoners so feeble, they must be left to the punishment inflicted
by Mr. Müller. On the other hand, students who regard the growth of the
idea of power, which is the predicate of every fetish, as a slow process, as
the result of various impressions and trains of early half-conscious reasoning,
cannot be disposed of by the charge that they think that 'every human
being was miraculously endowed' with any concept whatever. They, at
least, will agree with Mr. Max Müller that there are fetiches and fetiches,
that to one reverence is assigned for one reason, to another for another.
Unfortunately, it is less easy to admit that Mr. Max Müller has been happy
in his choice of ancient instances. He writes (p. 99): 'Sometimes a stock or
a stone was worshipped because it was a forsaken altar or an ancient place
of judgment, sometimes because it marked the place of a great battle or a
murder, or the burial of a king.' Here he refers to Pausanias, book i. 28, 5,

and viii. 13, 3.* In both of these passages, Pausanias, it is true, mentions stones – in the first passage stones on which men stood ὅσοι δίκας ὑπέ χουσι καὶ οἱ διωκοντες,³ in the second, barrows heaped up in honour of men who fell in battle. In neither case, however, do I find anything to show that the stones were worshipped. These stones, then, have no more to do with the argument than the milestones which certainly exist on the Dover road, but which are not the objects of superstitious reverence.⁴ No! the fetich-stones of Greece were those which occupied the holy of holies of the most ancient temples, the mysterious fanes within dark cedar or cypress groves, to which men were hardly admitted. They were the stones and blocks which bore the names of gods, Hera, or Apollo, names perhaps given, as De Brosses says, to the old fetichistic objects of worship, *after* the anthropomorphic gods entered Hellas. This, at least, is the natural conclusion from the fact that the Apollo and Hera of untouched wood or stone were confessedly the *oldest*. Religion, possessing an old fetich did not run the risk of breaking the run of luck by discarding it, but wisely retained and renamed it. Mr. Max Müller says that the unhewn lump may indicate a higher power of abstraction than the worship paid to the work of Phidias;⁵ but in that case all the savage adorers of rough stones *may* be in a stage of more abstract thought than these contemporaries of Phidias who had such very hard work to make Greek thought abstract.

Mr Müller founds a very curious argument on what he calls 'the ubiquity of fetichism.' Like De Brosses, he compiles (from Pausanias) a list of the rude stones worshipped by the early Greeks. He mentions various ex-

---

★ A third reference to Pausanias I have been unable to verify. There are several references to Greek fetich-stones in Theophrastus's account of the Superstitious Man. A number of Greek sacred stones named by Pausanias may be worth noticing. In Boeotia (ix. 16), the people believed that Alcmene, mother of Heracles, was changed into a stone. The Thespians worshipped, under the name of Eros, an unwrought stone, ἄγαλμα παλαιότατόν, 'their most ancient sacred object' (ix. 27). The people of Orchomenos 'paid extreme regard to certain stones,' said to have fallen from heaven, 'or to certain figures made of stone that descended from the sky' (ix. 38). Near Chaeronea, Rhea was said to have deceived Cronus, by offering him, in place of Zeus, a stone wrapped in swaddling bands. This stone, which Cronus vomited forth after having swallowed it, was seen by Pausanias at Delphi (ix. 41). By the roadside, near the city of the Panopeans, lay the stones out of which Prometheus made men (x. 4). The stone swallowed in place of Zeus by his father lay at the exit from the Delphian temple, and was anointed (compare the action of Jacob, Gen. xxviii. 18) with oil every day. The Phocians worshipped thirty squared stones, each named after a god (vii. xxii.). '*Among all the Greeks rude stones were worshipped before the images of the gods.*' Among the Troezenians a sacred stone lay in front of the temple, whereon the Troezenian elders sat, and purified Orestes from the murder of his mother. In Attica there was a conical stone worshipped as Apollo (i. xliv.). Near Argos was a stone called Zeus Cappotas, on which Orestes was said to have sat down, and so recovered peace of mind. Such are examples of the sacred stones, the oldest worshipful objects, of Greece.

amples of fetichistic superstitions in Rome. He detects the fetichism of popular Catholicism, and of Russian orthodoxy among the peasants. Here, he cries, in religions the history of which is known to us, fetichism is secondary, 'and why should fetiches in Africa, where we do not know the earlier development of religion, be considered as primary?'[6] What a singular argument! According to Pausanias, this fetichism (if fetichism it is) *was* primary, in Greece. The *oldest* temples, in their holiest place, held the oldest fetich. In Rome, it is at least probable that fetichism, as in Greece, was partly a survival, partly a new growth from the primal root of human superstitions. As to Catholicism, the records of Councils, the invectives of the Church, show us that, from the beginning, the secondary religion in point of time, the religion of the Church, laboured vainly to suppress, and had in part to tolerate, the primary religion of childish superstitions. The documents are before the world. As to the Russians, the history of their conversion is pretty well known. Jaroslaf, or Vladimir, or some other evangelist,[7] had whole villages baptized in groups, and the pagan peasants naturally kept up their primary semi-savage ways of thought and worship, under the secondary varnish of orthodoxy. In all Mr. Max Müller's examples, then, fetichism turns out to be *primary* in point of time; *secondary* only, as subordinate to some later development of faith, or to some lately superimposed religion. Accepting his statement that fetichism is ubiquitous, we have the most powerful *a priori* argument that fetichism is primitive. As religions become developed they are differentiated; it [is][8] only fetichism that you find the same everywhere. Thus the bow and arrow have a wide range of distribution: the musket, one not so wide; the Martini-Henry rifle, a still narrower range: it is the primitive stone weapons that are ubiquitous, that are found in the soil of England, Egypt, America, France, Greece, as in the hands of Dieyries and Admiralty Islanders. And just as rough stone knives are earlier than iron ones (though the same race often uses both), so fetichism is more primitive than higher and purer faiths, though the same race often combines fetichism and theism. No one will doubt the truth of this where weapons are concerned; but Mr. Max Müller will not look at religion in this way.

[…]

The end of the polemic against the primitiveness of fetichism deals with the question, 'Whence comes the supernatural predicate of the fetich?'[9] If a negro tells us his fetich is a god, whence got he the idea of 'god'? Many obvious answers occur. Mr. Müller says, speaking of the Indians (p. 205): 'The concept of *gods* was no doubt growing up while men were assuming a more and more definite attitude towards these semi-tangible and intangible objects'[10] – trees, rivers, hills, the sky, the sun, and so on, which he thinks suggested and developed, by aid of a kind of awe, the religious feeling of the infinite. We too would say that, among people who adore fetiches and ghosts, the concept of gods no doubt silently grew up, as men assumed a more and more definite attitude towards the tangible and intangible objects they held sacred.[11] Again, negroes have had the idea of god imported among them by Christians and Islamites, so that, even if they did not climb (as De Brosses grants that many of them do) to purer religious ideas unaided, these ideas are now familiar to them, and may well be used by them, when they have to explain a fetich to a European. Mr. Max Müller explains the origin of religion by a term ('the Infinite') which, he admits, the early people would not have comprehended. The negro, if he tells a white man that a fetich is a god, transposes terms in the same unscientific way. Mr. Müller asks, 'How do these people, when they have picked up their stone or their shell, pick up, at the same time, the concepts of a supernatural power, of spirit, of god, and of worship paid to some unseen being?'[12] But who says that men picked up these ideas *at the same time*? These ideas were evolved by a long, slow, complicated process. It is not at all impossible that the idea of a kind of 'luck' attached to this or that object, was evolved by dint of meditating on a mere series of lucky accidents. Such or such a man, having found such an object, succeeded in hunting, fishing, or war. By degrees, similar objects might be believed to command success. Thus burglars carry bits of coal in their pockets, 'for luck.' This random way of connecting causes and effects which have really no inter-relation, is a common error of early reasoning. Mr. Max Müller says that 'this process of reasoning is far more in accordance with modern thought';[13] if so, modern thought has little to be proud of. Herodotus, however, describes the process of thought as consecrated by custom among the Egyptians. But there are many other practical ways in which the idea of supernatural power is attached to fetiches. Some fetich-stones have a superficial resemblance to other objects, and thus (on the magical system of reasoning) are thought to influence these objects. Others, again, are pointed out as worthy of regard in dreams or by the ghosts of the dead.* To hold these views of the origin of the supernatural predicate of fetiches is not 'to take for granted that every human being was miraculously endowed with the concept of what forms the predicate of every fetich.'[14]

Thus we need not be convinced by Mr. Max Müller that fetichism (though it necessarily has its antecedents in the human mind) is 'a corrup-

---

* Here I may mention a case illustrating the motives of the fetich-worshipper. My friend, Mr. J.J. Atkinson, who has for many years studied the manners of the people of New Caledonia, asked a native *why* he treasured a certain fetich-stone. The man replied that, in one of the vigils which are practised beside the corpses of deceased friends, he saw a lizard. The lizard is a totem, a worshipful animal in New Caledonia. The native put out his hand to touch it, when it disappeared and left a stone in its place. This stone he therefore held sacred in the highest degree. Here then a fetich-stone was indicated as such by a spirit in the form of a lizard.

tion of religion.' It still appears to be one of the most primitive steps towards the idea of the supernatural.

What, then, is the subjective element of religion in man? How has he become capable of conceiving of the supernatural? What outward objects first awoke that dormant faculty in his breast? Mr. Max Müller answers, that man has 'the faculty of apprehending the infinite'[15] – that by dint of this faculty he is capable of religion, and that sensible objects, 'tangible, semi-tangible, intangible,' first roused the faculty to religious activity, at least among the natives of India. He means, however, by the 'infinite' which savages apprehend, not our metaphysical conception of the infinite, but the mere impression that there is 'something beyond.' 'Every thing of which his senses cannot perceive a limit, is to a primitive savage or to any man in an early stage of intellectual activity *unlimited* or *infinite*.'[16] Thus, in all experience, the idea of 'a beyond' is forced on men. If Mr. Max Müller would adhere to this theory, then we should suppose him to mean (what we hold to be more or less true) that savage religion, like savage science, is merely a fanciful explanation of what lies beyond the horizon of experience. For example, if the Australians mentioned by Mr. Max Müller believe in a being who created the world, a being whom they do not worship, and to whom they pay no regard (for, indeed, he has become 'decrepit'), their theory is scientific, not religious. They have looked for the causes of things, and are no more religious (in so doing) than Newton was when he worked out his theory of gravitation. The term 'infinite' is wrongly applied, because it is a term of advanced thought used in explanation of the ideas of men who, Mr. Max Müller says, were incapable of conceiving the meaning of such a concept. Again, it is wrongly applied, because it has some modern religious associations, which are covertly and fallaciously introduced to explain the supposed emotions of early men. Thus, Mr. Müller says (p. 177) – he is giving his account of the material things that awoke the religious faculty – 'the mere sight of the torrent or the stream would have been enough to call forth in the hearts of the early dwellers on the earth . . . a feeling that they were surrounded on all sides by powers invisible, infinite, or divine.'[17] Here, if I understand Mr. Müller, 'infinite' is used in our modern sense. The question is, How did men ever come to believe in powers infinite, invisible, divine? If Mr. Müller's words mean anything, they mean that a dormant feeling that there were such existences lay in the breast of man, and was wakened into active and conscious life, by the sight of a torrent or a stream. How, to use Mr. Müller's own manner, did these people, when they saw a stream, have mentally, at the same time, 'a feeling of *infinite* powers?' If this is not the expression of a theory of 'innate religion' (a theory which Mr. Müller disclaims), it is capable of being mistaken for that doctrine by even a careful reader. The feeling of 'powers infinite, invisible, divine,' *must* be in the heart, or the mere sight of a river could not call it forth. How did the feeling get into the heart? That is the question. The ordinary anthropologist distinguishes a multitude of causes, a variety of processes, which shade into each other and gradually produce the belief in powers invisible, infinite, and divine. What tribe is unacquainted with dreams, visions, magic, the apparitions of the dead? Add to these the slow action of thought, the conjectural inferences, the guesses of crude metaphysics, the theories of isolated men of religious and speculative genius. By all these and other forces manifold, that emotion of awe in presence of the hills, the stars, the sea, is developed. Mr. Max Müller cuts the matter shorter. The early inhabitants of earth saw a river, and the 'mere sight' of the torrent called forth the feelings which (to us) seem to demand ages of the operation of causes disregarded by Mr. Müller in his account of the origin of Indian religion.

The mainspring of Mr. Müller's doctrine is his theory about 'apprehending the infinite.' Early religion, or at least that of India, was, in his view, the extension of an idea of Vastness, a disinterested emotion of awe.* Elsewhere, we think, early religion has been a development of ideas of Force, an interested search, not for something wide and far and hard to conceive, but for something practically *strong* for good and evil. Mr. Müller (taking no count in this place of fetiches, ghosts, dreams and magic) explains that the sense of 'wonderment' was wakened by objects only semi-tangible, trees, which are *taller* than we are, 'whose roots are beyond our reach, and which have a kind of life in them.' 'We are dealing with a quarternary, it may be a tertiary troglodyte,' [18] says Mr. Müller. If a tertiary troglodyte was like a modern Andaman Islander, a Kaneka, a Dieyrie, would he stand and meditate in awe on the fact that a tree was taller than he, or had 'a kind of life,' 'an unknown and unknowable, yet undeniable something'?† [19] [20] Why, this is the sentiment of modern Germany, and perhaps of the Indian sages of a cultivated period! A troglodyte would look for a possum in the tree, he would tap the trunk for honey, he would poke about in the bark after grubs, or he would worship anything odd in the branches. Is Mr. Müller not unconsciously transporting a kind of modern malady of thought into the midst of people who wanted to find a dinner, and who might worship a tree if it had a grotesque shape, that, for them, had a magical meaning, or if *boilyas* lived in its boughs, but whose practical way of dealing with the problem of its life was to burn it round the stem, chop the charred wood with stone axes, and use the bark, branches, and leaves as they happened to come handy? [21]

[…]

---

* Much the same theory is propounded in Mr. Müller's lectures on 'The Science of Religion.'

† The idea is expressed in a well known parody of Wordsworth, about the tree which

Will grow ten times as tall as me
And live ten times as long.

'Anthropology and Religion' I,
The Making of Religion,
2nd edition

(Longmans, Green and Co., 1900)

[…]

Anthropology is concerned with man and what is in man – *humani nihil a se alienum putat.*[1] These researches, therefore, are within the anthropological province, especially as they bear on the prevalent anthropological theory of the Origin of Religion. By 'religion' we mean, for the purpose of this argument, the belief in the existence of an Intelligence, or Intelligences not human, and not dependent on a material mechanism of brain and nerves, which may, or may not, powerfully control men's fortunes and the nature of things. We also mean the additional belief that there is, in man, an element so far kindred to these Intelligences that it can transcend the knowledge obtained through the known bodily senses, and may possibly survive the death of the body. These two beliefs at present (though not necessarily in their origin) appear chiefly as the faith in God and in the Immortality of the Soul.

It is important, then, to trace, if possible, the origin of these two beliefs. If they arose in actual communion with Deity [sic] (as the first at least did, in the theory of the Hebrew Scriptures), or if they could be proved to arise in an unanalysable *sensus numinis*, or even in 'a perception of the Infinite' (Max Müller), religion would have a divine, or at least a necessary source.[2] To the Theist, what is inevitable cannot but be divinely ordained, therefore religion is divinely preordained, therefore, in essentials, though not in accidental details, religion is true. The atheist, or non-theist, of course draws no such inferences.

But if religion, as now understood among men, be the latest evolutionary form of a series of mistakes, fallacies, and illusions, if its germ be a blunder, and its present form only the result of progressive but unessential refinements on that blunder, the inference that religion is untrue – that nothing actual corresponds to its hypothesis – is very easily drawn.[3] The inference is not, perhaps, logical, for all our science itself is the result of progressive refinements upon hypotheses originally erroneous, fashioned to explain facts misconceived. Yet our science is true, within its limits, though very far from being exhaustive of the truth. In the same way, it might be argued, our religion, even granting that it arose out of primitive fallacies and false hypotheses, may yet have been refined, as science has been, through a multitude of causes, into an approximate truth.

Frequently as I am compelled to differ from Mr. Spencer both as to facts and their interpretation, I am happy to find that he has anticipated me here. Opponents will urge, he says, that 'if the primitive belief' (in ghosts) 'was absolutely false, all derived beliefs from it must be absolutely false?' Mr. Spencer replies: 'A germ of truth was contained in the primitive conception the truth, namely, that the power which manifests itself in consciousness is but a differently conditioned form of the power which manifests itself beyond consciousness.'[4] In fact, we find Mr. Spencer, like Faust as described by Marguerite,[5] saying much the same thing as the priests, but not quite in the same way. Of course, I allow for a much larger 'germ of truth' in the origin of the ghost theory than Mr. Spencer does. But we can both say 'the ultimate form of the religious consciousness is' (will be?) 'the final development of a consciousness which at the outset contained a germ of truth obscured by multitudinous errors.'[*] [6]

> 'One God, one law, one element,
> And one far-off divine event,
> To which the whole creation moves.'[7]

Coming at last to Mr. Tylor, we find that he begins by dismissing the idea that any known race of men is devoid of religious conceptions. He disproves, out of their own mouths, the allegations of several writers who have made this exploded assertion about 'godless tribes.' He says: 'The thoughts and principles of modern Christianity are attached to intellectual clues which run back through far pre-Christian ages to the very origin of human civilisation, *perhaps even of human existence.*'[†][8] So far we abound in Mr. Tylor's sense. 'As a minimum definition of religion' he gives 'the belief in spiritual beings,' which appears 'among all low races with whom we have attained to thoroughly intimate relations.'[9] The existence of this belief at present does not prove that no races were ever, at any time, destitute of all belief. But it prevents us from positing the existence of such creedless races, in any age, as a demonstrated fact. We have thus, in short, no opportunity of observing, *historically*, man's development from blank unbelief into even the minimum or most rudimentary form of belief. We can only theorise and

---

[*]   *Ecclesiastical Institutions*, 837–839.

[†]   *Primitive Culture*, i. 421, chapter xi.

make more or less plausible conjectures as to the first rudiments of human faith in God and in spiritual beings. We find no race whose mind, as to faith, is a *tabula rasa*.[10]

To the earliest faith Mr. Tylor gives the name of *Animism*, a term not wholly free from objection, though 'Spiritualism' is still less desirable, having been usurped by a form of modern superstitiousness. This Animism, 'in its full development, includes the belief in souls and in a future state, in controlling deities and subordinate spirits.'[11] In Mr. Tylor's opinion, as in Mr. Huxley's, Animism, in its lower (and earlier) forms, has scarcely any connection with ethics. Its 'spirits' do not 'make for righteousness.' This is a side issue to be examined later, but we may provisionally observe, in passing, that the ethical ideas, such as they are, even of Australian blacks are reported to be inculcated at the religious mysteries (*Bora*) of the tribes, which were instituted by and are performed in honour of the gods of their native belief. [...]

Mr. Tylor, however, is chiefly concerned with Animism as 'an ancient and world-wide philosophy, of which belief is the theory, and worship is the practice.'[12] Given Animism, then, or the belief in spiritual beings, as the earliest form and minimum of religious faith, what is the origin of Animism? It will be seen that, by Animism, Mr. Tylor does not mean the alleged early theory, implicitly if not explicitly and consciously held, that all things whatsoever are animated and are personalities.* Judging from the behaviour of little children, and from the myths of savages, early man may have half-consciously extended his own sense of personal and potent and animated existence to the whole of nature as known to him. Not only animals, but vegetables and inorganic objects, may have been looked on by him as persons, like what he felt himself to be. The child (perhaps merely because *taught* to do so) beats the naughty chair, and all objects are persons in early mythology. But this *feeling*, rather than theory, may conceivably have existed among early men, before they developed the hypothesis of 'spirits,' 'ghosts,' or souls. It is the origin of *that* hypothesis, 'Animism,' which Mr. Tylor investigates.

What, then, is the origin of Animism? It arose in the earliest traceable speculations on 'two groups of biological problems:'
(1) 'What is it that makes the difference between a living body and a dead one; what causes waking, sleep, trance, disease, and death?'
(2) 'What are those human shapes which appear in dreams and visions?'[†]

Here it should be noted that Mr. Tylor most properly takes a distinction between sleeping 'dreams' and waking 'visions,' or 'clear vision.' The distinction is made even by the blacks of Australia. Thus one of the Kurnai

---

* This theory is what Mr. Spencer calls 'Animism,' and does not believe in. What Mr. Tylor calls 'Animism' Mr. Spencer believes in, but he calls it the 'Ghost Theory'.

† *Primitive Culture*, i. 428.

announced that his *Yambo*, or soul, could 'go out' during sleep, and see the distant and the dead. But 'while any one might be able to communicate with the ghosts, *during sleep*, it was only the wizards who were able to do so in waking hours.' A wizard, in fact, is a person susceptible (or feigning to be susceptible) when awake to hallucinatory perceptions of phantasms of the dead. 'Among the Kulin of Wimmera River a man became a wizard who, as a boy, had seen his mother's ghost sitting at her grave.'* [13] These facts prove that a race of savages at the bottom of the scale of culture do take a formal distinction between normal dreams in sleep and waking hallucinations – a thing apt to be denied.

Thus Mr. Herbert Spencer offers the massive generalisation that savages do not possess a language enabling a man to say 'I dreamed that I saw,' instead of 'I saw' ('Principles of Sociology,' p. 150).[14] This could only be proved by giving examples of such highly deficient languages, which Mr. Spencer does not do.† In many savage speculations there occur ideas as subtly metaphysical as those of Hegel. Moreover, even the Australian languages have the verb 'to see,' and the substantive 'sleep.' Nothing, then, prevents a man from saying 'I saw in sleep' (*insomnium*, ἐνύπνιον).[15]

We have shown too, that the Australians take an essential distinction between waking hallucinations (ghosts seen by a man when awake) and the common hallucinations of slumber. Anybody can have these; the man who sees ghosts when awake is marked out for a wizard.

At the same time the vividness of dreams among certain savages, as recorded in Mr. Im Thurn's 'Indians of Guiana,' and the consequent confusion of dreaming and waking experiences, are certain facts. Wilson says the same of some negroes, and Mr. Spencer illustrates from the confusion of mind in dreamy children.[16] They, we know, are much more addicted to somnambulism than grown-up people. I am unaware that spontaneous somnambulism among savages has been studied as it ought to be. I have demonstrated, however, that very low savages can and do draw an essential distinction between sleeping and waking hallucinations.

[...] It was not only on the dreams of sleep, so easily forgotten as they are, that the savage pondered, in his early speculations about the life and the soul. He included in his materials the much more striking and memorable experiences of waking hours, as we and Mr. Tylor agree in holding.

Reflecting on these things, the earliest savage reasoners would decide: (1) that man has a 'life' (which leaves him temporarily in sleep, finally in death); (2) that man also possesses a 'phantom' (which appears to other people in their visions and dreams). The savage philosopher would then

---

★   Howitt, *Journal of Anthropological Institute*, xiii. 191–195.

†   The curious may consult, for savage words for 'dreams,' Mr. Scott's *Dictionary of the Mang'anja Language*, s.v. 'Lots,' or any glossary of any savage language.

'combine his information,' like a celebrated writer on Chinese metaphysics. He would merely 'combine the life and the phantom,' as 'manifestations of one and the same soul.' The result would be 'an apparitional soul,' or 'ghost-soul.'

This ghost-soul would be a highly accomplished creature, 'a vapour, film, or shadow,' yet conscious, capable of leaving the body, mostly invisible and impalpable, 'yet also manifesting physical power,' existing and appearing after the death of the body, able to act on the bodies of other men, beasts, and things.* [17]

When the earliest reasoners, in an age and in mental conditions of which we know nothing historically, had evolved the hypothesis of this conscious, powerful, separable soul, capable of surviving the death of the body, it was not difficult for them to develop the rest of Religion, as Mr. Tylor thinks. A powerful ghost of a dead man might thrive till, its original owner being long forgotten, it became a God. Again (souls once given) it would not be a very difficult logical leap, perhaps, to conceive of souls, or spirits, that had never been human at all. It is, we may say, only *le premier pas qui coûte*,[18] the step to the belief in a surviving separable soul. Nevertheless, when we remember that Mr. Tylor is theorising about savages in the dim background of human evolution, savages whom we know nothing of by experience, savages far behind Australians and Bushmen (who possess Gods), we must admit that he credits them with great ingenuity, and strong powers of abstract reasoning. He may be right in his opinion. In the same way, just as primitive men were keen reasoners, so early bees, more clever than modern bees, may have evolved the system of hexagonal cells, and only an early fish of genius could first have hit on the plan, now hereditary, of killing a fly by blowing water at it.

To this theory of metaphysical genius in very low savages I have no objection to offer. We shall find, later, astonishing examples of savage abstract speculation, certainly not derived from missionary sources, because wholly out of the missionary's line of duty and reflection.

As early beasts had genius, so the earliest reasoners appear to have been as logically gifted as the lowest savages now known to us, or even as some Biblical critics. By Mr. Tylor's hypothesis, they first conceived the extremely abstract idea of Life, 'that which makes the difference between a living body and a dead one.'† [19] This highly abstract conception must have been, however, the more difficult to early man, as, to him, *all* things, universally, are 'animated.'‡ [20] Mr. Tylor illustrates this theory of early man by the little child's idea that 'chairs, sticks, and wooden horses are actuated by the same

---

*   *Prim. Cult.* i. 429.

†   *Prim. Cult.* i. 428.

‡   *Ibid.* i. 285.

sort of personal will as nurses and children and kittens.... In such matters the savage mind well represents the childish stage.'* [21]

Now, nothing can be more certain than that, if children think sticks are animated, they don't think so because they have heard, or discovered, that they possess souls, and then transfer souls to sticks. We may doubt, then, if primitive man came, in this way, by reasoning on souls, to suppose that all things, universally, were animated. But if he did think *all* things animated – a corpse, to his mind, was just as much animated as anything else. Did he reason: 'All things are animated. A corpse is not animated. Therefore a corpse is not a thing (within the meaning of my General Law)'?

How, again, did early man conceive of Life, *before* he identified Life (1) with 'that which makes the difference between a living body and a dead one' (a difference which, *ex hypothesi*, he did not draw, *all* things being animated to his mind) and (2) with 'those human shapes which appear in dreams and visions'?[22] 'The ancient savage philosophers probably reached the obvious inference that every man had two things belonging to him, life and a phantom.' But everything was supposed to have 'a life,' as far one makes out, before the idea of separable soul was developed, at least if savages arrived at the theory of universal animation as children are said to do.

We are dealing here quite conjecturally with facts beyond our experience.

In any case, early man excogitated (by the hypothesis) the abstract idea of Life*, before* he first 'envisaged' it in material terms as 'breath,' or 'shadow.' He next decided that mere breath or shadow was not only identical with the more abstract conception of Life, but could also take on forms as real and full-bodied as, to him, are the hallucinations of dream or waking vision. His reasoning appears to have proceeded from the more abstract (the idea of Life) to the more concrete, to the life first shadowy and vaporous, then clothed in the very aspect of the real man.

Mr. Tylor has thus (whether we follow his logic or not) provided man with a theory of active, intelligent, separable souls, which can survive the death of the body. At this theory early man arrived by speculations on the nature of life, and on the causes of phantasms of the dead or living beheld in 'dreams and visions.' But our author by no means leaves out of sight the effects of alleged supernormal phenomena believed in by savages, with their parallels in modern civilisation. These supernormal phenomena, whether real or illusory, are, he conceives, facts in that mass of experiences from which savages constructed their belief in separable, enduring, intelligent souls or ghosts, the foundation of religion.

While we are, perhaps owing to our own want of capacity, puzzled by what seem to be two kinds of early philosophy – (1) a sort of instinctive or unreasoned belief in universal animation, which Mr. Spencer calls 'Animism'

---

*   *Ibid.* i. 285, 286.

and does not believe in, (2) the reasoned belief in separable and surviving souls of men (and in things), which Mr. Spencer believes in, and Mr. Tylor calls 'Animism' – we must also note another difficulty. Mr. Tylor may seem to be taking it for granted that the earliest, remote, unknown thinkers on life and the soul were existing on the same psychical plane as we ourselves, or, at least, as modern savages. Between modern savages and ourselves, in this regard, he takes certain differences, but takes none between modern savages and the remote founders of religion.

Thus Mr. Tylor observes:

> 'The condition of the modern ghost-seer, whose imagination passes on such slight excitement into positive hallucination, is rather the rule than the exception among uncultured and intensely imaginative tribes, whose minds may be thrown off their balance by a touch, a word, a gesture, an unaccustomed noise.'* [23]

I find evidence that low contemporary savages are *not* great ghost-seers, and, again, I cannot quite accept Mr. Tylor's psychology of the 'modern ghost-seer.' Most such favoured persons whom I have known were steady, unimaginative, unexcitable people, with just one odd experience. Lord Tennyson, too, after sleeping in the bed of his recently lost father on purpose to see his ghost, decided that ghosts 'are not seen by imaginative people.'[24]

We now examine, at greater length, the psychical conditions in which, according to Mr. Tylor, contemporary savages differ from civilised men. Later we shall ask what may be said as to possible or presumable psychical differences between modern savages and the datelessly distant founders of the belief in souls. Mr. Tylor attributes to the lower races, and even to races high above their level, 'morbid ecstasy, brought on by meditation, fasting, narcotics, excitement, or disease.'[25] Now, we may still 'meditate' – and how far the result is 'morbid' is a matter for psychologists and pathologists to determine. Fasting we do not practise voluntarily, nor would we easily accept evidence from an Englishman as to the veracity of voluntary fasting visions, like those of Cotton Mather. The visions of disease we should set aside, as a rule, with those of 'excitement,' produced, for instance, by 'dev-il-dances.' Narcotic and alcoholic visions are not in question.† For our purpose the *induced* trances of savages (in whatever way voluntarily brought on) are analogous to the modern induced hypnotic trance. Any supernormal acquisitions of knowledge in these induced conditions, among savages, would be on a par with similar alleged experiences of persons under hypnotism.

We do not differ from known savages in being able to bring on non-nor-

---

*   *Primitive Culture*, i. 446.

†   See, however, Dr. Von Schrenck-Notzing, *Die Beobachtung narcolischer Mittel für den Hypnotismus*, and S.P.R. *Proceedings*, x. 292–299.

mal psychological conditions, but we produce these, as a rule, by other methods than theirs, and such experiments are not made on *all* of us, as they were on all Red Indian boys and girls in the 'medicine-fast,' at the age of puberty.

Further, in their normal state, known savages, or some of them, are more 'suggestible' than educated Europeans at least.* [26] They can be more easily hallucinated in their normal waking state by suggestion. Once more, their intervals of hunger, followed by gorges of food, and their lack of artificial light, combine to make savages more apt to see what is not there than are comfortable educated white men. But Mr. Tylor goes too far when he says 'where the savage could see *phantasms*, the civilised man has come to amuse himself with fancies.'† [27] The civilised man, beyond all doubt, is capable of being *enfantosmé*.[28]

In all that he says on this point, the point of psychical condition, Mr. Tylor is writing about known savages as they differ from ourselves. But the savages who *ex hypothesi* evolved the doctrine of souls lie beyond our ken, far behind the modern savages, among whom we find belief not only in souls and ghosts, but in moral gods. About the psychical condition of the savages who worked out the theory of souls and founded religion we necessarily know nothing. If there be such experiences as clairvoyance, telepathy, and so on, these unknown ancestors of ours may (for all that we can tell) have been peculiarly open to them, and therefore peculiarly apt to believe in separable souls. In fact, when we write about these far-off founders of religion, we guess in the dark, or by the flickering light of analogy. The lower animals have faculties (as in their power of finding their way home through new unknown regions, and in the ants' modes of acquiring and communicating knowledge to each other) which are mysteries to us. The terror of dogs in 'haunted houses' and of horses in passing 'haunted' scenes has often been reported, and is alluded to briefly by Mr. Tylor. Balaam's ass, and the dogs which crouched and whined before Athene, whom Eumaeus could not see, are 'classical' instances.[29]

The weakness of the anthropological argument here is, we must repeat, that we know little more about the mental condition and experiences of the early thinkers who developed the doctrine of Souls than we know about the mental condition and experiences of the lower animals. And the more firmly a philosopher believes in the Darwinian hypothesis, the less, he must admit, can he suppose himself to know about the twilight ages, between the lower animal and the fully evolved man. What kind of creature was man when he first conceived the germs, or received the light, of Religion? All is guess-work here! We may just allude to Hegel's theory that clairvoyance and hypnotic phenomena are produced in a kind of temporary *atavism*, or

---

*   *Primitive Culture*, i. 306–315.

†   i. 315.

'throwing back' to a remotely ancient condition of the 'sensitive soul' (*Fühlende Seele*). The 'sensitive' [unconditioned, clairvoyant][30] faculty or 'soul' is 'a disease when it becomes a state of the self-conscious, educated, self-possessed human being of civilisation.'* 'Second sight,' Hegel thinks, was a product of an earlier day and earlier mental condition than ours.[31]

Approaching this almost untouched subject – the early psychical condition of man – not from the side of metaphysical speculations like Hegel, but with the instruments of modern psychology and physiology, Dr. Max Dessoir, of Berlin, following, indeed, M. Taine, has arrived, as we saw, at somewhat similar conclusions.[32] 'This fully conscious life of the spirit,' in which we moderns now live, 'seems to rest upon a substratum of reflex action of a hallucinatory type.'[33] Our actual modern condition is *not* 'fundamental,' and 'hallucination represents, at least in its nascent condition, the main trunk of our psychical existence.'† [34]

Now, suppose that the remote and unknown ancestors of ours who first developed the doctrine of souls had not yet spread far from 'the main trunk of our psychical existence,' far from constant hallucination. In that case (at least, according to Dr. Dessoir's theory) their psychical experiences would be such as we cannot estimate, yet cannot leave, as a possibility influencing religion, out of our calculations.

If early men were ever in a condition in which telepathy and clairvoyance (granting their possibility) were prevalent, one might expect that faculties so useful would be developed in the struggle for existence. That they are deliberately cultivated by modern savages we know. The Indian foster-mother of John Tanner used, when food was needed, to suggest herself into an hypnotic condition, so that she became *clairvoyante* as to the whereabouts of game.[35] Tanner, an English boy, caught early by the Indians, was sceptical, but came to practise the same art, not unsuccessfully, himself.‡ His reminiscences, which he dictated on his return to civilisation, were certainly not feigned in the interests of any theories. But the most telepathic human stocks, it may be said, ought, *ceteris paribus*,[36] to have been the most successful in the struggle for existence. We may infer that the *cetera* were not *paria*, the clairvoyant state not being precisely the best for the practical business of life. But really we know nothing of the psychical state of the earliest men. They may have had experiences tending towards a belief in 'spirits,' of which we can tell nothing. We are obliged to guess, in considerable ignorance of the actual conditions, and this historical ignorance inevitably besets all anthropological speculation about the origin of religion.

The knowledge of our nescience as to the psychical condition of our

---

*   *Phil. des Geistes*, pp. 406, 408.

†   See also Mr. A.J. Balfour's Presidential Address to the Society for Psychical Research, *Proceedings*, vol. x. See, too, Taine, *De l'Intelligence*, i. 78, 100, 139.

‡   Tanner's *Narrative*, New York, 1830.

first thinking ancestors may suggest hesitation as to taking it for granted that early man was on our own or on the modern savage level in 'psychical' experience. Even savage races, as Mr. Tylor justly says, attribute superior psychical knowledge to neighbouring tribes on a yet lower level of culture than themselves. The Finn esteems the Lapp sorcerers above his own; the Lapp yields to the superior pretensions of the Samoyeds. There may be more ways than one of explaining this relative humility: there is Hegel's way and there is Mr. Tylor's way. We cannot be certain, *a priori*, that the earliest man knew no more of supernormal or apparently supernormal experiences than we commonly do, or that these did not influence his thoughts on animism.[37]
[...]

The ideas of Mr. Tylor on the causes of the origin of religion are now criticised, not from the point of view of spiritualism, but of experimental psychology. We hold that very probably there exist human faculties of un-known scope; that these conceivably were more powerful and prevalent among our very remote ancestors who founded religion; that they may still exist in savage as in civilised races, and that they may have confirmed, if they did not originate, the doctrine of separable souls. If they *do* exist, the cir-cumstance is important, in view of the fact that modern ideas rest on a denial of their existence.

Mr. Tylor next examines the savage and other *names* for the ghost-soul, such as shadow (*umbra*), breath (*spiritus*), and he gives cases in which the *shadow* of a man is regarded as equivalent to his *life*. Of course, the shadow in the sunlight does not resemble the phantasm in a dream. The two, how-ever, were combined and identified by early thinkers, while *breath* and *heart* were used as symbols of 'that in men which makes them live,' a phrase found among the natives of Nicaragua in 1528. The confessedly symbolical character of the phrase, 'it is *not* precisely the heart, but that in them which makes them live,'[38] proves that to the speaker life was *not* 'heart' or 'breath,' but that these terms were known to be material word-counters for the conception of life.* Whether the earliest thinkers identified heart, breath, shadow, with life, or whether they consciously used words of material origin to denote an immaterial conception, of course we do not know. But the word in the latter case would react on the thought, till the Roman inhaled (as his life?) the last breath of his dying kinsman, he well knowing that the Manes[39] of the said kinsman were elsewhere, and not to be inhaled.

Subdivisions and distinctions were then recognised, as of the Egyptian *Ka*, the 'double,' the Karen *kelah*, or 'personal life-phantom' (*wraith*), on one side, and the Karen *thah*, 'the responsible moral soul,' on the other. The Roman *umbra* hovers about the grave, the *manes* go to Orcus, the *spir-itus* seeks the stars.

We are next presented with a crowd of cases in which sickness or leth-

---

★   *Primitive Culture*, i. 432,433. Citing Oviedo, *Hist. De Nicaragua*, pp. 21–51.

argy is ascribed by savages to the absence of the patient's spirit, or of one of his spirits. This idea of migratory spirit is next used by savages to explain certain proceedings of the sorcerer, priest, or seer. His soul, or one of his souls is thought to go forth to distant places in quest of information, while the seer, perhaps, remains lethargic. Probably, in the struggle for existence, he lost more by being lethargic than he gained by being clairvoyant!

Now, here we touch the first point in Mr. Tylor's theory, where a critic may ask, Was this belief in the wandering abroad of the seer's spirit a theory not only false in its form (as probably it is), but also wholly unbased on experiences which might raise a presumption in favour of the existence of phenomena really supernormal? By 'supernormal' experiences I here mean such as the acquisition by a human mind of knowledge which could not be obtained by it through the recognised channels of sensation. Say, for the sake of argument, that a person, savage or civilised, obtains in trance infor- mation about distant places or events, to him unknown, and, through chan- nels of sense, unknowable. The savage will explain this by saying that the seer's soul, shadow, or spirit, wandered out of the body to the distant scene. This is, at present, an unverified theory. But still, for the sake of argument, suppose that the seer did honestly obtain this information in trance, lethar- gy, or hypnotic sleep, or any other condition. If so, the modern savage (or his more gifted ancestors) would have other grounds for his theory of the wandering soul than any ground presented by normal occurrences, ordi- nary dreams, shadows, and so forth. Again, in human nature there would be (if such things occur) a potentiality of experiences other and stranger than materialism will admit as possible. It will (granting the facts) be impos- sible to aver that there is *nihil in intellectu quod non prius in sensu*.[40] The soul will be not *ce qu'un vain peuple pense* under the new popular tradition,[41] and the savage's theory of the spirit will be, at least in part, based on other than normal and every-day facts. That condition in which the seer acquires in- formation, not otherwise accessible, about events remote in space, is what the mesmerists of the mid-century called 'travelling clairvoyance.'

If such an experience be *in rerum natura*,[42] it will not, of course, justify the savage's theory that the soul is a separable entity, capable of voyaging, and also capable of existing after the death of the body. But it will give the savage a better excuse for his theory than normal experiences provide; and will even raise a presumption that reflection on mere ordinary experiences – death, shadow, trance – is not the sole origin of his theory. For a savage so acute as Mr. Tylor's hypothetical early reasoner might decline to believe that his own or a friend's soul had been absent on an expedition, unless it brought back information not normally to be acquired. However, we cannot reason, *a priori*, as to how far the logic of a savage might or might not go on occasion.

In any case, a scientific reasoner might be expected to ask: 'Is this alleged acquisition of knowledge, *not* through the ordinary channels of sense, a thing *in rerum natura*?' Because, if it is, we must obviously increase our list of the savage's reasons for believing in a soul: we must make his reasons include 'psychical' experiences, and there must be an X region to investigate. [...][43]

I may seem to have outrun already the limits of permissible hypothesis. It may appear absurd to surmise that there can exist in man, savage or civilised, a faculty for acquiring information not accessible by the known channels of sense, a faculty attributed by savage philosophers to the wandering soul. But one may be permitted to quote the opinion of M. Charles Richet, Professor of Physiology in the Faculty of Medicine in Paris. It is not cited because M. Richet is a professor of physiology, but because he reached his conclusion after six years of minute experiment. He says: 'There exists in certain persons, at certain moments, a faculty of acquiring knowledge which has no *rapport* with our normal faculties of that kind.'* [44]

★   *Proceedings*, S.P.R. v. 167.

'On Religion',
from *The Making of Religion*,
2nd edition

(Longmans, Green and Co., 1900)

[From 'Evolution of the Idea of God']

To the anthropological philosopher 'a plain man' would naturally put the question: 'Having got your idea of spirit or soul – your theory of Animism – out of the idea of ghosts, and having got your idea of ghosts out of dreams and visions, how do you get at the Idea of God?'[1] Now by 'God' the proverbial 'plain man' of controversy means a primal eternal Being, author of all things, the father and friend of man, the invisible, omniscient guardian of morality.

The usual though not invariable reply of the anthropologist might be given in the words of Mr. Im Thurn, author of a most interesting work on the Indians of British Guiana:

> 'From the notion of ghosts,' says Mr. Im Thurn, 'a belief has arisen, but very gradually, in higher spirits, and eventually in a Highest Spirit and, keeping pace with the growth of these beliefs, a habit of reverence for, and worship of spirits.... The Indians of Guiana know no God.'[*] [2]

As another example of Mr. Im Thurn's hypothesis that God is a late development from the idea of spirit may be cited Mr. Payne's learned 'History of the New World,' a work of much research:[†]

> 'The lowest savages not only have no gods, but do not even recognise those lower beings usually called spirits, the conception of which has invariably preceded that of gods in the human mind.'[3]

---

[*] *Journal Anthrop. Inst.* xi. 374. We shall return to this passage.

[†] Vol. i. p. 389, 1892.

Mr. Payne here differs, *toto caelo*,[4] from Mr. Tylor, who finds no sufficient proof for wholly non-religious savages, and from Roskoff, who has disposed of the arguments of Sir John Lubbock.[5] Mr. Payne, then, for ethnological purposes, defines a god as 'a benevolent spirit, permanently embodied in some tangible object, usually an image, and to whom food, drink,' and so on, 'are regularly offered for the purpose of securing assistance in the affairs of life.'

On this theory 'the lowest savages' are devoid of the idea of god or of spirit. Later they develop the idea of spirit, and when they have secured the spirit, as it were, in a tangible object, and kept it on board wages, then the spirit has attained to the dignity and the savage to the conception of a god. But while a god of this kind is, in Mr. Payne's opinion, relatively a late flower of culture, for the hunting races generally (with some exceptions) have no gods, yet 'the conception of a creator or maker of all things ... obviously a great spirit' is 'one of the earliest efforts of primitive logic.'* [6]

Mr. Payne's own logic is not very clear. The 'primitive logic' of the savage leads him to seek for a cause or maker of things, which he finds in a great creative spirit. Yet the lowest savages have no idea even of spirit, and the hunting races, as a rule, have no god. Does Mr. Payne mean that a great creative spirit is *not* a god, while a spirit kept on board wages in a tangible object *is* a god? We are unable, by reason of evidence later to be given, to agree with Mr. Payne's view of the facts, while his reasoning appears somewhat inconsistent, the lowest savages having, in his opinion, no idea of spirit, though the idea of a creative spirit is, for all that, one of the earliest efforts of primitive logic.

On any such theories as these the belief in a moral Supreme Being is a very late (or a very early?) result of evolution, due to the action of advancing thought upon the original conception of ghosts. This opinion of Mr. Im Thurn's is, roughly stated, the usual theory of anthropologists. We wish, on the other hand, to show that the idea of God, as he is conceived of by our inquiring plain man, is shadowed forth (among contradictory fables) in the lowest-known grades of savagery, and therefore cannot arise from the later speculation of men, comparatively civilised and advanced, on the original datum of ghosts. We shall demonstrate, contrary to the opinion of Mr. Spencer, Mr. Huxley, and even Mr. Tylor, that the Supreme Being, and, in one case at least, the casual sprites of savage faith, are active moral influences. What is even more important, we shall make it undeniable that Anthropology has simplified her problem by neglecting or ignoring her facts. While the real problem is to account for the evolution out of ghosts of the eternal, creative moral god of the 'plain man,' the germ of such a god or being[7] in the creeds of the lowest savages is by anthropologists denied, or left out of sight, or accounted for by theories contradicted by facts, or, at

---

*   Payne, i. 458.

best, is explained away as a result of European or Islamite influences. Now, as the problem is to account for the evolution of the highest conception of God, as far as that conception exists among the most backward races, the problem can never be solved while that highest conception of God is practically ignored.

Thus, anthropologists, as a rule, in place of facing and solving their problem, have merely evaded it – doubtless unwittingly. This, of course, is not the practice of Mr. Tylor, though even his great work is professedly much more concerned with the development of the idea of spirit and with the lower forms of animism than with the real *crux* – the evolution of the idea (always obscured[8] by mythology) of a moral, uncreated, undying God among the lowest savages. This negligence of anthropologists has arisen from a single circumstance. They take it for granted that God is always (except where the word for God is applied to a living human being) regarded as Spirit. Thus, having accounted for the development of the idea of spirit, they regard God as that idea carried to its highest power, and as the final step in its evolution. But, if we can show that the early idea of an undying,[9] moral, creative being does not necessarily or logically imply the doctrine of spirit (or ghost),[10] then this idea of an eternal, moral, creative being may have existed even before the doctrine of spirit was evolved.

We may admit that Mr. Tylor's account of the process by which Gods were evolved out of ghosts is a little *touffu* – rather buried in facts. We 'can scarcely see the wood for the trees.' We want to know how Gods, makers of things (or of most things), fathers in heaven, and friends, guardians of morality, seeing what is good or bad in the hearts of men, were evolved, as is supposed, out of ghosts or surviving souls of the dead. That such moral, practically omniscient Gods are known to the very lowest savages – Bushmen, Fuegians, Australians – we shall demonstrate.

Here the inquirer must be careful not to adopt the common opinion that Gods improve, morally and otherwise, in direct ratio to the rising grades in the evolution of culture and civilisation. That is not necessarily the case; usually the reverse occurs. Still less must we take it for granted, following Mr. Tylor and Mr. Huxley, that the 'alliance [of religion and morality] belongs almost, or wholly, to religions above the savage level – not to the earlier and lower creeds;'[11] or that 'among the Australian savages,' and 'in its simplest condition,' 'theology is wholly independent of ethics.'* [12] These statements can be proved (by such evidence as anthropology is obliged to rely upon) to be erroneous. And, just because these statements are put forward, Anthropology has an easier task in explaining the origin of religion; while, just because these statements are incorrect, her conclusion, being deduced from premises so far false, is invalidated.

---

*   *Prim. Cult.* vol. ii. p. 381; *Science and Hebrew Tradition*, pp. 346, 372.

[…]

We shall select such savage examples of the idea of a Supreme Being as are attested by ancient native hymns, or are inculcated in the most sacred and secret savage institutions, the religious Mysteries (manifestly the last things to be touched by missionary influence), or are found among low insular races defended from European contact by the jealous ferocity and poison-ous jungles of people and soil. We also note cases in which missionaries found such native names as 'Father,' 'Ancient of Heaven,' 'Maker of All,' ready-made to their hands.

It is to be remarked that, while this branch of the inquiry is practically omitted by Mr. Spencer, Mr. Tylor can spare for it but some twenty pages out of his large work. He arranges the probable germs of the savage idea of a Supreme Being thus: A god of the polytheistic crowd is simply raised to the primacy, which, of course, cannot occur where there is no polytheism. Or the principle of Manes[13] worship may make a Supreme Deity out of 'a primeval ancestor,' say Unkulunkulu, who is so far from being supreme, that he is abject. Or, again, a great phenomenon or force in Nature-worship, say Sun, or Heaven, is raised to supremacy. Or speculative philosophy as-cends from the Many to the One by trying to discern through and beyond the universe a First Cause. Animistic conceptions thus reach their utmost limit in the notion of the Anima Mundi.[14] He may accumulate all powers of all polytheistic gods, or he may 'loom vast, shadowy, and calm…too benevolent to need human worship … too merely existent to concern himself with the petty race of men.'* [15] But he is always animistic.

Now, in addition to the objections already noted in passing, how can we tell that the Supreme Being of low savages was, in original conception, *animistic* at all? How can we know that he was envisaged, originally, as *Spirit*? We shall show that he probably was not, that the question 'spirit or not spirit' was not raised at all, that the Maker and Father in Heaven, prior to Death, was merely regarded as a deathless *Being*, no question of 'spirit' being raised. If so, Animism was not needed for the earliest idea of a moral Eternal. This hypothesis will be found to lead to some very singular conclusions.

It will be more fully stated and illustrated, presently, but I find that it had already occurred to Dr. Brinton.† [16] He is talking specially of a heaven-god; he says 'it came to pass that the idea of God was linked to the heavens *long ere man asked himself, Are the heavens material and God spiritual*?' Dr. Brinton, however, does not develop his idea, nor am I aware that it has been devel-oped previously.

The notion of a God about whose spirituality nobody has inquired is new to us. To ourselves, and doubtless or probably to barbarians on a certain

---

*   *Prim. Cult.* vol. ii. pp. 335, 336.

†   *Myths of the New World*, 1868, p. 47.

level of culture, such a Divine Being *must* be animistic, *must* be a 'spirit.' To take only one case, to which we shall return, the Banks Islanders (Melanesia) believe in ghosts, 'and in the existence of Beings who were not, and never had been, human. All alike might be called spirits,' says Dr. Codrington, but, *ex hypothesi*, the Beings 'who never were human' are only called 'spirits,' by us, because our habits of thought do not enable us to envisage them *except* as 'spirits.' They never were men, 'the natives will always maintain that he (the *Vui*) was *something different*, and deny to him the fleshly body of a man,' while resolute that he was *not a ghost*.[*] [17]

This point will be amply illustrated later, as we study that strangely neglected chapter, that essential chapter, the Higher beliefs of the Lowest savages. Of the existence of a belief in a Supreme Being, not as merely 'alleged,' there is as good evidence as we possess for any fact in the ethnographic region.

It is certain that savages, when first approached by curious travellers, and missionaries, have again and again recognised our God in theirs.

The mythical details and fables about the savage God are, indeed, different; the ethical, benevolent, admonishing, rewarding, and creative aspects of the Gods are apt to be the same.[†]

> There is no necessity for beginning to tell even the most degraded of these people of the existence of God, or of a future state, the facts being universally admitted.[‡]

'Intelligent men among the Bakwains have scouted the idea of any of them ever having been without a tolerably clear conception of good and evil, God and the future state; Nothing we indicate as sin ever appeared to them as otherwise,' except polygamy, says Livingstone.[18]

Now we may agree with Mr. Tylor that modern theologians, familiar with savage creeds, will scarcely argue that 'they are direct or nearly direct products of revelation' (vol. ii. p. 356).[19] But we may argue that, considering their nascent ethics[20] (denied or minimised by many anthropologists) and the distance which separates the high gods of savagery from the ghosts out of which they are said to have sprung; considering too, that the relatively pure and lofty element which, *ex hypothesi*, is most recent in evolution, is also, *not* the most honoured, but often just the reverse; remembering, above all, that we know nothing historically of the mental condition of the founders of religion, we may hesitate to accept the anthropological hypothesis *en*

---

[*]   I observed this point in *Myth, Ritual, and Religion*, while I did not see the implication, that the idea of 'spirit' was not necessarily present in the savage conception of the primal Beings, Creators, or Makers.

[†]   See one or two cases in *Prim. Cult.* vol. ii. p. 340.

[‡]   Livingstone, speaking of the Bakwain, *Missionary Travels*, p. 158.

masse. At best it is conjectural, and the facts are such that opponents have more justification than is commonly admitted for regarding the bulk of savage religion as degenerate, or corrupted, from its own highest elements. I am by no means, as yet, arguing positively in favour of that hypothesis, but I see what its advocates mean, or ought to mean, and the strength of their position. Mr. Tylor, with his unique fairness, says 'the degeneration theory, no doubt in some instances with justice, may claim such beliefs as mutilated and perverted remains of higher religion' (vol. ii. p. 336).[21]

I do not pretend to know how the lowest savages evolved the theory of a God who reads the heart and 'makes for righteousness.' It is as easy, almost, for me to believe that they 'were not left without a witness,' as to believe that this God of theirs was evolved out of the maleficent ghost of a dirty mischievous medicine-man.

[...]

It would appear then, on the whole, that the question of the plain man to the anthropologist, 'Having got your idea of spirit into the savage's mind, how does he develop out of it what I call God?' has not been answered. God cannot be a reflection from human kings where there have been no kings; nor a president elected out of a polytheistic society of gods where there is as yet no polytheism; nor an ideal first ancestor where men do not worship their ancestors; while, again, the spirit of a man who died, real or ideal, does not answer to a common savage conception of the Creator. All this will become much more obvious as we study in detail the highest gods of the lowest races.

Our study, of course, does not pretend to embrace the religion of all the savages in the world. We are content with typical, and, as a rule, well-observed examples. We range from the creeds of the most backward and worst-equipped nomad races, to those of peoples with an aristocracy, hereditary kings, houses and agriculture, ending with the Supreme Being of the highly civilised Incas, and with the Jehovah of the Hebrews.

[From 'High Gods of Low Races']

To avoid misconception we must repeat the necessary cautions about accepting evidence as to high gods of low races. The missionary who does not see in every alien god a devil is apt to welcome traces of an original supernatural revelation, darkened by all peoples but the Jews. We shall not, however, rely much on missionary evidence, and, when we do, we must now be equally on our guard against the anthropological bias in the missionary himself. Having read Mr. Spencer and Mr. Tylor, and finding himself among ancestor-worshippers (as he sometimes does), he is apt to think that ancestor-worship explains any traces of a belief in the Supreme Being. Against each and every bias of observers we must be watchful.

[...]

Of all races now extant, the Australians are probably lowest in culture, and, like the fauna of the continent, are nearest to the primitive model. They have neither metals, bows, pottery, agriculture, nor fixed habitations; and no traces of higher culture have anywhere been found above or in the soil of the continent. This is important, for in some respects their religious conceptions are so lofty that it would be natural to explain them as the result either of European influence, or as relics of a higher civilisation in the past. The former notion is discredited by the fact that their best religious ideas are imparted in connection with their ancient and secret mysteries, while for the second idea, that they are degenerate from a loftier civilisation, there is absolutely no evidence.

It has been suggested, indeed, by Mr. Spencer that the singularly complex marriage customs of the Australian blacks point to a more polite condition in their past history. Of this stage, as we said, no material traces have ever been discovered, nor can degeneration be recent. Our earliest account of the Australians is that of Dampier, who visited New Holland in the unhappy year 1688.[22] He found the natives 'the miserablest people in the world. The Hodmadods, of Mononamatapa, though a nasty people, yet for wealth are gentlemen to these: who have no houses, sheep, poultry, and fruits of the earth.... They have no houses, but lie in the open air.'[23] Curiously enough, Dampier attests their *unselfishness*: the main ethical feature in their religious teaching. 'Be it little or be it much they get, every one has his part, as well the young and tender as the old and feeble, who are not able to go abroad, as the strong and lusty.' Dampier saw no metals used, nor any bows, merely boomerangs ('wooden cutlasses'), and lances with points hardened in the fire. 'Their place of dwelling was only a fire with a few boughs before it' (the *gunyeh*).

This description remains accurate for most of the unsophisticated Australian tribes, but Dampier appears only to have seen ichthyophagous coast blacks.

[...]

The Australians have been very carefully studied by many observers, and the results entirely overthrow Mr. Huxley's bold statement that 'in its simplest condition, such as may be met with among the Australian savages, theology is a mere belief in the existence, powers, and dispositions (usually malignant) of ghost-like entities who may be propitiated or scared away;

but no cult can properly be said to exist. And in this stage theology is wholly independent of ethics.'[24]

Remarks more crudely in defiance of known facts could not be made. The Australians, assuredly, believe in 'spirits,' often malicious, and probably in most cases regarded as ghosts of men. These aid the wizard, and occasionally inspire him. That these ghosts are *worshipped* does not appear, and is denied by Waitz. Again, in the matter of cult, 'there is none' in the way of *sacrifice* to higher gods, as there should be if these gods were hungry ghosts. The cult among the Australians is the keeping of certain 'laws,' expressed in moral teaching, supposed to be in conformity with the institutes of their God. Worship takes the form, as at Eleusis, of tribal mysteries, originally instituted, as at Eleusis, by the God. The young men are initiated with many ceremonies, some of which are cruel and farcical, but the initiation includes ethical instruction, in conformity with the supposed commands of a God who watches over conduct. As among ourselves, the ethical ideal, with its theological sanction, is probably rather above the moral standard of ordinary practice. What conclusion we should draw from these facts is uncertain, but the facts, at least, cannot be disputed, and precisely contradict the statement of Mr. Huxley. He was wholly in the wrong when he said: 'The moral code, such as is implied by public opinion, derives no sanction from theological dogmas.'[*] It reposes, for its origin and sanction, on such dogmas.

[...][25]

I shall now demonstrate that the religion patronised by the Australian Supreme Being, and inculcated in his Mysteries, is actually used to counteract the immoral character which natives acquire by associating with Anglo-Saxon Christians.[†]

Mr. Howitt[‡] gives an account of the Jeraeil, or Mysteries of the Kurnai.[26] The old men deemed that through intercourse with whites 'the lads had become selfish and no longer inclined to share that which they obtained by their own exertions, or had given them, with their friends.' One need not

---

[*]   *Science and Hebrew Tradition*, p. 346.

[†]   From a brief account of the Fire Ceremony, or *Engwurra* of certain tribes in Central Australia, it seems that religious ceremonies connected with Totems are the most notable performances. Also 'certain mythical ancestors,' of the '*alcheringa*, or dream-times,' were celebrated; these real or ideal human beings appear to 'sink their identity in that of the object with which they are associated, and from which they are supposed to have originated.' There appear also to be places haunted by 'spirit individuals,' in some way mixed up with Totems, but nothing is said of sacrifice to these Manes. The brief account is by Professor Baldwin Spencer and Mr. F.J. Gillen, *Proc. Royal Soc.Victoria*, July 1897. This Fire Ceremony is not for lads – not a kind of confirmation in the savage church – but is intended for adults.

[‡]   *J. Anthrop. Inst.* 1885, p. 310.

say that selflessness is the very essence of goodness, and the central moral doctrine of Christianity. So it is in the religious Mysteries of the African Yao; a selfish man, we shall see, is spoken of as 'uninitiated.' So it is with the Australian Kurnai, whose mysteries and ethical teaching are under the sanction of their Supreme Being. So much for the anthropological dogma that early theology has no ethics.

The Kurnai began by kneading the stomachs of the lads about to be initiated (that is, if they have been associating with Christians), to expel selfishness and greed. The chief rite, later, is to blindfold every lad, with a blanket closely drawn over his head, to make whirring sounds with the *tundun*, or Greek *rhombos*, then to pluck off the blankets, and bid the initiate raise their faces to the sky. The initiator points to it, calling out, 'Look there, look there, look there!' They have seen in this solemn way the home of the Supreme Being, 'Our Father,' Mungan-ngaur (Mungan = 'Father,' ngaur = 'our'), whose doctrine is then unfolded by the old initiator ('headman') 'in an impressive manner.'* 'Long ago there was a great Being, Mungan-ngaur, who lived on the earth.' His son Tundun is *direct ancestor* of the Kurnai. Mungan initiated the rites, and destroyed earth by water when they were impiously revealed. 'Mungan left the earth, and ascended to the sky, where he still remains.'

Here Mungan-ngaur, a Being not defined as spirit, but immortal, and dwelling in heaven, is Father, or rather grandfather, not maker, of the Kurnai. This *may* be interpreted as ancestor-worship, but the opposite myth, of making or creating, is of frequent occurrence in many widely-severed Australian districts, and co-exists with evolutionary myths. Mungan-ngaur's precepts are:

1. *To listen to and obey the old men.*
2. *To share everything they have with their friends.*
3. *To live peaceably with their friends.*
4. *Not to interfere with girls or married women.*
5. *To obey the food restrictions until they are released from them by the old men.*[27]

Mr. Howitt concludes: 'I venture to assert that it can no longer be maintained that the Australians have no belief which can be called religious, that is, in the sense of beliefs which govern tribal and individual morality under a supernatural sanction.'[28] On this topic Mr. Howitt's opinion became more affirmative the more deeply he was initiated.†

The Australians are the lowest, most primitive savages, yet no propitiation by food is made to their moral Ruler, in heaven, as if he were a ghost.

---

*   *J. Anthrop. Inst.* 1885, p. 313.

†   *J. Anthrop. Inst.* xiii. p. 459.

The laws of these Australian divine beings apply to ritual as well as to ethics, as might naturally be expected. But the moral element is conspicuous, the reverence is conspicuous: we have here no mere ghost, propitiated by food or sacrifice, or by purely magical rites. His very image (modelled on a large scale in earth) is no vulgar idol: to make such a thing, except on the rare sacred occasions, is a capital offence. Meanwhile the mythology of the God has often, in or out of the rites, nothing rational about it.

On the whole it is evident that Mr. Herbert Spencer, for example, underrates the nature of Australian religion. He cites a case of addressing the ghost of a man recently dead, which is asked not to bring sickness, 'or make loud noises in the night,' and says: 'Here we may recognise the essential elements of a cult.' But Mr. Spencer does not allude to the much more essentially religious elements which he might have found in the very authority whom he cites, Mr. Brough Smyth.* 29 This appears, as far as my scrutiny goes, to be Mr. Spencer's solitary reference to Australia in the work on 'Ecclesiastical Institutions.'30 Yet the facts which he and Mr. Huxley ignore throw a light very different from theirs on what they consider 'the simplest condition of theology.'

Among the causes of confusion in thought upon religion, Mr. Tylor mentions 'the partial and one-sided application of the historical method of inquiry into theological doctrines.'† 31Here, perhaps, we have examples. In its highest aspect that 'simplest theology' of Australia is free from the faults of popular theology in Greece. The God discourages sin, though, in myth, he is far from impeccable. He is almost too revered to be named (except in mythology) and is not to be represented by idols. He is not moved by sacrifice; he has not the chance; like Death in Greece, 'he only, of all Gods, loves not gifts.' Thus the status of theology does not correspond to what we look for in very low culture. It would scarcely be a paradox to say that the popular Zeus, or Ares, is degenerate from Mungan-ngaur, or the Fuegian being who forbids the slaying of an enemy, and almost literally 'marks the sparrow's fall.'

If we knew all the mythology of Darumulun, we should probably find it (like much of the myth of Pundjel or Bunjil) on a very different level from the theology. There are two currents, the religious and the mythical, flowing together through religion. The former current, religious, even among very low savages, is pure from the magical ghost-propitiating habit. The latter current, mythological, is full of magic, mummery, and scandalous legend. Sometimes the latter stream quite pollutes the former, sometimes they flow side by side, perfectly distinguishable, as in Aztec ethical piety, compared with the bloody Aztec ritualism. Anthropology has mainly kept her eyes fixed on the impure stream, the lusts, mummeries, conjurings, and frauds of

*   *Ecclesiastical Institutions*, p. 674.

†   *Prim. Cult.* ii. 450.

priesthoods, while relatively, or altogether, neglecting (as we have shown) what is honest and of good report.

The worse side of religion is the less sacred, and therefore the more conspicuous. Both elements are found co-existing, in almost all races, and nobody, in our total lack of historical information about the beginnings, can say which, if either, element is the earlier, or which, if either, is derived from the other. To suppose that propitiation of corpses and then of ghosts came first is agreeable, and seems logical, to some writers who are not without a bias against all religion as an unscientific superstition. But we know so little!

[...]

From all this evidence it does not appear how non-polytheistic, non-monarchical, non-Manes-worshipping savages evolved the idea of a relatively supreme, moral, and benevolent Creator, unborn, undying, watching men's lives. 'He can go everywhere, and do everything.'*

[From 'Supreme Gods Not Necessarily Developed Out of "Spirits"']

[...]One cause of our blindness to the point appears to be this: We have from childhood been taught that 'God is a Spirit.' We, now, can only conceive of an eternal being as a 'spirit.' We know that legions of savage gods are now regarded as spirits. And therefore we have never remarked that there is no reason why we should take it for granted that the earliest deities of the earliest men were supposed by them to be 'spirits' at all. These gods might most judiciously be spoken of, not as 'spirits,' but as 'undefined eternal beings.' To us, such a being is necessarily a spirit, but he was by no means necessarily so to an early thinker, who may not yet have reached the conception of a ghost.

A ghost is said, by anthropologists, to have developed into a god. Now, the very idea of a ghost (apart from a wraith or fetch) implies the previous *death* of his proprietor. A ghost is the phantasm of a *dead* man. But anthropologists continually tell us, with truth, that the idea of death as a universal ordinance is unknown to the savage. Diseases and death are things that once did not exist, and that, normally, ought not to occur, the savage thinks. They are, in his opinion, supernormally caused by magicians and spirits. Death came into the world by a blunder, an accident, an error in ritual, a

---

* In Mr. Carr's work, *The Australian Race*, reports of 'godless' natives are given, for instance, in the Mary River country and in Gippsland. These reports are usually the result of the ignorance or contempt of white observers, cf. Tylor, i. 419. [...]

decision of a god who was before Death was. Scores of myths are told everywhere on this subject.[*]

The savage Supreme Being, with added power, omniscience, and morality, is the idealisation of the savage, as conceived of by himself, *minus* fleshly body (as a rule), and *minus* Death. He is not necessarily a 'spirit,' though that term may now be applied to him. He was not originally differentiated as 'spirit' or 'not spirit.' He is a Being, conceived of without the question of 'spirit,' or 'no spirit' being raised; perhaps he was originally conceived of before that question could be raised by men. When we call the Supreme Being of savages a 'spirit' we introduce our own animistic ideas into a conception where it may not have originally existed. If the God is 'the savage himself raised to the nth power' so much the less of a spirit is he.[32] Mr. Matthew Arnold might as well have said: 'The British Philistine has no knowledge of God. He believes that the Creator is a magnified non-natural man, living in the sky.'[33] The Gippsland or Fuegian or Blackfoot Supreme Being is just a *Being*, anthropomorphic, not a *mrart*, or 'spirit.' The Supreme Being is a *wesen*, Being, *Vui*; we have hardly a term for an immortal existence so undefined. If the being is an idealised first ancestor (as among the Kurnai), he is not, on that account, either man or ghost of man. In the original conception he is a powerful intelligence who was from the first: who was already active long before, by a breach of his laws, an error in the delivery of a message, a breach of ritual, or what not, death entered the world. He was not affected by the entry of death, he still exists.

Modern minds need to become familiar with this indeterminate idea of the savage Supreme Being, which, logically, may be prior to the evolution of the notion of ghost or spirit.

But how does it apply when, as by the Kurnai, the Supreme Being is reckoned an ancestor?

It can very readily be shown that, when the Supreme Being of a savage people is thus the idealised First Ancestor, he can never have been envisaged by his worshippers as at any time a *ghost*; or, at least, cannot logically have been so envisaged where the nearly universal belief occurs that death came into the world by accident, or needlessly.

Adam is the mythical first ancestor of the Hebrews, but he died, ὑπὲρ μόρον,[34] and was not worshipped. Yama, the first of Aryan men who died, was worshipped by Vedic Aryans, but *confessedly* as a ghost-god. Mr. Tylor gives a list[35] of first ancestors deified. The Ancestor of the Mandans did not die, consequently is no ghost; *emigravit*, he 'moved west.' Where the First Ancestor is also the Creator (Dog-rib Indians), he can hardly be, and is not, regarded as a mortal. Tamoi, of the Guaranis, was 'the ancient of heaven,' clearly no mortal man. The Maori Maui was the first who died, but he is

---

[*]   I have published a chapter on Myths on the Origin of Death in *Modern Mythology*.

not one of the original Maori gods. Haetsh, among the Kamchadals, precisely answers to Yama. Unkulunkulu will be described later.*

This is the list: Where the First Ancestor is equivalent to the Creator, and
is supreme, he is – from the first – deathless and immortal. When he dies he
is a confessed ghost-god.

Now, ghost-worship and dead ancestor-worship are impossible before
the ancestor is dead and is a ghost. But the essential idea of Mungan-ngaur,
and Baiame, and most of the high gods of Australia, and of other low races,
is that *they never died at all.* They belong to the period before death came
into the world, like Qat among the Melanesians. They arise in an age that
knew not death, and had not reflected on phantasms nor evolved ghosts.
They could have been conceived of, in the nature of the case, by a race of
immortals who never dreamed of such a thing as a ghost. For these gods,
the ghost-theory is not required, and is superfluous, even contradictory. The
early thinkers who developed these beings did not need to know that men
die (though, of course, they did know it in practice), still less did they need
to have conceived by abstract speculation the hypothesis of ghosts. Baiame,
Cagn, Bunjil, in their adorers' belief, were *there*; death later intruded among
men, but did not affect these divine beings in any way.

The ghost-theory, therefore, by the evidence of anthropology itself, is
not needed for the evolution of the high gods of savages. It is only needed
for the evolution of ghost-propitiation and genuine dead-ancestor worship.
Therefore, the high gods described were not necessarily once ghosts – were
not idealised *mortal* ancestors. They were, naturally, from the beginning,
from before the coming in of death, immortal Fathers, now dwelling on
high. Between them and apotheosised mortal ancestors there is a great gulf
fixed – the river of death.

The explicitly stated distinction that the high creative gods never were
mortal men, while other gods are spirits of mortal men, is made in every
quarter. 'Ancestors *known* to be human were *not* worshipped as [original]
gods, and ancestors worshipped as [original] gods were not believed to have
been human.'† 36

Both kinds may have a generic name, such as *kalou*, or *wakan*, but the
specific distinction is universally made by low savages. On one hand, original gods; on the other, non-original gods that were once ghosts. Now, this
distinction is often calmly ignored; whereas, when any race has developed
(like late Scandinavians) the Euhemeristic hypothesis ('all gods were once
men'), that hypothesis is accepted as an historical statement of fact by some
writers.

It is part of my theory that the more popular ghost-worship of souls of
people whom men have loved, invaded the possibly older religion of the

---

*   *Prim. Cult.* ii. 311–316.

†   Jevons, *Introduction*, p. 197.

Supreme Father. Mighty beings, whether originally conceived of as 'spirits' or not, came, later, under the Animistic theory, to be reckoned as spirits. They even (but not among the lowest savages) came to be propitiated by food and sacrifice. The alternative, for a Supreme Being, when once Animism prevailed, was sacrifice (as to more popular ghost deities) or neglect. We shall find examples of both alternatives. But sacrifice does not prove that a God was, in original conception, a ghost, or even a spirit. 'The common doctrine of the Old Testament is not that God is spirit, but that the spirit [rûah = 'wind,' 'living breath'] of Jehovah, going forth from him, works in the world and among men.'* [37]

[…] It may be retorted that this makes no real difference. If savages did not invent gods in consequence of a fallacious belief in spirit and soul, still, in some other equally illogical way they came to indulge the hypothesis that they had a Judge and Father in heaven. But, if the ghost theory of the high Gods is wrong, as it is conspicuously superfluous, that *does* make some difference. It proves that a widely preached scientific conclusion may be as spectral as Bathybius.[38] On other more important points, therefore, we may differ from the newest scientific opinion without too much diffident apprehensiveness.

[From 'Savage Supreme Beings']

[…] Anthropological study of religion has hitherto almost entirely overlooked the mysteries of various races, except in so far as they confirm the entry of the young people into the ranks of the adult. Their esoteric moral and religious teaching is nearly unknown to us, save in a few instances. It is certain that the mysteries of Greece were survivals of savage ceremonies, because we know that they included specific savage rites, such as the use of the *rhombos* to make a whirring noise, and the custom of ritual daubing with dirt; and the sacred *ballets d'action*, in which, as Lucian and Qing say,[39] mystic facts are 'danced out.'† But, while Greece retained these relics of savagery, there was something taught at Eleusis which filled minds like Plato's and Pindar's with a happy religious awe. Now, similar 'softening of the heart' was the result of the teaching in the Australian *Bora*: the Yao mysteries inculcate the victory over self; and, till we are admitted to the secrets of all other savage mysteries throughout the world, we cannot tell whether, among mummeries, frivolities, and even license, high ethical doctrines are not presented under the sanction of religion. The New Life, and perhaps the future life, are undeniably indicated in the Australian mysteries by the simulated Resurrection.

---

*   Robertson Smith. *The Prophets of Israel*, p. 61.

†   *Myth, Ritual, and Religion*, i. 281–288.

I would therefore no longer say, as in 1887, that the Hellenic genius must have added to 'an old medicine dance' all that the Eleusinian mysteries possessed of beauty, counsel, and consolation.* [40] These elements, as well as the barbaric factors in the rites, may have been developed out of such savage doctrine as softens the hearts of Australians and Yaos. That this kind of doctrine receives religious sanction is certain, where we know the secret of savage mysteries. It is therefore quite incorrect, and strangely presumptuous, to deny, with almost all anthropologists, the alliance of ethics with religion among the most backward races. We must always remember their secrecy about their inner religion, their frankness about their mythological tales. These we know: the inner religion we ought to begin to recognise that we do not know.

[…]

It is impossible to prove, historically, which of the two main elements in belief – the idea of an Eternal Being or Beings, or the idea of surviving ghosts – came first into the minds of men. The idea of primeval Eternal Beings, as understood by savages, does not depend on, or require, the ghost theory. But, as we almost always find ghosts and a Supreme Being together, where we find either, among the lowest savages, we have no historical ground for asserting that either is prior to the other. Where we have no evidence to the belief in the Maker, we must not conclude that no such belief exists. Our knowledge is confused and scanty; often it is derived from men who do not know the native language, or the native sacred language, or have not been trusted with what the savage treasures as his secret. Moreover, if anywhere ghosts are found without gods, it is an inference from the argument that an idea familiar to very low savage tribes, like the Australians, and falling more and more into the background elsewhere, though still extant and traceable, might, in certain cases, be lost and forgotten altogether.

[…]

If a people like the Andamanese, or the Australian tribes whom we have studied, had such a conception as that of Puluga, or Baiame, or Mungan-ngaur[41] and then, *later*, developed ancestor-worship with its propitiatory sacrifices and ceremonies, ancestor-worship, as the newest evolved and infinitely the most practical form of cult, would gradually thrust the belief in a Puluga, or Mungan-ngaur, or Cagn into the shade. The ancestral spirit, to speak quite plainly, can be 'squared' by the people in whom he takes a special interest for family reasons. The equal Father of all men cannot be

* Lobeck, *Aglaophamus*, 133.

'squared,' and declines (till corrupted by the bad example of ancestral ghosts) to make himself useful to one man rather than to another. For these very intelligible, simple, and practical reasons, if the belief in a Mungan-ngaur came first in evolution, and the belief in a practicable bribable family ghost came second, the ghost-cult would inevitably crowd out the God-cult.* The name of the Father and Maker would become a mere survival, *nominis umbra*,[42] worship and sacrifice going to the ancestral ghost. [...]

But, if the idea of a universal Father and Maker came last in evolution, as a refinement, then, of course, it ought to be the newest, and therefore the most fashionable and potent of Guianese cults. Precisely the reverse is said to be the case. Nor can the belief indicated in such names as Father and Maker be satisfactorily explained as a refinement of ancestor-worship, because, we repeat, it occurs where ancestors are not worshipped.

These considerations, however unpleasant to the devotees of Animism, or the ghost theory, are not, in themselves, illogical, nor contradictory of the theory of evolution, which, on the other hand, fits them perfectly well. That god thrives best who is most suited to his environment. Whether an easy-going, hungry ghost-god with a liking for his family, or a moral Creator not to be bribed, is better suited to an environment of not especially scrupulous savages, any man can decide. Whether a set of not particularly scrupulous savages will readily evolve a moral unbribable Creator, when they have a serviceable family ghost-god eager to oblige, is a question as easily resolved.

[From 'The Old Degeneration Theory']

[....] Not only is there degeneration from the Australian conception of Mungan-gnaur, at its best, to the conception of the Semitic gods in general, but, 'humanly speaking,' if religion began in a pure form among low savages, degeneration was inevitable. Advancing social conditions compelled men into degeneration. Mungan-ngaur is, so far, in line with our own ideas of divinity because he is not localised. He dwelleth not in temples made with hands; it is not likely that he should, when his worshippers have neither house, tent, nor tabernacle. As Mr. Robertson Smith says,[43] 'where the God had a house or a temple, we recognise the work of men who were no longer pure nomads, but had begun to form fixed homes.' By the nature of Australian society, a deity could not be tied to a temple, and temple-ritual, and consequent myths to explain that ritual, could not arise. Nor could Darumulun be attached to a district, just as 'the nomad Arabs could not assimilate the conception of a god as a land-owner, and apply it to their

---

*   Obviously there could be no Family God before there was the institution of the Family.

own tribal deities, for the simple reason that in the desert private property in land was unknown.'*

Darumulun is thus not capable of degenerating into 'a local god, as *Baal*, or lord of the land,' because this 'involves a series of ideas unknown to the primitive life of the savage huntsman,' like the widely spread Murring tribes.†

Nor could Darumulun be tied down to a place in Semitic fashion, first by manifesting himself there, therefore by receiving an altar of sacrifice there, and in the end a sanctuary, for Darumulun receives no sacrifice at all.

Again, the scene of the Bora could not become a permanent home of Darumulun, because, when the rites are over, the effigy of the god is scrupulously destroyed. Thus Darumulun, in his own abode 'beyond the sky,' can 'go everywhere and do everything' (is omnipresent and omnipotent), dwells in no earthly places, has no temple, nor tabernacle, nor sacred mount, nor, like Jehovah, any limit of land.‡

The early Hebrew conception of Jehovah, then, is infinitely more conditioned, practically, by space, than the Supreme Being, 'The Master,' in the conception of some Australian blacks.

> By a prophet like Isaiah the residence of Jehovah in Zion is almost wholly dematerialised.... Conceiving Jehovah as the King of Israel, he[44] necessarily conceives His kingly activity as going forth from the capital of the nation.§

But nomad hunter tribes, with no ancestor-worship, no king and no capital, cannot lower their deity by the conditions, or limit him by the limitations, of an earthly monarchy.

In precisely the same way, Major Ellis proves the degeneration of deity in Africa, so far as being localised in place of being the Universal God, implies degeneration, as it certainly does to our minds.[45] By being attached to a given hill or river 'the gods, instead of being regarded as being interested in the whole of mankind, would eventually come to be regarded as being interested in separate tribes or nations alone.'[46]

To us Milton seems nobly Chauvinistic when he talks of what God has done by 'His English.'[47] But this localised and essentially degenerate conception was inevitable, as soon as, in advancing civilisation, the god who had been 'interested in the whole of [known] mankind' was settled on a hill, river, or lagoon, amidst a nation of worshippers.

In the course of the education of mankind, this form of degeneration

---

* Robertson Smith, *Religion of the Semites*, pp. 104, 105.

† Op. cit. p. 106.

‡ On the Glenolg some caves and mountain tops are haunted or holy. Waitz, vi. 804. No authority cited.

§ *Religion of Semites*, p. 110.

(abstractly so considered) was to work, as nothing else could have worked, towards the lofty conception of universal Deity. For that conception was only brought into practical religion (as apart from philosophic speculation) by the union between Israel and the God of Sinai and Zion. The Prophets, recognising in the God of Sinai, their nation's God – One to whom righteousness was infinitely dearer than even his Chosen People – freed the conception of God from local ties, and made it overspread the world.

Mr. Robertson Smith has pointed out, again, the manner in which the different political development of East and West affected the religion of Greece and of the Semites. In Greece, monarchy fell, at an early period, before the aristocratic houses. The result was 'a divine aristocracy of many gods, only modified by a weak reminiscence of the old kingship in the not very effective sovereignty' (or *prytany*) 'of Zeus. In the East the national god tended to acquire a really monarchic sway.'* [48] Australia escaped polytheistic degeneracy by having no aristocracy, as in Polynesia, where aristocracy, as in early Greece, had developed polytheism. Ghosts and spirits the Australians knew, but not polytheistic gods, nor departmental deities, as of war, agriculture, art. The savage had no agriculture, and his social condition was not departmental. In yet another way, political advance produces religious degeneration, if polytheism be degeneration from the conception of one relatively supreme moral being. To make a nation, several tribes must unite. Each has its god, and the nation is apt to receive them all, equally, into its Pantheon. Thus, if worshippers of Baiame, Pundjel, and Darumulun coalesced into a nation, we might find all three gods living together in a new polytheism. In fact, granting a relatively pure starting-point, degeneration from it must accompany every step of civilisation, to a certain distance.

★ *Rel. Sem.* p. 71.

'Science and Superstition',
Magic and Religion
(Longmans, Green and Co., 1901)

We all know what we mean by science; science is 'organised common sense.' Her aim is the acquisition of reasoned and orderly knowledge. Presented with a collection of verified facts, it is the part of science to reduce them to order, and to account for their existence in accordance with her recognised theory of things. If the facts cannot be fitted into the theory, it must be expanded or altered; for we must admit that, if the facts are verified, there is need for change and expansion in the theory. The 'colligation' of facts demands hypotheses, and these may not, at the moment of their construction, be verifiable. The deflections of a planet from its apparently normal course may be accounted for by the hypothesis of the attraction of another heavenly body not yet discovered. The hypothesis is legitimate, for such bodies are known to exist, and to produce such effects. When the body is discovered, the hypothesis becomes a certainty. On the other hand, the hypothesis that some capricious and conscious agency pushed the planet into deflections would be illegitimate, for the existence of such a freakish agency is not demonstrated. Our hypotheses then must be consistent with our actual knowledge of nature and of human nature, and our conjectured causes must be adequate to the production of the effects. Thus, science gradually acquires and organises new regions of knowledge.

Superstition is a word of much less definite meaning. When we call a man 'superstitious' we usually mean that evidence which satisfies him does not satisfy us. We see examples daily of the dependence of belief on bias. One man believes a story about cruelties committed by our adversaries; another, disbelieving the tale, credits a narrative about the misconduct of our own party. Probably the evidence in neither case would satisfy the historian, or be accepted by a jury. A man in a tavern tells another how the

Boers, retreating from a position, buried their own wounded. 'I don't believe that,' says the other. 'Then you are a pro-Boer.'[1]

The sceptic reasoned from his general knowledge of human nature. The believer reasoned from his own prejudiced and mythopoeic conception of people whom he disliked. If the question had been one of religion the believer might be called superstitious; the sceptic might be called scientific, if he was ready to yield his doubts to the evidence of capable observers of the alleged fact.

Superstition, like science, has her hypotheses, and, like science, she reasons from experience. But her experience is usually fantastic, unreal, or if real capable of explanation by causes other than those alleged by superstition. A man comes in at night, and says he has seen a ghost in white. That is merely his hypothesis; the existence of ghosts in white is not demonstrated. You accompany him to the scene of the experience, and prove to him that he has seen a post, not a ghost. His experience was real, but was misinterpreted by dint of an hypothesis resting on no demonstrated fact of knowledge.

The hypotheses of superstition are familiar. Thus, an event has happened: say you have lost your button-hook. You presently hear of a death in your family. Ever afterwards you go anxiously about when you have lost a button-hook. You are confusing a casual sequence of facts with a causal connection of facts. Sequence in time is mistaken for sequence of what we commonly style cause and effect. In the same way, superstition cherishes the hypothesis that like affects like. Thus, the sun is round, and a ball of clay is round. Therefore, if an Australian native wishes to delay the course of the round sun in the heavens, he fixes a round ball of clay on the bough of a tree; or so books on anthropology tell us. Acting on the hypothesis that like affects like, a man makes a clay or waxen image of an enemy, and sticks it full of pins or thorns. He expects his enemy to suffer agony in consequence, and so powerful is 'suggestion' that, if the enemy knows about the image, he sometimes falls ill and dies. This experience corroborates the superstitious hypothesis, and so the experiment with the image is of world-wide diffusion. Everything is done, or attempted, on these lines by superstition. Men imitate the killing of foes or game, and expect, as a result, to kill them in war or in the chase. They mimic the gathering of clouds and the fall of rain, and expect rain to fall in consequence. They imitate the evolution of an edible grub from the larva, and expect grubs to multiply; and so on.

All this is quite rational, if you grant the hypotheses of superstition. Her practices are magic. We are later to discuss a theory that men had magic before they had religion, and only invented gods because they found that magic did not work. Still later they invented science, which is only magic with a legitimate hypothesis, using real, not fanciful, experience. In the long run magic and religion are to die out, perhaps, and science is to have the whole field to herself.[2]

This may be a glorious though a remote prospect. But surely it is above all things needful that our science should be scientific. She must not blink facts, merely because they do not fit into her scheme or hypothesis of the nature of things, or of religion. She really must give as much prominence to the evidence which contradicts as to that which supports her theory in each instance.[3] Not only must she not shut her eyes to this evidence, but she must diligently search for it, must seek for what Bacon calls *instantiae contradictoriae*, since, if these exist, the theory which ignores them is useless.[4] If she advances an hypothesis, it must not be contradictory of the whole mass of human experience. If science finds that her hypothesis contradicts experience, she must seek for an hypothesis which is in accordance with experience, and, if that cannot be found, she must wait till it is found. Again, science must not pile one unverified hypothesis upon another unverified hypothesis till her edifice rivals the Tower of Babel. She must not make a conjecture on p. 35, and on p. 210 treat the conjecture as a fact. Because, if one story in the card-castle is destroyed by being proved impossible, all the other stories will 'come tumbling after.' It seems hardly necessary, but it is not superfluous, to add that, in her castle of hypotheses, one must not contradict, and therefore destroy, another. We must not be asked to believe that an event occurred at one date, and also that it occurred at another; or that an institution was both borrowed by a people at one period, and was also possessed, unborrowed, by the same people, at an earlier period. We cannot permit science to assure us that a certain fact was well known, and that the knowledge produced important consequences; while we are no less solemnly told that the fact was wholly unknown, whence it would seem that the results alleged to spring from the knowledge could not be produced.

This kind of reasoning, with its inferring of inferences from other inferences, themselves inferred from conjectures as to the existence of facts of which no proof is adduced, must be called superstitious rather than scientific. The results may be interesting, but they are the reverse of science.

It is perhaps chiefly in the nascent science of the anthropological study of institutions, and above all of religion, that this kind of reasoning prevails. The topic attracts ingenious and curious minds. System after system has been constructed, unstinted in material, elegant in aspect, has been launched, and has been wrecked, or been drifted by the careless winds to the forlorn shore where Bryant's ark, with all its crew, divine or human, lies in decay. No mortal student believes in the arkite system of Bryant, though his ark, on the match-boxes of Messrs. Bryant and May, perhaps denotes loyalty to the ancestral idea.[5]

The world of modern readers has watched sun myths, and dawn myths, and storm myths, and wind myths come in and go out: *autant en emporte le vent*.[6] Totems and taboos succeeded, and we are bewildered by the contending theories of the origins of taboos and totems. Deities of vegetation now are all in all, and may it be far from us to say that any one from Ouranos to Pan, from the Persian King to the horses of Virbius, is not a spirit of vegetable life. Yet perhaps the deity has higher aspects and nobler functions than the pursuit of his 'vapid vegetable loves;'[7] and these deserve occasional attention.[8]

The result, however, of scurrying hypotheses and hasty generalisations is that the nascent science of religious origins is received with distrust. We may review the brief history of the modern science.

Some twenty years ago, when the 'Principles of Sociology,' by Mr. Herbert Spencer, was first published, the book was reviewed, in 'Mind,' by the author of 'Primitive Culture.'[9] That work, again, was published in 1871. In 1890 appeared the 'Golden Bough,' by Mr. J. G. Frazer, and the second edition of the book, with changes and much new matter, was given to the world in 1900.

Here, then, we have a whole generation, a space of thirty years, during which English philosophers or scholars have been studying the science of the Origins of Religion. In the latest edition of the 'Golden Bough,' Mr. Frazer has even penetrated into the remote region where man neither had, nor wanted, any religion at all. We naturally ask ourselves to what point we have arrived after the labours of a generation. Twenty years ago, when reviewing Mr. Spencer, Mr. Tylor said that a time of great public excitement as to these topics was at hand. The clamour and contest aroused by Mr. Darwin's theory of the Origin of Species and the Descent of Man would be outdone by the coming war over the question of the Evolution of Religion. But there has been no general excitement; there has been little display of public interest in these questions. They have been left to 'the curious' and 'the learned,' classes not absolutely identical. Mr. Frazer, indeed, assures us that the comparative study of human beliefs and institutions is 'fitted to be much more than a means of satisfying an enlightened curiosity, and of furnishing materials for the researches of the learned.'* [10] But enlightened curiosity seems to be easily satisfied, and only very few of the learned concern themselves with these researches, which Mr. Tylor expected to be so generally exciting.

A member of the University of Oxford informed me that the study of beliefs, and of anthropology in general, is almost entirely neglected by the undergraduates, and when I asked him 'Why?' he replied 'There is no money in it.' Another said that anthropology 'had no evidence.' In the language of the economists there is no supply provided at Oxford because there is no demand. Classics, philology, history, physical science, and even literature, are studied, because 'there is money in them,' not much money indeed, but a competence, if the student is successful. For the study of the evolution of beliefs there is no demand, or very little. Yet, says Mr. Frazer, 'well handled, it may become a powerful instrument to expedite progress, if

---

★   *Golden Bough*, i. xxi., 1900.

it lays bare certain weak spots in the foundations on which modern society is built.'[11] We all desire progress (in the right direction), we all pine to lay bare weak spots, and yet we do not seem to be concerned about the services which might be done for progress by the study of the evolution of religion. 'It is indeed a melancholy and, in some respects, thankless task,' says Mr. Frazer, 'to strike at the foundations of beliefs in which, as in a strong tower, the hopes and aspirations of humanity through long ages have sought a refuge from the storm and stress of life.'[12] 'Thankless,' indeed, these operations are. 'Yet sooner or later,' Mr. Frazer adds, 'it is inevitable that the battery of the comparative method should breach these venerable walls, mantled over with the ivy and mosses and wild flowers of a thousand tender and sacred associations. At present we are only dragging the guns into position; they have hardly yet begun to speak.'[13]

Mr. Frazer is too modest: he has dragged into position a work of immense learning and eloquent style in three siege guns, we may say, three volumes of the largest calibre, and they have spoken about 500,000 words. No man, to continue the metaphor, is better supplied than he with the ammunition of learning, with the knowledge of facts of every kind. Yet the venerable walls, with their pleasing growth of ivy, mosses, wild flowers, and other mural vegetation, do not, to myself, seem in the least degree impaired by the artillery, and I try to show cause for my opinion.

Why is this, and why is the portion of the public which lives within or without the venerable walls mainly indifferent?

Several sufficient reasons might be given. In the first place many people have, or think they have, so many other grounds for disbelief, that additional grounds, provided by the comparative method, are regarded rather as a luxury than as supplying a felt want. Again, but very few persons have leisure, or inclination, or power of mind enough to follow an elaborate argument through fifteen hundred pages, not to speak of other works on the same theme. Once more, only a minute minority are capable of testing and weighing the evidence, and criticising the tangled hypotheses on which the argument rests, or in which it is involved.

But there is another and perhaps a sounder argument for indifference. The learned are aware that the evidence for all these speculations is not of the nature to which they are accustomed, either in historical or scientific studies. More and more the age insists on strictness in appreciating evidence, and on economy in conjecture. But the study of the evolution of myth and belief has always been, and still is, marked by an extraordinary use, or abuse, of conjecture. The 'perhapses,' the 'we may supposes,' the 'we must infers' are countless.

As in too much of the so-called 'Higher Criticism'[14] hypothesis is piled, by many anthropologists, upon hypothesis, guess upon guess, while, if only one guess is wrong, the main argument falls to pieces. Moreover, it is the easiest thing, in certain cases, to explain the alleged facts by a counter hypothesis, not a complex hypothesis, but at least as plausible as the many combined conjectures of the castle architects, though perhaps as far from the truth, and as incapable of verification. Of these statements examples shall be given in the course of this book.

We are all, we who work at these topics, engaged in science, the science of man, or rather we are painfully labouring to lay the foundations of that science. We are all trying 'to expedite progress.' But our science cannot expedite progress if our science is not scientific. We must, therefore, however pedantic our process may seem, keep insisting on the rejection of all evidence which is not valid, on the sparing use of conjecture, and on the futility of piling up hypothesis upon unproved hypothesis. To me it seems, as I have already said, that a legitimate hypothesis must 'colligate the facts', that it must do so more successfully than any counter hypothesis, and that it must, for every link in its chain, have evidence which will stand the tests of criticism.

But the chief cause of indifference is the character of our evidence. We can find anything we want to find people say — not only 'the man in the street' but the learned say — among reports of the doings of savage and barbarous races. We find what we want, and to what we do not want we are often blind. For example, nothing in savage religion is better vouched for than the belief in a being whom narrators of every sort call 'a Creator who holds all in his power.' I take the first instance of this kind that comes to hand in opening Mr. Tylor's 'Primitive Culture.' The being is he whom the natives of Canada 'call "Andouagni," without, however, having any form or method of prayer to him.'[15] The date of this evidence is 1558. It is obvious that Andouagni (to take one case out of a multitude) was not invented in the despair of magic. Mysticism has been called the despair of philosophy, and Mr. Frazer, as we shall see, regards religion as the despair of magic. By his theory man, originally without religion, and trusting in magic found by experience that magic could not really control the weather and the food supply. Man therefore dreamed that 'there were other beings, like himself, but far stronger,' who, unseen, controlled what his magic could not control. 'To these mighty beings … man now addressed himself … beseeching them of their mercy to furnish him with all good things ….'*

But nobody beseeched Andouagni to do anything. The Canadians had 'no method or form of prayer to him.'† [16] Therefore Andouagni was not invented because magic failed, and therefore this great power was dreamed of, and his mercy was beseeched with prayers for good things. That was not the process by which Andouagni was evolved, because nobody prayed to him in 1558, nor have we reason to believe that any one ever did.

---

*   G.B. i. 77.

†   Tylor, *Prim. Cult*, ii. 309, citing Thevet, *Singularitez de la France Antarctique*, Paris, 1558, ch. 77.

From every part of the globe, but chiefly from among very low savage and barbaric races, the existence of beings powerful as Andouagni, but, like him, not addressed in prayer, or but seldom so addressed, is reported by travellers of many ages, races, creeds, and professions. The existence of the belief in such beings, often not approached by prayer or sacrifice, is fatal to several modern theories of the origin and evolution of religion. But these facts, resting on the best evidence which anthropology can offer, and corroborated by the undesigned coincidence of testimony from every quarter, are not what most students in this science want to find. Therefore these facts have been ignored or hastily slurred over, or the beliefs are ascribed to European or Islamite influence. Yet, first, Christians or Islamites, with the god they introduced would introduce prayer to him, and prayer, in many cases, there is none. Next, in the case of Andouagni, what missionary influence could exist in Canada before 1558? Thirdly, if missionaries, amateur or professional, there were in Canada before 1558 they would be Catholics, and would introduce, not a Creator never addressed in prayer, but crosses, beads, the Madonna, the Saints, and such Catholic rites as would leave material traces.

In spite of all these obvious considerations, I am unacquainted with any book on this phase of savage religion, and scarcely know any book, except Mr. Tylor's 'Primitive Culture,' in which the facts are prominently stated.

The evidence for the facts, let me repeat, is of the best character that anthropology can supply, for it rests on testimony undesignedly coincident, given from most parts of the world by men of every kind of education, creed, and bias. Contradictory evidence, the denial of the existence of the beliefs, is also abundant: to such eternal contradictions of testimony anthropology must make up her mind. We can only test and examine, in each instance, the bias of the witness, if he has a bias, and his opportunities of acquiring knowledge. If the belief does exist, it can seldom attest itself, or never, by material objects, such as idols, altars, sacrifices, and the sound of prayers, for a being like Andouagni is not prayed to or propitiated: one proof that he is not of Christian introduction. We have thus little but the reports of Europeans intimately acquainted with the peoples, savage or barbaric, and, if possible, with their language, to serve as a proof of the existence of the savage belief in a supreme being, a maker or creator of things.

This fact warns us to be cautious, but occasionally we have such evidence as is supplied by Europeans initiated into the mysteries of savage religion. Our best proof, however, of the existence of this exalted, usually neglected belief, is the coincidence of testimony, from that of the companions of Columbus, and the earliest traders visiting America, to that of Mr. A. W. Howitt, a *mystes* of the Australian Eleusinia, or of the latest travellers among the Fangs, the remote Masai, and other scarcely 'contaminated' races.*

If we can raise, at least, a case for consideration in favour of this non-utilitarian belief in a deity not approached with prayer or sacrifice, we also raise a presumption against the theory that gods were invented, in the despair of magic, as powers out of whom something useful could be got: powers with good things in their gift, things which men were ceasing to believe that they could obtain by their own magical machinery. The strong primal gods, unvexed by prayer, were not invented as recipients of prayer.

To ignore this chapter of early religion, to dismiss it as a tissue of borrowed ideas — though its existence is attested by the first Europeans on the spot, and its originality is vouched for by the very absence of prayer, and by observers like Mr. A. W. Howitt, Miss Kingsley, and Sir A. B. Ellis,[17] who proposed, but withdrew, a theory of 'loan-gods' — is not scientific.

My own early readings in early religion did not bring me acquainted [sic] with this chapter in the book of beliefs. When I first noticed an example of it, in the reports of the Benedictine Mission at Nursia, in Australia, I conceived, that some mistake had been made in 1845, by the missionary who sent in the report.[†][18] But later, when I began to notice the coincidence of testimony from many quarters, in many ages, then I could not conceal from myself that this chapter must be read. It is in conflict with our prevalent theories of the development of gods out of worshipped ancestral spirits: for the maker of things, not approached in prayer as a rule, is said to exist where ancestral spirits are not reported to be worshipped. But science (in other fields) specially studies exceptional cases, and contradictory instances, and all that seems out of accord with her theory. In this case science has glanced at what goes contrary to her theory, and has explained it by bias in the reporters, by error in the reporters, and by the theory of borrowing. But such coincidence in misreporting is a dangerous thing for anthropology to admit, as it damages her evidence in general. Again, the theory of borrowing seems to be contradicted by the early dates of many reports, made prior to the arrival of missionaries, and by the secrecy in which the beliefs are often veiled by the savages; as also by the absence of prayer to the most potent being.

We are all naturally apt to insist on and be prepossessed in favour of an idea which has come to ourselves unexpectedly, and has appeared to be corroborated by wider research, and, perhaps, above all, which runs contrary to the current of scientific opinion. We make a pet of the relatively new idea; let it be the origin of mythology in 'a disease of language;'[19] or the vast religious importance of totems; or our theory of the origin of totemism; or the tremendous part played in religion by gods of plants. We insist on the idea too exclusively; we find it where it is not — in fact, we are very human,

* *Journal of Anthropological Institute*, Oct.–Dec. 1900 and N.S. II., Nos. 1, 2, p. 85.

† Max Müller, *Hibbert Lectures*, p. 16.

very unscientific, very apt to become one-idea'd. It is even more natural that we should be regarded in this light by our brethren (*est-il embêtant avec son Etre Suprême!*),[20] whose own systems will be imperilled if our favourite idea can be established.

I risk this interpretation when I keep maintaining — what? — that the chapter of otiose or unworshipped superior beings in the 'Early History of Religion' deserves perusal. Not to cut its pages, to go on making systems as if it did not exist, is, I venture to think, less than scientific, and borders on the superstitious. For to build and defend a theory, without looking closely to whatever may imperil it, is precisely the fault of the superstitious Khond, who used to manure his field with a thumb, or a collop from the flank of a human victim, and did not try sowing a field without a collop of man's flesh, to see what the comparative crops would be. Or science of this kind is like Don Quixote, who, having cleft his helmet with one experimental sword-stroke, repaired it, but did not test it again.[21]

Like other martyrs of science, I must expect to be thought importunate, tedious, a fellow of one idea, and that idea wrong. To resent this would show great want of humour, and a plentiful lack of knowledge of human nature. Meanwhile, I am about to permit myself to criticise some recent hypotheses in the field of religious origins, in the interests of anthropology, not of orthodoxy.

'First-fruits and Taboos',
Magic and Religion
(Longmans, Green and Co., 1901)

Taboo is one of the few savage words which have struck root in England. Introduced from New Zealand (*tapu*) and other Polynesian islands, it is used in English to denote a prohibition. This, that, or the other thing, or person, or book is 'tabooed.' Many of the Ten Commandments are, in this sense, taboos. But, in anthropological language, 'taboo' generally denotes something more than a prohibition. It commonly means a prohibition for which, to the civilised mind, there is no very obvious meaning. In this way the prohibitive Commandments are not precisely taboos; it is pretty obvious why we ought not to steal or kill, though the *raison d'être* of the Seventh Commandment is obscure to some advanced intelligences.[1] But the reasons why a Sinclair must not cross the Ord on a certain 'lawful day,' or why on another 'lawful day' the fishermen of St. Andrews might not go a-fishing, resemble many savage taboos in the lack of a manifest reason why.[2] Secondly, the infraction of the savage taboo generally, unlike that of the decalogue,[3] carries its own punishment. Forbidden food is poison, tabooed land is dangerous to tread upon, to handle tabooed property may mean death; nobody knows what awful cosmic catastrophe might occur if a tabooed woman saw the sun; many words and names are taboo, and no luck will come of using them – for instance, you must not name 'salmon,' 'pigs,' or the minister when out fishing in some parts of Scotland.

In many cases the reason of this or that taboo is easily discovered. A day is unlucky because all the fishers, as at St. Andrews, were lost on that day in a past century through a storm; or the Sinclairs on another day were cut off in an expedition. Most of us have our lucky or unlucky days, clothes, and other vanities. Again, things are taboo for some reason in that kind of faith which holds that things connected in the association of ideas are mystically connected in fact. You must not mention salmon, lest they hear you and escape; or tin in Malay tin mining, lest the tin should literally 'make itself scarce.' You may not name the fairies, a jealous folk. Therefore you say 'the people of peace,' and so on. But many other taboos have good practical reasons. If women, among ourselves, were tabooed from salmon-fishing, eating oysters, or entering smoking-rooms (all of which things are greatly to be desired), the reason would be the convenience of the men, who wish a sanctuary or asylum in the smoking-room, and want to keep oysters and fishing to themselves. It is pretty plain why the sight of the royal treasury is tabooed to a West African king: to speak colloquially, if admitted to see the hoards he 'would blue the lot.' A taboo often protects by a supernatural sanction the property and persons of the privileged classes. If the umbrella of a bishop or a baronet were taboo, it would not be taken away from the club by accident.

This simple explanation covers the case of many taboos.

Brother and sister may scarcely ever see each other, still less speak to or name each other, where the law against brother and sister marriage or amour is the one most definite law of the community. 'It is not, therefore, surprising,' says Mr. Jevons, 'that the earlier students of the custom' (of taboo) 'regarded it as an artificial invention, a piece of statecraft, cunningly devised in the interests of the nobility and the priests. This view is, however, now generally abandoned,' because taboo 'is most at home in communities which have no state organisation, and flourishes where there are no priests or no priesthood. Above all the belief is not artificial and imposed, but spontaneous and natural.'* [4]

I hesitate about this theory. Taboo can hardly flourish more than it does in Polynesia and West Africa, where there are kings and priests. Moreover, though there are human societies without kings or priests (as in Australia), there are no societies in which artificial rules are not propagated, instituted, and enforced by the adult males meeting in councils. The Arunta of Central Australia are, of course, far from 'primitive.' They have institutions, cere-monies, weapons, rules, and a complete system of philosophy, which must have needed unknown ages to develop. They have local head-men, or Alatunjas, whose office passes always in the male line: from father to son, if the son be of age to succeed, or, if he is not, to the brother, on whose death it reverts to the son. An Alatunja dying without a son nominates a brother or nephew to succeed him. Messrs. Spencer and Gillen know no equivalent to this law among other Australian tribes, and it indicates, among the so-called 'primitive' Arunta, a marked advance beyond other tribes in social evolution. The Alatunja is hereditary Convener of Council, and if an able man has considerable power. He is guardian of the Sacra of the group, determines the date of the cessation of close-time for certain sorts of game,

---

★   *Introduction to the History of Religion*, p. 82.

the date of the magical ceremonies for fostering the game or edible plants, and directs the ceremonies. In the councils called by the Alatunja it appears that changes in stereotyped custom may be introduced. Men learned in the customs and skilled in magic 'settle everything.' Definite proof of fundamental innovations thus introduced Messrs. Spencer and Gillen do not possess; but tradition indicates alterations of custom, and it is quite possible that a strong Alatunja, well backed, might bring in even a radical reform.* There are also recognised grades of skill among the medicine-men and the dealers with spirits, who must have their own share of social influence.[5]

In brief, though without priests or kings these backward tribes have councils, and conveners, and directors whose office is hereditary in the male line. These persons, through unknown ages, have moulded customs and taboos, which are just as much sanctioned by tradition and authority, just as little 'spontaneous and universal,' as if kings and priests had invented them for purposes of statecraft. Mr. Jevons next argues that taboo 'cannot have been derived from experience. It is prior to and even contradictory of experience. In fine, it is an inherent tendency of the human mind.'[6] In the same way Gibbon's ancestor, Blue Gown herald,[7] when among North American Indians, declared that heraldry is an inherent tendency of the human mind, an innate idea.

An opinion is not necessarily erroneous because it is obsolete, nor a view wrong because 'it is generally abandoned.' I am here supporting the 'generally abandoned' hypothesis that many taboos, at least, are artificial and imposed, against Mr. Jevons's idea that the taboo, like armorial bearings, results from 'an inherent tendency of the human mind' 'prior to and even contradictory of experience.'† That 'a new-born baby is dangerous,' or that 'the water in which a holy person has washed is dangerous,' my private experience does not tell me; in fact, I never made either experiment: never tubbed in the water previously used by a bishop. But I am prepared to admit that neither babies nor bishops are proved by our experience to be dangerous. That is not the question. The savage argued, not from unbiassed and impartial scientific experiment, but from *fancied* experience. Thus Mr. Jevons mentions a Maori who died after finding out that he had eaten, unawares, the remains of the luncheon of a holy person, a chief.[8] There was experience produced by suggestion. The suggestion was suggested in the interests of holy chiefs; they were 'tabooed an inch thick,' as Mr. Manning writes.[9] As to the baby, the Dyaks, as in our own fairy belief, hold that 'new-born children are the especial prey of evil spirits,' just as corpses were in Scotland, where, if the door was left ajar, the corpse sat up, and mopped and mowed. If the watchers left it, and dined in the 'but,' an awful *vacarme* arose in the 'ben.' The minister entered, stilled the tumult, asked for the

---

*   Spencer and Gillen, pp. 10–16.

†   Jevons, p. 85.

tongs, and came back holding in the tongs *a bloody glove*! This he dropped into the fire.

This kind of thing is contradictory to the experience of Mr. Jevons, but not to the *fancied* experience of Dyaks, Scots, and other races. Opinion therefore makes taboos in accordance with experience, or what is believed to be experience, and the belief is fortified by suggestion, which produces death or disease when the taboo is broken. On the analogy of infectious diseases, the mischief of the tabooed thing is held to be contagious.

Thus I cannot hold with Mr. Jevons that the human mind is provided with an *a priori* categorical imperative 'that there are some things which must not be done,' 'a feeling' 'independent of sense experience.'* If the choice of what things are 'not to be done' seems to us 'irrational' that is merely because our reason is more enlightened than that of the savage. He prohibited just such things as his philosophy, and what he believed to be his experience, showed him to be dangerous for obscure reasons. Any fool could see that it was dangerous to eat poison berries or frolic with a bear. But it took reflection to discover that a baby or a corpse was dangerous by reason of evil spirits, *Iruntarinia*, whom the *Alkna Buma*, or clairvoyant, could see, and describe, though Mr. Jevons and I could not discern them.† These Iruntarinia notoriously carry off women, and probably, like the fairies, have their best chance in the hour of child-birth: at all events, the fairies have.‡ The belief is socially useful: it prevents young Arunta women from wandering off alone, and philandering out of bounds.

Thus these taboos are sanctioned by the tribal counsellors as the results of experience, not their own perhaps, but that of the *Alkna Buma*, or clairvoyant, or 'sensitive,' or 'medium,' or habitually hallucinated person. Other taboos, as to women, are imposed for very good reasons, though not for the reasons alleged, and broken taboos are not (in actual ordinary experience) attended by the penalties which, however, suggestion may produce.

Taboo, then, is not imposed irrationally, nor in deference to 'an inherent tendency of the human mind' (that Mrs. Harris of philosophy),[10] but for a very good reason, as savage reasoning goes, and in accordance with what is believed to be experience, and, by dint of suggestion, really does become experience.

It was 'irrational' in Dr. Johnson to touch certain posts, and avoid certain stones, and enter a door twice, if he first entered it with the wrong foot. All my life I have had similar private taboos, though nobody knows better that they are nonsense. But some solitary experience in childhood probably suggested a relation of cause and effect, where there was only a fortuitous

---

*   Jevons, pp. 85–87.

†   Spencer and Gillen, pp. 15, 515.

‡   Ibid, p. 517.

sequence of antecedent and consequent, and so Dr. Johnson and I (though not so conspicuously as the Doctor) imposed taboos on ourselves in deference to (fancied) experience.[11] Early man has acted in the same way on a large scale, obeying no categorical a priori imperative, but merely acting on his philosophy and experience which is real to him, though not to civilised men. They usually do not understand it, but educated persons with a survival of savagery in their mental constitutions find the affair intelligible.

But the reason in actual practical experience for some taboos must be plain to the most civilised minds, except those of Radical voters for the Border Boroughs.[12] Man, in the hunter stage, *must* have game laws and a close-time for edible animals and plants. The Border Radical will not permit a close-time for trout, preferring to destroy them, and with them their offspring, when gravid and unfit for human food, or before they recover condition.

The 'primitive' Arunta are not so irrational, and have a close-time, protected by taboo, or, at least, by ceremonies of a nature more or less magical. In these ceremonies of a people not pastoral or agricultural, we seem to see the germs of the offerings of first-fruits to gods or spirits, though the Australian produce is offered neither to spirits nor to gods. These tribes recognise a great spirit, indeed, Twanyirika, but that he plays any other part in religion or society than presiding over the tribal mysteries we have at present no evidence to prove. Similar figures, associated with the mysteries, are, in other parts of Australia, provided with an ample mythology, and are subject to a being more august and remote. But either the Arunta are advanced thinkers who have passed beyond such ideas, or they have not yet attained to them, or our witnesses are uninformed on the subject.* In any case, the first-fruits of the game, grubs, and plants of the Arunta are not offered to Twanyirika, or to the minor sprites, *Iruntarinia*.

The ceremonies, partly intended to make the creatures used for food prolific, and partly, I think, to indicate that the close-time is over and that the creatures may be taken and eaten, are called Intichiuma. On the mummeries expected to make animals and plants plentiful we need not dwell. In each case the men who belong to the totem of the beast, grub, or plant perform the ceremonies. There is believed to be a close and essential connection between a man of the kangaroo totem and all kangaroos, between a man of the grub totem and all grubs, so each totem group does the magic to propagate its ally among beasts or plants. How these ideas arose we do not know. But if a local group was originally called kangaroos or grubs (and some name it must have), the association of names would inevitably lead, by association of ideas, to the notion that a mysterious connection existed between the men of a totem name and the plant, animal, or

---

*   Spencer and Gillen, pp. 222, 246.

what not which gave the name. These men, therefore, would work the magic for propagating their kindred in the animal and vegetable world. But the existence of this connection would also suggest that, in common decency, a man should not kill and eat his animal or vegetable relations. In most parts of the world he abstains from this uncousinly behaviour: among the Arunta he may eat sparingly of his totem, and must do so at the end of the close-time or beginning of the season.

He thus, as a near relation of the actual kangaroos or grubs, declares the season open, and gives his neighbours of other totems a lead. Now they may begin to eat grubs or kangaroos; the taboo is off. Thus, in 1745, Gask ta-booed the corn of his tenants;[13] they must not reap it, because they refused 'to rise and follow Charlie.' Prince Charles, hearing of this, cut a few ears with his claymore, thus removing the taboo. In the same way the grub or kangaroo men publicly eat a little of their own totem, after which the tribesmen and other totems may fall to and devour. When the grub or whatever it is becomes plentiful, after the magic doings for its propagation, it is collected and placed before some members of the grub totem. The *Alatunja*, or convener, grinds up some of the grub, he and his fellow to-temists eat a little, and hand the mass back to the members of other totems. They eat a little of their own totem, partly, Messrs. Spencer and Gillen say, to strengthen their mystic connection with the creature.[14] This, in a way, is a 'sacramental' idea, though no religious regard is paid to the plants and animals. But the men also partake, to remove the taboo, and to let the rest of the community gorge themselves legally.*

The rite has thus a practical purpose. The grubs or other creatures are not prematurely destroyed, like trout on the Border.

[...]

After writing this paper, I found that Mr. Robert Louis Stevenson's experience of *tapu*, in the Pacific, led him to form the same opinions as are here expressed. 'The devil-fish, it seems, were growing scarce upon the reef; it was judged fit to interpose what we should call a close season ... a tapu had to be declared.' The tapus described 'are for thoroughly sensible ends.' There are tapus which, to us, appear absurd, 'but the tapu is more often the instrument of wise and needful restrictions.'†[15]

---

* The Arunta eating of the totem, at the magic ceremony, is not religious. Mr. Jevons, however, adduces it as proof of 'the existence of the totem-sacrament,' surviving 'in an etiolated form.' But what proof have we that the totems were once 'totem gods,' or in any way divine, among the Arunta? Jevons, 'The Science of Religion,' *International Monthly*, p. 489, April 1901.

† *In the South Seas*, pp. 47–50.

These taboos are imposed from above, by Government. In other cases, where the taboo expresses an inference from savage superstition (say that a baby or a corpse is dangerous), the taboo is not imposed except by public opinion. That opinion is sanctioned (as in the case of first-fruits) by the action of the Alatunja, or headman: in more advanced societies, by the king. In many cases, taboos are imposed on the king himself by the priestly colleges. But the greatest authority is tradition, resting on fancied experience.

'Australian Problems',
Anthropological Essays Presented to Edward Burnett Tylor in Honour of his 75th Birthday

(Oxford: Clarendon, 1907), pp. 203–18

[...]

When heaven, to punish the sins of the learned, permitted Messrs. Spencer and Gillen[1] to discover and describe the institutions of the Arunta nation, it was found that these tribes practised an unheard-of kind of totemism. The totem was not hereditary, the totem-set of people in each case was not exogamous; a man who was a Dog might marry a woman who was a Dog, and their children might be Rat, Cat, and Frog.

Instantly some of the learned (A) averred that this unheard-of form of totemism was the oldest extant and the nearest to the primitive model; while others (B) declared that the Arunta totemism was a decadent 'sport', and showed how it arose, or might have arisen, out of exogamous totemism and hereditary totems. I was of the second party, the B division, from the first.

The A division, who regarded Arunta totemism as the earliest, naturally tried to show that, in other matters, the Arunta nation was the most primitive. The Arunta wore no clothes, and they were ignorant of the fact that sexual connexions are the cause of conception and birth – what could be more primitive? They also practised co-operative totemic magic; and co-operation, duly organized, may be more primitive than individual effort; the division of labour being also primitive.

To this the opposite faction (B) replied that the Arunta (1) exhibited confessedly the most complex, and, as had hitherto been agreed, the latest form of matrimonial rules, the 'eight-class system'. Next (2), they reckon descent and transmit hereditable property in the male line, and hitherto we had unanimously supposed reckoning in the female line to be the earlier. Next (3), they had lost the names of their primary exogamous divisions (phratries), and, hitherto, these names had been looked on as very early. Next

(4), they practised the bloody rites of initiation which Mr. Spencer thinks posterior in evolution to the south-eastern dentistry. (5) The Arunta have no 'All Father', and while the A disputants thought this a proof of primitiveness, the B party held that the animistic philosophy of the Arunta had left no logical *raison d'etre* for a creative 'All Father'. (6) The B faction held that co-operation and division of labour, each totem-set doing magic for its own totem, were not primitive, but much the reverse.

The A party admitted the social advance of the Arunta to the eight-class system. Advance, however, is not uniform; a tribe might reach the eight-class system, but be primitive in other respects. As to Arunta male descent (hitherto looked on as a proof of advance), the A party suggested that one tribe might begin with male descent, and another with female descent, though we have irrefutable proof that, in other northern tribes of the eight-class system, female descent has left indelible traces, and no proof that male descent has ever become female descent.

The Arunta philosophy of reincarnated spirits, entertained, with modifications, by tribes of female descent near Lake Eyre, and by the northern tribes, with male descent, is entirely animistic. Among the Arunta, at the beginning of things, rudimentary animated bulks of lacustrine environment were converted by two beings named 'Self-existing' or 'Made out of Nothing' (Ungambikula) into animal forms of known species. One of these beings might be styled either 'a man-kangaroo' or 'a kangaroo-man'. They went about playing their pranks and founding rites and institutions, carrying decorated stone *plaques*, called *churinga*, still used by the Arunta. Their bodies died, but their immortal part haunted the stone *churinga*. These immortal spirits, the Arunta say, cause conception by entering into women who pass the places where the *churinga* were deposited. Thus every Arunta has been, in the spirit, from the beginning, and will endlessly be reincarnated. Consequently sexual connexion does not cause conception and birth.[*][2] How could it? A baby is to the Arunta only a being who has been from the beginning – now in the flesh, and now out of it – and who will so continue to be. Such a spiritual entity cannot conceivably owe his existence to gross material amours. The thing, to an Arunta philosopher, is unthinkable. For this philosophic reason, says party B, the Arunta ignore procreation. A man cannot beget an everlasting spirit. 'No,' says party A; 'the Arunta are too primitive to understand physical processes which are sufficiently understood by other savages.'

For example, certain tribes of south-eastern Australia, including some who reckon descent in the female line, hold that 'children originate solely from the male parent, and only owe their infantine nurture to their mother'. 'A woman is only a nurse who takes care of a man's children for him.'[†][3]

---

[*]   Spencer and Gillen, *Central Tribes*, p. 265.

[†]   Howitt, *J.A.I.*, 1882, p. 502; *N.T.S.E.A.*, pp. 283–4.

But matrimonial life, among the Arunta, is supposed, at most, only to prepare a woman for the entrance of a spirit which has existed from the beginning, the *Alcheringa*. Therefore the Arunta are in pristine ignorance of physiology.

I have argued, often and in many places, that the Arunta nescience of the part of the male in procreation need not be a proof of absolute ignorant 'primitiveness', but merely the logical result of their animistic philosophy. Their psychology has clouded their physiology. Every one of them, according to their elaborate philosophy (which surely no mortal can think 'primitive'), has existed since the beginning and can never cease to exist.

No efforts of men and women can produce a spirit which, they say, is pre-existent and of endless existence. The logical black fellow, granting his premises, can come to no other conclusion than that human beings – incarnate spirits – do not beget pre-existing spirits. Their speculations deal with the spirit, *forma formans*,[4] neglecting to account for the body of flesh. There is nothing 'primitive' in all this; there is only logic working on the basis of animism, or so it seems to me.

As far as I am aware, nobody except M. van Gennep, who believes in Arunta 'primitiveness' has tried to meet my argument, or even made it the subject of an allusion.[*] [5] But I have seen many grateful references to Dr. Roth's discovery of denial of human procreation by other tribes, a discovery set forth in his Bulletins on *North Queensland Ethnography* (No. 5, 1903). In most references to Dr. Roth which I have seen, the details of his discoveries were not fully discussed. I therefore discuss them; they show that an animistic philosophy, differing in many points from that of the Arunta, colours and even causes the Northern Queensland denial of procreation. When North Queensland peoples say that the lower animals have no spirits or souls, and that *they* may be and are the result of procreation; whereas mankind, having spirits, are not and cannot be procreated, but are made or created, then we have to confess that, in the case of mankind, the North Queensland psychology has clouded the Queensland physiology. The North Queensland tribes know the method of the procreation of the lower animals. What they deny is that physical procreative processes can produce man, who has a soul, who is a living spirit. I have been unaware that the Queensland blacks draw this essential and illuminating distinction between man and beast, because, till lately, I had never been able to procure Dr. Roth's *Bulletin* No. 5.

Dr. Roth says, 'Animals and plants are not regarded as having any "Koi" – spirit or soul.'[†] 'Although sexual connection as a cause of conception is

---

[*] M. van Gennep, indeed, urges that the spirits of the Alcheringa folk have not existed from the beginning. They are as old as the beginning, for the Alcheringa is the beginning. (*Mythes et Légendes d'Australie*, p. lxv, note 3.)

[†] *Bulletin* No. 5, pp. 17, § 64.

not recognized among the Tully River blacks so far as they themselves are concerned, it is admitted as true for all animals; indeed this idea confirms them in their belief of superiority over the brute creation.' Connexion can make a brute; 'to make a *man's* beyond its might,' as Burns says, for man is a living spirit.*

These passages prove, I hold, beyond possibility of doubt, that the animistic or spiritual philosophy of these blacks, and nothing else, causes them to deny that sexual connexion is the agency in the making of man. They have to invent other ways.

[...]

This philosophy is the reverse of 'primitive'; it does not indicate pristine ignorance, but the logical invention of the spiritualist philosopher. It took him long, doubtless, to evolve the idea of spirit from his experiences of dreams, trances, coincidental death-wraiths, hallucinatory phantasms of the dead, crystal-gazing, *vue à distance*, or clairvoyance, and hypnotism. Man was not 'primitive' when he had amassed and speculated on all these experiences, and had recognized himself as a spiritual being, encased in clay. He was not primitive when he patiently and logically worked out his complex animistic philosophies, varying in different tribes. Some south-eastern tribes have not worked out their psychology to its necessary conclusions; they have discovered the physical causes of procreation, and do not trouble to inquire, 'Whence and how comes the informing spirit?' The northern nations, on the other hand, have resolutely pushed their animism to its necessary conclusion, and deny that material processes produce the spirit of man. [...]

---

* *Bulletin* No. 5, pp. 22, § 81.

5
ANTHROPOLOGY
AND
PSYCHICAL RESEARCH

There are many examples of Lang's keenness to assert that psychical research and anthropology were part of the same investigative impulse and
needed to share methods and evidence. However, as Lang laments in his
preface to the second edition of *The Making of Religion* (London: Longmans,
Green and Co.,1900), it was a struggle convincing either psychical researchers or anthropologists of this. Anthropologists were on the whole dismissive
of contemporary accounts of such experiences as evidence, and psychical
researchers doubted the evidential value of historical accounts. Nevertheless,
across a wide selection of his work – from his serious anthropology through
to more popular works such as *Cock Lane and Common Sense* (London:
Longman's, Green and Co.,1894) and again and again in his journalism –
Lang makes the case for the relation between the two. The selections here
cover the range of places in which Lang made this argument.

In 'The Comparative Study of Ghost Stories' we see Lang constructing
a position distinct from, and challenging to, not only anthropologists and
psychical researchers, but also folklorists. Here stories, rather than just being
examples of Tylor's 'survivals', are valued for their links to experience and
practice, for what can they tell us about the material reality of cultures
widely dispersed historically and temporally. Here and in the following
piece, 'Superstition and Fact', we can see Lang developing ideas on both
supernatural phenomenon and that relation to anthropology that will finally
lead to the position set out in *The Making of Religion*.

The 'Preface' to *Cock Lane and Common Sense* is from the second edition,
published in 1895, in which Lang responds to critical responses to the first
edition from both sides, from anthropology and from psychical research.
His sense of being between two camps which want little to do with each
other is clear here, as it is in the later 'Preface' to the second (1900) edition
of *The Making of Religion*. As is often the case in Lang's work, here he explicitly eschews the idea of constructing theories based on the evidence he
presents. The subsequent chapters of *Cock Lane and Common Sense* pile up
the evidence for universal experience of certain supernatural phenomena,
but Lang does not account for this, rather he just asserts it as evidence, and
that it needs to be noted by both anthropologists and psychical researchers.

In 'Anthropology and Religion' II, from the second edition of *The
Making of Religion*, Lang sets out the case he will make in the first half of
that book for the connections between accounts of supernatural events
across time and space. Crucially, he suggests that, as anthropology was once
seen as a pseudo-science but has recently been accepted into the institutions
of science, so psychical research will follow the same trajectory.

'The Comparative Study
of Ghost Stories',
Nineteenth Century 17

(April 1885), pp. 623–32

W e seem to need a name for a new branch of the science of Man, the Comparative Study of Ghost Stories. Neither sciology, from σκιά, nor idolology, from εἴδωλον,[1] appears a very convenient term, and as the science is yet in its infancy, perhaps it may go unnamed, for the time, like a colt before it has won its maiden race. But, though nameless, the researches which I wish to introduce are by no means lacking in curious interest. It may be objected that the comparative study of ghost stories is already well known, and practised by two very different sets of inquirers, anthropologists and the Society for Psychical Research; but neither Mr. Tylor and Mr. Herbert Spencer nor 'those about' Mr. Gurney and Mr. Myers work, as it seems to me, exactly on the topics and in the manner which I wish to indicate. Mr. Herbert Spencer, as we all know, traces religion to the belief in and worship of the ghosts of ancestors. Mr. Tylor, again, has learnedly examined the probable origin of the belief in ghosts, deriving that belief from the phenomena of dreams, of fainting, of shadows, of visions induced by hunger or by narcotics, and of death.[2] To state Mr. Tylor's theory briefly, and by way of an example, men reasoned themselves into a theory of ghosts after the manner of Achilles in the *Iliad*, (xxiii.70–110). The unburied Patroclus appeared to his friend in a dream, and passed away, 'And Achilles sprang up marvelling, and smote his hands together, and spake a word of woe: "Ay me, there remaineth then even in the house of Hades a spirit and phantom of the dead, albeit the life be not anywise therein; for all night long hath the spirit of hapless Patroclus stood over me, wailing and making moan, and charged me everything that I should do, and wondrous like his living self it seemed."'[3]

Here we find Achilles in the moment of inferring from his dream the actual existence of a spirit surviving the death of the body. No doubt a belief in ghosts might well have been developed by early thinkers, as Mr. Tylor holds, out of arguments like these of Achilles. It is certain, too, that many of the social and religious institutions of savages (if writers in the English language are to be allowed the use of that word) have been based on the opinion that the spirits of the dead are still active among the living. All this branch of the subject has been exhaustively treated by Mr. Tylor in his *Primitive Culture*. But I do not observe that Mr. Tylor has paid very much attention to what we may call the actual ghost stories of savages — that is, the more or less well-authenticated cases in which savages have seen the ordinary ghost of modern society. Here, for the purposes of clearness, I will discriminate certain kinds of ghost stories, all of them current among races as low as the Australians, and lower than the Fijians, all of them current, too, in contemporary European civilisation. First, let us place the well-known savage belief that the spirits of the dead reappear in the form of the lower animals, often of that animal which is the totem or ancestral friend and guardian of the kinship. This kind of ghost story one seldom or never hears in drawing-rooms, but it is the prevalent and fashionable kind among the peasantry, for example, in Shropshire. In the second class, we may reckon the more or less professional ghosts that appear obedient to the medium's or conjurer's command at *séances*. These spirits, which come 'when you do call them,' behave in much the same manner, and perform the same sorts of antics or miracles, in Australian *gunyehs*, in Maori *pahs*, and at the exhibition of Mr. Sludge, or of the esoteric Buddhists.[4] Thirdly, we arrange the non-professional ghost, which does not come at the magician's call, but appears unexpected, and apparently irresponsible. This sort also haunts houses and forests; other members of the species manifest themselves at the moment of death, or become visible for the purpose of warning friends of their own approaching decease. Such phenomena as a sudden flash of supernatural light, or the presence of a white bird, or other ghostly creatures prophesying death, may perhaps be allotted to this class of apparitions.

These things are as well known to contemporary savages as they were to the classical people of Lucian's day, or as they are, doubtless, to the secretaries of the Society for Psychical Research.[5] Once more, we ought to notice the 'well-authenticated' modern ghost story, which on examination proves to be really a parallel to the William Tell myth,[6] and to recur in many ages, always attached to different names, and provided with fresh properties. To look into these ghost stories cannot be wholly idle. Apparently there is either some internal groundwork of fact at the bottom of a belief which savages share with Fellows of the Royal Society, or liability to certain recurring hallucinations must be inherited by civilised man from his untutored ancestors, or the mythopoeic faculty, to use no harder term, is common to all stages of culture. As to habits of hasty inference and false reasoning, these, of course, were bequeathed to us by our pre-scientific parents, and these, with our own vain hopes and foolish fears, afford the stuff for most ghosts and ghost stories. The whole topic, in the meanwhile, has only been touched at either end, so to speak. The anthropologists have established their own theory of the origin of a belief in ghosts, without asking whether the actual appearance of apparitions may not have helped to start or confirm that belief. The friends of psychical research have collected modern stories of the actual appearance of apparitions without paying much attention, as far as I am aware, to their parallels among the most backward races, or to their mediaeval and classical variants.

[…]

The second class of ghost stories, tales of what we may call 'professional' spirits that come and go at the sorcerer's command, need not detain us long. This branch of the subject has been examined by the anthropologists. Mr. Tylor has provided many examples of the savage *séance*, the Shaman or medicine man bound and tied in a darkened room, and then released by the spirits whose voices are heard chattering around him. 'Suppose a wild North American Indian looking on at a spirit *séance* in London. As to the presence of disembodied spirits manifesting themselves by raps, noises, voices, and other physical actions, the savage would be perfectly at home in the proceedings, for such things are part and parcel of his recognised system of nature.'[7] I doubt if any modern medium could quite rival the following feat of an Australian Birraark or sorcerer, as vouched for by one of the Tatungolung tribe. 'The fires were allowed to go down,' the Birraark began his invocation. At intervals he uttered the cry, *Coo'ee!* 'At length a distant reply was heard, and shortly afterwards the sound as of persons jumping on the ground in succession. This was supposed to be the spirit Baukan followed by the ghosts. A voice was then heard in the gloom asking in a strange intonation, "What is wanted?" Questions were put by the Birraark, and replies given. At the termination of the *séance*, the spirit voices said, "We are going." Finally the Birraark was found in the *top of an almost inaccessible tree, apparently asleep*. It was alleged that the ghosts had transported him there at their departure.'*[8] If as good a *séance* could be given in Hyde Park, and if Mr. Sludge could be found at the close in the top of one of the Scotch pines in Kensington Gardens, we might admit that the civilised is on a level with savage spiritualism. Yet even this *séance* was very much less impressive than what the author of Old New Zealand witnessed in a Maori pah, when the spirit of a dead native friend of his own was present and 'manifested' rarely.[9]

The curious coincidences between savage and civilised 'spiritualism' have still to be explained. Mr. Tylor says that 'the ethnographic view' finds

---

★   *Kamilaroi and Kurnai*, p. 254.

'modern spiritualism to be in great measure a direct revival from the regions of savage philosophy and peasant folklore.'[10] But in a really comparative study of the topic, this theory would need to be proved by historical facts. Let us grant that Eskimo and Australian spiritualism are a savage imposture. Let us grant that peasants, little advanced from the savage intellectual condition, retained a good deal of savage spiritualism. To complete the proof it would be necessary to adduce many examples of peasant *séances*, to show that these were nearly identical with savage *séances*, and then to demonstrate that the introducers of the civilised modern *séance* had been in touch with the savage or peasant performances. For the better explanation of the facts, the Psychical Society might send missionaries to investigate and test the exhibitions of Australian Birraarks, and Maori Tohungas, and Eskimo Angekoks. Mr. Im Thurn, in Guiana, has made experiments in Peayism, or local magic, but felt no more than a drowsy mesmeric sensation, and a headache, after the treatment. While those things are neglected, psychical research is remiss in attention to her elevating task.

In the third class of ghosts we propose to place those which are independent of the invocations of the sorcerer, which come and go, or stay, at their own will. As to 'haunted houses,' savages, who have no houses, are naturally not much troubled by them. It is easy to leave one *gungeh* or bark shelter for another; and this is generally done after a death among the Australians. Races with more permanent habitations have other ways of exorcising the haunters — by feeding the ghosts, for example, at their graves, so that they are comfortable there, and do not wish to emerge.

[...]

The ghosts which at present excite most interest are ghosts beheld at the moment of their owner's decease by persons at a distance from the scene of death. Thus Baronius relates how 'that eximious Platonist, Marsilius Ficinus,' appeared at the hour of his death on a white horse to Michael Mercatus, and rode away, crying 'Michael, Michael, vera, vera sunt illa,' that is, the doctrine of a future life is true.[11] Lord Brougham[12] was similarly favoured. Among savages I have not encountered more than one example, and that rather sketchy, of a warning conveyed to a man by a ghost as to the death of a friend. The tale is in FitzRoy's[13] *Voyage of the 'Adventurer' and the 'Beagle'* (ii. 118). Jemmy Button was a young Fuegian whom his uncle had sold to the 'Beagle' for a few buttons.

> While at sea, on board the 'Beagle' about the middle of the year 1843, he said one morning to Mr. Byno, that in the night some man came to the side of his hammock, and whispered in his ear that his father was dead. Mr. Byno tried to laugh him out of the idea, but ineffectually. He fully believed that such was the case, and maintained his opinion up to the time of finding his relations in Beagle Channel, when, I regret to say, he found that his father had died some months previously.[14]

Another kind of ghost, again, that of a dead relative who comes to warn a man of his own approaching decease, appears to be quite common among savages. In his interesting account of the Kurnai, an Australian tribe, Mr. Howitt writes: —

> Mr. C. J. Du Vé, a gentleman of much experience with the Aborigines, tells me that, in the year 1860, a Maneroo black fellow died while with him. The day before he died, having been ill for some time, he said that, in the night, his father, his father's friend, and a female spirit he could not recognise, had come to him, and said that he would die next day, and that they would wait for him.[15]

To this statement the Rev. Lorimer Fison appends a note which ought to interest psychical inquirers. 'I could give many similar instances which have come within my own knowledge among the Fijians, and, strange to say, the dying man, in all these cases, kept his appointment with the ghosts to the very day.'[16] A civilised example recorded by Henry More is printed in the *Remains* of the late Dr. Symonds. In that narrative a young lady was wakened by a bright light in her bedroom. Her dead mother appeared to her, exactly as the father of the Maneroo black fellow did, and warned her that she was to die on the following midnight. The girl made all her preparations, and, with Fijian punctuality, 'kept her appointment with the ghosts to the very day.'[17] The peculiarity of More's tale seems to be the brilliance of the light which attended the presence of the supernatural. This strange fire is widely diffused in folk-lore. If we look at the Eskimo we find them convinced that the Inue, or powerful spirits, 'generally have the appearance of a fire or bright light, and to see them is very dangerous...*partly as foreshadowing the death of a relation*.'[*18] In the story repeated by More, not a kinsman of the visionary, but the visionary herself was in danger. In the *Odyssey*, when Athene was mystically present as Odysseus and Telemachus were moving the weapons out of the hall (xix. 21-50), Telemachus exclaims, 'Father, surely a great marvel is this I behold! Meseemeth that the walls of the hall, and the fair spaces between the pillars, and the beams of pine, and the columns that run aloft are bright as it were with flaming fire. Verily some god is within of them that hold the wide heaven.' Odysseus answers, 'Lo, this is the wont of the gods that possess Olympus.'[19] Again, in Theocritus, when Hera sends the snakes to attack the infant Heracles, a mysterious flame shines forth, φάος δ' ἀνὰ οἶκον ἐτύχθη.[†] The same phenomenon occurs in the saga of Burnt Njal when Gunner sings within his tomb. Philosophers may dispute whether any objective fact lies at the bottom of this belief, or whether a savage superstition has survived into

---

[*] Rink, *Tales and Traditions of the Eskimo*, p. 43.

[†] 'And all the house showed clear as in the light of dawn.' – Theoc. xix. 30–40, ed. Ahrens.

Greek epic and idyll, and into modern ghost stories. Into Scotch legend, too, this faith in a mysterious and ominous fire found its way—

> Seemed all on fire that chapel proud,
> Where Roslin's chiefs uncoffined lie,
> Each baron, for a sable shroud,
> Sheathed in his iron panoply. [20]

Scott derives the idea from the tomb fires of the Sagas, but we have shown the wide diffusion of the belief.

[…]

Though this sketch of a new comparative science does not perhaps prove or disprove any psychical or mythological theory, it demonstrates that there is a good deal of human nature in man. From the Eskimo, Fuegians, Fijians, and Kurnai, to Homer, Henry More, Theocritus, and Lady Betty Cobb, we mortals are 'all in a tale,' and share coincident beliefs or delusions. What the value of the coincidence of testimony may be, how far it attests facts, how far it merely indicates the survival of savage conceptions, Mr. Tylor and Mr. Edmund Gurney may be left to decide. Readers of the *Philopseudes* of Lucian[21] will remember how the Samosatene settled the inquiries of the psychical researchers of his age, and in that dialogue there are abundant materials for the comparative student of ghost stories.

'Superstition and Fact',
Contemporary Review 64
(December 1893), pp. 882–92

A remark of M. Richet, the eminent French psychologist, may be said to strike the key-note of the following essay. Richet is arguing (in 1884) for the genuine character of 'Somnambulism' by which he means provoked somnambulism, hypnotic phenomena.[1] 'If the phenomena are simulated,' says M. Richet, 'then the skill, the perfection, the universality of the imposture, everywhere and always, constitute one of the most extraordinary phenomena in the records of science.'[2] This I chanced to read, after publishing an article on 'Comparative Psychical Research' in the *Contemporary* for September, 1893.[3] In that paper, having given a selection of reported 'spiritualistic phenomena,' from various ancient sources, including 'spirit-rapping' and a 'medium' of 1526, I argued, like M. Richet, that the universal similarity of the imposture, granting imposture, is a most curious phenomenon. But M. Richet was thinking of the ordinary and familiar features of hypnotism, which, as I understand, are now denied by no competent authority. The alleged occurrences which interest *my* inquiry are different from these, and include ghosts, physical movements of untouched objects, unexplained noises and disturbances, clairvoyance, the divining rod, crystal vision, and so forth.

The accounts of these have not been accepted by science, far from it; nor can one do otherwise than applaud science for being 'sober and distrustful.' However, M. Richet's contention applies to these outlying phenomena, ghosts, disturbances, clairvoyance, as much as to the accepted facts of hypnotism. The imposture in these affairs (if imposture there be, as a rule) is as uniform, and as widely diffused, as the supposed 'simulation' of hypnotic facts. Further, we must note that many of the contested and disdained phenomena notoriously accompany persons subject to trance, to convulsive movements, and other abnormal nervous conditions. This is said to be so at present, and can it be by accident that this was always said to be so in the past? We hear of clairvoyance, of physical movements of objects, of commands transferred and obeyed from a distance, of 'telepathic' hallucinations voluntarily produced, among the very people who display the ordinary and accepted phenomena of hypnotism. Now in old witch-trials, in old ghost and bogie stories, in the reports of anthropological observers among savages, we find the ordinary and accepted phenomena of hypnotism occurring among the witches, the 'possessed,' the ghost-seers, the savage medicine-men. They, too, are not only subject to convulsion and rigidity, and trance, but they are clairvoyant. They produce phantasms of themselves at a distance, their presence is attended by unexplained noises and physical movements of objects. Now there must be some cause for this remarkable coincidence — namely, the uniformity of modern and ancient reports of phenomena still unaccepted by science – always accompanying other phenomena which science, since Puységur, Braid, Esdaile, Charcot, and others, has been content to accept.[4] At the lowest there must be a traditional system of imposture, or a common persistent sympathy in hallucination.

[…]

The most popular superstition is, of course, the belief in ghosts. Hence Mr. Tylor derives, ultimately, the whole of religion. His theory is very well known. Thinking savages 'were deeply impressed by two groups of biological phenomena.' They asked, what makes the difference between a living body and a dead one? Again, what causes waking, sleep, trance, disease, death? Next, what are the human shapes that appear in dreams and visions? They concluded that life can go away, and leave a man insensible or dead, while a phantom of the living man can appear [in dreams, one presumes] to people at a distance from him.[5] The savage philosopher then mentally combines and identifies the life and the phantom. The result is, life is a soul, when at home, in the body; a ghost when abroad, out of the body. This wandering life is 'shadow,' or 'breath,' σκιά, πνεύμα, umbra, spiritus, anima. Having decided that shadows, dreams, trances, when reflected on, suggest the belief in wandering phantasms, separable selves, Mr. Tylor's duty is done. He gives abundant accounts of 'veridical hallucinations,' and of 'clairvoyance;' but he expressly does not ask, Are these tales true, and if so, what do they mean? Now it is evident that, if clairvoyance does occur, and if the phantasm of the clairvoyant is actually seen, in the place which he fancies that he visits, and if appearances of men at the hour of death are, verily, beheld at a distance, then the savage's philosophy had more to go upon than mere dreams, shadows, sleeping, waking, and the contemplation of death. He was really in touch with disputed, unaccepted phenomena, and these phenomena are of high importance. They would not, indeed, justify the savage theory that phantasm and life are identical, that life is soul at home and is ghost abroad. But, if accepted, they would demonstrate the existence of a new range of human faculties. These phenomena, the discarded – much more than sleep, dreams, drugs, and so forth, the accepted – would be the real basis of the savage theory of life, and death, and spirits. Take the Eskimo, and Pawnee, and Scandinavian superstition of a 'sending' — the sorcerer's power to project his volition, unaccompanied by a phantasm. If Jung Stilling, whom, Mr. Tylor cites, did not fable in his tales of 'sick persons who, longing to see absent friends, have fallen into a swoon, during which they appeared to the distant objects of their affection,' and, if any one of many such stories is true, then friendly 'sending' is possible. A French physician vouches for such 'sendings,' by a hospital nurse, as having been visible to himself.* [6] An instance given by St. Augustine is well known.†[7] About Catholic legends of 'bilocation' — the visible presence of a man at a distance from the point where he really is — Mr. Tylor says that these things 'fit perfectly in with the primitive animistic theory of apparitions.'[8] Probably they do, if the theory was founded on just such hallucinations, which do undeniably occur.

[...]

To explain these appearances as 'ghosts,' which, again are the visible life and spirit of a man, was a natural speculation: the facts exist, though the theory does not hold water. The modern explanation of those who think that the idea of a mere chance coincidence of death on one aide and hallucination on the other does not hold water, is 'telepathy.' At a distance the healthy man feels, from a distance the dying man causes, some mental 'impact,' which results in a hallucination of the dying man's presence. This is modern, but perhaps not quite so recent as some suppose. It is, in effect, the hypothesis of Herbert Mayo, M.D., Professor of Anatomy and Physiology in King's College, and of Comparative Anatomy in the Royal College of Surgeons, London, F.R.S., F.G.S., &c. He sets it forth in his book on 'The Truth contained in Popular Superstitions' (Blackwood. London, 1851). In the fallow leisure of his life Dr. Mayo took up Reichenbach's writings, and believed in 'Od force,' animal magnetism, and other very dim and dubious theories. Starting from Zschokke's amazing anecdotes about his own power of occasionally seeing, when he met a stranger, minute facts in the stranger's life, Dr. Mayo 'assumed it to be proved that the mind, or soul, of one human being can be brought, in the natural course of things, and under

---

*   Tylor, 'Primitive Culture,' i. 440. 'Proceedings of the Society for Psychical Research, 1892.'

†   'De Civ. Dei,' xviii. 18.

physiological laws hereafter to be determined, into immediate relation with the mind of another person.'*9 'Suppose our new principle brought into play; the soul of the dying person is to be supposed to have come into direct communication with the mind of his friend, with the effect of suggesting his present condition,' which the reported visions, however, seldom or never do. If the seer be awake, the contact 'originates a sensorial illusion.'[10] Mayo says that his theory will be held to rest on 'few and trivial instances.' 'That,' he replies, 'is only because the subject has not been attended to. For how many centuries were the laws of electricity preindicated by the single fact that a piece of amber, when rubbed, would attract light bodies!'[11] Messrs. Gurney and Myers have used the same illustration. It is clear that Mayo is the modern inventor of 'telepathy,' whatever we may think of the value of his theory. But cases are not really few. They abound through all history, and among all tribes of men, in all known conditions of culture. There are the facts; the savage and the ordinary citizen explain them by speaking of ghosts; *raffinés*,[12] of 'veridical hallucinations'; many people talk of 'chance coincidence,' and the question is, Have we not too many coincidences for the doctrine of probabilities?

Unluckily, good evidence is becoming more difficult of attainment. The public are learning what the, so to say, genuine symptoms of telepathy and of psychical experience are. Fictitious ghost-stories are being written, as by Fitzjames O'Brien,[13] on correct psychical lines; thus uniformity of evidence is no longer a good test of honesty, when some semi-hysterical lady chooses to vouch for a bogie. Our best chances are among the uneducated and savages. Their evidence is unsophisticated, but, alas, it has other conspicuous drawbacks! Consequently one is inclined to believe that the testimony for abnormal occurrences is least likely to be contaminated when it is found in the works of men who (another drawback!) are dead, and cannot be cross-examined. I do not attempt to disguise the difficulties in the way of collecting evidence. They may even prove fatal to the study. Yet, only yesterday, I met three sane and healthy English people who had simultaneously seen a ghost, in broad daylight, *sans le savoir!*[14] They had each remarked on the presence of a young and pretty girl in a room where (as was incontestably demonstrated) there was only an old and plain woman, whom, of course, they also beheld. It was not till next day that they woke and found themselves famous, for what they had seen, though they knew it not, was the right thing to see — the traditional 'ghost' of the place. But about this legend they were absolutely ignorant.

These are the kind of experiences, I fancy, on which 'the primitive philosophy of animism' is really based, or these, at least, must have confirmed it. The essence of the evidence is just what we regard as the essence of the evidence in anthropological studies at large — the undesigned uniformity of testimony. Defending anthropological evidence, Mr. Tylor says:

---

* 'Truth contained in Pop. Sup.' Second edition, p. 66.

> It is a matter worthy of consideration that the accounts of similar
> phenomena of culture, recurring in different parts of the world, actually
> supply incidental proof of their own authenticity. ... *The test of recurrence*
> *comes in* ... . The possibility of intentional or unintentional mystification is
> often barred by such a state of things as that a similar statement is made in
> two remote lands by two witnesses, of whom A. lived a century before B.,
> and B. appears never to have heard of A.[15]

Substitute 'similar abnormal experiences' for 'similar phenomena of culture,'
and Mr. Tylor's argument is identical with my own. I shall substitute another word in the next sentence. 'How distant are the countries, how wide apart
are the dates, how different the creeds and characters of the observers in the
catalogue of the facts of *psychical phenomena*, needs no farther showings,'[16] to
readers of Mr. Tylor's foot-notes. Here I only put 'psychical phenomena'
in place of 'facts of civilisation.' As to the said psychical phenomena identical with those of modern tales, Mr. Tylor himself quotes stories on the
authority of heathen philosophers, as Cicero, Christian fathers, Catholic
histories of saints, Maoris, Malagassies, modern Germans, Shetland ladies,
English people, and so forth. One can add vastly to Mr. Tylor a cloud of
instances, but they are various enough, and distant enough from each other
in creed, country, climate, and culture. 'Narratives of this class,' of the
'veridical hallucination,' or common deathbed-wraith, 'which I can only
specify without arguing on them, are abundantly in circulation,' says
Mr. Tylor.* [17] But the truth or falsity of these narratives makes the whole
difference in the discussion of the origin of religion. If they are false, Mr.
Tylor (if we accept his argument) traces religion to mistaken savage theories
of *normal* facts. If they are true (and if we accept Mr. Tylor's hypothesis),
religion is based on savage theories of *abnormal* facts— facts which show in
man transcendent faculties beyond what can be explained by physiological
causes as at present recognised.

We have touched on 'physical manifestations,' abnormal movements of
objects, and on the common deathbed-wraith. We may now turn to 'clairvoyance,' or the alleged power of beholding places and events distant in
space. Mayo and, of course, many other writers accept the existence of
clairvoyance — 'the patient discerns objects through any obstruction —
partitions, walls, or houses — and at an indefinite distance.'[18] Of course
science does not swallow this, though cases in abundance have been recorded between Mesmer's time and our own, by physicians who seem, otherwise, sane and competent. Even inquirers who admit the facts, in certain
cases, do not necessarily admit clairvoyance, but prefer a theory of
thought-reading.

[...][19]

★   *Op. cit.*, i. 449.

Here it may be as well to dismiss the idea that I take the Angekok, and his savage friends in general, at their own valuation. They are, no doubt, impostors, and their trick of being tied up (which they practise even when aiming at clairvoyance for their own ends) interests us because it has been revived by civilised quacks. But I am inclined to believe that, if no cases of clairvoyance had ever occurred, savage mediums would not so universally lay claim to that accomplishment.

In the same way, I doubt if 'veridical death-wraiths' would be so commonly attested, in all stages of culture, if such things were never observed. The same remarks apply to the noisy rapping *Poltergeist*, 'the elf who goes knocking and routing about the house at night.' [...]

The similarity of physiological condition among the persons in whose presence these impressions of noises, movements, and so forth are most common, has already been noticed. These people 'suffer from hysterical, convulsive, and epileptic affections.'* [20] Tasmanians, Karens, Zulus, Patagonians, Siberians, all, when selected as 'medicine men' have such 'jerks' as modern mediums display, and as afflict some young ladies when they dabble in table-turning and 'the willing game.'

Mr. Tylor asks whether it is probable that savages and charlatans have some method or knowledge, lost by the civilised; for this loss would be a case of degeneration. But, first, there is nothing odd in such degeneration of faculty: the Australian black has senses of sight and hearing, and powers of inference from what he sees and hears, which notoriously excel those of civilised man, and make the native 'tracker' a rival of Sherlock Holmes. The cultivation of these senses to the highest point enables the black to survive his condition of society. In the same way the cultivation of trance, and of whatever uncanny powers trance may lend, is highly serviceable to the savage. This accomplishment leads straight to wealth and power; it is a notable factor in chiefship, and in the evolution of rank. The chief often develops out of the medicine man, and supernatural attributes clung to royalty as late as the days when 'Charles III.' touched for scrofula in Italy (1761-86).[21]

Now, in civilised society of the Middle Ages, convulsions and trance led either to the stake or to canonisation; while since 1710, or so, they have been medically treated, and would not even qualify a man for knighthood, still less increase his wealth and political power. Thus the abnormal phenomena, if any, have been neglected. Yet, in fact, the savage and the charlatan, such as Mesmer, did hold, darkly, a secret, a piece of knowledge, namely, hypnotism, which civilised science has, at last, deemed worthy of recognition. Perhaps the savage and the quack knew even more than science has yet recognised. Certainly sane and educated men testify that certain patients display faculties as abnormal as any of those claimed for his own by the Angekok.

★   *Ibid.*, ii., 181.

Among these is what used to be called 'divination by the mirror' or crystal, and is now called 'crystal-gazing.' Nobody knows how far back the practice of looking for visions in a clear deep may go: the Egyptians have long used a drop of ink, the Maoris a drop of blood; wells of water have been employed, and in the Dordogne, a black hole in an old wall serves as a background for visions of the Virgin. The polished coal ball of Kelly and Dr. Dee still exists, similar things have ever been an element in popular superstition.[22]

In this case the explanation of old was, naturally, animistic. Dee believed that there was a spirit, or a crowd of spirits, in his various *specula*. An old writer tells us 'how to get a fairy' into one of these crystal balls. Folly, and superfluous rites, clustered about the crystals. Now it is an ascertained matter of fact that a certain proportion of men and women, educated, healthy, with no belief in 'spiritualism,' can produce hallucinations, pictures, by looking into a crystal ball.

[...] Where savage belief, and popular superstition, and, we must add, ecclesiastical opinion went wrong, was, not in accepting the existence of certain abnormal phenomena, but in the animistic interpretation of these phenomena. The Angekok who claims possession of a *tornak*, the witch who believes she has a familiar spirit, the magistrate who burns her for having one, the modern medium with his 'control,' are all in the primitive animistic stage of philosophy, with the seers of hallucinations who believe in 'ghosts.' What nucleus of fact there may be in their theory we cannot at present determine; we can only say that 'there are visions about,' and wait for time to bring clearer information, or once more to wipe out the whole interest in such matters among the educated. At present we seem to be gaining a little free space for the flight of fancy, a brief escape, perhaps, from an iron philosophy of the hard and fast. This is quite enough to be thankful for while it lasts; if it does not last, why, 'things must be as they may,' and we can endure our limited destiny.

The chief reason for believing that an accepted extension of human faculty may be imminent is this: A certain set of phenomena, long laughed at, but always alleged to exist, has been accepted. Consequently the still stranger phenomena — uniformly said to accompany those now welcomed within the scientific fold – may also have a measure of fact as a basis for the consentient reports.

'Preface to the Second Edition',
Cock Lane and Common Sense
(1894; Longmans, Green and Co., 1895)

Since the first publication of *Cock Lane and Common-Sense* in 1894, nothing has occurred to alter greatly the author's opinions. He has tried to make the Folklore Society[1] see that such things as modern reports of wraiths, ghosts, 'fire-walking,' 'corpse-lights,' 'crystal-gazing,' and so on, are within their province, and within the province of anthropology. In this attempt he has not quite succeeded. As he understands the situation, folklorists and anthropologists will hear gladly about wraiths, ghosts, corpse-candles, hauntings, crystal-gazing, and walking unharmed through fire, as long as these things are part of vague rural tradition, or of savage belief. But, as soon as there is first-hand evidence of honourable men and women for the apparent existence of any of the phenomena enumerated, then Folklore officially refuses to have anything to do with the subject. Folklore will register and compare vague savage or popular beliefs; but when educated living persons vouch for phenomena which (if truly stated) account in part for the origin of these popular or savage beliefs, then Folklore turns a deaf ear. The logic of this attitude does not commend itself to the author of *Cock Lane and Common-Sense*.

On the other side, the Society for Psychical Research, while anxiously examining all the modern instances which Folklore rejects, has hitherto neglected, on the whole, that evidence from history, tradition, savage superstition, saintly legend, and so forth, which Folklore deigns to regard with interest. The neglect is not universal, and the historical aspect of these beliefs has been dealt with by Mr. Gurney (on Witchcraft), by Mr. Myers (on the Classical Oracles), and by Miss X. (on Crystal-Gazing).[2] Still, the savage and traditional evidence is nearly as much eschewed by psychical research, as the living and contemporary evidence is by Folklore. The truth is that anthropology and Folklore have a ready-made theory as to the savage and illusory origin of all belief in the spiritual, from ghosts to God. The reported occurrence, therefore, of phenomena which suggest the possible existence of causes of belief *not* accepted by anthropology, is a distasteful thing, and is avoided. On the other hand, psychical research averts its gaze, as a rule, from tradition, because the testimony of tradition is not 'evidential,' not at first hand.

In *Cock Lane and Common-Sense* an attempt is made to reconcile these rather hostile sisters in science. Anthropology ought to think *humani nihil a se alienum*.[3] Now the abnormal and more or less inexplicable experiences vouched for by countless living persons of honour and sanity, are, at all events, *human*. As they usually coincide in character with the testimony of the lower races all over the world; with historical evidence from the past, and with rural Folklore now and always, it really seems hard to understand how anthropology can turn her back on this large human province.[…] The present writer has no theory, except the theory that these experiences (or these modern myths, if any one pleases), are part of the province of anthropology and Folklore.

He would add one obvious yet neglected truth. If a 'ghost-story' be found to contain some slight discrepancy between the narratives of two witnesses, it is at once rejected, both by science and common-sense, as obviously and necessarily and essentially false. Yet no story of the most normal incident in daily life, can well be told without *some* discrepancies in the relations of witnesses. None the less such stories are accepted even by juries and judges. We cannot expect human testimony suddenly to become impeccable and infallible in all details, just because a 'ghost' is concerned. Nor is it logical to demand here a degree of congruity in testimony, which daily experience of human evidence proves to be impossible, even in ordinary matters.

[…]

In answer to all that has been urged here, anthropologists are wont to ejaculate that blessed word 'Survival'. Our savage, and mediæval, and Puritan ancestors were ignorant and superstitious; and we, or some of us, inherit their beliefs, as we may inherit their complexions. They have bequeathed to us a tendency to see the viewless things, and hear the airy tongues which they saw and heard; and they have left us the legacy of their animistic or spiritualistic explanation of these subjective experiences.

Well, be it so; what does anthropology study with so much zest as survivals? When, then, we find plenty of sane and honest people ready with tales of their own 'abnormal' experiences, anthropologists ought to feel fortunate. Here, in the persons of witnesses, say, to 'death-bed wraiths,' are 'survivals' of the liveliest and most interesting kind. Here are parsons, solicitors, soldiers, actors, men of letters, peers, honourable women not a few, all (as far as wraiths go), in exactly the mental condition of a Maori. Anthropology then will seek out these witnesses, these contemporary survivals, these examples of the truth of its own hypothesis, and listen to them as lovingly as it listens to a garrulous old village wife, or to an untutored Mincopi.

This is what we expect; but anthropology, never glancing at our 'survivals,' never interrogating them, goes to the Aquarium to study a friendly Zulu. The consistency of this method *laisse a désirer!*[4] One says to anthropologists: 'If all educated men who have had, or believe they have had "psychical experiences" are mere "survivals," why don't you friends of "survivals" examine them and cross examine them? Their psychology ought to be a most interesting proof of the correctness of your theory. But, far from studying the cases of these gentlemen, some of you actually denounce, for doing so, the Society for Psychical Research.'

The real explanation of these singular scientific inconsistencies is probably this. Many men of science have, consciously or unconsciously, adopted the belief that the whole subject of the 'abnormal,' or, let us say, the 'psychical,' is closed. Every phenomenon admits of an already ascertained physical explanation. Therefore, when a man (however apparently free from superstitious prejudice) investigates a reported abnormal phenomenon, he is instantly accused of *wanting to believe* in a 'supernatural explanation'. Wanting (*ex hypothesi*) to believe, he is unfit to investigate, all his conclusions will be affirmative, and all will be worthless.

This scientific argument is exactly the old argument of the pulpit against the atheist who 'does not believe because he does not want to believe'. The writer is only too well aware that even scientific minds, when bent on these topics, are apt to lose balance and sanity. But this tendency, like any other mental bad habit, is to be overcome, and may be vanquished.

Manifestly it is as fair for a psychical researcher to say to Mr. Clodd, 'You won't examine my haunted house because you are afraid of being obliged to believe in spirits,' as it is fair for Mr. Clodd to say to a psychical researcher, 'You only examine a haunted house because you want to believe in spirits; and, therefore, if you *do* see a spook, it does not count'.

We have recently seen an instructive example. Many continental savants, some of them bred in the straitest sect of materialists, examined, and were puzzled by an Italian female 'medium'. Effects apparently abnormal were attested. In the autumn of 1895 this woman was brought to England by the Society for Psychical Research. They, of course, as they, *ex hypothesi*, 'wish to believe,' should, *ex hypothesi*, have gone on believing. But, in fact, they detected the medium in the act of cheating, and publicly denounced her as an impostor. The argument, therefore, that investigation implies credulity, and that credulity implies inevitable and final deception, scarcely holds water.[5]

[...]

Mr. J. W. Maskelyne,[6] the eminent expert in conjuring, has remarked to the author that the old historical reports of 'physical phenomena,' such as those which were said to accompany D. D. Home, do not impress him at all. For, as Mr. Maskelyne justly remarks, their antiquity and world-wide diffusion [...] may be accounted for with ease. Like other myths, equally uniform and widely diffused, they represent the natural play of human fancy. Inanimate objects are stationary, therefore let us say that they move about. Men do not float in the air. Let us say that they do. Then we have the 'physical phenomena' of spiritualism. This objection had already occurred to, and been stated by, the author. But the difficulty of accounting for the large body of respectable evidence as to the real occurrence of the alleged phenomena remains. Consequently the author has little doubt that there is a genuine substratum of fact, probably fact of conjuring, and of more or less hallucinatory experience. If so, the great antiquity and uniformity of the tricks, make them proper subjects of anthropological inquiry, like other matters of human tradition. Where conditions of darkness and so on are imposed, he does not think that it is worth while to waste time in examination.

Finally, the author has often been asked: 'But what do you believe yourself?'

He believes that all these matters are legitimate subjects of anthropological inquiry.

'Anthropology and Religion' II, *The Making of Religion*, 2nd edition

(Longmans, Green and Co., 1900)

A mong the various forms of science which are reaching and affecting the new popular tradition, we have reckoned Anthropology. Pleasantly enough, Anthropology has herself but recently emerged from that limbo of the unrecognised in which Psychical Research is pining. The British Association[1] used to reject anthropological papers as 'vain dreams based on travellers' tales.' No doubt the British Association would reject a paper on clairvoyance as a vain dream based on old wives' fables, or on hysterical imposture. Undeniably the study of such themes is hampered by fable and fraud, just as anthropology has to be ceaselessly on its guard against 'travellers' tales,' against European misunderstandings of savage ideas, and against civilised notions and scientific theories unconsciously read into barbaric customs, rites, traditions, and usages. Man, *ondoyant et divers*,[2] is the subject alike of anthropology and of psychical research. Man (especially savage man) cannot be secluded from disturbing influences, and watched, like the materials of a chemical experiment in a laboratory. Nor can man be caught in a 'primitive' state: his intellectual beginnings lie very far behind the stage of culture in which we find the lowest known races. Consequently the matter on which anthropology works is fluctuating; the evidence on which it rests needs the most sceptical criticism, and many of its conclusions, in the necessary absence of historical testimony as to times far behind the lowest known savages, must be hypothetical.

For these sound reasons official science long looked askance on Anthropology. Her followers were not regarded as genuine scholars, and, perhaps as a result of this contempt, they were often 'broken men,' intellectual outlaws, people of one wild idea. To the scientific mind, anthropologists or ethnologists were a horde who darkly muttered of serpent worship, phallus worship, Arkite doctrines,[3] and the Ten Lost Tribes that kept turning up in the most unexpected places. Anthropologists were said to gloat over dirty rites of dirty savages, and to seek reason where there was none. The exiled, the outcast, the pariah of Science, is, indeed, apt to find himself in odd company. Round the camp-fire of Psychical Research too, in the unofficial, unstaked waste of Science, hover odd, menacing figures of Esoteric Buddhists,[4] *Satanistes*, Occultists, Christian Scientists, Spiritualists, and Astrologers, as the Arkites and Lost Tribesmen haunted the cradle of anthropology.

But there was found at last to be reason in the thing, and method in the madness. Evolution was in it. The acceptance, after long ridicule, of palaeolithic weapons as relics of human culture,[5] probably helped to bring Anthropology within the sacred circle of permitted knowledge. Her topic was full of illustrations of the doctrine of Mr. Darwin. Modern writers on the theme had been anticipated by the less systematic students of the eighteenth century – Goguet, de Brosses, Millar, Fontenelle, Lafitau, Boulanger, or even Hume and Voltaire.[6] As pioneers these writers answer to the early mesmerists and magnetists, Puységur, Amoretti, Ritter, Elliotson, Mayo, Gregory, in the history of Psychical Research.[7] They were on the same track, in each case, as Lubbock, Tylor, Spencer, Bastian, and Frazer, or as Gurney, Richet, Myers, Janet, Dessoir, and Von Schrenck-Notzing.[8] But the earlier students were less careful of method and evidence.

Evidence! that was the stumbling block of anthropology. We still hear, in the later works of Mr. Max Müller, the echo of the old complaints. Anything you please, Mr. Max Müller says, you may find among your useful savages, and (in regard to some anthropologists) his criticism is just. You have but to skim a few books of travel, pencil in hand, and pick out what suits your case. Suppose, as regards our present theme, your theory is that savages possess broken lights of the belief in a Supreme Being. You can find evidence for that. Or suppose you want to show that they have no religious ideas at all; you can find evidence for that also. Your testimony is often derived from observers ignorant of the language of the people whom they talk about, or who are themselves prejudiced by one or other theory or bias. How can you pretend to raise a science on such foundations, especially as the savage informants wish to please or to mystify inquirers, or they answer at random, or deliberately conceal their most sacred institutions, or have never paid any attention to the subject?

To all these perfectly natural objections Mr. Tylor has replied.* Evidence must be collected, sifted, tested, as in any other branch of inquiry. A writer, 'of course, is bound to use his best judgment as to the trustworthiness of all authors he quotes, and, if possible, to obtain several accounts to certify each point in each locality.' Mr. Tylor then adduces 'the test of recurrence,' of

---

*   *Primitive Culture*, i. 9, 10.

undesigned coincidence in testimony, as Millar had already argued in the last century.* ⁹ If a mediaeval Mahommedan in Tartary, a Jesuit in Brazil, a Wesleyan in Fiji, one may add a police magistrate in Australia, a Presbyterian in Central Africa, a trapper in Canada, agree in describing some analogous rite or myth in these diverse lands and ages, we cannot set down the coincidence to chance or fraud. 'Now, the most important facts of ethnography are vouched for in this way.'¹⁰

[...]Though but recently crept forth, *vix aut ne vix quidem*,¹¹ from the chill shade of scientific disdain, Anthropology adopts the airs of her elder sisters among the sciences, and is as severe as they to the Cinderella of the family, Psychical Research. She must murmur of her fairies among the cinders of the hearth, while they go forth to the ball, and dance with provincial mayors at the festivities of the British Association. This is ungenerous, and unfortunate, as the records of anthropology are rich in unexamined materials of psychical research. I am unacquainted with any work devoted by an anthropologist of renown to the hypnotic and kindred practices of the lower races, except Herr Bastian's very meagre tract, 'Über psychische Beobachtungen bei Naturvölkern.'† We possess, none the less, a mass of scattered information on this topic, the savage side of psychical phenomena, in works of travel, and in Mr. Tylor's monumental 'Primitive Culture.' Mr. Tylor, however, as we shall see, regards it as a matter of indifference, or, at least, as a matter beyond the scope of his essay, to decide whether the parallel supernormal phenomena believed in by savages, and said to recur in civilisation, are facts of actual experience, or not.

Now, this question is not otiose. Mr. Tylor, like other anthropologists, Mr. Huxley, Mr. Herbert Spencer, and their followers and popularisers, constructs on anthropological grounds, a theory of the Origin of Religion. That origin anthropology explains as the result of early and fallacious reasonings on a number of biological and psychological phenomena, both normal and (as is alleged by savages) supernormal. These reasonings led to the belief in souls and spirits. Now, first, anthropology has taken for granted that the Supreme Deities of savages are envisaged by them as 'spirits.' This, paradoxical as the statement may appear, is just what does not seem to be proved, as we shall show. Next, if the supernormal phenomena (clairvoyance, thought-transference, phantasms of the dead, phantasms of the dying, and others) be real matters of experience, the inferences drawn from them by early savage philosophy may be, in some degree, erroneous. But the inferences drawn by materialists who reject the supernormal phenomena will also, perhaps, be, let us say, incomplete. Religion will have been, in part, developed out of facts, perhaps inconsistent with materialism in its present

---

*   *Origin of Ranks.*

†   Published for the Berlin Society of Experimental Psychology, Günther, Leipzig, 1890.

dogmatic form. To put it less trenchantly, and perhaps more accurately, the alleged facts 'are not merely dramatically strange, they are not merely extraordinary and striking, but they are "odd" in the sense that they will not easily fit in with the views which physicists and men of science generally give us of the universe in which we live' (Mr. A.J. Balfour, President's Address, 'Proceedings', S.P.R. vol. x. p. 8, 1894).[12]

As this is the case, it might seem to be the business of Anthropology, the Science of Man, to examine, among other things, the evidence for the actual existence of those alleged unusual and supernormal phenomena, belief in which is given as one of the origins of religion.

To make this examination, in the ethnographic field, is almost a new labour. As we shall see, anthropologists have not hitherto investigated such things as the 'Fire-walk' of savages, uninjured in the flames, like the Three Holy Children.[13] The world-wide savage practice of divining by hallucinations induced through gazing into a smooth deep (crystal-gazing) has been studied, I think, by no anthropologist. The veracity of 'messages' uttered by savage seers when (as they suppose) 'possessed' or 'inspired' has not been criticised, and probably cannot be, for lack of detailed information. The 'physical phenomena' which answer among savages to the use of the 'divining rod,' and to 'spiritist' marvels in modern times, have only been glanced at. In short, all the savage parallels to the so-called 'psychical phenomena' now under discussion in England, America, Germany, Italy, and France, have escaped critical analysis and comparison with their civilised counterparts.

An exception among anthropologists is Mr. Tylor. He has not suppressed the existence of these barbaric parallels to our modern problems of this kind. But his interest in them practically ends when he has shown that the phenomena helped to originate the savage belief in 'spirits,' and when he has displayed the 'survival' of that belief in later culture. He does not ask 'Are the phenomena real?' he is concerned only with the savage philosophy of the phenomena and with its relics in modern spiritism and religion. My purpose is to do, by way only of *ébauche*,[14] what neither anthropology nor psychical research nor psychology has done: to put the savage and modern phenomena side by side. Such evidence as we can give for the actuality of the modern experiences will, so far as it goes, raise a presumption that the savage beliefs, however erroneous, however darkened by fraud and fancy, repose on a basis of real observation of actual phenomena.

[...]

It is an example of the chameleon-like changes of science (even of 'science falsely so called' if you please) that when he wrote his book, in 1871, Mr. Tylor could not possibly have anticipated this line of argument. 'Psychical planes' had not been invented; hypnotism, with its problems, had not been much noticed in England. But 'Spiritualism' was flourishing. Mr. Tylor did not ignore this revival of savage philosophy. He saw very well that the end of the century was beholding the partial rehabilitation of beliefs which were scouted from 1660 to 1850. Seventy years ago, as Mr. Tylor says,[15] Dr. Macculloch,[16] in his 'Description of the Western Islands of Scotland,' wrote of 'the famous Highland second sight' that 'ceasing to be believed it has ceased to exist.'*

Dr. Macculloch was mistaken in his facts. 'Second sight' has never ceased to exist (or to be believed to exist), and it has recently been investigated in the 'Journal' of the Caledonian Medical Society. Mr. Tylor himself says that it has been 'reinstated in a far larger range of society, and under far better circumstances of learning and prosperity.' This fact he ascribes generally to 'a direct revival from the regions of savage philosophy and peasant folklore,'[17] a revival brought about in great part by the writings of Swedenborg. To-day things have altered. The students now interested in this whole class of alleged supernormal phenomena are seldom believers in the philosophy of Spiritualism in the American sense of the word.[†]

Mr. Tylor, as we have seen, attributes the revival of interest in this obscure class of subjects to the influence of Swedenborg. It is true[…]that Swedenborg attracted the attention of Kant.[18] But modern interest has chiefly been aroused and kept alive by the phenomena of hypnotism. The interest is now, among educated students, really scientific.

Thus Mr. William James, Professor of Psychology in the University of Harvard, writes:

> 'I was attracted to this subject (Psychical Research) some years ago by my love of fair play in Science.'[‡] [19]

Mr. Tylor is not incapable of appreciating this attitude. Even the so-called 'spirit manifestations,' he says, 'should be discussed on their merits,' and the investigation 'would seem apt to throw light on some most interesting psychological questions.'[20] Nothing can be more remote from the logic of Hume.[21]

[…]

These considerations did not fail to present themselves to Mr. Tylor. But his manner of dealing with them is peculiar. With his unequalled knowledge of the lower races, it was easy for him to examine travellers' tales about

---

* *Primitive Culture*, i. 143.

† As 'spiritualism' is often used in opposition to 'materialism,' and with no reference to rapping 'spirits,' the modern belief in that class of intelligences may here be called spiritism.

‡ *The Will to Believe*, preface, p. xiv.

savage seers who beheld distant events in vision, and to allow them what weight he thought proper, after discounting possibilities of falsehood and collusion. He might then have examined modern narratives of similar performances among the civilised, which are abundant. It is obvious and undeniable that if the supernormal acquisition of knowledge in trance is a *vera causa*, a real process, however rare, Mr. Tylor's theory needs modifications; while the character of the savage's reasoning becomes more creditable to the savage, and appears as better bottomed than we had been asked to suppose. But Mr. Tylor does not examine this large body of evidence at all, or, at least, does not offer us the details of his examination. He merely writes in this place:

> 'A typical spiritualistic instance may be quoted from Jung-Stilling, who says that examples have come to his knowledge of sick persons who, longing to see absent friends, have fallen into a swoon, during which they have appeared to the distant objects of their affection.'* [22]

Jung-Stilling[23] (though he wrote before modern 'Spiritualism' came in) is not a very valid authority; there is plenty of better evidence than his, but Mr. Tylor passes it by, merely remarking that 'modern Europe has kept closely enough to the lines of early philosophy.'[24] Modern Europe has indeed done so, if it explains the supernormal acquisition of knowledge, or the hallucinatory appearance of a distant person to his friend by a theory of wandering 'spirits.' But facts do not cease to be facts because wrong interpretations have been put upon them by savages, by Jung-Stilling, or by anyone else. The real question is, Do such events occur among lower and higher races, beyond explanation by fraud and fortuitous coincidence? We gladly grant that the belief in Animism, when it takes the form of a theory of 'wandering spirits,' is probably untenable, as it is assuredly of savage origin. But we are not absolutely so sure that in this aspect the theory is not based on actual experiences, not of a normal and ordinary kind. If so, the savage philosophy and its supposed survivals in belief will appear in a new light. And we are inclined to hold that an examination of the mass of evidence to which Mr. Tylor offers here so slight an allusion will at least make it wise to suspend our judgment, not only as to the origins of the savage theory of spirits, but as to the materialistic hypothesis of the absence of a psychical element in man.

---

*   *Primitive Culture*, i. 440. Citing Stilling after Dale Owen, and quoting Mr. Alfred Russel Wallace's *Scientific Aspect of the Supernatural*, p. 43. Mr. Tylor also adds folk-lore practices of ghost-seeing, as on St. John's Eve. St. Mark's Eve, too, is in point, as far as folk-lore goes.

6

PSYCHICAL RESEARCH

By the end of his life, Lang had come to be strongly associated with psychical research, and was by many credited with bringing it such credibility and respectability as it had. A selection of his interventions in the topics of psychical research are presented here, although the selection makes clear how integrated his interest was with his other work and interests – with his anthropological work and his history in particular. His defence of Jeanne d'Arc in 'Three Seeresses', for example, links his absolute insistence on rigour and logic in the use of historical evidence, as in his challenges to Anatole France's history of Jeanne (see Volume 2, pp. 236–48), to his belief that psychical experiences can be genuine, rather than fraudulent or the result of fantasy. 'Science and "Miracles"' uses his reading in the intellectual history of Europe to challenge contemporary scientific disdain for interest in psychical phenomenon as part of his argument that anthropology needs to consider all the evidence.

The selection makes clear also Lang's vacillation between insider and outside status with regard to psychical research. In 'Ghosts Up to Date', part of the material of which also appears in 'Apparitions, Ghosts, and Hallucinations' in *Cock Lane and Common Sense* (London: Longmans, Green and Co.,1894), Lang jumps between the methods and assumptions of folklore, mainstream science, psychical research and the literary, playing one off against the other in order to be constrained and held by the boundaries of none of them. In 'Science and Demonology' too Lang resists the already existing positions in the debate – those represented by T. H. Huxley and Alfred Russel Wallace – and forges instead a third position beyond the limits of these.

Lang wrote a number of times on crystal-gazing, and of all the psychical phenomenon he considers throughout his work, it seems to be the one he was most convinced by. His most extensive considerations of it are 'Magic Mirrors and Crystal Gazing', reproduced here; 'Crystal Visions, Savage and Civilised', chapter 5 of the second edition of *The Making of Religion* (1898; London: Longmans, Green and Co., 2nd edition 1900); and in his 'Introduction' to Northcote W. Thomas, *Crystal Gazing: Its History and Practice* (London: Alexander More Ltd, The De La More Press, 1905), pp. ix–xlvii.

'Human Personality After Death' and the 'Presidential Address' together indicate Lang's complex position vis-à-vis the institutions of psychical research. Frederic Myers's posthumously published *Human Personality and Its Survival of Bodily Death*, 2 vols (London: Longmans, Green and Co., 1903) demonstrated over hundreds of closely argued pages the evidence for survival, and the work was seen in many ways as the magnum opus, not just of Myers but of psychical research as a whole. Lang's review of it clearly outlines his scepticism about some of Myers's central claims, and his 'Presidential Address', given on his acceptance of the presidency of the Society for Psychical Research in 1911, while of course in some ways finally placing him at the centre of the SPR and its methods, seeks to retain an outsider's position.

The letters selected here – to Oliver Lodge, William James and E. B. Tylor – give a very different insight into Lang's relation to psychical research. The letters to Lodge in particular show the intense mixture of fascination and repulsion in his attitude. Lang rarely wrote a year on his letters, but suggestions for the year of writing for the letters reproduced here is given below.

The SPR Archive held at Cambridge University Library holds sixty-two letters from Lang to Oliver Lodge and these are dominated by the subject of psychical research. The Archive lists these letters as having been received between 1905 and 1911, but internal evidence suggests that some are much earlier. Marysa Demoor, in her thesis, doesn't date any of the letters included here, although she does suggest a year for other letters from Lang to Lodge. The letters reproduced here are broadly in two lots, the first from around the first part of 1895, the second from around 1909. In the first Lang is mostly concerned with trying to arrange for the stage magician J. N. Maskelyne to sit with the medium Eusapia Palladino and with the question of Robert Browning's relation to the medium D. D. Home. In particular, he discusses the question of whether Home had purported to communicate to the Brownings messages from a lost child of theirs.

At the beginning of 1895 J. N. Maskelyne began to suggest that the Society for Psychical Research should bring Palladino to the UK, to test those things claimed about her after sittings with her in France in the late summer of 1894. He began, in his own words, 'a controversy about her with Mr. Andrew Lang' at this time (quoted in 'Another Good Ghost Gone Wrong', *Tuapeka Times* XXVII:4304 (1895), p. 3). Maskelyne was very famous by this time, and his challenge and the subsequent sitting with Palladino were widely reported in the mainstream press. At the beginning of 1895 it was reported in the *Newcastle Weekly Courant* (2 February), that '[a]n interesting correspondence has been going on between Mr Andrew Lang and Mr Maskelyne on the subject of spooks'. In the first set of letters Lang often refers to his conversations and correspondence with Maskelyne, and his belief that Maskelyne should sit with Palladino to see if he could catch her out in using tricks to produce her phenomena. The SPR eventually arranged for Palladino to come to the UK, and she stayed in Cambridge with Frederic Myers during the August and September of 1895. The results were described in detail in the November issue of the SPR's *Journal* of that year (Alice Johnson, 'Eusapia Paladino' [sic], *Journal of the Society for Psychical Research* 7 (November 1895), pp. 148–59). While Johnson admits that the Cambridge experiments revealed that Palladino used tricks, she does not mention the presence of Maskelyne at all. However, Maskelyne's attendance at one of the sittings, and his discovery of fraud, was widely reported in the press (see 'The Weekly Times', *Manchester Times*, 1 November 1895).

Maskelyne himself wrote of his experience to the *Daily Chronicle* on 29 October 1895. This letter prompted letters to the paper by Alfred Russel Wallace (1 November) and Frederic Myers (4 November), both challenging Maskelyne's assumption that his detection of fraud meant that none of Palladino's phenomena could be genuine. A fuller account of Maskelyne's involvement and precisely what he found was later published by SPR insider Hereward Carrington as *Eusapia Palladino and Her Phenomena* (New York: B. W. Dodge, 1909).

While the letters show the extent of Lang's involvement in bringing together Maskelyne and Eusapia Palladino, and his belief that a 'conjurer' was the best person to test her, following her exposure by Maskelyne at the Cambridge sittings Lang complained in his column 'At the Sign of the Ship', in *Longman's Magazine* that Maskelyne had not acknowledged the role of the psychical researcher Richard Hodgson in exposing her: 'months before Mr. Maskelyne ever saw Eusapia Dr Hodgson published a long and minute forecast of what her dodges were likely to be, and then demonstrated, in practice, that his forecast was correct' ('At the Sign of the Ship', *Longman's Magazine* 27:158 (December 1895), p. 209).

The question of the relation between the Brownings and Daniel Dunglas Home was raised a number of times in SPR circles following Robert Browning's death in 1889. In 1889 an anonymous account appeared in the SPR's journal ('Appendix D', *Journal of the Society for Psychical Research* 4 (July 1889), pp. 120–1) which gave a full description of the Browning's sitting in 1855 with Home. This volume of the *Journal* also contains a review by William Barrett and Frederic Myers of a book on Home written by his wife (p. 101–6). The review contains an account of a conversation Myers had with Browning on the subject. On 28 November 1902 a letter was sent to the *Times Literary Supplement* by F. Merrifield in response to a review in the magazine of Frank Podmore's *Modern Spiritualism* (1902). Merrifield enclosed letters by both Browning and Elizabeth Barrett Browning on the subject. These letters were reproduced in the *Journal of the Society for Psychical Research* 11 (January 1903), pp. 11–16, along with the revelation that Merrifield had been the author of the account in the *Journal* in 1889. The Brownings' son, Pen, wrote to the *TLS* in response to Merrifield's letters. At the heart of the dispute was whether Browning had detected Home in fraud. The question of Home's supposed message from a dead child, and subsequent questions around possible miscarriages suffered by Barrett Browning, unsurprisingly, do not appear in this public discussion. However, Lang's discussion of this subject in his letters to Lodge is often interwined with his discussion of his conversations with Maskelyne, which date the letters reasonably precisely to 1895.

In the second set of letters Lang is concerned centrally with the cross-correspondences, of which Oliver Lodge was one of the chief investigators. The cross-correspondences were a series of messages obtained through a number of mediums between 1901 and 1930 which were particularly cryptic and fragmented. Investigators began to believe that their elliptical nature was part of a plan on the part of a number of now-dead psychical investigators, principally Frederic Myers, Henry Sidgwick and Edmund Gurney, to finally prove survival beyond death. Messages from individual mediums, the investigators believed, only made sense when they were put together with those from other mediums, and their correspondences interpreted. The letters on the cross-correspondences must, then, have been written after 1901. Lang also mentions Eusapia Palladino in these letters, however. Between 1901, when the cross-correspondences began, and 1909, neither the *Journal* nor the *Proceedings* of the SPR mention Palladino. In 1909 interest in her on the part of the Society revived. In an article from the *Journal* in that year ('Some Sittings With Eusapia Palladino', *Journal of the Society for Psychical Research* 14, pp. 115–32), the psychical researcher Everard Feilding admits that it has been 'a very long time since the subject of these physical phenomena has been considered at meetings of this Society' (p. 115). These circumstances, along with more detailed evidence given below, suggest that the second set of letters to Lodge is from 1909.

Only seven letters from Lang to William James are so far known to exist, and these are held in the Houghton Library, Harvard University. The letters reproduced here are particularly concerned with James's involvement with the medium Mrs Leonora Piper. James began investigating Mrs Piper in 1885, but his interest in her began to wane in the early twentieth century, particularly after the death of the main investigator, Richard Hodgson, in 1905 (see letter to Theodore Flournoy, 9 February 1906, in *The Letters of William James*, edited by his son Henry James, two vols (London: Longmans, Green and Co.), vol. 2, p. 242). James wrote late in his life that his family had hardly sat with Mrs Piper from about 1898 until the death of Hodgson (see letter to J. G. Piddington, 21 May 1910, in *The Selected Letter of William James*, edited and with an introduction by Elizabeth Hardwick (Boston: Nonpareil Books, 1980), p. 258). The first letter mentions June 1896 as in the past, and the following letter mentions that *Pickle the Spy: Or, The Incognito of Prince Charles* (1897) has already been published, suggesting that the book was published between the first and second letters, and that they are from 1897. In addition, in the second letter Lang refers to his recent experiment with crystal gazing, and his successful experiments with a young woman who previously knew nothing of scrying. He writes about the experiments with this 'seer' in 'Crystal Visions, Savage and Civilised' in *The Making of Religion* (Longmans, Green and Co., 1898), and dates his meeting and his experiments with her as '[e]arly in the present year (1897)' (p. 94). Marysa Demoor dates all but one of the letters included here as 1897. For a letter dated 1896 by her, see this volume p. 439, n.17 (Marysa Demoor, *Friends Over the Ocean: Andrew Lang's American Correspondents, 1881–1912*, Ghent: Ruksuniversiteit Gent, 1989).

The Pitt Rivers Museum, which holds Tylor's archive, has twenty-seven letters from Lang to Tylor. These mostly concern details of their anthropological work. Lang often criticised Tylor, in however a respectful way, for dismissing contemporary accounts of psychical phenomena as mere 'survivals'. In the letter included here, however, Lang involves Tylor too in the discussion of the Brownings' involvement with D. D. Home. In the Pitt Rivers Archive, where the letters to Tylor have an envelope with them, so can be dated in terms of year, the year has been added in pencil to the letter. If the attribution of the date to this letter, 1904, is correct, Lang was clearly still interested in what had occurred between Browning and D. D. Home nearly ten years after his letters to Lodge reproduced in this volume. The fact that Lang doesn't mention the miscarriages suffered by the Brownings, however, may suggest that the letter was written before his letters to Lodge of 1895, that is, before Lang knew of them, but of course it may be that his relations with Tylor were not intimate enough for the discussion of such events.

'Ghosts Up To Date',
Blackwood's Edinburgh Magazine 155:939

(January 1894), pp. 47–58

The most frivolous pastimes have now a habit of degenerating into scientific exercises. Croquet was ruined, as a form of lounging, by the
precision attained by some players; lawn-tennis is a serious affair; and even
ghost stories, the delight of Christmas Eve, have been ravaged and annexed
by psychology. True, there are some who aver that the science of the Psychical Society does not hold water; but, in any case, it is as dull and difficult
as if it were some orthodox research dear to Mr Herbert Spencer. To prove
this fact, I had marked for quotation some remarks, by eminent ghost-hunt-
ers, on the provinces and parts of the brain, on the subjective and the objective, the conscious, the reflex, the automatic, – *tout le tremblement*, as we
may well say, – which would frighten off the most intrepid amateurs. 'The
oldest aunt' would forget 'the saddest tale,' if plied with remarks on the
'dextro-cerebral hemisphere' of the brain. If we must understand all that
kind of thing before we can enjoy a ghost story, we who are middle-aged
may despair. But I hope to give the gist of what psychological science (if it
is a science) has to say about the existence of a bogie, and to do so without
overtaxing intellects about the average. Science has tackled this theme
before. By aid of about two cases of hallucination, Nicolai's and 'Mrs A.'s'[1]
(whoever Mrs A. may have been), Ferrier and Hibbert[2] decided that ghosts
were merely 'hallucinations,' 'revived impressions.' Very good; but hallucinations caused by what? and wherefore so frequently coincident with the
death of the person who seems to be seen? I ventured to ask these questions
long ago in the article on 'Apparitions' in the 'Encyclopædia Britannica.'[3]
A good many years have elapsed since I bleated out my artless amateur
theories of the ghostly, and incurred the censure, I think, of Dr Maudsley
and other serious persons.[4] Yet I was serious enough in holding that the

explanation of *all* ghosts as casual hallucinations was too attenuated. Materials were scanty then, – mere tales of one's grandmother, and legends in old books concerned with what was called 'the Supernatural.' In the interval hypnotism has been accepted as a fact by science, the Psychical Society has been founded, a great collection of some six hundred stories of 'phantasms of the living' has been printed;[5] phantasms of the dead are also brought forward in considerable numbers; committees have reported on haunted houses in a friendly sense; and Mrs Besant has acquired a creditable number of beliefs.[6] Thirty-three years ago, a writer in 'Chambers Encyclopædia' said, 'If psychological study were more in repute, and if the phenomena of dreams, in particular, were diligently examined, there might be a hope of a satisfactory theory of what are called apparitions ere the world was many years older.' Psychological study has increased, the world is a many years older; but a satisfactory theory of apparitions is still sadly to seek.

What are we to answer now when people ask, 'Do you believe in ghosts?' No reply can be made (except by a downright sceptic) till we have defined the term 'ghost.' Even popular usage has made one step towards a definition by employing the word 'wraith' to denote the phantasm of a living person, while 'ghost' means the phantasm of a dead person. But the difficulty begins when we inquire what *is* the phantasm in either case?

> 'Gin a body meet a body,'[7]

who actually is not there, but elsewhere, and in life, what is the thing met? The old idea was that the thing is a spiritual double of its living owner, a separable self, or, as the Esoteric Buddhists[8] do vainly talk, an 'astral body.' That body, or double, is an actual entity, filling space, and, as it seems, is really material, and capable of exercising an influence on matter. That phantasm of a dead person, the ghost, again, was regarded as the surviving soul, made visible, and was really material, as far as being ponderable and able to affect matter – for example, to draw the bed-curtains – involves materiality. We may argue about matter and spirit as we please, but wraiths, and ghosts, and souls, on the old theory, are obviously matter, though matter of a refined sort: the soul, for example, was capable of material pains and pleasures, could touch a harp, or rejoice in the society of houris, or burn in material fire, or freeze in material ice.

Now there are many educated persons, who, if asked, 'Do you believe in ghosts?' would answer, 'We believe in apparitions; but we do not believe that the apparition is the separable or surviving soul of a living or a dead man. We believe that it is a hallucination, projected by the brain of the percipient, which, again, in some instances, is influenced so as to project that hallucination, by some agency not at present understood.' To this experience of the percipient, who is sensible, by emotion, by sight, hearing, or touch, or by all these at once, of the presence of the absent, or of the dead, the name *telepathy* (feeling produced from a distance) is given. Any one may believe, and many do believe, in telepathy, yet not believe in the old-fashioned ghost. True, if you admit that an influence from a dead man may beget a hallucination of his presence, you must also believe in the continued existence of the dead, or else in the survival of some mood of the dead man's while he was alive – a mood powerful enough to beget a hallucination in the living, or in some of them. To believe even in this is to run counter to old-fashioned common-sense; but it is not to believe in the *ghost*, or perceivable spirit of the departed. The human race, then, at present, may be divided into certain categories of sceptics and believers. The sceptics, probably the large majority in civilised countries, say, 'Mere stuff and nonsense!' According to them, all who report a phantasm as in their own experiences, are liars, drunkards, or maniacs; or they mistook a dream for waking reality, or they are 'excitable' and 'imaginative,' or they were under an illusion, and placed a false interpretation on some actual perception – for example, they took a post for a ghost, or, by a mistake of identity, recognised in one person, who was actually present, another who was absent or dead. Finally, the percipient may have really had a hallucination, caused by indigestion, overwork, or what not. In no case does a real ghost or wraith appear. In no case does a man, living or dead, 'telepathically' cause a hallucination in another man.

This is the theory of the sceptic, who also asks, 'What is the use of a ghost?' as if nothing useless, or of unascertained use, could exist in the nature of things. The sturdy sceptic is a very serviceable character, though he is generally quite ignorant of his subject, or perhaps is the dupe of his own character for sound common-sense. Thus, Scott had actually seen a phantasm for which he could not account (the story is in Gillies, not in Lockhart),[9] and had heard disturbances coincident with the death of a friend, which deeply affected him. Yet he persuaded himself to publish statements of the most thoroughly unbelieving kind, and throughout his life endeavoured to regard himself as a true unbeliever in the abnormal. The other way lay madness, he thought; for two of his friends, who had believed in ghostly experiences of their own, lost their reason many years later. Alas! the sturdiest profession of unbelief is no guarantee that we shall keep our reasoning faculties to the end.

To the sceptic *à outrance*,[10] believers of both kinds, believers in ghosts and believers in telepathy, must grant that many people who report abnormal experiences may fall under the uncomplimentary categories of mad, drunk, knave, fool, visionary, and so forth. But it is urged that there are hundreds of other cases in which men and women of good character, sober, sane, not in a condition of expectancy, not excited in any way, declare themselves to have had abnormal experiences. These, again, might be classed as empty hallucinations; but the experiences have coincided with some crisis, usually death, in the history of the person whose apparition was perceived. Further, these experiences, as a rule, have been *unique* in the case of the percipients. If a man is in the habit of seeing the absent, and if one of the people he fancies he sees happens to die, that is clearly a mere accident. But if a man sees an absent acquaintance only once in his life, and if, at that moment, the acquaintance is dying; still more, if this unique experience, with the coincident death, be comparatively common, – then the theory of chance hallucination becomes untenable. The spokesmen of the Psychical Society have made statistical researches, not, of course, on the scale of a national census, and they have convinced themselves that the ratio of empty to veridical hallucinations, to apparitions coincident with death, does not justify the hypothesis of mere accident. They must be credited with very considerable assiduity in the collection and comparison of evidence, and, though I am not certain that they have been zealous enough in setting forth the particulars of the empty hallucinations of the sane, I must confess that the coincidence of events with apparitions does seem to me to exceed what the laws of chance allow. Only the advanced mathematical student can understand Mr Edgeworth's 'Calculus of Probabilities applied to Psychical Research.'[11] But the impression is left on one's mind that, though empty hallucinations of great vividness are well attested, the number of hallucinations corresponding with death, or some other crisis, is too great to be regarded as merely casual. That the coincidence is merely casual – a *quantité négligeable* – is the essence of the theory of Ferrier and Hibbert. I am acquainted with one case in which a dripping apparition announced its owner's death by drowning; with another in which a ghost pronounced a blessing on its widow (the owner of the ghost giving out that he had died of cholera); and with a third case in which a dead kinswoman appeared to an acquaintance of my own and predicted her decease. The last incident exactly answered to the anecdote recorded, in 1662, by the Bishop of Gloucester, concerning the daughter of Sir Charles Lee, whose dead mother appeared to her, and predicted her death at noon the next day. Miss Lee punctually expired at noon; but my friend is living yet, very many years after the prophecy of her dead kinswoman. Moreover, the owner of the first ghost of these three was *not* drowned; nor did the owner of the second ghost die of the cholera, as the spectre averred. Every one of these three apparitions was an empty hallucination, every one of them profoundly affected the spirits of the percipients, and I find none of them in the voluminous records of the Psychical Society.

[...]

None of these apparitions coincided with any distinguishable event, or with any excitement on the part of the owners of the phantasms. Of course, granting telepathy, we do not know but that an unobserved and unremembered thought or mood of the agent *may* affect the percipient so as to cause a hallucination. This topic has not been, and can hardly be studied. But, vivid as were the merely casual hallucinations known to me at first hand, the phantasms, known to me at first hand, which did coincide with events are about double in number. Therefore I am inclined, not to dogmatise, indeed, but to consider it probable enough that coincidental hallucinations are too numerous to be explained as mere 'flukes,' while the evidence for phantasms of the dead cannot always be rejected as the offspring of mendacity or illusion.

Nobody has a right to condemn these opinions summarily who has not made a study of the evidence, old and new, and who is unaware of the very strange uniformity which, in all ages, marks the reports of the abnormal. Modern inquirers are apt to neglect this uniformity. They urge that the old-fashioned ghosts always, or usually, appeared with a practical purpose: they had a wrong to redress, a secret to reveal, a message to deliver, or the like. The recent ghosts, it is said, are aimless and purposeless, and vague, flitting like a dream. Now, if there are any such things as apparitions, we may take it that they are pretty conservative: that they were not all purposeful up to, say, 1830, and are all purposeless now. The more probable theory is, that the old believers in the old-fashioned ghost chiefly collected and recorded the more striking and interesting cases – those in which the ghost showed a purpose (as a few modern ghosts do still) – while these anecdotes were, doubtless, improved upon and embellished. The early students would scarcely think the aimless ghosts worthy of mention, though they do mention some of them.

In other provinces of the abnormal, such as spirit-rappings, and noisy hauntings, the early phenomena, since 1856 (when a rapping goblin disturbed a convent, as we read in the Chronicles of Richard of Fulda), have been very much akin to modern 'spiritualistic manifestations.' This uniformity is, indeed, at once monotonous and interesting, proving either the reality of strange occurrences, or unanimity in imposture or in imagination. All this agreement of evidence – in fact, all the evidence – is habitually neglected by the sceptic, who pronounces an opinion in complete ignorance of the subject. It is by no means necessary that every one should study the topic; but an opinion founded on confessed and contemptuous nescience is of no more value as regards apparitions than as regards chemistry or Biblical criticism.

When the student has arrived at these conclusions – namely, that even common-sense may err when it pronounces a verdict based on ignorance, and again, that the testimony for apparitions is not wholly valueless – the moment has come when one or other view of ghosts, or both views, must be adopted, or an agnostic attitude must be assumed. A man may say, 'There is *something* in this ancient belief. That something may be explained by telepathy, by the power which one mind has of producing hallucinations in another mind.' Or he may say, '"A ghost's a ghost for a' that," – a spectre which can be seen, and heard, and touched, which can lay a cold hand on me, or drag my bed-curtains aside, is an existing actual being, the double of a living, or the ghost of a dead person.' There remains the third position which may be taken by one who is not a complete sceptic; he may say that he knows nothing about the matter: that apparitions do appear, but that nothing like a satisfactory theory of apparitions has been put forward. Probably neither the old nor the new believers can quarrel with this position, for the facts (as we may call them by courtesy) cannot be fitted into any harmonious hypothesis.

The difficulties of theory may be illustrated later by convenient examples. As to the sceptical doctrine of hallucinations, which merely fortuitously coincide with death and other crises, enough has been said. The coincidences are too numerous, unless we decline to receive the evidence. The telepathic hypothesis has been urged with great candour and ingenuity by the late Mr Edmund Gurney, and by Mr Myers. They first maintain that the minds of some people can be impressed, where none of the known senses is made use of, by the idea present in the mind of another person. Thus A. concentrates his thoughts on a triangle, let us say, and B. discerns and designs such a figure. Very great pains have been bestowed on these experiments in 'thought transference,' and very monotonous and uninteresting they are. But if once it be admitted that the experiments do succeed in a proportion of cases greater than chance can account for, then there is such a thing as telepathy, and one mind may affect another by means not familiar to common experience. Again, hypnotic experiment shows that the mind of one person can be strangely influenced by that of another – for example, that if told when hypnotised that he is to see a phantasm on a given day, while wide awake, a man *does* see it. Further, a few cases are on record in which men have voluntarily impressed persons at a distance, expecting nothing of the sort, with the phantasm of their presence. Granting that the testimony for all this is authentic, there is less to marvel at in the *spontaneous* production of phantasms of themselves, caused by people dying, or in some other crisis. The dead, especially the recent dead, are supposed, in rare cases, to exercise the same power; but both the dead and the living do so in a vague way. The phantasm is occasionally seen, so to speak, by the wrong person. The appearance of an old gentleman, for instance, displayed itself in the room above that where his daughter lay dead, and merely frightened a casual lodger. In truth, the phenomena have the very intermittent lucidity of dreams. A ghost is a dead man's dream, the phantasm of the departed is walking in his sleep, and a wraith is seldom much more purposeful and intelligent than a ghost.

The hypothesis thus summarily stated* has the merit, if it be one, of cutting down the marvellous to the lowest point.[12] Once admit that when A. stares at a circle B. sees a circle – once admit the accuracy of hypnotic experiment, and what follows is comparatively easy. One mind works on another mind in all the cases; in none is present any ghost, any actual *being*.

---

*   *Proceedings of the Society for Psychical Research*, Part vi.

But if we accept the facts, the facts do not really seem to be accounted for by this hypothesis. For example, if the phantasm ever produces any effect on material objects, an effect which endures after the phantasm has vanished, then there was an actual agent, a real being, on the scene.[…] Thus, the best and most valid proof that an abnormal being is actually present was that devised by the ghost of Sir Richard of Coldinghame in the ballad, and by the Beresford ghost, who threw a heavy curtain over the pole.[13] Unluckily, Sir Richard is a poetical figment, and the Beresford ghost is a myth, like William Tell:[14] he may be traced back through various medieval authorities almost to the date of the Normal Conquest. I have examined the story in a little book of folk-lore, 'Études Traditionistes.' Always there is a compact to appear, always the ghost burns or injures the hand or wrist of the spectator. A version occurs in William of Malmesbury.

What we need, to disprove an *exclusively* telepathic theory, is a ghost who is not only seen, heard, and even touched, but a ghost who produces some change in physical objects. Most provokingly, there are agencies at every spiritualistic *séance* and in every affair of the *Poltergeist* who do lift tables, chairs, beds, bookcases, candles, and so forth, while others play accordions. But then nobody *sees* these agencies at work, while the spontaneous phantasms which are *seen* do not so much as lift a loo-table, generally speaking. In the spiritualistic cases, we have the effect, with no visible cause; in ghost stories, we have the visible presence, but he very seldom indeed causes any physical change in any object. No ghost who does not do this has any strict legal claim to be regarded as other than a telepathic hallucination at best, though, as we shall see, some presumptions exist in favour of some ghosts being real entities.

[…]

Hallucinations (which are all in one's eye) cannot draw curtains, or open doors, or pick up books, or tuck in bed-clothes, or cause thumps – not real thumps, hallucinatory thumps are different. Consequently, if the stories are true, *some apparitions are ghosts*, real objective entities, filling space. The senses of a hallucinated person may be deceived as to touch, and as to feeling the breath of a phantasm (a likely story), as well as in sight and hearing. But a visible ghost which produces changes in the visible world cannot be a hallucination.[…]

These arguments, then, make in favour of the old-fashioned theory of ghosts and wraiths, as things objectively existing, which is very comforting to a conservative philosopher. Unluckily, just as many, or more, anecdotes look quite the other way.[…] On the whole, if the evidence is worth anything, there are real objective ghosts, and there are also telepathic hallucinations: so that the scientific attitude is to believe in both, if in either.[…] The alternative is to believe in neither, and I have already remarked on the difficulty of this very ordinary mental position. But the difficulty is only felt by the infinitesimal minority of people who are acquainted with the evidence for and the history of apparitions.

And why take all this trouble, and write all this drearihead? some one may ask. Well, the argument *is* dreary: all arguments are, especially those which verge on metaphysics. But, on the other hand, the facts are of the highest curiosity; or, if any one denies the facts *in toto*, then the indubitable fact that so many sane and commonly truthful persons agree in suffering similar delusions, or inventing similar falsehoods, is in itself a phenomenon which well deserves examination. For it is not the 'imaginative' only, or the ignorant, or the unhealthy, or the timid and nervous, who report their abnormal experiences. If only schoolgirls, or poets like Shelley (a small class), or uneducated persons, or cowards, or fools came forward with their tales, we might contemptuously reject them. But the witnesses are very often honourable men, honourable women, brave, sane, healthy, not fanciful, not in a state of 'expectancy' (which, in fact, is usually fatal to ghost-seeing); and these persons have nothing to gain, and some consideration to lose, by reporting their experience. It is absurd to say that these reports are not curious, and do not deserve careful study, by all who have leisure to interest themselves in anthropology, the science of man. As to the bearing of the whole discussion on the awful subject of personal immortality, we may say that at present psychical studies do not bear on that problem at all, except as raising a presumption that we do not know everything about human life, and about the mystic elements deep-seated in our nature. And perhaps this is the real attraction to the theme: it is so natural to wish for a *terra incognita*, 'the land not yet meted out' by science – the free space where Romance may still try an unimpeded flight. When we do really know all about everything, then (and perhaps not till then) Life will cease to be worth living, and mankind, like Mr Darwin, will find Shakespeare nauseously dull.[15] But that can never happen while unexplained apparitions continue to remind us of what Hamlet said about the philosophy of Horatio.[16] And yet the 'common steadfast dunce' asks, 'What is the use of apparitions?'

Perhaps too boldly I began by expressing a modest belief that I could explain, to intellects rather above the average, how ghosts now stand in the philosophical market. They are 'inquired for'; they are not scouted by *all* those brilliantly gifted men of genius who can sign themselves F.R.S. This is a position which ghosts have not enjoyed since the Blessed Restoration. Common-sense (or common ignorance and dulness) is no longer all supreme here. The ghost may come to his own again; but this can hardly happen while we do not know whether he is 'a sort of something,' or whether he merely represents the impression made on the mind of the percipient, A., by the mind of B., who may be dead, or at Jericho, when he appears, say, in Bond Street. This is a question which nobody can answer:

we have given reasons for believing that some ghosts are 'a sort of a some-thing,' while others are mere hallucinations.

[...]

As to the sounds, thumps, lights, I still cling fondly to my theory, stated by a ghost in a little tale called 'Castle Perilous,'* that there are examples of a kind of *aphasia* in ghosts. They are doing their best to appear, but just as the aphasiac patient cannot get hold of the words he wants, so they cannot quite show us what they want to show. But all this relies on the suppressed prem-iss, *sunt aliquid manes*, – ghosts are *something*,[17] and have a purpose. Now, that is just the question at issue.

---

* 'In the Wrong Paradise.'

'Science and Demonology',

Illustrated London News CIV:2880
(30 June 1894), p. 822

There are moments, I confess, when it seems to me that we place science on too high a pedestal. By 'science,' of course, I do not mean knowledge 'in the abstract'; but just the opinion, or *obiter dictum*,[1] of this, that, or the other scientific gentleman. In England, when people say 'science' they commonly mean an article for Professor Huxley in the *Nineteenth Century*. The learned Professor has lately collected in 'Science and Christian Tradition' (Macmillan) a number of his Homeric combats with Mr. Gladstone and the Duke of Argyll, battles waged over such themes as demonology and coral islands.[2] 'I'm no caring,' as the Scotch say, but about demonology it is notoriously difficult. 'Demonology is doomed,' says Professor Huxley (p. 347).[3] Now, in 1858, M. Littré wrote, in the *Revue des Deux Mondes*, an essay in which he said that the study of demoniacal affections had, as yet, scarcely been sketched out.[4] M. Littré was a considerable man of science, and his notable scepticism stood in the way of his election to the French Academy.

About 'demoniacal affections' he gave forth a very uncertain sound, as was natural and right, seeing that the subject had never, in his opinion, been properly investigated. If, in the thirty-six years that have intervened, science has completed what, in Littré's time, was a mere sketch, I wish I could be informed about the works in which the task is done, and about the new researches on the strength of which demonology is 'doomed.' My difficulty is increased by another saying of Professor Huxley's (pp. 391, 392). He has been warring with Mr. Gladstone, and quotes a criticism of that philosopher's 'grossest exaggerations,' his 'arguments based upon the slightest hypotheses,' and so remarkable for their 'intrinsic hollowness.'[5] The critic was Mr. A.J. Balfour. Mr. Balfour, cries Mr. Huxley, 'has science in the blood' (which Mr. Gladstone has not), 'and has the advantage of a natural, as well as a highly cultivated, aptitude for the use of methods of precision in investigation.'

Très bien. But then Mr. Balfour, with science in his blood, does not seem to hold that demonology is doomed. On the contrary, he is president of a society for the investigation of demonology, among other matters; and I gather, from a summary of his speech to the society, that he 'thinks there is something in it.'[6] If this be so, Science, in the blood too, has not spoken her last word on demonology from the lips of Professor Huxley.

This might be gratifying to the superstitious, but if we turn to a scientific believer in demonology, Mr. Alfred Russel Wallace, I fear that we are but little comforted. Science is, no doubt, in Mr. Wallace's blood, and, as to original investigation and discovery, I am given to understand that he has done more than Professor Huxley, for the Professor's 'Bathybius' is scratched out of all his engagements.[7] Now, Mr. Wallace, in 1875, wrote a little work on 'Miracles and Modern Spiritualism,' where we might expect an application of 'methods of precision' to the theme. But we are sadly disappointed. Mr. Wallace writes (p. 7): 'Lord Orrery and Mr. Valentine Greatrak both informed Dr. Henry More and Mr. Glanvil that, at Lord Conway's house at Ragley, in Ireland (!), a gentleman's butler, in their presence and in broad daylight, rose into the air and floated about the room above their heads. This is related by Glanvil in his "Sadducismus Triumphatus".'[8]

I am sorry to contradict a man of science on a matter of easily ascertainable fact, but Mr. Wallace is wrong. Ragley is so far from being 'in Ireland' that Greatrak was brought over from Ireland, at very considerable expense, to heal Lady Conway, in which he failed. The gentleman's butler floated in Lord Orrery's house in Ireland. He had gone out of a Sunday to buy playing-cards, he met the fairies, and it was they who made him float in the air, after Lord Orrery took him in, to protect him from 'the good people.' Mr. Wallace states incompletely and very inaccurately facts which we may pardon Professor Huxley for discarding. Now, surely we do expect science, in one of its most distinguished votaries, to tell a plain tale correctly. Mr. Wallace may have read 'Sadducismus Triumphatus,' but in other cases he takes his facts at second hand from Mr. Dale Owen, in place of going to the very accessible authorities.[9] These authorities are infinitely more valuable for his purpose, and Mr. Dale Owen gives a very inadequate summary of their contents. Thus, on this side, science, in the person of Mr. Wallace, has not applied the ordinary historical 'methods of precision.'

To a mere looker-on, Mr. Wallace seems to exhibit the same unscientific method in another curious question. Mr. G.H. Lewes, in 'Problems of Life and Mind,' remarked on a most interesting theme – the identity of hallucinations among the insane, in England and Germany and in all ranks of life.[10] All believe in 'invisible enemies,' who 'strike them with galvanic batteries hidden under the table,' and so on.[11] If I am not misinformed, a not uncommon symptom of epilepsy is the vision of a person in red, who strikes down the patient. Mr. Lewes explains the identity of hallucination by 'identity of congestion'[12] of the brain, as most people would naturally do; but Mr. Wallace urges that 'race, nation, education, lifelong habits and associations and ideas being *all* different,'[13] the explanation of identity of hallucination, as caused by identity of cerebral disease, is very inadequate. It seems adequate enough, granting that the patients are really mad. Of course a mad Australian black will not talk of galvanic batteries, but about 'invisible enemies' he will talk, and explain his morbid sensations, perhaps, by invisible boomerangs. Differing from Mr. Lewes, Mr. Wallace would apparently regard the 'so-called spectral' as 'often actual objective forms.'[14] The maniacs, on this theory, are sane enough, though terrified by 'invisible enemies,' which are 'actual.' Surely a 'mad doctor' should know a madman by this time when he sees one, though perhaps the public has reason to be sceptical about that point. However (p. 196), Mr. Wallace thinks that 'perhaps' the eternal Nicolai, of Berlin, 'saw real things, after all,' and that, had photography been invented, they might have been photographed![15] Clearly, if Mr. Wallace thinks *that*, the scientific thing to do is to photograph madmen who see hallucinatory foes or friends. There is no lack of subjects! Again, after Nicolai had been let blood, as was his custom, and became easier in his mind (which had been agitated) he did not see his spectral friends any more. It will hardly be argued that they only appeared, if they were actual objective beings, while he was ill and troubled in spirit, departing when he took his usual medical precautions. These methods of precision seem to lack preciseness, which leads to the conclusion that on both sides of this question men of science may be unscientific.

Mr. Wallace mentions one fact to which I can give him a pleasing parallel. He speaks of a lady medium whose chair was drawn away from her, apparently by spiritual power.[16] Now, according to Mrs. Parson's 'Life of Saint Colette,' the nuns would see the saint's chair dragged away as by an invisible schoolboy, and the saint come a cropper.[17] 'He often treats me so,' said St. Colette, as she got up and rubbed the part affected. Saint Colette, who founded the Clarisses, or Poor Clares, in France, lived about 1485–1545, roughly speaking, which shows that the schoolboy trick is an old one of the Enemy's. The saint so often floated in the air at Mass that the service had to be conducted privately for her, as the spectacle of her elevation disturbed the minds of the faithful. Unluckily, Professor Huxley will only say 'Fudge!' also 'Sludge!' and he rejects poor old Sludge's performance, without, perhaps, explaining why many honourable and living men say that they witnessed it.[18] Yet some of these, too, 'have science in their blood.'

'Science and "Miracles"',
The Making of Religion,
2nd edition

(Longmans, Green and Co., 1900)

Historical Sketch

Research in the X region[1] is not a new thing under the sun. When Saul disguised himself before his conference with the Witch of Endor, he made an elementary attempt at a scientific test of the supernormal. Croesus, the king, went much further, when he tested the clairvoyance of the oracles of Greece, by sending an embassy to ask what he was doing at a given hour on a given day, and by then doing something very *bizarre*. We do not know how the Delphic oracle found out the right answer, but various easy methods of fraud at once occur to the mind. However, the procedure of Croesus, if he took certain precautions, was relatively scientific. Relatively scientific also was the inquiry of Porphyry, with whose position our own is not unlikely to be compared.[2] Unable, or reluctant, to accept Christianity, Porphyry 'sought after a sign' of an element of supernormal truth in Paganism. But he began at the wrong end, namely at Pagan spiritualistic *séances*, with the usual accompaniments of darkness and fraud. His perplexed letter to Anebo, with the reply attributed to Iamblichus, reveal Porphyry wandering puzzled among mediums, floating lights, odd noises, queer dubious 'physical phenomena.' He did not begin with accurate experiments as to the existence of rare, and apparently supernormal human faculties, and he seems to have attained no conclusion except that 'spirits' are 'deceitful.'*

Something more akin to modern research began about the time of the Reformation, and lasted till about 1680. The fury for burning witches led men of sense, learning, and humanity to ask whether there was any reality

---

* See Mr. Myers's paper on the 'Ancient Oracles,' in *Classical Essays*, and the author's 'Ancient Spiritualism,' in *Cock Lane and Common Sense*.

in witchcraft, and, generally, in the marvels of popular belief. The inquiries of Thyraeus, Lavaterus, Bodinus, Wierus, Le Loyer, Reginald Scot, and many others,[3] tended on the whole to the negative side as regards the wilder fables about witches, but left the problems of ghosts and haunted houses pretty much where they were before. It may be observed that Lavaterus (*circ.* 1580) already put forth a form of the hypothesis of telepathy (that 'ghosts' are hallucinations produced by the direct action of one mind, or brain, upon another), while Thyraeus doubted whether the noises heard in 'haunted houses' were not mere hallucinations of the sense of hearing. But all these early writers, like Cardan, were very careless of first-hand evidence, and, indeed, preferred ghosts vouched for by classical authority, Pliny, Plutarch, or Suetonius. With the Rev. Joseph Glanvil, F.R.S. (*circ.* 1666), a more careful examination of evidence came into use. Among the marvels of Glanvil's and other tracts usually published together in his 'Sadducismus Triumphatus' will be found letters which show that he and his friends, like Henry More and Boyle, laboured to collect first-hand evidence for second sight, haunted houses, ghosts, and wraiths. The confessed object was to procure a 'Whip for the Droll,' a reply to the laughing scepticism of the Restoration. The result was to bring on Glanvil a throng of bores – he was 'worse haunted than Mr. Mompesson's house,' he says – and Mr. Pepys found his arguments 'not very convincing.' Mr. Pepys, however, was alarmed by 'our young gib-cat,' which he mistook for a 'spright.'[4] With Henry More, Baxter, and Glanvil practically died, for the time, the attempt to investigate these topics scientifically, though an impression of doubt was left on the mind of Addison.[5] Witchcraft ceased to win belief, and was abolished, as a crime, in 1736. Some of the Scottish clergy, and John Wesley, clung fondly to the old faith, but Wodrow, and Cotton Mather (about 1710–1730) were singularly careless and unlucky in producing anything like evidence for their narratives.[6] Ghost stories continued to be told, but not to be investigated.

Then one of the most acute of philosophers decided that investigation ought never to be attempted. This scientific attitude towards X phenomena, that of refusing to examine them, and denying them without examination, was fixed by David Hume in his celebrated essay on 'Miracles.'[7] Hume derided the observation and study of what he called 'Miracles,' in the field of experience, and he looked for an *a priori* argument which would for ever settle the question without examination of facts. In an age of experimental philosophy, which derided *a priori* methods, this was Hume's great contribution to knowledge. His famous argument, the joy of many an honest breast, is a tissue of fallacies which might be given for exposure to beginners in logic, as an elementary exercise. In announcing his discovery, Hume amusingly displays the self-complacency and the want of humour with which we Scots are commonly charged by our critics:

'I flatter myself that I have discovered an argument which, if just, will, with the wise and learned, be an everlasting check to all kinds of superstitious delusions, and consequently will be useful as long as the world endures.'[8]

He does not expect, however, to convince the multitude. Till the end of the world, 'accounts of miracles and prodigies, I suppose, will be found in all histories, sacred and profane.'[9] Without saying here what he means by a miracle, Hume argues that 'experience is our only guide in reasoning.'[10] He then defines a miracle as 'a violation of the laws of nature.'[11] By a 'law of nature' he means a uniformity, not of all experience, but of each experience as he will deign to admit; while he excludes, without examination, all evidence for experience of the absence of such uniformity. That kind of experience cannot be considered. 'There must be a uniform experience against every miraculous event, otherwise the event would not merit that appellation.'[12] If there be any experience in favour of the event, that experience does not count. A miracle is counter to universal experience, no event is counter to universal experience, therefore no event is a miracle. If you produce evidence to what Hume calls a miracle (we shall see examples) he replies that the evidence is not valid, unless its falsehood would be more miraculous than the fact. Now no error of human evidence can be more miraculous than a 'miracle.' Therefore there can be no valid evidence for 'miracles.' Fortunately, Hume now gives an example of what he means by 'miracles.' He says:--

'For, first, there is *not to be found*, in *all history*, any miracle attested by a *sufficient number* of men, of such unquestioned *good sense, education*, and *learning*, as to secure us against all delusion in themselves; of such undoubted *integrity*, as to place them beyond all suspicion of any design to deceive others; of such credit and reputation in the eyes of mankind, as to have a great deal to lose in case of their being detected in any falsehood; and at the same time attesting facts performed in such a *public manner*, and in so *celebrated a part of the world*, as to render the detection unavoidable; all which circumstances are requisite to give us a full assurance in the testimony of men.'* [13]

Hume added a note at the end of his book, in which he contradicted every assertion which he had made in the passage just cited; indeed, he contradicted himself before he had written six pages.

'There surely never was a greater number of miracles ascribed to one person than those which were lately said to have been wrought in France upon the tomb of Abbé Paris, the famous Jansenist, with whose sanctity the people were so long deluded. The curing of the sick, giving hearing to the deaf, and sight to the blind, were everywhere talked of as the usual effects of that holy sepulchre. But what is more extraordinary, many of the miracles were *immediately proved upon the spot*, before *judges of unquestioned integrity*, attested

---

*   The italics here are those of Mr. Alfred Russell [sic] Wallace, in his *Miracles and Modern Science*. Mr. Huxley, in his exposure of Hume's fallacies (in his Life of Hume), did not examine the Jansenist 'miracles' which Hume was criticising.

by *witnesses* of *credit and distinction*, in *a learned age*, and on the most *eminent theatre* that is *now in the world*. Nor is this all. A relation of them was published and dispersed everywhere; nor were the Jesuits, though a learned body, supported by the civil magistrate, and determined enemies to those opinions, in whose favour the miracles were said to have been wrought, ever able *distinctly to refute or detect them*. Where shall we find such a number of circumstances, agreeing to the corroboration of one fact? And what have we to oppose to such a cloud of witnesses, but the absolute *impossibility*, or *miraculous nature* of the events which they relate? And this, surely, in the eyes of all reasonable people, will alone be regarded as a sufficient refutation.'[14]

Thus Hume first denies the existence of such evidence, given in such circumstances as he demands, and then he produces an example of that very kind of evidence. Having done this, he abandons (as Mr. Wallace observes) his original assertion that the evidence does not exist, and takes refuge in alleging 'the absolute impossibility' of the events which the evidence supports. Thus Hume poses as a perfect judge of the possible, in a kind of omniscience. He takes his stand on the uniformity of all experience that is not hostile to his idea of the possible, and dismisses all testimony to other experience, even when it reaches his standard of evidence. He is remote indeed from Virchow's position 'that what we call the laws of nature must vary according to our frequent new experiences.'* In his note, Hume buttresses and confirms his evidence for the Jansenist miracles. They have even a martyr, M. Montgeron, who wrote an account of the events, and, says Hume lightly, 'is now said to be somewhere in a dungeon on account of his book.' Many of the miracles of the Abbé Paris were proved immediately by witnesses before the Bishop's court at Paris, under the eye of Cardinal Noailles.... 'His successor was an enemy to the Jansenists, yet twenty-two *curés* of Paris...pressed him to examine these miracles.... *But he wisely forbore.*'[15] Hume adds his testimony to the character of these *curés*. Thus it is wisdom, according to Hume, to dismiss the most public and well-attested 'miracles' without examination. This is experimental science of an odd kind.

The phenomena were cases of healing, many of them surprising, of cataleptic rigidity, and of insensibility to pain, among visitors to the tomb of the Abbé Paris (1731). Had the cases been judicially examined (all medical evidence was in their favour), and had they been proved false, the cause of Hume would have profited enormously. A strong presumption would have been raised against the miracles of Christianity. But Hume applauds the wisdom of not giving his own theory this chance of a triumph. The cataleptic seizures were of the sort now familiar to science. These have, therefore, emerged from the miraculous. In fact, the phenomena which occurred at the tomb of the Abbé Paris have emerged almost too far, and now seem in danger of being too readily and too easily accepted. In 1887

★   Moll, *Hypnotism*, p. 357.

MM. Binet and Féré, of the school of the Salpêtrière, published in English a popular manual styled 'Animal Magnetism.' These authors write with great caution about such alleged phenomena as the reading, by the hypnotised patient, of the thoughts in the mind of the hypnotiser. But as to the phenomena at the tomb of the Abbé Paris, they say that 'suggestion explains them.'* That is, in the opinion of MM. Binet and Féré the so-called 'miracles' really occurred, and were worked by 'the imagination,' by 'self-suggestion.'[16]

[...]

We return to Hume. He next argues that the pleasures of wonder make all accounts of 'miracles' worthless. He has just given an example of the equivalent pleasures of dogmatic disbelief. Then Religion is a disturbing force; but so, manifestly, is irreligion. 'The wise and learned are content to deride the absurdity, without informing themselves of the particular facts.'[17] The wise and learned are applauded for their scientific attitude. Again, miracles destroy each other, for all religions have their miracles, but all religions cannot be true. This argument is no longer of force with people who look on 'miracles' as = 'X phenomena,' not as divine evidences to the truth of this or that creed. 'The gazing populace receives, without examination, whatever soothes superstition,' and Hume's whole purpose is to make the wise and learned imitate the gazing populace by rejecting alleged facts 'without examination.'[18] The populace investigated more than did the wise and learned.

Hume has an alternative definition of a miracle – 'a miracle is a transgression of a law of nature by a particular volition of the Deity, or by the interposition of some invisible agent.'[19] We reply that what Hume calls a 'miracle' may result from the operation of some as yet unascertained law of nature (say self-suggestion), and that our business, at present, is to examine such events, not to account for them.

It may fairly be said that Hume is arguing against men who wished to make so-called 'miracles' a test of the truth of Jansenism,[20] for example, and that he could not be expected to answer, by anticipation, ideas not current in his day. But he remains guilty of denouncing the investigation of apparent facts. No attitude can be less scientific than his, or more common among many men of science.

According to the humorous wont of things in this world, the whole question of the marvellous had no sooner been settled for ever by David Hume than it was reopened by Emanuel Swedenborg. Now, Kant was familiar with certain of the works of Hume, whether he had read his 'Essay on Miracles' or not. Far from declining to examine the portentous 'visions'

---

*   *Animal Magnetism*, p. 355.

of Swedenborg, Kant interested himself deeply in the topic.[21] As early as 1758 he wrote his first remarks on the seer, containing some reports of stories or legends about Swedenborg's 'clairvoyance.' In the true spirit of psychical research, Kant wrote a letter to Swedenborg, asking for information at first hand. The seer got the letter, but he never answered it. Kant, however, prints one or two examples of Swedenborg's successes.

[...]

Kant's real position about all these matters is, I venture to say, almost identical with that of Sir Walter Scott. A Scot himself, by descent, Kant may have heard tales of second-sight and bogles. Like Scott, he dearly loved a ghost-story; like Scott he was canny enough to laugh, publicly, at them and at himself for his interest in them. Yet both would take trouble to inquire. As Kant vainly wrote to Swedenborg and others – as he vainly spent 7l. on 'Arcana Coelestia,' so Sir Walter was anxious to go to Egypt to examine the facts of ink-gazing clairvoyance. Kant confesses that each individual ghost-story found him sceptical, whereas the cumulative mass made a considerable impression.*

The first seventy pages of the 'Träume' are devoted to a perfectly serious discussion of the metaphysics of 'Spirits.' On page 73 he pleasantly remarks, 'Now we shall understand that all said hitherto is superfluous,' and he will not reproach the reader who regards seers *not* as citizens of two worlds (Plotinus), but as candidates for Bedlam.

Kant's irony is peculiarly Scottish. He does not himself know how far he is in earnest, and, to save his self-respect and character for canniness, he 'jocks wi' deeficulty.' He amuses himself with trying how far he can carry speculations on metaphysics (not yet reformed by himself) into the realm of the ghostly. He makes admissions about his own tendency to think that he has an immaterial soul, and that these points are, or may be, or some day will be, scientifically solved. These admissions are eagerly welcomed by Du Prel in his 'Philosophy of Mysticism;'[22] but they are only part of Kant's joke, and how far they are serious, Kant himself does not know. If spiritualists knew their own business, they would translate and publish Kant's first seventy pages of 'Träume.' Something like telepathy, action of spirit, even discarnate, on spirit, is alluded to, but the idea is as old as Lavaterus at least (p. 52). Kant has a good deal to say, like Scott in his 'Demonology,' on the physics of Hallucination, but it is antiquated matter.[23] He thinks the whole topic of spiritual being only important as bearing on hopes of a future life. As speculation, all is 'in the air,' and as in such matters the learned and unlearned are on a level of ignorance, science will not discuss them. He then repeats the Swedenborg stories, and thinks it would be useful to pos-

---

*   *Träume*, p. 76.

terity if some one would investigate them while witnesses are alive and memories are fresh.

In fact, Kant asks for psychical research.

As for Swedenborg's so costly book, Kant laughs at it. There is in it no evidence, only assertion. Kant ends, having pleased nobody, he says, and as ignorant as when he began, by citing *cultivons notre jardin*.[24]

[…]

On the whole Kant is interested, but despairing. He wants facts, and no facts are given to him but the book of the Prophet Emanuel. But, as it happened, a new, or a revived, order of facts was just about to solicit scientific attention. Kant had (1766) heard rumours of healing by magnetism, and of the alleged effect of the magnet on the human frame. The subject was in the air, and had already won the attention of Mesmer, about whom Kant had information. It were superfluous to tell again the familiar story of Mesmer's performances at Paris. While Mesmer's theory of 'magnetism' was denounced by contemporary science, the discovery of the hypnotic sleep was made by his pupil, Puységur. This gentleman was persuaded that instances of 'thought-transference' (not through known channels of sense) occurred between the patient and the magnetiser, and he also believed that he had witnessed cases of 'clairvoyance,' 'lucidity,' *vue à distance*, in which the patient apparently beheld places and events remote in space. These things would now be explained by 'unconscious suggestion' in the more sceptical schools of psychological science. The Revolution interrupted scientific study in France to a great degree, but 'somnambulism' (the hypnotic sleep) and 'magnetism' were eagerly examined in Germany. Modern manuals, for some reason, are apt to overlook these German researches and speculations. (Compare Mr. Vincent's 'Elements of Hypnotism,' p. 34.)[25] The Schellings were interested; Ritter thought he had detected a new force, 'Siderism.'[26] Mr. Wallace, in his preface to Hegel's 'Philosophie des Geistes,' speaks as if Ritter had made experiments in telepathy.[27] He may have done so, but his 'Siderismus' (Tübingen, 1808) is a Report undertaken for the Academy of Munich, on the doings of an Italian water-finder, or 'dowser.' Ritter gives details of seventy-four experiments in 'dowsing' for water, metals, or coal. He believes in the faculty, but not in 'psychic' explanations, or the Devil. He talks about 'electricity' (pp. 170, 190). He describes his precautions to avoid vulgar fraud, but he took no precautions against unconscious thought-transference. He reckoned the faculty 'temperamental' and useful.

[…]

Probably the most important philosophical result of the early German researches into the hypnotic slumber is to be found in the writings of Hegel.

Owing to his peculiar use of a terminology, or scientific language, all his own, it is extremely difficult to make Hegel's meaning even moderately clear. Perhaps we may partly elucidate it by a similitude of Mr. Frederic Myers. Suppose we compare the ordinary everyday consciousness of each of us to a *spectrum*, whose ends towards each extremity fade out of our view.

Beyond the range of sight there may be imagined a lower or physiological end: for our ordinary consciousness, of course, is unaware of many physiological processes which are eternally going on within us. Digestion, so long as it is healthy, is an obvious example. But hypnotic experiment makes it certain that a patient, in the *hypnotic* condition, can consciously, or at least purposefully, affect physiological processes to which the *ordinary* consciousness is blind – for example, by raising a blister, when it is suggested that a blister must be raised. Again (granting the facts hypothetically and merely for the sake of argument), at the *upper* end of the spectrum, beyond the view of ordinary everyday consciousness, knowledge may be acquired of things which are out of the view of the consciousness of every day. For example (for the sake of argument let us admit it), unknown and remote people and places may be seen and described by clairvoyance, or *vue à distance*.

Now Hegel accepted as genuine the facts which we here adduce merely for the sake of argument, and by way of illustrations. But he did not regard the clairvoyant consciousness (or whatever we call it) which, *ex hypothesi*, is untrammelled by space, or even by time, as occupying what we style the *upper* end of the psychical spectrum. On the contrary, he placed it at the *lower* end. Hegel's upper end 'loses itself in light;' the lower end, *qui voit tant de choses*,[28] as La Fontaine's shepherd says, is *not* 'a sublime mental phase, and capable of conveying general truths.'[29] Time and space do not thwart the consciousness at Hegel's *lower* end, which springs from 'the great soul of nature.' But that lower end, though it may see for Jeanne d'Arc at Valcouleurs a battle at Rouvray, a hundred leagues away, does not communicate any lofty philosophic truths.* The phenomena of clairvoyance, in Hegel's opinion, merely indicate that the 'material' is really 'ideal,' which, perhaps, is as much as we can ask from them. 'The somnambulist and clairvoyant see without eyes, and carry their visions directly into regions where the waiting consciousness of orderly intelligence cannot enter' (Wallace).[30] Hegel admits, however, that 'in ordinary self-possessed conscious life' there are traces of the 'magic tie,' 'especially between female friends of delicate nerves,' to whom he adds husband and wife, and members of the same family.[31] He gives (without date or source) a case of a girl in Germany who saw her brother lying dead in a hospital at Valladolid. Her brother was at the time in the hospital, but it was another man in the next bed who was dead. 'It is thus impossible to make out whether what the clairvoyants really see preponderates over what they deceive themselves in.'[32]

---

*   Hegel accepts the clairvoyance of the Pucelle.

As long as the facts which Hegel accepted are not officially welcomed by science, it may seem superfluous to dispute as to whether they are attained by the lower or the higher stratum of our consciousness. But perhaps the question here at issue may be elucidated by some remarks of Dr. Max Dessoir. Psychology, he says, has proved that in every conception and idea an image or group of images must be present. These mental images are the recrudescence or recurrence of perceptions. We see a tree, or a man, or a dog, and whenever we have before our minds the conception or idea of any of these things the original perception of them returns, though of course more faintly. But in Dr. Dessoir's opinion these revived mental images would reach the height of actual hallucinations (so that the man, dog, or tree would seem visibly present) if other memories and new sensations did not compete with them and check their development.

Suppose, to use Mlle. Ferrand's metaphor, a human body, living, but with all its channels of sensation hitherto unopened.[33] Open the sense of sight to receive a flash of green colour, and close it again. Apparently, whenever the mind informing this body had the conception of green (and it could have no other) it would also have an hallucination of green, thus

'Annihilating all that's made,
To a green thought in a green shade.'[34]

Now, in sleep or hypnotic trance the competition of new sensations and other memories is removed or diminished, and therefore the idea of a man, dog, or tree once suggested to the hypnotised patient, does become an actual hallucination. The hypnotised patient sees the absent object which he is told to see, the sleeper sees things not really present.

Our primitive state, before the enormous competition of other memories and new sensations set in, would thus be a state of hallucination. Our normal present condition, in which hallucination is checked by competing memories and new sensations, is a suppression of our original, primitive, natural tendencies. Hallucination represents 'the main trunk of our psychical existence.'* [35] In Dr. Dessoir's theory this condition of hallucination is man's original and most primitive condition, but it is not a *higher*, rather a lower state of spiritual activity than the everyday practical unhallucinated consciousness.

This is also the opinion of Hegel, who supposes our primitive mental condition to be capable of descrying objects remote in space and time. Mr. Myers, as we saw, is of the opposite opinion, as to the relative dignity and relative reality of the present everyday self, and the old original fundamental Self. Dr. Dessoir refrains from pronouncing a decided opinion as to whether the original, primitive, hallucinated self within us does 'preside

---

* See Dr. Dessoir, in *Das Doppel Ich*, as quoted by Mr. Myers, *Proceedings*, vol. vi. 213.

over powers and actions at a distance,' such as clairvoyance; but he believes in hypnotisation at a distance. His theory, like Hegel's, is that of 'atavism,' or 'throwing back' to some very remote ancestral condition. This will prove of interest later.

Hegel, at all events, believed in the fact of clairvoyance (though deeming it of little practical use); he accepted telepathy ('the magic tie'); he accepted interchange of sensations between the hypnotiser and the hypnotised; he believed in the divining rod, and, unlike Kant, even in 'Scottish second-sight.' 'The intuitive soul oversteps the conditions of time and space; it beholds things remote, things long past, and things to come.'*

The pendulum of thought has swung back a long way from the point whither it was urged by David Hume. Hegel remarks: 'The facts, it might seem, first of all call for verification. But such verification would be superfluous to those on whose account it was called for, since they facilitate the inquiry for themselves by declaring the narratives, infinitely numerous though they be, and accredited by the education and character of the witnesses, to be mere deception and imposture. Their *a priori* conceptions are so rooted that no testimony can avail against them, and they have even denied what they have seen with their own eyes,'[36] and reported under their own hands, like Sir David Brewster.[37] Hegel, it will be observed, takes the facts as given, and works them into his general theory of the Sensitive Soul (*fühlende Seele*). He does not try to establish the facts; but to establish, or at least to examine them, is the first business of Psychical Research. Theorising comes later.

The years which have passed between the date of Hegel's 'Philosophy of Mind' and our own time have witnessed the long dispute over the existence, the nature, and the causes of the hypnotic condition, and over the reality and limitations of the phenomena. Thus the Academy of Medicine in Paris appointed a Committee to examine the subject in 1825. The Report on 'Animal Magnetism,' as it was then styled, was presented in 1831.[38] The Academy lacked the courage to publish it, for the Report was favourable even to certain of the still disputed phenomena. At that time, in accordance with a survival of the theory of Mesmer, the agent in hypnotic cases was believed to be a kind of efflux of a cosmic fluid from the 'magnetiser' to the patient. There was 'a magnetic connection.'

Though no distinction between mesmerism and hypnotism is taken in popular language, 'mesmerism' is a word implying this theory of 'magnetic' or other unknown personal influence. 'Hypnotism,' as will presently be seen, implies no such theory. The Academy's Report (1831) attested the development, under 'magnetism,' of 'new faculties,' such as clairvoyance and intuition, also the production of 'great changes in the physical econo-

---

*   *Philosophie des Geistes*, Werke, vol. vii. 179. Berlin, 1845. The examples and much of the philosophising are in the *Zusätze*, not translated in Mr. Wallace's version, Oxford, 1894.

my,'[39] such as insensibility, and sudden increase of strength. The Report declared it to be 'demonstrated' that sleep could be produced 'without suggestion,' as we say now, though the term was not then in use. 'Sleep has been produced in circumstances in which the persons could not see or were ignorant of the means employed to produce it.'[40]

The Academy did its best to suppress this Report, which attests the phenomena that Hegel accepted, phenomena still disputed. Six years later (1837), a Committee reported against the pretensions of a certain Berna, a 'magnetiser.' No person acted on both Committees, and this Report was accepted. Later, a number of people tried to read a letter in a box, and failed. 'This,' says Mr. Vincent, 'settled the question with regard to clairvoy-ance;'[41] though it might be more logical to say that it settled the pretensions of the competitors on that occasion. The Academy now decided that, be-cause certain persons did not satisfy the expectations raised by their prelim-inary advertisements, therefore the question of magnetism was definitely closed.

We have often to regret that scientific eminence is not always accompa-nied by scientific logic. Where science neglects a subject, charlatans and dupes take it up. In England 'animal magnetism' had been abandoned to this class of enthusiasts, till Thackeray's friend, Dr. Elliotson, devoted him-self to the topic. He was persecuted as doctors know how to persecute; but in 1841, Braid, of Manchester, discovered that the so-called 'magnetic sleep' could be produced without any 'magnetism.' He made his patients stare fixedly at an object, and encouraged them to expect to go to sleep. He called his method 'Hypnotism,' a term which begs no question. Seeming to cease to be mysterious, hypnotism became all but respectable, and was being used in surgical operations, till it was superseded by chloroform. In England, the study has been, and remains, rather *suspect*, while on the Continent hypno-tism is used both for healing purposes and in the inquiries of experimental psychology. Wide differences of opinion still exist, as to the nature of the hypnotic sleep, as to its physiological concomitants, and as to the limits of the faculties exercised in or out of the slumber. It is not even absolutely certain that the exercise of the stranger faculties – for instance, that the production of anaesthesia and rigidity – are the results merely of 'suggestion' and expectancy. A hypnotised patient is told that the middle finger of his left hand will become rigid and incapable of sensation. This occurs, and is explained by 'suggestion,' though *how* 'suggestion' produces the astonishing effect is another problem. The late Mr. Gurney, however, made a number of experiments in which no suggestion was pronounced, nor did the pa-tients know which of their fingers was to become rigid and incapable of pain.[42] The patient's hands were thrust through a screen; on the other side of which the hypnotist made passes above the finger which was to become rigid. The lookers-on selected the finger, and the insensibility was tested by a strong electric current. The effect was also produced *without* passes, the operator merely pointing at the selected finger, and 'willing' the result. If he did not 'will' it, nothing occurred, nor did anything occur if he willed without pointing. The proximity of the operator's hand produced no effect if he did not 'will,' nor was his 'willing' successful if he did not bring his hand near that of the patient. Other people's hands, similarly situated, produced no effect.

Experiments in transferring taste, as of salt, sugar, cayenne pepper, from operator to subject, were also successful. Drs. Janet and Gibert also produced sleep in a woman at a distance, by 'willing' it, at hours which were selected by a system of drawing lots.* These facts, of course, rather point to an element of truth in the old mesmeric hypothesis of some specific influence in the operator. They cannot very well be explained by suggestion and expectancy. But these facts and facts of clairvoyance and thought-transference will be rejected as superstitious delusions by people who have not met them in their own experience. This need not prevent us from examining them, because *all* the facts, including those now universally accepted by Continental and scarcely impeached by British science, have been noisily rejected again and again on Hume's principles.

The rarer facts, as Mr. Gurney remarks, 'still go through the hollow form of taking place.'[43] Here is an example of the mode in which these phenomena are treated by popular science. Mr. Vincent says that 'clairvoyance and phrenology were Elliotson's constant stock in trade.' (Phrenology was also Braid's stock in trade.) 'It is a matter of congratulation to have been so soon delivered from what Dr. Lloyd Tuckey has well called "a mass of superincumbent rubbish."'† [44] Clairvoyance is part of a mass of rubbish, on page 57. On page 67, Mr. Vincent says: 'There are many interesting questions, such as telepathy, thought-reading, clairvoyance, upon which it would be perhaps rash to give any decided opinion.... All these strange psychical conditions present problems of great interest,' and are only omitted because 'they have not a sufficient bearing on the normal states of hypnosis....'[45] Thus what was 'rubbish' in one page 'presents problems of great interest' ten pages later, and, after offering a decided opinion that clairvoyance is rubbish, Mr. Vincent thinks it rash to give any decided opinion. It is rather rash to give a decided opinion, and then to say that it is rash to do so.‡ [46]

This brief sketch shows that science is confronted by certain facts, which, in his time, Hume dismissed as incredible miracles, beneath the contempt of the wise and learned. We also see that the stranger and rarer phenomena

* *Proceedings*, S.P.R., vol. ii. pp. 201–207, 390–392.

† *Elements of Hypnotism*, p. 57.

‡ Possibly Mr. Vincent only means that Elliotson's experiments, 'little more than sober fooling' (p. 57), with the sisters Okey, were rubbish. But whether the sisters Okey were or were not honest is a question on which we cannot enter here.

which Hegel accepted as facts, and interwove with his general philosophy, are still matters of dispute. Admitted by some men of science, they are doubted by others; by others, again, are denied, while most of the journalists and authors of cheap primers, who inspire popular tradition, regard the phenomena as frauds or fables of superstition. But it is plain that these phenomena, like the more ordinary facts of hypnotism, *may* finally be admitted by science. The scientific world laughed, not so long ago, at Ogham inscriptions, meteorites, and at palaeolithic weapons as impostures, or freaks of nature.[47] Now nobody has any doubt on these matters, and clairvoyance, thought-transference, and telepathy may, not inconceivably, be as fortunate in the long run as meteorites, or as the more usual phenomena of hypnotism.

It is only Lord Kelvin who now maintains, or lately maintained, that in hypnotism there is nothing at all but fraud and malobservation.[48] In years to come it may be that only some similar belated voice will cry that in thought-transference there is nothing but malobservation and fraud. At present the serious attention and careful experiment needed for the establishment of the facts are more common among French than among English men of science. When published, these experiments, if they contain any affirmative instances, are denounced as 'superstitious,' or criticized after what we must charitably deem to be a very hasty glance, by the guides of popular opinion. Examples of this method will be later quoted. Meanwhile the disputes as to these alleged facts are noticed here, because of their supposed relation to the Origin of Religion.

'Three Seeresses
(1880–1900, 1424–1431)',
Anglo-Saxon Review 6

(September 1900), pp. 63–73

'Under the black volcanic peak of Moreh' (says Colonel Conder)[1] the witch of Endor had her habitation. It seems an appropriate abode. Saul had 'smelled out' the witches, as Panda and Cetewayo are wont to do in Zululand, and the witch of Endor had to lurk in the hills, a persecuted seeress.[2] The seeress is now more common in the land. But yesterday I read a long report from a lady in Boston, Mass. She was sent by the mother of two lost boys to consult a clairvoyante. The first two clairvoyantes to whom she applied were engaged in prophesying to earlier visitors; the third, though busy, proved to be a prophetess with a vengeance. Such things are done not far from Salem, where so many mediums were burned two centuries ago. London is full of seeresses; in Bond Street, not under black volcanic cones, they have their habitations. I once consulted one by proxy; I sent a young lady to ask the simple question, 'Who was Mademoiselle Luci?'[3] The seeress knew no means of magic art whereby to unriddle a purely historical problem, and my guinea was wasted. But often, at dinner, ladies talk to me about wonderful Bond Street seeresses, who tell them 'all that ever they did.' One was tested by the Society for Psychical Research, and failed to satisfy that sceptical clan.

Modern seeresses are of two classes: the Bond Street class, who divine for the fair sex; and the class who are studied by eminent psychologists, like Professor James, Professor Richet, and Professor Flournoy. Books are published about them, full of strange words, as *promnesic*, *subliminal*, *telaesthetic*, and, for all I know, *proparoxytonic*. These are difficult phrases, and in writing about seeresses I shall shun them as far as possible. But I cannot avoid the word *hallucination*, which means an impression of sight, sound, or hearing, so vivid that it seems to the patient to be real, though it is the reverse. I confine myself to three examples of women having a spirit of divination. Boston (U.S.), Geneva, and Domremy have produced these three seeresses of unequal interest and reputation. Two of them are still alive, Mrs. Piper and Mademoiselle 'Hélène Smith.'[4] We have to ask whether their achievements throw any light on the visions and voices of the third, the immortal Jeanne d'Arc.[5] The reader need not, I should say at once, be under any anxiety lest the reputation of La Pucelle may suffer from this example of the Comparative Method.

Mrs. Piper, the first seeress on our list, has been discussed at prodigious length in the 'Proceedings' of the Society for Psychical Research. I do not advise persons of ordinary applications to attempt the adventure of reading through the mass of evidence about Mrs. Piper. Assuredly they would faint by the way. In many cases the inspired utterances of Mrs. Piper, with the conversation of her clients, have been taken down in shorthand; and more dreary chatter has never been thus recorded. But the object of science is not amusement, is not literary interest, but sternly assiduous investigation of facts, and accurate record of the same. Mrs. Piper is a married woman, who, in these many years, has fully persuaded her examiners of her simplicity and honesty, when in her natural everyday condition. But, at her *séances*, she falls into a kind of trance, after sitting in quiet abstraction for a short time. She is then, in her own opinion, the mouthpiece of divers spirits of the dead. They speak through her lips, or employ her hand in writing, or (what is really remarkable) they sometimes do both at once, one spirit writing the message, another speaking a different message, simultaneously. In this accomplishment (which is shared by some hypnotised patients) Mrs. Piper exceeds the skill of the savage mediums, in many quarters, who deliver spirit messages after falling into trances. In old days, when Professor William James first inspected Mrs. Piper, she was mainly possessed by a spirit giving his name as Phinuit, and averring that he had been a French physician at Metz. He speaks in a French accent, but does not know French. He revels in diagnosing the complaints of the living, and in describing the diseases of the dead. His medicine is popular medicine, such as may be found in rural practice by housewives.

[…]

If we had only Phinuit to consider, I, for one, should feel certain that Phinuit was only Mrs. Piper talking in her sleep, and keeping up an impersonation of a French doctor who never existed. The successes I would attribute to a lucky set of guesses craftily conducted, to 'muscle-reading' (as Mrs. Piper, in many cases, holds the sitter's hand), to facility of recognitions on the sitter's part, and, perhaps, to telepathy, or thought transference, between the sitter and Mrs. Piper.

In recent years Mrs. Piper has been much inspired by the spirit of 'G.P.,' a dead man of letters, and by that of the Rev. Mr. Moses, who, in his day, was a medium.[6] In his time Mr. Moses had a crowd of controlling spirits of the mighty dead, whom he called by such assumed names as 'Mentor,' 'Rector,' and 'Imperator.' The real names are known; but they are not known to Rector, Mentor, and Imperator when they speak through the mouth of Mrs. Piper. As to Mr. Moses himself, this is the kind of thing that he says (through Mrs. Piper): 'When you see my friend Sidgwick kindly ask him if he remembers the evening we spent together at his home.'

Now, Mr. Sidgwick does not 'remember the evening': there was, indeed, no such evening: Mr. Moses never entered Mr. Sidgwick's door.

Mr. Moses, the posthumous Mr. Moses, in short, is, as Mr. Pickwick said, 'a humbug,' or, to put it more plainly, as Mr. Pickwick went on to do, is 'an impostor.'

But, it may be argued, 'G.P.' is certainly 'G.P.' He tells his friends, through Mrs. Piper, things that are true, though Mrs. Piper could not know them; and things too intimate to be reported; and even things that are found to be true, though unknown to the sitters themselves. Therefore 'G.P.' is a genuine spirit; and *he* vouches for it that Phinuit and Mr. Moses are also genuine. But they certainly are *not*: they are dreams of Mrs. Piper's, and, far from being aided by G.P.'s recognition, that recognition only damages G.P. Mr. Moses's character is 'totally lost,' and G.P. 'has not sufficient for two.' Indeed Rector (who does not know his own name) candidly advises us 'not to rely too much on the statements made as tests, so called, by your friend George' – that is, G.P. As Mrs. Sidgwick asks, 'if the guaranteed spirits throw doubt on the genuineness of the guarantors, where are we?'[7] Where indeed? One affable spirit said he was Dr. Wiltze, who 'was dead, and his body was in the water.' Dr. Wiltze was not in the water, and he remains in robust health. 'G.P.' in life was addicted to certain metaphysical speculations. Mr. Moses knew Greek. He has forgotten his Greek. G.P. is all at sea in his metaphysics.

[...]

It is proper to add that some inquirers who have studied Mrs. Piper for several years with scientific thoroughness do believe in her spirits, and that Mrs. Sidgwick by no means abandons, though she greatly restricts the limits of, the spiritualistic hypothesis. The opinion of a mere student of the reports of the case, like myself, must be taken 'with all reserves.' That opinion is negative.

We now approach the second, the Genevan, seeress. What has to be said about her is based on a work much less tedious than the Reports on Mrs. Piper. It is entitled 'Des Indes à la Planète Mars. Etude sur un Cas de Somnambulisme avec Glossalalie. Par Th. Flournoy, Professeur de Psychologie à la Faculté des Sciences de l'Université de Genève. Alcan. Paris: 1900.'

'From India to Mars'! The title of Professor Flournoy's book is romantic. In fact, the work is a minute study of 'a woman having a spirit of divination': that is, of a girl of Geneva, in excellent health, who has, like Mrs. Piper, curious accesses of somnambulism. In these she sees and hears a being calling himself 'Leopold,' and professing to have been Cagliostro in a former life.[8] Leopold is very much akin to Phinuit, and, like him, is fond of amateur doctoring, to which the mother of Miss Smith of greatly addicted. The lady herself has had, and remembers, as many previous existences as She:[9] has been Marie Antoinette, and, earlier, an Arab princess, wife of a Hindu monarch of the fifteenth century A.D. She also visits, occasionally, the planet Mars. She talks and writes 'Martian' (a jargon based on French), and, what is more curious, she talks and writes, as an Arab princess, a sort of Sanskrit gibberish. She is an assistant in a large shop, works – always standing up, as is the cruel rule – for eleven hours a day, and has only a week's holiday in the year. Her case has analogies with those of the ignorant girls who, in unauthenticated legends dear to writers of psychological manuals, speak Greek and Hebrew. She is much akin to Mrs. Piper: her Cagliostro does not know Italian, as Mrs. Piper's Phinuit does not know French. Both Cagliostro and Phinuit, as I have said, give medical advice, based on popular, not scientific, medicine. In fact, both characters are 'secondary personalities' – fragments of the personalities of Mrs. Piper and Mlle. 'Hélène Smith.' Both exhibit talents and possess information beyond the range of Mrs. Piper and Miss Smith when in their normal condition. Both ladies look on their familiars as real guiding spirits, which, of course, is not the view of Professor Flournoy. Unlike Mrs. Piper, Miss Smith does not accept money for her *séances*. She appears to be an exemplary character, and have given M. Flournoy every facility for studying her case, though, being a spiritualist, she utterly disagrees with his diagnosis. Miss Smith was, as a child and a young girl, good, quiet, rather dull at her lessons, and dreamy. Her leisure was passed in building castles in Spain, and in weaving interminable romances, where she took the leading part. De Quincey, Scott, Sir James Mackintosh, George Sand, Louis Stevenson, and many other people, have had the same custom of romance-building in childhood. Like George Sand, Miss Smith in early youth was subject to hallucinations. Leopold began to appear at the critical period of youth, like the spirits of Jeanne d'Arc: the Leopolds, as it were, of a child of inspired genius, which, of course, Miss Smith does not possess. She always felt herself to be 'better born and bred than the rest of her family;' had longings for a rich, decorative existence; and embroidered designs of a bizarre Oriental quality.

[…]

The Oriental part of these reveries is the most curious. The theory of M. Flournoy (demonstrated in many cases by facts) is that Miss Smith, in her trances, reproduces many facts of which, in her normal state, she has no knowledge. An extremely bad linguist when awake, she can, in sleep, reproduce words and characters (such as Sanskrit or Hindu) which may only have passed under her eyes when in a 'suggestible' condition, between awake and asleep. In her Oriental fable she was the daughter of an Arab prince, wedded to King Sivrouka, who in 1401 (she says) reigned in Kanara, and built the fortress of Tchandraguizi. On his death she was burned. Sivrouka is now – Professor Flournoy! Him she suddenly recognised with the endearing cry of *Aitêyâ Ganapatinâmâ*! This was peculiarly appropriate, as is the equivalent of *Ganesâ*, the elephant-headed god, the patron of professors and men of literature. M. Flournoy took down, as well as he and his friends were able, the Oriental jargon of Miss Smith, and submitted it to Orientalists, including M.F. de Saussure, M. Barth, and M. Michel of Liège. The speech is of no idiom known to these specialists, but contains disfigured words and roots more akin to Sanskrit than to the living languages of India. 'The sense corresponds fairly well with the situations in which the words were spoken.'[10] Thus nobody has interpreted *aitêyâ*; but *ganapatinâmá* is part, I understand, of an invocation with which most Sanskrit MSS. open. In a love scene (with M. Flournoy-Sivrouka) Miss Smith used the words *mama priya, mama sadiva* (it should be *sâdhô*), which means, in Sanskrit, 'My dear, *mon bien aimé, mon excellent!*' Other Sanskritoid words were incomprehensible. On the whole, M. Michel (a most distinguished scholar and editor of Greek inscriptions) finds in the Oriental talk a jargon interlarded with *appropriate* fragments of Sanskrit. M. de Saussure is of the same opinion. A few real Sanskrit words are rightly used. The rest is an imitative babble.

[...] As to the 'supranormal,' in Miss Smith's case, M. Flournoy has found none. Physical marvels are reported of her before M. Flournoy made her acquaintance. At present, and provisionally, M. Flournoy believes that material objects *do* move without contact, in the presence of Eusapia, whom he studied *after* her exposure at Cambridge. He is ready to throw over this opinion as soon as proof of trickery or illusion is given. But he has seen none of these minor miracles when studying Miss Smith. Nor has he caught her in the fact of telepathy, though other persons appear to have been more lucky. Her best case of 'clairvoyance' (finding a lost object in picturesque circumstances) looks like a revival of an unconscious memory ('cryptomnesia'). In the same way, the historical 'retrocognitions' contain nothing that Miss Smith may not have known or heard mentioned. The evidence for that kind of thing is good only when the vision has been formally recorded before the discovery of the existence of the authenticating manuscript. Of this combination, perhaps, only one example is known; and that instance, though curious, does not compel belief.

M. Flournoy's theory of Hélène regards her as a centre of dream-selves who have access to things forgotten by her in her normal state. Again, what to another person might be a vague 'presentiment' (say to avoid a certain path in her walks) takes, for Hélène, the form of a warning in an audible *voice* (that of Leopold) or of a vision of Leopold barring the way. The source of the presentiment is obscure, as in the case of presentiments in general; the rare fact is its expression in an audible or visual hallucination of a guiding spirit, a merely fanciful being. The hallucinations of eye or ear answers to the visionary chess-boards on which great chess-players exercise themselves blindfold, but is not voluntarily called up, like these, and is more distinct – in fact, is mistaken for a real voice or figure.

These peculiarities of Miss Smith's voices and visions lead us to the case of Jeanne d'Arc. Her honesty, at all events, is unimpeachable. Mrs. Piper and Miss Smith believe that they converse with the dead. But Jeanne d'Arc, by the assertion of the men who burned her, went to the death of fire unshaken in the same opinion. Even when, before her martyrdom, she is said to have doubted whether the spirits with whom she talked were souls of saints, she still maintained that 'she really had revelations and apparitions of *spirits.*' At the stake she returned to her happier faith, and called on her familiar saints.

Now, just as there never was a real Dr. Phinuit, and as there never was a Leopold, so, as far as existing evidence gores, there never was a real St. Catherine of Alexandria. Into the legend of St. Margaret I have not made much inquiry; but there is certainly no known evidence for an historical St. Catherine of Alexandria. Still, Jeanne saw, heard, and touched her, and acted on her advice. It may, therefore, be argued that St. Catherine was but a dream-self of the Maid, an hallucination which, through channels of the eye and ear, conveyed knowledge and wisdom latent in the soul of the Maid herself. Just as Leopold, by voice or gesture, warns Miss Smith not to take this path, or try to move that weight, expressing in visible or audible form a presentiment latent in Miss Smith's mind, so did the glorious vision of St. Catherine, by word or gesture, make manifest to Jeanne knowledge of great duties and momentous events, which had reached her mind – we know not how. In her dream-selves, and through their voices, was knowledge made manifest to her. The marvel is none the less, the mystery is not more intelligible, if we disbelieve in an historical St. Margaret or St. Catherine. These figures, these dream-selves, were but the symbols through which the Maid was instructed. As Leopold is a suggestion from a novel, so Margaret and Catherine may have been suggestions from the storied glass of Domremy Church, or from sacred pictures and images. The question is – not what were they, but – what messages did they communicate? They were such messages as could not come from the everyday mind of the child of twelve. We do not, let us admit, know how Mrs. Piper acquires some parts of her trivial information about people dead or living; and we can only guess how

Miss Smith learns that she had better not take this path or try to lift that weight. But the knowledge which somehow reached the child of Domremy was of a much more important character. The evidence is as good as at this distance of time – four hundred and seventy years – it can be. It consists of contemporary letters, and depositions on oath, made by Jeanne at her trial, and recorded by her enemies, or made by persons who had known her, at a second trial, eighteen years later.

All the evidence proves that Jeanne was physically strong and healthy to an unusual degree. She was gay, humorous, tender, and, as her exploits in war and her answers to a crowd of any theologians prove, had a genius and intellect which may be called 'miraculous' in an illiterate girl who died at nineteen. As to her visions and voices, she does not seem to have given any details about them, except to a board of theologians who examined her in 1429, before she was admitted to serve her King, and later, in 1431, at her trial. From reports in letters of 1429, and from the record of her trial, we learn that Jeanne, like Miss Smith, began to see visions and hear voices when between twelve and fourteen. As in Miss Smith's case, the voices seemed to come from one quarter, the right. According to a letter to the Duke of Milan (June 21, 1429, two months after Jeanne's first examination by the theologians), her first voice and visions occurred after she had been racing with other children in the fields. She was 'rapt and distraught in her senses,' says the writer; but, unlike Miss Smith and Mrs. Piper, she was never, so far as we hear, *entranced*. She summoned her Saints in a brief and touching prayer to God, which is recorded. She herself said nothing about running and jumping before her first experience of a light and a voice. The Voice bade her to be a good girl and go to church, and later, in spite of her strenuous opposition (her sensible normal self resisting her adventurous dream-self), compelled her to fare to Court and do what she did. The idea of rescuing a kingdom and crowning a king may, perhaps, be not unnatural to an enthusiastic child. The difficulty was to *do* it. Jeanne could not have done it without the Voices of the dream-selves.[…] Not to dwell on other instances, the great historian of the Maid, M. Quicherat, though not one of her devout Catholic admirers, felt obliged to say that thought-reading or telepathy, clairvoyance (*lucidité*) and prescience, in the case of Jeanne, were as well attested as any facts of normal history.[11] The practical value of such experiences was to win national confidence for Jeanne and to enable her to work, by 'suggestion,' on the national spirit. Thus, though belief waxed faint, it lived long enough to turn the tide of English conquest. Jeanne's inspirations were not about popular medicine, details of diseases, or lost brooches. They were on the level of her extraordinary intellect and character. The mechanism may have been, as in vulgar modern examples, that of the dream-self: *not* in conditions of trance, as far as our evidence goes. But the knowledge at the command of the dream-self was concerned with higher themes that those of ordinary presentiments, true or false. How that knowledge reached the dream-self of Jeanne, expressing itself in the symbolic hallucinations of Saints and Voices, is a question as to which any opinion must be premature. Certainly these things are not without the will of Heaven. This at least must remain my theory, though I feel obliged to recognise that the apparitions themselves were not more real, more objective, than such beings as Leopold and Phinuit.

'Magic Mirrors and Crystal Gazing', *Monthly Review* 5:15

(December 1901), pp. 115–29

M r. Yeats recently instructed the readers of this magazine in magic and spells, of which he is a master.[1] My humbler purpose is to show the inquiring student how he may (perhaps) make experiments for himself in what was once thought a branch of magic, but is now an outlying province of experimental psychology. These are long words, but the experiments are as easy and simple as brushing one's hair before a glass. History and romance, ancient and modern, are full of anecdotes and legends of 'magic mirrors,' magic crystals, 'show stones,' like those of Dr. Dee,[2] in Queen Elizabeth's time, and so forth. Conspirators have, in various ages, been accused of trying to discern, say, the period of the King's life, by looking into 'magic mirrors.' The early Church denounced *specularii*, people who peeped into these forbidden glasses with the purpose of 'spotting' winners in the chariot races. The Earl of Surrey, the poet, was shown his distant Geraldine in a mirror: 'My Aunt Margaret's Mirror,' by Sir Walter Scott, narrates a similar tradition in the Rosebery family. The ink-gazing of the modern Egyptians puzzled Lane, keenly interested Scott, and was laughed at by Kinglake in 'Eothen.'[3] The experiments of the Regent d'Orleans are recorded by Saint Simon, and those of Cagliostro by Carlyle.[4] There is, in short, a chain of examples, from the Greece of the fourth century B.C., to the cases observed by Dr. Mayo and Dr. Gregory, in the middle of the nineteenth century, and to those which Mrs. de Morgan wished to explain by 'spiritualism.'[5]

In spite of all these examples, I, for one, had always regarded crystal gazing and the use of 'magic mirrors' as purely superstitious or poetical fancies. I did not believe that any sane and truthful person could see more, say in a glass ball, than the fancy pictures we construct in the fire or the clouds, or from the stains of a damp wall. There would be reflections in the glass, which anybody, even I, could fancifully construe into, let us say, landscapes of rivers, hills, and sheets of water. In this practical, sane, and scientific mood, forswearing all examination of the subject, I remained, till I read Miss Goodrich Freer's article (signed 'X.'), on crystal gazing.[*6] Miss Goodrich Freer gave an excellent account of the history of the hallucinations, or let us say fancy pictures, induced by gazing into any clear deep. Then I remembered George Sand's account of the visions which, as a child, she used to see, and could not get any one else to see, in the back of a polished screen. George Sand had no motive for invention here, she did not seem to have heard of, or to be interested in, the general question of such fancy pictures.[7] As Miss Goodrich Freer adduced many contemporary examples in her own experience, and among her acquaintance, I fell from my scientific pinnacle so far as to suggest experiments. Of course, to make such experiments was, scientifically speaking, mere superstition. But a common glass ball was bought, and I, with a number of persons at a country house, began to stare at it. We saw reflections of our noses, and of other adjacent objects. However, our hostess was at first rather startled by beholding pictures in the ball. A man lying in bed, his face like that of the actor who takes the chief part in the Ammergau mystery play, was the first picture, others followed, faces and places, and scenes, as it were, out of romantic novels, which she was not aware of having read. None of these 'led to anything'; no information of any kind was derived from them: in fact, they soon bored the lady. Here I may remark that, with perhaps two exceptions, crystal gazing does not interest any of the many people of all sorts and ages whom I have since found able to see, what I cannot see, pictures of persons in motion and other pictures in a glass ball, a ring stone, a teaspoonful of ink, a glass jug of water, or what not. Of the two exceptions, one is a student of psychology; the other, out of good nature, made regular notes, to oblige myself and the late Mr. F.W.H. Myers. As the gazers were persons of undoubted veracity, my intimate friends, near relations, or casual acquaintances, and as they were not 'hysterical,' nor ghost seers (except in three or four cases), and as the numbers of persons with the faculty proved to be large, I have been obliged to abandon the obvious and popular hypothesis that they are all engaged in a practical joke. One of them, Mr. B., had a rare opportunity.[8] I had sent him (without any comments) an object, an inch of leather shoe-tie, found beside an unidentified corpse that lay for years under the Chancellor rock at Glencoe. I asked Mr. B. to look in a glass ball for information about the piece of leather. He replied, by letter, that he saw nothing. But, by a mere chance, he knew what the scrap of leather was, and whence it came. The temptation to play on my credulity by seeing the corpse in Glencoe, Mr. B. overcame; in his case I should have succumbed to it!

---

[*] *Proceedings of the Psychical Society*, vol. v. p. 486, *et seq.*

Having satisfied myself that some people really would see hallucinatory pictures in a glass ball or in water, I examined the ethnological side of the question.[9] I found, by studying works of travel and anthropology, that many savage and barbarous races gaze into the water, polished basalt, rock crystals, and so on, for the purpose of seeing distant events, foreseeing the future, detecting criminals, and so forth. Polynesians, Hurons, Iroquios, Apaches, the Huille-che, the people of Madagascar, the Zulus, the Siberians, the people of Fez, the Arabs, the Australian black fellows, the Maoris, the Incas, not to forget the Hindoos, all unite in the same practice. It does not seem to me credible that so many and so widely separated peoples should agree with ancient Greeks and the races of Western Europe, in staring away, if they did *not* see hallucinatory pictures. So I believe that some people do see them: nor is the fact now denied by professors of psychology. Here I ought to meet the current objections, such as occur to everybody.

(1) If anybody can see such pictures, everybody ought to see them. 'If it is a law of Nature it is universal,' a fair logician said to me to-day.

But it is not everybody who even dreams, or, at least, wakens with any conscious recollection of having dreamed. Again, not everybody has experiences of *illusions hypnagogiques*: visions of faces and places, and other things, seen with closed eyes on the borderland of sleep. These are very common and much discussed by writers on psychological science. But I have remarked that persons of common sense, unfamiliar themselves with the experience (only too customary with myself), do not believe in the existence of *illusions hypnagogiques*, yet no professor of psychology has any doubt on the matter. If as small a percentage of people dreamed as the percentage that see crystal pictures, the majority of mankind would deny the existence of dreams.

One may also cite the 'mind's eye' visions of figures (numerals) coloured and arranged in diagrams on which Mr. Galton has written.[10] Many scientific men did deny the existence of pictures 'in the mind's eye.' They do not occur to myself, but nobody, thanks to Mr. Galton, now doubts that they do occur. My own nearest approach to anything like crystal gazing is the *illusion hypnagogique*. A few days ago I was drowsy before dinner; I sat between two friends who were talking, and, with shut eyes, I contemplated a very complex pattern in red of a wall paper till I rose and dressed for dinner. I could have copied the pattern, but I could not consciously have designed it. Now the ordinary crystal picture has more than the vividness and distinctness with all the unexpected, unsummonsed character of the *illusion hypnagogique*, only it is seen with open eyes by people in a fully wide-awake condition. The pictures obey a law of Nature no doubt, but we are not all endowed with the faculty of seeing the pictures, any more than we all dream or all see *illusions hypnagogiques*, or numerals arranged in coloured diagrams.

(2) 'Hypnotism' is not the explanation. I never studied a crystal gazer who was not wide awake and in the full possession of all his or her normal faculties. The fixed gaze at the glass ball may hypnotise some people, but I never met such a case.

(3) It is often argued that the pictures are merely imaginative readings of the reflections and lights and shadows in the glass ball or jug of water. This may sometimes, or often, be the case. You may see pictures in the embers, where I see none, and also in the reflections in the ball. My friend, Mr. B. already spoken of, believed in the reflection theory. So did the Misses A., ladies entirely unknown to Mr. B. I therefore took him to the house where they were staying, and seated Mr. B. with his back to the wall, facing the light, in one corner of the room. Miss C.A. sat with her back to the light, in the opposite corner. Each looked at the glass ball. I then left the room with Mr. B. He had seen a picture of an old woman. We returned and asked Miss C.A. if she had seen any picture? She had seen an old woman writing. There was no old woman, nor any picture of one in the room, and the reflections, in the circumstances described, could not, within reasonable probability, have coincided in representing the old woman. Nor was collusion possible, not to mention that Mr. B. was the last person likely to 'collude.' Again he and Miss C.A. wished to maintain the theory of reflections, which the experiment, as far as it went, tended to confute.

[…]

(4) If all my many friends and acquaintances who see crystal pictures are not hoaxing me, if the argument (1) about law being universal does not constitute a valid objection (because our faculties are not identical in all individuals), if the theory of reflection is, to say the least, not exhaustive – pictures being seen where no reflections exist – I may be told that 'it is all imagination.' Perhaps the philosophers who say this will ask themselves what they mean by 'imagination'? If they mean invention, or 'poetic imagination,' one must remark that most of the seers are not inventive or poetical, and that the inventive and poetical usually see – their own noses, at least, as far as I have questioned them. But if by 'imagination' is meant the power of consciously calling up a vivid 'mind's eye' picture of a selected object – of 'visualising' things – I agree that most crystal seers (as far as I know) are good visualisers, though many good visualisers are incapable of seeing crystal pictures. But the crystal pictures are not consciously selected and created mental pictures of a known object (except in certain cases). They come, and go, and change, like figures in a dream, or in *illusions hypnagogiques*, to the surprise of the gazer, and with *conscious* choice or effort on his part. For my part my pictures, seen with closed eyes on the frontier of sleep, represent no objects selected by or even, as a rule, consciously

known to me. They may be intensely vivid, but, when completely awake, I can scarcely 'visualise,' or form a 'mind-picture' at all. When I try, between awake and asleep, to call up a picture of a face, I never succeed: never once have I succeeded. But a bright picture may arise of a face that I never saw, or of a wall paper, or of a landscape unknown to my conscious self, or of something that I remember having seen, but this is very rare.

For all these reasons, though I do not deny that 'imagination' is concerned in making the pictures appear, I infer that it is a peculiar sort of 'imagination,' not consciously exerted. Some crystal gazers can, and others cannot, purposely put into the ball a picture of a familiar person or object. As a rule, they no more call up the pictures on purpose than they can choose their own dreams. Thus we cannot dismiss the pictures as 'all imagination,' or 'all fancy.' Our business, on the other hand, is to examine and try to understand the processes of this peculiar species of 'imagination.' To show that it is not the usual sort of exercise of the fancy, I may mention two cases; both of maidservants who had never heard of the topic. One of them picked up a glass ball, looked at it, and said: 'That is a pretty picture of a ship.' She then turned the ball round, expecting to find that a picture was pasted on the back. The other girl was asked by a friend of mine to look at a glass ball. She did so, said that she saw a piece of paper covered with writing, and then laid the ball down. 'She thought the ball was one of those toy things where you see views and things, and that the writing was there, and at any moment she could pick the ball up and read it.' But she could not see the writing again, though she was able to describe the characteristics of the hand. 'The girl had never heard of this harmless scientific amusement,' my friend adds.

These two cases are cited to show that the kind of 'imagination' at work is not the usual kind. The gazers believed what they saw to be real or objective, a material picture, an actual piece of written paper, fixed in, or at the back of a glass ball.

(5) It may be said that the people who can see such pictures are 'hysterical.' That they are usually 'hysterical' appears to be the theory of Dr. Janet.* Dr. Janet had experimented on 'neurotic' patients. In my own experience the subjects have been healthy British subjects, often vigorous athletes, sportsmen and sportswomen, golfers, tennis players, bicyclists, and salmon fishers. I would not attend to the descriptions of crystal pictures given by hysterical patients, who are eminently and cunningly mendacious.

(6) People almost always object – 'But, if the faculty exists, what is the use of it?' The suppressed premise is that, if anything has no known use, that thing does not exist. But what is the use of argon in the atmosphere? What is the use of dreams, or of *illusions hypnagogiques*, or of the appendix in the

---

*   *Les Névroses et les Idées Fixes.* Bleau, Paris. 1898.

human organism? The last, we are told, is a rudimentary survival of some organ that was useful to man when his ancestors were another kind of animals [sic]. Perhaps the faculty of crystal gazing is also a survival of some earlier mental equipment. I have no theory, but there the faculty is.

[...]

I have now discussed the *a priori* objections to the existence of the faculty of crystal gazing. It is dull work, 'tedious and inartistic,' as a reviewer of mine remarks. But I am not treating the subject as a drawing-room amusement. People, if not sceptical, are apt to be superstitious. They expect crystal gazers to read the future, and they go to professional seers, who, like other extorters of money on false pretences, ought to be locked up. Other people say that the devil, or 'spirits of the dead,' are the causes of the phenomena. That was the savage and the mediaeval theory; I know no single fact which lends to it any reason of plausibility.

On the other hand (and here I must expect to be regarded as credulously superstitious), I cannot deny that I have met many cases in which the crystal gazer appeared to see, in the glass ball, pictures of what was in the mind of another person present. And, what was more curious, say that A. (a stranger to B., the gazer) was thinking of C., at a distance, B. would behold C., and describe him or her, dressed and occupied as C., on inquiry, proved to have been. I have published a collection of these and other singular results.* In the work cited I exhausted such ingenuity as I possess, in the way of inventing ordinary explanations, such as those of imposture, collusion, eager recognition of persons from vague descriptions, and chance coincidence. None of these theories, nor all of them together (one for one case, others for others), proved satisfactory. The gazer was a visitor among strangers; I had never met her before; she had never heard of crystal gazing before I lent her a glass ball; she could not have 'crammed' the history and family connections of the people among whom she found herself, and then made lucky guesses; she could not have anticipated the contents of letters which had not arrived. The witnesses were usually old friends of my own, who made signed depositions. I myself was 'scried for,' with more than the usual precautions, and with astonishing success. The descriptions of persons seen were extremely minute, and eked out by pantomimic imitation of gait and manner. As to chance coincidence, it seemed to be excluded by the fact that the people seen in the pictures were sometimes described as in unusual situations, which it was found they had occupied. On the other hand, in one case for myself, and in others known to me, the gazer either saw nothing, or nothing to the purpose. Obviously a certain conclusion could only be reached by a long series of experiments, with many people, conducted

---

* 'The Making of Religion.' Second edition. Longmans & Co. 1900. Chapter V.

in a psychological laboratory. For my own part, I was, and am, personally convinced that a more than normal faculty was exhibited, both by this gazer and by others of my acquaintance, including Mr. B. (already mentioned as almost too disdainful of a practical joke, and as a partisan of the theory that the pictures are constructed out of the reflections in the ball).

[…]

I have never been able to foresee from character, complexion, habit of mind, and other indications, what persons would prove capable of descrying even fancy pictures in a glass ball. The best gazers of my acquaintance (those who hit on pictures coincidental with actual events unknown to them, or with the secret thoughts of a companion), are, both of them, not unfamiliar with other curious experiences. But I have tried with a glass ball two or three other friends who have seen what are vulgarly called 'ghosts,' in haunted houses, and, in the glass ball, they can see nothing, while people who never saw ghosts, do see 'coincidental' pictures in the glass ball. In another case, a 'ghost-seer,' known to me, can occasionally see pictures in the ball, but, as a rule, fails. The vast majority of the successful gazers have had no other hallucinations of any kind. A cook, a school master, a golfer, a barrister, may succeed; a poet, painter, or novelist may try in vain: to my knowledge.

If any readers care to make experiments, they can begin by purchasing a ball (from half a crown to four shillings) from the Secretary of the Society for Psychical Research, 19 Buckingham Street, Adelphi, Strand, W.C. As a rule, the public declines to take this initial trouble and expense, and I am obliged to buy the balls for friends who wish to try their luck. Of course a glass jug of water will do, or even a teasponful of ink, in some cases, but both are inconvenient and may spill.

Having got the ball, the neophyte may read the accompanying instructions. It is best to go, alone, into a room, sit down with the back to the light, place the ball, at a just focus, in the lap on a dark dress, or a dark piece of cloth, try to exclude reflections, think of anything you please, and stare for, say, five minutes, in the ball. That is all. If, after two or three trials, you see nothing in the way of pictures in the ball (which *may* seem to vanish, leaving only the pictures), you will probably never succeed. But you may have acquaintances who will succeed. If you, or your friends, are successful, you would oblige by making contemporary notes. If anything like pictures correctly representing what is, unknown to you, in the mind of a 'sitter' appears, or if events are represented which later prove to have been actually occurring, the sitter, or other witnesses, ought to write down and sign their statements. But it is very unlikely that you or they will take so much trouble. If the trouble is not taken, mere anecdotes, orally reported later, are of no kind of use as evidence.

Many psychologists, at least in France, now admit the reality of the faculty of crystal gazing. But that the pictures can convey intelligence as to what is, unknown to the gazer, in another person's mind, or is actually occurring at a distance, *that* science will not believe in our time: will not even consider the question. It is my humble aspiration to collect evidence copious and strong enough to induce official professors to give it consideration, a pious desire! In my opinion any two persons who can see pictures in the ball might try careful and carefully watched and recorded experiments in simultaneously gazing. It would be interesting to learn in what proportion of cases their experiences coincide: that is, they see the same hallucinatory picture. Of course, the usual difficulty of securing the good faith of the experimenters is glaringly obvious. But *that* difficulty occurs in all cases where psychologists rest (as they frequently do) on the reports which people give of their own mental experiences.

I shall be happy to receive (at 1 Marloes Road, Kensington, W.) any carefully recorded, dated, and well attested accounts of experiments in crystal gazing; though it would be simpler to send them to the Secretary of the Society for Psychical Research, at the address already given.

The experiments ought to be recorded on the day of their occurrence. If any one has two or three successes in divining thoughts, or descrying things unknown and distant, he or she should also record all failures. But, alas, one cannot expect even the busiest and most energetic of people to 'have time for' all this writing.

My own position, let me repeat, is the opinion that crystal gazing, in my experience, has yielded apparent traces of the existence of unexplored regions of human faculty. But evidence which, provisionally, satisfies me is, of course, not nearly sufficient to satisfy those who do not personally know the gazers and the other witnesses. But let us not be deterred by the oppositions of writers of popular science, who never examine evidence in these fields; or, at best, misread, misquote, mistake, and mislead, in too many instances. I have never known trance or self-hypnotisation result from the experiments, and in only one case have I heard of a repulsively ghastly picture being seen.

'Human Personality After Death'*,
Monthly Review 30:X.3

(March 1903), pp. 94–109

M r. Frederick Myers's[1] book, 'Human Personality,' sums up the effort of a lifetime.[2] The author was perhaps the most elegant, certainly the most poetical of modern classical scholars. His English poetry had its original music, its personal note, its expression of a singular character. He was a hard-working Inspector of Schools. He was fond of social intercourse, and most interesting in conversation. But what lay nearest his heart was the problem of human immortality, or rather of the survival of the conscious life of the soul or spirit, using that word 'without prejudice,' till a better term is adopted. In Mr. Myers's opinion this question of survival after death was 'the most momentous of all.' Here I must differ from him to a certain extent. The question may be the most momentous, but it is not so regarded. Our race has always 'jumped the life to come.' The belief in it, when most generally held, had next to no influence on morality, on conduct. At the time of the Reformation the Catholic believed; but he could propitiate the Lord of Death and Life by gifts, penances, masses, and so forth. The Calvinist believed; but he was 'elect,' – and then could do as he pleased; or he was reprobate, – and then it did not matter. Black Ormistoun, before he was hanged for unnumbered offences (about 1574), announced that he was elect, and certain to sup that night in Paradise. Gilles de Rais entertained similar expectations.[3]

If immortality was as absolutely certain as Mr. Myers himself believed it to be, people would, I think, behave exactly as they do at present. In short,

---

*   'Human Personality and Its Survival of Bodily Death.' By F.W.H. Myers. Longmans, 1903. 'Modern Spiritualism' By Frank Podmore. Methuen. 1902.

the idea of immortality, as it does not affect conduct, is not the most momentous of all possible ideas.

The emotions with which Mr. Myers regarded immortality were very
unlike those of men in general. In what I have to say of his book I shall be
as frank as if he were yet with us, for he knew what I thought, and listened
to objection with imperturbable humour and good humour. It is an objection that he had the strongest possible bias towards belief; just as most of
our instructors in cheap popular science have precisely the opposite bias.
This bias makes them criticise such works as Mr. Myers's without taking
the trouble to read them; this bias enables them freely to advance statements
in which truth is not art and part. On the other hand, Mr. Myers, in certain
cases, was able to accept as valid and as probatory evidence (chiefly of so-
called trance-speakers) which I and certain official students of psychical
research look on as inadequate, or even as fraudulent. Unluckily such evidence, notably that of Mrs. Piper and the Rev. Stainton Moses,[4] plays a great
part in Mr. Myers's theory, as it evolved itself after the regretted death of Mr.
Edmund Gurney. There is no orthodoxy in Psychical Research. Each student has his own provisional conclusions. Mr. Podmore, in his 'Modern
Spiritualism,' can get no farther than a qualified opinion that there is such
a phenomenon as telepathy, not necessarily implying the existence of anything 'spiritual.' I myself, regarding the words 'matter' and 'spirit' as mere
metaphysical counters with which we pay ourselves, think (religious faith
apart) that human faculty lends a fairly strong presumption in favour of the
survival of human consciousness. Mr. Myers went all the way with the
Socrates of the *Phædo*.

I shall try to give a brief and inevitably inadequate account of Mr.
Myers's work, though I am totally ignorant of the science of brain, nerves,
'neurons,' and so forth, in which he was deeply versed. Let us take it that we
have no evidence of the existence of mind apart from a fleshly mechanism;
that thought, in our experience, is universally a concomitant of certain
cerebral changes. The lowest savage knows that, when a man is sufficiently
knocked on the head, his mind does not work in his body, though, for more
caution, it may be as well to tie his body up tightly, bury it, and light a fire
on the top. Science can add nothing to this certainty; it can only give details
about the physical machinery of thought. But the savage, by reflection on
dreams, sleep, visions, hallucinations, and the rest, has come to the conclusion that there is in man a spirit, or shadow, which can go abroad while the
man lives, can see, and be seen, at a distance from the body, and can survive
death. Mr. Myers, to some degree, accepted this 'palæolithic psychology,' as
he styles it; and I rather think that I suggested the phrase. It is my humble
belief that civilisation has developed no theory of religion, evolution, creation, or the soul, which low savages have not anticipated in their rude way.
The faith of the Mincopie or of the Gourn-ditcha is based on observed facts,
and on speculation about the facts.

'There is *much* speculation in these eyes
That he doth glare withal.'[5]

Among the alleged facts are many with which the savage and the popular minds have always been familiar, but which science has either ignored
or 'explained away,' or, at most, has but recently and gingerly begun to
scrutinise. These facts, such as in hypnotism, are unusual examples of human
faculty, long ago familiar to savages. It is these things that Mr. Myers persistently claimed as highly deserving of examination, and as, conceivably,
inconsistent with what is called 'materialism' – one of the counters used in
the game of metaphysics. In this opinion Mr. Myers was at one with Hegel.
Here I may remark that, at Oxford, we were dosed with Hegel in lectures;
but that I never heard the late Mr. T.H. Green[6] drop a word about Hegel's
belief in these 'supernormal' examples of human faculty which are the basis
of Mr. Myers's argument. 'The intuitive soul,' say the Teuton sage at whose
shadowy feet we reluctantly sat, 'oversteps the conditions of time and space;
it beholds things remote, things long past, and things to come.'* [7] Hegel, like
Mr. Myers, and Quicherat,[8] the great historian and palæographer, believed
in the 'clairvoyance' of Jeanne d'Arc. Concerning all this of Hegel we were
not told one word at Oxford. The motto of science, physical or metaphysical, as to all these matters, has been 'Keep it dark!' Mr. Myers, Mr. Gurney,
Mr. Sidgwick were resolved that such things should be kept dark no longer;
but examined so far as 'a *nascent* science…in its dim and poor beginnings'
could examine them, 'simply by observation and experiment.'[9]

Is this common sense or not? Is this not part of the provinces of anthropology, and of mythology, and of psychology? When Lord Kelvin tells us
that 'clairvoyance and the like are the result of bad observation, chiefly,
somewhat mixed up, however, with the effects of wilful imposture acting
on an innocent, trusting mind,' we want to know whether Lord Kelvin
speaks after long and conscientious investigation, at first hand, of cases of
so-called clairvoyance?[10] If not, is his dogmatic statement strictly scientific?
In any case, the founders of the Society for Psychical Research resolved to
investigate the whole subject. That the minds of Mr. Sidgwick, Mrs.
Sidgwick, Mr. Gurney, and Mr. Podmore were peculiarly 'innocent and
trusting' – or trusting, at any rate, (Lord Kelvin's mind, probably, is 'innocent') only prejudice can assert. That Mr. Myers's mind was 'trusting' (in
this matter) I have already averred: I think it was too trusting; though, when
fraud or error was proved, he candidly confessed the fact.

[…]

★ '*Philosophie des Geistes*,' Werke, VII. 179, Berlin, 1845. See Mr. Wallace's
translation (1894), which does not include the *Zusätze*, most copious on these
points.

Mr. Myers has tried to show, in the chapters on Dreams, Sleep, Hypnotism, and Genius, that there is something much cleverer and more potent in a region of our nature usually submerged and out of view, than in our normal waking consciousness. To take a mild example. A person is hypnotised, and is told to see a tiger. Now we can all, in various degrees, make a mind-picture of a tiger, but the hypnotised person, in Mr. Myers's opinion, sees it infinitely more vividly, as a real presence, than he could do when awake. Here the sceptic will remark that the hypnotised person sees nothing at all, but only behaves dramatically as if he did. Experiment may illustrate this question. There seems no doubt about the actuality of post-hypnotic hallucinations.

Next Mr. Myers supposes an 'inner vision.' As you certainly see with your eyes shut in dreams, and in *illusions hypnagogiques*, so what you see in the way of hallucination, when awake, may be by virtue of 'a central hyperæsthesia' not dependent on the open bodily eye.* Ibn Kaldoun, an Arab of the thirteenth century, applied this theory to the pictures seen by the crystal gazer. 'They do not see what is really to be seen in the mirror' (reflections of surrounding objects), 'theirs is another form of perception which awakes *within them*, not by means of the sense of sight, but of the soul, though the perceptions of the soul, as far as the seers are concerned, have a deceptive resemblance to the perceptions of the ocular sense.'† Mr. Myers is in accord with my Arabian author. He goes on to say that, in certain cases, these hallucinations (really internal, but in appearance external visions or hallucinations of the sane) 'are in some way generated by some agent outside the percipient's mind':[11] say a death, a battle, a mere thought of an absent person, and so on.

Now we have always heard of this kind of vision as 'telepathic,' caused merely by some unknown action of distant brain on distant brain. Wait awhile. Mr. Myers mentions crystal-gazing as 'an empirical method of developing internal vision,'[12] as when all sense of the presence of the glass ball is lost, and the seer appears to be looking at a real occurrence among actual people. But when the vision is spontaneous, and corresponds with an unknown distant event, or unknown experience of a distant person, Mr. Myers gives his reasons for dissenting from Sir William Crookes's theory of 'ether waves of even smaller amplitude and greater frequency than those which carry the X rays.'[13] The syntonisation of the cerebral coherers (these are bonny scientific words!) is rather too good for Sir William

---

* The *illusion hypnagogique* is the vision, in half sleep, with shut eyes, of faces, places, and other things, usually unknown to the waking self. Thus I, who can scarcely form the faintest mental picture, when awake, can see, with shut eyes, on the border of sleep, very vivid presentations of objects of all kinds. But I cannot voluntarily introduce the presentation of an object which I want to see. The vivid 'inner sight' has its own way of choosing objects to be presented.

† 'Notices et Extraits des MSS. de la Bib. Imp.' I. xix. pp. 643–645.

Crookes's theory, and also rather too bad. Jones, in Australia, unconsciously transmits waves which only his friend Brown, in Bayswater, picks up. But sometimes Smith and Green, strangers to Jones, but in Brown's company, pick them up too. How to explain these syntonisations?

Now comes Mr. Myers's novelty, bearing on our occasional observations of the subliminal self at a distance from his organism, whether living or decaying. Jones's subliminal self has actually made a 'psychical excursion,' or 'invasion' has actually set up a 'phantasmogenetic centre' in 'the percipient's surroundings' which are also the surroundings of Smith and Green. All perceive the phantasm generated by the subliminal self of Jones, installed by him, during his psychical excursion, say, from Australia. As Mr. Myers admits, this is rather like 'palæolithic psychology.'[14] But it is not really more akin to palæolithic psychology than the Australian Arunta theory of evolution is akin to that of Dr. A.R. Wallace; than the Gourn-ditcha theology is akin to that of the Church; than the Dieri theory of the Origin of Totemism is akin to that of Mr. Fison; than other savage theory is akin to that of Dr. Haddon; and so on. Primitive man, like Brookes of Sheffield,[15] is sharp; and I cannot scout a civilised theory of evolution, theology, totemism, or phantasms merely because it had occurred to neolithic man: of palæolithic man we know little. He was an admirable artist, and quite clever enough to have a theory of phantasms.

Now let us apply Mr. Myers's theory to my own observations of the subliminal self apart from his organism. Two years ago I was sitting, and making copy, where I am sitting now. I was opposite the window, two paces from my writing-table. The window looks out on a path through a little garden. The path is fourteen paces long, it is closed at the farther end by an iron gate, giving on to the road from Leuchars to St. Andrews. I looked up from my work (on Scottish History) and saw Mr. Q. He was just within my gate, and ran up the path to my door. He was dressed in a grey cloth cap, and a greyish or brownish ulster, and was smiling. I went to open the front door and welcome him. The process occupies seven seconds. There was nobody at the door, in the garden, or within sight. Tradespeople do not enter by that gate, nor by that door. Again, I do not remember that Mr. Q. ever did come into my house, except in my own company, in the afternoon. I dined out that evening and met Mrs. Q. without her husband. He had a cold, or other malady, and was not going out. Now, on Mr. Myers's theory, I presume that Mr. Q.'s unifying principle, or subliminal self, had made an 'excursion,' and set up a phantasmogenetic agency in my garden. Perhaps he was asleep at the time (says 3.30 P.M.), but the owner of another self, whose phantasm I saw and spoke to once, was only on the other side of a door, and wide awake: and not in the dress in which I saw her *eidolon*.[16]

Mr. Myers says that, unlike palæolithic man, he finds his own theory 'credible with difficulty.'[17] So do I, who have no theory. Mr. Myers's theory does not imply that Jones, say, is *consciously* trying to make an excursion and set up a phantasmogenetic agency. 'Different fractions of the personality can act so far independently of each other that the one is not conscious of the other's action.'[18] Mr. Myers's theory implies some relation of the subliminal self to space; the space in our surroundings is, somehow, modified by that self's excursions. If so, that accounts for *collective* observation of phantasms, by a group of people, of which several examples are given. In fact, when one of a group sees a phantasm, I think that the experience is frequently collective. Any person may try the experiment of saying, 'Hullo, there's Jones!' and may discover how often his companions also see Jones – by 'suggestion' (the popular science explanation). This is quite a scientific experiment, but may lead to strong opinions as to the sanity of the experimenter. Mr. Myers offers large numbers of anecdotes of phantasms which coincided with crises in the lives of their distant owners. These tales are mainly borrowed from 'Phantasms of the Living,'[19] now difficult to procure, and from the archives, mainly in print, of the S.P.R.

[…]

But Mr. Myers's general theory was this. The ghosts in well-attested cases are almost invariably flitting, evasive, motiveless phantasms – to look at much like somnambulists, still more like phantasms of the living. These last, on Mr. Myers's theory, are not set up, as a rule, by any *conscious* action of their living owners. If they are created by the unconscious phantasmogenetic agencies of their owners, so, by parity of reasoning, are the phantasms of the dead, whose selves, therefore, somehow survive. Now that the phantasms of the living are not always mere psychological freaks on the part of their observers, or 'percipients,' Mr. Myers argues, first from the numerous cases in which phantasm synchronises with the death, or other crisis of the owner of the phantasm. In the 'Census of Hallucinations' the statistical conclusion was that the phantasm coincided with the death of his owner 440 times oftener than he ought to do, by the laws of chance, after every conceivable deduction had been made.[20] Now these statistics are an unknown number of degrees better than what Mr. E.B. Tylor produced in his statistical examination of the laws regulating marriage among savage and barbarian peoples.* Thus Mr. Tylor, out of 350 peoples, would give a fact occurring twenty-two times 'where accident might fairly have given eleven.'[21] The eleven against twenty-two – it is two to one. But the S.P.R., out of 17,000 persons, gets the fact of the coincident phantasm occurring in the ratio of 440 times, where accident should produce 1.

---

* *Journal of the Anthropological Institute*, February 1889, pp. 245–269.

Thus, Mr. Myers regarded phantasms of the living, or rather dying, as having an origin in their owners; moreover, the appearances were often seen by several persons at once, so he could not deem them mere psychological freaks on the side of the observer. As to phantasms of the dead, there could not be the evidence of a coincidence with any posthumous crisis of the dead. The evidence, practically, could only be that the phantasm, in one way or other, conveyed information unknown to the living observers, and this point is illustrated in a number of instances.

To myself, after reading the evidence, it appears that a fairly strong presumption is raised in favour of a 'phantasmogenetic agency' set at work, in a vague unconscious way, by the deceased, and I say this after considering the adverse arguments of Mr. Podmore, for example, in favour of telepathy from living minds, and all the hypotheses of hoaxing, exaggerative memory, malobservation, and so forth – not to mention the popular nonsense about 'What is the use of it?' 'Why is it permitted?' and the rest of it. What is the use of *argon*, why are cockroaches 'permitted'?

So far I can go, a long way, with Mr. Myers. I do firmly believe that there are human faculties, as yet unexplained, as yet inconsistent with popular scientific 'materialism.' But when Mr. Myers goes farther, and expresses a belief that messages from the dead are uttered by Mrs. Piper, or were written by the late Rev. Stainton Moses, or given by table-tilting, or automatic writing, I cannot march with him. The curious may compare Mr. Myers's reverential treatment of Mr. Moses with the account of Mr. Podmore, who also knew him, in 'Modern Spiritualism.' Mr. Moses got a third class in Moderations, a pass in Greats. He was a clergyman of stainless character, and a schoolmaster, mainly teaching English Literature. His performances were given only before a little flock of intimate friends. But I agree with Mr. Podmore that his 'controls' or 'guides' were mere freaks of his own brain, and that his 'messages' from the dead contained nothing that he could not pick up in newspapers and works of reference. His 'physical' marvels were not observed under test conditions, and, if fraudulent, were deliberately fraudulent. This implies almost a moral miracle (for the man was otherwise upright); but who can calculate the excesses of an hysterical temperament overwrought?

On the other hand, I am unable to accept Mr. Podmore's theory of the world-wide phenomena of the Poltergeist – the noises, and flights of objects – as always mere results of fraud, and collective hallucination, and exaggerative memory.* [22] I cannot believe that a 'circle' mainly composed of men in the Oxford Eleven and Football team was of the sort to be easily 'hallucinated' collectively, or to abstain from 'ragging' the medium (who

---

* In the new number of the *Proceedings of the Society for Psychical Research*, Mr. Podmore and I wrangle on this point.

shone in Rugby football) if they found him cheating.* When the bowler and wicket-keeper of the Eleven told me what they did tell me, both being clear-headed sceptics who cared for none of these things, when the wicket-keeper (in whose rooms the men met) averred that the *vacarme*[23] persisted through the night, after all the men had gone, I cannot repose easily on Mr. Podmore's explanation. But I have none of my own. Mr. Podmore, having a theory, is well content, but I think he is rather easily satisfied, and happily impermeable to adverse arguments in favour of suspense of judgment. At all events, it is salutary to compare his book with that of Mr. Myers, and to try to discount the bias of either author. We must not allow ourselves to be prejudiced by the unfortunate circumstance that Mr. Podmore writes about 'happenings.'

To end with a confession of opinion: I entirely agree with Mr. Myers, and Hegel, that we, or many of us, are in something, or that something is in us, which 'does not know the bonds of time, or feel the manacles of space.'[24] Mr. Myers knew, in detail, and I know, in gross, the reply of popular science, about living automata; consciousness as an 'epiphenomenon,' and the rest of it. The reply does not meet with the facts which Mr. Myers produces; some of them win my belief, others do not. I do not believe that educated English people after death pick up American idioms. The controversy therefore, turns on these facts, and though well aware of the methods by which popular science explains them away, I am also much alive to the futility of these methods. You can explain no facts by first egregiously misstating them, and then accounting for the circumstances as given in your misstatement.

---

* I am well aware of what is sure to be said about my acceptance, as far as it goes, of the evidence of young English athletes, my friends, and, in two cases, my near kinsman. But they were keen-sighted and agile, they were neither enthusiasts, nor theorists, nor women: nor mere scientific characters, like Messrs. Crookes and Huggins, and Lord Crawford. They had no point to make, they drew no inferences, and so I take their evidence to be good.

'Presidential Address, Delivered on May 16th, 1911',
Proceedings of the Society for Psychical Research 25: LXIV

(August 1911), pp. 364–76

[…]

M y qualities, in the field of study, are first, I venture to think, a fixed desire to be sportsmanlike – 'at least as far as I am able' – and, in the second place, familiarity with the historical, the folk-lorish, and the anthropological aspects of the topics which we study.

These aspects do not greatly interest the Society, for what the Society desires is 'modern instances,' fresh evidence from just persons ready to submit to cross-examination. But in my own mind the enormous volume of historical and anthropological reports of supernormal phenomena, and their striking uniformity with alleged modern experiences, produces the conviction that so much smoke can only be explained by the existence of some fire. I must not speak of the psychical experiences of savages; these, for want of contemporary records duly attested, are illustrative, not evidential. Nor must I, for the same reason, dilate on the strange stories of the psychical experiences of men of genius. This is a most curious theme. Among such cases, in various degrees, I have observed those in the wraith Byron, seen by Sir Robert Peel; of incidents in the lives of George Sand, Goethe, Dickens, Thackeray, Lord Nelson, Dr. Donne, Shelley; the last words of de Quincey – a most pathetic story; – the experiences of Sir Walter Scott;[1] and – a record, from his own pen, of the Duke of Wellington. But this is 'the blue smoke' of literature; and of history, you will say. Still, with this blue smoke there is some fire, as the cause thereof. The Duke of Wellington, in a private letter of his, published in Sir Herbert Maxwell's *Life* of that great man, could not guess that he was playing into the hands of Mr. Myers's theory of the Subliminal Self, and Mr. Myers obviously never read the letter.

To be fair is the first thing of all, and I dare to say that the Society has been fair. It is not in human nature not to make mistakes, and never to be inclined to accept evidence which examination proves to be erroneous;

never to indulge in hypotheses which criticism demonstrates to be worthless. But when the Society has been deceived, it has not concealed the fact, and, as to hypotheses, as a Society we have none. The Society, as such, has no views, no beliefs, no hypotheses, except perhaps the opinion that there is an open field of inquiry; that not all the faculties and potentialities of man have been studied and explained, up to date, in terms of nerve and brain. Now this opinion is also, I presume, entertained by the most stalwart and emancipated 'rationalists.' Their belief, however, I suppose, is that everything in human nature can be, and probably will be, explained on terms chemical and biological, satisfactory to themselves. The members of the Society, as a rule, perhaps, though not necessarily, are not absolutely sure of *that*: perhaps there are other things to be discovered, though what these other things may be, at present we know not. This mere conception of the possibility of the existence of faculties not readily to be explained in terms of what, in the airy currency of speech, we call 'matter,' is, I think, that in the Society which irritates so many people. If other members of the Society agree with me in the hope (in my own case the belief) that many orthodox theories of all kinds are apt to be upset in the course of time, that new fields of knowledge are perhaps to be annexed, our attitude may, doubtless, be called Romantic. Yet in other fields I have seen my early romantic aspirations made actual; I have seen a vast region of the historic past, in which from boyhood I fervently believed, thrown open by the spade of the excavator. I have seen Homer's 'golden Mycenae' and 'Crete of the Hundred Cities' won from the realm of dreams by Dr. Schliemann, and by Mr. Arthur Evans, and their followers.[2]

Therefore I may not live to see, but I hope that later generations will see, certain world-old world-wide beliefs find scientific recognition. Hegel believed in almost all the 'supernormal' phenomena which we, not necessarily believing in them, have the audacity to study: and the brain of Hegel was not, as Mr. Carlyle said of Mr. Keble's, 'the brain of a rabbit.'[3]

I spoke of my desire to be fair, and in my desire to be fair I have deliberately exhibited my bias, my romantic prepossessions. I would, as a matter of taste, prefer certain facts to be established, rather than not. I would even welcome with pleasure an indisputable *Poltergeist*; not that I think *him* a desirable inmate of the universe – far from it. When I say *Poltergeist*, I mean an authenticated instance of the queer disturbances and movements of objects, of which history is so full.[4] Thus in a very early Life of St. Dunstan we find that, as a boy, he was a Somnambule, in mature life was a centre of flying and falling stones, and, before death, was bodily levitated, bed and all, before the eyes of the bewildered monks. These are not saintly miracles. Men would rather conceal than invent them about a holy man, and they are parallel in character to those modern instances on with Mr. Barrett[5] lately read a paper, and to Claire Claremount's[6] case, as given in the journals of herself and Shelley. In short I am not certain that this kind of thing never occurs. But to suggest to little poltergeistish boys, by a gentle correction, that they should not be mediums, appears a sagacious measure. I have lived to see so many so-called scientific certainties proved to be fleeting phantasms of hypothesis, and more of them, I think, will go by the primrose path to the gulf and grave of Lachmann – and other learned persons! But these expressions of bias are only made in a spirit of fairness, and I must not, dare not, say that the scientifically orthodox would rather prefer that there were no *Poltergeist*; even nothing corresponding to what we call 'Telepathy.' The orthodox believe themselves, I am aware, to be wholly destitute of bias and prejudice, – and surely they ought to know! But were I to think myself destitute of bias, I would be mournfully bereft of humour; and, were I to conceal the circumstance, I would be equally devoid of honour.

None the less, I do not, at present, believe in a *Poltergeist*: in fact, for the moment, you have a sceptical President, who gives the *coup de pouce* [7] against his inclinations. Other prejudices possess me which I shall later divulge. As they are on the sceptical side, perhaps they ought not to be called 'prejudices,' but 'the intuitive monitions of stalwart common-sense, and genuine inductive science.' (I have always heard that Inductive science is 'true and tender,' and Deductive science 'an old offender.')

Meanwhile, though entirely destitute of hostile bias, our critics are, certainly, a little careless and inaccurate. Perhaps this error springs from a strong consciousness of intellectual superiority. They should remember that their native genius can scarcely be superior to that of the great Napoleon, who fell, to the regret of the Whig party, and of Lord Byron and Mr. Hazlitt, by plunging into wintry Russia without waiting for the arrival of his supplies, and without even providing instruments calculated to prevent his cavalry from slipping about on the frozen roads. With the same Napoleonic confidence in their own intellectual superiority, our adversaries criticise us without taking the trouble to read what we have written; or even to re-read what they have written themselves. This negligence can only arise from their sense of intellectual greatness.

[...]

This kind of criticism 'is not cricket,' perhaps; but nobody is ever *consciously* unfair. We are all only subject to the hallucinations of our bias, to Bacon's 'spectres of the cave' (*idola specus*), and men of science, like Sir David Brewster,[8] have before now given, not the *coup de pouce*, but the *coup de botte*,[9] to their own signed and written statements of their own strange experiences. Almost equally painful examples of this error, the error of superior persons in thinking themselves infallible, may be gleaned from a work no older than yesteryear, *Studies in Spiritism*, by Miss Amy E. Tanner, Ph.D.*

---

*   Appleton & Co., London and New York, 1910.

Miss Tanner is a Doctor of Philosophy, of what University I know not.[10] On some points I think, against my bias, that she is right in her criticisms, but am open to conviction if she can be proved to be wrong. On her first page she states that 'the Psychical Researchers' (under correction I suppose her to mean the Society for Psychical Research) 'have printed voluminously, persistently calling their work "scientific" and maintaining that they have "proved" certain facts bearing in the most fundamental way upon personal survival after death.' 'Whereby we have' drawn to ourselves 'a large following,' and so forth, and so forth. Dr. Tanner must have overlooked, 'In the mad pride of intellectuality,' as her country's chief poet says,[11] the perpetual protests of the Society that, as a Society, it never expresses any collective opinion. No Society does. The Folk-Lore Society may publish my theories of Totemism. But they also publish those of several benighted members who are so misguided as to reject my views. The British Academy publishes, but is not committed to, the opinions of Mr. Ridgeway as to who the Romans really were, – and so on, in every case. If Mr. Feilding and other observers thought that Eusapia did some inexplicable things in their presence, and said so in our *Proceedings*, other members of our Society arose and said, in the same work, that the performances might be very easily explained by the old familiar tricks.[12] But so superior are our critics that this simple fact – every member may air his own opinions, and the Society has contracted itself out of all responsibility for every opinion – is unknown to our censors. By sheer force of native genius, *they* may say what they please, quite independent of the simple truth. Not only does the Society abstain from offering any opinion as to the Society's having 'proved' certain facts bearing in the most fundamental way upon personal survival after death, or any other facts, but the Society continually publishes the essays of members who maintain, in certain cases, that no such proofs have been produced. A member is very welcome to disprove, if he thinks he can, all evidence even for Telepathy. The members who argue on the negative side, as regards communication with the dead, in the *Proceedings* of the Society are, I think, more numerous than the members – if any such members exist – who argue in the affirmative: who say that such communications are proved. Of course if our critics say 'you should not publish the observations of members with whom *we* do not agree,' of members who take the affirmative side, I understand them, and partly sympathise with them. But, unluckily, the constitution of the Society obliges us to hear all parties, and to side with none.

My own bias, to proceed in the path of confession, curls away from Mrs. Piper and from all professional mediums. A case of abnormal psychology so curious as hers is worthy, indeed, of the study of orthodox psychologists, and I would be the last to complain if our Society left her for three or four years in the hands of *savants* who think, like Dr. Hall, that they might succeed in exorcising all her 'sub-personalities,' all her 'communicators,' and making her a perfectly normal human being; which she is, apparently, when she does not voluntarily pass into a very curious and enigmatic mental condition. As to the real nature of that condition – as to whether, when apparently entranced, she is acutely conscious – the reports of Dr. Hall and Dr. Tanner are too self-contradictory and too casual to enable me to form any opinion. One cannot even be certain that on all occasions the condition is absolutely the same.

My own opinions are almost identical with the hesitations of the late Professor William James as described by him in the *Proceedings*. Much more evidence than has been published is needed before I can enter into the way of belief in the identity of Mrs. Piper's 'communicators' with the dead men that they profess to be. As at present instructed, I believe in nothing of the sort. In the matter of experiments I prefer to deal with highly-educated British subjects, such as the ladies to whom we are obliged for so many automatic writings. I have read with much interest and some agreement Dr. Tanner's criticisms of what are called 'Cross-Correspondences.'[13] But criticism of her criticisms in detail I must leave to writers better acquainted than myself with those perplexing documents. At the lowest they illustrate the singular workings of the subconscious mind, especially in the matter of impersonation. I have read, for example, passages in the documents which bring to my ears the very accents of the voice of one of the 'communicators,' and imitations of his style which, I think, the conscious self of the most consummate parodist could not compose.[14] In short, there are cases in which communicators are at once so perfectly impersonated and so thoroughly false, that our rude forefathers would have regarded the subconscious self as a synonym for the Devil. If this view were correct it would give a great shock to the Rationalist.

After prolonged study of the documents, I find myself in complete bewilderments over the Cross-Correspondences, with a tendency to think that, in matters so vast, so various, and so incoherent, it must needs be that patient ingenuity will discover correspondences which some minds will accept as the result of design, and others as the result of fortuitous coincidence.

Between chance coincidences, and subconscious memories; by supposing, for example, that Mrs. Verrall[15] had read the Neo-platonists though she believed she had not, Dr. Tanner can explain away most things. Yet if she has herself read Plotinus, Porphyry and Iamblichus in the original Greek, I am sure she will admit that she could not entirely forget the circumstance; these writers demand more serious application than an ordinary novel.

When it comes to three cases of predictions automatically written, Dr. Tanner is puzzled. Subconscious memory will not explain, but why not try chance coincidence? Apparently Dr. Tanner does perceive, though many other critics do not, that the theory of chance coincidence may be overworked.

On one 'supernormal' point I have to confess myself resolutely credulous, namely telepathy. The word 'telepathy,' of course, is a merely technical term to cover a variety of incidents, some of which, but not all, might be explained on the hypothesis that minds may intercommunicate by other means than the channels of the senses. On this point I am convinced by personal experience, by experiments, made in my presence, and by others, carefully and contemporaneously recorded by friends whom I can entirely trust, and my spontaneous experiments of the same and other friends. Of course the evidence which, in the circumstances, is sufficient for me, need not be convincing to, or, perhaps, need not even be thought worthy of a moment's consideration by other people.

Still, I am wholly convinced. When Dr. Tanner's ally, Dr. Stanley Hall, writes, 'only when conditions can be so controlled that, *e.g.*, a teacher can announce beforehand that, on such a day, hour, and place he will demonstrate these things, can or will they be accepted by any sound scientific mind,' one is merely amazed by the learned Doctor's attitude.[16] For my part I should at once regard the 'teacher' as a humbug. If either Keats or Wordsworth had announced that, in a teacher's lecture-room, on January 29, 1820, at three forty-five P.M., he would write an ode of immortal merit, and if he *did* write it, – we all see that he must have composed his poem before he made his promise, and committed it to memory. 'The wind' of poetic inspiration 'bloweth where it listeth,' and so does the telepathic breeze, which requires a harmony of an unguessed-at kind between two or more minds. The experimenters may now hit on the 'heaven-sent moment,' and now miss it. If 'sound scientific minds' will not believe in telepathy till its conditions can be punctually produced to order, they can never believe in it at all. I see no reason to suppose that the existence of telepathy can ever be demonstrated to the satisfaction of this order of scientific intellect. But, believing in telepathy myself, I take pleasure in the opinion that we do not yet know all about everything; that, if we persevere, we may discover numbers of curious and interesting things.

Letters to Oliver Lodge

'Very secret'.
(Foreign [?] Office Papers. Passim [?])
8 Gibson Place
St Andrews
Scotland
Jan 4[1]

Dear Mr Lodge

I ground-baited the stream, and tried to lower Prof. Tait's moral tone,[2] some, by throwing in my book, <u>Cock Lane</u>, and he rose freely, saying, in the kindest manner, that it entertained him. But he did not bite at your point at all. Please destroy this note and keep the contents dark, as I like the Professor, who is a capital fellow, and I don't want to make sport of him. But he takes <u>no</u> interest in Eusapia. He talks of Slade[3] and D.D. Home[4] (who are not quite on a level) and he quotes poetry about charlatans and rapping tables, which rapping tables are no great part of the show. He says that he can dimly conceive a 'purpose' in second sight, (if there were any second sight) and so on.

You may possibly have remarked that training in physical science, and genius for it, do not invariably bring the philosophic mind. For example, Mr A.R. Wallace's writings on Spookology are conspicuous for lack of logic, and for historical inaccuracy of a flagrant kind.[5] I don't, myself, see what 'purpose' has got to do with the matter in hand. The idea is pre-Lucretian, in science, though, for my part, I have no doubt that 'an unceasing purpose runs'. But that is manifestly not the question at issue. So, on the whole, the worthy Professor is <u>not</u> interested in Madame Paladino. I confess that I think professional conjurers would be the best critics, though they, like General Councils, 'may err and have erred.'[6] I am sorry this is all there is of it, and that Tait did not come over here and play Golf. He had expected, I fancy, something in the line of Hertz's and Clerk Maxwell's ideas,[7] – whatever they may be, – not a physical examination of Madame Palladino.

He says the more precautions are taken, the more one confides [?] in them, and is, ergo, the more easily a victim. But if you <u>don't</u> take precautions, the other argument of 'careless idiot' is generally produced.

Such is the scientific intellect and the discovery of Truth must be left to men of letters, who are destitute of scientific training.

The human mind is a poor machine.

Sincerely yours
    A Lang

★ ★ ★ ★ ★

8 Gibson Place
St Andrews
Scotland
Jan 11[8]

Dear Mr Lodge

I never saw anything funnier than the <u>Post's</u> suggestion of a bogus Ochorowicz[9] and a bogus Schrenck Notzing. Somebody sent it to me. And the real gentlemen not protesting: and the confederates, who take it in turns!

Mrs P. Of course no one but a damn Yankee could be so vulgar as her Phinuit.[10] But, call him only a 'personality', he 'fishes' so much, that I regard him as her perfectly every day personality. And I could see no out-of-the way successes in her tentative shots. Any one, in so many innumerable queries, might have guessed moderately right, (very moderately) now and again. Most boys have been nearly drowned, and have killed cats, to take her best performance.[11] However, I never saw her, and don't want to. And, of course, as I do not suppose you to be more superstitious than myself (nobody is) I presume that, when with her, there is something impressive that is lost in print. I can (and do) believe in very much more extraordinary things, she is not extraordinary enough, but very ordinary on paper. I must look at Nature, which I occasionally consult for tales of clever dogs, and cats.

Yours very sincerely
  A Lang

★ ★ ★ ★ ★

8 Gibson Place
St Andrews
Scotland
Jan 14[12]

  Dear Mr Lodge
  I did not see Greenwood's remarks.[13] Home was Sludge. Browning loathed him, Mrs B. being a believer. You can read it in Mrs Sutherland Orr; I have a private letter too, from a friend of Home's, which I gave to Myers.[14] I am aware that some stories of his kidding are 'not evidential'. I once was on the tracks of one, but could get nothing solid. The narrator was a Mr Linksils [?], to whom I think Myers should apply at Cambridge, as I saw L's letter (I think) he had nobbled a phosphorescent jest. But this is merely my recollection.
  I know Maskelyne can't do the things, and his excuse is childish.
  In re. Madame Piper, I am prejudiced, her familiar is such an odious cad. Fancy a future life where we can be interviewed! This is my argument, and I admit that the nicks on the watch handle were telling.[15] But 'the [illegible word] business 'and all the other [illegible]' and the fishing and not finding out, do suggest to me the Mrs. Piper of everyday life. However my mind is open, even to that extent. Kellar seems to be a liar, so it does not matter what he says.[16] Nothing would induce me to see Mrs. P. The bare idea of the dead being brought into contact with her (supposing it conceivable) makes me sick. This, however, is unscientific, very,

Sincerely yours
> A Lang

I wrote to Greenwood[17] asking if he has evidence to go to a jury. Of course less evidence is wanted for a familiar than for an unfamiliar fact, but I think it should be <u>good</u>, what there is of it. I am <u>certain</u> about Sludge being Home, Home himself said so.

★ ★ ★ ★ ★

8 Gibson Place
Jan [illegible][18]

Dear Mr Lodge
Many thanks. I can hardly fancy R.B.[19] lying in wait in the dark for the ghost of his child, especially if there <u>was</u> no such child. What is Evidence? said Testing Pilate.[20]

Yours very truly
> A Lang

★ ★ ★ ★ ★

27 Palmerston Place
Edinburgh
Jan 20 [21]

Dear Lodge
Here we have Maskelyne in much better form. He has a perfect right to say that he cannot compete with a mere description, unless that is precisely what he always does. Apart from that <u>argumentum ad hominem</u>[22] it is perfectly [illegible word] that he should see her before he competes. There is no getting around that.

I wrote to him a private letter, as he seems rather hurt, and I said, (on my own authority), that I myself thought if you would meet each other, you might learn something from each other.

The Browning affair: there was (to Mrs Orr's[23] knowledge) no such 'child lost by death' but several miscarriages. I can't discuss whether two sane people would try to evoke the ghost of what was never born. It would be indecent.

Yours very truly
A Lang

★ ★ ★ ★ ★

Jan [illegible][24]
St Andrews

Dear Mr Lodge
Mrs Orr never heard (supraliminally) of a dead child of Browning's. This is a little crushing. I see an AII [?] writing on you &C, in the <u>Edinburgh</u>.[25] He is too jolly stupid to make any odds, only I <u>don't</u> like Mrs Piper. […]
However, that dead kid, unlamented by two parental bards, is very agreeable.

Sincerely yours
A Lang

★ ★ ★ ★ ★

27 Palmerston Place
Edinburgh
Jan 28[26]

Dear Lodge
I jumped at any point of agreement with J.N.M.[27] and merely said that any one would impose <u>tests</u>, and I thought the fair

plan was for him to study the conditions, under which she worked, and to try to produce identical impressions, in conditions which he and his Committee regarded as identical.

I added that I was afraid it was almost impossible to do away, on one side or other, with the suspicion of quibbling. His side would never allow themselves beaten, and spiritualists would be equally unsportsmanlike. It would, I fear, be like the competition of Sandow and Sampson in strength, though before a small circle.[28] Again, I don't think you'd get any cock sure man of science to umpire in the dark, (I would not, if I were asked) so I have no great hope of anything coming of it. However to bring it even to a point of agreement that J.N.M. should see (as far as we can say 'see') Eusapia is something. I observed his hint of a confederate, but as you had discounted that, I said nothing. The skill, of course, would lie in always securing a confederate. I suppose you have seen the enclosed Mrs Mellon business.[29] I never heard of her before. In the cage trick, it is natural to suppose that the whole cage lifted bodily off its woodenbase, and that the judge was a confederate. I think Stevenson should have used the donnée[30] in Jekyll & Hyde, instead of the mechanical dodge with the powder. But this is another business. On the whole I think Maskelyne's letter much to his credit for logic and sense. He put his name to a book called 'The Supernatural?' but it was much worse written, and very crude.[31]

As to Home, I have not read Lord Dunraven,[32] the other writing, I have read. On one side I was struck by the coincidence with Iamblichus, on the other, Mrs Orr too has a vague recollection of the Home's foot anecdote. Browning must have told it, Greenwood[33] assures me that, when he put inverted commas ' ' he used Browning's identical words, and I believe him. If we grant that Home was ever in an abnormal state of consciousness he might play the foot trick, especially when asked for the ghost of an abortion. But it requires a deal of good will to advance such a remark!

If there are spirits that play these pliskies,[34] I'd like to see the fact established, and then I would cut their acquaintance; I wouldn't go near Eusapia, myself. They may be catching, and the Bible takes them in a very bad sense.

Yours very truly
    A Lang

★ ★ ★ ★ ★

1 Marloes Road
London
W
Jan 29[35]

Dear Lodge

Maskelyne will be glad to see you whenever you chance to be up. He writes to me a very frank and logical letter which I would send with his permission. His belief clearly is that there is some one 'in' with E.P. that some one <u>not</u> an investigator. Now I do think you made this impossible, so where are we landed? 'There is bear leader[36] somewhere if not more than one' he says, but <u>how</u> on the island?[37] Such power of concealing an accomplice borders on the supernatural. In brief, he thinks that, on the whole, you all saw &c what you saw &c, that the events occurred, <u>plus</u> an accomplice. That is clearly his conclusion, however this is private of course.

He explains that his cocksureness is the result of long experience in imposture, and must seen unscientific to you. Nothing can be fairer, in fact.

Yours very truly
A Lang

★ ★ ★ ★ ★

1 Marloes Road
Kensington. W
Feb 5[38]

Dear Lodge

I saw Maskelyne today, and his show amused me. I am convinced that he won't to do [sic] Eusapia's tricks, but he may as well see her. He seems to believe in a pal under a divan, how fed and concealed I don't know. He had not read your Report when he wrote![39] He is a very good kind of soul, but clearly knows nothing of the subject. He has a tendency to think Telepathy may be somewhat. I believe he thinks Sidgwick is a spiritualist! On the whole I don't expect much from him – for this confederate idea is pure bosh. However he was very agreeable and entertaining, if rather remote from the point of view. But I sat next to a most curious person, a fat American with an English accent, who knew Slade and [illegible name] &c and told me mountains and marvels, a professional, obviously. I wish I knew who he was. Maskelyne speaks of a 'test', but admits that you holding on to E.P. is 'better than ropes.'

Yours very truly
    A Lang

* * * * *

1 Marloes Road
Kensington W
Feb 5 [40]

Dear Lodge

[...]
    Really your society should examine that Browning and Home story. Home says he only saw Browning twice, and only séanced with him once, at a Mrs Rymer's.
    He published this in 1871, uncontradicted by R.B. as far as I know. The Dictionary of National Biography says they met at Garth Wilkinson's, in 1855.[41] Some Wilkinson and Rymer may be alive.[42] The miscarriages, I understand, were before 1849, and who would be bothering after their non existent ghosts in 1855. The whole story is very fishy. Mrs Hawthorne,[43] like Mrs Orr,[44] bears witness that Mrs Browning kept on believing. You could not hang a cat on such evidence, but I can't go into it. Perhaps nobody can.

Yours very truly
A Lang

* * * * *

1 Marloes Road
Kensington. W.
Feb 6[45]

Dear Lodge

  I think I would not send the Home Letter for I told
Greenwood[46] that I would not raise the question of the child, and
as I suggested it to you, I'd have a feeling of <u>qui facit per alium</u>.[47]
  What I'd like to see done is a thorough examination of
the Browning Home incident and their relations. This I would do,
had I opportunity. But that wretched foetus bars the way to any
thing short of a full inquest.
  The Table is most ingenious. Not glass supports,
I suppose?[48] I have had a very odd crystal ball affair which I sent
to Myers.[49] I return photographs, which no doubt would interest
Maskelyne much.
  Greenwood I know, he quoted R.B.'s words to himself,
but he would only reply to you that I know why he is not
explicit. At the same time, when he wrote, he clearly believed in
a genuine dead child. The weakness of <u>that</u> belief struck me at
once.

Yours very truly
  A Lang

★ ★ ★ ★ ★

1 Marloes Road
Kensington. W.
Feb 27[50]

Dear Lodge

  I suppose Minot <u>must</u> be scientific because, (as Horace
Darwin once said to me) he 'despised literature.' Podmore wrote
a reply for the North American Review, and was fair for the
cause, some time ago, but there have been delays, so I gather from
Myers.[51]
  Allen is a fanatic and a sciolist, but has very good private
qualities.[52] He is certainly the queerest fish I know. He wants to
upset everything; <u>olista principicis</u>, down with the Principia! Of

course he is infallible! He used to rave about Herbert Spencer, who is a most irritating sciolist also, as far as Primitive Man goes. Allen wrote an article to prove that Jehovah was an old tombstone, and I fear I rather vexed him by going about to prove that he knew nothing about the matter. I was mean enough to get Robertson Smith to coach me in the Hebrew department. This skittles [?] about holy [illegible] in my [?] he has been bulging with for a long time: hinting that he could and if he would. As a novel, it is beneath contempt, and I'm too old to 'go to [illegible] with a very dear friend', so I take no interest in the apologia for that practice. However, Allen is almost the only person whom I ever knew that behaved like a Christian on occasion, on an irritating occasion, I suppose, of course, he is the most dogmatic of all atheists. He was a past Master [?] of Merton, and a classical man. So he hated classical, and went in for being a popular prophet of Darwin. As popular science does not pay much, he writes novels and stories, and some of the short stories are very good. In fact I don't know why he has never taken up Psychical Research[…]!

Yours very truly
    A Lang

★ ★ ★ ★ ★

Alleyne House
St Andrews
Scotland
Feb 9 [53]

Dear Lodge
    I need not bore you with my notes on your address in detail. My own feeble mind is dead against all metaphysics, a sweeping conjecture about world souls. I am only pretty certain that there is a neglected field of human experiences […] and our business is to make this circumstance certain, if we can, without bothering about how it comes to be, or how it affects human 'futures'.
    Personally, if I <u>am</u> to guess, I guess much like you and Virgil. But the practice of history shows us that the cleverest guesses are upset by the discovery of a manuscript containing the real facts,

which no mortal genius could have conjectured to be what they actually were.

We have got to make Telepathy a thing certain, not to you or me, but to the dullest and most prejudiced prophets of popular science, before we speculate on the why and wherefore of it. Besides, we can't find out the why and wherefore of anything at all. However, I am saying what you know better than I do.

Yours very truly
    A Lang

* * * * *

Alleyne House
St Andrews
Scotland
Feb 12[54]

Dear Lodge

Of course we must guess about, till we find out. But the guesses ought to be in verifiable matters. We can't guess why the Rex Nemorensis[55] had to slay the slayer, there is no possibility of verification, despite Frazer's three volumes, and I offered a cheaper guess, involving the simplest elements.[56] But the [illegible] soul is not a guess in verifiable matters. You guess that something is the cause of something in natural affairs, and then you can try if it will work, or wait to see if it will come off, but that is very different from soul, and worlds.

I enclose the most philistine comments I can think of. But, more seriously, I really do not think the exposition as clear as crystal, or the materializings and Piper spooks worth mentioning, or the guesses of Plato & Co. at the unverifiable. I am also on this side, I feel sure there are unexplained faculties, but I don't want to guess.

Yours very truly
    A Lang

* * * * *

Nov 21 [?][57]
Alleyne House

Dear Lodge

I am afraid that though Mrs P. certainly knows now more of
the classics than Yankees generally do Mr Dorr [?][58] knows, and
also has forgotten, enough to account for the knowledge of the
supposed Myers. Would it be possible to ask it what it used to
consider the three greatest love lyrics in the world? Myers said
something about this to me, which I thought in very bad taste, but
I never mentioned the fact to mortal. Of course he may have made
the same remarks to other people.

I think you have got beyond Mrs P but not beyond Mr
Dorr in the way of possible telepathy.

I would like to review you in a serious place, but don't
suppose that I shall have a chance, serious places don't like it – not
from me.

I think Mrs V's[59] [illegible] the most staggering thing yet. By
the way look at Proc. vol XXI p. 379 March 25 1901.[60]

The Latin, I am sure, is meant to say this [...]

Look at Mrs V's translation, it is nonsense [...]

Yours very sincerely
A Lang

★ ★ ★ ★ ★

Alleyne House
St Andrews
Scotland
Nov 21[61]

Dear Lodge

In reading Mrs Holland, the communicators strike me as
almost impossibly like the real persons.[62] That about your thought
'even lions do not lecture in the winter months,' and a thing F says
about 'the Backs in May' are almost beyond even the cunning of
the S.S.[63] The lions look like a memory of a waggery of [illegible
name] Smith's about lions meeting and growling out their social
ideas.

Either Mrs H or F[64] quotes me in 'The Shameful Hills', some lines of mine [illegible] about Ian Hamilton at Majuba.[65] But Mrs H. is a whale [?] for minor poetry. The university use of men's initials, 'A.L' &c, is also clever in the S.S. I suppose these sorts of things strike you too.[66]

Yours very truly
    A Lang

★ ★ ★ ★ ★

1 Marloes Road
Kensington. W.
Sep 21[67]

Dear Lodge
    As you will see in Journal SPR a fial [?] Mr Dorr [?] has nailed E.P., top [?] nailed her.[68] I hope this happy incident will make you steer clear of her. I quite believe that Home did some good things; I do fervently believe in the common Poltergeist; in E.P., no.
    Yes, your new C.C.[69] [illegible] seems good but why can't F.W.H. M.[70] be <u>explicit</u>?
    Let him answer a single question of mine, or two, for that matter, and the supernormality of the things is certain. It is a good chance for me, I know the answers probably – unluckily we can never be <u>quite</u> sure [illegible] him when he saw me last. That is simple. Of course he & [?] any fellow may forget. Ask him what he said on a certain river bank. And no minor or major poetry.

Yours very truly
    A Lang

Ask him what line of Virgil he quoted about the Venezuela [illegible]

★ ★ ★ ★ ★

Alleyne House
St Andrews
Scotland
Dec 18[71]

Dear Lodge

I am in fact, apt to believe on historical grounds that <u>est aliquid Poltergeist</u>,[72] and even of E.P.s best things I do not see that the explanation explains them. But as neither human nor mechanical controls are evidential, (and my own experiences would never convince me, if I had them) and as the lady is a noted cheat, I own that I think she should be fought shy of; as an offence to weak brethren and a strong card in the hands of opponents. I do believer she is better let alone.

When a thing cannot be proved I see nothing to be gained and a good deal to lose by expressing any personal conviction based on experience. I don't mind saying anywhere that I believe in Old Jefferies,[73] but E.P. is too much [illegible].

I daresay my position is illogical, but I'm not sure, for it is not illogical to disbelieve in one's own experiences or rather in a supernormal theory of them.

Yours very sincerely
A Lang

Letters to William James

8 Gibson Place
St Andrews
Scotland
Feb 19[1]

Dear Mr James

     If Mrs Piper will give me any verifiable news about Mlle Luci (Ferrand) (<u>ob</u>. 1752) <u>not already known to me</u>, I will be open to convictions and pay her fees. As a psychologue you probably know about <u>Mlle Ferrand</u>, but I am an ignoramus.[2]

     In June 1896, I was reading the m.s. letters of Prince Charles, in the Queen's collection – (1749–1752).[3] I found that H.R.H. was 'run' by a mysterious 'Mlle Luci.' Unable to find out anything about her, I asked Miss X, who looked in a common inkpot, and saw a pleasing young woman, say of 28, dark, like Madame Patti, 18th century costume (I forget details of costume) and, on her shoulder, another lady's long white hand with a <u>marquise</u> diamond ring.[4] Now please look at Condillac, <u>Traité des Sensations</u>, and read the initial chapter, a letter to Madame de Vassé.[5] My Mlle Luci, I found by various hints, was the Mademoiselle Ferrand, mentioned in that chapter, who coached Condillac: she was the bosom friend of Madame de Vassé; they called each other sisters. The <u>hand</u>, we shall call Madame de Vassé's, who, in the Prince's secret corresponds [sic], is always called 'La Grande <u>main</u>.' It is picturesque, though not 'evidential.'[6] But read Condillac's chapter. The pair kept the Prince hidden in their rooms in a convent: they call Condillac 'le philosophe.' I thought it was Montesquieu, but I was wrong.[7]

Now if Mrs Piper can go one better, it won't be evidence, for <u>you</u> know the facts, but it will be useful. And I'm sure a girl who could coach Condillac and mother Prince Charlie was no ordinary young woman. Miss X. knew nothing, for <u>I</u> didn't when I asked her, and the name 'Luci' was a cypher name: all we knew: and I only said 'look for Mlle Luci', without saying why. And what does Mrs Piper know of Mlle Luci?

Your theory of <u>singular</u> taboos is the same as mine; Dr Johnson being a case.[8] But taboos of wider prevelance have usually a discernible reason, if we know the run of the early mind: Jevons does not, I fancy. Alas, I forgot the Spencerian lunch: he is an old dear, but 'knows nothing, and is nowhere.' A keeper told me Spencer asked him why we got sea trout in a loch where a burn came in. 'Looking for food' said the keeper, which, of course, is the reason. Herbert said 'no,' difference of temperature in the water! Skittles: I don't think he had tried the temperature, and then naturally got what the burn brings down. Besides their idea is to go up and spawn. H.S. dressed his flies against the grain, not ⬱ but ⬱, and was no bad fisher, but it would not do with dry fly on a chalk stream: any bunch of fibre would do for sea trout, if on the take. Excuse this medley of philosophies, but if H.S. knows no more about other things than he does of Primitive Culture, it is all a prismatic soap bubble. He does not even know Greek.

Sincerely yours A Lang

Pray draw Madame Piper about Luci.

★ ★ ★ ★ ★

1 Marloes Road
Kensington. W.
Apr 4[9]

Dear Mr James

Mlle Luci is no longer evidential, as I have written about her in <u>Pickle</u>.[10] I think, therefore, we can't consult Mrs Piper. Besides I would subject no lady, alive or dead, to a chance of contact with such a bounder as Dr Phinuit.

I have just left Miss X, in a haunted house, which, as such, is a failure, I think.[11] I found a girl who certainly staggered me by what looked uncommonly like clairvoyance in a glass ball which I gave her, she being ignorant of these things.[12] It was exactly as if she had Prince Ali's telescope, she picked out and described to me and others (strangers) people whom she really could not have heard of, with a detail, (in my case) which I did not know, but found to be correct. But she could not see Henry Goring (<u>ob.</u> 1794).[13] I can't get a portrait of Luci in France. I have ordered your new book, but it has not yet arrived.[14]

You'll hear about the haunted house, it may be haunted, but I doubt it extremely.

Yours very sincerely
A Lang

Miss Freer takes no stock in Moses,[15] and probably never heard of George Pellew.[16] But you can ask Mrs P. 'Who was J.N.'? If she knows, I cave in.

★ ★ ★ ★ ★

St Andrews
Fife
Dec [?][17]

> Dear Mr James
>
> I don't know if it is of any interest to you <u>à propos</u> of Binet, (in your book II, 128)[18] that I know a barrister, a man who had also made a literary success, who can 'scry.' I saw his first attempts, and can vouch for his honesty and ability. He wrote to me lately that his spectacles affect his view of everything he looks at <u>except</u> crystal visions, which he sees in the same way and degree with spectacles as without them.
>
> They are fancy pictures – people often in picturesque situations, and he sees them more vivid than actual things. The indifference to spectacles looks rather against Binet's theory of *points de repère*,[19] especially as he would naturally <u>expect</u> his glasses to make a difference. I tried a girl who came here, with a glass ball, and expect to publish some of her experiments. She had never heard of scrying before (I had the ball) and was, in half a dozen cases or more, among total strangers of whom she knew nothing. (I was one of them.)[20] But the result beat me, now I suppose I must swallow 'thought transference'. One very good case could not be given, but they were all much of a muchness. Of course she was an amateur, why I fancied she would be useful.
>
> Yours very sincerely
> A Lang

'Letter to E. B. Tylor on Home and the Brownings'[1]

1, Marloes Road,
Kensington. W.
Nov 8 (1904)[2]

Dear Tylor

Have you found your note of what Browning told you?
He told Greenwood[3] (1) that he caught hold above a table[4] of
Home's naked foot which Home was passing off as the ghost of
a dead child of his R.B.'s[5] and Mrs Browning.

They had no dead child and were only once at a <u>séance</u>
with Home. Several other people were present, and a
contemporary letter of Mrs Browning's give a favourable account
of it, but protests against the notion of meeting dead people.[6]

(2) Browning told F. Myers and another that he knew two
people who had caught Home experimenting on a wall with
phosphorous.

He told his son (3) that he had 'exposed Home by catching
hold of his foot under the table.' What he told you (4) sounds like
a variant of 2. As the only meet of Home with the Brownings, at a
séance, was in June or July 1855, and as the <u>contemporary </u>letters
of both Brownings exist, the date can be fixed.[7] In thirty or forty
years the poet's memory seems to have become mythopoeic,
which is interesting. Of course the memories of Greenwood[8] and
of Pen Browning[9] may have added their quota of myth, so your
contemporary note would be valuable. There is <u>contemporary</u>
record of the fake (as it seemed to the observers) by Home, in a

moonless July night. H. is still alive and thinks the Pigat was good enough.

If a fake, it was childishly cheap and obvious. Home said that Thackeray was the most sceptical observer he ever met, but Thackeray could find out nothing.

Yours very truly
    A Lang

APPENDIX I:
Names frequently cited by Lang

Andersen, Hans Christian (1805–1875). Danish author of novels, plays, poems, travel narratives and short stories. In fairy tale collections published between 1835 and 1870 Andersen fused materials borrowed from traditional Danish folklore with his own elaborate literary inventions, creating a distinctive form of literary fairy tale. His stories include 'The Little Mermaid', 'The Princess and the Pea', 'The Emperor's New Clothes', 'The Ugly Duckling' and 'The Snow Queen'.

Apollonius Rhodius (now more commonly anglicised as Apollonius of Rhodes) third century BCE Greek author of the epic poem *The Argonautica* (*Voyage of Argo*) upon which Lang partially relies for his account of the Jason myth.

Apuleius (*c.*125–*c.*180) (sometimes given the forename Lucius) a Roman traveller and writer of Berber descent from the colony of Numidia in North Africa. He is best known as the author of the satirical prose romance, *Metamorphoses*, generally referred to as *The Golden Ass*, in which the protagonist undergoes a series of picaresque adventures after having accidentally transformed himself into a donkey through the practice of witchcraft. *The Golden Ass* includes a number of intercalated narratives, amongst them the story of Cupid and Psyche in Books 4–6, narrated by an old woman to comfort a young woman who has been abducted by thieves.

Aulnoy, Marie-Catherine D' (1650/1–1705), French novelist, travel writer and fairy tale writer. She was married at 16 to a much older man, and forced to flee France following a scandal relating to her marriage. During her exile she claimed to have travelled in Spain and England, and later published memoirs of her experiences, including the popular *Memoires de la cour d'Espagne, Relation du voyage d'Espagne* (1690/1; *Memoirs of the Court of Spain, Account of the Voyage to Spain*). By 1690 she had been allowed to return to Paris, and set up a salon at which various regular entertainments took place, including the reading of fairy tales. D'Aulnoy published two collections of fairy tales *Les Contes des Fées* (1697; Tales of Fairies) and *Contes Nouveaux, ou Les Fées à la Mode* (1698; New Tales, or Fairies in Fashion). She is credited with having initiated the seventeenth- and eighteenth-century French vogue for fairy tale writing, and with introducing the term 'Fairy Tale', courtesy of a translation of the French phrase 'contes des fées' into English. Her elaborate courtly tales include five stories that Lang offered versions of (translated and adapted by Minnie Wright) in his *Blue Fairy* Book (London: Longmans, Green and Co., 1889): 'La chatte blanche' (The White Cat), 'Fortunée' (in Lang as 'Felicia and the Pot of Pinks'), 'Le mouton' (The Ram, in Lang as 'The Wonderful Sheep'), 'Le nain jaune' ('The Yellow Dwarf'), and 'La belle aux cheveux d'or' (Beauty with the Golden Hair, in Lang as 'The Story of Pretty Goldilocks'). Lang was especially fond of d'Aulnoy's 'The Yellow Dwarf', and borrowed the narrative's eponymous villain for his own villain in *Prince Ricardo of Pantouflia* (1893).

Balfour, Arthur (1848–1930). The 1st Earl of Balfour, was a politician, philosopher and scientist. He was President of the Society for Psychical Research in 1893, was an early member of the society, and was the brother of two of the Society's most active members, Eleanor Sidgwick and Gerald Balfour. One of the supposed stories at the heart of the cross-correspondences concerned the attempts of Mary Lyttleton, whom Balfour had intended to marry before her early death from typhus in 1875, to contact him from beyond the grave. He was Conservative prime minister between 1902 and 1905.

Benfey, Theodor (1809–81). German philologist, who specialised in the study of Hebrew and Sanskrit. He is now best known for his monumental *Sanskrit–English Dictionary* (1862), and for his scholarly edition and translation of the ancient Indian fable collection, the *Panchatantra* (1859). Benfey's edition of the *Panchatantra* is prefaced by an extended essay on the story collection, in which he makes the argument with which he is now associated: that India was the source of a great number of the world's folk tales, and that these stories originating in India were disseminated throughout the world as a result, primarily, of gradual literary transmission.

Blavatsky, Helena (1831–91) was the co-founder of Theosophy in New York in 1875. She was investigated, in India, by Richard Hodgson on behalf of the SPR in 1884–5. The subsequent report concluded that she was a fraud (see Edmund Gurney et al., 'Report of Committee Appointed to Investigate Phenomena in Connection with the Theosopical Society', *Proceedings of the Society for Psychical Research* 3 (1885), pp. 201–400).

Bleek, Wilhelm (1827–75). German philologist who worked on South African languages and culture. After extensive interviews with representatives of the Xan people (then referred to as 'Bushmen') he published *A Comparative Grammar of South African Languages* in two parts in 1862 and 1869. He also preserved Xan folklore and customs in the collections *Reynard the Fox in South Africa; or Hottentot Fables and Tales* (1864) and *A Brief Account of Bushman Folklore and Other Texts* (1875). After his death, his collaborator and sister-in-law Lucy Lloyd continued their work, seeing *Specimens of Bushman Folklore* to publication in 1911.

Boccaccio, Giovanni (1313–75) major writer, poet and dramatist of the Italian Renaissance, and best known as the author of the highly influential collection of prose tales (or novella), *The Decameron*, composed *circa* 1350–3. The tales are set in a frame narrative in which ten young people of Florence, having fled the city to the countryside to avoid the plague of 1348, pass the time by telling ten tales each for ten days (amounting to 100 tales in total). The collection was a significant influence on later writers such as Chaucer and Shakespeare, and is sometimes regarded as having provided a model for the transformation of popular folk traditions into literature.

Boileau-Despréaux, Nicholas (1636–1711); French poet, literary critic and aesthetic theorist; his works include *L'Art poétique* (1674; The Art of Poetry), modelled upon Horace's *Ars Poetica*, that seeks to define poetic genres and supply some rules of poetry. Boileau was given an official role at the court of Louis XIV in 1677, and was admitted to the Académie française in 1684. As an academician he became the leading combatant in the passionately fought debate known as the 'querelle des Anciens et des Modernes' (Quarrel of the Ancients and the Moderns), advocating the position of the 'ancients', who argued for the superiority of classical literary models. Charles Perrault was an advocate for the counter-position: that modern poetry could improve on the models of the ancients.

Braid, James (1795–1860) is seen by many as the 'father of hypnotism'. He was a Scottish surgeon, and began to investigate the claims of the followers of Anton Mesmer in the 1840s. While he continued to doubt the more fantastic claims of mesmerists, he did find that the symptoms of nervous disorders were alleviated through trance. He was the first to use the term 'hypnotism' to name a psycho-physiological practice rather than an occult one.

Brosses, Charles de (1709–77), French scholar and author of works on archaeology, exploration, religion and language. De Brosse's third book, *Du culte des dieux fétiches ou Parallèle de l'ancienne religion de l'Egypte avec la religion actuelle de Nigritie* (1760; Of the Cult of God Fetishes; or, a Comparative Study of Ancient Egyptian Religion with Current Negro Religion), anticipates the methods used by nineteenth-century comparative anthropologists by using contemporary African religious practices to explain the religious practices of Ancient Egypt.

Callaway, Henry (1817–90), missionary to South Africa and, ultimately, Bishop of Kaffraria (now King Williams Town). From 1858, influenced by his extensive reading in ethnology, anthropology and folklore, he made records of Zulu customs and religious practices, later publishing the material he collected in *Nursery Tales, Traditions, and Histories of the Zulus* (1868) and *The Religious System of the Amazulu* (1870). Lang makes extensive use of the Zulu tales in Callaway's collection.

Campbell, John Francis (1821–85), also known as Campbell of Islay; a scholar of Gaelic languages and Celtic culture, who, in addition to fulfilling various government roles (for instance, as secretary to the Lighthouse Commission) devoted himself to the preservation of storytelling from the Highlands and Western Isles of Scotland. He revolutionised the field collection of oral traditions by using a team of trained local collectors to interview storytellers and preserve their narratives – sometimes making use of early recording devices. By 1862 he had received a total of 791 stories, a selection of which were published in the four volumes of *Popular Tales of the West Highlands, Orally Collected* (1862).

Castrén, Matthias Alexander (1813–52); Finnish philologist and ethnologist. After extensive fieldwork in Siberia he published a number of studies of the language and culture of the Uraic and Altaic peoples, including *Ethnologische Vorlesungen über die Altaischen Völker* (Ethnological Lectures on the Altaic People) (St Petersburg: Buchdrucherei der Kaiserlichen Academie, 1857). Lang made use of the collection of Samoyed *märchen* that was included in this volume (pp. 151–81). Influenced by the Romantic Nationalist ideas of the Brothers Grimm in Germany, and Elias Lönnrot in his native Finland, Castrén argued for the original linguistic and cultural unity of the Uraic-Altaic peoples, and used his studies in language and myth to demonstrate that unity.

Charcot, Jean-Martin (1825–93) was a French neurologist who taught and worked at the Salpêtrière, Paris for over thirty years. He is particularly known for his work with hysterics and with hypnosis. He believed hysteria was a neurological disorder, and that susceptibility to hypnosis was synonymous with the disease.

Chastenet, Armand-Marie-Jacques, Marquis de Puységur de (1751–1825) made experiments in inducing hypnotic sleep and set up the Société Harmonique des Amis Réunis. His work was rediscovered by Charles Richet in the 1880s.

Clodd, Edward (1840–1930), English anthropologist and folklorist. Clodd was an early follower of Darwin, and wrote biographies of Darwin, T. H. Huxley and Herbert Spencer, as well as popularising works on evolution. He joined the Folklore Society at its foundation in 1878, and was its president in 1896. He wrote anthropological works from the 1890s, including *The Story of 'Primitive' Man* (1895) and *The Childhood of Religions* (1896).

Codrington, Robert Henry (1830–1922); teacher, Anglican missionary and anthropologist who worked in Melanesia and published numerous studies of Melanesian culture, language and society. His works include *The*

Melanesian Languages (1885) and *The Melanesians: Studies in their Anthropology and Folk-Lore* (1891) which constitute the first systematic study of Melanesian society and culture. Lang knew of his work from publications in the *Journal of the Anthropological Institute*.

Cosquin, Emmanuel (1841–1921), French folklorist who, influenced by Theodor Benfey, argued that India was a major source of the world's folk tales. Recognising the evidence that there were folk tales in ancient Egypt that predated any possible borrowing from India, Cosquin proposed that whilst India was the major reservoir of world folk tales it was not, as Benfey had maintained, the sole source. Cosquin's works include *Contes Populaires de Lorraine* (Popular Tales of Lorraine) which has an introductory essay 'Sur l'origine et la propagation des contes populaires européens' (On the Origin and Dissemination of the Popular Tales of Europe).

Coulanges, Numa Denis Festel de (1830–89), French archaeologist and historian of Greece, Rome and ancient France. He published *La Cité antique* (1864) which argued for the centrality of religion in the development of Greece and Rome.

Cox, George (1827–1902), English disciple of Max Müller, who developed Müller's theories concerning the Aryan origin of folk narratives and their solar significances in his two-volume work *The Mythology of the Aryan Nations* (1870). Cox's arguments are one of Lang's principal targets in the essay 'Household Tales' (Introduction to Margaret Hunt (ed.), *Grimm's Household Tales* (London: George Bell and Sons, 1884), pp. xi–lxx).

Darmancour, Pierre Perrault (1678–?); (sometimes d'Armancour) son of Charles Perrault. Perrault's *Contes* were initially presented under the name of his son, for reasons that remain a subject of debate. Lang's theory was that the work was a collaboration between father and son.

Dasent, George Webbe (1817–96); English scholar, journalist and civil servant; known especially for his translations of Norse and Icelandic texts. His works include a translation of the Prose Edda (1842), *Popular Tales from the Norse* (1859, translated from Peter Christen Asbjørnsen and Jørgen Moe's *Norske Folkeeventyr*), and *The Story of Burnt Njal* (1861; from the Icelandic *Njal's Saga*). *Popular Tales from the Norse* was extremely popular and went into a second edition in the same year as its first publication (1859). It is this expanded edition that is used by Lang. In a long introductory essay to *Popular Tales*, Dasent supports the arguments for an Aryan origin of popular traditions advanced by the Brothers Grimm.

Davey, S. J. (1863–90) was an amateur conjurer who worked with Richard Hodgson and the SPR to reproduce the slate-writing phenomena claimed as supernormal by the medium William Eglinton. Their experiments were reported in 'The Possibilities of Mal-Observation and Lapse of Memory From A Practical Point of View', *Proceedings of the Society for Psychical Research* 4 (1886–7), pp. 381–495.

Dessoir, Max (1867–1947), German philosopher and psychologist, coined the term 'parapsychology'. His *Das Doppel Ich* (The Double Ego) was published in 1890.

Deulin, Charles (Charlemagne) (1827–77); French novelist, fairy-tale writer, journalist and critic. Deulin wrote three collections of fairy tales, including *Contes du roi Cambrinus* (1874; Tales of King Cambrinus) which Lang makes occasional reference to (citing the title as *Contes du roi Gambrinus*). Deulin also wrote a posthumously published study of the tale types used by Perrault, *Les Contes de ma mère l'Oye, avant Perrault* (1878; Tales of Mother Goose, before Perrault) in which he traces numerous variants of the stories. This study had a significant influence on Lang's analysis of the same tale types in his introduction to *Perrault's Popular Tales* (1888).

Elliotson, John (1791–1868), a physician at University College Hospital in London, experimented with the use of mesmerism in the 1830s, eventually giving up his position after his experiments were challenged in *The Lancet*.

Esdaile, James (1808–59), British physician who pioneered the use of mesmerism in the management of pain during surgery.

Eusebius of Caesarea (*c.*263 CE–339 CE), Roman theological writer and author of *Historia Ecclesiastica* (Church History), *De Martyribus Palestinae* (On the Martyrs of Palestine), *Praeparatio Evangelica* (Preparation for the Gospel), and *Demonstratio Evangelica* (Demonstration of the Gospel). In *Praeparatio Evangelica* Eusebius rejects the argument that heathen myths anticipate Christian morality, and maintains instead that pre-Christian myths 'descend from a period when men in their lawless barbarism knew no better than to tell such tales' (Lang, *Myth, Ritual and Religion* (Longmans, Green and Co., second edition, 1899), vol. 1, p. 21). In *Myth, Ritual and Religion* (vol. 1, pp. 19–22) Lang uses Eusebius's argument to support his own view that myths originate as narratives told by primitive tribes.

Fénelon, François de Salignac de la Mothe (1651–1715); French Roman Catholic churchman, courtier and writer; from 1689 to 1697 he was tutor to Louis, Duke of Burgundy, a grandchild of Louis XIV and future Dauphin of France. In his capacity as tutor, Fénelon composed a series of imaginary dialogues between dead literary and historical figures, and a collection of instructive fables, both designed to impart moral lessons to his young charge. The former was published towards the end of Fénelon's life as *Dialogues des morts composés pour l'éducation d'un prince* (1712; Dialogues of the Dead Composed for the Education of a Prince), the latter was published posthumously as *Recueil des fables composées pour l'éducation de feu Monseigneur le duc de Bourgogne* (1718; Collection of Fables Written for the Education of the late Monseigneur the Duke of Burgundy). Fénelon was also the author of the extremely popular allegorical narrative *Les aventures de Télémaque, fils d'Ulysse* (The Adventures of Telemachus, the Son of Ulysses), published in 1699.

Fison, Lorimer (1832–1907); a Wesleyan missionary and anthropologist. Fison travelled to Australia from England in the late 1850s to become a prospector in the goldfields, but following religious conversion travelled to Fiji to conduct missionary work. Whilst working in Fiji he responded to a request from the American anthropologist Lewis Henry Morgan to supply an account of Fijian and Tongan kinship systems. This was published in Morgan's *Systems of Consanguinity and Affinity* in 1871. After his return from Fiji to Australia in 1871, Fison conducted a similar investigation with Alfred Howitt of the kinship systems of the aborigines of Australia. This investigation resulted in the publication of *Kamilaroi and Kurnai* in 1880. Fison was brother to the British fairy tale writer Anna Walter Thomas, whose story 'Tom Tit Tot' was celebrated by the Folk-Lore society whilst Lang was President.

Fontaine, Jean de la (1621–95) was a French poet who produced several volumes of fables between 1668 and 1669 under the title *Fables choisies, mises en vers* (Choice Fables, Put into Verse). In some instances the fables were adapted from existing sources, particularly Aesop, in others they were original. La Fontaine's fables are notable for their moral and satirical significances.

Frazer, Sir James George (1854–1941); Scottish anthropologist; his major work *The Golden Bough: A Study in Comparative Religion* (1890) has been extremely influential, both within the field of anthropology and more widely. Inspired by E. B. Tylor's *Primitive Culture: Researches into the Development of Mythology, Pholosophy, Religion, Languages, Art and Customs* (1871), Frazer assembled quantities of data about ritual practices from across the globe, and through comparative analysis of this data claimed to have discovered universal patterns in religious practices. Frazer also developed his own theory of cultural evolution, maintaining that societies progress through three stages: belief in magic, faith in religion and explanation by science. While Lang was initially favourable in his reception of Frazer's work, his response to the second edition of *The Golden Bough*, now subtitled 'A Study in Magic and Religion' (1900), was very critical, and he challenged the basis of Frazer's work in *Magic and Religion* (London: Longmans, Green and Co., 1901).

Freer, Ada Goodrich (1857–1913) was an American medium and writer. She published much of her work on psychical research under the name 'Miss X.' Lang often cited her essay on crystal gazing which appeared as 'Recent Experiments in Crystal Vision', *Proceedings of the Society for Psychical Research* V (1888–9), p. 486–521.

Fontenelle, Bernard le Bovier de (1657–1757), French author of literary satires, scientific treatises and philosophical works. Lang was especially interested in Fontenelle's essay *Sur l'Origine des Fables* (On the Origin of Fables), which proposed that myths are developed by primitive peoples as a means of explaining phenomena that they lack the scientific capacity to understand. Fontenelle also anticipates Lang's arguments by suggesting that commonalities in the myths and stories of diverse peoples and diverse periods are the result of universal commonalities in human developmental processes. A summary of this essay is provided by Lang in an appendix to *Myth, Ritual and Religion* (London: Longmans, Green and Co., second edition, 1899), vol. 2, pp. 339–43.

Gill, William Wyatt (1828–96). British Anglican minister who conducted missionary work at Mangaia, in the Cook Islands, between 1852 and 1872. He wrote several ethnographical works, including *Life in the Southern Isles; or, Scenes and Incidents in the South Pacific and New Guinea* (1876) and *Myths and Songs from the South Pacific* (1876). The latter work was proposed for publication and introduced by Max Müller.

Glanvil, Joseph (1636–80) was an English clergyman and philosopher. He was close to the Cambridge Platonists. He was the main contributor to *Sadducismus Triumphatus* (1681) which included a collection of folklore about witches and asserted the existence of the supernatural in general. Lang often quotes the work as an important link in the continuity of experience of and 'scientific' interest in such phenomena.

Grimm, Jacob (1785–1863) **and Wilhelm** (1786–1859); German brothers, compilers and editors of the seminal collections of German traditions: *Deutsche Sagen* (1816–18; German Legends), *Deutsche Mythologie* (1835; German Mythology), and, above all in influence and importance, *Kinder- und Hausmärchen* (Children's and Household Tales), first published in two volumes in 1812 and 1815. The Grimms were strongly influenced by the

Romantic Nationalist movement of late eighteenth- and early nine-teenth-century Germany, and sought to collect popular traditions as a means of preserving what they saw as an authentic and ancient Germanic legacy. As well as being narrative collectors, the Grimms were also scholars, and in supplementary essays and prefaces to their collections promoted the view that household tales were the remains of ancient Aryan myths. Lang makes extensive use of the Grimms' work, both in his own theoretical approaches to fairy tales, and in his collections of international tales (there are seven tales from Grimm in the *Blue Fairy Book*), though he disagrees with the Grimms about the Aryan sources of the stories.

Gubernatis, Angelo De (1840–1913), Italian philologist, mythologist, poet and playwright. Lang was highly critical of the solar mythological argu-ments formulated by de Gubernatis in his best-known work *Zoological Mythology; or, The Legends of Animals*, 2 vols (1872).

Gurney, Edmund (1847–88) wrote philosophy and musical theory, and worked for the Society for Psychical Research from its beginnings. He was co-writer of the Society's first major work, *Phantasms of the Living* (1886), and carried out the Society's first experiments in telepathy. He was found dead in circumstances that suggested suicide. Lang wrote the entry on Gurney for the 1911 edition of the *Encyclopaedia Britannica*.

Hahn, Johann Georg Von (1811–69); Austrian diplomat and linguist who worked as a consul in Greece and Albania. He made a lifelong study of Albanian culture and language, and in various works sought to prove that Albanian belonged to the Indo-European family of languages described by Max Müller. In 1864 he published his folk narrative collection *Griechische und Albanesiche Märchen* (Greek and Albanian Tales) which Lang regularly cites, though he disputes von Hahn's contention that folk tales are the de-generate myths of an earlier civilisation.

Hearne, Samuel (1745–92), English explorer, trader and naturalist. Hearne was the first European to cross northern Canada and reach the Arctic Ocean. He worked for the Hudson Bay Company. His *A Journey From Prince of Wales's Fort in Hudson's Bay to the Northern Ocean* was published posthu-mously, in 1795.

Heritier, Marie-Jeanne de Villandon L' (*c*.1664–1734); (the surname is now more usually rendered L'héritier) French aristocrat, salon owner, and author who published courtly fairy tales in her collection *Bigarrures Ingenieuses* (1696; Ingenious Variations). She also makes a defence of the practice of writing and modifying traditional tales in a letter included in the collection: 'Lettre à Madame de G★★★'. Lang states the common Victorian opinion that L'héritier spoiled traditional fairy tales, whilst Perrault preserved traditions in more authentic form. For a contemporary examination of these assumptions, however, see Elizabeth Wanning Harries, *Twice Upon a Time: Women Writers and the History of the Fairy Tale* (Princeton: Princeton University Press, 2001).

Herodotus (*c*.484 BCE – 425 BCE), Ancient Greek historian and author of *Histories* (*c*.450–420 BCE). Lang is especially interested in the *Histories* of Herodotus because of the wealth of ethnographic information they include concerning early Persian, Greek, and Egyptian culture.

Hesiod. Greek poet believed to have been active between the seventh and eighth centuries BCE. The two surviving works with which he is principally associated are *Works and Days* and *Theogony*, both of which Lang knew well. The *Theogony* in particular is an important source of information about ancient Greek mythology and culture.

Hodgson, Richard (1855–1905) was a psychical researcher. He moved to Cambridge from Australia in the early 1880s, where he met Henry Sidgwick. He joined the SPR in the year of its founding, and went on to lead some of the Society's most important investigations of the late nineteenth and early twentieth centuries, including those of Helena Blavatsky and Leonora Piper.

Home, Daniel Dunglas (1833–86) (sometimes spelled Hume) was the most famous physical medium of the nineteenth century. He was born in Scotland and emigrated to the US with his family as a child. He held his first séance as a young man in 1851 and thereafter his phenomena included levitation, moving furniture, rappings, and moving unharmed through fire. Home came to London in 1855, and then travelled through Europe. While he was feted by many prominent people, he was also criticised by many, including Thackeray, Michael Faraday and T. H. Huxley. Robert Browning's poem 'Mr. Sludge, "the Medium"' (1864) was based on Home.

Homer. Name conventionally given to the poet of the *Iliad* and the *Odyssey*, although his date, authorship and even his existence are still debated. The poems are usually thought to date from the eighth century BCE, though perhaps existing in oral form from considerably earlier. No evidence of Homer exists, though many versions of his life have been proposed since times of antiquity. A consensus that Homer was the single author of the poems first emerged in about 350 BCE, but this has been continually under question since then. During the nineteenth century the general view was that the poems were works of multiple authorship produced over an extended period of time, so Lang's position that Homer was one person and the author of both epics was unusual.

Howitt, Alfred William (1830–1908), English explorer and natural scientist. He went with his father and brother to Australia in 1852, where he travelled to previously unexplored areas, got to know the fauna, flora and geology of the country, and worked in various official positions. He began to collect anthropological information in the 1860s, and published, with Lorimer Fison, *Kamilaroi and Kurnai* in 1880. He continued to write papers on Australian culture until his death.

Hume, David (1711–76) was a Scottish philosopher, historian and economist. His work contributed importantly to the development of scepticism and empiricism. He challenged belief in the supernatural, particularly in the section 'Of Miracles' in his enormously influential *An Enquiry Concerning Human Understanding* (1748).

Hunt, Margaret (1831–1912) (*née* Raine), British novelist, mother of Violet Hunt, with whom she wrote *The Governess* (1912) and wife of the painter Alfred William Hunt. Her first three novels were written under the pseudonym Averil Beaumont. In 1884 she published a complete two-volume translation of the tales of the Brothers Grimm, which included the notes and additional scholarly materials appended by the Grimms to their 1857 edition. This translation, introduced by Lang, was the definitive English version of the Grimms' tales in the late nineteenth century, and remains the only translation to include their scholarly materials.

Husson, Hyacinthe (*c*.1830–?), an adherent of the solar-mythological school who argued in *La Chaine Traditionelle: Contes et Légendes au Point de vue Mythique* (1874; The Chain of Tradition: Tales and Legends from the Mythological Perspective) that Vedic legend offers a precedent for the identification of the wolf in Little Red Riding Hood as a symbol of 'le soleil *dévorateur*' (the devouring sun) that intercepts the dawn. The 'M' in Lang's attribution stands for Monsieur (Hyacinthe in France in this period was a name given to boys).

Huxley, Thomas Henry (1825–95) was a biologist and at the time the most famous scientist in Britain. He was known as 'Darwin's bulldog' for his powerful defence of the theory of evolution, and he coined the term 'agnostic'. He was Professor of Natural History at the Royal School of Mines, President of the British Association for the Advancement of Science and President of the Royal Society. His collection of essays, *Science and the Christian Tradition*, was first published in 1894. These essays, and those in *Science and the Hebrew Tradition* (1893), were the result of his very public debate, between 1885 and 1891, with W. E. Gladstone in the pages of the *Nineteenth Century* over evolutionary science and its implications for the status of biblical truth. He taught H. G. Wells, who credited the idea of the Eloi and the Morlocks in his novel *The Time Machine* (1895) to Huxley's lecture on evolution and degeneration.

Iamblichus (*c.*245 CE–325 CE) was a Syrian Neoplatonist philosopher. He engaged in a debate with Porphyry, whose disciple he had been, over the practice of magic for the achievement of salvation. His response to Porphyry's criticisms is contained in *On the Egyptian Mysteries*.

James, William (1842–1910) was an American psychologist and an important contributor to pragmatism in philosophy. He was president of the SPR in 1894–5 and co-founder of the American SPR. James initiated the investigations into the mediumship of the Boston trance medium Leonora Piper that were so central to the work of the SPR during the late nineteenth and early twentieth centuries. Lang corresponded with James (whose brother, the novelist Henry James, he knew well), and Lang was particularly concerned to contribute to the investigation of Mrs Piper.

Jeanne d'Arc (*c.*1412–31), usually known as Joan of Arc in English, became a heroine in her native France though her interventions in the Hundred Years War between France and England over the control of the French throne. From a peasant background, she believed that the voices of a number of saints were urging her to aid the French cause. She led a number of successful military campaigns, but was arrested by the Burgundians and sold on to the English in 1430, tried and then burned at the stake as a heretic in 1431. A second trial, authorised by the Pope in the 1450s, found her innocent of the original charges. In the late nineteenth century a campaign began for her canonisation, which finally occurred in 1920.

Jeune, Paul Le (1591–1664), French Jesuit Missionary who was superior of the Jesuit mission in Canada from 1631 to 1639. He learned several Native American languages, and in the *Relations des Jésuites de la Nouvelle-France* of 1634 published a detailed ethnographic account of the Innu people of Quebec. Le Jeune was the first editor of the Jesuit *Relations* that chronicled missionary activity amongst Native American tribes from 1632 to 1672.

Jevons, Frank Byron (1858–1936), Professor of Philosophy and administrator of Durham University. *An Introduction to the History of Religion* was published in 1896, and he went on to publish *An Introduction to the Study of Comparative Religion* (1908), *The Idea of God in Early Religions* (1910) and *Comparative Religion* (1913).

Kuhn, Franz Felix Adalbert (1812–81), German mythologist and philologist. Influenced by the Grimms, he developed a method of comparative mythology that sought to demonstrate the existence of a source civilisation for Indo-Germanic peoples. Like Müller, Kuhn used philological analysis of words and names to make arguments about the belief systems of an originary Germanic race, though, revealingly in Lang's view, his conclusions differ from Müller's. Lang's principal source of information about Kuhn's arguments was *Die Herabkunft des Feuers und des Göttertranks* (1859; The Descent of Fire and the Nectar of the Gods).

Lafitau, Joseph-François (1681–1746), French Jesuit missionary and ethnologist, who made a detailed study of the Iroquois people whilst appointed to the mission of Sault Saint-Louis (Caughnawaga) in New France (Canada) between 1712 and 1717. On his return to France he published the influential study *Moeurs des Sauvages Amériquains* (1724; Customs of the American Indians). Lafitau's work is notable in the history of anthropology because of its early use of comparative methods, and because of its dependence upon extensive observational field work.

Lobeck, Christian Augustus (1781–1860), German scholar who specialised in ancient Greek language and culture. In his major work *Aglaophamus* (1829) he maintained that ancient Greek religion can be explained by reference to primitive practices. In *Myth, Ritual and Religion* (Longmans, Green and Co., 1887; second edition 1899), Lang identifies Lobeck as an intellectual ally.

Lockhart, John Gibson (1794–1854). Scottish lawyer who became an important critic and translator. He was one of the main contributors to *Blackwood's Edinburgh Magazine*, where he published his attacks on the 'Cockney School': Keats, Hazlitt and Leigh Hunt. His translations of German Romantic theory were influential, as were his essays on German literature. His reputation as a fierce critic was cemented during his long editorship of the *Quarterly Review* (1825–53). Lang became interested in him through his biography of Walter Scott, and declared his own biography *The Life and Letters of John Gibson Lockhart* (2 vols, 1896) a defence of Lockhart's character and reputation.

Lodge, Oliver (1851–1940) was a British physicist involved in the development of wireless telegraphy. In 1901 he became the first principal of the University of Birmingham and he was knighted in 1902. He first became interested in psychical phenomena in the 1880s, and was President of the SPR in 1901, 1902, and 1932, and was involved in all the major investigations of the SPR in the late nineteenth and early twentieth centuries. Lodge was one of the key SPR investigators of the cross-correspondences, a huge series of linked messages, obtained through mediums by automatic speech and writing, from 1901 to 1930. The SPR believed that these messages were the result, in part, of an attempt to prove life beyond death by the posthumous leading psychical researchers, in particular F. W. H. Myers.

McLennan, John Ferguson (1827–81) was a Scottish ethnologist and lawyer. His disagreement with Sir Henry Maine on the subject of legal reform led eventually to his *Primitive Marriage* (1865). This, plus a later work on kinship in ancient Greece and other essays were published in 1876 as *Studies in Ancient History*. In his 'The Worship of Animals and Plants' (1869–70) he coined the term 'totemism'. His work was influential in establishing the comparative method in anthropology.

Mannhardt, Wilhelm (1831–80), German folklorist and librarian. He is particularly known for his solar theory, that sun worship is behind all myths of gods who die and are then resurrected. Mannhardt was an important influence on James Frazer.

Maskelyne, John Nevil (1839–1917) was a stage magician who ran the famous Egyptian Hall between 1873 and 1904. With his partners (first George Alfred Cooke and then David Devant), he produced magical shows, invented many famous illusions, and attempted to show that spiritualist phenomena could be normally, rather than supernaturally, produced. He set up the Occult Committee of the Magic Circle in 1914 in order to investigate claims of supernatural power and, more importantly, to expose fraud. His son, Nevil Maskelyne (1863–1924), ran the Egyptian Hall with him, and wrote numerous books on stage magic.

Mayo, Herbert (1796–1852) was the author of *Letters on The Truths Contained in Popular Superstition* (1849). The book is made up of a series of letters each on a separate subject, including the divining rod, second sight, and possession, which first appeared in *Blackwood's Edinburgh Magazine* in 1847.

Mesmer, Franz Anton (1734–1815), German physician who developed the theory of animal magnetism, positing the existence of an invisible fluid in the human body that acted according to the laws of magnetism. Mesmer used his ideas as a therapeutic practice; diseases were obstacles to the flow of the fluid and trances were induced in patients in order to unblock it.

Moetjens, Adrian (*fl. c.*1650–1700), seventeenth-century Dutch publisher based in the Hague. He was the editor of a periodical miscellany titled *Recueil de pièces curieuses et nouvelles, tant en prose qu'en vers* (Collection of Curious and New Pieces, both in Prose and Verse), in which Charles

Perrault's tales were published. Perrault's tales in verse appeared in the *Recueil* in 1694, the tales in prose between 1696 and 1697.

Morgan, Lewis H. (1818–81), American anthropologist, who saw kinship systems as being fundamental to social structure and change. He wrote a large number of anthropological works, including *Ancient Society* (1877), which influenced both Karl Marx and Friedrich Engels.

Müller, Friedrich Max (1823–1900), German philologist and Sanskrit specialist who was instrumental in founding the study of India and of comparative religion. He spent his academic career in England, at Oxford University, writing both academic and popular works on religion, India and the Sanskrit Vedas. Müller's solar theories were first developed fully in his *Oxford Essays* of 1856, specifically in the essay 'Comparative Mythology' which was to become the principal focus of Lang's intellectual dispute with him. Müller gave the Hibbert lectures, the first to be given, in 1878.

Myers, Frederic William Henry (1843–1901) was a classicist, poet, schools inspector and psychical researcher. He attended Trinity College, Cambridge and was involved in the creation of the Society for Psychical Research in 1882. He was involved, with Edmund Gurney and Frank Podmore, with the Society's early investigation into telepathy, and in the collection of material for the Society's first major work, *Phantasm's of the Living* (1886). His huge work, *Human Personality and Its Survival of Bodily Death*, was published posthumously in 1903. Myers work contained in this was influential for a number of psychologists, including William James and Theodore Flournoy. After Myers's death, the messages via automatic speech and writing that eventually became known as the cross-correspondences began, and Myers was believed to have been, posthumously, one of their authors.

Palladino (sometimes written as Paladino), **Eusapia** (1854–1918), an Italian spirit medium. Palladino was subject to a number of investigations by a variety of scientists including Cesare Lombroso, Charles Richet, Oliver Lodge, Frederic Myers and Nicolas Flammarion. Following investigations with Charles Richet in France in 1894, the Society for Psychical Research investigated her in 1895 at the Cambridge home of Frederic Myers, at one of which the stage magician J. N. Maskelyne was present, and decided she was a fraud. Other European scientists continued to examine her in the early twentieth century, making her perhaps the most investigated medium in history. The SPR lost interest in her until, in 1908, it began new investigations, leading to Hereward Carrington's *Eusapia Palladino and Her Phenomena* (New York: B. W. Dodge, 1909), which on the whole sees her phenomena as authentic.

Pausanias (*c.*110 CE–180 CE), ancient Greek geographer, and author of *Description of Greece*. Lang was especially interested in this detailed account of the regions of ancient Greece because of Pausanias's practice of recording mythological narratives and ritual customs.

Payne, Edward John (1844–1904), barrister and historian. Two volumes of his *A History of the New World Called America* were published (1892 and 1899), but the work remained unfinished at his death.

Perrault, Charles (1628–1703) French court official, poet and fairy tale writer. For the bulk of his working life he was secretary to Jean-Baptiste Colbert, the controller general of Louis XIV's finances. In 1671 he was elected to the *Académie française*, and became one of the main disputants in the 'Querelle des ancients et des modernes' (Quarrel of the Ancients and the Moderns), arguing, against Nicholas Boileau, that modern writers could improve upon the models established by ancient writers, chiefly because they were informed by Christian moral precepts. Perrault's first fairy tales were written in verse and published together in 1694. He also published a collection of prose tales in 1697, *Histoires ou contes du temps passé avec des moralités* (Stories or Tales of Past Times with Morals), under the name of his son Pierre Perrault Darmancour. This collection contains eight stories which have subsequently become very well-known internationally, establishing Perrault as one of the major figures in the development of the literary fairy tale. Lang published an edition of Perrault's tales in 1888 which includes a substantial dissertation on his life and work. He also included all but one of Perrualt's prose tales in *The Blue Fairy Book* (London: Longmans, Green and Co., 1889).

Piper, Leonora (1857–1950) was a trance medium from Boston, USA. While working as a paid medium, she was visited by William James in 1885, a meeting which began a long and not always happy relation with the Society for Psychical Research in both the US and the UK. Piper was investigated by the psychical researcher Richard Hodgson on behalf of the SPR from 1887 until his death in 1905. She was one of the central mediums in the cross-correspondences, producing messages first through automatic speech and later through automatic writing.

Podmore, Frank (1856–1910) was a psychical researcher and one of the founding members of the Fabian Society. He joined the Society for Psychical Research in 1882, co-wrote its first major work, *Phantasms of the Living* (1886), with Edmund Gurney and Frederic Myers, and was involved in the early investigations of telepathy. He was always more sceptical of spiritualist explanations than the other central psychical researchers, as can be seen in his *Studies in Psychical* Research (1897) and *Modern Spiritualism: A History* *and a Criticism* (1902). He died by drowning and is believed to have committed suicide.

Porphyry (*c*.234 CE–*c*.305 CE) was a Neoplatonic philosopher and disciple of Plotinus, with whom he studied in Rome. He engaged in a public debate with Iamblichus over the use of theurgical practices to attain salvation.

Richet, Charles (1850–1935), French physiologist and psychical researcher. He was Professor of Physiology at the Collège de France and won the Nobel Prize in Physiology and Medicine in 1913. Richet had a strong interest in hypnosis and an interest in spiritualist phenomena. He was involved in the investigations of Eusapia Palladino in the 1890s. He was president of the SPR in 1905, and coined the term 'ectoplasm'.

Rink, Hinrich (sometimes Henry in translations) (1819–93); Danish geologist. Between 1848 and 1868 he made numerous trips to Greenland to conduct geological surveys, and simultaneously collected ethnological information about the indigenous people of Greenland. Lang makes frequent use of Rink's collection *Tales and Traditions of the Eskimo* (1866) which combines traditional tales with anthropological data.

Robertson Smith, William (1846–94), Scottish theologian, ethnologist and scholar of Hebrew and Arabic. His works include *The Prophets of Israel* (1882), *Kinship and Marriage in Early Arabia* (1885) and *Lectures on the Religion of the Semites* (1889). He was editor of the *Encyclopaedia Britannica* whilst Lang was contributing articles to it.

Roth, Rudolf von (1821–95); German philologist and Sanskrit scholar. In common with Müller, he argued that Vedic texts derived from nature myths and used etymological analysis of names to support his speculations. His main work on this subject was *Zur Litteratur und Geschichte des Veda* (1846; On the Literature and History of the Vedas).

Roth, Walter E. (1861–1933) was an English anthropologist and physician, and was appointed the first Northern Protector of Aborigines in 1898. He was Chief Protector of Aborigines between 1904 and 1906. His Bulletins on North Queensland, published between 1901 and 1910, were based on his official reports.

Schrenck-Notzing, Baron Albert von (1862–1929), German physician, sexologist and psychical reseacher. He was much involved in the investigations of Eusapia Palladino, and became notorious just before the First World War on the publication of his *Materialisations-Phaenomene*, his investigation, using photography, of the ectoplasmic phenomena of the medium Eva C.

Scott, Sir Walter (1771–1832). Scott wrote in different genres but is generally regarded as having established the historical novel as a form. He was deeply interested in traditional Scottish culture and was important in collecting and preserving old ballads and stories of the Border country, many of which feature in his works. He was a prolific writer, beginning with verse and then publishing the first of his many novels, *Waverley*, in 1817. Lang was devoted to Scott's work and shared his conservative views as well as claiming a common ancestor with him from his own Border lineage.

Sévigné, Marie de Rabutin-Chantal, Marquise de (1626–96); French aristocrat, salonniere, and prolific letter writer. Her letters, renowned for their wit, style, and force of observation, were circulated at court during her lifetime, and published posthumously. The primary recipient was her married daughter Françoise-Marguerite de Sévigné, Comtesse de Grignan.

Sidgwick, Eleanor (1845–1936) was active in the campaign for women's higher eduction and a prominent psychical researcher. She was born Eleanor Balfour, and was the brother of the future Conservative prime minister, Arthur Balfour. She met the moral philosopher Henry Sidgwick at Newnham College, Cambridge, and they were married in 1876. She went on to become principal of Newnham, and the Sidgwicks together were instrumental in the founding of the Society for Psychical Research. She was a central figure in the Society for over thirty years, and was president in 1908.

Sidgwick, Henry (1838–1900) was an English classicist, philosopher and economist at Trinity College, Cambridge. He was active in promoting higher education for women, and was one of the founders of Newnham College in 1875. He was also one of the founders of the SPR in 1882. He and his wife, Eleanor Sidgwick, were central to the Society in the late nineteenth century.

Spencer, Herbert (1820–1903) English philosopher and social theorist, whose thinking ranged across numerous subjects, including sociology, anthropology, natural science, politics, biology, literature and psychology. Spencer argued that the evolutionary theories that Darwin applied to the natural world could also be used to understand the development of other phenomena, including human culture, the human mind, and social and political systems. He also sought to establish a universal set of laws that would show that all phenomena, biological, physical and cultural, were involved in a process of gradual, progressive evolutionary development. Lang frequently refers to the first volume of Spencer's study *The Principles of Sociology* (3 vols, published 1874–1896; vol. I, 1874–5), and, in his earlier anthropological writings, uses Spencer's arguments to support his own view that society develops progressively from a stage of savagery towards a stage of civilisation. In later writings, however, Lang disputed Spencer's arguments concerning savage animism and religion.

Spencer, John (1630–93). English minister and theological writer, Master of Corpus Christi College, Cambridge from 1667 to his death, and author of *De Legibus Hebraeorum Ritualibus* (The Laws of Jewish Rituals), published in 1685. In *De Legibus* Spencer makes use of the comparative method to support his argument that Hebrew ritual was a development of existing pagan belief systems, especially those of the ancient Egyptians. Lang approved of Spencer's use of comparative methods.

Stevenson, Robert Louis (1850–94). Born in Edinburgh and trained for the profession of law, Stevenson was drawn to writing from an early age. He wrote some plays including *Deacon Brodie* (1880) the story of which would become part of the inspiration for his best-known work *The Strange Case of Dr Jekyll and Mr Hyde* (1886). His first novel, *Treasure Island* (1883) made him famous and those that followed, such as *Kidnapped* (1886) and *The Master of Ballantrae* (1889) were equally popular. He and Lang knew each other and when Stevenson left Britain to live in the South Seas to improve his health, Lang continued to send him ideas and material for novels.

Swedenborg, Emanuel (1688–1772), Swedish philosopher, scientist and mystic, began to experience visions in the 1740s, and believed that God had revealed to him in these visions truths about the future, and about the need to reform Christianity. His most well-known work is *Heaven and Hell* (1758).

Thackeray, William Makepeace (1811–63). Trained for the law, he never practised but became a journalist instead, working in London and in Paris. From the 1830s he was a regular contributor to periodicals; his novel *Vanity Fair* was published in serial form 1847–8 and was followed by many others. Becky Sharp, the vivacious but unprincipled heroine of *Vanity Fair*, was a favourite character of Lang's, who also liked his other novels and his depictions of journalism and journalists. Thackeray's novel for children, *The Rose and the Ring* (1855), was also much admired by Lang and provided a model for his 'Chronicles of Pantouflia'.

Thurn, Everard Ferdinand Im (1852–1932) was a British explorer, botanist, photographer and anthropologist. He was the curator of the British Guiana Museum between 1877 and 1882 and held positions in the colonial administrations of Guiana, Ceylon and Fiji. From 1919–20 he was also president of the Royal Anthropological Institute. His major anthropological work, *Among the Indians of Guiana*, was published in 1883.

Tylor, E. B. (1832–1917); the most influential British anthropologist of the late Victorian period, and proponent of a number of theories that significantly influenced Lang's approach to mythology and folklore. Tylor's ideas were formulated in his study *Researches into the Early History of Mankind and the Development of Civilization* (1865) and his extremely influential *Primitive Culture: Researches into the Development of Mythology, Pholosophy, Religion, Languages, Art and Customs*, 2 vols (1871), which Lang read in 1872, meeting Tylor at about the same time. Here Lang found the inspiration for his arguments about cultural evolution, primitive animism and folkloric survivals. Whilst Lang's anthropological writings were significantly influenced by Tylor, however, he also disagreed with Tylor in some crucial respects, notably in his assessment of the value of survivals in civilised societies, and in his arguments about belief in spirits. Tylor became the first Professor of Anthropology at Oxford University in 1896 and was knighted in 1912.

Waitz, Theodor (1821–64), German anthropologist and psychologist. His six-volume *Die Anthropologie der Naturvölker* (The Anthropology of Indigenous Peoples) was published between 1859 and 1872, the last two volumes being published posthumously. Waitz, alongside Tylor and McLennan, is identified by Lang in *Myth, Ritual and Religion* (Longmans, Green and Co., 1887; second edition 1899) as one of the most significant influences on his own anthropological method.

Wallace, Alfred Russel (1823–1913) was a biologist, geographer and anthropologist and the co-discoverer with Darwin of evolution by natural selection. By the end of the nineteenth century he was one of the most famous scientists in Britain, and indeed in the world. He was a socialist and a spiritualist, and in *Miracles and Modern Spiritualism* (1874) he challenged the definition of miracles famously given by David Hume in *An Enquiry Concerning Human Understanding* (1748).

APPENDIX II:
Ethnic groups cited by Lang

Algonkins: now more commonly Algonquin; a first nation people from the region of Quebec in modern Canada.

Arunta: also known as the Aranda, Arrernte or Arrarnta; an Aboriginal people whose traditional lands consist of Mparntwe (Alice Springs) and surrounding areas in Central Australia.

Basutos: now called the Sotho people; an ethnic group from Lesotho and South Africa.

Bushmen: a term used for the San or Xan people of Southern Africa.

Caribs: indigenous people of the Americas, from whom the Caribbean takes its name. The Caribs originated in South America, and settled the islands of the Lesser Antilles in the first millennium CE.

Cingalese: now more commonly Sinhalese; the largest ethnic group of the island of Sri Lanka (given the colonial name Ceylon until 1972).

Circassians: also called Adyghe; people of the Northern Caucasus, conquered and occupied by Russia in the nineteenth century.

Digger Indians: name given by European settlers to the indigenous Paiute people of south-western United States (Arizona, Nevada and California). The term is now considered derogatory.

Epirote: people from the Epirus region of north-western Greece, which also lies partially in modern Albania.

Eskimo: generic term, now generally seen as pejorative, for the Inuit and Yupik peoples of the Northern Polar regions of Alaska, Canada, Siberia and Greenland.

Fuegians: indigenous peoples of the Tierra del Fuego, an archipelago at the southernmost point of South America.

Futa: more commonly Fula or Fulani; an African ethnic group, found predominantly in West Africa.

Hottentots: see Nama

Huron: the name given by French settlers to indigenous Americans of the Wyandot league of tribes.

Iroquois: a league of indigenous American peoples deriving from what is now New York state.

Maoris: indigenous Polynesian people who settled in New Zealand in the thirteenth century CE.

Murri: a collection of aboriginal Australian peoples from what is now the state of Queensland.

Nama: an ethnic group from Southern Africa. European colonisers gave them the derogatory name Hottentots in imitation of the sound of their language.

Namaquas: see Nama.

Nootka: now called Nuu-chah-nulth; first nation American peoples from the Northwest coast of Canada.

Odjibwas: see Ojibbeway.

Ojibbeway: now more commonly Ojibwa or Ojibway, also called Chippewa and Anishinaabe; an indigenous American and first nation people, inhabiting the area covered by the southern states of Canada and the northern states of the United States.

Ovahereroes: also Herero; an ethnic group of southern Africa, predominantly inhabiting what is now Namibia, Botswana and Angola.

Samoyeds: generic term for the Nenet, Selkup and Nganasan peoples of the Arctic regions of Northern Russia (Siberia). The term is now considered derogatory because it suggests cannibalism in Russian.

Turkomans: also spelled Turkmens; an ethnic group of Iraq, descended from the Turks.

Wolufs: more commonly Wolof; a West African ethnic group, inhabiting the modern republics of Senegal, the Gambia and Mauritania. In Senegal they are the largest ethnic group.

Yorubas: West African ethnic group, predominantly from Nigeria and Benin. They are one of the largest single ethnic groups in Africa.

Zulu: The largest ethnic group in Southern Africa, primarily located in what is now the South African province of KwaZulu-Natal.

EXPLANATORY NOTES

General Introduction

1   Henry James to Edmund Gosse, 19 November 1912. *Selected Letters of Henry James to Edmund Gosse 1882–1915*, ed. Rayburn S. Moore (Baton Rouge: Louisiana State University Press, 1988), p. 284.

2   The lectures in his name at St Andrews were stipulated in the will of a Professor of Mathematics at St Salvator and St Leonard, Sir Peter Redford Scott Lang, a friend of Lang's but no relation. They were annual from 1927 until 1934, then more intermittent, given in 1937 and 1939 (which was J. R. R. Tolkein's lecture on fairy stories), 1947–51, 1955, 1956, 1978, 1988, 2004 and revived again for the centenary of Lang's death in 2012.

3   A. Blyth Webster, 'Introduction', *Concerning Andrew Lang: Being the Andrew Lang Lectures Delivered Before the University of St. Andrews 1927–1937, with a Preface by J. B. Salmond and an introduction by A. Blyth Webster* (Oxford: Clarendon Press, 1949), p. xi.

4   George Saintsbury, 'Andrew Lang in the 'Seventies – and After', in Harley Granville-Barker (ed.), *The Eighteen-Seventies: Essays by Fellows of the Royal Society of Literature* (London: Cambridge University Press, 1929). p. 94.

5   Ibid., p. 95.

6   Roger Lancelyn Green calculates that Lang wrote eighty-six reviews for *The Academy* alone between 10 January 1870 and 11 June 1887. Roger Lancelyn Green, *Andrew Lang: A Critical Biography with a Short-title Bibliography of the Works of Andrew Lang* (Leicester: Edmund Ward, 1946), p. 254.

7   The only other attempt at a bibliography seems to have been C. M. Falconer, *The Writings of Andrew Lang M.A., LL.D. Arranged in the Form of a Bibliography with Notes by C.M. Falconer* (Dundee: 1894). A hundred copies were privately printed by Winter, Duncan & Co. Falconer was a Dundee man (Green describes him as a rope-spinner) who had probably a complete collection of Lang's work from 1863 to 1906 when he died in 1907. The collection was sold in one lot, but even the indefatigable Green was not able to locate it. See Green, *Andrew Lang*, p. 196.

8   Written by Douglas Young, recorded on 12 September 1962 and broadcast at 8.45pm on 13 September 1962. The script is in the Roger Lancelyn Green collection in St Andrews University Library. PR4877. ms38257.

9   John Gross, *The Rise and Fall of the Man of Letters* (London: Weidenfeld & Nicolson, 1969), p. 139.

10   Harold Orel, *Victorian Literary Critics* (London: Macmillan, 1984), p. 150.

11   Despite his frequently repeated exhortations to his correspondents to destroy his letters, a very large number remain, mostly in the archives of those correspondents. Demoor's PhD thesis 'Andrew Lang (1844–1912): Late Victorian Humanist and Journalistic Critic: with a Descriptive Checklist of the Lang Letters' (Ghent University, 1983) is in two volumes, the second being a catalogue of the letters. There are discussions of groups of the letters in Demoor, 'Andrew Lang on Gissing: A Late Victorian Point of View', *Gissing Newsletter* 20:2 (April 1984), pp. 23–8; Demoor, 'Andrew Lang's Letters to Edmund Gosse: The Record of a Fruitful Collaboration as Poets, Critics and Biographers', *Review of English Studies* 38:152 (1987), pp. 492–509; Demoor, 'Andrew Lang versus W. D. Howells: A Late Victorian Literary Duel', *Journal of American Studies* 21:3 (December 1987), pp. 416–22; Demoor, 'Andrew Lang's Letters to H. Rider Haggard: the Record of a Harmonious Friendship', *Etudes Anglaises* 40:3

(1987), pp. 313–22; Demoor, 'Andrew Lang's Causeries 1874–1912', *Victorian Periodicals Review* 21:1 (Spring 1988), pp. 15–22 and Demoor, *Friends Over the Ocean: Andrew Lang's American Correspondents, 1881–1912* (Ghent: Rijksuniversiteit Gent, 1989).

12   This includes the PhD thesis by Antonius De Cocq, 'Andrew Lang: A Nineteenth Century Anthropologist' (University of Utrecht, 1968) and Louise McKinnell's PhD thesis 'Andrew Lang: Anthropologist, Classicist, Folklorist and Victorian Critic' (Toronto, 1993).

13   The only full-length book on Lang other than Green's critical biography is *Andrew Lang* by Eleanor de Selms Langstaff (Boston: Twayne, 1978). It is quite poorly researched and contains many inaccuracies. A special issue of *Romanticism and Victorianism on the Net* 64 (October 2013) http://ravonjournal.org/ appeared in April 2014 containing six articles on Lang.

14   George Gordon, *Andrew Lang* (Oxford: Oxford University Press, 1928), p. 12.

15   James to Edmund Gosse, 19 November 1912. *Selected Letters of Henry James to Edmund Gosse*, p. 285.

16   Margaret Beetham, '"The Agony Aunt, the Romancing Uncle and the Family of Empire": Defining the Sixpenny Reading Public in the 1890s', in Laurel Brake, Bill Bell and David Finkelstein (eds), *Nineteenth-century Media and the Construction of Identities* (Basingstoke: Palgrave, 2000), p. 266.

17   'Introduction' to J. Vyrnwy Morgan, *A Study in Nationality*, see Volume 2, pp. 207–13.

18   This was published in *St Andrews University Magazine* in April 1863.

19   Demoor, 'Andrew Lang', vol. 1, p. 79.

20   Lang never discusses why he chose to give up his Fellowship beyond a single reference where he says 'Things go wrong somehow' in *Adventures Among Books* (London:, Green and Co., 1905), p. 34. He married, but Merton allowed married Fellows to remain in college so this could not have been the reason. For further discussion see Green, *Andrew Lang*, pp. 39–41.

21   Green, *Andrew Lang*, p. 202.

22   This claim is made by J. B. Salmond in *Andrew Lang and Journalism* (Edinburgh: Thomas Nelson, 1951), p. 17.

23   For more detailed discussion see the Introduction to Volume 2.

24   See recollections in for example: H. Rider Haggard, *The Days of My Life: An Autobiography* (London: Longmans, Green and Co., 1926); Max Beerbohm, 'Two Glimpses of Andrew Lang', *Life and Letters* 1:1 (June 1928), pp. 2–13; Richard le Gallienne, *The Romantic Nineties* (London: G. P. Putnam's Sons, 1925); Edmund Gosse, *Portraits and Sketches* (London: William Heinemann, 1912); Rudyard Kipling, *Something of Myself* (London: Macmillan, 1937).

25   Letter to E. H. Coleridge (no year) cited in Demoor, 'Andrew Lang', vol. 1, p. v.

26   Green, *Andrew Lang*, p. ix.

27   Lang to Henry Rider Haggard, 26 April 1892. Roger Lancelyn Green Collection, St Andrews University Library. PR4877. ms38260.

28   Lang to Anna Hills, 31 December [1891]. Roger Lancelyn Green Collection, St Andrews University Library. PR4876. C7.ms3286.

29 See Philip Waller, *Writers, Readers and Reputations: Literary Life in Britain 1870–1918* (Oxford: Oxford University Press, 2006), pp. 456–63 on its formation.

30 Lang to Clement K. Shorter, 13 September [no year is given but from internal evidence it is certainly later than 1897]. Roger Lancelyn Green Collection, St Andrews University Library. PR4867.C7 ms1557.

31 Lang to Haggard, 26 December 1907. Roger Lancelyn Green Collection, St Andrews University Library. PR4877. ms38260.

32 Lang to Sir Oliver Lodge, 12 January [no year], in the archive of the Society for Psychical Research, Manuscripts Collection, University of Cambridge Library. SPR. MS 35/1022.

33 Demoor, *Friends Over the Ocean*, p. 17–18.

34 Green, *Andrew Lang*, p. 206.

35 Ibid., p. 207

36 Lang to Haggard, 2 June 1902, in the Roger Lancelyn Green Collection, St Andrews University Library. PR4877. ms38260.

Introduction to Volume 1

1 Andrew Lang, 'The Viking's Bones', *Illustrated London News* CII:2817 (15 April 1893), p. 462.

2 See, respectively, the following examples: 'The Ghastly Priest', in *Magic and Religion* (London: Longmans, Green and Co., 1901), pp. 205–23; 'Science and Demonology', this volume pp. 268–70; letter to Oliver Lodge, 27 February [no year], this volume pp. 322–3; *La Vie de Jeanne d'Arc De M. Anatole France* (Paris: Perrin, 1909).

3 Andrew Lang, 'Science and "Miracles"', this volume, p. 309.

4 Andrew Lang, 'Science and "Miracles"' (page not extracted in this volume), *The Making of Religion* (Longmans, Green and Co., 1898), p. 25.

5 See, for example, across a variety of disciplines: Ralph O'Connor, *The Earth on Show: Fossils and the Poetics of Popular Science, 1802–1856* (Chicago and London: University of Chicago Press, 2007); Jonathan Smith, *Fact and Feeling: Baconian Science and the Nineteenth-century Literary Imagination* (Madison: University of Wisconsin Press, 1994); Martin Willis, *Vision, Science and Literature, 1870–1920: Ocular Horizons* (London: Pickering & Chatto, 2011); Christopher Bracken, *Magical Criticism: The Recourse of Savage Philosophy* (Chicago: University of Chicago Press, 2007); Philippe-Alain Michaud, *Aby Warburg and the Image in Motion*, trans. Sophie Hawkes (New York: Zone Books, 2004); Joshua Landy and Michael Saler (eds), *The Re-enchantment of the World: Secular Magic in A Rational Age* (Stanford, CA: Stanford University Press, 2009); Leigh Wilson, *Modernism and Magic: Experiments with Spiritualism, Theosophy and the Occult* (Edinburgh: Edinburgh University Press, 2013).

6 James Frazer, *The Golden Bough: A Study in Magic and Religion* [1922], abridged edition (London: Penguin, 1996), pp. 13–14.

7 George Gordon, 'Andrew Lang', in *Concerning Andrew Lang: Being the Andrew Lang Lectures Delivered Before the University of St Andrews 1927–1937*, from the Andrew Lang Lecture delivered 1 December 1927 (Oxford: Clarendon Press, 1949), p. 6.

8   See Roger Lancelyn Green, *Andrew Lang: A Critical Biography, with a Short-title Bibliography of the Works of Andrew Lang* (Leicester: Edmund Ward, 1946), p. 23.

9   Lang to Clement Shorter, 13 September [no year], Roger Lancelyn Green Collection, St Andrews University Library, PR4867. C7 MS1557.

10 Marysa Demoor, 'Andrew Lang (1844–1912): Late Victorian Humanist and Journalistic Critic with a Descriptive Checklist of the Lang Letters', unpublished PhD thesis, 2 vols (University of Ghent, 1982–3), vol. 1, p. 79.

11 Andrew Lang, 'Edward Burnett Tylor' in W. H. R. Rivers, R. R. Marett and Northcote W. Thomas (eds), *Anthropological Essays Presented to Edward Burnett Tylor, In Honour of his 75th Birthday, October 2 1907* (Oxford: Clarendon Press, 1908), p. 8.

12 Andrew Lang, 'Anthropology and Religion' (page not extracted in this volume), *The Making of Religion*, p. 47.

13 Henrika Kuklick, 'The British Tradition', in Henrika Kuklick (ed.), *A New History of Anthropology* (Oxford: Blackwell, 2008), p. 52.

14 Ibid., pp. 52–3.

15 Ibid., p. 53. See James Cowles Prichard, *Researches in the Physical History of Man* (London: John and Arthur Arch, 1813), in particular chapter 4, section 4 on the 'negro' as the original human being.

16 Kuklick, 'The British Tradition', p. 54.

17 Ibid., p. 55.

18 Ibid.

19 Lang, 'Edward Burnett Tylor', p. 3

20 See, for example, Andrew Lang, 'The Bull-Roarer: A Study of the Mysteries', in *Custom and Myth* (London: Longmans, Green and Co., 1884), pp. 29–44 and '"Cup and Ring": An Old Problem Solved', in *Magic and Religion* (London: Longmans, Green and Co., 1901), pp. 241–56.

21 See for example, 'Australian Problems', this volume, pp. 223–6.

22 Andrew Lang, 'Cinderella and the Diffusion of Tales', *Folk-Lore* 4:4 (1893), pp. 419, 429. The stories have frequently been anthologised, adapted and republished. Lang's contemporary, Joseph Jacobs, changed their titles, eliminated the Scotch dialect, and published them as 'English' traditions in his collections *English Fairy Tales* (London: David Nutt, 1890) and *More English Fairy Tales* (London: David Nutt, 1894). Latterly, they can be found unadulterated in such major repositories of tradition as Katherine M. Briggs's (ed.), *A Dictionary of British Folk-Tales in the English Language*, 2 parts, 4 vols (London: Routledge, 1970–1), part A, vol. 1, pp. 424–6, 456–8.

23 For Lang's posing of these questions see 'Household Tales', this volume, pp. 89–90.

24 Nineteenth-century philologists had speculated, on the basis of linguistic evidence, that there might be an 'Aryan' civilisation from which all Indo-European civilisations had derived. The existence of this civilisation, however – and any stories that it may have told – remained a matter of speculation and philological reconstruction.

25 The Indo-European area is roughly encompassed by India in the East, Ireland in the West, Scandinavia in the North and the Mediterranean in the South.

26 See 'Introduction' to *Perrault's Popular Tales*, this volume, p. 150.

27 Ibid., pp. 150–1.

28 Ibid., p. 145.

29 Lang, 'Introduction', in *The Most Pleasant and Delectable Tale of the Marriage of Cupid and Psyche*, by Apuleius, trans. William Adlington (London: Nutt, 1887), p. xix.

30 Ibid., p. xxi.

31 'Mythology and Fairy Tales', *Fortnightly Review* 77 (May 1873), pp. 618–31.

32 Ibid., p. 620.

33 Ibid., p. 622.

34 Ibid.

35 Andrew Lang, 'Preface', in *Folk-Lore Record* 2 (1879), pp. i, vii.

36 Ibid.

37 See Max Müller, *Comparative Mythology:An Essay*, ed. A. Smythe Palmer (London: Routledge, 1909), pp. 126–7.

38 Andrew Lang, 'Mr. Max Müller's Philosophy of Mythology', *Fraser's Magazine* (August 1881), p. 171.

39 Andrew Lang, "Cupid, Psyche and the "Sun Frog"', this volume, p. 69.

40 Ibid., this volume, pp. 69–70.

41 Lang, *Modern Mythology* (London: Longmans, Green and Co., 1897), p. vii.

42 Ibid.

43 See Richard Dorson, 'The Eclipse of Solar Mythology', *Journal of American Folklore* 68:270 (1955), pp. 393–416.

44 See Eric Lawrence Montenyohl, 'Andrew Lang and the Fairy Tale', unpublished PhD thesis (Indiana University, 1986), p. 68.

45 For a systematic presentation of these answers by Lang see 'Household Tales', this volume, pp. 106–7. The phrase 'sphinx of popular tales' appears in Lang's Introduction to *Perrault's Popular Tales*. See this volume, p. 151.

46 Lang, 'Cinderella and the Diffusion of Tales', p. 431.

47 E. B. Tylor, *Primitive Culture: Researches into the Development of Mythology, Philosophy, Religion, Languages, Art and Customs*, 2 vols (1871; London: John Murray, 1920), vol. 1, p. 32.

48 In treating the subject of survivals Lang depends as much upon the work of McLennan as he does on Tylor. In his study *Primitive Marriage* (Edinburgh: Adam and Charles Black, 1865), McLennan had applied this doctrine systematically to the study of marriage, arguing that the recurrence around the world of marriage rituals that symbolise the act of bride-capture was likely to be a 'survival' of primitive practices in which bride-capture actually took place.

49 Tylor, *Primitive Culture*, vol. 1, p. 86.

50 See Andrew Lang, 'The Method of Folklore', this volume, p. 63.

51 This argument is made in 'Household Tales'. See this volume, pp. 116–17.

52 See Lang, 'Cupid, Psyche and the "Sun Frog"', this volume, p. 70.

53 See ibid., this volume, p. 77.

54 For further discussion of arguments concerning cultural evolutionism, see Robert Léonard Carneiro, *Evolutionism in Cultural Anthropology* (Boulder, CO: Westview, 2003).

55 Franz Boas, 'The Limitations of the Comparative Method of Anthropology', *Science* (December 1896), p. 901.

56 Ibid., p. 903.

57 Ibid., p. 905, 903.

58 Ibid., p. 903.

59 Ibid., p. 904.

60 Ibid.

61 Ibid., p. 905.

62 Ibid.

63 See 'New System Proposed', this volume, p. 83.

64 Dorson makes this argument in response to Lang's preoccupation with 'analogies': 'Today,' he writes, 'the anthropologist prefers to study the single culture in its totality, and shies away from superficial comparisons'. See 'Andrew Lang's Folklore Interests', p. 6.

65 Lang, 'Cinderella and the Diffusion of Tales', p. 429. '*Celte Celtisante*' implies that she is a Celtic expert on Celtic matters.

66 For a comparable (but briefer) discussion of 'Rashin Coatie' see Lang, 'At the Sign of the Ship', *Longman's Magazine* 13 (February 1889), p. 441.

67 Dorson, 'Andrew Lang's Folklore Interests', p. 5.

68 Joseph Jacobs, 'The Science of Folk-tales and the Problem of Diffusion', in *Transactions of the Second International Folk-Lore Congress* (London: Nutt, 1892), p. 76.

69 Joseph Jacobs, 'The Folk', *Folk-Lore* 4:2 (1893), p. 237.

70 Bronislaw Malinowski, 'Culture', in *The Encyclopedia of the Social Sciences* (New York: Macmillan, 1931), vol. 4, p. 624. For another consideration of Lang's approach to survivals see Jonah Siegel, 'Lang's Survivals' in *Romanticism and Victorianism on the Net*, Special Issue 'The Andrew Lang Effect: Network, Discipline, Method', guest eds Nathan Hensley and Molly Clark Hillard, 64 (October 2013) http://ravonjournal.org/issue/. Siegel argues that Lang's emphasis on 'survivals' represents a challenge to the Romantic idea of original authorship.

71 See also Molly Clark Hillard, 'Trysting Genres: Andrew Lang's Fairy Tale Methodologies' in *Romanticism and Victorianism on the Net*, 64 (October 2013) http://ravonjournal.org/issue/, pp. 15–21.

72 For a full listing of the tales and their sources see Montenyohl, 'Andrew Lang and the Fairy Tale', pp. 201–3.

73 Montenyohl gives a schematic breakdown of the motifs and tale types used in Lang's fairy-tale influenced fictions. See ibid., pp. 132–47.

74 For discussion see Jan Susina, '"Like the Fragments of Coloured Glass in a Kaleidoscope": Andrew Lang Mixes up Richard Doyle's *In Fairyland*', *Marvels and Tales* 17:1 (2003), pp. 100–19.

75 See Montenyohl, 'Andrew Lang and the Fairy Tale', pp. 204–5.

76 Green, *Andrew Lang*, p. vii.

77 *'children…of man'*: see p. 152

78 Quoted in Green, *Andrew Lang*, p. 100. 1 Marloes Road in Kensington, London was the Lang family residence.

79 See Lang 'Literary Anodynes' in Volume 2, pp. 104–11.

80 See 'Realism and Romance', Volume 2, p. 98.

81 See Sara Hines, 'Collecting the Empire: Andrew Lang's Fairy Books (1889–1910)', *Marvels and Tales* 24:1 (2010) pp. 39–56.

82 Grant Allen, 'Ghost Worship and Tree Worship', *Popular Science Monthly* (February 1893), p. 489.

83 Herbert Spencer, 'The Origins of Animal-worship', *Fortnightly Review* (May 1870), pp. 536–7.

84 Tylor, *Primitive Culture* (1871), vol. 1, p. 425.

85 Ibid., p. 426.

86 Ibid., p. 428.

87 Ivan Stenski, 'The Spiritual Dimension', in Henrika Kuklick (ed.), *A New History of Anthropology* (Oxford: Blackwell, 2008), p. 117.

88 Andrew Lang, *Cock Lane and Common Sense* (London: Longmans, Green and Co., 1894), p. 335.

89 Ibid., p. 338.

90 Andrew Lang, 'Preface', *The Making of Religion*, 2nd edition (London: Longmans, Green and Co., 1900), p. vii.

91 Lang, *Cock Lane and Common Sense*, p. 345.

92 Ibid., p. 355.

93 'Anthropology and Religion II', this volume, p. 246.

94 See, for example, 'Science and Superstition', in *Magic and Religion* (London: Longmans, Green and Co., 1901), where Lang goes so far as to suggest that valuing theories over the facts is itself an example of superstition. This volume, p. 214–15.

95 Andrew Lang, 'Preface', in *Custom and Myth*, second edition (London: Longmans, Green and Co., 1893), p. ix–x.

96 Andrew Lang, 'Theories of the Origins of Religion', in *The Origins of Religions and Other Essays* (London: Watts & Co., 1908), p. 127.

97 See, for example, Joseph Tracy, '"Immortality of the Soul" and Origin of the Idea of Gods and God', *American Catholic Quarterly Review* 24 (1899), p. 172ff. The work perhaps most directly influenced by this misreading of *The Making of Religion* was Wilhelm Schmidt's series of articles 'L'origine de l'Idée de Dieu' (1908–12), expanded into his *Der Ursprung der Gottesidee* (The Origin of the Idea of God) (12 vols, Münster: Aschendorffsche, 1912–55). Schmidt was a Catholic priest who argued for the existence of monotheism among 'primitive' peoples.

98 Quoted in R. R. Marett, 'The Raw Material of Religion', in *Concerning Andrew Lang*, from the Andrew Lang Lecture delivered 25 October 1929, p. 11.

99 See for example Andrew Lang, *Myth, Ritual and Religion*, 2nd edition, 2 vols (London: Longmans, Green and Co., 1889), vol. 1, pp. 334–5.

100 Lang, 'Theories of the Origins of Religion', p. 120.

101 Lang to Henry Rider Haggard, 3 July [1897], quoted in Marysa Demoor, 'Andrew Lang (1844–1912)', vol. 1, p. 89.

102 Eleven letters from Lang to Sir James Frazer are held in the Wren Library, Trinity College Library, Cambridge University.

103 Lang, 'Preface', *Custom and Myth* (2nd edition, 1893), p. vii.

104 Lang, 'Mr. Frazer's Theory of Totemism', *Fortnightly Review*, 65 (1899), pp. 1012–25.

105 Marett, 'The Raw Material of Religion', p. 16.

106 Lang, *Magic and Religion*, pp. 48–9.

107 Ibid., p. 60.

108 Frazer, *The Golden Bough*, p. 2.

109 Lang, *Magic and Religion*, p. 223.

110 Lang to Annie Hills, February 15 [1901], quoted in Marysa Demoor, 'Andrew Lang (1844–1912)', p. 90.

111 See Antonius de Cocq, *Andrew Lang: A Nineteenth Century Anthropologist* (Amsterdam: Uitg Zwijsen Tilburg, 1968), pp. 108ff.

112 See Robert Ackerman, 'Anthropology and the Classics', in Kuklick (ed.), *A New History of Anthropology*, p. 144.

113 George Gordon, 'Andrew Lang', in *Concerning Andrew Lang*, p. 11.

114 Lang, *Magic and Religion*, p. 240.

115 Lang, 'Theories of the Origins of Religion', p. 122.

116 G. K. Chesterton, 'Chesterton on Lang', *New York Times*, reprinted from *Illustrated London News* (11 August 1912), p. BR445.

117 Marett, 'The Raw Material of Religion', p. 7.

118 See in particular 'The Comparative Study of Ghost Stories', this volume, pp. 229–34 and 'Preface to the Second Edition', *Cock Lane and Common Sense*, this volume, pp. 242–5.

119 See, for example, Frazer, *The Golden Bough*, p. 13–14: 'it is to be borne in mind that the primitive magician knows only magic on its practical side; he never analyses the

mental processes on which his practice is based, never reflects on the abstract principles involved in his actions ... It is for the philosophic student to trace the train of thought which underlies the magician's practice ... '

120 Lang to Henry Sidgwick, 9 September [1898?], Marysa Demoor, 'Andrew Lang (1844–1912)', vol. 1, p. 94.

121 Lang to W. T. Stead, July 29 [1893? added in pencil], Roger Lancelyn Green Collection, St Andrews University Library. MS PR4877.58. ms1587.

122 Lang to William Blackwood, January 23 [1894], quoted in Marysa Demoor, 'Andrew Lang (1844–1912)', vol.1, p. 95.

123 Personal communication with Tom Ruffles, Society for Psychical Research. Lang's new membership is listed in the May 1904 issue of the *Journal*.

124 Andrew Lang, 'Premonitions', *Illustrated London News*, 18 January, CVIII:2961 (1896), p. 82.

125 Andrew Lang, 'Ghosts Up To Date', this volume, p. 259.

126 See Andrew Lang, 'The Voices of Jeanne d'Arc', *Proceedings of the Society for Psychical Research* 11 (1895), pp. 198–212 and 'Queen Mary's Diamonds', *Journal of the Society for Psychical Research* 7 (1895-6), pp. 116–19.

127 Louis Cazaman, 'Andrew Lang and the Maid of France', in *Concerning Andrew Lang*, from the Andrew Lang Lecture delivered 25 October 1908, p. 25.

128 See, for example, Andrew Lang, 'III. Discussion of the Trance Phenomena of Mrs. Piper. III Reflections on Mrs. Piper and Telepathy', *Proceedings of the Society for Psychical Research* 15 (1900–1), p. 43.

129 See his admission that he believes in telepathy at the end of his 1911 Presidential Address to the SPR (this volume, p. 313) and his recounting of his own experiments in crystal gazing in 'Magic Mirrors and Crystal Gazing' (this volume, pp. 292–9).

130 See, for example, Lang, 'Science and Superstition', this volume, pp. 207–15.

131 Lang, *The Making of Religion*, p. 44.

I   THE METHOD OF FOLKLORE

'The Method of Folklore', *Custom and Myth* (1884)

1   *'elf-shots'*: Neolithic flint arrow heads that, in popular superstition, were believed to be weapons shot by elves or fairies at cattle to make them sick. The use of the term in Scotland was noted by William Pennant in *A Tour in Scotland 1769*; see 4th edition (London: Benjamin White, 1776), p. 115. For a recent account of the superstition see Steve Roud, *The Penguin Guide to the Superstitions of Britain and Ireland* (London: Penguin, 2003), pp. 170–1.

2   *Etruria ... Etruscan*: in central Italy. Etruscan civilisation lasted from approximately the ninth century BCE to the sixth century BCE.

3   *spindle-whorls of stone*: stone weights with a central hole used on a spindle in textile making.

4   [footnote] *Mitchell's* Past and Present: the work partially cited by Lang here is Arthur
    Mitchell's *The Past in the Present: What is Civilisation?* (Edinburgh: David Douglas,
    1880). Lang's examples come from this study.

5   *stone of Scone*: an ancient limestone block used in coronation ceremonies in Scotland
    and, latterly, Britain.

6   *devinettes*: French, 'riddles'.

7   *'Recueil de Calembours'*: French, 'collection of puns'. Lang is probably referring to
    Grassottiana, recueil de calembours ... (Paris: Parmentier, 1856) assembled by the French
    actor Paul Grassot (1800–60).

8   'un père a douze fils?'—'l'an': French, 'a father with twelve children? – 'The year'.

9   *M. Rolland's 'Devinettes'*: Lang refers to *Devinettes, ou, Enigmes populaires de la France*
    (Riddles, or, Popular Enigmas of France) (Paris: F. Vieweg, 1877) collected by the
    French folklorist Eugène Rolland (1846–1909).

10 *Boilat*: Pierre Boilat (*c*.1810–53) was a Senegalese writer, teacher and Christian minister,
    educated in France so that he could return to Africa to conduct missionary work. His
    only published work, *Esquisses sénégalaises* (Senegalese Sketches) (Paris: P. Bertrand,
    1853), describes Senegalese culture for a French audience, and includes the riddles
    mentioned here.

11 *Turner's 'Samoa'*: *Samoa a Hundred Years Ago and Long Before'* (London: Macmillan, 1884)
    by the Scottish missionary George Turner (1818–91).

12 *Chambers*: Robert Chambers (1802–71); Scottish antiquarian and publisher; compiler of
    a number of important collections of Scottish traditions, including *Scottish Jests and
    Anecdotes* (Edinburgh: W. Tait, 1832), which includes the enigmas mentioned here.

13 *Sahagun*: Bernardino de Sahagún (1499–1590) was a Spanish missionary to New Spain
    (now Mexico) who documented Aztec culture, society and tradition in his *Historia
    general de las cosas de la Nueva España* (General History of the Things of New Spain)
    (1540–85), otherwise known, after the manuscript in which it is best preserved, as *The
    Florentine Codex*.

14 *Sahagun's account of the 'midnight axe'*: see Book 5 ('The Omens'), chapter 3, of the
    Historia general. Sahagún's record of Aztec culture is written in the Nahuatl (Aztec)
    language, with a simultaneous Spanish translation by Sahagun, which Lang translates
    into English, probably working from the edition published by Carlos Maria de
    Bustamante in 1829. A complete English translation was made of *The Florentine Codex*
    by Charles Dibble and Arthur J. O. Anderson between 1950 and 1982 (New Mexico:
    University of Utah). For Dibble and Anderson's rendering of this passage, accompanied
    by the original Nahuatl, see book 5, pp. 157–8.

15 *Tezeatlipoca*: more commonly rendered 'Tezcatlipoca' (Lang's 'e' in place of the 'c' is
    possibly a misprint), one of the principal Aztec deities.

16 Kernababy: harvest ornaments, more recently called 'corn dolls' or 'corn dollies'. For a
    recent account of this practice see Steve Roud, *The English Year: A Month-by-Month
    Guide to the Nation's Customs and Festivals, from May Day to Mischief Night* (London:
    Penguin, 2006), p. 280.

17 *Κόρη*: Ancient Greek, 'maiden'.

18 *daughter of Demeter*: Persephone (sometimes Prosperine), who is associated with Spring and the regeneration of the land. Demeter was the ancient Greek goddess of the harvest and fertility. See Ovid, *Metamorphoses* V. 386–563.

19 *Acosta*: José de Acosta (1540–1600) was a Spanish Jesuit missionary who worked in Peru and Mexico from 1572 to 1587. Acosta's *Historia natural y moral de las Indias* (1590), translated into English as *The Natural and Moral History of the Western Indies* by Edward Grimston in 1604, is one of the earliest authoritative accounts of the natural history of the New World and of Aztec and Inca culture.

20 *This feast is made ... Mama cora*: see Joseph de Acosta, *The Natural and Moral History of the Indies*, trans. Edward Grimston (London: Hakluyt Society, 1880), vol. 2, p. 374.

21 μήτηρ: Ancient Greek, 'mother'.

22 *They take a certaine portion ... Mays may not perish*: see De Acosta, *Natural and Moral History*, vol. 2, p. 374.

23 *'Lord, punish this man ... in dishonour'*: see Sahagun, *Historia general*, book 5, appendix, chapter 4; also rendered into English in Dibble and Anderson, *The Florentine Codex*, book 5, p. 184.

24 *Accad*: more commonly, Akkad; the city at the centre of an empire founded in Mesopotamia (now Iran) at the end of the third millennium BCE by Sargon the Great.

25 *Boris Godunof*: also, Godunov (*c.*1551–1605), Tsar of Russia from 1598.

26 *Mrs. Riddell*: Charlotte, or Mrs. J. H. Riddell (1832–1906); writer of popular Victorian novels and ghost stories.

27 *Aryan story*: Lang means a story found in the Indo-European area that may be presumed to have originated in the hypothetical source culture of the Indo-European peoples.

28 *mythopœic faculty*: a pre-scientific mode of thinking in which the phenomena of the world are explained by the use of poetic metaphors. These metaphors, Müller argued, gradually developed into complex myths.

29 *Pleiades*: a star cluster in the constellation of Taurus, also known as the Seven Sisters. In Greek mythology the Pleiades, the seven daughters of Atlas and the sea-nymph Pleione, were transformed into stars by Zeus in order to preserve them from rape by Orion. In the traditions of several indigenous Australian communities nearly identical stories are told about the star cluster. See, for instance, Mudrooroo, *Aboriginal Mythology* (London: Aquarian, 1994), p. 134.

30 *as the Aggry beads of Ashanti ... bone-cave in Poland*: Lang alludes to a series of archaeological discoveries made in the later nineteenth century that appeared to demonstrate the extensive migrations of peoples throughout the world. The discovery of the Indian Ocean shell in a Polish bone-cave was announced by Ferdinand Römer in *The Bone Caves of Ojcow in Poland*, published by Longmans, Green and Co. in 1884. The cowry, which is sometimes presented as Indian rather than African, was a minor cause célèbre in Lang's day, and also inspired the poem 'An Indian Cowrie (Found in a Cornish Barrow at the Land's End)' by William Canton (1887).

31 *The best way ... have in common*: Lang offers a more substantial consideration of astronomical names and customs in his essay 'Star Myths', also in *Custom and Myth*, pp. 121–42.

32 *In the following essays*: Lang introduces the essays that appear in *Custom and Myth*.

'Cupid, Psyche, and the "Sun Frog"', *Custom and Myth* (1884)

1   *Cupid and Psyche*: tale type ATU425 'Search for the Lost Husband'. See Note on the Text (this volume, p. 52–3) for the use of tale type references. See also Apuleius in Appendix I to this volume.

2   *Peau d'Ane*: French, 'Donkey Skin'; after Charles Perrault's story of that name.

3   *kraals*: in Dutch and Afrikaans, a cattle enclosure; frequently used to identify South African settlements.

4   *the method hitherto adopted*: in the other essays of *Custom and Myth*. See 'The Method of Folklore' this volume, pp. 57–65.

5   *the Rig Veda (x. 95)*: The *Rig Veda*, composed in Sanskrit between 1700 BCE and 1100 BCE, is one of the four ancient Indian *Vedas* that form the basis of the Hindu religion. Judging from later citations Lang was using the German translation made by Alfred Ludwig (1832–1912): *Der Rigveda oder die heiligen Hymnen der Brâhmana* (The Rigveda, or the Sacred Hymns of the Brahmans) (Prague: Altenberg, 1876–88).

6   folle maîtresse: French, 'mad mistress'.

7   *'ate once a day … went away'*: Rig Veda x.95.16.

8   *Persephone's tasting the pomegranate in Hades*: In Greek mythology, Persephone is condemned to remain a portion of the year in the underworld after eating pomegranate seeds. See Ovid, *Metamorphoses* V.535–51.

9   *'the language is coarse and the meaning is obscure'*: The reference is to Charles Dickens's *Dombey and Son* (1848). Lang misquotes slightly. Dickens has Mr Toots say to a chicken: 'your expressions are coarse, and your meaning is obscure'.

10 *'like the first of the dawns … joy of the festival'*: all Lang's references here are to *Rig Veda* x.95.

11 *Vishnu Purana*: the Puranas are theological and philosophical works devoted to the worship of Hindu deities. Both the *Vishnu Purana* (*c.*4th century CE) and the *Bhagavata Purana* (*c.*9th century CE) concern Vishnu and his avatars.

12 *'expresses the identity … evening twilight'*: Müller does not use precisely the words quoted. The specific essay by Müller that Lang refers to here is 'Comparative Mythology,' *Selected Essays on Language, Mythology and Religion* (two vols, London: Longmans, 1881), vol. I, pp. 299–424. The quotations from Müller that follow can all be found in this essay on pp. 405–12.

13 *Kuhn objects … sacred fire-lighting*: for this and the following observations see Adalbert Kuhn, *Die Herabkunft des Feuers und des Göttertranks* (The Descent of Fire and the Nectar of the Gods) (Berlin: Ferd. Dümmler, 1859), p. 79.

14 *Roth, again … 'Bull in rut'*: see Kuhn, *Die Herabkunft des Feuers*, p. 87.

15 *Schwartz sees storm and storm-myths*: see Wilhelm Schwartz, *Die Poetischen Naturanschauungen der Griechen, Römer und Deutschen in ihrer Beziehung zur Mythologie* (The Poetic Conceptions of Nature of the Greeks, Romans and Germans in Relation to Mythology) 2 vols (Berlin: Hertz, 1864–79).

16 custom of women: A footnote detailing another parallel from Liebrecht's *Zur Volkskunde* has been omitted here.

17 *lingers in the Welsh fairies*: John Rhys gives numerous examples of this in *Celtic Folklore* (Oxford: Clarendon, 1901).

18 *'tabooed'*: subject to ritualised prohibition. The term was introduced into English from the Tongan by James Cook in his observations on the practices of the Island (*A Voyage to the Pacific Ocean*, 1793). Herbert Spencer's comments on the uses of taboo in Tonga and New Zealand in *The Principles of Sociology* (published in various combinations of three volumes and eight parts between 1874 and 1896) (vol. 1, New York: Appleton, 1883, p. 272) influenced Lang's approach to the concept.

19 *Caillié*: René Caillié (1799–1838), French explorer, and student of Arabic language and Islamic culture. Between 1827 and 1828 he travelled from the coast of West Africa to Timbuktu, winning the 10,000 Franc award offered by the French Société de Géographie for being the first European to visit and return alive from the fabled city. He recorded his travels and his observations in *Journal d'un voyage à Temboctou et à Jenné dans l'Afrique Centrale* (Journal of a Voyage to Timbuktu and Jenné in Central Africa), 3 vols (Paris, 1830).

20 *'Ils n'osent … de la nuit'*: French, 'they do not dare go into the special huts in which their wives reside except in the darkness of night'.

21 *'Volkslied'*: German, 'folk song'.

22 *Grozdanka … marries thee*: See August Dozon, *Chansons Populaires Bulgares* (Paris: Maisonneuve, 1875), pp. 17–2.

23 *just as in the Welsh fairy tale … losing her for ever*: See Rhys, *Celtic Folklore*, vol. 2, p. 598. See also this volume, p. 377, n. 36.

24 *'Hlonipa'*: in Zulu tradition, when the use of a name is avoided out of respect. Lang's information comes partly from George McCall Theal, *Kaffir folk-lore* (1882; 2nd edition, London: Sonnenschein, 1886), p. 10.

25 *according to Dall … presence of others*: see William Dall, *Alaska and its Resources* (1870; Boston: Lee and Shepard, 1897), p. 396.

26 *Among the Turkomans … wife by stealth*: see John Lubbock, *The Origin of Civilisation* (1870; 3rd edition, London: Longmans, 1875), p. 75.

27 *Breton sailor's tale of the 'Cupid and Psyche'*: the story is called 'Le Pilote du Bologne' (The Pilot of Bologne). See Paul Sébillot, *Contes Populaires de la Haute-Bretagne* (Folk Tales of Upper Brittany) (Paris: Charpentier, 1882), p. 180–8.

28 *'C'est l'usage … mères'*: French, 'It is the custom in that country: husbands cannot see their wives unveiled until their wives have become mothers'. See Sébillot, *Contes Populaires*, p. 183.

29 dum ipsam nudam non viderit: Latin, 'as long as he did not see her naked'. See Gervaise of Tilbury, *Otia Imperialia*, ed. and trans. S. E. Banks and J. W. Binns (Oxford: Clarendon, 2002), p. 89.

30 Märchen: German, 'tale'; now commonly used by folklorists to designate 'fairy tale'.

31 *She will not come … come away*: see Matthew Arnold's poem, 'The Forsaken Merman' (1849) *Matthew Arnold: Major Works*, ed. Miriam Allott and Robert H. Super (Oxford: Oxford University Press, 1986), pp. 46–50.

32 *Mr. Max Müller ... his own method*: the following account appears in full in Müller, *Chips from a German Workshop* (London: Longmans, Green and Co., 1867) vol. 2, pp. 246–9.

33 *'belongs to ... civilisation'*: this quotation has not been located. Elsewhere, Lang's citations from M. Alexander Castrén are from *Ethnologische Vorlesungen* (Ethnological Lectures) (St. Petersburg: Kaiserlichen Akademie, 1857).

34 *an Ojibway parallel*: this story is recorded by the German geographer and travel writer Johann Georg Kohl (1808–78) in *Kitschi Gami oder Erzählungen vom Oberen See* (1859), translated in 1860 as *Kitchi-Gami: Wanderings Round Lake Superior* (London: Chapman and Hall). See pp. 92–104. Kohl gives the story the title 'The Good and Bad Squaw'. The quotations from the story that follow can all be found here, though Lang's rendering of them is often free.

35 *Kohl*: see note 34 above.

36 *published by Professor Rhys*: John Rhys (1840–1916) was a Welsh philologist, scholar of Celtic tradition, and Professor of Celtic at Oxford University from 1877. His works include *Lectures on Welsh Philology* (1877), *Celtic Britain* (1882) and a two-volume reflection upon traditional materials, *Celtic Folklore, Welsh and Manx* (1901). Lang had access to the materials that would contribute to this latter volume when he was writing *Custom and Myth* through Rhys's advance publication in the journals *Folk-Lore* and *Y Cymmrodor* (The Welshman).

37 *Welsh and German* Märchen: tale type ATU400. For an example see 'Von Drei Schwänen' (Three Swans) in Ernst Meier's *Deutsche Volksmärchen aus Schwaben* (German Folk Tales from Swabia) (Stuttgart: C. P. Scheitlin's Verlagshandlung, 1852), pp. 39–42.

38 *Mr. Farrer*: James Anson Farrer (1849–1925) author of *Primitive Manners and Customs* (London: Chatto and Windus, 1879).

39 *told by Schoolcraft in his 'Algic Researches'*: Henry Rowe Schoolcraft (1793–1864) was an American geographer, geologist and anthropologist, author of *Historical and Statistical Information Respecting ... the Indian Tribes of the United States* (6 vols, 1851–7) and *Algic Researches: Inquiries Respecting the Mental Condition of the North American Indians*, 2 vols (New York: Harper, 1839). For this story see 'The Celestial Sisters: A Shawnee Tale,' in *Algic Researches*, vol. 1, pp. 67–73. In the story as related by Schoolcraft the protagonist is Waupee, not 'Wampee'.

40 *Ludwig's rendering*: see this volume, p. 375, n. 5.

41 *'in the morning ... a shining shape'*: see Henry Callaway, *Nursery Tales, Traditions, and Histories of the Zulus* (London: Trübner, 1868) vol. 1, pp. 63–4. Lang gives a précis here, not a direct quotation as indicated by the speech marks.

42 *friends ... kill a tabooed animal*: see Callaway, *Nursery Tales*, vol. 1, pp. 118–22.

---

2 ANTHROPOLOGY AND FOLKLORE

'New System Proposed', *Myth, Ritual and Religion*, 2nd edition (1899)

1 *examines*: Lang has 'studies' here in the first edition (London: Longmans, Green and Co., 1887). The change has presumably been made for stylistic reasons.

2   *less perilous ground*: less perilous because Lang thereby avoids allying himself with the potentially blasphemous argument that current religions are formed as a result of the sublimation of pagan folk traditions.

3   Sur l'Origine des Fables: French, 'On the Origin of Fables'. Lang summarises this essay in an appendix to *Myth, Ritual and Religion*, 2nd edition, vol. 2, pp. 339–43.

4   *to be neglected*: a footnote has been omitted here directing readers to the précis of Fontenelle's essay which appears in the appendix of *Myth, Ritual and Religion*.

5   *'makes it manifest … fetichism and savagery'*: in a note (omitted here) Lang cites Mannhardt's '*Baum und Feld Kultus* xxiii', for this quotation. More precisely, the quotation appears in volume 1 of Mannhardt's *Wald- und Feldkulte* (Forest and Field Cults), titled *Der Baumkultus der Germanen und ihrer Nachbarstämme* (The Tree Cults of the Teutons and their Neighbour Tribes) (Berlin: Borntraeger, 1875).

6   *the puzzling qualities of*: Lang has added this clause to the second edition in order to make it clear that it is not myth per se that he seeks to explicate using the comparative anthropological method, but those elements of myth that have become incomprehensible because they are survivals of a savage world view.

7   *preface to the* Arabian Nights: see Edward William Lane, 'Translator's Preface,' *The Arabian Nights' Entertainments* (London: C. Knight and Co., 1839), vol. 1, p. xix. Lane (1801–76) published his translation of the *Arabian Nights* serially between 1838 and 1840. As he makes clear both in his preface and in his earlier ethnological study *Manners and Customs of the Modern Egyptians* (1836) he regarded the *Nights* as illustrative of Arab customs.

8   *Afreet*: in Arabic folklore, a powerful class of Jinn.

9   *historical information*: omitted here is a long footnote by Lang defining the savage.

10   *the fancy of*: this clause has been added in the second edition, possibly to make it clearer that it is exclusively imaginative materials that are under examination.

11   *though even then … morals and religion*: this clause has been added to the parenthesis in the second edition. Lang makes it clear that he regards myths as distinct from religion and morals even at their savage source.

12   [Footnote] *Myth, in Mr. Darwin's phrase … Descent of Man, p. 69*: the final sentence of the footnote, referencing Darwin, has been added in the second edition. Lang's references to Darwin increase in the second edition, but it nonetheless remains the case that this citation from Darwin's *The Descent of Man* (1871) is one of only a handful of passing references to Darwin in *Myth, Ritual and Religion*; surprisingly given the similarities of some of their subject matter, and the fact that Lang seeks explicitly to develop comparisons between Darwin's theory of biological evolution and his own theories of cultural evolution.

13   Coma Berenices: Latin, 'Berenice's hair'; a constellation named after Queen Berenice II of Egypt who cut off her hair in a sacrifice to the Goddess Aphrodite after her husband returned safe from war. When her severed locks disappeared from the temple where they had been stored, a royal astronomer announced that Aphrodite had transported the gift into the sky. Lang regards this explanatory myth as the product of 'a poet of a late age' because the story appears to derive from the poem *Coma Berenices* by the ancient Greek poet Callimachus (3rd Century BCE).

14   *sacerdotage*: priesthood.

15 *'let the ape and tiger die'*: the quotation is from Alfred Tennyson's poem *In Memoriam* (canto CXVIII) and refers to the capacity of the spiritual part of mankind to rise up and leave beastly elements behind.

16 *We are not compelled*: the first edition has a parenthesis here reading 'as will be shown later' and a note directing readers to Appendix B, which is Lang's 'Reply to Objections'. Appendix B appears in both editions, so Lang must simply have decided not to reference it at this point in the second edition.

17 *donnée*: the French for 'given'; Lang uses this term to designate the original idea that is supplied by savage culture.

18 *persistence of myths*: in the first edition Lang has here 'after their significance has become obsolete'. Lang has perhaps deleted this clause because he is arguing that only some elements of myths become obsolete.

19 *one aspect of*: this is Lang's most substantial change to the current extract in the second edition of *Myth, Ritual and Religion*. The clause 'one aspect of' has been added, as has the following explanatory sentence. In making these changes, Lang establishes that he does not believe that all aspects of savage culture are irrational and senseless, only those that have resulted in the apparently 'crazy' elements in myth. This change, and the change at p. 378 (n. 6), suggest a shift in Lang's thinking between 1887 and 1899, away from a straightforward presentation of savage culture as obsolete and absurd, towards a greater recognition of its positive values. These changes also reflect an increasing tendency in Lang's anthropological work to resist aspects of E. B. Tylor's argument in *Primitive Culture* (1871).

20 *Argo speaks with a human voice*: in the account of the voyage of the Argo given by Apollonius of Rhodes the ship speaks twice to the Argonauts because it has in its prow an enchanted timber from the forest of Dordonia, site of an ancient oracle. In his *Tanglewood Tales* (1853) Nataniel Hawthorne has the ship converse with Jason in the form of a talking figurehead.

21 *'giant who had no heart in his body'*: the best-known version of this story appears in Jorgen Moe and Peter Asbjornsen's *Norske Folkeeventyr (Norwegian Folk Tales)* (1841–4). For George Webbe Dasent's translation see *Popular Tales from the Norse*, 2nd edition (Edinburgh: Edmonston and Douglas, 1859), pp. 69–79.

22 *Dr. Tiele writes*: C. P. Tiele, (1830–1902) was a Dutch theological writer and Professor of the History of Religions at the University of Leiden from 1877. He makes these remarks in a long essay 'Le Mythe de Kronos' published in the journal *Revue de l'Histoire des Religions* 12 (1885), pp. 246–77. After seeing his words quoted in support of the anthropological school in the first edition of *Myth, Ritual and Religion*, Tiele sought to distance himself from Lang and his supporters, arguing that the anthropological folklorists were too narrow in their interpretations, lacked originality, and had an unhealthy attachment to parody and 'songs of triumph'. See Lang, *Modern Mythology* (London: Longmans, Green and Co., 1897), p. 28. Thus Lang notes in the second edition of *Myth, Ritual and Religion* (vol. 1, p. 46, note 1) that, though he had initially quoted Tiele as an ally, Tiele was not, in fact, 'a thorough adherent of our theory'. In the chapter 'The Question of Allies' in *Modern Mythology*, Lang gives further details of Tiele's responses to *Myth, Ritual and Religion*, and offers a reply to Tiele (pp. 22–40).

23 *'If I were obliged … degree of culture'*: Tiele, 'Le Mythe de Kronos,' pp. 253–4.

'Household Tales; Their Origin, Diffusion, and Relations to the Higher Myths',
Introduction to Margaret Hunt's *Grimm's Household Tales* (1884)

1   *Kinder- und Hausmärchen:* German, 'Children's and Household Tales'. The first edition
    was published in two volumes in 1812 and 1815.

2   *Aryan peoples*: peoples deriving from a presumed Indo-Aryan root culture.

3   *Jason and Medea … wizard king*: in Greek myth, Medea assists Jason in fulfilling the tasks
    set by her father Æetes. See Apollodorus, *Bibliotheca,* I.9.23. The motif is a common
    one in folk literature (H335.0.1. 'Bride helps suitor perform his tasks'), and is often
    found in the international tale type ATU313 'The Girl as Helper in the Hero's Flight'.

4   Berthe aux grans piés: more commonly *Li Romans de Berte aus grans piés*
    [The Romance of Broadfoot Bertha], a poem written by the French troubadour
    Adenes Le Roi in 1270. The poem concerns the life of Bertrada of Laon, the mother
    of Charlemagne.

5   *known to the Scythians*: in the account given of the Scythians by Herodotus in his
    Histories (*c.*440 BCE), a story is narrated about three brothers who endeavour to take
    hold of some burning gold that has fallen from heaven. The two elder brothers are
    unable to touch the gold, but when the younger brother approaches it the flames go
    out. It is from this youngest son that the royal line of the Scythians is said to descend.
    See Herodotus, *Histories*, IV.5–6.

6   Peau d'Ane … *saint of the Irish Church*: the story of St Dymphna, the daughter of an
    Irish king who is forced to flee from her father's court after he decides to marry her,
    has notable similarities to Charles Perrault's tale in verse, 'Peau d'âne' (Donkey Skin),
    published as 'Peau d'ane, conte' in Adrian Moetjen's *Receuil de pieces curieuses et nouvelles,
    tant en prose qu'en vers*, vol. 1 (1694), pp. 50–79.

7   *St. Tryphine*: Lang probably has in mind the plot of the Medieval Breton mystery play
    Sainte-Tryphine et le roi Arthur (St. Tryphine and King Arthur) published by the French
    folklorist François-Marie Luzel in 1863 (Quimperlé: A. C. Henry). In the play,
    Tryphine is forced to flee from the court of her husband, King Arthur, after she is
    falsely accused of murdering her son. She works in degrading circumstances as a
    servant for six years before she is returned to Arthur's court and her innocence
    accepted.

8   *The smith … Sisyphus in Greek*: in the ancient Greek story, Sisyphus evades capture by
    Thanatos, the God of Death, by trapping him with his own chain. In the folk story
    'The Blacksmith and the Devil', which appeared (amongst other places) in the 1812
    edition of the Grimm collection, a cunning Smith evades the Devil by trapping him in
    a magic sack that the Devil has himself supplied. See 'The Blacksmith and the Devil,'
    in *The Complete Fairy Tales of the Brothers Grimm*, ed. Jack Zipes (New York: Bantam,
    1992), pp. 672–4.

9   *Urvasi in the Rig Veda*: the immortal Urvasi consents to become the bride of the mortal
    King Pururavas on the condition that she never sees him without his clothes. The
    injunction is transgressed after Pururavas leaps from his bed to prevent Urvasi's pet
    rams from being stolen, and Urvasi immediately disappears. See *Rig Veda* X.95.1–18.

10 *oriental jade … Cornish barrow*: see this volume, p. 374, n. 30.

11 *sounding* loggia *of an Homeric house*: the loggia is an appended part of the house which
    is open to the elements. Lang is imagining the stories of Homer being told in this
    setting.

12 *Somadeva ... Perrault*: the collections referred to here are, respectively, the eleventh
century Sanskrit compendium *Kathasaritsagara* (The Ocean of Streams of Story) by
Bhatta Somadeva; the Middle Eastern story cycle *Alf layla wa-layla* (*The Thousand and
One Nights*); Giovan Francesco Straparola's *Piacevoli Notti* (Pleasant Nights) (1550–3);
Marguerite de Navarre's *Heptameron* (1558); and Charles Perrault's *Histoires, ou contes du
temps passé* (Stories, or Tales of Times Passed) (1697).

13 '*The Wolf and the Kids*': tale type ATU123 'The Wolf and the Kids'. For the Grimm
story that Lang was using, see Margaret Hunt (ed.), *Grimm's Household Tales, with the
Author's Notes*, 2 vols (London: George Bell and Sons, 1884), vol. 1, pp. 20–4.

14 *In a Kaffir tale ... cannibal*: see 'The Story of Demane and Demazana' in George
McCall Theal, *Kaffir Folk-lore, or, A Selection from the Traditional Tales Current Among the
People Living on the Eastern Border of the Cape Colony* (1882; 2nd edition, London:
Sonnenschein, 1886), pp. 118–21.

15 *Apparently the tale ... the whites*: the version of the story that Lang proceeds to
summarise is 'The Story of the Pigs' from Joel Chandler Harris, *Nights with Uncle
Remus: Myths and Legends of the Old Plantation* (Boston: Houghton Mifflin, 1883), pp.
38–43. This tale type is classified as ATU124 ('Blowing the House In').

16 *It is found ... Gargantua*: Stith Thompson classifies this motif as F913 'Victims Rescued
from the Swallower's Belly' and provides a fuller list of instances. See *The Motif Index of
Folk-Literature*, 2nd edition (Copenhagen: Rosenkilde and Bagger, 1957). For the
disgorgement in the story of Cronos (more commonly, Cronus) see Apollodorus,
Bibliotheca, I.1.7 and I.2.1. For the Gargantua story, see François Rabelais's *Gargantua
and Pantagruel* (1532–4), trans. J. M. Cohen (London: Penguin, 1955), book 1, chapter
38, pp. 120–2.

17 *Zulu examples ... Guiana*: see Callaway, *Nursery Tales, Traditions and Histories of the Zulus*
(London: Trübner, 1868) vol. 1, pp. 84–5 and p. 334. Callaway also cites the Native
American example, which concerns Hiawatha (vol. 1, p. 84, n. 12).

18 *Grimm ... examples of the incident*: Grimm's note is in Hunt (ed. and trans.), *Grimm's
Household Tales*, vol. 1, pp. 347–8. For Wilhelm Bleek's narratives of disgorgement
translated from the Xan language (South Africa) see *A Brief Account of Bushman Folklore
and Other Texts* (London: Trübner, 1875), p. 8 (story 12) and p. 11 (story 25).

19 *Cronus in Hesiod*: see *Theogony* 453–91. Cronus swallows, and later disgorges, a stone
that he believes to be his newborn son Zeus.

20 '*We can hardly doubt ... clocks*': Tylor does not use precisely these words, but expresses a
similar view.

21 *M. Husson*: See *La Chaine Traditionelle: Contes et Légendes au Point de vue Mythique* (The
Chain of Tradition: Tales and Legends from the Mythological Perspective) (Paris: A.
Franck, 1874), p. 8. For Müller's comments on Husson's work see *Selected Essays on
Language, Mythology and Religion*, 2 vols (London: Longmans, 1881), vol. 1, pp. 564–7.

22 '*The real evidence ... than we had taken it to be*': George Cox, *Mythology of the Aryan
Nations*, 2 vols (London: Longman Green and Co. 1870), vol. 1, p. 145.

23 '*years might pass ... the weakest analogy*': ibid., vol. 1, p. 41.

24 '*perhaps for ages ... never return*': ibid.

25 *Mr. Tylor, Mr. Im Thurn, Mr. Herbert Spencer*: see E. B. Tylor, *Primitive Culture: Researches
into the Development of Mythology, Philosophy, Religion, Languages, Art and Customs*, 2 vols

(London: John Murray, 1871), vol. 1, pp. 417–502; E. im Thurn, *Among the Indians of Guiana, Being Sketches, Chiefly Anthropologic, from the Interior of British Guiana* (London: Kegan Paul, Trench and Co., 1883), pp. 341–70; and H. Spencer, *The Principles of Sociology*, 3rd edition (London: Williams and Norgate, 1885), vol. 1, pp. 123–31.

26   *'He had life … conscious beings also?'*: Cox, *Mythology of the Aryan Nations*, vol. 1, p. 40.

27   *'a thousand phrases … original force of the name'*: Cox, *Mythology of the Aryan Nations*, vol. 1, p. 42. The italics have been added by Lang. Lang misquotes slightly; Cox has: 'a thousand phrases would be used …'

28   *Kephalos … Prokris*: in Greek myth Kephalos or Cephalus (meaning 'head') is the lover of Eos (Dawn) and the husband of Prokris (Dew). Kephalos accidentally slays Prokris with his javelin, prompting the argument summarised here by Lang that he symbolises the sun, the rays of which dry up the morning dew.

29   *supposed – by a folk-etymology – to be Apollo the Wolf*: because the Greek word for 'shining' or 'light' ($\lambda\varepsilon\upsilon\kappa\acute{o}\varsigma$) has at some stage in history been confused with the phonetically similar Greek word for 'wolf' ($\lambda\acute{u}\kappa\upsilon\varsigma$). See this volume, p. 104 for Lang's further analysis of this mistaken etymology.

30   *Aryan Peoples*: Lang mistakes Cox's title here, transposing 'Nations' with 'Peoples'. He mistakes the title twice more in this essay again on this page (see also this volume, p. 103).

31   *Husson, De Gubernatis*: see Husson, *La Chaine Traditionelle*, and A. de Gubernatis, *Zoological Mythology; or, The Legends of Animals*, 2 vols (London: Trübner, 1872).

32   *'The prominent characteristics … harshness of savages'*: Cox, *Mythology of the Aryan Nations*, vol. 1, p. 39. Lang misquotes this. Cox has 'Stubborn facts disclose as the prominent characteristics of that early time the selfishness and violence, the cruelty and slavishness of savages'.

33   *mythopoeic*: see this volume, p. 374, n. 28.

34   *'Animism,' 'personalism,'*: the concept of animism, as Lang uses it here, was developed by Tylor in *Primitive Culture* (1871) (see for instance vol. 1, p. 260). It refers to the practice, associated by Tylor and Lang with primitive thought, of regarding animals and objects as having a life force or spirit, although Tylor's own concept of animism goes beyond this. 'Personalism' in this context means a tendency to project personality onto animals and objects.

35   *'Animism'*: Cox describes a state of mind which 'threw the halo of a living reality over everything of which it spoke', but does not use the term 'animism'. Cox, *Mythology of the Aryan Nations*, vol. 1, p. 58.

36   *Early History of Man*: in full, *Researches into the Early History of Mankind and the Development of Civilization* (London: John Murray, 1865).

37   *'as for the loss … never return'*: Cox, *Mythology of the Aryan Nations*, vol. 1, p. 41.

38   Polyonymy … Synonymy: these terms were not invented by Müller, but Müller was the first to use them together as part of a systematic argument. In 1803 G. S. Faber used the concept of polyonymy in the course of an examination of Solar myths, a likely source for Müller's use of the word. See G. S. Faber, *Dissertation on the Mysteries of the Cabiri* (Oxford: Oxford University Press, 1803), vol. 1, p. 150.

39   ex hypothesi: Latin, 'from the hypothesis'.

40 *Maui or Tcha-ka-betch*: Maui is a trickster hero of Polynesian myth. Lang's information about stories of Maui comes from Richard Taylor's *Te Ika a Maui: Or, New Zealand and Its Inhabitants* (London: Wertheim and Macintosh, 1855). *Tcha-ka-betch* (now more commonly, Tshakapesh) is a trickster hero from Cree and Innu mythology.

41 *the myth … and died*: Lang's main sources for the story of Jason are the third century BCE *Argonautica* of Apollonius of Rhodes and the second century CE *Bibliotheca* of Pseudo-Apollodorus (I.9.16–28).

42 *Phrixus … son of the cloud*: Lang goes on to tell the story of Phrixus and Hellê more fully. See this volume, pp. 116–17.

43 *'must be classed … same root'*: Lang mistakes the volume here; the quote is in *Mythology of the Aryan Nations*, vol. 2, pp. 150–1.

44 *a loud colour*: Lang's satirical footnote here refers to an episode in William Makepeace Thackeray's novel *Pendennis* (1848–50).

45 *Decharme… 'a goddess of lightning!'*: Paul Decharme (1839–1905) was a French classical scholar and author of *Mythologie de la Grèce antique* (1879, Mythology of Ancient Greece) in which Greek myths are interpreted as nature allegories. For this quotation see *Mythologie de la Grèce antique* (1879; Paris: Garnier Frères Libraires-Éditeurs, 1886), p. 608.

46 *'It would be a bold assertion … red horses'*: Müller is here censuring arguments made by Husson in *La Chaine Traditionelle*, p. 7.

47 [footnote] *Mythological Philosophy of Mr. Max Müller*: the full and accurate citation for this article is: Andrew Lang, 'Mr. Max Müller's Philosophy of Mythology,' *Fraser's Magazine* (August 1881), pp. 166–87.

48 *a frog … is betrothed to a princess*: tale type ATU440, 'The Frog King'.

49 *'The frog prince … a lion, a swan' (Ar. Myth. i. 105.)*: this quotation in fact appears in Cox, *Mythology of the Aryan Nations*, vol. 1, p. 165, n. 3. The complex etymological shifts, for which, as Lang suggests, very little evidence is offered, are described by Cox on p. 47 of the same volume. The 'Seven Shiners' which are subsequently converted into a series of myths involving the number seven, are the seven brightest stars in the Ursa Major (Great Bear) constellation, popularly referred to as The Plough (UK) or the Big Dipper (USA).

50 *'is primeval … such transformations'*: Lang is using the second edition of George Webbe Dasent's *Popular Tales from the Norse* (Edinburgh: Edmonston and Douglas, 1859).

51 *'if this be an illustration … original meaning of words'*: Cox, *Mythology of the Aryan Nations*, vol. 1, p. 63 (continuation of note 3 from p. 62). The italics have been added by Lang.

52 *'so named .. this "coat,"'*: ibid.

53 *Alfred Lyall*: (1835–1911) minor British poet and historian; he spent his career working as a government official in India, and wrote several works on Indian culture and customs, including *Asiatic Studies: Religious and Social*, 2 vols (1882 and 1899).

54 Fortnightly Review: Lyall also included this essay ('On the Origin of Divine Myths in India') in *Asiatic Studies* (London: John Murray, 1882), p. 41 (note).

55 *'Bears, wolves … conquers the darkness'*: Cox, *Mythology of the Aryan Nations*, vol. 1, p. 405.

56 *'Phoibos Lykeios'*: ibid. 'Phoibos,' the Greek for 'radiant', was an epithet for Apollo, and derives from his identification as God of the sun; he is also associated with the figure of the wolf via his mother Leto, hence Phoibos Lykeios (radiant wolf). Cox suggests that the identification with the wolf derives from a corruption of phrases such as 'Phoibos Lyceus' ('radiant light'). See also this volume, p. 382 n. 29.

57 *'The mythology ... subsequent ages'*: Lang misquotes Scott slightly. Scott writes: 'The mythology of one period would then appear to pass into the romance of the next century, and that into the nursery-tale of the subsequent ages'. See *The Poetical Works of Sir Walter Scott*, ed. J. W. Lake (Boston: Phillips, Sampson and Co, 1855), p. 261.

58 *'The gods of ancient mythology ... our nursery tales'*: Lang's citation is inaccurate. The quotation may be found in Max Müller, *Chips from a German Workshop* (London: Longmans, Green and Co., 1867), vol. 2, p. 241.

59 *Griechische Märchen*, p. 5: the reference in full is J. G. von Hahn, *Griechische und Albanesiche Märchen* (Leipzig: W. Engelmann, 1864), vol. 1., p. 5.

60 *Leminkainen*: protagonist of the Finnish epic, The *Kalevala*. See this volume, p. 388, n. 115.

61 *Chips, ii. 233*: the quotation is in fact on p. 231 (of Müller's *Chips from a German Workshop*, vol. 2).

62 *'It has been said ... unnatural conceptions'*: see Müller, *Chips from a German Workshop*, vol. 2, p. 231.

63 *Vallauris*: in Southern France, known as a centre for fine pottery making.

64 *Uist or Barra*: islands in the Outer Hebrides, Scotland.

65 *façon:* French, 'something made', 'an ornament'.

66 *'witch-knots'*: the tying and untying of knots is used in the folk-magic rituals of numerous cultures. See Cyril Lawrence Day, *Quipus and Witches' Knots: The Role of the Knot in Primitive and Ancient Cultures* (Kansas: University of Kansas Press, 1967).

67 *Medea and Circe, of Odin and Loki*: Medea uses magic to assist Jason in the completion of his tasks (see this volume, p. 380, n. 3), Circe is an enchantress who captivates the crew of Odysseus and transforms them into swine (*The Odyssey*, X.135), and the Norse gods Odin and Loki are both associated with shape shifting and uses of magic.

68 *vera causa:* Latin, 'true cause'.

69 *Pitt Rivers's ... collection*: a collection of ethnological artefacts made by the Bitish army officer, anthropologist and archaeologist Augustus Pitt Rivers (1827–1900) and housed, since 1884 (the year of this essay), in the Pitt Rivers Museum, Oxford.

70 *considered by mythologists*: a footnote in which Lang notes the scantiness of the evidence is omitted here.

71 *Steere's* Swahili Tales: Edward Steere, *Swahili Tales: As Told by Natives of Zanzibar* (London: Bell and Daldy, 1870). Steere (1828–82) was a missionary to Central Africa and ultimately Bishop of Nyasaland in what is now Malawi. He wrote theological works and linguistic studies in addition to his collection of tales.

72 *James Sibree*: (1836–1929) architect and missionary who conducted missionary work in Madagascar, which included the building of numerous churches. Sibree published traditional material from Madagascar in successive issues of the *Folk-Lore Journal* (1883)

using the title 'The Oratory, Songs, Legends and Folk-Tales of the Malagasy'. In the following year (1884) he published further material under the title 'Malagasy Folk-Tales'.

73 *Casalis … 1860*: Eugène Casalis (1812–91) was a French missionary to Southern Africa from 1833 to 1855, working primarily amongst the Sotho people (also called Basutos, from that area that is now the Kingdom of Lesotho). On his return to France, he wrote and published the ethnographic work *The Basutos: or, Twenty-Three Years in South Africa* (London: James Nisbet, 1861), which includes a selection of folk tales (pp. 339–55).

74 *Ananzi* … Tales from the Norse: Ananzi (now more commonly, Anansi or Anancy) is a trickster protagonist in West African and West Indian storytelling. For the purposes of comparative analysis, Dasent includes thirteen Anansi stories in an Appendix of the second, enlarged edition of *Popular Tales from the Norse* (Edinburgh: Edmonston and Douglas, 1859), pp. 487–507.

75 *Sonnenschein, London, n.d.*: Theal's collection was first published in 1882.

76 *Folk Lore Society of South Africa*: Lang is probably referring to the South African Folklore Society and its *Folklore Journal*, established in 1879 by a team of folklorists including Lucy Lloyd.

77 *Jülg's* Kalmückische Märchen: Bernhard Jülg (1825–86) was a German comparative philologist who collected both Mongolian and Kalmyk Tales. *Kalmükische Märchen* (Kalmyk Tales) was published in 1866.

78 *Schoolcraft* … Algic Researches: see this volume, p. 377, n. 39.

79 Transactions … *vol. x*: this volume of *Transactions of the Asiatic Society of Japan* (1883) includes a supplement devoted to Basil Chamberlain's translation of the 'Ko-Ji-Ki,' or 'Records of Ancient Matters'. Chamberlain's translation was subsequently published independently.

80 *Taylor's* New Zealand: Richard Taylor (1805–73), *Te Ika a Maui: Or, New Zealand and Its Inhabitants* (London: Wertheim and Macintosh, 1855) which includes a section on myths and tales (pp. 12–54). Taylor was an Anglican missionary who worked primarily amongst the Maori in New Zealand.

81 *Mr. Codrington … Journal of the Anthropological Institute:* see for instance, R. Codrington, 'Religious Beliefs and Practices in Melanesia', *Journal of the Anthropological Institute* 10 (1880–1), pp. 261–316.

82 *Mr. Mitford*: A. B. Mitford, Baron of Redesdale (1837–1916); British diplomat and author. He translated and edited the collection *Tales of Old Japan* (London: Macmillan, 1871) whilst working as a diplomat in Japan.

83 *Indians on the Amazon*: Charles Frederick Hartt (1840–78) was a Canadian geologist who collected samples of Amazonian folklore during geological expeditions to Brazil. His major geological work before his early death from yellow fever was *Geology and Physical Geography of Brazil* (1870), but Lang's interest was in his pamphlet *Amazonian Tortoise Myths* (Rio de Janeiro: William Scully, 1875).

84 *Bancroft's*: Hubert Howe Bancroft (1832–1918). American publisher, book collector, ethnologist, and historian, compiler of *The Native Races of the Pacific States of North America*, 5 vols (San Francisco: A. C. Bancroft, 1875–6), and numerous volumes of history concerning the American states.

85   *old* Relations ... *other missionaries*: the Jesuit Relations were serial reports from Jesuit missionaries concerning their work in the Americas issued from the early seventeenth century to the early nineteenth century. The French Jesuit missionary Paul Le Jeune (1591–1664) was the first editor of *Relations des Jésuites de la Nouvelle-France* which included observations upon indigenous American tribes in Quebec.

86   *Maspero*: Gaston Maspero (1846–1916) was a French archaeologist, Egyptologist, and expert in hieroglyphic translation. He produced numerous works on Egyptian antiquity, including *Les Contes populaires de l'Égypte ancienne* (Popular Tales of Ancient Egypt) in 1882.

87   *India and what it can Teach us*: the full reference is: Müller, *India: What it can Teach Us* (1883; London: Longmans, Green and Co., 1892), p. 110.

88   Les religions ... non Civilisés: the reference in full is Albert Réville, *Les religions des peuples non-civilisés* (The Religions of Non-Civilised Peoples) (Paris: Librairie Fischbacher, 1883), p. 6. Réville (1826–1906) was a Protestant minister and theological writer who made use of recent anthropological data and comparativist methods of analysis.

89   *Aristotle ... Ptolemy*: Aristotle, Greek philosopher (4th century BCE), it is hard to determine precisely which works Lang has in mind here, but probably his writings on politics and ethics; Strabo, Greek geographer, author of *Geographica* (*c.*10 CE); Pliny (the Elder), Roman naturalist, author of *Naturalis Historia* (*c.*77 CE–79 CE); Plutarch, Greek historian, Lang perhaps has his *Moralia* in mind because of its emphasis on manners and customs; Ptolemy, Egyptian astronomer and mathematician, author of *Geographia* (2nd century CE).

90   *Marco Polo ... to Hawkins*: the travels of Marco Polo through Asia were recorded by Rustichello de Pisa in *Livres des merveilles du monde* (Books of the Marvels of the World) in approximately 1300; Bernal Diaz del Castillo (1492–1585) made a record of Aztec culture in his account of the Spanish conquest of Mexico, *Historia verdadera de la conquista de la Nueva España* (The True History of the Conquest of New Spain); Garcilasso de la Vega (known as El Inca) (1539–1616), the son of an Inca princess and a Spanish conquistador, recorded Inca traditions in his *Comentarios Reales de los Incas* (Royal Commentaries of the Incas) published in 1609; Sir John Hawkins (1532–95) was an Elizabethan naval officer, explorer and slave trader author of *A True Declaration of the Troublesome Voyadge of M. J. Haukins to the Parties of Guynea and the West Indies, in the Yeares of our Lord 1567 and 1568*. For Sahagun see this volume, p. 373, n. 14.

91   *Hakluyt's men*: Richard Hakluyt (*c.*1552–1616), English writer and churchman, author of *Divers Voyages Touching the Discoverie of America* (1582), and the monumental three-volume account of Elizabethan explorations, *The Principal Navigations, Voyages, Traffiques and Discoveries of the English Nation* (1589–1600) that remained a much-read and well-known text in the nineteenth century. His 'men' are the travellers described in his work.

92   Relations Edifiantes: French, 'Edifying Reports'. On the Jesuit Relations see n. 85 above.

93   *Nordenskiöld and Moseley*: Adolf Erik Nordenskiöld (1832–1901) was a Finnish arctic explorer and navigator of Northern coast of Europe and Asia. An account of his voyages appeared in English in 1881 under the tile *The Voyage of the Vega Round Asia and Europe, with a Historical Review of Previous Journeys Along the North Coast of the Old World*, trans. Alexander Leslie (1881; London: Macmillan, 1885). Henry Nottidge

Moseley (1844–91) was a British naturalist who sailed on the H. M. S. Challenger between 1872 and 1876 during its circumnavigation of the globe. The collection of scientific and ethnographical observations made by Moseley, Thomas Henry Tizard, J. Y. Buchanan, and John Murray after the voyage were published in 1885 as *Narrative of the Cruise of H. M. S. Challenger, with a General Account of the Scientific Results of the Expedition* (Edinburgh: Neil and Co.). Since these papers were published a year after this essay, Lang must have had access to material in advance.

94 Leviticus: Lang singles out the Old Testament Book of *Leviticus* (4th–6th century BCE) because of its emphasis upon the performance of ritual.

95 Cruise of the Challenger: see n. 93 above.

96 *Mariner*: William Mariner (1791–1853) was a ship's clerk who lived amongst Tongans on the island of Lifuka for four years (1806–10) after the ship upon which he was working was violently seized by a Ha'api chief. Upon his rescue and return to England, Mariner narrated to John Martin an account of his experiences: *An Account of the Natives of a Tonga Island in the South Pacific Ocean* (London: J. Murray, 1817).

97 *Rig-Veda*: see this volume, p. 375, n. 5.

98 *primitive methodist*: Lang offers examples in a footnote that has been omitted here.

99 *Dr. Bleek ... Dobrizhoffer*: ethnologists deemed reliable by Lang. See Appendix I for Bleek, Codrington, Gill and Rink. Joseph Millerd Orpen (1828–1923) was a British colonial administrator who recorded the traditions and cultures of the Xan people of Southern Africa in works such as 'A glimpse into the mythology of the Maluti Bushmen,' *Cape Monthly Magazine* 9 (1874), pp. 1–13; Hans Egede (1686–1758) was a Norwegian missionary to Greenland who recorded Inuit hero myths; Martin Dobrizhoffer (1717–91) was an Austrian missionary who wrote about the culture and traditions of the Gauranis and Abipones of Paraguay.

100 *Strabo*: see this volume, p. 386, n. 89.

101 *Müller or McLennan*: a footnote offering further illustration of the point has been omitted.

102 *stronger evidence*: a footnote clarifying the idea here has been omitted.

103 *animal shapes*: a footnote elaborating upon transformation of people into animals is omitted here.

104 *ii. 230*: the second quotation is a précis of Tylor's words rather than an exact rendering.

105 *We may now offer ... Household Tales*: Lang supports this list with a substantial appendix, listing authorities for the existence of these ideas, customs and beliefs, and giving references for the tales based, as Lang believes, upon these beliefs and customs. The list of authorities has been omitted here. See Lang's appendix in Margaret Hunt, ed., *Grimm's Household Tales*, 2 vols (London: George Bell and Sons, 1884), pp. 71–5.

106 *Helle*: elsewhere Lang gives Helle a circumflex on the final 'e'.

107 *The Scholiast ... Philostephanus*: Lang here refers to the marginal gloss upon *Iliad* VII.86 that appears in the tenth century 'Venetus A' manuscript. Philostephanus of Cyrene was a Greek writer of the third century BCE.

108 *'the sun ... horns come out'*: De Gubernatis, *Zoological Mythology*, vol. 1, p. 402.

109 *children ... series of adventures*: this is Thompson's motif S322, 'Children abandoned (driven forth, exposed) by hostile relative'.

110 *Castrén, p. 164*: the *Samodjedische Märchen* (Samoyed Tales) cited here appeared in M. Alexander Castrén's *Ethnologische Vorlesungen* (Ethnological Lectures) (St Petersburg: Buchdruchereu Kaiserlichen Academie, 1857), pp.155–81. This tale may be found (in German) on pp. 164–9.

111 *'Story of the Bird that made Milk'*: see George McCall Theal, *Kaffir Folk-lore* (1882; London: Sonnenschein, 1886), pp. 29–39.

112 *'Little brother took his little sister ... into the wide world'''*: see 'Brother and Sister' (Tale 11) in Hunt (ed. and trans.), *Grimm's Household Tales*, vol. 1, p. 44. Lang misquotes the opening of the story, omitting 'we have had no happiness' after 'Since our mother died'.

113 *Demane and Demazana*: see Theal, *Kaffir Folk-lore*, pp. 118–21.

114 *The companions of the hero ... gifted beasts*: this is motif D1820, 'Magic sight and hearing'. Lang includes a Slavonic version of this tale type 'Long, Broad and Quickeye' in his *Grey Fairy Book* (London: Longmans, Green and Co., 1900), pp. 366–81.

115 *the Kalewala ... of the Finns:* an epic Finnish poem based upon traditional Karelian songs published by Elias Lönnrot in two versions in 1835 and (substantially expanded) 1849. The Finnish title *Kalewala* is now commonly rendered in English as *Kalevala*. Lang's notes in *Myth, Ritual and Religion* (1887; London: Longmans, Green and Co., 2nd edition, 1899, vol. 1, p. 59) suggest that he was working from a French translation (titled Kalevala) made by Léouzon le Duc in *La Finlande* (Paris: Jules Labitte, 1845). The first complete translation of the *Kalevala* into English was published by John Martin Crawford in 1888, four years after Lang wrote this introduction.

116 *The fugitives ... and so forth*: Thompson classifies this motif as D672 'Obstacle Flight'. In Thompson's description: '[f]ugitives throw objects behind them which magically become obstacles in [the] pursuer's path'. The similarity of Lang and Thompson's language suggests that Thompson may have been influenced by Lang's account in his description of this motif.

117 *In Bleek's Hottentot Fables and Tales ... adventurous lover*: the story is 'How a Nama Woman Outwitted the Elephants,' in Bleek (ed.), *Reynard the Fox in South Africa* (London: Trübner, 1864), pp. 61–4.

118 *Gaelic and Zulu ... Russian tale*: see John Francis Campbell, *Popular Tales of the West Highlands* (1862; Paisley: Alexander Gardner, 1890), vol. 1, p. 56; Callaway, *Nursery Tales*, vol. 1, p. 64; and 'Vasilissa the Fair' in W. R. S. Ralston, *Russian Folk-Tales* (London: Smith, Elder and Co., 1873), pp. 150–8.

119 *In the Eskimo Tale ... cannibal too*: see Hinrich Rink, 'The Brothers Visit Their Sister' (Tale 9), *Tales and Traditions of the Eskimo* (1866; London: W. Blackwood and Sons, 1875), pp. 128–32. Lang erroneously cites this as Tale 7.

120 *'Two Girls' (Rink, 8)*: see Rink 'A Tale about Two Girls' (Tale 8), *Tales and Traditions of the Eskimo*, pp. 126–8.

121 *Castrén. 11*: it's not clear what the '11' refers to in Lang's citation. The story referenced is the same as that identified by Lang on p. 117 (this volume); see note 110 above.

122 *a story from Madagascar (Folk-lore Record, Aug. 1883)*: in full, James Sibree, 'The Oratory, Songs, Legends, and Folk-Tales of the Malagasy: The Three Sisters And Itrìmobé', *Folk-Lore Journal* 1:8 (Aug. 1883), pp. 233–43.

123 *'Nicht, Nocht, Nothing'*: collected by Lang from Miss Margaret Craig of Darliston in Morayshire and published, along with the story 'Rashin Coatie', under the slightly more Anglicised title of 'Nicht, Nought, Nothing' in *Revue Celtique*, vol. 3 (1876–8), pp. 365–78. Lang later incorporated the story into his essay 'A Far-Travelled Tale' (*Custom and Myth*, London: Longman's Green and Co., 1884, pp. 89–92), and Joseph Jacobs included a heavily adapted version of it in *English Fairy Tales* (1890) under the title 'Nix, Nought, Nothing'.

124 *'Tsar Morskoi'*: a mythological Russian Sea King. The story Lang alludes to here is 'The Water King and Vasilissa the Wise' which Lang read in Ralston, *Russian Folk-Tales*, pp. 120–32.

125 *'Battle of the Birds'*: the story appears in Campbell's *Popular Tales of the West Highlands*, (1862), told by a fisherman from Inverary named John Mackenzie in April 1859. See Campbell, *Popular Tales*, vol 1. pp. 25–38. Lang later included a modified version of this story in *The Lilac Fairy Book* (London: Longmans, Green and Co., 1910).

126 *in the Kalewala ... waters of forgetfulness:* this occurs in song 19. See E. Friberg, trans., *The Kalevala* (Helsinki: Otava, 1998), pp. 161–7.

127 *Callaway, 470*: Lang's page citation is an error. See Callaway, *Nursery Tales*, vol. 1, p. 170.

128 *Apollonius Rhodius contains ... performed by Jason*: after killing Apsyrtus Jason lops off his extremities, licks up some of his blood three times, and spits it out three times in order to expiate the murder.

129 *Grote (ed. 1869, i. 232)*: the reference is to the British historian George Grote's *History of Greece*. Grote (1794–1871) published his history in multiple volumes between 1846 and 1856.

130 *'a vivid image ... the encroaching darkness'*: Cox, *Mythology of the Aryan Nations*, vol. 2, p. 40–1.

131 *'the breath or motion of the air'*: Cox, *Mythology of the Aryan Nations*, vol. 2, p. 150. In a footnote omitted here Lang outlines conflicting solar interpretations of the same symbols.

132 *Mr. Farrer*: see this volume, p. 377, n. 38.

---

3   FAIRY TALES

'Literary Fairy Tales', Introduction to Frederick van Eeden's *Little Johannes* (1895)

1 Chansons de Geste: Old French, 'Songs of Deeds'; epic Medieval poems sung by minstrels.

2 fabliau *or the* conte: popular forms of story. The *fabliau* is a short comic tale, often bawdy, popular in Medieval and Renaissance Europe; the term *conte* ('tale') is commonly used to identify folk and fairy tales.

3 *a* Märchen *of world-wide renown*: tale type ATU425 'The Search for the Lost Husband' – particularly ATU425B, 'Son of the Witch'.

4   *Dr. Macdonald*: George MacDonald (1824–1905) was a British writer of fantasies,
     children's fictions and fairy tales; he was also a Church of England minister. His works
     include *Phantastes: A Faerie Romance for Men and Women* (1858), *At the Back of the North
     Wind* (1871) and *The Princess and the Goblin* (1872). In each of these works MacDonald
     uses the fairy tale as a basis for social and spiritual allegory.

5   *Jatakas … Ocean of the Stream of Stories*: ancient Sanskrit story collections. The
     Jatakas are a cycle of tales with a core group of narratives dating from around the
     fourth century BCE that narrate the experiences of Buddha in his previous incarnations.
     The *Ocean of the Streams of Story* (*Kathasaritsagara*) is a vast narrative compendium
     composed by the Kashmiri court poet Bhatta Somadeva in the eleventh century CE.

6   Précieuses: French term referring to the precocious aristocratic ladies of seventeenth-
     century French salon culture.

7   bouts-rimés: French, 'rhymed ends', a game in which the players are given rhyming
     words and must make a poem with the rhyming words at the end of the lines.

8   mitonnent: French, literally 'simmer'.

9   Pentamerone: Italian collection of fifty tales by Giambattista Basile, published between
     1634 and 1636.

10   *la Comtesse de M— (Murat)*: Henriette-Julie de Castelnau, Comtesse de Murat (1670–
     1716) was a French aristocrat and writer who published three collections of tales,
     Contes des fées (Fairy Tales) (1698), *Les nouveaux contes des fées* (New Fairy Tales) (1698),
     and *Histoires sublimes et allégoriques* (Sublime and Allegorical Stories) (1699). She
     published her autobiography under the title *Memoires de Madame la comtesse de M—*,
     hence Lang's use of the obscuring dash.

11   Cabinet des Fées: French, Cabinet of Fairies, a forty-one-volume compendium of
     French fairy tales assembled by Charles-Joseph de Mayer and published between 1785
     and 1789.

12   Le Mouton … Souris: French, 'The Ram', 'The Yellow Dwarf', 'Finette Cendron',
     'The Good Little Mouse'. For modern translations of these tales see Jack Zipes, ed. and
     trans., *Beauties, Beasts and Enchantments: Classic French Fairy Tales* (New York: Meridian,
     1991).

13   *the Hathors of Egypt, the Moerae who came to the birth of Meleager, the Norns of Scandinavian
     myth*: Hathor was an Ancient Egyptian goddess associated with women, children and
     childbirth; the Moerae were the three fates of Ancient Greek mythology who
     announced prophesies at the birth of the Argonaut Meleager, the third of which was
     that he would die when a burning brand in the fire was fully consumed; the Norns are
     the equivalent of the Moerae in Norse mythology.

14   *Sainte-Beuve … portraits*: the French literary critic Charles Augustin Sainte-Beuve
     (1804–69) published several collections of literary portraits of prominent figures,
     including *Portraits de femmes* (Portraits of Women) (1844).

15   *From Madame d'Aulnoy … Beauty and the Beast*: 'Beauty and the Beast' was not in fact
     written by d'Aulnoy, though she has many Beauty/Beast narratives. The 'very prolix
     novel' *La belle et la bête* was published by Gabrielle-Suzanne de Villeneuve (1685–1755)
     in 1740, and this was abbreviated by Jeanne-Marie Leprince De Beaumont (1711–80)
     in 1757.

16 *Caylus*: Anne Claude Philippe de Tubières-Grimoard de Pestels de Lévis, Comte de
    Caylus (1692–1765): French courtier, antiquarian and writer of fairy tales. Caylus
    experimented with the form of the fairy tale, producing self-conscious, parodic, and
    sometimes bawdy variations on traditional models. He was strongly influenced by
    Antoine Galland's French translation of *The Thousand and One Nights* (*Les Mille et une
    nuits*, 1704–17); and produced his own collection of pseudo-Oriental tales, *Contes
    orientaux* in 1743.

17 *Kingsley's* Water Babies: *The Water Babies: A Fairy Tale for a Land Baby* was published
    by the English writer Charles Kingsley (1819–75) in 1863. It is, as Lang suggests,
    an eclectic narrative that incorporates scientific observations, moral instruction and
    social satire.

18 *Captain Costigan, or Becky Sharpe*: characters from Thackeray's novels *Pendennis*
    (1848–50) and *Vanity Fair* (1847–8) respectively.

19 *Angelica is ... of the nursery*: Lang compares characters from Thackeray's *The Rose and the
    Ring* with characters from *Pendennis*.

20 *He laid his hands ... warming pan*: Lang misquotes here. King Valoroso says: 'But now he
    dared, with sacrilegious hand, to strike the sacred night-cap of a king—Hedzoff, and
    floor me with a warming-pan!' See Thackeray, *The Rose and the Ring* (Basingstoke:
    Macmillan, 1981), p. 57.

21 *Phantastes of Dr. Macdonald*: see this volume, p. 390, n. 4.

22 *the kind Academician ... gardens of the Louvre*: Perrault notes in his memoirs that he
    persuaded Jean-Baptiste Colbert to keep the Tuileries Garden open for the use of the
    public, rather than reserving it exclusively for the use of the King. See *Charles Perrault:
    Memoirs of My Life*, ed. and trans. Jeanne Morgan Zarucchi (Columbia: University of
    Missouri Press, 1989), pp. 107–8.

23 *Charles Nodier ... 'Othello of children'*: this is one of Lang's favourite observations and he
    quotes it a number of times. It appears in Nodier's essay 'Du Fantastique en Littérature'
    (The Fantastic in Literature) published in his *Oeuvres* vol. 5 ('Rêveries') (Brussels: J. P.
    Meline, 1832), pp. 59–98. For this observation see p. 86. Nodier (1780–1844) was a
    French Romantic writer whose own novels, plays and stories draw frequently on
    folklore and fairy tales.

24 *'win their way ... to the fabulous'*: the quotation is from Thucydides's *History of the
    Pelponnesian War* (see 1.21). Thucydides is making an unfavourable comparison
    between the writings of poets and the writings of the historian.

25 contes populaires: French, 'popular tales' or 'folk tales'.

26 conteurs: French, 'tale tellers' (masculine).

27 *'it needs ... this skill'*: the quotation is from Matthew Arnold, 'The Scholar Gipsy'
    (1852), stanza 5.

28 *stretch the bow ... till it breaks*: the ancient Greek God Apollo is associated with the bow;
    the allusion to it being bent until it breaks has not been identified.

29 *Madame d'Aulnoy, in* Ponce de Léon *... to put his price upon*: 'Dom Gabriel Ponce de
    Léon' is one of the frame narratives in d'Aulnoy's *Contes des Fées*. For this passage see
    Madame d'Aulnoy, *Les Contes des Fées* (Paris: Billois, 1810), vol. 2, pp. 216–17. Lang
    translates the whole, except *l'on peut badiner avec*: 'one can play around with [them]'.

30 faiseur … et moderns: French, 'maker of fairy tales old and modern'.

31 *'Vous y mettrez … donner la peine'*: French, 'you may value them as you please, but I must say that he who makes up tales is capable of the most weighty things, if he wants to take the trouble'. Lang misquotes; the original has 'ceux qui les composent'. D'Aulnoy, *Contes des Fées*, vol. 2, p. 217.

'Perrault's Popular Tales', Introduction to *Perrault's Popular Tales* (1888)

1 *Madame de Sévigné … August, 1676*: the letter is in fact of 6 August 1677. See *Lettres de Madame de Sévigné à sa fille et à ses amis*, ed. Ph. A. Grouvelle (Paris: Bossange, Masson et Besson, 1806), vol. 4, p. 260.

2 *mon habit … plus indifférentes*: French, 'my red velvet gown, and my English lace; my cloak with golden flowers and my diamond necklace which is not the most commonplace.'

3 Peau d'Ane: French, 'Donkey Skin', one of Perrault's stories.

4 *Cybele*: Anatolian mother goddess, and the focus of a cult that persisted in both Ancient Greece and Ancient Rome. Her appearance in this story draws attention to the themes of fertility and regeneration, and also introduces an exotic note.

5 *Saint Cyr*: a school for the daughters of impoverished aristocrats was established at Saint Cyr in 1684 at the request of Madame de Maintenon.

6 *'par simplicité … sur une table'*: French, 'Out of simplicity, I take the best thing; out of simplicity I praise myself; out of simplicity I want something at table that is far away from me.' These pert remarks are recorded by Madame de Maintenon in a letter to Madame de Fontaines, dated 20 September 1691. The translation is from Katharine Prescott Wormeley, *The Correspondence of Madame, Princess Palatine … Marie-Adélaide de Savoie … and of Madame de Maintenon, in relation to Saint-Cyr* (Boston: Hardy, Pratt & Co., 1899), p. 247.

7 *Madame de Maintenon*: Françoise d'Aubigné, Marquise de Maintenon (1635–1719) was the second wife of King Louis XIV of France, though the marriage was never publically recognised because of her relatively humble origins. Her school at Saint Cyr sought to inculcate strict moral and religious values.

8 *Œil de Bœuf*: French, 'bull's eye'. Lang's meaning is obscure.

9 *L'Heritier* in Bigarrures Ingénieuses: see Heritier in Appendix 1.

10 *'Les Romances modernes … Romances antiques'*: French, 'Modern Romances strive to imitate the simplicity of ancient Romances'.

11 demoiselles: French, 'young ladies'.

12 *'mais non … n'en veux point'*: French, 'but not fairy tales or Donkey Skin stories because I don't want them'.

13 Cendrillon, *and* La Belle au Bois Dormant: French, 'Cinderella' and 'Sleeping Beauty in the Woods'.

14 L'Esprit Fort: French, 'The Strong Spirit' or 'The Free Thinker'. André Lefèvre attributes this short poem he found in a collection of *contes en vers* published in Geneva

in 1774 to Perrault. Lefèvre also reprints the poem in full. See *Les contes de Charles Perrault* (Paris: Alphonse Lemerre, 1875), pp. xxxvi–xxxviii.

15 *La Marquise … nouvelle*: French, 'The Marquise of Salusses, or the Patience of Griselda, a novella'.

16 *from Boccaccio*: see *The Decameron* X.10.

17 *Rambouillet or Marly*: locations near Paris used by Louis XIV for leisure and hunting.

18 *'Clair de … son erreur'*: French, 'With its clear streams and shady foliage / Filled his spirit with secret awe; / Simple and unsullied nature / Showed itself so beautiful and so pure, / That a thousand times he blessed his error'.

19 *'Rempli de … prairies'*: French, 'Filled with sweet daydreams / Inspired by the great woods, the waters and the meadows'.

20 *feuille qui chante*: French, 'leaf which sings', or perhaps Singing Leaf. See *Lettres de Madame de Sévigné*, vol. 1, p. xiv.

21 *Chaucer veils them in his kindly courtesy*: see 'The Clerk's Tale' in *The Canterbury Tales*.

22 La Bibliothèque Bleue: French; literally, 'The Blue Library', inexpensive popular publications that circulated in France from the late sixteenth century, so named because they came wrapped in blue paper.

23 *'If I had taken out … so many years'*: for the original French and a recent translation of this essay (in fact a dedicatory letter) see Perrault, *The Complete Fairy Tales in Verse and Prose: A Dual Language Edition*, ed. and trans. Stanley Appelbaum (Mineola: Dover, 2002), pp. 60–7. This comment appears on pp. 60–1. It is likely that Lang read this dedicatory letter, along with the other prefatory material he refers to in his study of Perrault, in Lefèvre's *Les contes de Charles Perrault*.

24 *M. Maury*: Louis Ferdinand Alfred Maury (1817–92); French physician and scholar; author of works on dream theory, antiquarianism, archaeology and cultural history, including the text Lang cites here, *Les Fées du Moyen Age* (The Fairies of the Middle Ages).

25 *Elzevir collection:* the Dutch publishing firm of Elzevir stopped printing books in the early eighteenth century. They were much sought after by collectors and Lang may have owned Elzevir editions as he had been an enthusiastic book collector.

26 Recueil … prose qu'en vers: see Moetjens in Appendix I.

27 Les Souhaits Ridicules: French, 'The Foolish Wishes'.

28 *André Lefèvre*: (1834–1904); a prolific French author who wrote on philosophy, the classics, languages, architecture, ethnology and mythology. Lang draws heavily upon his study *Les contes de Charles Perrault* (Paris: Alphonse Lemerre, 1875).

29 *the* Parallèle: Perrault's work, *Parallèle des Anciens et des Modernes* (Parallel of the Ancients and the Moderns) (1688–92).

30 *Zoilus*: Greek philosopher who was said to have been critical of Homer in his lost work, *Homeric Questions*.

31 contes de Vieilles: French, 'old tales'.

32 *Van der Meer*: Noach Van der Meer, Dutch artist and etcher (1741–1822).

33 *the blind bard of Chios*: Homer, who is traditionally presented as being blind, and whose birthplace is identified by some commentators as the island of Chios.

34 '*I have to do … example of the Ancients*': see Perrault, *Complete Fairy Tales in Verse and Prose*, p. 2.

35 '*The Moral of … know what it is*': ibid., p. 4.

36 '*on les voit … bonheur arrive*': French, 'one sees them sad and despondent when the hero or the heroine of the story is in trouble, and crying out with joy when the time of their happiness arrives'.

37 Marmoisan ou l'Innocente Tromperie: French, 'Marmosian or The Innocent Trickery'.

38 '*the excellent education … led on to others*': see Marie-Jean L'Héritier de Villandon, *Bigarrures Ingenieuses* (Ingenious Variations) (Paris: Jean Guignard, 1696), p. 3.

39 '*avec quelque broderie … dans l'esprit*': French, 'with some embroidery that came to me spontaneously'.

40 *practically lost:* a footnote is omitted here giving some verses by L'Heritier.

41 '*à ce jeune Conteur … de son enfance*': French 'to this young storyteller, who makes such spirited use of the amusements of his childhood'. See *Bigarrures Ingenieuses*, p. 3.

42 '*handed to us … write them out*': this is at the start of the story 'Les Enchantemens de l'Eloquence' ('The Enchantments of Eloquence'), *Bigarrures Ingenieuses*, p. 112.

43 *known … to the Kaffirs*: see 'The Story of the Five Heads' in George McCall Theal, *Kaffir Folk-lore* (1882; London: Sonnenschein, 1886), pp. 48–55.

44 Eloquentia Nativa … Douceur: the name is Latin and means 'Native Eloquence', the story title is French and translates as 'The Enchantments of Eloquence, or The Effects of Sweetness'.

45 *Fables d'animaux*: a long footnote about the transformation of animal fables has been omitted here.

46 'Cent et Cent fois … Histoire surprenante': French 'Hundreds and Hundreds of times my Governess / Instead of animal Fables / Told me the instructive details / Of this remarkable History'. *Bigarrures Ingenieuses*, p. 227.

47 Privilége du Roy: French, 'privilege of the king'.

48 *an Academician*: a member of the prestigious French scholarly society *Académie française*, which would have entailed conformity to certain codes of conduct by its members.

49 '*fit parfaitement … même tems*': French, 'improved his place at Court at the same time'.

50 '*Quelquefois, cependant … la famille!*': French, 'Sometimes, however, it is this little monkey / Who will bring delight to the whole family!'

51 *Paul Lacroix*: (1806–84), a French cultural historian and novelist who edited and introduced a volume of Perrault's tales *Les Contes de Perrault* (Paris: Jouast, 1876) in which these arguments appear.

52 '*a mis depuis … tant d'agrément*': French, 'has recently put a few tales down on paper with such approval'. *Bigarrures Ingenieuses*, p. 3.

53 brodeuses: French, 'embroiderers', meaning those who elaborate upon traditional tales.

54 Esprit: French, 'spirit', with particular connotations of liveliness in wit and invention.

55 *Histoires et Contes du Tem[p]s passé*: French, 'Stories and Tales of Past Times', the title of Perrault's prose collection. Lang omits the 'p' in *Temps*.

56 *Maive Stokes*: (1867–?); she collected and translated the stories in *Indian Fairy Tales* (1880) at the age of 13, assisted by her mother, Mary Stokes, and her father, the noted scholar of Irish language and tradition, Whitley Stokes. Stokes records in her preface that the stories were told to her in Calcutta and Simla by two Ayahs and a male cook.

57 beau esprit: signifies a cultivated individual, literally 'beautiful spirit' or 'beautiful mind'.

58 '*Livre unique … candeur de l'enfant*': French, 'Book unique amongst all books, mixed with the wisdom of age and the innocence of youth'. This reflection on Perrault's work comes in Paul Bins Comte de St. Victor's essay 'Les Contes des Fées', published in the collection *Hommes et Dieux* (Men and Gods) (1867; Paris: Calmann Lévy, 1887), pp. 467–77, p. 475. St Victor (1827–81) was a French journalist and essayist admired by Lang.

59 Diaskeuast: one who revises and edits.

60 '*Elle commença … pareilles rencontres*': French 'She began by passing out (for that is the first recourse of almost all women in similar situations)'.

61 '*ce fut là … ce côté-là*': French, 'that's where he made his greatest profit. He found a few women who entrusted him with letters for their husbands, but they paid him so badly, and it came to so small a sum, that he didn't deign to take into consideration the money he gained in that way'.

62 '*de la nouvelle création pour sa famille*': French, 'of new invention for his family' (in fact, Perrault has 'for his father and brothers').

63 '*You never did that of your own wit*': the version of this story that Lang collected does not include this phrase, though the giant does say 'Shame for the wit that helped you'. See *Custom and Myth* (Longmans, Green and Co., 1884), p. 91.

64 '*Anne, ma sœur … encore plus loin*': French, 'Anne, my sister Anne, do you not see anything coming?' (Bluebeard), 'I see nothing but the sun dappling, and the grass growing green' (Bluebeard), 'Pull the latch and the catch will fall' (Little Red Riding Hood), 'So she travelled very far, very far, then even further' (Donkey Skin).

65 pulveris exigui jactu: Latin, 'the casting of a little dust'. The quotation is from Virgil's *Georgics* IV.87.

66 *Madame d'Epernon*: (1624–1701) a high-born society lady who later became a Carmelite nun.

67 *as Nodier says*: see this volume, p. 391, n. 23.

68 '*Aux jeunes gens … biens acquis*': French, 'Ordinarily for young men, / Industry and ability / will be more valuable than an inheritance'.

69 chevalier d'industrie: French, implying 'swindler'.

70 *George Cruikshank*: (1792–1878), English illustrator and political cartoonist of the Victorian period who provided illustrations for Dickens's works, the first English edition of Grimms' Tales, and Sterne's *Tristram Shandy*. He became an advocate for the temperance movement, and wrote four versions of fairy tales (*Puss in Boots, Hop O' My Thumb, Cinderella* and *Jack and the Bean Stalk*) designed to illustrate moral values,

including the values of temperance. These tales were published together under the title the *Fairy Library* in 1870.

71 *'When I came to look … the minds of children'*: Cruikshank's comment appears on p. 39 of the edition Lang cites at the end of the paragraph.

72 *'fraud on the fairies … flower-garden'*: see *Household Words* 8 (1853), p. 97.

73 Schwank: German, 'comic tale'.

74 *Minyan legend of Athamas and Ino*: see this volume, p. 398, n. 5.

75 rakshása: Hindu demon.

76 weendigo: more commonly 'wendigo', malevolent spirit in the mythology of the Algonquian peoples of North America.

77 *Dr. Jekyl … Dean Maitland*: popular novels by, respectively, Robert Louis Stevenson, H. Rider Haggard, F. Anstey and Maxwell Gray (pseudonym of Mary Gleed Tuttiett). Lang misspells Jekyll.

78 *'On n'inventerait … longtemps'*: French, 'We could not invent these things today if they had not been imagined long ago'.

79 [footnote] Schol. ad. Theog. *885*: Lang's footnote here is an abbreviation of *Scholia ad Theogony*, and probably refers to Thomas Gaisford's collection of ancient scholarly commentaries on Hesiod's *Theogony* titled *Scholia ad Hesiodum* (1823).

80 [footnote] *Thorpe's* Palace with Pillars of Gold: Lang's citation here refers to the story 'The Palace that Stood on Golden Pillars' in Benjamin Thorpe's *Yule-tide Stories: A Collection of Scandinavian and North German Tales and Traditions* (London: Henry G. Bohn, 1853), pp. 64–75.

81 [footnote] *Dasent's* Lord Peter: the story cited appears in George Webbe Dasent's *Popular Tales from the Norse*, 2nd edition (Edinburgh: Edmonston and Douglas, 1859), pp. 340–7.

82 *merely lets the cat do all the tricks*: see Charles Deulin, *Les contes de ma mère l'oye avant Perrault* (The Tales of Mother Goose before Perrault) (Paris: Dentu, 1879), p. 196. Lang's analysis of the tale is strongly influenced by Deulin's reading.

83 Straparola: Giovan Francesco Straparola (*c.*1480–*c.*1558), Italian writer of tales; he published the two–volume collection of novella cited here in 1550 and 1553, titled *Piacevoli Notti* (Pleasant Nights). His 'Puss in Boots' variant is 'Constantino Fortunato'.

84 *a popular version from Sicily*: Lang cites three versions of this Sicilian story: 'Don Giuseppe Piru', tale 88 (erroneously cited by Lang as 188) in Giuseppe Pitrè's *Fiabe, novelle e racconti popolari siciliani* (*Sicilian Fairy Tales, Stories, and Folk Tales*) (Palermo: Luigi Pedone Lauriel, 1875), vol. 2, pp. 273–9; Thomas Frederick Crane's translation of this tale 'Don Joseph Pear' in *Popular Italian Tales* (Boston: Houghton, Mifflin and Co.: 1885), pp. 127–31; and Laura Gonzenbach's German translation 'Dom Conte Piro' in *Sicilianische Märchen* (Sicilian Folk Tales) (Leipzig: Wilhelm Engelmann, 1870), vol. 1, pp. 59–65. Lang also included a version of this story in *The Crimson Fairy Book* under the title 'How the Beggar Boy Turned into Count Piro'.

85 *the story with the moral … the Caucasus*: for a full bibliography of variants see Hans-Jörg Uther, *The Types of International Tales*, FF Communications 284 (Helsinki: Suomalainen Tiedeakatemia Academia Scientiarum Fennica, 2004), ATU 545.

86 *June 29, 1876*: cited in Deulin, *Les contes*, p. 203.

87 Hitopadesa: a twelfth-century collection of Sanskrit fables designed, like the third-century collection, the *Panchatantra*, to give advice on statecraft to princes.

88 *Lal Behari Day's* Folk Tales of Bengal *(Macmillan)*: Lal Behari Day (1824–92), now more commonly Dey, was a Bengali writer, teacher, and Christian minister. In addition to writing novels and editing magazines in both English and Bengali, Dey published the collection of Bengali folk tales in English cited here in 1883.

89 *'remembering … compassion on him'*: for the references to this story see Day, *Folk-Tales of Bengal* (London: Macmillan, 1883) pp. 226–35.

90 zu haben: German, 'available'.

91 *'l'idée toute bouddhique … native de l'animal'*: French, 'the completely Buddhist idea of the ingratitude of man opposed to the natural generosity of animals'. The words cited here are Deulin's, see *Les contes*, p. 203. Deulin identifies Cosquin's article in *Le Français* (29 June 1876) as the source of the idea.

92 The Rat's Wedding: this appears in Flora Annie Steel's 1894 collection *Tales of the Punjab*, though Lang must have seen it when it was first published by Steel and R. C. Temple in *The Indian Antiquary* 11 (1882), pp. 226–30.

93 *Dr. Steere's* Swahili Tales: see this volume, p. 384, n. 71.

94 *'men of … origin'*: the observation is Steere's, though Steere has 'a Swahili is by definition a man of mixed Negro and Arab descent' (p. vi).

95 *'they have been … own language'*: Swahili Tales, p. viii.

96 *'Almighty God … more than I'*: references to the story are from Steere, pp. 11–137.

97 Five Heads: see Theal, *Kaffir Folk-lore*, pp. 48–55.

98 *'De riche appauvri … passé Richard'*: Lang gives a French translation of the lines from *Il Pentamerone*, originally in Neapolitan dialect. Nancy Canepa translates the original text as: '*May God save you from the rich who become poor and from the beggar who has worked his way up*'. See *Giambattista Basile's The Tale of Tales, or Entertainment for Little Ones* (Detroit: Wayne State University Press, 2007), p. 168 (italics in source).

99 *syllogism*: a kind of logical argument in which a conclusion is derived from two premises. In this case, the premise that a moral Arab form of *Puss in Boots* had a gazelle in place of a cat, combined with the premise that a certain Arab clan mourns gazelles, yields the conclusion that the Arab gazelle story is the original form of *Puss in Boots*. Lang compares this argument to the argument made by the proponents of Indian origin, and rejects both. In fact, Lang elsewhere makes arguments that resemble this in structure, as when he proposes that 1) the tale of 'Cupid and Psyche' codifies marriage taboos, 2) certain primitive cultures enforce marriage taboos, so 3) 'Cupid and Psyche' originated in those primitive cultures to illustrate the taboo.

100 *Lefèvre*: see this volume, p. 393, n. 23.

101 *'disease of language'*: the phrase is associated with Max Müller. For Lang's explanation of the concept see this volume, 'Cupid, Psyche and the "Sun Frog"', pp. 73–74 and 'Household Tales', p. 99.

102 ex hypothesi: see this volume, p. 382, n. 39.

103 *Ramses II*: Ramses II was Pharoh of Egypt from 127 BCE to 213 BCE. A manuscript survives on papyrus from around this period, which narrates a recognisable version of the 'Two Brothers' tale type (ATU303). Lang includes an account of this tale in *Myth, Ritual and Religion* (1887; London: Longmans, Green and Co., 2nd edition, 1899), vol. 2., pp. 318–20.

104 *Algonkin tales … by Mr. Leland*: see Charles Leland, *Algonquin Legends of New England* (Boston: Houghton Mifflin, 1884). Leland (1824–1903) was an American folklorist, ethnologist and translator, with a particular interest in gypsy lore and witchcraft.

'Introduction', *The Blue Fairy Book* (1889)

1 *The Scotch … a tale from the Norse*: tale type ATU425A 'The Search for the Lost Husband'. 'The Black Bull of Norroway' was taken by Lang from Robert Chambers's *Popular Rhymes of Scotland*, where a version of it appeared in 1842 as 'The Red Bull of Norroway'. It appeared under the present title from 1858. See Robert Chambers, *Popular Rhymes of Scotland,* 3rd edition, *Select Writings of Robert Chambers*, vol. 7 (Edinburgh: W. & R. Chambers, 1858), pp. 244–7. Lang included it as the thirty-sixth story in *The Blue Fairy Book*. 'East of the Sun, West of the Moon' is the third tale in *The Blue Fairy Book* and derives from Dasent's translation of Asbjørnsen and Moe's *Norske Folkeeventyr,* George Webbe Dasent, *Popular Tales from the* Norse, 2nd edition (Edinburgh: Edmonston and Douglas, 1859), pp. 25–40.

2 *'Beauty and the Beast' … 'Eros and Psyche'*: these stories are also instances of tale type ATU425. 'Beauty and the Beast' is classified under the subcategory ATU425C.

3 *'Bronze Ring'*: in his Preface to *The Blue Fairy Book* (London: Longmans Green and Co., 1889), p. vii, Lang notes that 'The Bronze Ring' was 'translated, or rather adapted' from Henri Carnoy's *Traditions Populaires de l'Asie Mineure* (Paris: Maisonneuve, 1889).

4 *The Finns … the Celts*: tale type ATU510A. Hans-Jörg Uther gives a comprehensive listing of the tale's international variations in *The Types of International Folktales*, FF Communications 284 (Helsinki: Suomalainen TiedeakatemiaAcademia Scientiarum Fennica, 2004). In *The Blue Fairy Book*, Lang uses an eighteenth-century English translation of Perrault's *Cendrillon*.

5 *'Hop o' my Thumb' … Phrixus, and Hellê*: 'Hop o' my Thumb' is a variant of tale type ATU327B. For *The Blue Fairy Book*, Lang uses an eighteenth-century English translation of Perrault's 'Le Petit Poucet' ('Little Thumbling' or 'The Little Thumb'). In Perrault's story, an ogre accidentally murders his own children during the night after Little Thumb places the golden crowns worn by the ogre's children upon the heads of himself and his brothers. In Euripides's account of the story of Athamas, his wife Themisto dresses her own children in white and the children of his former wife Ino in black, intending to murder Ino's children in revenge for Athamas's decision to abandon her and return to Ino. Ino switches the clothes, however, and Themisto murders her own children. See Hyginus, *Fabulæ* IV.

6 *Here we have a shadow … North American continent*: the tale type referred to is ATU313 'The Girl as Helper in the Hero's Flight'. 'The Master Maid', taken from Dasent's *Popular Tales from the Norse*, 2nd edition (pp. 81–102), is the twelfth story in *The Blue Fairy Book*. As in the story of Jason, it includes the motif of a girl who aids the hero in the completion of a series of tasks set by her father. See this volume, p. 380, n. 3.

7 *tales recognisably like ours*: see this volume, p. 398, n. 103.

8   Decies repetita placebit: Latin, 'though repeated ten times it continues to please'.

9   *'They all went to bed ... turn to me'*: this verse appears in 'The Black Bull of Norroway,' *The Blue Fairy Book*, pp. 383–4.

10   *'And she told him ... happened to him'*: see *The Blue Fairy Book*, p. 384.

11   *'to the rites of their ancient bed'*: see *The Odyssey* xxiii. v. 295. This specific formulation appears in Henry Cary's translation of *The Odyssey* (London: Whittaker, 1823), vol. 2.

'Introduction', *The Red Fairy Book* (1890)

1   *True Thomas*: protagonist of the ballad 'Thomas Rhymer' (and known also by that name). In the ballad tradition he becomes the lover of the Fairy Queen and is transported to Fairyland. See *The Penguin Book of Ballads*, ed. Geoffrey Grigson (Harmondsworth: Penguin, 1975), pp. 65–7.

2   *nonage*: youth.

3   Decies repetita placebit: see this volume, p. 399, n. 8.

'Preface', *The Yellow Fairy Book* (1894)

1   *president of ... the Folk Lore Society*: Gomme held this post from 1890 to 1894, immediately after Lang's tenure.

2   *they heard their president say .... blue fairy books!*: in his Presidential Address of 1894 Gomme observed 'folk-tale loses much of its old charm now that it has become the sport of literature. Maimed, altered, and distorted in one direction; clothed in red, blue, and green in another direction – of course, those who cannot see that these are not the doings of folk-lore will never give the folk-tale all the credit it really deserves as an element of the anthropology of civilised races.' These comments sparked a bitter internecine squabble in the Society, to which Lang's sally here contributed. See Gomme, 'Presidential Address,' *Folk-Lore* 5:1 (1894), pp. 43–69; quotation on p. 63.

3   *like Father William in the poem*: 'You are Old, Father William' by Lewis Carroll, in *Alice's Adventures in Wonderland* (1865).

4   *'Little Sioux ... Eskimo'*: Lang misquotes the start of Robert Louis Stevenson's poem 'Foreign Children' from *A Child's Garden of Verses* (London: John Lane, 1885), p. 51, which begins 'Little Indian, Sioux or Crow, / Little frosty Eskimo'.

5   Mr. Ford: Henry J. Ford (1860–1941), British illustrator.

6   *Professor Huxley thinks there are none*: the biologist, Thomas Henry Huxley (1825–95). This is probably a reference to the Romanes lecture, given at Oxford by Huxley in 1893, the year before this preface was published, in which fairy tales are alluded to. See Huxley, *Evolution and Ethics and other Essays* (1894; New York: Appleton, 1896), pp. 46–86.

7   *Mr. Baring-Gould ... the Troubadours*: see Sabine Baring-Gould, *In Troubadour Land: A Ramble in Provence and Languedoc* (1890; London: W. H. Allen & Co., 1891), p. 40.

8   *Claverhouse*: John Graham Claverhouse, 1st Viscount Dundee (1648–89), known as 'Bonnie Dundee'; led Jacobite rebels against the English forces and lost his life whilst helping secure a Jacobite victory at the Battle of Killiecrankie.

'**Preface**', *The Pink Fairy Book* (1897)

1   *Tanuki*: an animal known as the 'racoon dog' that features recurrently in Japanese folklore and is attributed certain supernatural characteristics. The story in *The Pink Fairy Book* is 'The Slaying of the Tanuki,' and concerns a peasant's efforts to revenge himself upon a disruptive Tanuki after it has tricked him into eating his own wife.

'**Preface**', *The Lilac Fairy Book* (1910)

1   *more about portraits of Queen Mary than he did*: see for instance Lang's essay 'Portraits and Jewels of Mary Stuart,' *Scottish Historical Review* 3:10 (1906), pp. 129–56. Lang is referring here to Mary Queen of Scots, not Mary Tudor.

2   *'Prince Prigio ... Fairy Court'*: see Introduction to Volume 1, pp. 31–2.

3   *Adam, according to Mark Twain, in the Garden of Eden*: Lang is referring to Twain's satirical short fiction *Eve's Diary* published in *Harper's Bazaar* for Christmas 1905.

4   *Miss Thackeray ... 'Five Old Friends'*: Anne Isabella Thackeray Ritchie (1837–1919), eldest daughter of William Makepeace Thackeray, published five reworked fairy tales and a fairy-tale inspired story in her collection *Five Old Friends, and a Young Prince* (London: Smith and Elder, 1868).

---

4   ANTHROPOLOGY, AND THE ORIGINS OF RELIGION

'**Anthropology and Ancient Literature**', *The Academy* (1883)

1   *the Vedas*: the Vedas are a large body of texts in Sanskrit. They are formed into four collections of canonical writing: the Rig Veda, the Sama Veda, the Yajur Veda and the Atharva Veda. The texts form the oldest layer of Sanskrit and constitute the primary texts of Hinduism. They contain hymns, incantations and rituals. Max Müller edited the fifty-volume English translation of the Vedas, among other texts, the *Sacred Books of the East Translated by Various Oriental Scholars* (Oxford: Oxford University Press, 1879–1910).

2   *the mangled Purusha*: in Hinduism, Purusha, meaning cosmic man, is the being who pervades the universe. In the Purusha sukta of the Rigveda, Purusha was dismembered by the devas, and his different parts made the moon, the sun, and the earth and so on.

3   *'If we mean ... are primitive'*: Friedrich Max Müller, *India: What Can It Teach Us?* (London: Longmans, Green, and Co., 1883), p. 123–4. This work was taken from a series of lectures first given at Cambridge. In this letter Lang is in the main contesting Müller's argument in these lectures.

4   *'do not ... have been'*: ibid., p. 123. Müller talks of critics who 'stand aloof and can do nothing but find fault, because these songs do not represent to us primitive men exactly as they think they ought to have been'.

5   *'as rude … weapon'*: Friedrich Max Müller, Lecture V, 'The Ideas of Infinity and Law', *Lectures on the Origin and Growth of Religion As Illustrated in the Religions of India*, Lectures delivered April–June 1878 (London: Longmans, Green and Co., 1878), p. 234: 'There are in the Vedas thoughts as rude and crude as any Paleolithic weapons, but by the side of them, we find thoughts with all the sharpness of iron and all the brilliancy of bronze'.

6   *Mr. Müller says, in his Cambridge Lectures*: these lectures were published as *India: What Can It Teach Us?* in 1883.

7   *'the first … and contract'*: Friedrich Max Müller, Lecture III, 'The Human Interest of Sanskrit Literature', *India: What Can It Teacher Us?*, p. 89.

8   *In Mr. Müller's new volume a chapter*: Lecture V of *India: What Can It Teach Us* is titled 'The Lessons of the Veda.'

9   *'no Indo-European or Semitic nation … the worship of the dead'*: Müller cites this quote without attribution in Lecture VII of *India: What Can It Teach Us?*, 'Veda and Vedanta'. He also uses it in one of his later Gifford Lectures, Lecture V, 'About the True Character of Ancestor Worship', published in Friedrich Max Müller *Anthropological Religion* (London: Longmans, Green and Co., 1892), pp.115–44.

10 *the Hibbert Lectures*: Max Müller inaugurated the annual Hibbert Lectures in 1878 with his lectures 'On the Origin and Growth of Religion.'

11 *'There are … of bronze'*: Friedrich Max Müller, *Lectures on the Origins and Growth of Religion*, p. 234 (not p. 232, as given by Lang).

12 *'If we find … primitive savage'*: Max Müller, Lecture III, 'The Human Interest of Sanskrit Literature', *India: What Can It Teach Us?*, p. 112.

'Fetichism and the Infinite', *Custom and Myth* (1884)

1   *'The Origin … of India'*: Friedrich Max Müller, *Lectures on the Origin and Growth of Religion As Illustrated in the Religions of India*, Lectures delivered April–June 1878, (London: Longmans, Green and Co., 1878).

2   *'have taken … or god*: ibid., p. 127.

3   ὅσοι δίκας ὑπέχουσι καὶ οἱ διώκοντες: Ancient Greek, 'as many as those prosecuting and defending the lawsuits'.

4   *These stones … reverence*: Lang uses milestones to satirise the philological theories of Max Müller and his followers as applied to questions of anthropology in his short story 'The Great Gladstone Myth', first published in *Macmillan's Magazine* in February 1886. Here a philologist from the far future attempts to explain the figure of Gladstone as deriving from a name for the sun. The narrator reads the inscription on a stone found between London and Bristol as 'GOM' and believes this stands for 'Gladstonio Optimo Maximo', rejecting the 'unscholarly' suggestion that it is in fact a milestone, and the inscription is actually '90 M'. See 'The Great Gladstone Myth', *In the Wrong Paradise and Other Stories* (London: Kegan Paul, Trench & Co., 1886).

5   *Phidias*: Phidias (or Pheidias) (*c*.480 BCE–430 BCE) is regarded as one of the greatest sculptors of classical Greece. His statue of Zeus at Olympia was one of the seven wonders of the ancient world.

6 *'and why … as primary?'*: Max Müller, Lecture II, 'Is Fetishism a Primitive Form of Religion?', *Lectures on the Origin and Growth of Religion*, p. 104.

7 *Jaroslaf, or Vladimir*: the conversion of Vladimir the Great (*c*.958–1015) to Christianity in the late tenth century was a crucial moment in the conversion of Russia. Following his own conversion, he ordered that his subjects be baptised. His son was Yaroslav the Wise (*c*.978–1054).

8 *it only fetichism*: 'is' is added in later editions.

9 *'Whence … fetich?'*: the title of a section towards the end of Müller's second lecture is 'Whence the Supernatural Predicate of a Fetish?', p. 121.

10 *'The concept … intangible objects'*: Max Müller, Lecture IV, 'The Worship of Tangible, Semi-Tangible, and Intangible Objects', *Lectures on the Origin and Growth of Religion*, p. 205.

11 *they held sacred*: Lang's position vis-à-vis the 'ghost theory' subsequently changed, and in *The Making of Religion* and elsewhere he later argued that the idea of God came, not from a belief in the spirits of the dead, but from an earlier conception of a single, powerful, creator god. See 'Anthropology and Religion I' (this volume, pp. 179–88) and 'On Religion' (this volume, pp. 189–206).

12 *'How do … unseen being?'*: Max Müller, Lecture II, 'Is Fetishism a Primitive Form of Religion?', *Lectures on the Origin and Growth of Religion*, p. 125.

13 *'this process … modern thought'*: Müller asks, as part of his challenge to other accounts of how objects become fetishes, 'Is not the whole process of reasoning, as here described, far more in accordance with modern than with ancient and primitive thoughts!', Lecture II, 'Is Fetishism a Primitive Form of Religion?', *Lectures on the Origin and Growth of Religion*, p. 123.

14 *'to take … every fetich'*: ibid., p. 127.

15 *'the faculty … infinite'*: Müller speaks of those who 'claim for man the possession of a faculty or potential energy for apprehending the infinite', Lecture I, 'The Perception of the Infinite', *Lectures on the Origin and Growth of Religion*, p. 31.

16 *'Every thing … infinite'*: ibid., p. 37. The emphasis is Lang's own.

17 *'the mere sight … or divine'*: Max Müller, Lecture IV, 'The Worship of Tangible, Semi-Tangible, and Intangible Objects', *Lectures on the Origin and Growth of Religion*, p. 177. The full quote is: 'the mere sight of the torrent or the stream, like a stranger coming they know not whence, and going they know not whither, would have been enough to call forth in the hearts of the early dwellers on earth, a feeling that there must be something beyond the small speck of earth which they called their own or their home, that they were surrounded on all sides by powers invisible, infinite, or divine.'

18 *'we are dealing…troglodyte'*: ibid., p. 172.

19 *'an unknown…something'*: ibid., p. 175.

20 [Footnote] *a well known parody of Wordsworth*: from Catherine Maria Fanshawe, 'Fragment in Imitation of Wordsworth' (1865). The original lines are: 'He'd be ten times as tall as me,/And live three times as long.'

21 *to come handy?*: in the next part of the essay, Lang goes on to challenge Müller further on the basis that his scheme does not work with what is known to be the development of society via kinship, rank and property.

'**Anthropology and Religion**' I, *The Making of Religion*, 2nd edition (1900)

1 humani nihil a se alienum putat: from Plautus (*c.*254 BCE–184 BCE), 'He thinks nothing human to be foreign to himself.'

2 *a necessary source*: Max Müller argued for an inherent 'perception of the infinite' in humans in numerous of his works including *Lectures on the Origin and Growth of Religion As Illustrated in the Religions of India*, Lectures delivered April–June 1878 (London: Longmans, Green and Co., 1878), and in his Gifford Lectures from 1888 published as *Natural Religion* (London: Longmans, Green and Co., 1899). Lang contested this, for example in his 'Fetichism and the Infinite', see this volume pp. 170-6.

3 *is very easily drawn*: as is implied in James Frazer's *Golden Bough*, the first edition of which was published in 1890.

4 *'was absolutely false … beyond consciousness'*: Herbert Spencer, *Ecclesiastical Institutions, Part VI of the Principles of Sociology* (London: Williams and Norgate, 1885), p. 838.

5 *Faust as described by Marguerite*: in Johann Wolfgang von Goethe's *Faust, Part I* (1808), Margarete (called Marguerite in Gounod's opera, *Faust*), after asking Faust if he believes in God, listens to his answer and replies, 'All well and good and as it should be. / The priest himself says much the same / Only a little bit differently', see Johann Wolfgang von Goethe, *Faust, Part I*, trans. and with an introduction and notes by David Constantine (London: Penguin, 2005), lines 3459–61.

6 *'the final … errors'*: Spencer, *Ecclesiastical Institutions,* p. 839.

7 *'One God … whole creation moves'*: from Alfred Tennyson (1809–92), *In Memoriam*, lines 141–4.

8 *'… perhaps even of human existence'*: the emphasis is Lang's.

9 *He says: 'The thoughts … intimate relations'*: E. B. Tylor, *Primitive Culture: Researches into the Development of Mythology, Philosophy, Religion, Art and Custom*, 2 vols (London: John Murray, 1871), vol. 1, pp. 381, 383, 384. The first edition has 'acquaintance' rather than 'relations'.

10 tabula rasa: Latin, 'blank slate'.

11 *'in its full … subordinate spirits'*: Tylor, *Primitive Culture*, vol. 1, p. 386.

12 *'an ancient … the practice'*: ibid.

13 *'Among the … her grave'*: A. W. Howitt, 'On Some Australian Beliefs', *Journal of the Anthropological Institute of Great Britain and Ireland*, 13 (1883), pp. 185–98.

14 *'I dreamed … saw'*: Herbert Spencer, *Principles of Sociology*, vol. I (New York: D. Appleton & Co., 1883), p. 150, § 69.

15 ἐνύπνιον: Ancient Greek, 'dream, vision.'

16 *Wilson*: Wilson unknown.

17 *'Reflecting on these…and things'*: throughout these two paragraphs Lang is quoting from Tylor, *Primitive Culture*, vol. 1, p. 387.

18 le premier … coûte: French, literally, 'the first step that counts.' The full French proverb is 'Il n'y a que le premier pas qui coûte'.

19 *'that which … dead one'*: Tylor, *Primitive Culture*, vol. 1, p. 387.

20 *'animated'*: 'First and foremost among the causes which transfigure in myths the facts of daily experience, is the belief in the animation of all nature, rising at its highest pitch to personification', ibid., p. 258.

21 *'chairs, sticks … childish stage'*: ibid.

22 *'those … visions'*: Lang is referring back to quotes from Tylor used earlier on p. 180–1, from *Primitive Culture*, vol. 1, p. 387.

23 *'The condition … unaccustomed noise'*: ibid., p. 403.

24 *Lord Tennyson*: an account of this is given in Hallam Tennyson, *Alfred Lord Tennyson: A Memoir by His Son*, 2 vols (London: Macmillan, 1897), vol. I, p. 72–3.

25 *'morbid … disease'*: Tylor, *Primitive Culture*, vol. 1, p. 277.

26 *Further … least:* Lang here refers to Tylor's argument at pp. 276–84 in the first edition (1871). In this section Tylor gives numerous accounts of the workings of what he calls 'mythic fancy'.

27 *'where … fancies'*: Tylor, *Primitive Culture*, vol. 1, p. 284.

28 enfantosmé: Old French, 'to be terrified by phantoms'.

29 *Balaam's ass … are 'classical' instances*: the story of Balaam's ass is given in Numbers 22:21–38. In book 16 of the *Odyssey*, Athene appears to Odysseus and the dogs cower and whine, but it is Telemachus, not Eumaeus, who is unable to see her.

30 *[unconditioned, clairvoyant]*: the brackets and contents are Lang's.

31 *We may just allude … than ours*: Lang has a full discussion of Hegel's theories of what Lang calls the 'X region' in chapter 2 of *The Making of Religion*, 'Science and "Miracles"', see this volume, pp. 271–83.

32 *M. Taine*: Hippolyte Adolphe Taine (1828–93) was an influential French historian and literary critic. His *De l'intelligence* was published in 1870.

33 *'This fully conscious … type'*: in the previous chapter of *The Making of Religion*, 'Science and "Miracles"' (see this volume, pp. 271–83), Lang has a longer discussion of Dessoir's ideas. The quote is from Dessoir, *Das Doppel Ich* (1890), using the translations from Frederic Myer's discussion of Dessoir in 'Das Doppel Ich', *Proceedings of the Society for Psychical Research* 6 (1889–90), pp. 207–15.

34 *' … psychical existence'*: Lang cites Balfour's work in the footnote here. A. J. Balfour was President of the SPR in 1893. His address appeared in *Proceedings of the Society for Psychical Research*, 10:26 (1894), pp. 2–13.

35 *foster-mother of John Tanner … game*: John Tanner (*c.*1780–*c.*1846) was captured by Shawnee Indians when he was 10 and grew up among the Ojibwa. He published *A Narrative of the Captivity and Adventures of John Tanner* (New York: G. & C. & H. Carvill, 1830).

36 ceteris paribus: Latin, 'all other things being equal'.

37 *his thoughts on animism*: the first edition has 'religion' rather than 'animism'.

38 *'it is not … live'*: Tylor, *Primitive Culture* , vol. 1, p. 390. The emphasis is Lang's.

39 *Manes*: in the religion of ancient Rome, the Manes are deities of the underworld which represent the souls of the dead.

40 nihil in intellectu quod non prius in sensu: Latin, 'Nothing is in the intellect that was not first in the senses', used by Thomas Aquinas, taken from the Peripatetic school of Greek philosophy.

41 ce qu'un vain peuple pense: French, from Voltaire's first play, Oedipe, first performed in 1718. The full line is 'Nos prêtres ne sont point ce qu'un vain peuple pense; / Notre credulité fait toute leur science' (The priests are not what we take them to be; / Their knowledge lies in our credulity).

42 in rerum natura: Latin, 'In the nature of things.'

43 X region to investigate: in the previous chapter in The Making of Religion, 'Science and "Miracles"' (see this volume, pp. 271–83), Lang charts the history of the investigation of the X region, that is, where science and the supernatural meet.

44 He says: ... kind : this is Lang's translation. The original reads: 'Il existe chez certaines personnes, à certains moments, une faculté de connaissance qui n'a pas de rapport avec nos facultés de connaissance normales', Charles Richet, 'Relation de diverses expériences sur la transmission mentale, la lucidité, et autres phénomènes non explicables par les données scientifiques actuelles', Proceedings of the Society for Psychical Research 5 (1888–9), p. 167, emphasis in original.

'On Religion', from The Making of Religion, 2nd edition (1900)

1   'Having got ... Idea of God?': Lang here glosses the theories of both Herbert Spencer and E. B. Tylor on the origin of religion. He deals more directly with these theories in 'Anthropology and Religion I', see this volume, pp. 177–88.

2   'From the notion ... know no God': Everard E. Im Thurn, 'On the Animism of the Indians of British Guiana', Journal of the Anthropological Institute of Great Britain and Ireland II (1882), pp. 360–82.

3   'The lowest ... human mind': the reference here should be John Payne, A History of the New World Called America, vol. I (Oxford: Clarendon and New York: Macmillan, 1892), p. 431, n. 4.

4   toto caelo: Latin, 'by the whole extent of the heavens', that is, 'totally, entirely'.

5   Mr. Payne here differs ... Lubbock: Georg Gustav Roskoff (1814–89), Austrian theologian. His History of the Devil (1869) traces the idea of the devil and of the concept of dualism from earlier human times on. Sir John Lubbock (1834–1913), Liberal politician who contributed to the new disciplines of anthropology and archaeology. In Prehistoric Times (1865), an incredibly influential work, and in Origin of Civilisation and the Primitive Condition of Man (1870), Lubbock suggested evidence for the existence of tribes, both in the past and contemporary, without any religion. Roskoff's Religionswesen der rohestern Naturvölker (1880) disputes Lubbock's theory based on the same evidence. Lang discusses this dispute in later editions of Myth, Ritual and Religion, vol. 2.

6   'the conception ... primitive logic': the reference should be to Payne, A History of the New World, vol. I, p. 509.

7   the germ of such a god or being: 'the existence of such a god or being' in the first edition.

8   always obscured: 'often obscured' in first edition.

9   undying: 'eternal' in first edition.

10 *(or ghost)*: the words in parentheses were added in the second edition.

11 *'alliance … lower creeds'*: E. B. Tylor, *Primitive Culture: Researches into the Development of Mythology, Philosophy, Religion, Art and Custom*, 2 vols (London: John Murray, 1871), vol. 2, p. 327.

12 *'among the Australian … of ethics'*: T. H. Huxley, 'The Evolution of Theology: An Anthropological Study' (1886), in *Science and the Hebrew Tradition: Essays*, London: Methuen, 1893, pp. 346–7.

13 *Manes*: see this volume, p. 404, n. 39.

14 *Anima Mundi*: Latin, 'world soul'.

15 *'loom vast … race of men'*: Tylor, *Primitive Culture*, vol. II, p. 305. The original reads 'looming vast'.

16 *Dr. Brinton*: Daniel G. Brinton, *Myths of the New World: A Treatise on the Symbolism and Mythology of the Red Race of America* (New York: Leypoldt and Holt, London: Trübner & Co., 1868). Emphasis in following quote is Lang's.

17 *'and in the … of a man'*: Rev. Robert Henry Codrington, 'Religious Beliefs and Practices in Melanesia', *Journal of the Anthropological Institute of Great Britain and Ireland*, 10 (1881), pp. 261–315, quote from p. 267. Emphasis is Lang's.

18 *'Intelligent men … says Livingstone*: David Livingstone (1817–73) was a medical missionary with the London Missionary Society and an explorer of Africa. The actual quote is 'On questioning intelligent men among the Bakwains as to their former knowledge of good and evil, of God, and the future state, they have scouted the idea of any of them ever having been without a tolerably clear conception on all these subjects. Respecting their sense of right and wrong, they profess that nothing we indicate as sin ever appeared to them as otherwise, except the statement that it was wrong to have more wives than one', David Livingstone, *Missionary Travels and Researches in South Africa* (London: John Murray, 1857), p. 158.

19 *'they are direct … revelation'*: Tylor, *Primitive Culture*, vol. 2, p. 323.

20 *their nascent ethics*: this was given as 'their ethical factors' in the first edition.

21 *'the degeneration … religion'*: Tylor, *Primitive Culture*, vol. 2, p. 305.

22 *Dampier*: William Dampier (1651–1751), privateer and explorer. He was the first Englishman to explore parts of Australia, and the first person to circumnavigate the globe three times. He published numerous books about his voyages, and was pilot of the ship which rescued the shipwrecked Alexander Selkirk, upon whom the narrator of Defoe's *Robinson Crusoe* (1719) was based, in 1709. The year is presumably an unhappy one for Lang as it saw the end of the Stuart monarchy in the 'Glorious Revolution'.

23 *'the miserablest people … open air'*: the phrase which opens this quote, from William Dampier, *A New Voyage Round the World*, (1697), has become notorious as an example of colonial discourse; William Dampier, *A New Voyage Round the World* (London: The Argonaut Press, 1927), p. 312.

24 *'in its simplest … of ethics'*: Huxley, 'The Evolution of Theology,' p. 346.

25 *[…]*: in the deleted section Lang uses examples of the existence of Australian religion taken from A. W. Howitt, 'On Some Australian Beliefs', *Journal of the Anthropological Institute of Great Britain and Ireland* 13 (1884), pp. 185–98.

26 *Mr. Howitt … Kurnai*: A. W. Howitt, 'The Jeraeil, or Initiation Ceremonies of the Kurnai Tribe', *Journal of the Anthropological Institute of Great Britain and Ireland* 14 (1885), pp. 301–28.

27 *1. To listen to … by the old men*: in the first edition Lang annotated this list to show the parallels between these precepts and various aspects of Hebraic law as given in the Old Testament.

28 *'I venture to assert … sanction'*: A. W. Howitt, 'On Some Australian Ceremonies of Initiation', *Journal of the Anthropological Institute of Great Britain and Ireland* 13 (1884), pp. 432–59.

29 *Mr. Brough Smyth*: Robert Brough Smyth (1830–99), geologist and goldminer in Australia. His *The Aborigines of Victoria: With Notes Relating to the Habits of the Natives of Other Parts of Australia and Tasmania* was published in 1878.

30 *'Ecclesiastical Institutions'*: Herbert Spencer, *Ecclesiastical Institutions, Part VI of The Principles of Sociology* (Edinburgh and London: Williams and Norgate, 1885).

31 *'the partial … doctrines'*: Tylor, *Primitive Culture*, vol. 2, p. 408.

32 *If the God is … a spirit is he*: this sentence was added in the 1900 edition. The first edition has instead a quote on the Gippsland tribes as having 'no knowledge of God … They believe the Creator was a gigantic black, living among the stars' quoting Edward M. Curr, *The Australian Race*, 4 vols (London: Trübner and Co., 1886–7).

33 *Mr. Matthew Arnold … living in the sky'*: Matthew Arnold (1822–88), British poet and critic. His *Culture and Anarchy* (1869) coined the term 'Philistine' to refer to the English middle class. Arnold lectured on poetry at Oxford while Lang was an undergraduate there.

34 ὑπὲρ μόρον: Ancient Greek, 'beyond/above fate.'

35 *Mr. Tylor gives a list:* Tylor, *Primitive Culture*, vol. 2, pp. 282–7.

36 *'Ancestors … been human'*: F. B. Jevons, *An Introduction to the History of Religion* (London: Methuen, New York: Macmillan, 1896). The emphasis is Lang's.

37 *'The common … among men'*: William Robertson Smith, *The Prophets of Israel and Their Place in History* (Edinburgh: A & C Black, 1882); the words in square brackets have been inserted by Lang.

38 *as spectral as Bathybius*: in 1868, after studying samples taken from the Atlantic seabed, T. H. Huxley believed that he had discovered an actual example of the until then hypothetical primordial matter, the protoplasm from which all organic life had evolved. Huxley named the substance *bathybius haeckelii*, after Ernst Haeckel. In the second half of the 1870s Huxley realised that he had been mistaken, and that the substance was in fact the product of a chemical reaction between the sample and the alcohol in which it was preserved. Huxley published his recantation in *Nature*.

39 *Lucian and Qing say*: Lucian of Samosata (*c.*125 CE–*c.*180 CE) was a rhetorician and satirist who wrote in Greek. Qing was a San ('Bushman') hunter, the informant of the anthropologist Joseph Millerd Orpen (1828–1923). Orpen believed Qing to be the last of his people, and recorded his beliefs and mythology. Lang detailed the beliefs of both in *Myth, Ritual and Religion*, vol.1.

40 *I would … and consolation*: the reference is to Christian Augustus Lobeck, *Aglaophamus* (Königsberg: Borntraeger, 1829).

41 *or Mungan-ngaur:* the name Darumulun was used in the place of Mungan-ngaur in the first edition.

42 nominis umbra: 'the shadow of a name.'

43 *As Mr. Robertson Smith says:* William Robertson Smith, *Lectures on the Religion of the Semites, First Series, The Fundamental Institutions* (Edinburgh: A & C Black, 1889). Lang's footnote reverses the order of the page numbers. The first quotation is from p. 105 and the second from p. 104.

44 *the King of Israel, he:* Lang has taken out a clause from the original, which reads: 'as the King of Israel, the supreme director of national policy, he necessarily …'.

45 *Major Ellis proves … our minds:* Colonel Alfred Burdon Ellis (1852–94), see this volume, p. 409, n. 17.

46 *'the gods … alone':* Alfred Burdon Ellis, *A History of the Tshi-Speaking Peoples of the Gold Coast of West Africa* (London: Chapman and Hall, 1887), p. 115.

47 *To us Milton seems:* John Milton (1608–74), English poet, author of *Paradise Lost* (1667).

48 *Of Zeus … sway':* Lang's page number for the quotation is incorrect. It is pp. 73–4 in both first and second editions.

'Science and Superstition', *Magic and Religion* (1901)

1 *a pro-Boer:* the Second Boer War (1899–1902) was taking place at the time of writing.

2 *In the long run … to herself:* the 'evolution' from magic to religion to science, sketched out by Lang here, is the theory put forward by Sir James Frazer in *The Golden Bough*. Frazer published the first edition in 1890, and by 1915 it had reached twelve volumes. The second edition of *The Golden Bough*, made up of three volumes, was published in 1900. An abridged version was published in 1922. Frazer argued that religion originated in the developing sense that magical thinking is a fallacy and that, as magic failed, people transferred an idea of power from their own control over the natural world to that of an exterior, supernatural being.

3 *in each instance:* Lang's private opinion of Frazer's 'scientific' method is given in an undated letter to E. B. Tylor, where he concludes that 'History is a more exact science than anthropology, as illustrated in the G.B.' See Tylor Papers, Pitt Rivers Museum Manuscript Collection, Box 13, Lang 23.

4 *Not only must she not … is useless:* in his *Novum Organum* (1620), Francis Bacon (1561–1626), the British philosopher and scientist, set out his inductive method of science against the methods used by the ancients. In the experimental, inductive method, the existence of facts or events which contradict an hypothesis or theory have to be acknowledged and tested and, if necessary, the hypothesis or theory must be abandoned. Bacon's '*instantia contradictoria*' is the fact, experience or event which contradicts what has been experienced to that point, and so necessitates a revision of existing theories and laws.

5 *the arkite system of Bryant:* Jacob Bryant (1715–1804) was an early scholar of myth. His *A New System or Analysis of Ancient Mythology* (1774–6) attempted to link the mythologies of the world to the stories recorded in Genesis. William Blake worked as engraver on the *A New System* and was influenced by Bryant's ideas.

6   autant en emporte le vent: French, 'gone with the wind'.

7   *'vapid vegetable loves'*: from 'The Talking Oak' (written 1837–8) by Alfred, Lord
     Tennyson in *Poems*, 2 vols (London: Edward Moxan, 1842), vol. 2, p. 75.

8   *The world of modern readers … occasional attention*: Lang here alludes first to the theories
     of Friedrich Max Müller and then to those of James Frazer. Theories of the existence
     and meaning of totems originated in the work of John McLennan in a series of articles
     entitled 'The Worship of Animals and Plants' published in the *Fortnightly Review*
     (October and November 1869, February 1870) and was continued by William
     Robertson Smith in *Lectures on the Religion of the Semites* (Edinburgh: Adam and
     Charles Black, 1889), and in Baldwin Spencer and F. J. Gillen's *The Native Tribes of
     Central Australia* (London: Macmillan,1899).

9   *the book was reviewed*: E. B. Tylor gave Spencer's work a favourable review in *Mind*. See
     Tylor, 'Mr. Spencer's *Principles of Sociology*', *Mind* 2:6 (April 1877), pp. 141–56.

10   *of the learned*: James Frazer, *The Golden Bough: A Study in Magic and Religion*, 2nd
     edition, 3 vols (London: Macmillan, 1900), vol. I, p. xxi.

11   *society is built*: ibid., pp. xxi–xxii.

12   *stress of life*: ibid., p. xxii.

13   *begun to speak*: ibid.

14   *the so-called 'Higher Criticism'*: Higher Criticism refers to the application to the Bible of
     scholarly methods used to interpret Classical literary works. The Higher Criticism
     began in Germany in the eighteenth century. Its wider dissemination in Britain in the
     nineteenth century through the translations of the work of scholars such as David
     Friedrich Strauss (1808–74) and Ludwig Feuerbach (1804–72) challenged the belief of
     many in the literal truth of the Bible. The phrase was also more widely used to mean
     critical work carried out in the same fashion of testing historical veracity.

15   *'call … prayer to him'*: E. B. Tylor, *Primitive Culture: Researches into the Development of
     Mythology, Philosophy, Religion, Art, and Custom*, 2 vols (London: John Murray, 1871),
     vol. 2, p. 309.

16   *'no method or form of prayer to him'*: Tylor's words are actually, as Lang quotes above, 'any
     form or method of prayer to him'.

17   *Miss Kingsley, and Sir A. B. Ellis*: Mary Kingsley (1862–1900) was an explorer and
     ethnographer of West Africa. Her *Travels in West Africa* (1897) and *West African Studies*
     (1899) had great influence on end-of-century views of Africa. She was the niece of the
     novelist Charles Kingsley. Colonel Alfred Burdon Ellis (1852–94), officer in the 1st
     West India Regiment, who wrote a number of anthropological works in the 1880s and
     1890s, including *The Land of the Fetish* (1883), *A History of the Tshi-Speaking Peoples of
     the Gold Coast of West Africa* (1887) and *The Yoruba-speaking Peoples of the Slave Coast of
     West Africa: Their Religion, Manners, Customs, Laws, Language, Etc. With an Appendix
     Containing a Comparison of the Tshi, Gã, Ew e, and Yoruba Languages* (1894).

18   *in the report*: Friedrich Max Müller, *Lectures on the Origin and Growth of Religion
     As Illustrated in the Religions of India*, Lectures delivered April–June 1878 (London:
     Longmans, Green and Co., 1878), p. 16. Müller used it as an example of a religion
     without any form of external worship.

19 *'a disease of language'*: the work of Friedrich Max Müller argued that myths were the result of a degenerated language. See 'Cupid, Psyche and the "Sun Frog"', pp. 66–77 and 'Household Tales', pp. 88–121, this volume.

20 *est-il … Suprême!*: French, 'Is he annoying with his Supreme Being!'

21 *Or science … test it again*: this is recounted in chapter 1 of *Don Quixote* (1605) by Miguel de Cervantes.

'First-Fruits and Taboos', *Magic and Religion* (1901)

1 *the Seventh Commandment*: Thou shalt not commit adultery.

2 *But the reasons why … lack of a manifest reason why*: the Ord is a coastal headland between Sutherland and Caithness in the Scottish Highlands. A superstition suggested that it would be fatal for a Sinclair to cross the Ord in green on a Monday, and is believed by some to originate in the battle of Flodden, between England and Scotland, in 1513, when a whole band of Sinclairs were killed. The source of the fishermen's practices has not been found, but in legend St Andrews is the resting place of the apostle St Andrew, the patron saint of Scotland, and originally a fisherman, so the ground is a fertile one for superstition.

3 *decalogue*: another name for the Ten Commandments of Moses which appear in the books of Exodus and Deuteronomy.

4 *'It is not, therefore, surprising … natural'*: F. B. Jevons, *An Introduction to the History of Religion* (London: Methuen, New York: Macmillan, 1896).

5 *but tradition indicates … social influence*: Lang takes the examples here from Baldwin Spencer and F. J. Gillen, *The Native Tribes of Central Australia* (London: Macmillan, 1899).

6 *Mr. Jevons next argues*: Jevons, *An Introduction to the History of Religion*, p. 85.

7 *Gibbon's ancestor, Blue Gown herald*: John Gibbon was an expert on heraldry in the seventeenth century, in which he apparently became interested when he saw body paint used by Native Americans in the colony of Virginia in 1659. In 1668 he became the Bluemantle Pursuivant-at-Arms for the College of Arms in London until his death in 1719. The relation of the historian Edward Gibbon (1737–94) to John Gibbon is disputed.

8 *Thus Mr. Jevons mentions*: Jevons, *An Introduction to the History of Religion*, p. 83.

9 *as Mr. Manning writes*: Frederick Edward Manning (1812–83), an early settler in New Zealand who wrote two books, *Old New Zealand* and *History of the War in the North of New Zealand*, under the pseudonym 'a Pakeha Maori'. He was very knowledgeable about Maori language, customs and beliefs. The quote is from *Old New Zealand By A Pakeha Maori* (London: Smith, Elder & Co., 1863), pp. 111–12. Manning attributes this saying to 'irreverent pakehas'.

10 *that Mrs. Harris of philosophy*: in *Martin Chuzzlewitt* (1843–4) by Charles Dickens, the bibulous and lazy nurse Mrs Gamp constantly refers to conversations with and the opinions of a Mrs Harris in order to justify herself. Mrs Harris is in fact a figment of her imagination.

11   *and so Dr. Johnson and I*: Samuel Johnson's superstitious behavior is described in James Boswell, *Life of Samuel Johnson* (1791) (Oxford: Oxford University Press, 1970), pp. 342–3.

12   *Radical voters for the Border Boroughs*: the Radicals constituted a parliamentary political grouping from the late eighteenth to the mid-nineteenth century. Radicals opposed the power of the traditional elites in the United Kingdom (represented in Parliament by the Tory party), and supported the extension of the franchise, free trade and the extension of individual rights more generally. In 1859 Radicals joined with the Whigs to form the Liberal Party. In the nineteenth century a borough was the name of an urban area (as opposed to the rural counties) that voted individuals into the House of Commons. The number of people eligible to vote in each varied very widely, depending on the kind of borough, and in some no voting took place at all. Such inequality and lack of real representation was challenged by Radicals throughout the century. In Scotland following the Act of Union in 1707 members were elected on the same model, but in very many countries and boroughs (or burghs) very few people could vote and the nomination and election of an individual was in the gift of the local landowner. Scottish representation was considered particularly corrupt during the period. The Border area (between England and Scotland) had been notorious as an area of political conflict and tension for centuries.

13   *Gask tabooed the corn of his tenants*: the Oliphants of Gask, in Perthshire, were staunch Jabobites, and fought with Prince Charles Edward Stuart at Culloden.

14   *Messrs. Spencer and Gillen say*: Spencer and Gillen, *Native Tribes of Central Australia*, p. 168.

15   *'After writing…needful restrictions'*: R.L Stevenson, *In the South Seas, The Works of Robert Louis Stevenson, Edinburgh Edition,* vol. 20, ed. Sidney Colvin (Edinburgh: Constable, 1896).

'Australian Problems', *Anthropological Essays Presented to Edward Burnett Tylor in Honour of his 75th Birthday* (1907)

1   *permitted Messrs. Spencer and Gillen*: Baldwin Spencer and F. J. Gillen, *The Native Tribes of Central Australia* (London: Macmillan, 1899).

2   [footnote] *conception and birth*: Lang's footnote here is misleading. The work referred to is Spencer and Gillen's *Native Tribes of Central Australia*.

3   *For example … for him'*: Lang's references to his quotes and examples here are to A. Howitt, 'Notes on the Australian Class System', *Journal of the Anthropological Institute of Great Britain and Ireland*, 12 (1882), pp. 496–512 and to Baldwin Spencer and F. J. Gillen, *Native Tribes of South-East Australia* (London: Macmillan, 1904).

4   forma formans: Latin, 'the forming figure/shape'.

5   *except M. Van Gennep*: Arnold van Gennep, *Mythes et Légendes d'Australie: Études D'Ethnologie et de Sociologie* (Paris: E. Guilmoto, 1906).

5 ANTHROPOLOGY AND PSYCHICAL RESEARCH

'The Comparative Study of Ghost Stories', *Nineteenth Century* (1885)

1 σκιά… εἴδωλον: Ancient Greek, 'shadow, darkness, ghost' and 'image, phantom, vision, idol.'

2 *Mr. Herbert Spencer…and of death*: see 'Anthropology and Religion I', this volume, pp. 177–88, where Lang both sets out and critiques the theories of Herbert Spencer and E. B. Tylor on the origins of religion.

3 *'And Achilles … it seemed'*: Lang is quoting his own translation; *The Iliad of Homer*, translated by Andrew Lang, Walter Leaf and Ernest Myers (London: Macmillan, 1883).

4 *Mr. Sludge, or of the esoteric Buddhists*: Mr. Sludge is the narrator, and fraudulent medium, of Browning's poem 'Mr Sludge, "the Medium"' (1864). By 'esoteric Buddhists', Lang means Theosophists. Theosophy was founded in 1875 by Mme Helena Blavatsky, and combined elements of spiritualism with an eclectic range of practices and beliefs from Hinduism and Buddhism.

5 *the Society for Psychical Research*: the SPR was founded in 1882 by a group consisting of scientists, spiritualists and Cambridge academics. Very soon many of the spiritualists left, offended at the scepticism inherent in the Society's pronouncements and practices. The Society carried out experiments, using what they believed to be scientific methods, to investigate occult and spiritualist phenomena and published them in their *Journal* and *Proceedings*. Lang published numerous articles in the *Proceedings*, although often in his journalism he critiques the SPR's methods and assumptions. He joined the Society, however, in 1904, and was President in 1911.

6 *William Tell myth*: William Tell is a folk hero of Switzerland. There are various versions of the legend, but the main elements are that in the early fourteenth century Tell, an expert with the crossbow, outwitted the representative of the hated Habsburg oppressors, Gessler, by shooting an apple off the head of his own young son. His actions led to his killing of Gessler, and to an uprising that eventually led to the freeing of Switzerland.

7 *'Suppose a wild North American Indian … his recognised system of nature'*: E. B. Tylor, *Primitive Culture: Researches into the Development of Mythology, Philosophy, Religion, Art and Custom*, 2 vols (London: John Murray, 1871), vol. 1, p. 156.

8 *'At length … at their departure'*: Lorimer Fison and A. W. Howitt, *Kamilaroi and Kurnai: Group-Marriage and Relationship, and Marriage by Elopement* (Melbourne, Sydney, Adelaide and Brisbane: George Robertson, 1880).

9 *the author of Old New Zealand…'manifested' rarely*: Frederick Manning, *Old New Zealand by a Pakeha Maori* (London: Smith, Elder & Co., 1863). Manning gives an account of this in chapter 10, pp. 143ff.

10 *'modern spiritualism to be … and peasant folklore'*: Tylor, *Primitive Culture*, vol. 1, p. 129.

11 *Thus Baronius … life is true*: Cesare Baronius (1538–1607) was a Cardinal and an ecclesiastical historian. His *Annales Ecclesiastici* appeared in twelve volumes between 1588 and 1607. This story was often cited in accounts of contact with the dead quoted from or written in the second half of the nineteenth century, as in for example Increase Mather's *Remarkable Providences* (1684; London: John Russell, 1856).

12 *Lord Brougham …*: Henry Peter Brougham (1778–1868), 1st Baron Brougham and Vaux, was a Scottish lawyer and statesman who was Lord Chancellor between 1830 and 1834.

His sighting of a friend at the moment of the latter's death a long way off is recounted by Lang in the preface to the first edition of *Cock Lane and Common Sense* (London: Longmans, Green and Co., 1894) and in chapter 5 of *The Book of Dreams and Ghosts* (London: Longmans, Green and Co., 1897).

13 *Fitzroy's*: Robert FitzRoy (1805–65) was a sea caption and meteorologist, captain of the *Beagle* during the voyage of Charles Darwin. He was the governor of New Zealand 1843–5.

14 *While at sea … previously*: Robert FitzRoy, *Narrative of the Surveying Voyages of HMS Adventure and Beagle*, 4 vols (London: Henry Colburn, 1839), vol. 2, p. 181. Benjamin Bynoe was the assistant surgeon of *The Beagle*. As well as the spelling of Bynoe's name, Lang also gets the year wrong in the first line of the quote; it is given as 1832 in the original.

15 *Mr. C.J. Du Vé … for him:* Fison and Howitt, *Kamilaroi and Kurnai*, p. 247.

16 *'I could give … the very day'*: ibid.

17 *A civilized example … the very day'*: Henry More (1614–1687) was an English philosopher and one of the Cambridge Platonists. He was in the circle of Lady Conway, whose Ragley became a centre of mystical thaumaturgists. More is believed to have edited, and certainly contributed to, Joseph Glanvill's *Saducismus Triumphatus* (1681), which is often referred to by Lang. Neither Dr Symonds nor his *Remains* could be traced.

18 *'generally have … death of a relation'*: Henry Rink, *Tales and Traditions of the Eskimo* (Edinburgh and London: William Blackwood, 1875). The section in the original reads: 'they generally have the appearance of a fire or a bright light; and to see them is in every case very dangerous, partly by causing *tatamingnek* – viz. frightening to death – partly as foreshadowing the death of a relative.' The emphasis is Lang's.

19 *'Father, surely … possess Olympus'*: this is, more or less, taken from the prose translation of the *Odyssey* Lang did with S. H. Butcher for the Harvard Classics Series in 1879.

20 *'Seemed all on fire … iron panoply*: these lines are from 'Rosabelle', in *The Lay of the Last Minstrel* by Sir Walter Scott (1805).

21 *Readers of the* Philopseudes *of Lucian*: Lucian (*c.* 125 CE–after 180 CE) was an Assyrian rhetoritician and satirist from Samosata. His *Philopseudes sive Incredulus* (The Lover of Lies, or the Doubter) is a collection of tall tales, including that of the Sorcerer's Apprentice.

'Superstition and Fact', *Contemporary Review* (1893)

1 *A Remark of M. Richet*: it is possible that Lang is here referring to Charles Richet's *L'homme et l'intelligence: fragments de physiologie et de psychologie* (Paris: F. Alcan, 1884), in chapter 4 of which, titled 'Le Somnambulisme provoqué', Richet discusses the credibility of such phenomena. However, see note 2 below.

2 *'If the phenomena … records of science'*: this sentence does not appear in the source suggested in note 1 above. However, Richet does make a similar claim in this source: '… il est déraisonnable de supposer partout et toujours le fraude et la fourberie. L'identié des phénomènes observes en divers pay et à diverses époques, et

l'impossibilité de certaines simulations rendent absurd l'hypothèse d'une mystification prolongé et universelle', *L'homme et l'intelligence*, p. 257.

3   *an article on 'Comparative Psychical Research'*: 'Comparative Psychical Research' also appears in *Cock Lane and Common Sense* (London: Longmans, Green and Co., 1894).

4   *Puységur … and others*: Lang here lists those foremost in the conceptualisation of mesmerism and hypnotism during the eighteenth and nineteenth centuries.

5   *Hence Mr. Tylor derives … distance from him*: Lang is here quoting from and closely paraphrasing E. B. Tylor, *Primitive Culture Researches into the Development of Mythology, Philosophy, Religion, Art and Custom*, 2 vols (London: John Murray, 1871), vol. 1, p. 428.

6   *If Jung Stilling … visible to himself*: Tylor, *Primitive Culture*, vol. 1, p. 397. Lang's footnote suggests that the story of the French doctor about a nurse who could 'send' is to be found in volume 8 of the *Proceedings of the Society for Psychical Research*. No such anecdote can be found in the volume, although many anecdotes of the same type are reproduced in F. W. H Myers, 'On Indications of Continuted Terrene Knowledge on the Part of Phantasms of the Dead', *Proceedings of the Society for Psychical Research* 8 (1892), pp. 170–252. For Jung-Stilling se p. 417, n. 23.

7   *St. Augustine is well known*: Tylor also quotes St. Augustine's story, *Primitive Culture*, vol. 1, p. 398.

8   *'fit perfectly … apparitions'*: Tylor, *Primitive Culture*, vol. 1, p. 404.

9   *'assumed … another person'*: Herbert Mayo, *On The Truth Contained in Popular Superstitions: With an Account of Mesmerism* (Edinburgh: Blackwood, 1st and 2nd editions, 1851). In the original the sentence is: 'And I shall assume it to be proved by the above crucial instance that the mind, or soul, of one human being can be brought, in the natural course of things, and under physiological laws hereafter to be determined, into immediate relation with the mind of another living person.'

10   *'Suppose our new … sensorial illusion'*: Mayo, *On The Truths Contained*, p. 67.

11   *Mayo says that his … light bodies!'*: ibid., p. 69.

12   raffinés: French, to be refined or sophisticated.

13   *as by Fitzjames O'Brien*: Fitz-James (sometimes Fitz James) O'Brien (1828–62) was an Irish-American writer. Some of his work is considered an important forerunner to the genre of science fiction.

14   sans le savoir!: French, 'unknowingly'.

15   *It is a matter … heard of A*: Tylor, *Primitive Culture*, vol. 1, pp. 8–9.

16   *'How distant … farther showings …'*: ibid., p. 9. The emphasis is Lang's.

17   *says Mr. Tylor*: *Primitive Culture*, vol. 1, p. 406.

18   *'the patient discerns … distance'*: Mayo, *On The Truths Contained*, p. 105. The original uses commas rather than dashes.

19   *[…]*: Lang gives numerous examples of clairvoyance, including that of Eskimo mediums known as Angakut.

20   *'suffer from … affections'*: Tylor, *Primitive Culture*, vol. 2, p. 119: 'The cases in which disease-possession passes into oracle-possession are especially connected with hysterical, convulsive, and epileptic affections.'

21 *clung to royalty … in Italy*: the belief that the monarchs of England and France had the 'royal touch' – that their touch could cure – began in around the eleventh century. From the sixteenth century on, the touch was believed to cure only tuberculous cervical lymphadenitis, known as scrofula. In England the practice climaxed with Charles II, and was discontinued by George I. Charles III (1716–88) ruled parts of Italy before ascending the Spanish throne in 1759, but evidence of his using the 'touch' could not be found. Lang repeats this information in his introduction to Kirk's *The Secret Commonwealth* (1893).

22 *coal ball of Kelly and Dr. Dee*: Sir Edward Kelly (1555–97) claimed to be a spirit medium, and to be able to communicate with spirits and angels via a reflective 'shew-stone'. He worked with John Dee (1527–1608), the mathematician, astronomer, alchemist and occultist, and Lang is probably referring to Dee's mirror, made from polished obsidian, and held by the British Museum.

'Preface to the Second Edition', *Cock Lane and Common Sense,* 2nd edition (1895)

1 *the Folklore Society*: the Folklore Society was established in 1878 to study traditional culture in all its varieties. Lang was involved in the foundation of the Society.

2 *Mr. Gurney … Miss X*: Edmund Gurney wrote on witchcraft in 'Note on Witchcraft', *Phantasms of the Living*, vol. I (1886). Frederic Myers wrote on classical oracles in relation to psychical research in 'Greek Oracles', in *Essays: Classical* (1883). Miss X. was Ada Goodrich Freer, as Lang acknowledges in his essay 'Magic Mirrors and Crystal Gazing' in the *Monthly Review* (see this volume, pp. 292–9).

3 humani nihil a se alienum: Latin, 'Nothing that is human is alien to me.'

4 laisse a désirer: French, the 'a' should have a grave accent, 'leaves something to be desired'.

5 *Many continental savants … hold water*: Lang is here referring to the case of Eusapia Palladino, the Italian physical medium who was investigated and tested by numerous scientists and psychical researchers in the late nineteenth and early twentieth centuries.

6 *Mr. J. W. Maskelyne*: Lang means J. N. Maskelyne. For more on Lang's relation with Maskelyne, see his letters to Oliver Lodge, this volume, pp. 314–27, and also pp. 255–6.

'Anthropology and Religion' II, *The Making of Religion,* 2nd edition (1900)

1 *The British Association*: the British Association for the Advancement of Science (BAAS) first met in 1831 with the aim of improving the practice, organisation and reputation of science in the United Kingdom. It held an annual meeting in different cities around the country and promoted relations with scientists abroad. It was important in promoting too the publication of scientific literature.

2 ondoyant et divers: this phrase was used by Montaigne – it literally means 'wavelike and varying' – to indicate the importance of inconsistency in human character.

3 *Arkite doctrines*: see 'Science and Superstition', this volume, p. 408, n. 5.

4 *Esoteric Buddhists:* see this volume, p. 412, n. 4.

5   *The acceptance…human culture*: see this volume, pp. 57–8.

6   *Goguet … Voltaire*: Antoine Yves Goguet (1716–58), Charles de Brosses (1709–77),
     possibly John Millar (1735–1801), Bernard le Bovier de Fontenelle (1657–1757),
     Joseph-Francois Lafitau (1681–1746), Nicolas Antoine Boulanger (1722–59), Voltaire
     (François-Marie Arouet) (1694–1778).

7   *Amoretti … Gregory*: Carlo Amoretti (1741–1816), Herbert Mayo (1796–1852), William
     Gregory (1803–58).

8   *Lubbock … and Von Schrenck-Notzing*: Lang is listing early pioneers of a rigorous,
     methodical anthropology and comparing them with contemporary psychical
     researchers.

9   *Mr. Tylor … last century*: E. B. Tylor, *Primitive Culture* (London: John Murray, 1871),
     vol. 1, p. 8. John Millar (1735–1801) was the author of *The Origin of the Distinction of
     Ranks* (1771).

10   *If a mediaeval … in this way'*: both the examples and the quotes used in this sentence
     come from Tylor, *Primitive Culture*, vol. 1, pp. 8–9.

11   vix aut ne vix quidem: Latin, 'scarcely or not even scarcely credible'.

12   *Mr. A .J. Balfour*: Lang discusses the place of Balfour in this debate in 'Science and
     Demonology', *Illustrated London News* (see this volume, pp. 268–9).

13   *the three Holy Children*: Daniel 3:12–30 tells the story of three young Jews, Hananiah,
     Mishael and Azariah, taken into slavery by King Nebuchadnezzar of Babylon, and
     given new names, Shadrach, Meshach and Abed-nego. The king had them thrown into
     a fiery furnace when they would not bow down to a statue of him, but was astonished
     when the fire did not touch them. As a result he promoted the three, and praised their
     god.

14   ébauche: French, 'an outline or sketch'.

15   *as Mr. Tylor says*: Tylor, *Primitive Culture*, vol. 1, p. 130.

16   *Dr. Macculloch*: John MacCulloch (1773–1835) was a Scottish geologist. His *Description
     of the Western Islands of Scotland* was published in 1819.

17   *'a direct revival … folklore'*: Tylor, *Primitive Culture*, vol. 1, p. 130.

18   *Mr. Tylor… Kant*: for more by Lang on Kant and his investigation of Swedenborg, see
     'Science and "Miracles"', this volume, pp. 271–83.

19   *Thus Mr. William James … in Science'*: William James, *The Will to Believe and Other Essays
     In Popular Philosophy* (New York: Longmans, Green and Co., 1897).This volume
     includes the essay 'What Psychical Research Has Already Accomplished', to which
     James is alluding in the part of his preface quoted by Lang. The original reads:
     'Attracted to this study some years ago by my love of sportsmanlike fairplay in science,
     I have seen enough to convince me of its great importance, and I wish to gain for it
     what interest I can.'

20   *'spirit manifestations … questions'*: Tylor, *Primitive Culture*, vol. 1, p. 129.

21   *the logic of Hume*: For Lang's critique of Hume, see his 'Science and "Miracles"', this
     volume, pp.271–83.

22   *'A typical…affection'*: Tylor, *Primitive Culture*, vol. 1, p. 397.

23 *Jung-Stilling:* Heinrich Jung-Stilling (1740-1817), German writer and scientist, wrote *Theorie der Geisterkunde* in 1808, which was translated in 1884 by Samuel Jackson as *Theory of Pneumatology.*

24 *'modern Europe ... philosophy':* ibid. The original reads: 'Modern Europe has indeed kept closely enough to the lines of early philosophy, for such ideas to have little strangeness in our own time.'

---

6 PSYCHICAL RESEARCH

'Ghosts Up To Date', *Blackwood's Edinburgh Magazine* (January 1894)

1 *Nicolai's and 'Mrs A.'s':* the cases of Nicolai and Mrs A. are dealt with by Lang in more detail in *Cock Lane and Common Sense* (London: Longmans, Green and Co.,1894). Nicolai was Christoph Friedrich Nicolai (1733–1811), a German scholar and bookseller, who gave a paper recounting his experiences of hallucination in 1799. An English translation of this was published in 1803 ('A Memoir on the Appearance of Spectres or Phantoms Occasioned by Disease, with Psychological Remarks: Read by Nicolai to the Royal Society of Berlin, on the 28th February, 1799', *Journal of Natural Philosophy, Chemistry and the Arts* 6 (1803), pp. 162–79) and his case went on to become paradigmatic in nineteenth-century psychology.

2 *Ferrier and Hibbert:* John Ferrier, *An Essay Towards a Theory of Apparitions* (London: Cadell and Davies, 1813) and Samuel Hibbert, *Sketches of the Philosophy of Apparitions* (London: Whittaker, 1824).

3 *'Apparitions' in the 'Encyclopædia Britannica':* this first appeared in 1875, in the ninth edition of the *Encyclopædia.*

4 *of Dr Maudsely:* Henry Maudsley (1835–1918) was a leading British psychiatrist. He believed that insanity had purely physiological causes, and criticised attempts to cure it. Late in his life he was instrumental in founding the Maudsley Hospital in south London.

5 *'phantasms of the living':* See 'Human Personality After Death', see this volume, p. 427, n. 19.

6 *Mrs Besant has acquired:* Annie Besant (1847–1933) was a writer and politician. She became a Theosophist in the 1890s, and the president of the Theosophical Society in 1907.

7 *'Gin a body meet a body':* from a traditional song of which there are many versions, one of which is Robert Burns' 'Comin' Thro' the Rye' (1782).

8 *Esoteric Buddhists:* See p. 412, n. 4.

9 *Gillies ... Lockhart:* the apparition is recorded in R. P. Gillies, *Recollections of Sir Walter Scott* (London: James Fraser, 1837), pp. 171–2; John Gibson Lockhart, *The Life of Sir Walter Scott* (7 vols, 1837–8). Lockhart was Scott's son-in-law, and Lang wrote *The Life of J. G. Lockhart* (2 vols, 1897).

10 *à outrance:* French, 'to the utmost'.

11 *Mr. Edgeworth's:* F. Y. Edgeworth, 'The Calculus of Probabilities Applied to Psychical Research', *Proceedings of the Society for Psychical Research* 3 (1885), pp. 190–9.

12   *The* hypothesis ... *lowest point: Proceedings of the Society for Psychical Research* 6 (1889–90), contains Frederic Myers, 'On Recognised Apparitions Occurring More Than A Year After Death', pp. 13–65, and a number of reports and articles on *Phantasms of the Living* and the *Census of Hallucinations.*

13   *ghost of Sir Richard ... the pole*: Sir Richard Coldinghame appears in the ballad 'The Eve of St John' (1799) by Sir Walter Scott. He is killed by the Baron of Smaylho'me, and his ghost appears before the Baron's lady, causing her to fall in love with him. The Beresford ghost was a very well-known Irish ghost story, in which, after a pact is made between two teenagers in the late seventeenth century or early eighteenth century, one of them, Lord Tyrone, returned after his death to visit the other, Lady Beresford, and predicted various events of her life and the year of her death.

14   *like William Tell*: see this volume, p. 412, n. 6.

15   *nauseously dull*: see volume 2, p. 401, n. 16.

16   *Hamlet said ... the philosophy of Horatio: Hamlet,* act 1, scene 5, lines166–7: 'There are more things in heaven and earth, Horatio / Than are dreamt of in your philosophy.'

17   sunt aliquid manes: Lang gives the translation of the Latin phrase here; it could be more powerfully translated as 'ghosts do exist!'. The phrase opens Elegy 4.7 by the Latin poet Sextus Propertius (*c.*50–45 BCE–*c.* 15 BCE), in which he is visited by the ghost of Cynthia.

'Science and Demonology', *Illustrated London News* (June 1894)

1   obiter dictum: Latin, 'said in passing'. The phrase is used to refer to the incidental comments or remarks of a judge that do not necessarily form part of the court's decision and form no precedent.

2   *The learned Professor ... and coral islands*: T. H. Huxley's essays, *Science and the Christian Tradition*, were first published in 1894. These essays, and those in *Science and the Hebrew Tradition* (1893), were the result of his very public debate, between 1885 and 1891, with W. E. Gladstone in the pages of the *Nineteenth Century* over evolutionary science and its implications for the status of biblical truth.

3   'Demonology is doomed': T. H. Huxley, 'Agnosticism and Christianity' in *Science and the Christian Tradition* (London: Macmillan, 1894), p. 347. Huxley's full claim is: 'But, I repeat my conviction that, whether Jesus sanctioned the demonology of his time and nation or not, it is doomed.'

4   *M. Littré wrote*: Emile Littré was a French lexicographer and philosopher. He completed his *Dictionnaire de la langue française* in 1873.

5   *'grossest ... hollowness'*: these are Balfour's phrases, quoted by Huxley.

6   *On the contrary ... in it'*: A. J. Balfour, 'Address By the President', *Proceedings of the Society for Psychical Research* 10 (1894), pp. 2–13.

7   *the Professor's 'Bathybius'*: See this vol., p. 407, n. 38.

8   *Now, Mr. Wallace ... Triumphatus'*: Alfred Russel Wallace, *On Miracles and Modern Spiritualism: Three Essays* (London: James Burns, 1875), p. 7. Lang has inserted the exclamation mark. Lang writes about this occurrence in 'Comparative Psychical Research' in *Cock Lane and Common Sense* (London: Longmans, Green and Co.,1894).

9   *from Mr. Dale Owen*: Robert Dale Owen was the son of the utopian socialist Robert Owen. He emigrated to the US as a young man to be part of his father's utopian community. He was a spiritualist and the author of *Footfalls on the Boundary of Another World* (Philadelphia: J. B.Lippincott & Co., 1859) and *The Debatable Land Between this World and the Next* (New York: W. G. Carleton & Co., 1872).

10 *Mr. G,H. Lewe s... in all ranks of Life*: G. H. Lewes (1817–78) was a philosopher and literary critic, and the companion of George Eliot. The multi-volume *Problems of Life and Mind* (1874–9) was unfinished at his death.

11 *All believe ... and so on*: G. H. Lewes, *Problems of Life and Mind*, first series, vol. 1 (London: Trübner, 1874), p. 225.

12 *'identity of congestion'*: ibid., p. 226.

13 *'race ... all different'*: Wallace, *On Miracles and Modern Spiritualism*, p. 197.

14 *'so-called ... forms'*: ibid.

15 *the eternal Nicolai ... might have been photographed!*: the case of Nicolai is dealt with by Lang in 'Apparitions, Ghosts, and Hallucinations' in *Cock Lane and Common Sense* and in 'A Reply to Dr. Andrew Wilson', *Illustrated London News* (27 January 1894), p. 114. See also this vol., p. 417, n. 1.

16 *He speaks ... power*: Wallace, *On Miracles and Modern Spiritualism*, p. 163.

17 *Now, according to Mrs. Parson's*: Gertrude Parsons, *The Life of St. Colette, the Reformer of the Three Orders of St. Francis* (London: Burns and Oates, 1879).

18 *Unluckily, Professor Huxley will only ... they witness it*: on Mr. Sludge, see 'The Comparative Study of Ghost Stories', this volume, p. 412, n. 4. On Browning and D. D. Home, see the letters to E. B Tylor and Oliver Lodge (this volume pp. 332–3 and pp. 314–27).

'Science and "Miracles"', *The Making of Religion*, 2nd edition (1900)

1   *the X region*: Lang uses this term to refer to the boundary between established scientific knowledge and the supernatural.

2   *When Saul disguised ... not unlikely to be compared*: the account of Saul and the witch of Endor is given in I Samuel 28: 3–25, see 'Three Seeresses (1880–1900, 1424–1431)' in this volume, p. 423, n. 2; Croesus' testing of the oracles is told by Herodotus in *The Histories*; Porphyry (234?–305?), a pupil of the Neoplatonist Plotinus, defended Paganism against early Christianity, but argued against the theurgy of his disciple, Iamblichus (245–325). Porphyry's arguments are set out in his *Letter to Anebo*, and Iamblichus's response is thought to be found in *On the Egyptian Mysteries*.

3   *The inquiries of Thyraeus ... and many others*: Lang here lists a number of writers on the supernatural, whose work he investigates in more detail in, for example, *Cock Lane and Common Sense* (London: Longman's, Green and Co., 1894).

4   *Mr. Pepys, however*: Samuel Pepys' (1633–1703) diary was first published in 1825. In his entry for 24 November 1666, he records going home to read 'the late printed discourse of witches by a member of Gresham College ... the discourse being well writ, in good stile, but methinks not very convincing'. On 29 November 1667, Pepys records that he and his wife were frightened by the noise of their 'young gibb-cat', and that they

'could not tell well whether it was the cat or a spirit, and do sometimes think this morning that the house might be haunted.'

5   *the mind of Addison*: Joseph Addison (1672–1719) founded *The Spectator* with Richard Steele.

6   *and John Wesley…for their narratives*: John Wesley (1703–91) was an Anglican cleric who, with his brother Charles, founded the Methodist Church. Robert Wodrow (1679–1734) wrote *The History of the Sufferings of the Church of Scotland from the Restoration to the Revolution* (1721–2). Cotton Mather (1663–1728) was a Puritan minister in New England who was involved in the Salem witch trials. He championed the use of the accounts of witnesses of supernatural events as 'evidence' during the trials.

7   *David Hume in his celebrated*: David Hume (1711–76) published 'On Miracles' as part of his *An Enquiry Concerning Human Understanding* (1748).

8   *'I flatter … world endures'*: Hume, *An Enquiry Concerning Human Understanding*, p. 174. Throughout the essay Lang's quotes from Hume are taken from Alfred Russel Wallace's *On Miracles and Modern Spiritualism: Three Essays* (London: James Burns, 1875). The volume contains a section on 'Miracles and Modern Science' (cf. Lang's footnote which gives this as the title of the volume itself), but Wallace's argument with and quotation from Hume comes mostly in the first section, 'An Answer to the Argument of Hume, Lecky, and Others, Against Miracles.' Where Wallace's, and consequently Lang's, quotations differ from the original, the sections as they appear in the 1748 first edition will be given with modern spelling. The original in this case reads: 'I flatter myself, that I have discovered an argument of a like nature, which, if just will, with the wise and learned, be an everlasting check to all kinds of superstitious delusion, and consequently, will be useful as long as the world endures.'

9   *'accounts … profane'*: Hume, *An Enquiry Concerning Human Understanding*, p. 174: 'For so long, I presume, will the Accounts of Miracles and Prodigies be found in all profane History.'

10 *'experience … reasoning'*: ibid., p. 174: 'Tho' Experience be our only Guide in reasoning concerning Matters of Fact.'

11 *'a violation … nature'*: ibid., p. 180.

12 *'There must…appellation'*: ibid., p. 180 –1: 'There must, therefore, be a uniform …'

13 *'For, first, … of men'*: ibid., p. 183.

14 *'There surely never … refutation'*: ibid., p. 195.

15 *In his note … forebore'*: Lang refers to and quotes from a note to a later edition of Hume's essay, David Hume, *Essays and Treatises on Several Subjects, Vol. II, Containing An Inquiry Concerning Human Understanding* (Dublin: J. Williams, 1779), p. 480–1. The emphasis is Wallace's. The original of the second quotation reads: 'His successor in the archbishopric was an enemy to the Jansenists, and for that reason promoted to the see by the Court. Yet 22 rectors or *curés* of Paris, with infinite earnestness, pressed him to examine those miracles, which they assert to be known to the whole world, and undisputably certain: But he wisely forbore.'

16 *in the opinion of MM. Binet and Féré*: Alfred Binet (1857–1911) was a French psychologist who did much work on children's development. He was a follower of Jean-Martin Charcot. With Charles Féré, Binet wrote *Animal Magnetism* (1887) after observing patients at the Salpêtrière hospital in Paris.

17 *'The wise … facts'*: Hume, *An Enquiry Concerning Human Understanding*, p. 188. The original reads: 'While the wise and learned are contented, in general, to deride its Absurdity, without informing themselves of the particular Facts.'

18 *'The gazing … examination'*: this statement from Hume only appears in this version in later editions as: 'The *avidum genus auricularum*, the gazing populace, receive greedily, without examination, whatever soothes superstition, and promotes wonder' (1779, p. 134). In the first edition the equivalent claim is: 'The *avidum genus auricularum*, swallow greedily, without Examination, whatever soothes Superstition, and promotes Wonder' (p. 197).

19 *'a miracle … agent'*: Hume, *An Enquiry Concerning Human Understanding*, p. 181: 'A Miracle maybe accurately defin'd, *a Transgression of a Law of Nature by a particular Volition of the Deity*, or *by the Interposal of some invisible Agent.*'

20 *Jansenism*: Jansenism was a theological movement, mostly in France, of the seventeenth and early eighteenth centuries, and based on the posthumously published work of the Dutch theologian Cornelius Jansen. Jansenists questioned the role of free will in salvation, and emphasised original sin and the primacy of God's divine grace. They were accused, particularly by Jesuits, of being Calvinist, and Jansenism was finally condemned outright by the Church and the French state in 1730.

21 *Kant was familiar*: Immanuel Kant (1724–1804), German philosopher, expressed interest in Swedenborg early in his career, but then refuted Swedenborg's claims in *Träume eines Geistersehers* (Dreams of a Spirit-Seer) (1766), although Kant's position in this work has sometimes been seen as ambiguous. The first English edition was published as *Dreams of a Spirit Seer Illustrated By Dreams of Metaphysics* in 1900; Lang's quotes are his own translations of the German original. Frank Sewall, who wrote the introduction to the first English translation, did publish, in 1898, *Kant and Swedenborg On Cognition: An Essay Introductory to a Forthcoming English Translation of the Traüme Eines Geistersehers*. This essay appears as chapter 4 in Frank Sewall, *Swedenborg and Modern Idealism: A Retrospective of Philosophy From Kant To The Present Time* (London: James Speirs, 1902).

22 *welcomed by Du Prel*: Carl Du Prel (1839–99), *The Philosophy of Mysticism*, 2 vols (London: George Redway,1889).

23 *like Scott in his 'Demonology'*: Sir Walter Scott, *Letters on Demonology and Witchcraft* (London: John Murray, 1830).

24 cultivons notre jardin: French, 'we must cultivate our garden'. Voltaire's short novel *Candide* (1759) follows a young man's journey from an innocent optimism to a painful knowledge of the world. At the end Candide's more pessimistic attitude to the world is that, rather than expecting a perfect world, 'il faut cultiver notre jardin', 'we must cultivate our garden'.

25 *(Compare … 34.)*: R. Harry Vincent, *The Elements of Hypnotis*m (London: Kegan Paul, Trench, Trübner & Co., 1893).

26 *The Schellings were interested; Ritter*: Friedrich Wilhelm Joseph Schelling (1775–1854), German philosopher of the *naturphilosophie* movement and contemporary of Hegel. Johann Wilhelm Ritter (1776–1810), German chemist, physicist and philosopher.

27 *Mr. Wallace, in his preface*: William Wallace translated the third part of Hegel's *Enzyklopädie der Philosophischen Wissenschaften Im Grundrisse* (1830), which contains *The Philosophy of Spirit*, as *Hegel's Philosophy of Mind: Translated from the Encyclopedia of the*

Philosophical Sciences, trans. William Wallace (Oxford: Clarendon, 1894). The edition includes five introductory lectures by Wallace. He refers to Ritter on pp. clxi and clxiii.

28 qui voit tant de choses: French, 'who sees many things'.

29 *'a sublime … truths'*: Hegel, *Hegel's Philosophy of Mind,* trans. William Wallace, p. 33.

30 *'The somnambulist … enter'*: ibid., p. clxvii.

31 *'especially … same family*: ibid., p. 29.

32 *He gives … themselves in'*: the quotation is from ibid., p. 33. The anecdote does not appear in Wallace's translation, but see *Hegel's Philosophy of Subjective Spirit*, ed. M. J. Petry, vol. 2, *Anthropology* (Dordrecht, Holland, and Boston: D. Reidel, 1978), p. 279 and note on p. 534.

33 *Suppose … unopened*: Elisabeth Ferrand (1700–52) was an intellectual of the French Enlightenment and corresponded with Charles Edward Stuart, Bonnie Prince Charlie. His letters to her were addressed to 'Mlle. Luci'. She lived with the Comtesse de Vassé and together the two harboured the prince from 1749. Mlle Luci Ferrand appears in Lang's *Pickle the Spy: Or the Incognito of Prince Charles* (London: Longmans, Green and Co.,1897), in which Lang calls her Prince Charles' 'most valuable friend and ally' (p. 72). In his *Traité des Sensations* (1754) de Condillac wrote that his new theory of the sensations was formed in response to Mlle Ferrand's criticisms of Locke's theory of the sensations. See also Lang's letter to William James, this volume, pp. 328–9.

34 *'Annihilating all … a green shade'*: Andrew Marvell (1621–78), 'The Garden'.

35 *[Footote] as quoted by Mr. Myers*: Frederic Myers, 'Das Doppel-Ich', *Proceedings of the Society for Psychical Research* vi (1889–90), pp. 207–15.

36 *'The facts … own eyes'*: Hegel, *Hegel's Philosophy of Mind: Translated from the Encyclopedia of the Philosophical Sciences*, trans. Wallace, pp. 30–1. The original reads: 'The facts, it might seem, first of all call for verification. But such verification would it must be added be superfluous for those on whose account if was called for: for they facilitate the inquiry for themselves by declaring the narratives – infinitely numerous though they be and accredited by the education and character of the witnesses – to be mere deception and imposture. The *a priori* conceptions are so rooted that no testimony can avail against them, and they have even denied what they have seen with their own eyes.'

37 *like Sir David Brewster*: Sir David Brewster (1781–1868) was a Scottish scientist whose work in the field of optics was particularly renowned. The earliest account of the production of a 'spirit photograph' is given in his *The Stereoscope: Its History, Theory and Construction* (1856). A biography of Brewster by his daughter, Margaret Maria Gordon, *The Home Life of Sir David Brewster,* was published in 1881, and recounts his ambiguous attitude to ghosts.

38 *The Report … in 1831*: for the first English translation of this report see J. C. Colquhoun, *Report of the Experiments on Animal Magnetism*, trans. and introduction by J. C. Colquhoun (Edinburgh: Robert Cadell, 1833).

39 *'new … economy'*: ibid., p. 194.

40 *'Sleep has … produce it'*: ibid.

41 *'This … clairvoyance'*: R. Harry Vincent, *The Elements of Hypnotism*, p. 61–2. The original reads: 'That this effectively settled the question of the super-normal states, with regard

to clairvoyance, is apparent, but it by no means decided the controversy with regard to animal magnetism.'

42 *The late Mr. Gurney ... pain*: Edmund Gurney, 'The Stages of Hypnotism', 'An Account of Some Experiments in Mesmerism', 'The Problems of Hypnotism', *Proceedings of the Society for Psychical Research* II (1884), pp. 61–72, 201–6, 265–92. The page spans in Lang's footnote are incorrect.

43 *'still go ... place'*: Edmund Gurney, 'The Problems of Hypnotism', *Proceedings of the Society for Psychical Research* II (1884), p. 289.

44 *'It is ... rubbish'*: Vincent, *Elements of Hypnotism*, p. 65.

45 *'There are ... hypnosis'*: ibid., p. 129.

46 *[Footnote] Possibly Mr. Vincent*: the quote in Lang's footnote is from Vincent, *The Elements of Hypnotism*, p. 65.

47 *at Ogham inscriptions*: Ogham is an alphabet, and is the earliest written form of ancient Irish. Its extant inscriptions are found on stone monuments scattered around southern Ireland, south west Wales, western Scotland, the Isle of Man and the Devon and Cornwall borders. The inscriptions are from between the fourth and the seventh centuries and comprise mostly proper names.

48 *It is only Lord Kelvin*: Lord Kelvin (William Thomson) (1824–1907) was a British mathematical physicist and engineer. He worked on the mathematical analysis of electricity, and on the formulation of the first and second law of thermodynamics.

'Three Seeresses (1880–1900, 1424–1431)', *Anglo-Saxon Review* (1900)

1 *(says Colonel Conder)*: Colonel Claude Reignier Conder (1848–1910) was a British soldier and explorer. He carried out numerous surveys in Palestine, and wrote many books on the geography and history of the area, among them *Tent Work in Palestine* (1879), *A Handbook To The Bible* (1880), *Bible Folk Lore: A Study in Comparative Mythology* (1884), *Heth and Moab: Explorations in Syria in 1882* (1885) and *Altaic Hieroglyphs and Hittite Inscriptions* (1889). While he often mentions the hill of Moreh, the quotation has not been traced.

2 *a persecuted seeress*: the story of the witch of Endor appears at 1 Samuel 28:3–25. Lang wrote a response to T. H. Huxley's reading of the story in 'The Witch of Endor and Prof. Huxley', *Contemporary Review* 66 (August 1894), pp. 165–76, in which he uses the case of Mrs. Piper as a contemporary comparison. He returned to a critique of Huxley's reading of the biblical story in his late essay, 'Theories of the Origins of Religion' in *The Origins of Religion, And Other Essays* (London: Watts & Co., 1908), pp. 112–15.

3 *'Who was Mademoiselle Luci?'*: see Lang's letter to William James 19 February, this volume, pp. 328–97, and p. 422, n. 33

4 *Mademoiselle 'Hélène Smith'*: 'Hélène Smith' was the pseudonym used by Théodore Flournoy (1854–1920), Professor of Psychology at the University of Geneva, in his account of his investigation of the medium Catherine-Elise Müller (1861–1921) in *Des Indes à la Planète Mars* (1900; the first English translation appeared the same year). The book was an immediate bestseller. Flournoy's account details Müller's claims to, among other things, be able to communicate with beings on Mars and to write in Martian.

Müller was estranged from Flournoy after the publication of his book. Made financially secure through the backing of rich American spiritualists, she went on to devote much time to painting, often of scenes of her Martian experiences. These caught the attention of the Surrealists in the 1920s.

5 *the immortal Jeanne d'Arc*: Jeanne d'Arc was something of an obsession for Lang. He published a privately printed pamphlet, *The Voices of Joan of Arc* (1895), and in the same year wrote on her in 'The Voices of Jeanne d'Arc', *Proceedings of the Society for Psychical* Research XI (1895), pp. 198–212, and went on to publish *The Story of Joan of Arc* (London, T. C. & E. C. Jack, 1906), and three replies to Anatole France's (1844–1924) critique of Jeanne, *La Vie de Jeanne d'Arc*, vol. 1 (Paris: Calmann Lévy, 1908): *The Maid of France: Being the Story of the Life and Death of Jeanne d'Arc* (1908; see Volume 2, pp. 249–58), 'M. Anatole France on Jeanne d'Arc' in the *Scottish Historical Review* (1908; see Volume 2, pp. 236–48) and *La Vie de Jeanne d'Arc de M. Anatole France* (Paris: Perrin, 1909). He also published *La Pucelle de France: histoire de la vie et de la mort de Jeanne d'Arc* (Paris: Nelson, 1911) and three poems on Jeanne, 'A Scot to Jeanne d'Arc' (*Ban and Arriére Ban: A Rally of Fugitive Rhymes*, London: Longmans, Green and Co., 1894), 'How the Maid Marched to Blois' and 'Jeanne d'Arc' (both in *New Collected Rhymes*, London: Longmans, Green, & Co., 1904). While Lang certainly saw in his historical work on Jeanne a chance to assert his ideas on historiography – the importance of a rigorous method and a scrupulous use of evidence – it is clearly the case too that Jeanne represented for him something more. As here, she seems to be for him one of a handful of cases which offered tangible evidence that human faculties are more than those assumed by materialist science.

6 *In recent years Mrs. Piper*: George Pellew, an American writer and member of the American SPR, became friends with Richard Hodgson, the SPR investigator who worked with Mrs. Piper. Pellew died suddenly in 1892 , and thereafter replaced Phinuit as Mrs Piper's main control. In the SPR records he is referred to by the pseudonym George Pelham, and was generally known as G. P. Rev. William Stainton Moses (1839–92) was introduced to spiritualism in the 1870s, and soon began to experience spiritualist phenomena himself. He wrote much on spiritualism, and especially on automatic writing. He was one of the founder members of the SPR. Lang assesses his credibility in 'Human Personality After Death', this volume, pp. 300–7.

7 *As Mrs. Sidgwick asks*: Eleanor Sidgwick actually asked: 'If the guaranteed spirits throw doubt on the trustworthiness of the guarantors, where are we?' Mrs Henry Sidgwick, 'II. Discussion of Trance Phenomena of Mrs. Piper', *Proceedings of the Society for Psychcial Research* 15 (1900–1), p. 24. This article by Eleanor Sidgwick was followed by Lang's own response to the supposed phenomena of Mrs Piper, 'III. Discussion of the Trance Phenomena of Mrs. Piper', pp. 39–52.

8 *Cagliostro in a former life*: the real name of the adventurer Alessandro Cagliostro (1743–95) was Guiseppe Balsamo, an occultist and shadowy figure. He was the subject of a two-volume novel by Alexandre Dumas, *Joseph Balsamo* (1846–8).

9 *as She:* Lang here refers to the long-lived heroine of the adventure novel *She* (1887) by his friend Henry Rider Haggard.

10 *'The sense … were spoken'*: this may well be Lang's translation from the French original. The original English translation has: 'the meaning of which often very well corresponds with the situations in which these words have been uttered', Théodore Flournoy, *From India to Planet Mars: A Study of a Case of Somnabulism with Glossolalia*, trans. Daniel B. Vermilye (New York and London: Harpers, 1900), p. 315.

11   *M. Quicherat:* Jules Étienne Joseph Quicherat (1814–82) was a French historian. He published the texts of Jeanne's two trials and much new evidence in *Procès de condamnation et de réhabilitation de Jeanne d'Arc* (1841–9) and *Aperçus nouveaux sur l'histoire de Jeanne d'Arc* (1850).

'Magic Mirrors and Crystal Gazing', *Monthly Review* (December 1901)

1   *Mr. Yeats recently instructed … master:* W. B. Yeats, 'Magic', *Monthly Review* 4:12 (September 1901), pp. 144–62. The Irish poet and playwright W. B. Yeats (1865–1935) was well known by the time this was published. He had a wide and also well-known interest in many areas of the occult.

2   *like those of Dr. Dee:* see this volume, p. 415, n. 22.

3   *Kinglake in 'Eothen':* Alexander William Kinglake (1809–91) was a lawyer who gave up his practice for literature. His first literary work was *Eothen, or Traces of Travel Brought Home From the East* (1844).

4   *those of Cagliostro:* see this volume, p. 424, n. 8. Thomas Carlyle (1795–1881) wrote an essay on him, 'Count Cagliostro, In Two Flights', first published in *Fraser's Magazine* (1833).

5   *to the cases observed by … by 'spiritualism':* William Gregory (1803–58) was a Scottish physician and chemist; Sophia de Morgan (1809–92) wrote *From Matter to Spirit: The Result of Ten Years' Experience in Spirit Manifestations* (London: Longmans, Green and Co., 1863).

6   *Miss Goodrich Freer's article:* 'Recent Experiments in Crystal Vision', *Proceedings of the Society for Psychical Research* 5 (1888–9), pp. 486–521. See this volume, p. 415, n. 2.

7   *George Sand:* George Sand was the pseudonym of the French novelist Amentine Lucile Aurole Dupin (1804–76).

8   *One of them, Mr. B:* in his 'Introduction' to Northcote W. Thomas, *Crystal Gazing: Its History and Practice* (1905), Lang names 'Mr. B.' as Mr. Balfour.

9   *I examined the ethnological side:* Lang included a chapter on 'Crystal Visions, Savage and Civilised' in *The Making of Religion* (London: Longmans, Green and Co.,1898).

10   *on which Mr. Galton has written:* Francis Galton (1822–1911) was an English polymath who worked in anthropology, eugenics, geography, meteorology and statistics, among other areas. Lang is referring here to his work in 'Visualised Numerals', *Journal of the Anthropological Institute* X:VIII (1881), pp. 85–102.

'Human Personality After Death', *Monthly Review* (March 1903)

1   *Mr. Frederick Myers's:* Lang misspells Myers's name here; it should be Frederic.

2   *of a lifetime:* while this review of Myers's book contains much criticism of his theory of personal survival, Lang later wrote a defence of Myers, which the *Nineteenth Century* refused to publish. It was published as '"The Nineteenth Century" and Mr F. Myers', *Proceedings of the Society for Psychical Research* 18 (1903–4), pp. 62–77. In it Lang defends Myers' against a critical review in *The Nineteenth Century and After* by W. H. Mallock, published in April 1903.

3   *Black Ormistoun …. Gilles de Rais*: James Black, Laird Ormiston (1522–73) was hanged for treason. He had been implicated in the murder of Lord Darnley, the husband of Mary, Queens of Scots, in 1567. Gilles de Montmorency-Laval (1404–40), Baron de Rais, was a knight in the French army and in 1429 fought alongside Jeanne d'Arc. He was hanged for the murder of scores of children, and is believed to be the figure on whom Bluebeard is based.

4   *Rev. Stainton Moses*: see this volume, pp. 424, n. 6.

5   *'There is much … glare withal'*: from *Macbeth*, Act 3, scene 4, lines 95–6, Macbeth to Banquo's ghost: 'Thou has no speculation in those eyes/Which thou doest glare with!'

6   *the late Mr. T.H. Green*: Thomas Hill Green (1836–82) was a British idealist philosopher who did much to influence the development of ethical socialism. He taught at Oxford from 1860 until his death.

7   [Footnote] *Mr. Wallace's translation*: see this volume, p. 421–2, n. 27.

8   *Quicherat …:* see this volume, p. 425, n. 11.

9   *'a nascent … and experiment'*: Frederic W. H. Myers, *Human Personality and Its Survival of Bodily Death*, 2 vols (London: Longmans, Green and Co., 1903), vol. I, p. 2. The original reads: 'Yet let me first explain that by the word "scientific," I signify an authority to which I submit myself – not a standard which I claim to attain. Any science of which I can here speak as possible must be a *nascent* science – not such as one of those vast systems of connected knowledge which thousands of experts now steadily push forward in laboratories in every land – but such as each one of those great sciences was in its dim and poor beginning, when a few monks groped among the properties of "the noble metals," or a few Chaldean shepherds outwatched the setting stars.'

10   *When Lord Kelvin … clairvoyance*: Lord Kelvin's 'Six Gateways of Knowledge' is quoted by Myers in *Human Personsality and its Survival,* vol. II, p. 533; Sir William Thomson (Baron Kelvin), *Popular Lectures and Addresses*, vol. I (London: Macmillan, 1889), p. 258. Lang also takes issue with Lord Kelvin in 'Science and "Miracles"', see this volume, pp. 271–83.

11   *'are in … mind'*: Frederic Myers, *Human Personality and Its Survival*, vol. I, p. 229.

12   *'an empirical … vision'*: ibid., p. xlii.

13   *'ether waves … X rays'*: ibid., p. 245. Sir William Crookes (1832–1919) was a chemist and physicist who did pioneering work on vacuum tubes and was the inventor of the Crookes radiometer. Crookes became interested in spiritualism in the late 1860s and conducted some of the earlier psychical research. He became well known, and perhaps notorious, for his interest in and championing of the materialisation medium Florence Cook.

14   *'palaeolithic psychology'*: ibid., p. 247.

15   *like Brookes of Sheffield*: in Charles Dickens' *David Copperfield* (1850), Mr Murdstone, in a conversation with other adults at which the young David is present, refers to an imaginary 'Mr Brooks of Sheffield' as being 'sharp' when in fact he means David, and wishes to warn the others to be careful of what they say.

16   eidolon: a transcription from Ancient Greek, 'apparition or image'.

17   *'credible … difficulty'*: Myers, *Human Personsality and its Survival,* vol. I, p. 249.

18   *'Different fractions … action'*: ibid.

19   *'Phantasms of the Living'*: Lang is here referring to *Phantasms of the Living*, a two-volume work edited by Edmund Gurney, Frederic W. H. Myers and Frank Podmore and published in 1886. This was the first major work to be produced through the investigative work of the recently formed Society for Psychical Research. In compiling it, the investigators had asked for experiences of seeing someone's 'ghost' coincident with a crisis in that person's life, most usually illness or death. They read and analysed thousands of accounts, and believed that the results showed that the accounts of coincident experiences were statistically significant. For many in the SPR this work was evidence of the existence of telepathy. Numerous scientists and writers disputed the findings. For example, C. S. Peirce disputed the statistical claims, and he and Edmund Gurney had a detailed argument in the pages of the *Proceedings* of the American Society for Psychical Research (see 'Criticism on "Phantasms of the Living": An Examination of an Argument of Messrs. Gurney, Myers, and Podmore' and 'Mr Peirce's Rejoinder', *Proceedings of the American Society for Psychical Research* 1/1–4 (1885–9), pp. 150–215).

20   *In the Census...been made*: The 'Census of Hallucinations' was carried out by the Society for Psychical Research between 1889 and 1892. The report on the census, written mostly by Eleanor Sidgwick, concluded that chance and coincidence could not account for the phenomena. See Henry Sidgwick et al., 'Report on the Census of Hallucinations', *Proceedings of the Society for Psychical Research*, 10 (1894), pp. 25–422.

21   *Thus Mr. Tylor ... eleven'*: E. B. Tylor, 'On A Method of Investigating the Development of Institutions: Applied to Laws of Marriage and Descent', *Journal of the Anthropological Institute of Great Britain and Ireland* 18 (1889), p. 248. The full page span is pp. 245–272; Lang's footnote gives the page span without the following discussion of Tylor's article.

22   *I am unable to accept Mr. Podmore's*: this comment, and Lang's footnote, refer to their debate about poltergeists in the *Proceedings of the Society for Psychical Research* 17 (1901–2), pp. 305–32.

23   vacarme: French, din or racket.

24   *'does not ... of space'*: Matthew Arnold's 'Morality' (1852) contains the lines: 'I knew not yet the gauge of time, / Nor wore the manacles of space...'

'Presidential Address, Delivered on May 16th, 1911', *Proceedings of the Society for Psychical Research* (August 1911)

1   *the experiences of Sir Walter Scott*: Lang often refers to and uses the experiences and experiments of Sir Walter Scott in the supernatural in his own work. Scott had a large library on occult subjects at this home, Abbotsford, and had been interested in the topic since childhood. In 1830 Scott published *Letters on Demonology and Witchcraft*, in which he argued for a non-supernatural explanation for such phenomena.

2   *I have seen ... their followers*: Heinrich Schliemann (1822–90) and Arthur Evans (1851–1941) were two of the most famous archaeologists of the late nineteenth and early twentieth centuries. Schliemann, believing he could find the sites mentioned in the *Iliad* and the *Odyssey*, which most classicists and archaeologists of the time took to be mythical, excavated a number of sites in the 1870s and 1880s. He dug at Hissarlik in Turkey, excavating the city of Troy, and in Ithaca and Mycenae. Arthur Evans, a British archaeologist, excavated Knossos, on Crete, between 1900 and 1905, and did much

work on translating tablets of writing found there, calling the two distinct scripts used on the tablets Linear A and Linear B.

3   *Hegel believed in almost all ... rabbit'*: see Lang's discussion of Hegel in 'Science and "Miracles"', this volume, pp. 271–83. Carlyle in fact said of Cardinal Newman (1801–90) that he had not the intellect of 'a moderate-sized rabbit'. John Keble (1792–1860), Newman's co-founder of the Oxford Movement, Carlyle described as a 'little ape'. Both of these comments appear in J. A. Froude, *Thomas Carlyle: A History of His Life in London 1834–1881*, 2 vols, (London: Longman, Green and Co, 1884), vol. II, p. 247–8. The first Froude says Carlyle said in conversation with him, the second is from a letter.

4   *When I say Poltergeist*: Lang wrote a fair amount about poltergeists, including 'The Poltergeist and His Explainers', in *The Making of Religion* (London: Longmans, Green and Co., 1898). For the dispute between Lang and Frank Podmore on the subject see this volume, p. 427, n. 22.

5   *Mr. Barrett*: William Fletcher Barrett (1844–1925), English physicist. He was the Professor of Experimental Physics at the Royal College of Science in Ireland. He became interested in spiritualist phenomena in the 1870s and was one of the co-founders of the Society for Psychical Research in 1882, and the American Society of Psychical Research in 1884. He edited the SPR *Journal* between 1884 and 1889, and was active in the Dublin SPR in the early twentieth century, and was president of the SPR in 1904. Like Lang, he had a special interest in divining rods, and published extensive work on them, see *Proceedings of the Society for Psychical Research* 13 (1897–8), pp. 2–282. He published *On the Threshold of the Unseen: An Examination of the the Phenomenon of Spiritualism and of the Evidence of Survival After Death* in 1917.

6   *Claire Claremount's*: Clara (or Claire) Claremont (1798–1879) was the stepsister of Mary Shelley and the sometime lover of Lord Byron, with whom she had a daughter, Allegra. She began to keep a journal in 1814 and continued it until 1826.

7   coup de pouce: French, 'helping hand'.

8   *Sir David Brewster*: see this volume, p. 422, n. 37.

9   coup de botte: French, 'kick'.

10   *Miss Tanner is a Doctor of Philosophy*: Amy Tanner was a psychologist. In 1909, accompanied by the psychologist Professor G. Stanley Hall, she attended six sittings with Mrs Piper. *Studies in Spiritism* is an account of these sittings, with an introduction by Hall. Tanner and Hall concluded that Mrs Piper suffered from multiple personalities, as well as not being above the use of straightforward deception.

11   *'In the mad pride of intellectuality'*: from 'To Marie Louise' (1829) by Edgar Allan Poe.

12   *If Mr. Feilding ... the old familiar tricks*: Everard Feilding was one of the main investigators of the Italian medium Eusapia Palladino during the SPR's second series of tests on her in 1908. He published, with others, a paper on Palladino in the *Proceedings of the Society for Psychical Research* in 1909, 'Report on a Series of Sittings with Eusapia Palladino', and his work on her was later published as *Sittings with Eusapia Palladino and Other Studies* (1963).

13   *what are called 'Cross-Correspondences'*: the cross-correspondences are a series of messages, communicated through a number of mediums, including Mrs Piper, between 1901 to around 1930. The messages became the main focus of the Society's work during this period, and investigators came to believe that the fragmented, elliptical messages were part of a cryptic puzzle created by the posthumous personalities of, among others,

Frederic Myers, in order to prove survival beyond death. The SPR devoted years of work to deciphering and testing the messages, and thousands of pages were written by the investigators on them.

14 *I have read … could not compose*: as is made clear in some of his letters to Oliver Lodge, Lang supplied questions to be put to the mediums involved in the cross-correspondences in order to test whether the posthumous personality of Frederic Myers was indeed one of the communicators. See 'Letters to Oliver Lodge', this volume, pp. 314–27.

15 *that Mrs. Verrall*: Margaret Verrall (1857–1916) was a Cambridge classicist, a member of the SPR, and a friend of Frederic Myers. It was her attempts at automatic writing soon after Myers' death in 1901 that initiated the cross-correspondences (see note 13 above). In a letter to Annie Hills from 1908, Lang describes experiments that his niece carried out with Mrs Verrall to try to reproduce the phenomena of the cross-correspondences. MS PR 4876.C7 ms 37240-10, Special Collections of the University of St Andrews Library.

16 *'only when … attitude*: Amy E. Tanner, *Studies in Spiritism* (London and New York: Appleton & Co., 1910), pp. xxxi–xxxii.

Letters to Oliver Lodge

1 *Jan 4*: letter SPR. MS 35/1018, SPR Archive, Manuscripts, Cambridge University Library. This letter is probably from 1895. See this volume, pp.255-7 for a full account of the dating of the letters to Lodge.

2 *Prof. Tait's moral tone*: this is probably Peter Guthrie Tait (1831–1901), Scottish mathematical physicist and Professor of Natural Philosophy at St Andrews. He was best known for his collaboration with Lord Kelvin on *Treatise on Natural Philosophy* (1867). While he publicly criticised spiritualist beliefs, he published, with Balfour Stewart, an early president of the SPR, *The Unseen Universe, or Physical Speculations on a Future State* in 1875 which attempted to reconcile contemporary science with orthodox Christian beliefs. The book was first published anonymously, and became a bestseller. The reference to Tait, who died in 1901, further suggests that this letter at least was written before the dates given in the SPR Archive.

3 *He talks of Slade*: Henry Slade (1835–1905) was an American psychic who performed throughout Europe and North America. He claimed to have discovered spirit slate writing in the 1860s. On coming to London in 1876 he was exposed by Edwin Ray Lankester, and was tried and found guilty of fraud.

4 *Slade and D.D. Home*: 'and' is circled in the original.

5 *Mr A.R. Wallace's … flagrant kind*: Wallace's major writings on 'spookology' began with a two-part article in *The Fortnightly Review*, 'A Defence of Spiritualism', in 1874 (15:89, pp. 630–57 and 15:90, pp. 785–807). This work was much quoted and anthologised, and was included in his *On Miracles and Modern Spiritualism: Three Essays* (London: James Burns, 1875). This book went on to two further editions (1881, 1896), in each of which more material was added. Wallace also wrote many articles, and letters, on the subject in both spiritualist periodicals and in the mainstream press. Lang critiques Wallace's arguments in some detail in 'Science and Demonology' (1894), see this volume, p. 268–70.

6   *I think that professional conjurers … erred'*: this seems to indicate the beginning of Lang's idea that a stage magician would be the best person to test those things claimed for Palladino.

7   *Hertz's and Clerk Maxwell's ideas*: Heinrich Rudolf Hertz (1857–94) was a German physicist who developed and proved the electromagnetic theory of light of the Scottish physicist James Clerk Maxwell (1831–79).

8   *Jan 11*: letter SPR.MS 35/1021, SPR Archive, Manuscripts, Cambridge University Library. This letter is likely to be from 1895. See in particular notes 9 and 11 below.

9   *a bogus Ochorowicz*: Julian Leopold Ochorowicz (1850–1917), Polish philosopher and psychologist, who did experiments in hypnosis and telepathy. It is likely that 'the Post' refers to the *Morning Post*, but nothing could be found in this about the impersonation of either of these psychical researchers. The various experiments with Eusapia Palladino in the first half of the 1890s often made the news, however, and both men had been involved with these. Ochorowicz was involved in séances given by Eusapia Palladino in Warsaw in 1893–4, and attended the sittings with her in Charles Richet's house on the Île Roubaud in France in 1894. More sittings took place a few weeks later with Richet in Toulon, this time attended by Albert von Schrenck-Notzing as well as Ochorowicz. Oliver Lodge attended both of these sets of sittings, and Lodge reported on them in 'Experience of Unusual Psychical Phenomena Occurring in the Presence of an Entranced Person (Eusapia Palladino)', *Journal of the Society for Psychical Research* 6 (1893–4), pp. 306–60.

10   *Mrs. P.*: Mrs Piper was investigated by the American Society for Psychical Research from 1887. She visited the UK in 1889 and Lodge was involved in the SPR investigations of her. Lang's public interest in Mrs Piper was at its peak between 1895 and 1900. He wrote on the investigations of her in his column 'At the Sign of the Ship', *Longman's Magazine*, December 1895, in 'Three Seeresses (1880–1900, 1424–1431)' (1900, see this volume, pp. 284–91), in 'Discussion of the Trance Phenomena of Mrs. Piper', *Proceedings of the Society for Psychical Research* 15 (1900–1), pp. 39–52, and in a response to Oliver Lodge's response to this article, 'Mrs Piper and Telepathy', *Journal of the Society for Psychical Research* 9 (1889–1900), pp 228–31. Lodge had written on Mrs Piper in the Society's *Proceedings* for 1894, which may have precipitated Lang's discussion of her here.

11   *Most boys … performance*: Lodge had twenty-two sittings with Mrs Piper during her visit to the UK in 1889–90. At one sitting he presented her with a watch which an uncle had just sent him. This led to messages which purported to be from a dead uncle, the original owner of the watch, reminiscing about the boyhood of Lodge's father and uncles. Lodge's report on these sittings ('A Record of Observations of Certain Phenomena of Trance', *Proceedings of the Society for Psychical Research* 6 (1889–90), pp. 436–659) reports that '"Uncle Jerry" recalled episodes such as swimming the creek when they were boys together, and running some risk of getting drowned; killing a cat in Smith's field …' (p. 459). While this might suggest that this letter is earlier than those around it which deal with Maskelyne and his proposed meeting with Palladino, its congruence in terms of month and place of residence suggests that the letter too is from 1895. In the next letter, which discusses Maskelyne's possible involvement with Palladino, locating the letter in 1895, Lang also goes back to the 1889–90 sittings with Mrs Piper in mentioning Lodge's watch.

12 *Jan 14*: SPR.MS 35/1023, SPR Archive, Manuscripts, Cambridge University Library. This letter is likely to be from 1895 in particular because it contains a reference to Lang's involvement with Maskelyne in arranging for his sitting with Eusapia Palladino.

13 *Greenwood's remarks*: this is probably Frederick Greenwood (1830–1909), a well-known British journalist and man of letters. He was editor of the *Cornhill Magazine* (1862–8), the *Pall Mall Gazette* (1865–80), and *St. James's Gazette* (1880–8). He knew Robert Browning well. While Lang's comment suggests that these remarks were written, no record of them has been found. In her 'Andrew Lang (1844–1912), Late Victorian Humanist and Journalistic Critic', 2 vols (dissertation, Ghent University, 1983), vol. 2, p. 280, Marysa Demoor suggests in her description of this letter that the Greenwood is G. G. (George) Greenwood (1850–1928), a lawyer and politician who published much on the controversy about Shakespearean authorship, believing that an unknown poet or poets wrote the work attributed to Shakespeare. He and Lang did spar publicly in print over this. However, there is no evidence that this Greenwood knew Browning, or was interested in the questions raised in the letter.

14 *which I gave to Myers*: in a number of letters to Lodge, Lang is keen to establish the fact that Browning's poem 'Mr Sludge, "the Medium"' (1864) is based on Daniel Dunglas Home, whose sittings both Browning and Elizabeth Barrett Browning attended in 1855. The question of Browning's 'exposure' of Home, and of the nature of Barrett Browning's belief, was the subject of correspondence in the *Times Literary Supplement* in 1902, following a review of Frank Podmore's *Modern Spiritualism* (see *Lives of Victorian Literary Figures II*, vol. I, *The Brownings*, edited by Simon Avery (London: Pickering & Chatto, 2004), pp. 327–30). Mrs Alexandra Sutherland Orr (1828–1903) had met Browning through her brother, Frederick Septimus Leighton, father of the painter, and they had remained good friends till his death. She wrote several books on Browning, including *Life and Letters of Robert Browning* (1891), published two years after his death. See also 'Letter to E. B. Tylor on Home and the Brownings', this volume, pp. 332–3.

15 *I admit that the nicks on the watch handle*: Lodge's sittings with Mrs Piper while she was in the UK in 1889–90 produced what Lodge believed to be evidential messages after he had presented her with a watch of his uncle's (see note 11 above). In his report on this, Lodge recounts that Mrs Piper's control 'told me to take the watch out of its case … and examine it in a good light afterwards, and I should see some nicks near the handle where Jerry said he had cut into it with his knife. Some faint nicks are there' (Part I of 'A Record of Observations of Certain Phenomena of Trance', *Proceedings of the Society for Psychical Research* 6 (1889–90), pp. 459–60).

16 *Kellar seems to be a liar*: probably Harry Kellar (1849–1922), an American magician known as the 'Dean of American Magicians'. Lang cites him with approval in 'Savage Spiritualism', *Cock Lane and Common Sense* (London: Longmans, Green and Co., 1894).

17 *Greenwood*: see note 13 above.

18 *Jan [illegible]*: letter SPR.MS 35/1025, SPR Archive, Manuscripts, Cambridge University Library. The congruence of month, residence and subject matter between this letter and others around it suggest a date of 1895.

19 *R.B.*: Robert Browning.

20 *Testing Pilate*: this is a pun on 'jesting Pilate'. Chapter 18, verse 38 of the Gospel of John is often referred to as 'jesting Pilate' or 'Truth? What is truth?' from the questions that Pontius Pilate puts to Jesus.

21 *Jan 20*: Letter SPR.MS 35/1026, SPR Archive, Manuscripts, Cambridge University Library. The discussion of Maskelyne needing to see Palladino before he could attempt to repeat her phenomena suggests 1895.

22 argumentum ad hominem: Latin, 'argument to the man', refers to an argument based on personal attacks against an opponent, rather than one based on a challenge to their arguments.

23 *Mrs Orr's*: see this volume, p. 431, n. 14.

24 *Jan [illegible]*: Letter SPR. MS 35/1027, SPR Archive, Manuscripts, Cambridge University Library. This letter may predate the previous, given the comments about Mrs Orr's knowledge of a dead child of the Brownings', but it is likely to be from late January 1895; see note 25 below on the *Edinburgh*.

25 *in the Edinburgh*: an article entitled 'Modern Magic' appeared in *The Edinburgh Review*, in January 1895 discussing, in a skeptical tone, recent publications of the Society for Psychical Research, among books on matters psychical, including Lang's *Cock Lane and Common Sense* (181:371, pp. 82–115). The article quotes widely from an article by Lodge from volume 10 of the *Proceedings*, during part of which he writes about Mrs Piper. The article ends by cautioning the reader against seeing what the SPR does as 'science'. While the article is unsigned, the Wellesley Index to Victorian Periodicals lists it as being by Arthur D. Elliot.

26 *Jan 28*: Letter SPR.MS 35/1028, SPR Archive, Manuscripts, Cambridge University Library. This letter discusses Lang's correspondence with Maskelyne and argues that he believes the magician needs to see Palladino face to face, suggesting it is from 1895.

27 *J.N.M.*: J. N. Maskelyne.

28 *Sandow and Sampson*: Eugene Sandow (Friedrich Müller) (1867–1925), Prussian bodybuilder, took on his rival Charles 'Samson' Sampson in a contest in London in 1889, at which he was victorious. He went on to write books on body-building, publish a magazine, and manufacture his own brand of cocoa. In 1901 a cast of his body was taken for the British Museum. Sampson published *Strength: A Treatise on the Development and Use of Muscle* in 1895.

29 *the enclosed Mrs Mellon business*: for an account of a test séance with a Mrs Mellon in Sydney, during which she was placed in a cage, see *The Argus* (Melbourne), Saturday 1 December 1894, p. 7.

30 donnée: French, 'a given', that is a set of principles upon which something is based.

31 *He put his name … very crude*: Lionel A. Weatherley and J. N. Maskelyne, *The Supernatural?* (London: Arrowsmith, 1891). Chapter 7 (pp. 153–232) is by Maskelyne, in which he gives away the secret techniques of a number of 'eastern' magic tricks, and questions the credibility of contemporary mediums such as Mme Helena Blavatsky and D. D. Home.

32 *I have not read Lord Dunraven*: Windham Thomas Wyndham-Quin, 4th Earl of Dunraven (1841–1926) was a landowner and Conservative politician. While he was still Viscount Adare, Dunraven wrote a detailed account of sittings with D. D. Home that he attended with his father, the 3rd Earl. These were privately printed as *Experiences in Spiritualism with Mr. D.D. Home* in 1869, but were subsequently withdrawn.

33 *Greenwood*: see note 13 above.

34 *pliskies*: Scottish, 'mischievous tricks, practical jokes'.

35 *Jan 29*: Letter SPR.MS 35/1029, SPR Archive, Manuscripts, Cambridge University Library. This letter continues Lang's attempts to organise a meeting between Maskelyne and Palladino, so is likely to be from 1895.

36 *bear leader*: from the description of men who trained bears in the Middle Ages by leading them around on a chain, this term was used to refer to a tutor that would take charge of a young man on the Grand Tour.

37 *but how on the island?*: the Île Roubaud, where Charles Richet's home was, and where the experiments with Eusapia Palladino, which Lodge attended, took place in the summer of 1894. See note 9 above.

38 *Feb 5*: Letter SRP.MS 35/1031, SPR Archive, Manuscripts, Cambridge University Library. The first lines of the letter suggest it was written before Maskelyne's sitting with Palladino, during the time that Lang was trying to broker a meeting, so it is likely to be from 1895.

39 *your Report when he wrote!*: that is, Lodge's report on the experiments with Eusapia Palladino, headed by Charles Richet, in France in 1894. See note 9 above.

40 *Feb 5*: Letter SPR. MS 35/1032, SPR Archive, Manuscripts, Cambridge University Library. In this letter Lang continues his discussion of the meeting between the Brownings and D.D. Home, suggesting that it is part of the 1895 series.

41 *The Dictionary of National Biography … Garth Wilkinson's*: the Brownings did indeed first attend a sitting with Home at the Rymers' in Ealing, west London.

42 *Some Wilkinson … may be alive*: An anonymous account of this sitting appeared in the *Journal* of the Society for Psychical Research in 1889 but the identity of the writer, who had attended the sitting in 1855 with the Brownings, was not revealed until 1902. See this volume, p. 256.

43 *Mrs. Hawthorne*: Sophia Hawthorne (1809–71) was the wife of the American writer Nathaniel Hawthorne. The Hawthornes visited the Brownings during their travels in Italy in the late 1850s. Sophia Hawthorne wrote about these meetings in *Notes in England and Italy* (1869).

44 *Mrs Orr*: see this volume, p. 431, n. 14.

45 *Feb 6*: Letter SPR. MS 35/1033, SPR Archive, Manuscripts, Cambridge University Library. The discussion of both the Browning/Home question and of Eusapia Palladino suggests this is from the same series as the preceding letters, and is therefore from 1895.

46 *Greenwood*: see note 13 above.

47 *qui facit per alium*: Latin, a legal term: 'He who acts through another does the act himself.'

48 *The Table is most ingenious*: in his report on his sittings with Eusapia Palladino in France in 1894 ('Experience of Unusual Psychical Phenomena', see note 9 above), Lodge recounts in some detail descriptions of the tables used in the sittings, in particular a 'Large Table' constructed especially for the purpose by Charles Richet (pp. 308–9). Lodge goes on to describe how, during a sitting, this large table, while they were all sitting at a smaller one, was turned upside down (pp. 310–11). It is likely that Lang had just read this report, suggesting that the letter is from early 1895.

49 *I have had a very odd … Myers*: Lang wrote about his own experiences with crystal balls in chapter 5 of *The Making of Religion* (London: Longmans, Green and Co., 1898),

where he recounts an experience early in 1897 with a young woman who could see visions in a crystal ball. In a later article, 'Magic Mirrors and Crystal Gazing' (1901, see this volume, pp. 292–9), he says that his mind began to change, from outright skepticism, regarding crystal visions after he read an article by Ada Goodrich Freer, published anonymously, in the *Proceedings* of the Society for Psychical Research. This article appeared in the 1888–9 volume. However, Lang may have read it much later. He goes on to recount an experiment with a glass ball that is clearly earlier than that in 1897. In his 'Introduction' to Northcote W. Thomas's *Crystal Gazing: Its History and Practice* (London: Alexander Moring Ltd, The De La More Press, 1905), Lang's account of his experiences suggest that some time elapsed between reading Freer's article, his first experiments, and his more productive experiments in 1897. This, along with the fact that this letter continues so closely on a subject, that of Browning and Home, discussed in the 1895 letters, suggests that it is of a piece with them.

50   *Feb 27*: Letter SPR. MS 35/1044, SPR Archive, Manuscripts, Cambridge University Library. The reference to Minot (see note 51 below) in particular places this letter in 1895.

51   *I suppose Minot … so I gather from Myers*: Charles Sedgwick Minot (1852–1914) was an American anatomist. Minot published a critical article on psychical research at the beginning of 1895: 'The Psychical Comedy', *North American Review,* February 1895, pp. 217–31. In response, Frank Podmore published 'What Psychical Research Has Accomplished', *North American Review*, March 1895, pp. 331–45. Podmore challenged Minot's criticism of the work done by the SPR on thought-transference, including a challenge to Minot's assertion that the leaders of the SPR are 'literary men' (p. 343) and therefore unlikely to grasp the nuances of scientific method. Lang's letter was clearly written after the publication of Minot's article and before the publication of Podmore's response. Lang himself also published a reply to Minot, 'On A Certain Condescension in Scientific Men', *Illustrated London News* CVI:2917 (16 March 1895), p. 327. Horace Darwin (1851–1928) was a son of Charles Darwin, and a civil engineer.

52   *Allen is a fanatic*: Grant Allen (1848–99) was a Canadian-born writer whose first published books were on philosophy and who was influenced by the sociological evolutionary theories of Herbert Spencer. He published articles on scientific subjects in journals such the *Cornhill,* and in the 1880s began writing fiction. His bestseller was *The Woman Who Did* (1895), a serious novel with an anti-marriage heroine that caused controversy on publication. Allen was a friend of Lang's; they were writing for the *Illustrated London News* during the same period, and sometimes directly challenged and responded to the other's work. See Lang's columns, *Illustrated London News* CV:2883 (21 July 1894), p. 78 and CVIII:2982 (13 June 1896), p. 751.

53   *Feb 9*: Letter SPR.MS 35/1036, SPR Archive, Manuscripts, Cambridge University Library. This letter is different in tone from the 1895 letters, but similar in tone – speculative and rather abstract – to the following letter which is probably from the early years of the twentieth century; see note 54 below.

54   *Feb 12*: Letter SPR.MS 35/1039, SPR Archive, Manuscripts, Cambridge University Library. In this letter Lang mentions Frazer's three-volume work (see note 55 below). The second edition of *The Golden Bough* was published in three volumes in 1900, and the third in twelve volumes between 1906 and 1915. Lang published his own response to Frazer's second edition (see note 56 below), all of which suggests that the letter is from between 1901 and 1906.

55 *the Rex Nemorensis*: Sir James Frazer's *The Golden Bough* (1890–1915) began with the question about the meaning of the myth of the *Rex Nemorensis*, the King of the Wood, who guarded the grove of Diana at Nemi, and in particular the sacred golden bough. This priest was constantly on guard, as the rule of the grove said that any man who murdered the incumbent would then become the *Rex Nemorensis*, until he too was murdered by his successor. As Frazer said, the rule had 'no parallel in classical antiquity, and cannot be explained from it. To find an explanation we must go farther afield' (*The Golden Bough*, 1922, p. 2), so beginning his huge study of worldwide mythical beliefs and practices.

56 *I offered a cheaper guess*: in 'The Ghastly Priest', chapter 11 of *Magic and Religion* (London: Longmans, Green and Co.,1901).

57 *Nov 21 [?]*: Letter SPR. MS 35/1060, SPR Archive, Manuscripts, Cambridge University Library. The report on the cross-correspondences by Alice Johnson which Lang mentions in this letter was published in June 1908 (see note 60 below) and the investigations of Mrs Piper connected with the cross-correspondences were carried out in 1908 (see note 60 below), both of which suggest the letter could be from late 1908, although it could be later.

58 *… Mr Dorr*: George Dorr, a vice-president of the SPR, conducted investigations into the cross-correspondences with Mrs Piper in 1908.

59 *I think Mrs V's …* Margaret Verrall, see this volume, p. 429, n. 15.

60 *March 25 1901*: In June 1908 a long article by Alice Johnson appeared in the *Proceedings* of the SPR on the cross-correspondences ('On the Automatic Writing of Mrs Holland', *Proceedings of the Society for Psychical Research* 21 (1908–9), pp. 166–391). On p. 379, which Lang references in this letter, Johnson gives Mrs Verrall's translations of the Greek and Latin passages that had appeared in her own automatic writing which was believed to be part of the cross-correspondences. The messages are dated; there is no message from 25 March 1901, but there are messages on this page from 21 and 28 March 1901. The translation for the 21 March 1901 message (from Latin) reads: 'Oh, if you cannot weave together pertinaciously, write all you know. Soon will come the inviolate light of the Sibyl. Either one of the two receiving will choose. Do not fail her who asks.' The translation for the 28 March 1901 message (from Latin) reads: 'What you have done is always dissociated; improve it by denying folds, weave together, weave together always.'

61 *Nov 21*. Letter SPR.MS.35/1061, SPR Archive, Manuscripts, Cambridge University Library. This letter too makes reference to the report on the cross-correspondences between Mrs Holland and Mrs Verrall published in June 1908 (see note 60 above), suggesting that it is from also from late 1908.

62 *In reading Mrs Holland*: Mrs Holland, one of the main mediums involved in the cross-correspondences, was the pseudonym for Alice Kipling Fleming (1868–1948), sister of Rudyard Kipling. She lived in India, wrote poetry and experimented with automatic writing. After reading Myers' *Human Personality and Its Survival of Bodily Death*, she began a correspondence with Alice Johnson (1860–1940), secretary of the SPR, and began to produces messages that were believed to be part of the cross-correspondences.

63 *That about your thought … S.S*: in Alice Johnson's report from June 1908 ('On the Automatic Writing of Mrs Holland', see note 60 above), she writes that Mrs Holland produced some messages which predicted that Oliver Lodge will have 'throat trouble' and that he 'ought to abstain from speaking so much in the winter months – He may

he as strong as a lion but lions never give lectures during the winter and the strain is tremendous' (pp. 277–8). Lodge did apparently go on to get a cold, and had to cancel several speaking engagements (p. 278). Alice Johnson has added a note to the original letter in the margin which reads: 'I have often tried to read this as "Backs", but it can't be done without perjury. I expect the things meant "Backs", but it wrote "Banks" A.J.' However, in the report from June 1908, 'Backs in May' is said to have occurred in Mrs Holland's script of 1 March 1905 (p. 252). The 'Backs' refer to the rear of several colleges in Cambridge that back on to the River Cam, including that of Trinity, Myers's college. S.S. stands for 'subliminal self', Frederic Myers's term for the part of the self that is below consciousness.

64   *or F*: Mrs Forbes, another medium involved in the cross-correspondences, and mentioned in Alice Johnson's report from June 1908 (see note 60 above).

65   *Either Mrs H or F ... at Majuba*: Lang's poem 'The Deeds of Men' was dedicated to 'Colonel Ian Hamilton', and contains the line 'The mist crept o'er the Shameful Hill'. General Sir Ian Hamilton (1853–1947) was wounded at the Battle of Majuba in the First Boer War. Henry Rider Haggard, in *The Days of My Life: An Autobiography* (1926), remembers a dinner organised by Lang in 1886 or 1887, at which the diners were Lang, Arthur Balfour, Haggard and Sir Ian Hamilton. According to Haggard, Hamilton and Lang were cousins.

66   *The university use of men's*: in Alice Johnson's report from June 1908 (see note 60 above), Mrs Verrall is quoted as saying that the use of initials in the cross-correspondences of Mrs Holland is 'characteristic in the case of Cambridge friends and especially Mr. Myers' (Johnson, 'On the Automatic Writing of Mrs Holland', p. 188).

67   *Sep 21*: Letter SPR.MS 35/1051, SPR Archive, Manuscripts, Cambridge University Library. This letter mentions the cross-correspondences and an exposure of Eusapia Palladino (see note 68 below), which suggests that it is from 1910.

68   *As you will see ... nailed her.* in April 1910 the *Journal* of the Society for Psychical Research published a report from the American psychical researcher G. B. Dorr. This was an account of three sittings with Eusapia Palladino during which he could see how some of her phenomena were produced. He concludes that, regarding the cabinet she used, 'there was nothing that took place in connection with the cabinet that could not easily be explained by a free foot or hand, used skilfully; and that she does use both, and skilfully, there now can be no doubt' (G. B. Dorr, 'Eusapia Palladino in America', *Journal of the Society for Psychical Research* 14, 1909–10, p. 272.)

69   *C.C.*: Cross-correspondence.

70   *F.W.H.M.*: F. W. H. Myers, one of the supposed main communicators of the cross-correspondences.

71   *Dec 18*: Letter SPR.MS.35/1067, SPR Archive, Manuscripts, Cambridge University Library. This letter is difficult to date. As the other letters show, Lang concerned himself with the believability of Eusapia Palladino's phenomena in both the 1895 letters, and those from around 1908. The letter is, however, a nice summation of Lang's complex position regarding psychical phenomena.

72   *est aliquid Poltergeist*: this is Lang's rewriting of the Latin phrase '*sunt aliquid manes*', 'ghosts do exist!'. The phrase opens Elegy 4.7 by the Latin poet Sextus Propertius (*c*.50–5 BCE–*c*.15 BCE), in which he is visited by the ghost of Cynthia. Here Lang is asserting the existence of poltergeists.

73 *in Old Jeffries*: 'Old Jeffrey' was the name given by the Wesley family to a poltergeist that inhabited their home, Epworth Rectory, in the early eighteenth century. Lang writes about the experience of the Wesley family (which included John Wesley, the founder of Methodism) in various places, including in *Cock Lane and Common Sense* and in his article, 'Poltergeist', in the 1911 edition of the *Encyclopaedia Britannica*.

Letters to William James

1   *Feb 19*: MS Am 1092 (490–493), William James Papers, Houghton Library, Harvard University. The letter is probably from 1897. For more details on the dating of the letters to James see this volume, p.257

2   *If Mrs Piper … an ignoramus*: for Mlle Luci Ferrand, see this volume p. 422, n. 33.

3   *In June 1896*: this research was for Lang's *Pickle the Spy: Or The Incognito of Prince Charles* (London: Longmans, Green and Co., 1897), a work of history uncovering the identity of a spy working for the English during the Jacobite rebellion.

4   *Unable to find out … diamond ring*: Lang also writes about experimenting with the name 'Mlle Luci' in 'The Three Seeresses (1880–1900, 1424–1431)', see this volume p. 285–91.

5   *Now please look at Condillac*: Étienne Bonnot de Condillac (1714–80), French philosopher of mind. His *Traité des sensations* is from 1754. See also this volume p. 422, n. 33 for Mlle Luci's intellectual influence on Condillac.

6   *though not 'evidential'*: Lang relates his new knowledge about Mlle Luci, and this experiment with Miss X, in the sequel to *Pickle the Spy*, *The Companions of Pickle* (London: Longmans, Green and Co., 1898), pp. 92–6.

7   *I thought it was Montesquieu*: in *Pickle the Spy* (1897) Lang suggests that Montesquieu is the 'philosophe' mentioned by Mlle Luci and Mme de Vassé (p. 88).

8   *Dr Johnson being a case*: See this volume p. 411, n. 11.

9   *Apr 4*: MS Am 1092 (490–493), William James Papers, Houghton Library, Harvard University. This letter is probably from 1897.

10 *in Pickle*: Lang's work of history, *Pickle the Spy* (1897).

11 *I have … I think*: Ada Goodrich Freer wrote about her experiences in a haunted house in 'Psychical Research and an Allegedly "Haunted House"', *Nineteenth Century*, April 1897, pp. 217–234.

12 *I found a girl … ignorant of these things*: Lang wrote about his experiments with crystal gazing, and the young woman 'seer', in various places, including 'Magic Mirrors and Crystal Gazing', see this volume, pp. 292–9, and his 'Introduction' to Northcote W. Thomas, *Crystal Gazing: Its History and Practice* (London: Alexander Moring Ltd, The De La More Press, 1905), as well as in the chapter on crystal visions in *The Making of Religion* (London: Longmans, Green and Co., 1898).

13 *Henry Goring (ob. 1794)*: Henry Goring was equerry to Prince Charles Edward Stuart (Bonnie Prince Charlie), and was spied on by Alexander MacDonnell, known as 'Pickle', for the English.

14 *I have ordered … yet arrived*: William James, *The Will to Believe, and Other Essays in Popular Philosophy* (London and New York: Longmans, Green and Co., 1897). In James's

ANDREW LANG, VOL. I

essay included in this, 'What Psychical Research has accomplished', he discusses the phenomena of Stainton Moses (see note 15 below) and concludes that they 'appear to force upon us what Mr. Lang calls a choice between a moral and a physical miracle' (p. 314).

15 *no stock in Moses*: William Stainton Moses (1839–92) was an English cleric and spiritualist. He was one of the founders of the Society for Psychical Research, practised automatic writing and claimed to have had an experience of levitation.

16 *George Pellew*: See this volume p. 424, n. 6. In the SPR records Pellew is referred to by the pseudonym George Pelham, and was generally known as G. P.

17 *Dec [?]*: MS Am 1092 (490–493), William James Papers, Houghton Library, Harvard University. Marysa Demoor dates this letter as 1896, and the others included here as 1897. Lang's reference to his experiment with the young woman who could scry, which he dates at the beginning of 1897 in *The Making of Religion*, and the fact that in December 1897 he would have been writing this work, so would have known by then that these experiments would indeed be published, suggests that it may be from 1897. See Marysa Demoor, *Friends Over the Ocean: Andrew Lang's American Correspondents, 1881–1912* (Ghent: Ruksuniversiteit Gent, 1989), p. 201.

18 *I don't know if it is of any interest*: William James discusses the theories of hallucinations put forward by Alfred Binet (see this volume p. 420, n. 16) in his *Principles of Psychology*, 2 vols (New York: Henry Holt, 1890), vol. 2, pp. 128ff.

19 *points de repère*: Alfred Binet introduced this term in 1884 to describe a reference point, often visual, which gives objectivity to hallucinatory experiences. James discusses this idea in his *Principles of Psychology*, see note 18 above.

20 *I tried a girl who came here*: Lang here refers to the young woman whose abilities at scrying he recounts in 'Crystal Visions, Savage and Civilised', in *The Making of Religion*. In the account he says he first experimented with her in early 1897 (*The Making of Religion*, p. 94).

'Letter to E. B. Tylor on Home and the Brownings'

1 *'Letter to E. B. Tylor …'*: Tylor Papers, Pitt Rivers Museum Manuscript Collection, Box 13, Lang 18. See also Lang's letters to Oliver Lodge on the subject, this volume, pp. 314–27. For more on this letter see p. 258.

2 *(1904)*: the year has been added in pencil by a hand other than Lang's.

3 *Greenwood*: see this volume p. 431, n. 13.

4 *above a table*: this phrase has been added by Lang in superscript.

5 *R.B.'s*: this has been added in superscript by Lang above 'his'.

6 *They had no dead child … dead people*: see this volume p. 256 for more details.

7 *the date can be fixed*: For an account of this séance in letters by both Robert Browning and Elizabeth Barrett Browning, see *Lives of Victorian Literary Figures II*, vol. 1, *The Brownings*, edited by Simon Avery (London: Pickering & Chatto, 2004), pp. 327–30.

8 Greenwood: see p. 431, n.13.

9 *Pen Browning*: Robert Wiedeman Barrett Browning (1849–1912), known as 'Pen', was the only son of Robert Browning and Elizabeth Barrett Browning.

INDEX

Numbers in the form 100n
signal a footnote by Lang on
the page indicated; numbers in
the form 100 n.1 indicate an
explanatory endnote.

C

D

Jesuits 110, 111, 248, 274, 347, 348, 374, 386
n.85, 421 n.20
Jeune, Paul le 347, 386 n.85
Jevons, Frank Byron 207n, 217, 218–19, 221n,
327, 347
Jewish tradition 63, 81, 177, 194, 196n, 200, 205,
354, 407 n.27, 416 n.13, 418 n.2
Joan of Arc see Jeanne d'Arc
Johnson, Alice 255–6, 435 n.57 n.60 n.62 n.63,
436 n.66
Johnson, Samuel 219–20, 329, 411 n.11
Jülg, Bernhard 110, 385 n.77
Jung-Stilling, Heinrich 237, 251, 417 n.23

K

Kalevala, the 106, 118, 119, 388 n.115
Kant, Immanuel 250, 275–7, 280, 421 n.21
Kathasaritsagara see Ocean of Streams of Story, the
Keats, John 313, 348
Kellar, Harry 316, 431 n.16
Kelly, Edward 241, 415 n.22
Kelvin, Lord 283, 302, 423 n.48, 426 n.10, 429
n.10
Kephalos 95, 382 n.28
king's touch, the 240, 415 n.21
Kinglake, A. W. 292, 425 n.3
Kingsley, Charles 128, 391 n.17, 409 n.17
Kingsley, Mary 214, 409 n.17
Kipling, Rudyard 13, 365 n.24, 435 n.62
Kirk, Robert, of Aberfoyle 49, 415 n.21
Kohl, Johann Georg 74–5, 377 n.34
Kuhn, Franz Felix Adalbert 25, 68, 69, 70, 73n,
77, 348
Kuklick, Henrika 20, 21
Kurnai, the see Australian Aboriginal cultures

L

Lacroix, Paul 137, 394 n.51
Lafitau, Joseph-François 71, 247, 348
Lamb, Charles 124, 153n
Lane, Edward William 82, 292, 378 n.7
Lang Lectures, the 10, 364 n.3
Lang, Andrew 9–15, 17–44, 56, 80, 124–5, 166–7,
228, 254–8; use of anthropology 12–13,
19–21, 22, 24–5, 26–31, 33–9, 42, 44, 56,
166–7; his birth 11; critique of Max Müller
23–6, 40, 44, 68–74, 77, 80, 96–112, 166–7,
170–6, 247; his death 9, 14; and folklore 12,
22–33, 56, 80, 124–5; and ghosts 17, 34–6,
40, 42, 166–7, 178, 228, 254, 402 n.11;

influence of E. B. Tylor on 12, 19, 20, 26–30,
33, 36–7, 38–9, 166–7, 255, 258, 279 n.19;
interest in magic 18–19; his journalism 10,
12, 17; and psychical research 11–12, 14, 17,
19, 27, 33, 34–5, 254–8, 308–13; and religion
17, 19, 33–7, 39, 166–7; his reputation 9–15,
17; his Scottish identity 11–12, 29–30, 38,
32–3, 167; works: 'At the Sign of the Ship'
256, 430 n.10; Adventures among Books 365
n.20; Ballads and Lyrics of Old France 22;
Ban and Arrière Ban 424 n.5; The Book of
Dreams and Ghosts 412 n.12; Cock Lane and
Common Sense 34–5, 42, 228, 242–5, 254,
271n, 314, 412n, 417 n.1, 418 n.8, 419 n.15
n.3, 431 n.16, 342 n.25, 437 n.73; the
Coloured Fairy Books 31–2, 124–5, 152–64,
336, 344, 351, 388 n.114, 389 n.155, 396 n.84;
Custom and Myth 22, 25, 26, 27, 30, 32, 34,
35, 36, 37, 56, 57–77, 84n, 103n, 116n, 120n,
166, 170–6, 367 n.20, 374 n.31, 377 n.36, 389
n.123; Encyclopaedia Britannica entries 17, 26,
259, 344, 352, 437 n.73; The Gold of Fairnilee
31, 32; on Homer 12–13, 41–2, 345–6,
412 n.3; How to Fail in Literature 13; on
Jeanne d'Arc 254, 424 n.5; Kirk's Secret
Commonwealth 415 n.21; The Life and Letters
of John Gibson Lockhart 348, 417 n.9; Life of
Sir Walter Scott 348; Magic and Religion
37–8, 167, 207–15, 216–22, 343, 366 n.2,
367 n.20, 370 n.94; The Making of Religion
18, 20, 35–6, 40–1, 166–7, 177–88, 109–215,
228, 246–51, 254, 257, 271–83, 297n, 402
n.11, 404 n.31 n.33, 425 n.9, 428 n.4;
Method in the Study of Totemism 12; Modern
Mythology 26, 200n, 379 n.22; 'Mr Max
Muller's Philosophy of Mythology' 25,
102n; Myth, Ritual and Religion 22, 26, 34,
36, 80, 81–7, 341, 343, 348, 355, 378 n.12,
379 n.19 n.22, 398 n.103, 405 n.5,
407 n.39; 'Mythology and Fairy Tales' 24;
Perrault's Popular Tales 124, 131–51; Pickle
the Spy 257, 330, 422 n.33, 437 n.3 n.6
n.13; Prince Prigio 31, 128n, 164; Prince
Ricardo of Pantouflia 31, 164, 337; The Princess
Nobody 31, 370 n.74; Tales of a Fairy Court
31, 164; In the Wrong Paradise 267n, 401 n.4
Lang, John 14
Lang, Leonora Blanche (née Alleyne) 14, 46, 51,
164
Langstaff, Eleanor de Selms 365 n.13,
Lavaterus, Ludovicus 272, 276
Leaf, Walter 41–2, 47, 412 n.3
Leland, Charles Godfrey 151, 398 n.104
Lewes, G. H. 269–70, 419 n.10,

305; influence on Lang 12, 19, 20, 26–30, 33, 36–7, 38–9, 166–7, 255, 258, 279 n.19; letter from Lang to Tylor 332–3; on mythology 82, 84–5, 91, 92, 101, 113; and religion 186–7, 190–3, 194–5, 198, 200, 210, 212, 213, 236–7, 238–9, 247–9 *see also* anthropology; comparative method, the

U

Uncle Remus stories 91, 148, 381 n.15
Urvasi and Pururavas (story of) 25, 67–70, 72–3, 76–7, 89, 120, 380 n.9
Uther, H-J 53, 396 n.85, 398 n.4

V

vedas, the 25, 67–8, 77, 83, 89, 98n, 100, 103, 111, 168–9, 170–1, 350, 352, 375 n.5, 400 n.1 *see also* Urvasi and Pururavas (story of)
Vega, Garcilasso de la 111, 386 n.90
Verrall, Margaret 312, 325, 429 n.15, 435 n.60 n.61, 436 n.66
Versailles, Palace of 127, 131, 138
Victorian period 10–11, 22, 31, 33
Vincent, R. Harry 277, 281, 282
Virgil 326, 395 n.64
Voltaire 187, 247, 277, 405 n.41, 421 n.24
voyages of discovery *see* exploration

W

Waitz, Theodor 82, 196, 355
Wallace, Alfred Russel 18, 251n, 254, 256, 269–70, 273n, 304, 314, 355, 420 n.8, 429 n.5
Wallace, William 274, 277, 278, 280n, 302n
Waller, Philip 366 n.29
Weatherley, Lionel A. 319, 432 n.31
Webster, Adam Blyth 9
Welsh traditions 27, 70, 71, 75, 88, 377 n.36
werewolves 95, 104
Wesley, John 248, 272, 342, 420 n.6, 437 n.73
William Tell (legend) 230, 265, 412 n.6
witches 108, 158, 236, 241, 271, 284, 389 n.3, 319 n.2, 423 n.2
Wodrow, Robert 272, 420 n.6
'Wolf and the Kids, The' 90–2, 381 n.13
Wolof people 59, 360
Woluf people *see* Wolof people
wolves (in folklore) 90–2, 95, 99, 104, 114, 119, 346, 381 n.13, 382, 384 n.56

Wordsworth, William 176n, 313
working classes, the 24, 57–8, 65, 72, 85, 90, 105, 106, 108, 121, 126, 138, 156, 173, 230, 232, 250
wraiths 17, 186, 199, 226, 239, 240, 242–3, 260–1, 264, 265, 272, 308

X

Xan people 83, 91, 107, 108, 109, 110, 181, 191, 337, 358, 381 n.18, 387 n.99

Y

Yeats, W. B. 292, 425 n.1
Yoruba people 71, 360, 409 n.17
Young, Douglas 364 n.8

Z

Zoilus 134, 393 n.30
Zola, Émile 12, 15
Zulu people 24, 27, 59, 71, 76, 77, 91, 107, 108, 109, 118, 119, 121, 139, 140–1, 142, 151, 156, 240, 244, 284, 294, 338, 360, 376 n.24